# IMPROVING STUDENT LEARNING SKILLS

## A NEW EDITION

Martha Maxwell, Ph.D.

H&H Publishing Company, Inc.
Clearwater, Florida

# H&H Publishing Company, Inc.

1231 Kapp Drive
Clearwater, FL 33765
(727) 442-7760
(800) 366-4079
FAX (727) 442-2195
hhservice@hhpublishing.com
www.hhpublishing.com

---

# IMPROVING STUDENT LEARNING SKILLS

## A NEW EDITION

Martha Maxwell, Ph.D.

---

**Copyright © 1997 by H&H Publishing Company, Inc.**

**Production Supervisor**
Robert D. Hackworth

**Editing/Production**
Karen Hackworth

**Editorial Assistant**
Priscilla Trimmier

**Business Operations**
Mike Ealy, Sally Marston

ISBN 0-943202-61-2

Library of Congress Catalog Number 96-079453

Printing is the lowest number: 10 9 8 7 6 5 4 3

# IMPROVING STUDENT LEARNING SKILLS

## INTRODUCTION

This is the first chance I've had to update this book since it first came out more than 15 years ago, and needless to say, there have been many changes in the learning assistance/developmental skills field. It's not that the basic philosophy and ideas have changed, but rather there is new terminology and new applications. Some topics I wrote about in the 70s now have new names—for example, the Scholastic Aptitude Test (SAT) is now called the Scholastic Assessment Test, and it has been renormed to reflect the lower scores of today's entering college students. The Freshman Year Experience is a new version of freshman orientation courses for all students, emphasizing small seminars where traditional study skills, career planning, and other topics are introduced to help students adapt to the college milieu. Supplemental Instruction (SI) is the University of Missouri-Kansas City's prototype program related to adjunct skills classes, a highly structured group program where student leaders serve as mentors and model study skills strategies to students enrolled in a difficult course. Management techniques too are changing as TQM (Total Quality Management), QAM (Quality Assurance Model), Benchmarking, etc., replace older methods such as Management by Objectives (MBO), Zero-Based Budgeting, etc.

But perhaps the most impressive changes have been in the increased diversity of students and how instructors have responded in developing new ways to teach. As students have become more diverse, courses have become more integrated. Now paired courses such as math/physics, math/chemistry, freshman English and biology, and developmental courses combining reading, writing, and sometimes mathematics skills are offered more frequently. Basic reading, writing, and mathematics are viewed as processes, not as separate courses. Writing has been integrated into math and reading courses by requiring students to keep journals, write reports, and build portfolios. Team taught courses such as physics/mathematics or chemistry/mathematics are increasing. Though these logical pairings were not unheard of in the past, they were often temporary arrangements soon abandoned as a result of the feudalistic philosophy that kept people in their own departmental fiefdoms. So today, perhaps the artificial boundaries between disciplines are beginning to breakdown.

We now talk about the need for early intervention efforts as if students would academically self-destruct if we did not step in, but college administrators are realizing the importance of "front-loading" (Tinto, 1993)—that is, providing special programs for freshmen as an important way to reduce attrition.

Integrated programs have proved to be more effective in developmental skills than services and courses dispersed through traditional academic departments. Underpreparedness is only one of the problems of today's at-risk students in open-admission colleges. As Roueche and Roueche, in their 1993 book *Between a Rock and a Hard Place* point out, "By at-risk we are describing students who are not only underprepared for college, but who are also working 30 or more hours each week, who have little if any support from key family members, who are first-generation college attendees, who have what some have described as 'failure expectations,' and who have little academic success as they begin their postsecondary experience. These harsh social, economic, and educational realities have merged to create an unprecedented pressure on community colleges for effective basic-skills training—a need that creates such a daunting challenge to American community colleges that some have called their response nothing less than a 'mission impossible,'" (p. 1).

On the other hand, new technology and new methodology have made it possible to substantiate many of the ideas we had about improving teaching and to demonstrate the complexities of learning in our research. Teaching strategies that were embryonic and rare in the 1970s are mature and mainstream today. For example, collaborative learning is now widely accepted as a learning tool in college classrooms as faculty recognize the importance of student communication in learning. More experimentation is being carried on in cooperative learning, interactive video sessions, and group decision-making. Although we have been aware of the limitations of lectures for many decades, it's been only

recently that significant efforts have been made to improve lectures through other methods and the use of classroom assessment methods (Angelo and Cross, 1993).

Assessment and evaluation continue to be important functions that administrators and the public expect college programs to perform. However, testing is changing. Traditional multiple-choice standardized exams have been computerized, making them easier to administer and easier to take and score. On the other hand, there is also a strong movement to deemphasize objective exams and return to qualitative measures such as essay exams, portfolios, and protocols. Yet it will be a long time before colleges change their requirements. Students will still need to make good scores on standardized tests to be accepted by selective colleges and to place in regular freshman courses.

The use of educational technology in the classroom to aid learning is increasing as more sophisticated hardware and software becomes available. Although we had self-paced courses in the 60s, today's courses use much more varied materials and activities—students keep journals, build portfolios of their work, use multi-media to prepare reports, and have many choices as to the activities they must complete to meet course standards.

Although we have always recognized that motivation is important to learning, in the past we have been limited in what we could do about it. Recent research on motivation and the emotional aspects of learning suggests better ways to teach courses and holds out the promise that we will be able to reach more students and help them learn more effectively.

Colleges that face declining enrollments are emphasizing retention as costs surge. They continue to accept underprepared adults to fill their classes, and they need strong developmental programs. Other colleges in areas experiencing the baby boom echo have too many applicants and are reducing or closing down developmental/remedial programs.

Gradually those who teach developmental education and provide learning assistance are being recognized as academic professionals. The National Association for Developmental Education (NADE) has grown into a large professional group and the National Center for Developmental Education, financed by the Kellogg Foundation, publishes journals and offers occasional conferences on research. New professional standards and guidelines have been written and adopted for learning assistance centers, tutoring programs, adjunct skills courses, teaching and learning, and developmental courses that reflect a consensus of professionals on those factors essential to successful programs. Tutor training too has assumed more importance as the College Reading and Learning Association (CRLA) sponsors an International Tutor Certification Program, and a new National Tutor Association (East Stroudsburg State University, PA) has been formed.

State-mandated basic skills testing for entering college students and mandatory skills courses for those who fail the test have largely replaced voluntary enrollment practices for developmental courses. Furthermore, there is concerted pressure to relocate developmental courses to the two-year colleges, as evidenced by plans in New York City and California. Other four-year institutions are phasing out developmental/remedial courses as a result of budget cuts.

Public criticism, ever rising costs, and financial cutbacks suggest that many more changes lie ahead.

The long expected decline in funding for higher education hit most institutions in the mid-90s as reengineering, cutbacks, and faculty downsizing became the norm. This same kind of fiscal crisis occurred in the 50s and in the 70s (where they called it faculty retrenchment), and it undoubtedly will reoccur in the future since academic recessions seem to be cyclical. Rising costs and declining enrollments govern the situation, and although there is a surge of young college aged students in some sections of the country, the competition for admission to the most prestigious colleges has become even more intense. As a result, today's cutbacks may spur greater and more appropriate use of the new technology for teaching/learning. The rapidly advancing improvements in technology have threatened to challenge traditional college teaching methods for decades, but so far their effects have been minimal. Technology has yet to fulfill its promise of providing the way for any motivated student to learn the skills and absorb the knowledge that has been available to only the most brilliant minds in the past, but today this is fast becoming a possibility.

The purpose of this book is to address the state of the art of learning assistance and developmental education programs in the 90s, and I dedicate this work to the many, many people who have so generously shared their experiences with me. I am especially grateful to Jennifer Conley and Jan Norton of Missouri Western State College for their careful review, comments, and suggestions on Chapter 8 and Chapter 9 and to my husband Walter Spieth, who patiently proofread the chapters after I lost most of my eyesight. I also want to thank Karen Hackworth and Priscilla Trimmier for their careful editing and their support throughout this endeavor.

*Martha Maxwell*

# ABOUT THE AUTHOR

Martha Maxwell, formerly academic coordinator of the Student Learning Center and lecturer in education at the University of California–Berkeley, founded learning centers and reading and study skills programs at the American University and the University of Maryland. She was awarded the bachelor's degree in psychology (1946), the master's degree in psychology (1948), and the doctor's degree in education and psychology (1960)—all from the University of Maryland. From 1976-1980 she coordinated Berkeley's Summer Institute for Directors and Staff of College Learning Centers and has participated in recent summer institutes, including those at MCLCA, Kellogg, and the Winter Institute (University of Arizona–Tucson). She represents the College Reading and Learning Association in the Council for the Advancement of Standards. Since retiring from Berkeley in 1979, she has continued to write and work as a consultant and lecturer.

Maxwell has published over 150 professional articles in educational and psychological journals and is the author of *Skimming and Scanning Improvement* (McGraw-Hill, 1968), *Improving Student Learning Skills* (Jossey-Bass, 1978), and *Evaluating Academic Skills Programs: A Sourcebook* (MM Associates, 1991, 1996). She edited *When Tutor Meets Student* (University of Michigan Press, 1994) and *From Access to Success: A Book of Readings on College Developmental Education and Learning Assistance Programs* (H&H Publishing, 1994). She is presently working on the book, *Improving the Academic Performance of Undergraduates: A Faculty Guide to Programs and Strategies*. She has had extensive experience in college positions, having served for many years as a teacher, scholar, researcher, counselor, administrator, diagnostician, and academic adviser. Her major professional interests are in college reading, program evaluation, the motivational problems of college students, and problem solving. Her major avocational interest is ethno-biology of tropical jungles.

# TABLE OF CONTENTS

# CHAPTER 1

## THE BACKGROUND, HISTORY AND RATIONALE FOR COLLEGE SKILLS PROGRAMS

This book focuses on the difficulties students have in adjusting to the academic demands of college, the nature of these difficulties, their causes, strategies for their prevention and treatment, and the programs that have been developed to ameliorate them. Certainly academic skills are not the only problems college students face, for they must make personal and social adjustments to a new environment, and they are just as susceptible to problems with their families, health, and finances as others in their age group. The increasing number of adult students returning, most on a part-time basis, is changing the profile of the typical freshman, and these adult students face new challenges in trying to balance study with the rest of life's demands.

However, I believe that the central concern of college students is success in academic work; if faced with academic difficulties, they are overwhelmed. They feel inadequate and fear failure, and these feelings affect all spheres of their lives. Conversely, when students are able to overcome learning difficulties, they gain confidence in themselves, and this confidence enables them to cope more effectively with other conflicts. In contrast to previous eras, never before have so many students from such diverse backgrounds entered our institutions of higher learning as is true today, and with them they bring a variety of learning needs and expectations.

Many students have difficulty adjusting to college academic demands. Most, if not all, entering students experience problems in adjusting to college courses. In contrast to high school, where attendance is required, college gives students greater freedom, for professors assume that they have the self-direction and self-discipline to attend class, study, and learn on their own. Furthermore, college students are expected to develop new and higher-level skills. Students often find that the skills that earned them good grades in high school are not enough to enable them to succeed in college. College courses demand that they think critically in their reading, writing, and study assignments as well as complete homework regularly. Whether they attend Harvard or an open-admission college, freshmen share a common problem—learning how to manage their own time.

Recently, Weinstein and others (1988) identified six categories of differences between high school and college that affect the success of first year students: academic environment, grading, knowledge acquisition, support, stress, and responsibility. College students have less support from family, friends, and teachers, and more difficult academic work leads to higher stress. In college, too, they are faced with increased responsibility for their own learning and increased responsibility for making life decisions. Thus it is not surprising that many freshman students withdraw from college since they have to contend with so many important life changes.

These observations are not new. In 1948 I wrote a paper called "Improving the Articulation Between High School and College," and I was far from the first to do so. It is sad that despite many years of effort to help students adjust to college, today's students still face the same struggles. In fact, they seem to need even more help in adjusting to college than did their predecessors, for the changes we've made in the past fifty years have not reduced the gap between learning in high school and college. In fact, as colleges admit larger numbers of at-risk students, that gap has widened. Perhaps one reason is that both high school teachers and college professors are subject matter specialists and have not been as concerned with teaching students how to learn their subjects. As a result, many of today's high school students graduate convinced of one thing—that they can't learn some subjects—perhaps it's math or science or writing or another course. Today, we call this having low self-efficacy, and it means that college instructors must first somehow find a way to convince students that they are capable of learning before they can teach them how to improve their skills.

The permissive environment of today's high schools, their lowered standards as reflected in high absentee rates and grade inflation, and their deemphasis of traditional college preparatory courses have produced a generation of students who are weaker in skills than students of earlier decades. Faculty members and administrators in colleges throughout the country continue to be deeply concerned about the continuing decline in college entrance test scores and in basic skills proficiency. As increasing numbers of students from poverty backgrounds and with weak academic preparation enter college, supported by federal and state financial aid, the pool of highly qualified college applicants seems to grow smaller each year. The problem of underprepared students affects every institution—indeed, it is viewed as a national crisis. Newspapers regularly report on the crisis in the three R's, the illiteracy of today's college students, and the fact that providing the necessary basic skills instruction is taxing college budgets and resources. Many colleges today require freshmen to take skills placement tests and, if they fail, strongly encourage or require them to enroll in basic reading, writing, and mathematics courses before beginning their mainstream college courses. In fact, a number of states mandate placement tests and remedial courses for those who fail the tests. Some colleges still struggle with the question whether credit should be awarded for preparatory work that faculty members (and state legislators) insist should have been taught in high school. Recent studies suggest that 40% of freshmen need basic skills courses, and some surveys report even higher rates, particularly in remedial mathematics. So the need for more preparation is increasing and there is no end in sight.

## DEVELOPMENTAL STUDENTS OR AT-RISK STUDENTS?

In an earlier edition of this book, I defined developmental students as those whose skills, knowledge, motivation, and/or academic ability are significantly below those of the "typical" student in the college or curriculum in which they are enrolled. By this definition, whether students are underprepared for higher education depends on the particular institution they attend—its entrance standards, the expectations of its faculty, and the characteristics of its average student. The more than 2000 institutions of higher education in the United States vary tremendously in their goals, their programs, and the students they attract. Students who are underprepared for the University of California or the University of Wisconsin may be adequately prepared to enter a community college. Thus, "underpreparedness" is relative. The further students fall below the college's norm, the more likely they are to have serious academic difficulties, and the harder it becomes to help them succeed.

There are also wide differences in the preparation and skills required for success in different majors within the same institution. If students admitted to a college with high standards have very weak reading and writing skills, then I would consider them underprepared for the regular freshman literature course and would think it most unlikely that a one-term basic writing course would prepare many of them for it. Or if an engineering program in a university accepts minority and women students who have not taken the prerequisite mathematics courses in high school (or have done poorly in them), then I would consider these students underprepared for engineering. They might, however, be adequately prepared for other programs that do not require college-level mathematics.

The terms underprepared and underachieving, as I use them, also encompass students who are labeled "misprepared," meaning that although they earned high grades in high school, either they did not take college preparatory courses or their courses were academically weak, resulting in inflated grades. National surveys show that today approximately 30 percent of high school students take college preparatory work, while over 50 percent of high school graduates eventually attend college.

However, today's developmental classes contain even more diverse students than those previously described and hence the term "at-risk" is used more frequently than "underprepared." Roueche and Roueche (1993) explain that today's community college students are at risk in a number of ways that complicate and make obsolete the old definition of college student, and they are not only underprepared for college, but are working 30 or more hours a week, have little support from key family members, are the first-generation in their families to attend college, have had little previous success, and often expect to fail in college courses. In their book, *Between a Rock and a Hard Place*, the Roueches describe the educational task of the open-admission college as a "mission impossible."

All of the at-risk students need effective basic skills improvement, but certainly their needs are broader and more varied than those we used to call underprepared. Hardin (1988) describes seven categories of developmental students including two types of "poor chooser"—those who chose to drop out of high school before they graduated and those who chose the wrong type of high school curriculum but are now returning to finish their education. She also includes adult learners who have been away from school for a long time and need to brush up their rusty skills, and the "ignored"—the student who has academic or physical weaknesses that were never detected in high school. She mentions that these students spent a great deal of time staying out of the teacher's way so that they were ignored and never really learned how to learn or even that they might be capable of learning. Their disabilities may include vision, hearing, emotional problems, and other factors that can interfere with learning. But their main characteristic has been that their problems have been ignored.

**ESL Students**. A fifth category of developmental students are those who acquired their elementary and/or secondary education in a non-English speaking country. Not only must they master formal English writing and reading conventions but also the rituals and traditions of American colleges that are vastly different from those in their home country. Even though some of these students may have attended elementary and high school in the United States, they have never overcome their linguistic deficiencies in English.

**The Learning Disabled.** Another type of developmental student includes those who have physical or learning disabilities that may have prevented them from becoming part of a mainstream secondary education and succeeding in pre-college courses. If the problem stems from a recent injury, the student's previous learning may have been lost and s/he must relearn the basics—a most frustrating experience. Learning disabled students' academic difficulties are exacerbated when parents and teachers view learning disabled students as lazy and unmotivated and impossible. On the other hand, faculty usually go out of their way to help students with overtly physical disabilities. Learning disabled students are among the most difficult developmental students for teachers to help, especially since colleges often lack the support services that were available to these students who were diagnosed and helped in high school. What is clear, however, is that the number of learning disabled students entering college will continue to increase.

Last, but not least, are **The Users**, those developmental students who lack clear cut academic goals and intend to use the educational system for their own purposes. In other words, their main reason for being in college is to receive financial aid and other benefits. They tend to aspire to the minimum grades that will enable them to continue in school. Obvi-

ously they need more than academic assistance; they need counseling. Interestingly enough, if these system-abusers can become excited about the prospect of learning, they can become excellent students, but they are most difficult to work with (Hardin, 1988).

Not only do developmental students differ from each other, but what constitutes "basic skills" at the college level is also subject to different interpretations. Some administrators and faculty members insist that "basic skills" refers to the reading, writing, computational, speech, and listening skills that should have been mastered in elementary school. Others, in more selective institutions, use the term "basic skills" to describe skills and knowledge normally acquired in high school, and some colleges (such as Harvard) include computer literacy as a "basic skill."

Sometimes professors confuse immaturity and inadequate knowledge of new subjects with skill deficiencies. Students cannot understand textbooks if they have not grasped the concepts, are unfamiliar with the technical vocabulary, or lack the information necessary to interpret the examples and references. Similarly, students cannot write skillful essays on topics about which they know little. Some professors may overlook the gaps in students' preparation for college as well as their skills limitations. A professor who assumes that all students in the class have completed high school chemistry may attribute the student's difficulties to poor skills when, in truth, the student may not have taken high school chemistry. Faculty members hold common, but erroneous beliefs about "appropriate" college-level work, materials, and courses. Because of our grade levels in public schools, many assume that college students should be able to read books written at the Grade 13 level. However, to implement a universal standard, such as requiring all students reading below the Grade 12 level on a standardized test to take a course in remedial reading, ignores the great variability among college populations. For example, in the 1970s, entering freshmen at Stanford averaged 615 on the verbal part of the Scholastic Aptitude Test (SAT), while those entering Coppin State College (Baltimore, Maryland) averaged 273. It stands to reason that the entry-level reading and composition courses at the two institutions should be markedly different. Each college must decide on the essential skills required for its curriculums, and each must take a cold, hard look at the characteristics of the students it enrolls. If most of the applicants lack the skills and preparation for the basic courses offered, then new programs and courses must be instituted unless the college is satisfied that it has a large enough pool of applicants that it need not be concerned about very high attrition rates.

## The Problem of Naming Programs

In the early 50s, I taught in a program for students who were accepted at the University of Maryland "on trial" because their high school averages were below "C." We called them "marginal" students and required them to take a general orientation course called College Aims, which included information about university rules and regulations, study skills, planning educational and vocational goals, and so on. In addition, they were offered counseling and tutoring. Initially about 27% of these students graduated when the group was small (under 30) and motivated (mostly ex-GIs), but as the numbers increased to three hundred, the course was taught in one section as a large lecture, and the percent of students graduating shrank to 20%. Students who failed to get a 2.5 GPA their first semester remained on trial and were required to take a reading improvement course their second semester. These students were not "happy campers." They resented taking the required courses, tried to cheat on exams, and, in general, behaved the way reluctant learners always have.

At that point, I changed jobs and started a reading and study skills program open to all students operating under the counseling center. By the late 50s counseling psychologists were trying to apply the philosophy of student development which involved "educating the whole person," as exemplified by the American Council on Education's publication in 1937 of *The Student Personnel Point of View*. This work set forth the idea of college learning and adjustment as a developmental process. I considered my program "developmental," in that any student, at whatever level they might be, could volunteer and receive individualized help to improve their reading and study skills. In fact, I was proud that my program attracted equal numbers of students who scored in each quartile of the college admissions test—from the highest to the lowest. Students at all levels of ability sought help from the center voluntarily, yet at the same time some students were referred by concerned faculty members and administrators. This is not to suggest that there was no stigma attached to attending the services, for I vividly remember a scene where two sorority girls literally dragged a reluctant pledge, kicking and screaming, into our center. They wanted to make sure she got help in improving her grades. It took me a while to calm them all down and explain that their referral technique was not appropriate and to reassure the pledge that we were not going to harm her.

The term developmental education evolved from the student personnel movement's attempts to merge academic and student affairs personnel to support student learning. As opposed to the negative connotations of remedial and compensatory education which view the learner as inadequate, the programs of the 1960s and 70s stressed the value and worth of each individual and focused on the potential of continuing growth and change. The goal is to have everyone involved master increasingly complex developmental tasks, achieve self-direction, and become interdependent. This establishes developmental education as a series of major life choices and processes through which all students must pass, rather than programs that are appropriate only for the weakest students. Learning centers that offer academic support services to all students epitomize the developmental viewpoint.

However, over the years, the definition of developmental education has changed so that today, unfortunately, it has become a synonym for remedial. For many years the term "developmental" enabled programs to avoid the stigma of calling a program "remedial," and in the 70s, when state legislators in the midwest became concerned about the number of remedial courses offered in community colleges and tried to reduce them, institutions quickly renamed their courses "developmental" and continued to offer them. Gradually, use of the term "developmental" to describe more advanced reading and study skills courses involving critical thinking skills and college-level materials declined so that by 1989, most accepted Tomlinson's description: "Developmental programs at institutions of higher education encompass a variety of courses and services that are conducted to provide assistance to individuals who have been denied regular admission to the institution because of failure to meet specified admission and placement requirements or because of predicted risk in meeting the requirements of college-level courses."

The term "remedial" was borrowed from medicine and implies that the course will fix some weaknesses in the student's academic background; and, according to Clowes (1980), "In its most restricted sense, (remedial) refers to work with academically backward and less able students." This negative connotation would, he felt, be also applied to the student who was viewed as a patient to be diagnosed, prescribed for, treated, and then retested. Current examples of remedial programs include the many required courses in basic reading, mathematics, and writing that a number of states and colleges mandate for entering students in public institutions who have failed college-level skills placement exams. In those programs, until students complete the required remedial course(s) and/or pass the post-test, they are prevented from enrolling in further college courses. I believe that the term "remedial" is the worst thing we can call a college program. It inevitably invites failure. Although most racial epithets have been eliminated from our vocabulary, the intellectual epithet "remedial college courses" is alive and well in many states, even though we should know better. As Urie Triesman, in describing successful college programs in math and science for disadvantaged students, warns, "Don't call them remedial. Call them 'intensive' or 'honors programs' or anything else if you want students to succeed."

Clowes (1980) further explains that the term compensatory education was introduced in the period following WWII, when federal legislation for elementary and secondary education formalized school efforts to make up for the debilitating consequences of discrimination and poverty. In other words, compensatory education was associated with cognitive deficiencies that were thought to be environmentally induced, as exemplified by President Johnson's War on Poverty. TRIO programs are examples of compensatory programs with their Special Services programs addressing the needs of college age students. In addition to providing help in basic skills (reading, writing, mathematics), compensatory education tries to counter balance a non-supportive home environment by providing a cultural enriching experience. The traditional black colleges provided a compensatory model of education in which the college assumed a strong "in loco parentis" role.

Clowes (1980) pointed out that remedial, compensatory, and developmental programs existed in colleges and universities, and often the same institution offered all three programs, yet the tendency was to consider them as the same. He explains that it is important to understand the differences between these approaches in order to articulate purposes and goals and to be clearer about expectations and desired outcomes. However, times have changed and definitions have changed as "developmental" has taken on the opprobrium of remedial.

Mary Rubin (1991), who chaired a CRLA (College Learning and Reading Association) committee to clarify terminology in the field and to develop a glossary of terms, reported that terms like developmental education have contradictory definitions and multiple meanings. When she asked program directors how they described their program in budget requests, "academic skills courses" was used most frequently; developmental courses ranked fifth. This suggests that there is still confusion about the term developmental college courses in the minds of college administrators.

In 1981 I recommended that the National Association for Remedial and Developmental Services in Post-Secondary Education (NARDSPE) drop the term "Remedial" from their name because it was pejorative and stigmatized students enrolled in those classes. Someone must have been listening, because the association did change their name to NADE (National Association of Developmental Education). Ten

years later I addressed the group, again noting that "developmental" had become a synonym of remedial, and suggested that perhaps it is fruitless to keep thinking up euphemisms for developmental education and instead find ways of changing our programs so that they are more closely integrated with main stream courses and not stand-alone courses with stigmatizing names. After all, team-taught or adjunct skills or Supplemental Instruction (SI) courses have been the most consistently successful programs we've offered.

Currently, some colleges are using the term "transitional" to refer not only to freshman programs for high-risk students, but also for services that help community college transfer students adapt to the academic rigors of four year colleges and programs that rehabilitate students who are on academic probation. Perhaps this will replace "developmental" until our courses are eventually assimilated into the academic mainstream so they won't need a special name.

The term "learning assistance" has long been the preferred term of learning centers that offer services to all students, and many practitioners prefer to refer to their services as learning assistance or academic support programs rather than calling them developmental programs.

Kerstiens (1995) classified college learning assistance into five categories, adding two more to Clowes framework, and delineating the differences between student needs, assessment methods, and prescriptions associated with each type of assistance. Although this model oversimplifies the issues because, in practice, these categories almost always overlap and certainly the professional associations that represent these practitioners share many of the same concerns, it can serve as a way of conceptualizing the different viewpoints.

# Five Models of Learning Assistance

(Copyrighted 1995 by Gene Kerstiens, Andragogy Associates; reprinted by permission of the author.)

## Developmental Studies

**Student**: Needs basic skills: reading, writing, and/or math before mainstreaming.

**Assessment**: Basic skills test battery: reading, writing, math.

**Prescription**: Mandatory placement in developmental semester/quarter classes. Confidence that assessing students' proficiencies early on and improving specific skills before the student is exposed to a rigorous curriculum provides the rationale. Accordingly, directors and staff are usually enlisted from the ranks of instructors in the college and are more likely to be housed in their own department and/or as a separate instructional unit. Developmental services incline toward a course/curricular avenue to enrollment in courses with prerequisites.

## Learning Assistance

**Student**: Needs basic skills and/or learning skills improvement, at any time in academic career.

**Assessment**: Basic skills battery and other instruments.

**Prescription**: Discretionary referral or voluntary referral rather than mandatory referral to: On-going workshops or mini-courses in studying, reading, writing, listening, notetaking, test taking, time management, tutoring, and other strategies; individual skills counseling; tutoring; Supplemental Instruction; CAI; or other mediated materials. Services tend to be open-ended and open-exit, and the variety of learning resources and democratic clientele mixing synergistically promotes motivation and minimizes the stigma sometimes attached to segregated classes. Programs tend to be separate units but not instructional departments.

## Learning Resources

**Student**: Needs alternative instructional delivery system.

**Assessment**: Learning styles survey and client/faculty referral.

**Prescription**: Voluntary, mediated learning (often with course credit); course delivery via cassette, video, CAI, multimedia; distance learning via TV courses, teleconferencing, local modem or Internet. Enrollment is voluntary and courses completed through mediated delivery are awarded with weight equal to traditional courses. Staff tend to be librarians or persons specifically trained to administer learning resources. (Note: Learning Resources Services also involve providing media and materials to faculty and what are currently called teaching/learning services.)

## Student Development

**Student**: Needs personal and social accommodation to academic life before and/or during instruction.

**Assessment**: Psychometric testing including vocational/professional preferences, personality type indicators—self/faculty referral.

**Prescription**: Voluntary individual or group counseling; orientation, re-entry, self concept, text anxiety, reality therapy sessions, alcohol/drug abuse, learning communities, collaborative learning programs and services. Personnel are typically enlisted from student affairs, counseling and guidance, and their mission is often related to that of the director of enrollment management or retention.

## Compensatory

(State and federally funded programs such as TRIO, EOP, etc.)

**Student**: Needs cultural enrichment to correct cognitive deficiencies brought about by the debilitating consequences of discrimination and poverty.

**Assessment**: Students selected on basis of economic need; first generation to enter college, under-represented ethnic group, etc.

**Prescription**: Students are given intensive help on basic skills (reading, writing, math) through tutoring, counseling, and culturally enriching activities such as field trips to art galleries, the theater, music concerts, museums, etc. Programs are designed to successfully sustain minority students in the life of the institution by providing financial, personal, and academic support. Directors and staff coordinate retention strategies in conjunction with the faculty and non-teaching personnel.

Professional Associations whose programs and publications are of interest to practitioners in the above types of programs include the National Association of Developmental Educators (NADE), College Reading and Learning Association (CRLA), American College Personnel Association (ACPA Commission XVI), Media Library Education Association (MLEA), and National Councils of Equal Opportunity Association (NCEOA).

## An Integrated Model Proposal

The five models briefly described previously are incomplete and usually are supplemented by other services such as writing centers, math labs, reading labs, computer labs, tutoring services, and supplemental instruction. Sometimes these services are integrated, but usually they are dispersed throughout the campus—depending on changing centers of institutional power, turf rivalries, political climate or even campus architectural limitations.

Ideally the complete array of services needed on a campus should be integrated to provide the most efficient and effective support for students.

The Learning Assistance Program Model by Burns (1991), reproduced in Fig. 1-1 below, represents such an integrated program.

### Fig. 1-1. The Learning Assistance Program Model

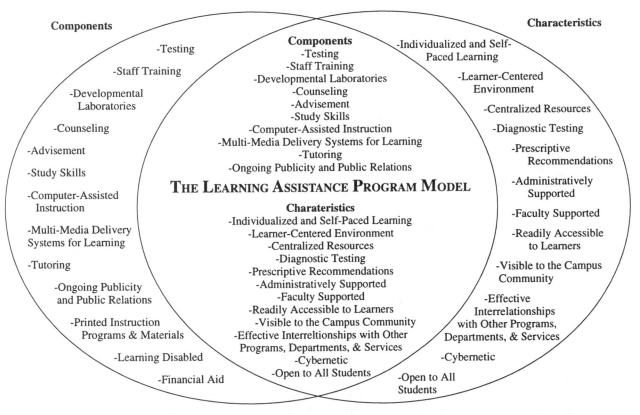

Marie-Elaine Burns (1991) *A Study to Formulate a Learning Assistance Model for the California Community College*, Dissertation, Pepperdine Univeristy, Graduate School of Education and Psychology, p. 184.

In this book, I will use "learning assistance" in describing general academic skills programs that serve all students and are based on a developmental philosophy, but I will use developmental to describe mandatory programs that are offered to the weakest students, referring occasionally to remedial programs when that is their official title. The term "learning assistance programs," I feel, includes both remedial, compensatory programs, developmental, learning resources and transitional programs but is not limited to them, and offers a variety of services to other student clients including advanced undergraduates as well as graduate students.

Are today's at-risk students different from their predecessors? The current euphemisms applied to underprepared college students (like "new students" or "non traditional students" or even "at-risk students") disturb me, for they imply that we are dealing with a new species of student. We have always had academically weak, poorly prepared college students. Certainly we have them in greater numbers today, but then, more students are currently attending college than ever before. I recall the first university course I taught in 1948—an English course called "Reading Improvement." Of the twenty-six students who enrolled, four would be considered barely literate even by today's standards. Two were recent graduates of rural black high schools, one a student from Appalachia, and the other a first-generation college student of Lithuanian ancestry from a coal mining district in Pennsylvania. The other students in the class ranged from government clerks to a navy captain. Individualizing instruction was a necessity, and each student needed his or her own special assignments and goals.

Today we label students culturally or educationally disadvantaged or learning-disabled, but they share the traits of poor achievers of previous eras as

Pitcher and Blaushild, (1970, pp. 107-108) note:

*"Cultural deprivation is now accepted as a fact by most people. Still the feeling persists that deprivation belongs only to a special ghetto population and has nothing in common with the learning problems of the white, middle class and upper economic classes of America's children who go to college. Although it is generally accepted that emotional problems can interfere with learning and cut across every class, economic, and color line, the idea of cultural deprivation cutting across these lines is new. Yet the same symptoms found in ghetto populations are found in the wealthy. Both the underachieving wealthy and the deprived student can share the same inability to plan long-range goals and the same indifference to grades; both groups can remain in worlds that are cut off from the academic, the wealthy in his car-filled playground, the ghetto student in his street gang. Both groups can show reading, writing, or speaking problems in the academic sense, and have the same ups and downs in academic performance. Both can be exclusively involved and preoccupied with the activities of their own pocket-cultures and uninterested in the values and goals of the larger society."*

One fact that is easily forgotten with the matriculation of each new freshman class is that the need to provide intensive basic skills services for college students is not a recent phenomenon but has deep historical roots. To put our present problem in perspective, we should remember that American higher education has historically had an egalitarian thrust. College has provided the principal way for children of immigrants and the poor to advance socially and economically, while it has also served to preserve the status of the children of the rich. Private colleges, from their beginnings, have admitted the talented children of the poor and given them scholarships. Furthermore, working one's way through college is a time-honored American custom for students whose families could not afford to support their college aspirations. In addition, our most prestigious private colleges have always found places in their freshman classes for the untalented scions of their wealthiest alumni. So teaching students from diverse academic backgrounds is certainly not a new experience for college faculties. Unfortunately, it is one that faculty do not expect to have to deal with, so it comes as a surprise to each new teacher. However, it is true that professors in the past rarely taught classes consisting of students representing such wide differences as we have in many of our colleges today.

## THE HISTORICAL BACKGROUND OF TEACHING AT-RISK COLLEGE STUDENTS

For those who insist that college students in the old days were somehow superior to present students—and for those who are too young to remember—a glimpse at some of the milestones in the history of American higher education may be enlightening (sources: Brubacher and Willis, 1976; Boylan and White, 1987; Losak and Miles, 1991; Spann and McCrimmon, 1994).

From the beginning of higher education in the United States, the faculty who founded Harvard University for the purpose of training ministers found few students capable of mastering college courses because books were written in Latin and Greek and courses were taught in Latin. Students preparing for college would apprentice themselves to ministers to learn Latin and Greek, but many entered the college inadequately versed in classical languages, so tutors were provided to ensure that students understood the lectures and could read the books.

Later, after the American Revolution, when English became the accepted academic language, faculty still complained about student writing, but it was not until 1874 that Harvard first offered fresh-man English at the request of faculty members who were dissatisfied with students' preparation in formal writing.

As new institutions were founded, the preparation of students became an increasing problem, and the University of Wisconsin established a preparatory department in 1849. This practice was frowned upon by educators like Henry P. Tappan, who in 1852 in his inaugural address as president of the University of Michigan, stated that American colleges were too much involved in teaching rudimentary courses that belonged in intermediate or even primary schools and that universities were lowering their standards by admitting poorly prepared students. He asked, "Of what avail could the learned professors and preparations of a University be to juvenile students? . . . To turn raw, undisciplined youth into the University to study the Professions, to study the Learned Languages and the Higher Sciences is a palpable absurdity."

But by 1862, when President Lincoln signed the Morrill Act, establishing land-grant colleges to teach agricultural and mechanical courses, a flood of "new" students entered colleges. Not only were they not prepared for studying the classics nor the professions, most had not attended high school and were not prepared for the basic skills required for learning practical agricultural and mechanical courses. A few years later, Iowa State College required that entering freshmen be fourteen years old and able to read, write, and do arithmetic. If they lacked these skills, they were placed in the college's preparatory department.

Although Oberlin College accepted the first woman student in 1832, their decision to admit women was motivated by their intent to use them to provide laundry and cleaning services for the young male students who were living away from home—a decision today's feminists would deplore. There were few opportunities for higher education for women until after the Civil War when women's colleges were initially established. But even then the early women's colleges served primarily as high schools since few women attended secondary schools. Some colleges like Vassar had preparatory programs from their inception, but by the 1890s Vassar's trustees were questioning whether underprepared women should be accepted at all, although in truth, they continued to accept such students as they do today. However, women's colleges continued to be considered academically inferior to male institutions until well into the 20th century.

In 1890, the Second Morrill Act increased federal aid to colleges for implementing programs in applied science and mechanical arts. This act freed American colleges from their classical and formal tradition. The rationale of the bill was that every American citizen was entitled to receive some form of higher education. This act initially brought many more unprepared students into colleges, but faculty were unprepared as well, for they had to develop curricula and write textbooks for these new programs.

In 1890 the College Entrance Examination Board was founded, representing an attempt to make college admission requirements uniform. Yet in 1907, over half the students who matriculated at Harvard, Yale, Princeton, and Columbia failed to meet entrance requirements. (Since colleges were competing fiercely for students, they were willing to admit those who did not meet their standards in order to fill their classes.)

By 1915, three hundred fifty colleges in the United States reported to the U.S. commissioner of education that they had college preparatory depart-

ments, suggesting even in this era that a gap remained between high school preparation and the expectations of colleges. Historians attribute this gap to the fact that states were spending most of their money for elementary education and little on high school education.

The number of colleges with preparatory programs began to decline rapidly after 1915, but as Losak and Miles (1991) report, this might not indicate that freshmen were better prepared for college. Some institutions, such as Wabash College, resolved the problem by simply changing the course numbers and titles on their preparatory courses, thereby translating all of the preparatory courses into college courses (p.9).

From 1930 to 1939, remedial reading programs were emphasized in the public schools, and by the end of the decade, colleges and universities were establishing remedial reading clinics. New York University's Reading Laboratory began in 1936, Harvard instituted a remedial reading course for its students in 1938, and Francis Triggs founded a reading clinic at the University of Minnesota in the same year. (I suspect that one impetus for the development of college reading services came from the introduction of general survey courses in 1929, when courses that required lengthy reading assignments, like "Introduction to Contemporary Civilization," became popular.)

During the depression there was another surge in college enrollment, since jobs for high school graduates were scarce. In times of economic stress, the brighter and most capable high school students can get jobs, while the others—such as those from farm families in the Dust Bowl and in other distressed areas—go to college—albeit on a shoe string. One of my friends from the midwest who attended college during the depression lived on less than eight dollars a week. You'll not be surprised to learn that he was very, very thin when he started graduate school.

In 1932 the University of Minnesota established a separate General College in response to the state legislature's mandate that the university accept all state high school graduates. (During the 1930s, public school graduates who realized they were unprepared for state college sometimes took a postgraduate year in high school or, if their families were wealthier, enrolled in a private preparatory school for a year or more before entering college, as wealthier students still do.)

From 1941 to 1945, during World War II, colleges reduced the time required to complete college degrees by shortening courses and adding intensive summer sessions. (My first husband completed medical school in three years during the war.) Frank Robinson of Ohio State University developed his SQ3R method for reading textbooks to help servicemen learn more quickly and effectively in their condensed, eight-week college courses. Later SQ3R became the basic method taught almost universally in college reading and study skills courses.

## FROM 1944 TO 1955

After the war, the G.I. Bill enabled millions of former servicemen to attend college regardless of their previous preparation. Government funding allowed colleges to establish veterans' guidance centers, reading and study skills programs, and tutoring services. As the number of veterans attending college declined, these services became institutionalized and were offered to all students.

The development and growth of community col-

leges in the thirties and forties made it possible for state universities to set higher admission standards, as two-year colleges served as preparation for the last two years of college, as well as serving many other purposes. Each state also had teachers' colleges, many with two year programs, so there were a number of options for post-secondary education other than universities. During the 1950s, college programs continued to expand, and community colleges grew tremendously in number and size. Following the launching of Sputnik, education in general, and colleges in particular, received federal funding for improving mathematics and science courses. These programs emphasized the identification and training of the most intellectually able students. (Having tried repeatedly to get funding for training marginally qualified college students during that period, I can attest to the number of federal agencies that turned a deaf ear to programs that did not involve the upper 10 percent of the college population.)

But despite the emphasis on quality, college students of the 1950s had similar difficulties. Experts complained about the reading problems of college students in the late fifties in language almost as strong as that used today, describing the alarming prevalence of reading and study skills deficiencies of college freshmen, and citing statistics that two-thirds of entering classes lacked the reading skills necessary for college success. The poor quality of high school preparation was blamed for college students' deficiencies, and many colleges offered reading and study skills programs to help students succeed.

These few facts suggest the complex and difficult development of U.S. higher institutions and point to some of the reasons for their tremendous variability in purpose and clientele. Educational historians have attributed the choppy history of developmental education to various causes. The egalitarian thrust of American education through the decades is one—although there is evidence that after institutions become established, whether they are agricultural, vocational, or technical, they tend to pull up the ladder and attempt to become elitist in choosing students and in the programs they offer. Other writers have noted the importance of developmental education to institutional financing—when the economy is tight, students are admitted who can pay, and sometimes course titles are changed, elevating what has been considered a remedial course to the regular curriculum. There are also indications that, because developmental courses are considered an unwelcome stepchild to the main business of college teaching, faculty members tend to view them as a short-term expediency—always hoping that "Next year's students will be better and not need all this costly help." Whenever the opportunity arises and they attract enough well-prepared students, colleges drop preparatory or developmental courses.

From the mid 1960s to 1980, colleges, aided by government funding and pressured by the politics of the day, opened their doors to low-income groups, especially minorities and women who were underrepresented in academic and other professional careers. Open-admissions policies were adopted by most two-year and many four-year colleges. Prestigious universities enlarged their special-admissions programs to include educationally disadvantaged minority students. In 1964 the federally funded Upward Bound program started, marking the beginning of efforts to identify large numbers of disadvantaged minority students in high school and encourage them to prepare for college. Other federal programs soon followed.

By 1970, one half million students—one seventh of those enrolled in U.S. colleges—came from poverty backgrounds. Open-admissions policies were implemented in the large City University of New York (CUNY) system, a program that lasted six years. Throughout the country, colleges instituted learning centers and tutorial programs to aid the disadvantaged minority students. Although accepting underprepared students was not a new idea in higher education, the large numbers of disadvantaged minorities who attended college in the 60s and 70s overwhelmed many campuses, where they were often welcomed by faculty as if they were hordes of barbarians attacking urban Rome. They represented people from a different social status, with different values, and different cultural backgrounds from the traditional college student. Colleges, albeit reluctantly, tried to prepare these students for traditional courses, while campuses faced the turmoil of students protesting the Vietnamese War, demonstrating for civil rights, and also demanding that women be given equal opportunity in higher education.

## THE CHAOS OF OPEN-ADMISSION

Despite the fact that colleges have always had some underprepared students and found ways to deal with them—whether they were prospective football players, band members, minorities, or scions of wealthy alumni—those who drafted the designs for open-admission colleges in the 60s and 70s managed to ignore this fact. Although some colleges embraced open admissions policies earlier, the rapid and traumatic experiences of the City University of New York (CUNY) were the most controversial, best publicized, and most heavily documented. [Note: For specific references on CUNY's experiences, see the 1978 edition of this book.]

When CUNY implemented open admissions policies in 1970, the system's ten senior colleges and eight two-year colleges, all CUNY colleges, were required to accept students with poor high school records. Many of these students were deficient in English, mathematics, and other basic skills. Open-admissions students traumatized both faculty members and their traditionally prepared student peers. Faculty members in four-year colleges, where open-admissions students were fewer, were generally indifferent to their needs or uncooperative, although some tried very hard to teach them. Even in community colleges with a decade or more of experience with disadvantaged students, there were serious problems because faculty members found the massive numbers of unprepared students enrolled in their classes unmanageable.

Although each institution developed its own methods for dealing with the educational deficiencies of the low-achieving enrollees, ranging from additional remedial work and tutoring within the department to assigning advisers to each individual student, some colleges treated open-admissions students like their regular students and assumed that they would seek help from faculty members when they needed it. They didn't.

In brief, the initial year of open admissions at CUNY showed clearly that all the programs that depended on large-scale faculty support and involvement failed. During the second year, all colleges implemented remedial programs, but funding was inadequate. Even if more funds had been available, the faculty did not know what might work with these students.

Follow-up studies of the CUNY freshmen who entered during the first year of open admissions reported that there was no evidence that the large-scale admission of low-achieving and economically disadvantaged students had produced either significant changes in the instructional methodology used or higher retention and success rates of students than would have been predicted from high school records and socioeconomic backgrounds. No relation between the number of required noncredit remedial courses offered to low-achieving students and their persistence was found—in fact, a negative relation was suggested. Over the four-year period studied, retention of all students—from high, average, or low socioeconomic backgrounds—declined at a small but significant rate. Colleges that had longer experience with underprepared students fared no better in retaining them; indeed, they did less well than selective colleges with no experience.

Every four-year college graduated or retained a higher proportion of its lower-achieving students than any community college did. To be sure, selective colleges did not have to deal with the massive numbers of open-admissions students, but there may be other reasons for the difference in graduation/retention rates. Perhaps the underprepared students who entered senior colleges were more highly motivated than those who entered junior colleges, or perhaps the expectations of the faculty in four-year colleges that students will complete college made a difference, or perhaps the student support services were better and more readily accepted by students. [Author's note: Later studies have consistently shown that underprepared minority students who enter selective four-year colleges or research universities have a significantly higher success rate than those who attend two-year colleges (Kulik & Kulik, 1991, Boylan & Bonham, 1992).]

Furthermore, the open-admissions efforts, particularly those at CUNY, were underfunded and considered tainted by expediency. Although this may be true, CUNY's experiences illustrate the problems most colleges faced, though CUNY's efforts and failures were on a grander scale.

In the 60s and 70s the greatest burden to provide access to underrepresented groups fell on our most selective institutions. They had always admitted underprepared students in small numbers, but not in the quantities that they accepted in the sixties. Black scholar Thomas Sowell (1974) points out that the special pressures that governmental affirmative-action demands placed on prestigious institutions created a demand for black students at precisely those institutions least fitted to the students' educational preparation—that is, at research-oriented universities more concerned with filling their quotas, or "doing their part," than with seeing that the students were appropriately prepared and interested in their programs. The mismatch between students and colleges, as Sowell describes it, worsened when prestigious institutions were convinced that they should adapt to serve students who did not meet their highly specialized requirements, and the possibility of sending black students to institutions whose normal standards they could meet was almost totally ignored (Sowell, 1974). Even worse, by government edict, prestigious colleges established special programs to admit black students who could not meet the colleges' normal standards: "Those institutions which most rapidly increased their enrollments were those in which the great majority of white Americans could not qualify" (1974, p. 180). In fact, regulations for the Educational Opportunity Program (EOP) and other programs specified that the students selected should have substandard academic performance as well as lower socioeconomic status. Sowell reports that black students themselves have said they are afraid to perform at their best in high school for fear of reducing their chances of getting the financial aid they need to go to college.

The question of whether black and other minority students received covertly given special treatment at selective white institutions is still controversial. Sowell (1974, p. 184) reports:

*"As for the prevalence of dishonest and clandestine double standards, its nature is such that it can only be estimated impressionistically. My interviews with academics from coast to coast convince me that double standards are a fact of life on virtually every campus, but not necessarily in a majority of courses. This situation may in fact present the maximum academic danger to the black student: enough double standards to give him a false sense of security and enough rigid-standards courses to produce academic disasters."*

Other critics have questioned the assumption underlying the programs for disadvantaged students: that they need less of the verbal ability measured by the SAT than the more advantaged students do. The proponents of accepting high-risk students into selective institutions seemed to imply that students from the ghettos would study harder and more effectively than advantaged students, or perhaps would have developed more effective coping skills that would serve them well in college, despite their previous difficulties in elementary and secondary school. Selective colleges seemed to place more emphasis on the high-risk students' persisting in college than in their earning high grades, and some experts questioned this, pointing out that a degree from a usually selective college means little if it is not in one's preferred field, if it represents little real educational achievement, or if the recipients have falsely convinced themselves that they are stupid.

## THE DISMAL SAGA OF REMEDIAL INSTRUCTION IN THE 70s

One might think that the CUNY experience represented the rock bottom experience faced by open-admission colleges, but CUNY was not alone; other institutions failed too.

For example, in 1979, the National Institute of Education provided grants to the Arizona State University and the University of Texas at Austin to conduct in-depth, longitudinal investigations of literacy development activities in selected Arizona and Texas community colleges. The investigators examined literacy requirements in all courses, not just developmental courses, and although conducted independently, the major findings were "remarkably similar." Both studies reported that students were expected to read, write and figure more in remedial courses than they were ever required to do in regular college courses (Roueche & Comstock, 1981; Richardson & Martens, 1982). Students rarely purchased textbooks for the courses they were enrolled in because they knew that reading and comprehending material was not required in order to pass the course. Many instructors never mentioned the textbook name nor made reading assignments. Teachers taught in bits—providing the information students needed to pass tests in small chunks; students were tested on giving back information in fragmented, disjointed pieces of information acquired from instructors' one page handouts (Roueche & Roueche, 1993). Faculty were satisfied with the most minimal information skills—not at all like the skills that were typically required in normal college coursework.

Indeed, remedial programs were such obvious failures that college administrators deliberately avoided evaluating them, knowing that they would reflect adversely on their institutions. The problems were attributed to poorly prepared, disinterested teachers, lack of commitment on the part of the institution, and a general disregard for the importance of the programs. Non-traditional students were foisted upon colleges who did not want nor need them and whose main consideration was how fast they could get rid of them. Some programs were established deliberately as holding tanks—that is,

they enrolled weak students in sequences of remedial courses, effectively removing them from the classes regular faculty taught, and hoped that they would eventually give up. Indeed, colleges saw their role as trying to force these new students into the typical mold of the traditional college student as quickly as possible—an effort that was doomed to fail.

Has anything changed since the 70s? In the 70s critics maintained that traditional college remedial courses were failures and were not the best way to help underprepared students gain the skills and knowledge they needed. In fact, many experts agree that such courses are the worst possible way to deal with the needs of academically weak freshmen because they kill student motivation and are not cost-effective—indeed they are considered a waste of college funding and staff (Keimig, 1983).

The seventies probably marked the lowest point for developmental education and, despite the money and resources devoted, there were few successes. What research was done yielded discouraging results. Losak (1972) evaluated the remedial reading-writing courses at a community college by randomly assigning students to the remedial course or to a control group who took regular college courses. Although the remedial students made higher grades in their first semester when they were taking the easier remedial courses, he found that taking the remedial course made no difference on their subsequent GPAs or test scores. Richard C. Richardson, Jr. put it more strongly, when he said in an interview that remedial students in community colleges were better off taking the regular English course, flunking it, and retaking it, than taking the remedial program.

In surveying the results of studies on developmental education in the 70s, Grant and Hoeber (1978) asked the question, "Are basic skills programs working?" and answered it by stating that the basic skills teaching staff members are working very hard indeed, but there is no hard evidence that the programs are succeeding in accomplishing their mission.

Reasons for the perceived failures of remedial courses cited above are not hard to find. The decline in Scholastic Assessment Test (SAT) scores on college admission tests is another symptom of the changes that have occurred in higher education. SAT scores began to drop in 1960 and have not recouped their losses since. Although the causes for the drop are complex, the basic reason is that more students are finishing high school, and more, regardless of their type of high school preparation, are going to college. As educational opportunities for educationally disadvantaged and minority students have expanded, more have sought college and therefore taken the SAT. For example, one half of U.S. high school graduates in 1970 went on to college, compared with one quarter in 1960. Blacks and students from low-income families have traditionally averaged 100 points lower on the SAT than whites and students from high-income families—and the greatest increase in college attendance in the 1970s occurred among low-income black students. Moreover, the percentage of women in college showed steady increases, and white women's SAT scores in mathematics averaged 50 points lower than the scores of white males.

The Advisory Panel on the Scholastic Aptitude Score Decline, established by the College Entrance Examination Board, analyzed the reasons for the decline in average scores during two periods—the 1960s, when they found that three-fourths of the decline could be explained by the changing population who took the test, and the 1970s, when they concluded that the causes were more complex. Absenteeism slowed classroom progress and made for repeated lessons and student boredom. Other suspected causes include such factors as the declining reading level of high school textbooks, the drop in enrollment in high school English courses when students were permitted to substitute other courses for English, automatic promotion, grade inflation, the decline in homework assignments, and the increase in time spent watching television. Reexamining this question, researchers in 1995 point out that the failure of teachers to assign homework assignments is an even more important factor than the amount of television watched.

## THE 80S: AN ERA WHEN DEVELOPMENTAL EDUCATION CAME OUT OF THE CLOSET AND BEGAN TO CHANGE FOR THE BETTER

In the 80s and 90s, concern mounted about retaining students in college, for the declining birthrate boded ill for the institutions competing for young high school graduates to fill their classrooms. Since colleges were overbuilt in the 60s and 70s, college administrators heeded the warnings about the baby bust generation that were due in colleges in the 80s and conducted aggressive recruiting campaigns to attract students and keep their institutions viable. Community college recruiters were said to sweep the streets of cities and beat the bushes of rural areas to fill their classrooms. One result of this, of course, is the current diversity of students who attend college. But today's classrooms also are more reflective of the different kinds of people we find in society at large than were college classrooms a generation ago.

Prior to 1960, remedial programs in colleges were widespread, but they were generally small and not acknowledged by their institutions ("sub-rosa" was what administrators in elitist colleges called them when I surveyed colleges in the early 1970s), and there was minimal research on their populations, except for the occasional education doctoral student doing a dissertation, needing a captive audience to sample for studies on reading skills. However, since the 60s, studies on the characteristics of underprepared students and what instructional strategies work best with them has increased as developmental educators are slowly being accepted as academic professionals (Clowes, 1994).

Forewarned by population specialists that the low birthrate in the 60s and 70s meant fewer traditional eighteen year olds in the 80s and 90s, colleges changed their attitudes toward underprepared students. Administrators realized that they needed to recruit large numbers of non-traditional students to fill their classes. The open admission movement persisted. Many colleges had no choice but to open their doors if they were to survive. But this time placement tests were instituted, and administrators recognized the need to demonstrate that the students they accepted could improve and meet the institution's academic standards. Miami-Dade Community College implemented its "systems for success model" in the early 80s, stressing four points: 1) open-access had to be maintained; 2) if success were to be achieved, the college had to be much more directive; 3) the college had to be much more supportive to students; and finally 4) high academic standards had to be maintained (Roueche & Baker, 1987, p. 63).

In their book *From Access to Excellence*, Roueche and Baker (1987) describe how Robert McCabe, then president of Miami-Dade Community College, created an institutional climate that enabled students to succeed and supported the faculty in making drastic policy changes—e.g., prescribing that a

limited number of required courses must be completed by all students; admitting no students to the college after classes started; requiring that students who worked full-time be limited in the number of courses they could carry; and prescribing that student progress was continually monitored and that students understood what was expected of them by the college, among many other rules. The program was a success. Miami-Dade's entering students, who scored at the bottom of state institutions on skills placement tests as freshmen, held their own with students from local universities on the sophomore level post-tests.

Increasingly, studies today are showing that developmental programs can be effective in increasing student retention and graduation rates (Boylan & Bonham, 1992; Clowes, 1994; New Jersey Basic Skills Council Report, 1991). In fact, the New Jersey Board of Higher Education reported that community college students who completed remedial math courses remained longer in subsequent math courses than their peers who were not held for remediation (New Jersey Basic Skills Council Report, 1991).

Additionally, recent studies at research universities suggest that learning assistance efforts are increasing the retention and graduation rates for minority students. For example, UC Berkeley's attempts to admit and retain large numbers of affirmative action students to diversify the student body have paid off in significantly increasing the number of African-American, American Indian, and Chicano/Latino graduates. A six-year follow up showed that Berkeley graduated 27 percent more of these underrepresented groups than the national averages of other colleges (Robert & Thompson, 1994). The dramatic gains in retaining underrepresented minority groups were attributed to the summer bridge program, careful selection and training of faculty and group leaders, and the services of the Student Learning Center—including tutor training among other support services. However, the major factor underlying these efforts was the institution's commitment to educating and retaining minority students.

The Gateway Program at Rutgers University is credited with Rutgers' ability to retain nearly 90% of their freshmen for the second year. This program gives faculty in ten departments both the financial support and incentive to develop special courses to prepare students that satisfy the departmental criteria for regular, credited coursework (Kluepful & others, 1994).

Other successful approaches include freshman seminars—e.g., the University of South Carolina has succeeded in retaining more Afro-Americans than white freshmen for many years as a result of its version of John Gardner's Freshman Year program (Fidler & Godwin, 1994), summer transition programs like the one for engineers at the University of Virginia (Simmons, 1994), and Supplemental Instruction programs for high risk courses (Martin & Arendale, 1992), among many others.

Programs in some open-admission community colleges are showing positive results, despite the difficult task they face. Roueche and Roueche (1993) identified 12 community colleges judged as having outstanding programs. The features of successful programs were based on a survey of the student identification, orientation and involvement procedures, instructional strategies, policies and programs, and evaluation procedures. Represented in this study were A Starting Point, the Minority Transfer Program at De Anza College (CA), the Athletic Advising Program at William Rainey Harper College (IL), the Academic Information Monitoring System at

Highland Community College, the Basic Skills Testing Program at Illinois Central College, the Black/Hispanic Student Opportunity Program at Miami-Dade Community College (FL), the Freshman Seminar and Course Clusters Program at Middlesex Community College (MA), and the Advantage Program at North Lake College (TX).

Along with research results that affirm that students enrolled in developmental/remedial programs can succeed in college, the 1980s marked the emergence of professionalism and professional recognition of those who work in the field. The National Center for Developmental Education at Appalachian State University has sponsored research, conferences, and publishes two journals—*The Journal of Developmental Education* and *Review of Research in Developmental Education*. Two large professional associations, NADE (The National Association of Developmental Education) and CRLA (The College Reading and Learning Association), each sponsor regional and state meetings as well as national conferences. In addition, professional workers in the field have started other groups such as the National Tutor Association, Midwest College Learning Center Association, and others. Under the aegis of Division 16 of the American Personnel and Guidance Association, a set of standards and guidelines for learning assistance programs were developed and adopted by the Council for the Advancement of Standards (CAS). NADE (1994) has also published self-study standards and guidelines for tutoring programs, adjunct skills programs, developmental courses, and teaching and learning activities (see references).

These changes reflect the fact that colleges are increasingly committed to educating and retaining students who do not meet traditional institutional standards, although the methods used and the program components differ very little from those used in the past. Summer bridge programs, all freshman orientation courses, and other strategies have been tried many times before. For example, The Freshman Experience Program is a fresh way of presenting traditional orientation courses that involves tutoring and counseling and skills development. Whereas, traditionally only graduate students and sometimes seniors were offered seminars, now freshmen seminars are prevalent. And there is one major difference between the old and the new: in today's successful programs, both the institutions and the faculty members are committed to empowering students and getting them involved in college life. And there seems to be a higher level of hope and expectation on the part of both students and instructors that former programs lacked. Colleges have made systematic efforts to reduce the stigma associated with remedial work and to assure students that they can succeed—positions that reflect our knowledge of the vital importance of students' attitudes and emotions in making programs with at-risk students successful. Certainly problems still remain, such as the continued underrepresentation of African-American males in higher education, but we have come a long way.

## INTERNATIONAL ASPECTS OF DEVELOPMENTAL EDUCATION

To put the American efforts at affirmative action and open-admission into proper perspective, it is important to recognize that the United States is not alone in trying to provide higher education to a greater segment of its population. Almost all developed nations are making efforts to include underrepresented groups in their college and university programs, and even African countries are committed to bringing wider access to higher education to their people, although the hurdles are great in a continent where less than ten percent of the people attend post-secondary institutions. A recent publication, *Issues in Access to Higher Education*, Proceedings of the 1994 International Access Network Conference held at the University of Southern Maine, contains a series of thirty-five papers describing access efforts in countries including the U.S., India, Eastern and Central Europe, among others. (For information about this publication and the International Access Network (IAN), contact: Robert E. Lemclin, University of Southern Maine, 90 Falmouth St., Portland, ME 04103.)

These international efforts range from Australia's program to provide college access and equity for aboriginal and Torres Islander groups, through access programs in Great Britain, France and Germany, to efforts by the Netherlands aimed at providing college access to ethnic minorities comprised mostly of immigrants and refugee people of color (who comprise ten percent of the population in large cities). Most countries also have programs to increase the opportunities for women to enter science and engineering careers.

Another article describes Russia's attempt to maintain free education while keeping competitive exams in an economy suffering under conditions of destabilization and hyperinflation. One example: Udmurt University in Izhevsk, Russia offers to admit students who pass entrance examinations and pay the university two and a half million rubles for education shares. (Note: At the present rate of 3,125 rubles = $1.00 U.S., that's not very much!) Each of the students who buys shares has a chance to get a free education if he/she qualifies by earning high grades in the freshman year. American readers will recognize many of the same problems that their institutions face in increasing college access to underrepresented groups, in defining their constituents, and in identifying the factors that make such programs successful as they read through these papers from other countries.

So affirmative action efforts are likely to endure in some form, not only in the United States but throughout the world, but these programs face major changes.

There have been other radical changes in the college environment as a result of the demographic changes in those who attend college. Ideas about political correctness have been accepted on most campuses, endangering the existence of campus humor magazines, and diverse student groups changed other college traditions. In 1976 I predicted, "Although today's Betty Coed is not as likely to be a grandmother as an eighteen-year-old, the day is fast approaching when grandma coed may be the norm." Well, today we do see grandmothers being chosen as homecoming queens, but perhaps the most radical change in perception of the college coed occurred in 1994, when New Mexico Highlands University chose as homecoming queen a 45-year-old graduate student who is wheel-chair bound because of rheumatoid arthritis, has impaired vision, and is a lesbian. She describes herself as the oldest, fattest, shortest competitor in the contest and the one with the highest GPA (4.0) and will no doubt be long remembered for her commitment to the motto that adults in college deserve to have fun too.

Today's many single-parent households have produced young male adults, now entering college, who grew up with few male role models. Their deference and dependency toward older males represent a new challenge to the male professorate.

Open admissions and other efforts to bring disadvantaged students into higher education have led to major changes in U.S. higher education, including declines in scores on traditional measures of college aptitude, and grade inflation, which, at the time, seemed peripheral to the major social changes and student protests that brought violence into the halls of ivy. A generation before, the G.I. Bill had changed U.S. higher education by enabling massive numbers of young men from all walks of life to participate in higher education. But the veterans had returned to classes peacefully, while the masses of disadvantaged and minority students entered at a time when campuses were erupting and emotions were high. In the long run, the events of the 1960s and early 1970s may be viewed as having a greater impact on higher education in this country than any other event. College entrance, except in the most prestigious institutions, is not as competitive today, and many small private colleges are actively seeking students—any students—to fill their classrooms. They also are awakening to the realization that admitting students is not enough. Institutions must be committed to providing the services and programs students need and to the expectation that students can learn and succeed. Or as one recent conference on diversity describes it, colleges are beginning to focus on students as assets rather than complaining about their limitations. Professors who see their role as teaching only to the top 10 percent of their classes are currently considered out-of-touch with reality.

Furthermore, administrators and faculty members are recognizing the importance of the freshman year in their efforts to attract and retain students. As Tinto writes, "Institutions should front-load their efforts in behalf of student retention" (Tinto, 1993, p. 152), and they are doing just that through Freshman Year Programs and many other efforts.

By the mid-nineties, fiscal constraints forced some smaller colleges to close and jeopardized developmental education programs and their staff's salaries in both public and private institutions. In some districts, budget cuts have forced community colleges to abandon placement testing, advising and counseling services, and cut back on remedial courses. Hopefully, this situation is temporary, and vital services will be restored so that the gains we've made in the 90s won't be erased. What seems inevitable is that programs will have fewer staff members and fewer resources and will be expected to teach more students.

## Conclusion

Of the many changes that have occurred in American higher education since 1960, four complex and interrelated events are probably the most important: open admissions, federal policies mandating increased access to higher education for educationally disadvantaged students and women, opportunities for the physically challenged, increasing numbers of older college students, declining basic skills of college students (as exemplified by the lower scores on college admissions tests) coupled with state mandated tests, mandated remedial courses, and grade inflation. For example, the average age of college students changed dramatically between 1980, when 25% were age 25 or older, and 1990, when over 40% were over age 25. This change may be the result of two factors: 1) more adults are returning to college and 2) college students in general are taking longer to complete degrees as a result of the continually increasing cost of attending college. Also we find that fewer entering freshmen rank in the top of their high school graduating classes.

In the 90s, colleges continued to recruit adult students, especially women, to fill classrooms depleted when the lower birth rate of the 70s resulted in fewer college-age students in the 80s and 90s. Today it is harder to encourage adults to return to college, and current recruitment efforts in some parts of the country may not be enough to save many small colleges from bankruptcy, particularly if federal and state scholarship funding continues to decline.

Out of the failures of the 1960s and 1970s, successful programs emerged in the 80s. In this book we will examine the concepts and strategies that have proved successful and discuss ideas that will help us avoid past mistakes and plan more realistic programs in the future.

At-risk students will not disappear from college classrooms, nor can most colleges expect to restrict admissions to the best prepared—there are too few of them to fill the classes of the many colleges established for the baby-boomers. Furthermore, average students' skills have deteriorated also. However, today the pools of prospective students vary with the different geographic regions of the country. In the northeast, there are too few students available for the number of college places. As a result, private colleges who have priced themselves above the level that middle-class families can afford are now facing severe financial problems, and even formerly prestigious schools are having trouble filling freshmen classes as lower priced public universities attract larger numbers of the best-prepared students. This has engendered increased pressure to restrict developmental courses to community colleges, as students entering four-year colleges have less need for the services.

## Should Developmental Courses Be Relegated to the Two-Year Colleges?

Since the early 80s, legislators and college presidents have placed great pressure on state universities to divest themselves of developmental courses and require students needing additional skills work to attend community colleges before matriculating in four-year institutions. Some say this will not work because research studies spanning many years have shown that developmental programs in four-year colleges and universities are more successful than those in two-year colleges. It is true, of course, that community colleges usually lack the extensive support services and other resources that developmental students need and that they enroll many more students who need intensive help. However, Boylan (1995) argues that moving all developmental courses to the two-year colleges in order to raise standards in public four-year colleges would exacerbate rather than improve the problem. First, unless resources currently assigned to universities for developmental education were reassigned to two-year colleges (a most unlikely event), two-year colleges could not handle the load and would be forced to exclude many students who need and can profit from developmental education. Furthermore, two-year colleges can't adequately prepare both the neediest students and those who are getting ready to go on to universities. Thus, fewer potentially successful students would survive. Some would counter these arguments by declaring that two-year colleges are quite capable of preparing students for upper-division courses, as that is what their transfer programs have been doing for generations.

What Boylan and others are overlooking is that better prepared students are beginning to enter college, a result of the education reforms in high school curricula following the publication of "A Nation at Risk," and public universities are planning to reduce their developmental/remedial courses significantly as they find that there are sufficient "college ready" freshmen to fill their mainstream courses.

## THE RETURN OF THE "COLLEGE-READY" STUDENT

There is increasing evidence that freshmen who entered public universities in 1995 were better prepared than their predecessors, an outcome that had been forecast in studies by the Rand Corporation and ETS. Certainly, the gap between the test scores of minority and white students had narrowed, and record numbers of college-ready students sought college admission in states where the population of 18 year olds was burgeoning. For example, new students entering the CUNY colleges in the fall of 1995 were reported to be the best prepared freshmen admitted in twenty years, based on their high school transcripts. More had completed four years of English and more had college preparatory mathematics. In addition, they were described as "knowing how to learn," a result of higher standards for high school graduation and a program called the College Preparatory Initiative. Another result was that fewer were held for non-credit remedial courses; in fact, 2300 fewer CUNY students took remedial courses in 1995 than in 1994. Also, the fact that the CUNY system has recently increased its tuition may have discouraged some poorer and possibly less prepared students from attending college.

Universities in sunbelt states also reported accepting more "college-ready" freshmen. The University of Georgia admitted the best qualified freshmen class in its history in terms of high school preparation and test scores; the University of Florida was swamped with applicants and turned away students who would have been readily accepted in previous years. The enthusiasm for higher academic standards was even felt in states such as Nebraska and Massachusetts, where universities admitted almost all applicants. They have tightened their belts and raised entrance requirements despite the effects on reducing freshmen classes.

Regardless of how selective and restrictive colleges become, many students will continue to need learning assistance since the gap between high school and college learning strategies remains a formidable hurdle for even the best prepared students. Our commitment to educate disadvantaged and ethnic groups that are underrepresented in academe and society's ever increasing need for better educated workers will ensure that developmental programs will continue, although the number of students they serve may be smaller and there may be fewer programs offered at four-year schools. Rising admission standards are often accompanied by tougher grading standards, inducing anxieties that motivate students to seek learning assistance. Better prepared students know they need better learning skills because graduating from college is not automatic. It is imperative that we develop and maintain quality programs that insure that students master the skills necessary for success.

# CHAPTER 2

## DIAGNOSING THE BASIC SKILLS DIFFICULTIES OF STUDENTS

Colleges and universities differ widely in the procedures they use to determine which students will take basic skills programs. Programs may be for credit or noncredit; enrollment may be required or voluntary. Specific policies reflect the philosophy and standards of the college and the number of students accepted who are considered underprepared.

Some colleges do not accept obviously underprepared students, carefully monitoring the qualifications of the students they admit. At the same time, they offer special reading and study skills programs, tutoring, and other academic support services for students who turn out to have difficulties or for targeted groups such as athletes, underrepresented minorities, and so on.

Some selective institutions limit admission of underprepared students to a fixed number or percentage within each entering class, while holding higher admissions standards for the majority of their freshmen. These "special admits" may be (1) required to take remedial courses with or without credit, (2) accepted into regular courses and given intensive tutoring and other help, and then, if they fail to make progress, be required to take remedial courses, (3) permitted, required, or encouraged to take reduced course loads, or (4) required or encouraged to attend special summer bridge programs; or some combination of these policies may be applied.

Public open-admission colleges, by law, must accept every student who applies, although they are not usually required to provide any course that students may want or need. Most open-admissions colleges require weak students to take basic skills courses, but some allow students to enroll in regular courses whether or not they have the prerequisite skills. However, even in open-admission colleges, students are usually required to have completed prerequisite courses or passed skills tests to enroll in traditional college courses like English. If students insist on taking a course that they are considered unprepared for, they may be allowed in if they sign a waiver indicating that they have been advised against enrolling but choose to go ahead anyway.

### SKILLS COURSES—REQUIRED OR VOLUNTARY?

The question whether basic skills courses should be required or voluntary has been debated by college educators for many years. In the past, educators argued that students would only succeed if the skills programs were voluntary—that forcing students to take a course did not work. Others insisted that if colleges admit students who have deficient skills, they should require skills improvement courses for the weakest students. Still others took a middle position, arguing that it was a mistake to assume that all beginning freshmen have the insight to know that they need a skills course, but that if they objected, they should be allowed to drop it.

In practice today, some colleges require skills courses, some counsel certain students to take them, and others open them to all students as electives. Each policy has advantages and disadvantages.

## PROS AND CONS OF REQUIRED SKILLS COURSES

Most four-year college programs today have mandatory reading, writing, and/or math courses for entering freshmen who fail college skills placement tests. Mandatory skills courses have a number of advantages. First, identifying and placing students with skills deficiencies is automatic. A formula of grades and test scores or a cutoff score is programmed into a computer, and all students scoring in the designated category are given enrollment cards for the skills courses. Compulsory enrollment in skills courses is cheap, simple for administrators and advisers, and efficient.

If skills classes are filled by the registrar under a college requirement, skills instructors need not worry about attracting students to their classes, for this is done automatically. Besides, their task is easier in that they teach groups of students who are relatively homogeneous in ability. Many instructors prefer teaching this type of class. However, students who are merely sectioned into remedial skills courses without being counseled may be very resentful.

Many faculty members and administrators view requiring basic skills courses as fairer and more objective than other methods of selecting students into these courses, because the placement criteria (test scores and prior grades) are specific and measurable. In addition, administrators can be certain that those students who need help the most will get it, for underprepared students may not volunteer to take basic skills courses. Another advantage is that compulsory basic skills courses protect the faculty members, who teach regular freshman courses, from having to teach underprepared students and deal with their needs in the same classes as better-prepared students, and certainly it reduces the needs of students taking advanced courses.

Roueche & Roueche (1994) include mandatory testing and placement in appropriate skills courses on their list of factors of major importance in successful developmental programs. (For a discussion of the rationale for mandatory assessment and placement, see Morante, E. A. (Spring 1982). "Selecting tests and placing students." *Journal of Developmental Education*, *13*(2), 1-6. Also reprinted in Maxwell, M. (Ed.). 1994. *From access to success*. H&H Publishing Co: Clearwater, FL.)

Mandating enrollment in basic skills courses has an equal number of disadvantages. Since requiring remedial courses has been the most common placement policy, and since many have been viewed as failures, one should carefully consider the problems and plan strategies to avoid them if one decides to require these courses.

First, the psychological effects of being required to take a remedial course and being stigmatized as dumb are shared by both students and instructors. As Felton and Biggs (1977, p. 7) point out, "Remediation, as it is sometimes practiced, may help the student to label herself as stupid, and this may in turn affect the teacher's attitudinal responses to that individual. This means that underachievement often is caused directly in the classroom and in the 'helping' provided there. This is a painful irony." Requiring students to take special, unchallenging courses is equivalent to creating an intellectual ghetto for a subgroup of students and instructors. Second, the task of instruction is made more difficult, in that instructors must bear the responsibility for motivating unmotivated and often quite resistant students. As a result, instructors must fight against developing a self-fulfilling, pessimistic prognosis for their students.

Third, without realistic role models to show what the regular college students are like, remedial students may not make the progress they should. Their instructors too may lose perspective of the skills and intellectual knowledge that the institution requires of its students, because they are teaching only the lowest. As a result, they may dilute their course material to make it easier and more palatable to their resisting students, thus effectively pushing the students further from their goals.

Fourth, segregating students into basic skills courses, particularly when those courses do not fit into a clear sequence of advanced courses, may lead to a proliferation of remedial courses. Skills instructors identify their weakest students and request that those students be assigned to a separate, simpler, more intensive class. As Malvina Reynolds' song goes, "Hit bottom? Oh, no! There's a bottom below." So the skills instructor focuses on the bottom group and finds more and more layers of deficiency. Soon the writing instructors are offering a series of courses from essay writing down to paragraph writing down to sentence writing. The reading instructors begin to specialize, too. Starting with a course in improving speed and comprehension, they add courses in basic comprehension skills, vocabulary building, word-attack skills, and finally basic phonics and decoding skills. The inevitable result—and it has occurred in some community colleges—is that students are required to take as many as fifteen noncredit remedial courses before being permitted to register for any regular college classes.

They are, in effect, majoring in being remediated. Invariably, this results in high student attrition.

Proliferation of remedial courses usually occurs when the faculty rigidly adheres to traditional curriculums and standards, while the institution admits large numbers of unqualified students. The basic skills instructors, who cannot hope to advance to teaching higher-level courses, respond by specializing. They plan new, preliminary courses in order to build a power base and compete with other departments for student full-time equivalent (FTE) and funding. Thrust into a role in which they must teach students who cannot expect to qualify for the institution's normal programs, they too play the traditional academic game—that is, identify a topic, label it, and expand it into a full-term course. Then they demand that students get credit for taking it. (If this trend continues, I expect that there will come a time when college students will get credit for three separate courses—one in prefixes, another in suffixes, and a third in roots.) By fragmenting and oversimplifying skills courses, instructors are actually pushing students further from their college goals intellectually, as well as setting up imposing time hurdles. For the weakest students—those who, even if they persist through the remedial series, will never be able to compete in traditional programs—the effect is tragic. Unfortunately, those who offer such courses do not see it that way. They are convinced that they are meeting their students' needs. To be sure, there are fewer practitioners with these beliefs today than there were 20 years ago, however there remain some programs that are so insular and so cut-off from the rest of the curriculum that they continue to abuse the system.

In summary, compulsory programs, by definition, permit students no options. Some students may not be motivated to improve their basic skills. In teaching mandatory basic skills courses, instructors play a dual role, that of motivating students as well as teaching them. Counselors can provide some assistance to resistant students but are usually placed in a reactive position—that is, they must explain and justify the rationale for the courses—and students may feel that their individual needs are not being considered. Required remedial courses protect the faculty from the need to modify its courses and curriculums, but if a college has large numbers of underprepared students, the remedial programs will proliferate. The remedial/developmental skills department grows in size, but few students are able to make the transition from remedial work to regular majors. What makes the difference is whether the students admitted have skills close to those demanded by the professors for their specialties and whether the remedial courses are closely articulated with advanced courses.

In light of the above problems, policymakers who are deciding whether to implement required remedial courses should consider their decision very carefully. Another book that sheds light on this decision is Ruth Keimig's (1983), *Raising Academic Standards: A Guide to Learning Improvement,* Association for the Study of Higher Education, Washingon D.C. Keimig argues that isolated remedial courses are the poorest way to improve grades and retention in underprepared students and the least cost-effective. This means that if you offer separate remedial/developmental courses, great care must be given to integrate these into your mainstream curriculum.

Results from the EXXON Study, where a national sample of developmental college students were followed for 5 years, indicated that voluntary programs were more successful than required studies in retaining students (Boylan and Bonham, 1992).

However, this may result from the fact that academically weak students, when given a choice, seldom volunteer for skills courses, or it may reflect the fact that volunteers are more realistic about their own abilities and more highly motivated to complete college courses.

## PLACEMENT THROUGH COUNSELOR RECOMMENDATION

Another approach to identifying students for placement in basic skills courses involves counseling. This technique might be viewed as midway between compulsory and voluntary enrollment. A voluntary program assumes that students are motivated to improve their skills and will choose to do so. To choose wisely, however, students need solid information about their skills and how they compare with the demands and expectations of the faculty. The counseling approaches address this problem.

One method is to have advisers identify students with weak high school backgrounds and low entrance-test scores, and encourage them to enroll in basic skills courses. Encouragement may range in intensity from a gentle nudge to a strong shove. I recall how advisers in a small, selective, liberal arts college used to do it. Entering freshmen were required to take a standardized reading test, and their percentile ranks were recorded on their permanent grade records. It took little urging from advisers to persuade students with low scores to volunteer for the reading-improvement course, for they were told that if they completed the reading improvement program they could retake the test and raise their scores. Since these students aspired to attend graduate and professional schools, they were highly motivated to get those low scores off their transcripts so as not to jeopardize their chances for getting into advanced programs.

Open-admission colleges, where basic skills courses are not mandated, report that only about ten percent of those who need them voluntarily enroll in the courses. This can pose major problems for instructors teaching courses where reading, mathematics, and/or writing skills are essential for learning the subject.

In some colleges, advisers refer students with low entrance test scores or weak high school grades to the testing service for diagnostic testing. A learning-skills counselor interprets the results of this testing and encourages those who need skills help to enroll in the program, but the student has the option of refusing. Most counseling and learning-support programs that offer diagnostic testing encourage students to come in on their own for skills testing as well as accepting referrals from faculty members. The self-referred student who needs skills courses will be encouraged to enroll in the program.

SKILLS COURSES AS ELECTIVES

In a few colleges, the skills courses are open to any student who wishes to take them. Underprepared and even learning-disabled students are channeled into these programs. For example, in the comprehensive program at West Valley College (Saratoga, California), a reading course is offered as an elective to any student (Peterson and others, 1978). West Valley College, an open-admissions community college, does not require students to take entrance tests for admission. Students learn about the reading course through friends, advertising, counselors, advisers, faculty members, and other means. During the first two class meetings, students enrolled in the reading course are given reading tests and, on the basis of their scores, are divided into two sections. This is easily accomplished, as two sections of the course are scheduled each hour of the school day in adjoining classrooms. Instructors use different criteria to assess the progress of the high- and low-scoring sections.

The advantages of mainstreaming are that it ensures that students enrolling in the class are motivated and it minimizes the remedial stigma. Instructor morale is higher too, reflecting the level of motivation of the students. A disadvantage is that the program may not reach all students who need it. Without entrance tests, there is no systematic way to determine how many students avoid the class, but as classes fill regularly, one can conclude that the program is popular with students.

Since instructors offering elective skills courses must compete with those offering other kinds of courses, their success in attracting students depends on having a strong public relations program to convince both students and faculty of the value of their courses. In addition, a successful course must provide ancillary services for the weakest students—diagnostic services, counseling, and individualized intensive practice in a learning laboratory. The qualities of the staff, of course, are important in attracting students and in developing and maintaining the support of other faculty members. If markedly deviant students, such as those with severe learning disabilities, are enrolled in the course, then flexible procedures that permit students to repeat the course are needed. To summarize, a successful elective basic skills course must be part of a comprehensive, well-coordinated program of student services.

OTHER WAYS TO ORGANIZE AND PRESENT BASIC SKILLS SERVICES

Basic skills may be presented to students as part of their regular courses, as by incorporating reading and study skills units into freshman English or requiring students in a course to complete learning modules on particular skills in a learning center as part of their assigned work. Adjunct skills or Supplemental Instruction classes—programs, generally noncredit, that parallel the work in a given subject and focus on the skills needed throughout the term—are another way of ensuring that students learn needed skills. (See Chapter 6 for descriptions of adjunct skills courses and Supplemental Instruction.) These techniques may require special skills of the faculty, or at least a willingness to refer students to support services, but they have the advantage of relating basic skills to what students consider real learning—that is, to the content of regular college courses.

## Summer Bridge Programs

Special summer bridge programs are another way of organizing basic skills and other support services for underprepared students and are widely used by both undergraduate and graduate institutions. Entering students with weak academic backgrounds are identified before enrolling in college and encouraged to attend a special summer school session. Most summer bridge programs include tutoring, counseling, advising, skills programs, and regular academic courses. If students are required to attend a summer session in order to qualify for fall admission, the number of applications for admission and enrollments of underprepared students will drop sharply. (In programs I have observed where summer attendance was mandatory, only about half of those who applied for admission attended the summer session.) Special programs for disadvantaged students attending graduate and professional schools usually do not show reduced enrollments in a summer bridge program, but these students tend to be very highly motivated. In undergraduate programs, a higher percentage of students will attend the summer session if

scholarships and financial aid are included and if some credit is offered.

One advantage of summer bridge programs is that they give students an opportunity to test out college courses and receive intensive skills help at the same time. Further, they offer students an opportunity to adjust to college at a time when the pace is less hectic. Some argue that summer programs are advantageous to underprepared students because they enable them to start at a slower pace. I disagree, because most summer courses are condensed into intensive six- or eight-week sessions, in which students must cover a full semester's worth of work in a shorter time. At any rate, summer-session enrollment is much lighter at most colleges and universities than during the academic year, so bridge students can be taught in smaller classes where they find the atmosphere less competitive than in the fall and spring terms.

Another advantage of summer bridge programs is that they employ the skills staff in the summer, when there is otherwise very little demand for its services. It also enables the institution to hire additional instructors for the summer only, as well as insuring that dormitory space is available.

On the negative side, summer bridge programs can be expensive, particularly when they offer scholarships, personal counseling, tutoring, skills assistance, and instruction in regular academic subjects. Whether this expense is an important consideration to a college depends on the reasons for the program and the functions it fulfills. If a large number of freshmen fail or drop out of the institution at the end of every fall term, then a summer bridge program designed to prevent attrition may be viewed by the administration as cost-effective. Even if the program only screens out those students who would leave college anyway, this can cut many costs—for instance, the cost of dormitory rooms that fill in the fall and are half-filled in the spring or the cost of hiring instructors by the year for freshman courses who have few courses to teach in the spring. If a college is mandated by the federal government to accept larger numbers of minority students, summer bridge programs are used to attract them and improve their skills.

However, there is little evidence that summer bridge programs are any more effective than programs offered during the academic year. Indeed, they may generate special problems for the students who attend them. As an example, one selective private university, which recruited minority students from Harlem ghettos, abandoned its special summer programs for EOP students when it discovered the culture shock these students experienced when they returned to college in the fall. Although the summer bridge program offered a full range of services, only disadvantaged students (EOP and Upward Bound) enrolled in campus courses during the summer session. When the regular student body returned in the fall, the small group of minority students found themselves like a few peas in a bushel of apples. Outnumbered and outdistanced in background by their peers, many of the disadvantaged students became discouraged and dropped out of college.

Attending summer school drains students' energies and financial resources, even when scholarships are given. Conscientious, underprepared students invest a tremendous amount of energy and time in succeeding in the summer program. When, after a few weeks' vacation, they enroll again in more rigorous, competitive fall classes, they may be tempted to relax and enjoy the social and other extracurricular activities the college offers, with the result being that they do not study, and they make low grades or fail.

In other words, if you are planning a summer bridge program, be sure to extend it to the other side of the river and continue your services in the fall or else students will drop off the end of the bridge.

(For an example of a successful summer bridge program, see Robert, E. R., & Thompson, G. (Spring 1994). Learning assistance and the success of underprepared students at Berkeley. *Journal of Developmental Education*, *17*(3), 4-15.)

## REDUCED-COURSE-LOAD PROGRAMS

An alternative—or an adjunct—to summer bridge programs is to permit underprepared students to take a lighter course load than regular students. Study units—ungraded credits that do not count toward graduation—are given for participation in basic skills programs so that the student may qualify for financial aid or veterans' benefits. Reduced course-load programs may be required or voluntary. If students are tested and counseled and work out contracts with their counselors or advisers that specify the skills courses and/or other activities they will complete, this type of program can be beneficial. Since students with poor preparation for college generally take longer to complete degrees, if they graduate at all, building a longer time span into their college plans seems realistic. Some colleges call these programs "extended degree programs" or "ninth semesters."

## THE FRESHMAN YEAR PROGRAM

### ALL FRESHMEN SKILLS COURSES

Some highly selective colleges, as well as many open-admissions colleges, require that all freshmen take basic skills courses such as composition, reading and study skills, and general mathematics and do not differentiate sections as remedial. A small number of outstanding students may be exempted from this requirement, but the rest of the freshmen are held for the course. High-risk freshmen are enrolled in the same classes as better-prepared students. Special services such as study skills specialists, tutors, and learning laboratories are available for students who need or want to use them. The Freshman Year Experience, promoted by the University of South Carolina, has rejuvenated freshman orientation courses, and they are currently popular in both two and four-year institutions.

One advantage of the all-freshman skills course is that it lacks the stigma associated with separate remedial courses. As a result, underprepared students are not so hesitant and resistant about taking it. (Of course, some students resent taking any required course, and they will object to this one too, but they are usually few.) Instructors are less likely to water down or simplify the course, since a wide range of students are enrolled in it. It is therefore easier to keep the course requirements consistent with the level of the college's other freshman courses. A further advantage is that faculty and student morale can generally be maintained at a higher level, and students are less subject to instructors' negative expectations. Research suggests that freshman seminars encourage student bonding and increase retention.

A disadvantage is that there are limits to the number of students and the range of abilities that some teachers can handle effectively in a single classroom, so that this method requires better and more sophisticated instructors than when students are segregated by ability. Another disadvantage is that some students who need extra help will not use the services provided and may fail the course or receive grades of incomplete and need to repeat it.

Of course, many other factors are involved, and some colleges have found that retention of underprepared students is higher when they are placed in regular courses than when they are segregated into separate remedial programs.

It should be obvious that an all-freshmen skills course in which a handful of nonreaders are registered amidst a group of students who read at the thirteenth-grade level or higher will not help the nonreaders and may drive the instructor up the wall. If a selective institution must admit students with very low skills, then special programs and curriculums for them are needed, not mainstreaming. Since the present accuracy of our best predictors of college grades are far from perfect, enrolling students who may not need the course or who can quickly improve their skills in a full term course may be a waste of students' time, the institution's time, and the resources of the college.

## SKILLS COURSES—CREDIT OR NONCREDIT?

Another often-debated issue about basic skills courses is whether credit should be given. The issue is still argued but should be moot because if students do not receive credit for skills courses, they will not qualify for financial aid as full-time students. Experts argue that disadvantaged students need the immediate and tangible reward of credit, and skills specialists insist that without credit, academically weak students will not attend classes (Cross (1976), Roueche & Snow (1977)). On the other hand, faculty members, administrators and politicians maintain that educationally disadvantaged students are being shortchanged when they are awarded credit toward graduation for skills training they should have had in high school or earlier, for they can't fulfill the breadth requirements or take as many courses in their majors as other students.

The reason most often cited for an institution's not awarding credit for skills courses is that the faculty feels that giving credit for remedial courses would lower standards. Although this attitude among the faculty may indeed play a part, the major determinants of whether a college awards credit for basic skills courses are more pragmatic: where the program gets its funding and who teaches the courses. If the basic skills instructors are paid by academic departments or developmental skills departments funded by monies earmarked for instruction, the college is apt to give credit. But if the skills courses are offered by nonacademic units, such as counseling centers, learning centers without departmental affiliations, and library services, the program generally does not carry credit. (There are exceptions, of course.)

Who teaches the course makes a difference. If a senior faculty member in a prestigious university becomes discouraged with the math preparation of his students and develops a course to re-educate students from the beginning up to college, he usually can get credit approved by his department. A lowly teaching associate who develops a precalculus course may find it much harder to secure departmental approval to offer the course for credit. However, if the topic is pursued long enough and students support credit for the course, the department may be persuaded to grant at least partial credit for the course.

The point is that credit courses in most institutions are taught by faculty members in academic departments, and if offering skills courses for credit will increase departmental student FTE (or, in private colleges, their tuition income), then it is to the department's advantage to offer courses for credit

developed and taught within their own departments. Programs staffed by counselors or learning-skills specialists are often budgeted from a different fund than academic departments and are less likely to secure approval to award credit for their courses.

Colleges must recognize the units which students take in order for them to qualify for financial aid, and that includes remedial courses. Whether the credit will count toward graduation or transfer to other institutions is another issue. A closer look at the way colleges grant credit for skills courses reveals some interesting facts. The credit awarded may be temporary, as for a precalculus course in a university. The student earns up to two credits for completing precalculus, but if he or she completes calculus, the credits for precalculus are removed. Similarly, in community colleges a reading course may carry credit that counts for an Associate of Arts degree but not for transfer to a senior college.

The student-as-consumer movement and pressures to admit and retain disadvantaged students led many institutions to award credit for skills courses that had traditionally been noncredit. Currently, faculty members seem more willing to grant credit for skills work as graduate enrollments shrink and as administrators scrutinize their workload measures and set arbitrary faculty/student ratios. Offering basic skills courses to freshmen is one way an education department, for instance, can attract enough students to offset the declining enrollments in graduate courses.

In recent years, even highly selective colleges have begun to offer partial credit for adjunct skills courses (UC Berkeley), Supplementary Instruction courses (California State University at Long Beach), and reading and study skills courses (West Point). But let me add that in prestigious schools it may take a very long time to get partial credit—at UC Berkeley the wait time was over 20 years. The rationale for credit was to encourage disadvantaged minority students to take supplemental courses and the combination of early identification, strong advising, and credit works.

In summary, the number of colleges and universities offering academic credit for basic skills courses has increased greatly since the mid sixties. However, such courses may carry partial credit—for instance, two credits may be awarded for a course requiring the same amount of time as a three-credit regular course—or disappearing credit, which is good for financial aid and veterans' benefits but not for graduation or transfer to a senior college or which is removed if the student completes a more advanced course.

Noncredit basic skills courses are often offered in large universities and in states where basic skills standards are mandated. Requiring remedial courses is an effective way to reduce the number of unqualified students who enroll in an institution and will increase freshman attrition. One university requires students who fail a qualifying mathematics test to take three sequential noncredit math courses in order to be eligible for general calculus. They must take algebra, solid geometry, and trigonometry, and the student who has a few gaps in one of the subjects must still complete all three. Only the most highly motivated do.

## Identifying Students with Weak Skills

Whether basic skills courses are required or voluntary, credit or noncredit, the key to a successful program is early identification of students with weak skills, preferably before they are accepted by the college. Precollege screening and counseling are essential. Prospective students must be evaluated in light of the college's existing programs and the characteristics of current students on the following points:

**Reading** — Are prospective students able to read well enough to understand freshman textbooks and hold their own with other students?

**Writing** — Can they expect to succeed in the lowest-level writing course the college offers?

**Mathematics** — Have they the skills to handle the basic math course? For example, if the college's mathematics course assumes that students have had algebra, then those who are deficient in basic arithmetic and have had no algebra should not be admitted until they have completed courses elsewhere and can qualify.

**Science** — If students aspire to science majors, have they adequate mathematics skills, prior courses in chemistry, and the analytic thinking skills needed to succeed in beginning courses?

**Expectations and Motivation** — Are students interested in and knowledgeable about the courses and majors offered by the institution? For example, if a student expects that a university business administration major prepares students to be clerk-typists, she is likely to be disappointed in the freshman courses she takes.

Are students aware of the time and effort it takes to learn in college, and are they willing and able to make this investment? If a college admits students whose skills and background are far below the level of the average student in that college or the level expected by the faculty, there will be high attrition among the underprepared group, dissatisfied faculty members, and/or lowered standards.

Colleges use different ways to determine the skills and motivation of their prospective students. Private schools will send out teams of interviewers and also use their local alumni to contact prospective students and evaluate them. Most institutions require admissions tests and have special summer orientation programs, which often include parents. Currently, community colleges are trying the same approaches—that is, loading new students into a bus for a weekend retreat to orient them to the demands and expectations of the faculty, to get to know them, and to give them a head start on skills they will need. (I know of few colleges that invite spouses to orientation, but I feel that it would be an excellent idea because so many of today's college students are married, and the spouse's attitude can make a great difference in the student's success.)

In addition to information about programs offered by and skills needed for a particular college, students need information about themselves. Testing assesses students skills and provides information for them. Colleges and universities use standardized tests, locally built tests, and informal instruments to place or guide freshmen into appropriate skills courses in mathematics, reading, and writing. (See Appendix 2-1 for a list and descriptions of frequently used tests.)

## READING TESTS

Ninety-five percent of the college reading programs in the 1960s used standardized tests to evaluate students' reading skills, and this is probably as true today. The Nelson-Denny Reading Test is still the test most often used for pre- and post-testing, probably because it takes less time to administer than most reading tests (30 minutes) and its subscores —speed, comprehension, and vocabulary—readily reflect students' gains in rate of reading. However, it continues to be criticized as inappropriate for measuring college reading skills since it tests the ability to answer questions quickly based on short passages. College reading demands that students read lengthy textbooks and other difficult materials and read them in a sustained manner so that the information can be the basis for further learning and be retained for future examinations. For more information on the limitations of standardized reading tests, you'll want to read:

Sternberg, R. J. (April 1991). Are we reading too much into reading comprehension tests? *Journal of Reading*, *34*(7), 539-544.

Kerstiens, G. (1990). A slow look at speeded comprehension. *Review of Research in Developmental Education*. 7(3).

The value of self-assessment inventories such as the LASSI or the Brown-Holtzman SSHA, SBI SR/SE, and PEEK to identify students who have study skills problems, depends on the student's willingness to answer honestly. Their main use is for counseling purposes, but they are also often used in studies of reading and study skills programs. Students find them helpful as pre and post-test indicators of their progress. Some instructors find that a simple checklist of problem areas works as well as a published attitude questionnaire, and as a result many learning centers have developed their own study-problem checklists. (For further information on study skills instruments see Appendix 2-1 and Chapter 10.)

## OTHER SELF-ASSESSMENT INSTRUMENTS

Rather than submitting a large group of new students to a mass testing program and waiting for the results to come from the computer-processing service (or because they can't afford computer placement testing), some educators use self-rating and self-analysis instruments so that students are involved in making their own decisions about courses and placement. For example, as part of their orientation program, students may be asked to rate their likes and dislikes, abilities, and high school grades in reading, mathematics, and writing. Their responses are weighted, and they can determine from a chart whether they can probably do the reading for such courses as psychology and history or whether they should take developmental reading, and also what courses in mathematics and writing would be most appropriate. Although students also take standardized tests as part of orientation, the self assessment gives them an understanding of how their backgrounds and skills fit with the demands of freshman courses and whether they should enroll in remedial/developmental courses. They are guided through the process by a counselor. Having access to this information, students make better choices and are less likely to drop out, and the system is reported to improve faculty morale as well.

Whether a college uses standardized tests, computerized placement tests, or self-assessment instruments to guide students to appropriate basic skills courses or sections, it is important that the instruments have local norms and validity for the purposes for which they are used. Too often, instructors use standardized tests and national norms to place students without knowing the distribution of scores within the college. When the test is not appropriate for the student population, this practice can lead to assignment of too many students to remedial courses or, more rarely, too few.

## WHO VOLUNTARILY SEEKS HELP?

With so many colleges expending so much effort to identify underprepared students for placement in remedial/developmental courses, the average student can be overlooked. Other students, who are neither underprepared nor disadvantaged, often need skills help too. So let us look briefly at the problems of students who volunteer for special help in basic skills and some of the ways their problems can be diagnosed and these students supported.

To diagnose students' learning problems, the learning-skills specialist (counselor) must recognize and understand their expectations, symptoms, self-diagnosis, and the conditions that lead students to seek help. Diagnosing a learning problem does not take place in a vacuum, nor can it be done solely by administering a battery of tests. The counselor must have a thorough understanding of the academic context in which the student's problems occur—the dynamics of the interaction between the student's needs, skills, attitudes, knowledge, and abilities and the instructors' expectations, teaching strategies, and characteristics. Factors such as peer competition and the institution's policies and standards must also be considered and weighed. To achieve the insights which must precede and accompany successful treatment, students must be helped to identify the most important causes of their problems and differentiate between those factors that are intrinsic and those that stem from extrinsic conditions. Intrinsic causes refer to personal limitations, such as attitudes, visual defects, or lack of background. Some intrinsic limitations can be improved; others cannot and the student must find ways to compensate for these if he is to remain in college. Extrinsic factors refer to conditions imposed by the academic environment over which the student has little control and with which he must learn to cope if he is to succeed. Another integral part of the diagnostic process is to help the student examine alternative programs and choices.

So the question that must be addressed is how to differentiate between the environmental factors that create problems for students and the subjective causes (such as lack of preparation, fear, or limited skills). The solution may involve three alternatives: (1) modifying the external conditions; (2) changing the student's behavior; and (3) changing the student's goals or plans.

It takes a certain kind of courage and a touch of desperation for students to seek help voluntarily from an academic support service, because doing so means that they admit they have a problem. It also implies that they realize that they are not up to the level of their peers. Superstrivers, who are very anxious about their ability to compete in college, are usually the first to volunteer for help—a fortunate circumstance for the image of the service. At the beginning of the fall term, anxious new freshmen, transfer students, and even beginning graduate students come for assistance in large numbers. Academically weak students, particularly those who have negative attitudes toward their previous teachers, may avoid learning-assistance services at the beginning of the term—unless they have been personally counseled concerning their needs and have met the staff. If weak students do not seek help early in the school term, their problems may be intensified, and, when they realize they are failing, they are angry and difficult to help.

## EXTERNAL REASONS FOR STUDENTS' PROBLEMS

The academic situations that cause problems for average and above-average students are not different in kind from those that cause problems for underprepared students. However, well-prepared students are usually more aware of and often more sensitive to the institution's standards and requirements. They have stronger fears that they will fail than their less well-prepared peers. (When learning skills services are available, average and above-average students often seek help in greater numbers than do academically weak students.) Getting into college may have been such a struggle for underprepared students that they may not be aware of or concerned about what is expected from them now that they are admitted.

Most students who seek learning assistance recognize that they are facing new demands on their abilities. This recognition may take the form of a feeling that college courses generally are going to be harder than high school courses were or that a particular professor's standards are so high that the skills that earned high grades in the past are not sufficient to succeed in this course. Coming for assistance may reflect a student's concern about succeeding in a new subject—such as philosophy or economics—in which the ideas are strange and the textbook hard to read. Or it may reflect the student's reactions to the amount of work expected—for instance, longer reading lists than he or she has ever been assigned before—or confusion about how to approach a particular assignment. New vocabulary, complex syntax, erudite lecturers who assume their students are familiar with the terms and ideas in their subjects are other factors that exacerbate the student's insecurity. (See Figure 2-1 for a model of some of the factors that lead students to seek help.)

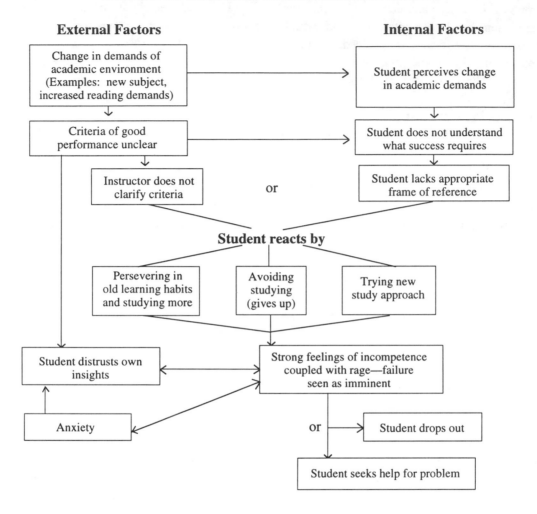

**FIGURE 2-1. PRECIPITATING FACTORS THAT LEAD A STUDENT TO SEEK HELP FOR A LEARNING PROBLEM**

**External Factors**

Change in demands of academic environment (Examples: new subject, increased reading demands)

Criteria of good performance unclear

Instructor does not clarify criteria

**Internal Factors**

Student perceives change in academic demands

Student does not understand what success requires

Student lacks appropriate frame of reference

or

**Student reacts by**

Persevering in old learning habits and studying more

Avoiding studying (gives up)

Trying new study approach

Student distrusts own insights

Strong feelings of incompetence coupled with rage—failure seen as imminent

Anxiety

or

Student drops out

Student seeks help for problem

A second, very common problem occurs when students find they do not understand the professor's criteria for grading and standards for judging good performance. Instructors may not clarify their expectation, or they may make vague statements that grades will be based on a paper and class participation, or say only, "There will be three midterms and a final in this course." Such statements may be sufficient for the experienced student, who can find out about the course from friends or who is willing to meet with the professor. But new students hesitate to ask for clarification for fear of being judged dumb. Professors too may become frustrated when students ask basic questions about how to tackle an assignment. For example, Jonathan, a freshman, came into the learning center to improve his reading speed after asking his geography professor how to approach the ten books assigned in the course. The professor had replied impatiently, "Read every word, of course. You will be responsible for all the material." I asked Jonathan what he had to do with the information he would collect from reading all the books, and he responded that he had an hour exam the following week covering four of the books. Then I discussed with him how much he felt he could write about four books on an hour exam, what questions the instructor was likely to ask, and which concepts, theories, and information he must know to answer the questions.

Some instructors espouse the philosophy that college students need to find their own way through life's maze. These instructors appear to revel in the role of maze builders who deliberately obfuscate the path with unstructured lectures and vague assignments. Others are so deeply committed to their own intellectual interests that they fail to recognize that students lack the background to understand them. Textbooks, too, are sometimes written as if the author considered it a disservice to the reader to present ideas in clear, explicit prose.

Another strategy that provokes anxiety in students is that faculty members' frequently do not provide constructive information to students about their progress. Uncertain of the professor's expectations, students find themselves unable to judge the quality of their own work, particularly when only one paper is assigned and it is due at the end of the term. In such situations even very well-prepared students may seek help, while less-prepared students procrastinate and, if they seek help, are likely to do so at the last minute. Similarly, if the instructor assigns only letter grades to papers, without comments, students have no basis for assessing their work and no guidelines for future papers. A grade of "B," the most common grade given currently, is particularly devastating if given without comments. It gives students no hint of what they need to do to improve. Instructors may not recognize that students do not share their

frame of reference or do not have the conceptual framework necessary to learn and retain the course content. For example, engineering students taking their first economics course may not understand that the formulas in economics are mere metaphors and cannot be solved like the formulas in engineering courses. Or an English teacher tells her class, "Write a theme on a controversial topic." The physical education major does not understand that the controversial issues that concern his swimming coach are not considered controversies by his English teacher, and so she fails him.

Absorbing the instructional traditions and learning the foibles of individual professors are situations that create problems for college students. Perhaps these problems could be termed communication difficulties, for the student must be indoctrinated into another language and different customs in order to communicate with his instructors. Faculty members, who are usually knowledgeable about the differences and schisms in their own fields, may be naive about the viewpoints of students, who make errors because they are using a different reference base than their instructors.

Unless the instructor presents a conceptual framework for her subject or helps students build their own, the information she presents in lectures may become an indigestible mass of facts that the student cannot organize, learn, or retain. As a result, students revert to memorization and, when asked to discuss issues, implications, or assumptions of the course, cannot. Asking and answering "why" questions is not a widely practiced skill in high school courses. So students who lack this experience become frustrated at their inability to perform well on tests that require them to generalize, compare different viewpoints, and draw inferences. Indeed, they become enraged.

Few faculty members realize how their instructional strategies and general teaching approaches adversely affect student attitudes and performance. Nor do they recognize how their teaching styles increase the anxiety that lowers performance, although they may be aware that their students are anxious.

But faculty members have been trained in the content of their disciplines, not in teaching techniques. Most are convinced that they are good teachers, but even those who students rate most competent have some class members who complain about the teacher's strategies and who seek assistance because they cannot learn. The student's problem may reflect poor or inappropriate teaching strategies, or it may represent the student's perception of poor teaching. Either way, the result is the same—the student becomes discouraged and angry, compounding his other difficulties.

In addition to the problems that result from faculty expectations and teaching methods, students may be burdened further by rigid institutional rules and policies, such as the requirement to carry a full schedule of classes to maintain financial aid or to remain in a major. Scheduling difficulties and poor academic advising may add extra burdens on the student who enrolls in inappropriate courses.

## INTERNAL REASONS FOR STUDENTS' PROBLEMS

There are many kinds of personal limitations that may cause learning problems for college students—physical disabilities such as poor vision, speech impediments, hearing losses, or poor health; weak learning skills; inadequate high school preparation; social adjustment difficulties; limited intellectual ability; or emotional and attitudinal problems. Sometimes physical limitations are overlooked by the learning counselor in his zeal to search for psychological explanations or to place the student in remedial courses. For instance, concentration problems, spelling problems, and slow reading may result from poor visual acuity. If the student's vision can be corrected, glasses may be more effective in treating the problem than counseling or remedial courses.

Other conditions that are unique to the student—that is, those not a function of the academic environment—may distract the student from learning or impair his efficiency. Such activities as holding down a full-time job (or working several part-time jobs), family pressures, and difficulties with roommates or friends are among the many situations that may prevent the student from achieving in college.

Frequently, however, the students' learning problems stem from their own attitudes, expectations and emotional outlook. If students have an unrealistically high estimate of the level of performance that professors expect or if their expectations of themselves are unrealistically high, then each two-page paper becomes an impossible struggle as they strive to write one of Nobel Prize-winning caliber.

By setting impossibly high standards for themselves, students ensure that they will never meet their goals. Whether their problem arises from not understanding what the instructor expects, from having an inappropriate frame of reference, or from misperceiving what they should be able to accomplish, students who are motivated to succeed in college will react. Some react by studying harder but using the same ineffective methods. Others try a new study approach, but even if it seems to be working well, they are still insecure if they have no way of verifying their intuitive feelings without feedback from their instructor in the form of comments or grades. Still others become discouraged and give up, stop studying, and stop attending the class. Each of these responses reflects the student's strong feelings of incompetence. Increased frustration, anxiety, and rage ensue. Students—at least freshmen—seldom direct their rage at their instructors. More often they are angry and disillusioned with themselves. When they seek help from the learning center, however, their frustrations may spill over on the receptionist or some other staff member.

## THE STUDENT'S SELF-DIAGNOSIS

Students seek learning-assistance services anxiously with more or less well-defined symptoms that they label as rather specific—not being able to read fast enough, poor comprehension, inability to concentrate or remember, problems in writing, spelling, or vocabulary. (See Figure 2-2, next page.) In general, students tend to blame themselves for their difficulties, and the more symptoms they list, the greater their anxiety. However, one should realize that students who seek help do not differ in their symptoms from those who do not seek help. I have given study-problem checklists to my graduate classes and found that they check the same problems with about the same frequency as learning-center students do. (I have tried the checklist on only a few faculty members, but I suspect that they too would indicate they had problems in concentration, remembering, reading rate, and comprehension.)

The reasons students give for their problems are revealing. Many attribute their present difficulties to gaps in their educational background. They say things like, "I've always had trouble with reading because I was never taught phonics." "No one ever showed me how to diagram sentences." "I was ill in third grade and missed most of the year. Since then I have always felt behind in school." Another common self-diagnosis—or rationalization, if you prefer—occurs when a student feels that his intellectual functioning is impaired by some neurological or physical disability. "My eyes won't move fast enough." "I think I'm developing a brain tumor like my mother (or other relative) had." "Perhaps I have chronic fatigue syndrome (or mono, or hypoglycemia or some other condition), which would explain why I'm so tired." To make sure there is no medical cause, it is extremely important that students be referred for medical screening. Occasionally students do have medical problems and treatment can improve their academic performance. The slowest reader I ever worked with was an overweight freshman with a very low energy level. I referred her to a physician, who discovered a hypothyroid condition. When she began taking medication, her reading rate increased dramatically. Some students, however, prefer a medical label for their difficulties because it helps them save face. It is more socially acceptable to give a medical reason for one's problem than to admit that one cannot stand up under the competition or that one lacks ability. Students faced with the threat of failure may diagnose themselves as having rare disorders like dyslexia or brain tumors.

# FIGURE 2-2. THE DIAGNOSTIC PARADIGM

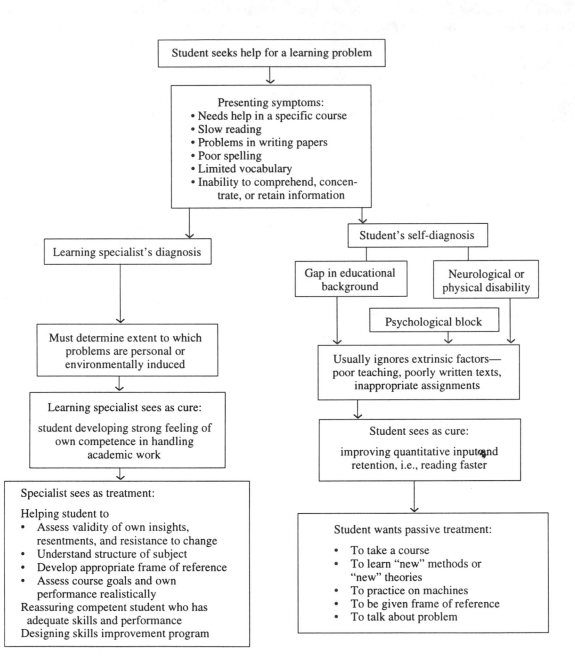

Students are usually quite willing to discuss their psychological blocks to learning. (Today, people prefer to call these same symptoms "anxieties." Consequently, we have math anxiety, writing anxiety, test anxiety, and so on.) Generally students who block on a subject or are anxious about it have avoided taking courses that require the skill. They expend great effort in finding ways to escape the subject, and so I think it more appropriate, in most cases, to call their problem math avoidance or writing avoidance. If the student blocks and avoids the subject, he does not have an opportunity to engage in the practice necessary to develop skills and acquire understanding. People who claim to have math anxiety have usually excluded mathematics from their personal universe.

Inevitably, anxious students can recall some embarrassing or traumatic incident in elementary school which they feel triggered their emotional block. For example, Jake recalled being forced to take a remedial reading course in summer school when he was in the fourth grade. He said that he could remember little about it, except that he had to cross town to get to the class. On further questioning, he recalled that once when he had been asked to read orally in front of the class, he fainted. He awoke to find himself lying on the floor, looking up at the faces of the other children who were staring down at him—a most humiliating experience. At age twenty-five, he still saw himself as a retarded reader although he was making excellent grades in science courses. His reading block prevented him, he felt, from doing well in nonscience courses.

If a student is helped to recall the emotional event that precipitated the learning block, he has taken the first step toward overcoming it. However, this will not cure the problem. Students with this kind of problem must practice and, in most cases, learn or relearn the fundamentals. One does not expect to become a professional musician in three or four hours of practice (or even as a result of a few hours of psychotherapy). One should not expect to remedy five or ten years of deficiencies in the basic skills in a few hours, but sometimes students expect miracles.

Many students are unable to differentiate those problems that stem from their own limitations (or avoidance) from those that result from poor teaching, poorly written textbooks, or other factors in their academic environment.

## WHAT DOES THE STUDENT SEE AS THE CURE?

Students usually seek simple cures and are convinced that the cure is a formula, short course, or technique that will alleviate their symptoms and one that will require minimal effort and time. Some seem to have an almost mystical faith in a magic cure. "If only," they say, "I could read a thousand words per minute. I could absorb more information and get A's on all my exams." Or, "Isn't there a new law of learning (or new drug) that will help me increase my memory so I can retain all the facts in my biology book?" Many students see the cure for their problems as finding a way to increase the quantity of information they can absorb, retain, and regurgitate; they fail to see that remembering requires them to organize and understand the major concepts, not just cram in the facts. Others, who are convinced they have a psychological block, are sure their problems will be cured if they can just talk about them with a counselor, even though practice and intensive effort may be needed if these students are to develop skills commensurate with their peers. The treatments students suggest usually reflect their desire to remain in a passive, receptive role and to let the skills counselor provide the effort and the cure. (See Figure 2-2.)

## The Role of the Skills Counselor

Faced with a student who suppresses his anger, presents a variety of symptoms, has an oversimplified diagnosis of his difficulty, and expects a quick cure, what does the learning-skills counselor do? The skills counselor must explore the basic question, "To what extent are this student's problems due to his own educational deficiencies and attitudinal or motivational confusion, and to what extent due to the constraints and stress created by the academic environment in which he struggles?" Some students willingly assume the blame for their problems and feel helpless, stupid, and discouraged. Others blame the instructor, the textbook, or the academic policies of the college. The learning skills counselor must help the student with a problem determine realistically how much of his difficulty stems from his own limitations and how much is a function of the academic situation. Although usually little can be done to change instructors' teaching strategies or assignments (or to improve textbooks), it is therapeutic for the student to be reassured that he is not to blame. Often when this happens, he finds ways to cope. However, when students' problems stem from their own limitations, the counselor must hold out hope that they can catch up on the skills or knowledge needed to achieve and show the student how this can be accomplished. If the student can develop better insight into the real causes of his problem and the steps that must be taken to solve it, he is on his way to a solution.

Inevitably, the college student who seeks help for a learning problem also has an emotional problem, which may be a low self image, resentment of authority, resistance to change, or simply an active hatred of the college environment. But even if the student understands and changes his emotional outlook, he still must learn to cope with academic realities. For some well-prepared students, this may mean that the skills counselor must provide reassurance that their new study approaches will work. For the less prepared and for those whose anxieties mask a weakness, it means that the skills counselor must help them recognize the need for, and embark on, a skills program that will take time and effort. Convincing the student that he can improve and that improving will make it easier for him to attain his goal is crucial. The skills counselor must provide support and encouragement as the student works. The skills counselor must help him learn to recognize his own progress and the ways he can apply the skills in his other course work.

Michelle's case serves as an example. An archeology major, Michelle was having difficulty in the history of archeology and complained that she was unable to comprehend and retain the information in the textbook. She felt very depressed, as she had done well in previous courses in her major. As I quickly skimmed the book, I commented that it was poorly organized. In fact, it looked as if the author had handed his secretary an outline and dumped a stack of note cards down the stairs, gathered them up, and given them to his secretary with instructions to type ten cards under each heading. After noting other limitations, I watched Michelle breathe a sigh of relief and exclaim, "Yes, I wondered how the author managed to pass freshman English." Since her professor presented well-organized lectures, I asked her whether she felt it essential to read the textbook. She felt she must read it, because her study ritual dictated that one always read the textbook before going to lectures. We were able to work out a compromise of sorts in that she agreed to take lecture notes first and then skim the textbook for further ideas that might fit into her notes. Common sense? Perhaps, but even the brightest students are often quite rigid and superstitious about their study methods. Would Michelle's problem have been revealed by a standardized reading test? I doubt it, as she was an excellent reader.

In diagnosing specific difficulties in college courses, the skills counselor must play a detective-like role, examining both the materials students read and the study methods they use.

The key to effective treatment of learning problems is to thoroughly assess the task the student must perform and help him or her understand not only what is being asked, but the steps that should be followed to complete the task. This assessment includes determining what skills and information the student needs and aiding her or him to assess the validity of his/her own insights, resentments, and resistances within the class context. Once students are realistically aware of the tasks required to suc-ceed, they are in a position to determine how much effort and time they must invest to learn what they want to know and to attain the goal to which they aspire.

College learning services should adhere to the old maxim and offer different strokes to different folks. Students with very poor preparation for col-lege—those who don't know that they don't know—need required skills courses since they won't volun-teer, but these services should be provided for other students too. The required skills courses, however, must be thoroughly integrated into mainstream cur-ricula. Those who slip in climbing the academic ladder, if encouraged, may come in voluntarily—some reluctantly and some desperately. Others who are doing quite well may want to increase their study efficiency and improve their grades. The compre-hensive learning service offers help to all.

# CHAPTER 3

## CREATING TUTORING SERVICES

Tutoring is individualized instruction. Group instruction, even under ideal conditions, must be supplemented by individualized instruction if all students are to learn well. In college classrooms where group instruction through lectures is the norm, some students will need intensive help, and most students, even the brightest and most highly motivated, may need individual instruction at various times as a supplement to group instruction. If the instructor is unable to provide individual instruction (owing to the large size of the class or for other reasons), then tutoring can fill the gap. Peer tutoring is considered by both students and experts alike to be one of the most important ingredients of a successful learning assistance program—students expect it and most colleges offer it.

## HISTORICAL BACKGROUND

Historically, the wealthy and elite have always hired tutors for their children, and in some historical eras, tutoring was the main avenue to learning. Apprenticeships predated schooling, and even today complex skills from surgery to sculpture are still taught one to one by master tutors. Since the Middle Ages, going to a European university has usually meant traveling to a city, renting a room, hiring a tutor, studying for years, attending lectures, and taking the examinations for a degree when one felt prepared.

Oxford and Cambridge, after which Harvard and other early colleges in the United States were modeled, have had a somewhat different arrangement. There, students lived in residential units with tutors and dons, a setting in which study and social life were merged. The English dons did not have the responsibility of examining, grading, and disciplining students, so that they were able to provide a supportive, collegial atmosphere and develop close, personal relationships with students. The early United States colleges, however, never quite achieved the same collegial atmosphere. Even in colonial days, American professors assumed disciplinary and examining roles and did not live with their students.

In the nineteenth century, when Harvard attempted a residential system with tutors, the program was modeled after the British system but was not a replica. American tutors and professors preferred not to live with their students, and providing individual tutors for each student soon proved too expensive. During a later period, President Lowell of Harvard, determined to excite superior students to their maximum attainment and avoid mediocrity, implemented rigorous examinations to challenge the students. This policy created a need for tutors, and so professors, graduate assistants, and undergraduates helped younger students prepare for the tests.

Woodrow Wilson, when he was president of Princeton, introduced preceptors (typically graduate students) whose function was to establish informal associations with students and stimulate and guide their intellectual endeavors. Whereas most of the earlier Harvard tutors had been members of the faculty, the Princeton preceptors were predominantly students.

Tutors have long been available in public colleges and universities for students who could afford to hire them. Academic departments usually keep lists of qualified tutors, and some departments, particularly in the sciences and mathematics, pay upperclassmen and women to tutor lower-division students. Tutoring has also been a way for economically poor students to work their way through college, as my father did at Berkeley in 1911. A tutor then earned thirty cents an hour. Student members of honor societies, motivated by a sense of noblesse oblige, also have a long history of offering free tutoring to their less academically successful peers. Student-athletes, too, have traditionally received intensive tutoring along with their athletic scholarships, and since World War II, the G.I. Bill package of services for veterans has included funds for tutoring. To summarize, tutoring has long been an accepted part of academic life, but it is still considered a low-paying, low prestige, entry-level position for teachers, despite the needs it fills.

Tutoring continues to be a service contracted for by students with money; for example, the Arabian princess whose father arranged with the University of Houston to send two women professors, books, films, tapes, and other learning materials to the princess' quarters in the palace in Riyadh, Saudi Arabia—an event that may mark the most expensive college education ever arranged and the ultimate in individualized instruction. However, it does signal a breakthrough in the education of Arabian women, where few females enter high school and even fewer attend college.

In the 1960s, as U.S. colleges and universities began to admit large numbers of low-income, educationally disadvantaged students, tutorial services were among the first programs organized on a large scale to help these students. Although figures from national surveys vary because of differences in the colleges sampled, there is clear evidence that formal, cross-disciplinary tutorial programs have increased. While sixty-three percent of the colleges and universities surveyed in an Educational Testing Service study in 1971-72 reported having special tutoring for educationally disadvantaged students by faculty members or students, more recent surveys show that almost all institutions today offer peer tutoring.

Some tutors are paid, some are volunteers, and others tutor for credit or room and board. In some very large universities such as Texas A&M, tutoring is a big business with private tutoring companies competing for students' dollars. It is reported that many of the A&M students use these commercial tutors for help in large lecture courses. On the other hand, at University of Texas–Austin, tutoring is offered by the Learning Skills Center which selects, trains, and supervises tutors, but requires most students receiving tutoring to pay by the hour, unless they are in a special program that funds tutoring.

## WHY USE PEER-TUTORS TO HELP ACADEMICALLY WEAK STUDENTS?

Professors often argue that using peer tutors to help academically weak students is like "the blind leading the blind" or, as I once said, asking pre-med students to do heart-transplants. But—I was wrong, for if students are adequately trained and supervised they can be very helpful tutors for at-risk students. College freshmen, especially high-risk students, usually feel more comfortable with and prefer working with peer tutors than with graduate students or faculty members. Similarly, those who specialize in working with learning disabled students have learned that an important part of their job is to recruit, select, train, and supervise peer tutors. It's a good idea to encourage former tutees to become tutors themselves, as they may have the patience and ability to explain concepts to struggling students.

## SPECIAL PROBLEMS OF PEER TUTORING

Peer tutoring as an educational support program presents special problems—peer tutors, by definition, are students themselves and need training and careful supervision to be most effective. In addition, tutors are transitory and do not generally remain as tutors long—especially in two-year institutions. Therefore training must be ongoing and continuous. Training programs run the gamut in types and amount of training, and informal arrangements are probably still the norm. But this is changing as professional associations and institutions begin to recognize the importance of tutoring and tutor training.

### WHAT COMPRISES A SUCCESSFUL PEER TUTORING PROGRAM?

Despite the differences in policies, people, and philosophies, most experts agree that a successful peer tutoring program should have, at a minimum, the following characteristics:

◊ tutors are recommended by a faculty member in the subject they are to tutor;

◊ tutors are carefully screened and selected on the basis of performance criteria and knowledge of the subject;

◊ tutors are given a tutor training program where

they learn techniques of working with under-prepared students before they start tutoring and are offered on-going training, supervision, and support as they continue to tutor students; and

◊ tutors are evaluated regularly by their coordinators, their supervisors, and their students.

Lou Tripodi (1987) says that it takes recruiting, training, delivery of services, and equal measures of persistence and patience to make a tutoring program successful. Developing rapport with faculty members and finding out what they need provides a necessary foundation; getting their recommendations and recruiting and selecting tutors is the next step. Training should include, at a minimum, orientation to the service, student types, student characteristics, communication skills, and professionalism (including ethics and confidentiality in the tutoring situation, rights of clients, importance of keeping accurate records, and developing a professional relationship). Then advertising to draw students and networking with faculty and administrators to keep them informed are essential for maintaining the program.

## RECRUITING AND SELECTING PEER TUTORS

A peer tutor is defined as a person having a minimum of special training who helps one or more students learn a particular skill or body of information in a course under the guidance of an instructor or supervisor. For tutoring to be both effective in enhancing student learning and cost-efficient, tutors should be carefully selected so that those who have a good background in the subject, a natural predisposition for working with students, good communication skills, and appropriate personality traits can be hired. The goal should be to minimize the amount of training and supervision necessary to prepare tutors to work independently and effectively with students. However, this is not to suggest that beginning tutors do not need training and careful supervision, but selecting responsible tutors can reduce the amount of training required. When tutors are enrolled in the same courses as the students they are tutoring (a true peer-tutoring situation), they need intensive supervision and monitoring.

As mentioned earlier, college tutoring programs use many kinds of people as tutors—faculty members, undergraduate and graduate students, students on work-study or taking courses in tutoring for credit as field study experiences, high school teachers, paraprofessionals from the community, and volunteers. Volunteers may include students or ex-students, housewives (including faculty wives), local business people who are released by their employers for social service work, and the elderly (retired professors, former school teachers, or retired persons from other professional fields). Increasingly, librarians are serving as skills specialists and tutors, as libraries often house learning centers and tutorial programs. Most tutors work part time, whether paid or volunteers. Tutoring college students is not a field that is conducive to full-time work unless other duties are included, such as administration and supervision, teaching, materials development, or research.

Most tutoring programs have a mixture of paid tutors and volunteers, and increasingly, programs are offering tutoring-for-credit courses both as a way to train tutors and as a way to extend services to more students. Some programs use special incentives to entice volunteer tutors. For example, the Learning Assistance Center at California State University at Long Beach offered volunteer tutors, who were not students, the title of "Adjunct Professor," paid them a token $1 a term, gave them parking and library privileges, required them to participate in staff de-

velopment activities, and considered them regular staff members.

Recruitment practices vary, but most programs solicit recommendations from academic departments for prospective tutors. If a program needs large numbers of tutors, they may use other recruiting methods such as listing positions in student employment offices, advertising in local college and/or community newspapers, soliciting recommendations from student organizations (especially ethnic organizations), and recruiting tutors from among former tutees of the program who are succeeding academically. To recruit volunteers from the community, program directors advertise in newspapers and through public service announcements on radio and television, obtain lists of community organizations and businesses that offer volunteer services and contact them, or enlist the support of the alumni association and campus faculty and staff organizations.

At the Student Learning Center at Berkeley, we relied heavily on advertisements in the student newspaper, on referrals from a network of minority faculty and staff members, from academic departments, and from student organizations—ethnic student associations and the work-study and student employment services. Posters and notices were put up around campus in places where student traffic was heavy and on department bulletin boards. The tutor-for-credit program was extensively advertised. Once the program was well established, student tutors referred their friends, and students who had been tutored volunteered to tutor others. Experienced tutors also recruited new tutor applicants by making announcements in advanced classes.

When prospective tutors applied, they were given a brief description of the center's programs and objectives and written information on qualifications, personal characteristics, and duties. They filled out an application form which contained questions about their class, their major, courses taken, and grades they received in the courses they wished to tutor, their ethnic background, any previous tutoring or teaching experiences, the reasons they wanted to tutor, and their attitudes toward and understanding of underprepared or low-achieving students. Students seeking paid tutoring positions were required to have a letter of recommendation from a faculty member in the subject they wanted to tutor. This letter served two functions: it protected us from complaints by faculty members that we were hiring tutors who were not sufficiently knowledgeable in the course, and it helped publicize the tutoring service to the faculty. We found faculty letters generally honest and helpful. Faculty members were given the option of phoning the tutor supervisor instead of writing a recommendation.

The applicants for paid tutoring positions whose applications and recommendations looked most promising were screened by a team of three persons: a learning specialist in the appropriate subject, a senior tutor or learning specialist (who may be in another field), and a member of the clerical staff. We tried to include at least one woman and one minority-group member on each screening team. During the screening interview, the applicant was presented with a role-playing situation planned in advance, involving a typical student problem. One of the team members, who need not be an expert in the subject, role played the tutee. Using the applicant's performance in the screening situation, the team rated the applicant on three major factors: knowledge of the subject, ability to explain and communicate this knowledge to the tutee, and sensitivity to students' problems.

Knowledge of the subject is the first prerequisite most tutorial directors look for in selecting tu-

tors. As I've said before, some tutor coordinators insist that only outstanding, straight-A graduate students should be selected, but we found that many of our freshman clients relate well to undergraduate peer tutors who have average to good grades in the course and can explain the subject well. Often tutees categorized graduate students or A students as "experts," and found them intimidating. A study by Brown (1989) supports this, for he found that the best predictor of problem-solving behavior in tutees was the class of the tutor. That is, the closer the tutor was to the student in college class, the more problem-solving occurred in the session. In other words, students who were freshmen and were tutored by sophomores engaged in more problem-solving during the tutoring session than freshmen who were tutored by seniors.

Some students prefer to work with tutors who come from their own ethnic background and reject tutors from other ethnic groups. Many students have difficulty working with tutors of the opposite sex. It requires intensive recruitment to find bilingual, minority, or even women tutors in the sciences and mathematics. In general, we looked for tutors who were supportive and flexible enough to work with the different types of clients that we saw. We tried to staff enough tutors in each subject so that students had a choice, but often found it impossible to find tutors from each ethnic group for each subject. For example, it was not easy to find a female Native-American tutor able to tutor introductory physics—we did finally find one but her heavy course schedule limited the amount of time she could give us. When this situation was explained to students and they were given options both in tutors and in types of service—i.e., study groups, self-paced instruction, drop-in tutoring as well as regularly scheduled tutoring sessions with the same tutor—they usually understood and accepted the situation. However, tutor coordinators must be sensitive to the needs of their students and try to find tutors who are representative of the ethnic and gender distribution of their clientele.

It is vital that tutors be sensitive, empathetic (not sympathetic), nonjudgmental people who can accept students as they are and who do not have unrealistically high expectations of what the tutee should have had in high school or should be able to do in college. Effective tutors must also have a clear understanding of the academic realities of the courses and instructional practices of the college.

Other traits we considered in screening tutors were willingness to undergo training, reliability, acceptance of continual evaluation by students and supervisors, commitment to making the learning success of their tutees the central concern of the relationship, interest in understanding students' problems and backgrounds, and ability to establish a supportive relationship. Obviously, some of these traits are hard to assess in a screening interview or from an application blank. However, if tutors are closely supervised during their initial training, supervisors usually can pinpoint those who are having problems relating to students.

We used similar, though less rigorous, procedures in selecting students admitted to our tutoring-for-credit courses and volunteer tutors. They too needed faculty recommendations and were interviewed by a supervisor, who considered their background and motivation. We found that students who took the course just to earn a credit often did not become good tutors. (Note: Is it just a coincidence that Sheets (1994) recently found that those tutors who said their main reason for tutoring was the money did not learn to make appropriate responses to students during the time they worked as tutors?)

## TUTORING FOR CREDIT

Tutors-for-credit, who must have junior standing, signed up each term for the course. Although we encouraged them to continue in the course for a full year, often they were unable to because they had to take required courses in their major. Supervisors of the tutors-for-credit course attempted to match students with tutors during their first term, met with the tutors regularly, and required them to keep logs or journals describing each session with their tutees and records of the time spent in each tutoring session. (Note: A complete description of the UCB tutoring-for-credit course in writing can be found in the Appendix of *When Tutor Meets Student*. M. Maxwell (Ed.), 1994, Ann Arbor: University of Michigan Press—a book of 51 stories written by tutors describing their experiences in working with students. Also see Treuer's 1995 book listed in Appendix 3-1.)

Students who spent a term in our tutoring-for-credit program made good candidates for our paid tutoring positions. Often tutors wrote on their course evaluation forms that the tutoring-for-credit course was the most valuable course they had taken at UC Berkeley, a not uncommon response to tutor training courses at any college.

Well-meaning but untrained tutors can do more harm than good. They can intimidate students, overprotect them, and do the work for the student, causing them to become dependent on tutoring. That training makes a difference is supported by the findings of the Exxon Grant, a recent national follow-up study of 6000 developmental education students, which found that tutor training was the one programmatic factor that differentiated between successful and unsuccessful developmental education programs. Successful programs, those with high graduation rates, were more likely to have tutor training programs than those where few developmental students graduated (Boylan and Bonham, 1992).

The expansion in the number of college programs certified under the College Reading and Learning Association's (CRLA's) International Tutor Training Certification Program attests to the increasing recognition of the field. (For information about CRLA's program, contact: Ms. Gladys Shaw, Coordinator CRLA International Tutor Certification Program, Tutoring and Learning Center, 300 Library, University of Texas at El Paso, El Paso, Texas 79968-0611. Phone (915) 747-5366 or FAX (915) 747-5486.) Other indications of the growing professionalization of college tutoring programs are the publication of the NADE *Self-Evaluation Guides* which include Tutoring Programs (H&H Publishing Co., 1994) and the emergence of the National Tutor Association founded at East Stroudsburg University, East Stroudsburg, PA 18301.

Rick Sheets (1994) studied 70 adult tutors in Arizona community colleges and reported that those who had 10 or more hours of training were able to respond appropriately in tutoring situations while those with fewer training hours were not able to identify an appropriate course of action. An appropriate course of action in the tutor situations was defined by the responses of twenty experts on the same instruments. "Active listening and paraphrasing was the one topic investigated in which one or more hours of training made a significant difference in tutor responses," (Sheets, p. iii). Note: Constructivism was the underlying theoretical framework for tutor training enabling students to use problem-solving, self-monitoring, and other meta-cognitive strategies to accurately construct new information adding to their previous knowledge.

Sheets reports that tutors did not learn to make appropriate responses on the post-test just because they gained experience by tutoring. This is contrary to what some program directors believe and supports the importance of tutor training in changing tutor behavior. His conclusion that as few as ten hours of training make a difference supports the College Reading and Learning Association's (CRLA) International Tutor Certification Program which requires a minimum of 10 hours of training for the lowest level of certification. Another finding was that the responses "Making money" and "Giving something back," as answers to questions on the rewards of tutoring, were negatively related to learning to make appropriate responses to clients. This finding has implications for those who select tutors.

## A Model Tutor-Training Program

Here are some guidelines for an effective tutor-training program based on a survey of current literature and my own experiences. Tutors need:

1. Knowledge of the goals and objectives of the program, knowledge of appropriate behavior for a tutor, and the opportunity to demonstrate these in practice (for example, in a role-playing or modeling situation).

2. Training in using appropriate materials and structured activities.

3. Training in conducting sessions: opening the session; establishing rapport; diagnosing or clarifying the student's problem; creating a supportive learning situation in which the tutee can demonstrate his learning; closing the session; determining when the student is progressing and helping the student focus on the task.

4. Training in listening.

5.  Training in how to develop a working relationship with faculty members.

6.  Ways of explaining, presenting, and clarifying the basic concepts in the subject.

7.  Strategies for helping students master concepts and basic skills.

8.  An awareness of some of the typical tutoring problems they will encounter and ways of working with them (see Appendix 3-2, "Difficult Tutoring Situations").

9.  An understanding of the record keeping and other procedures of the program and its organizational structure.

10. An opportunity to develop sensitivity to students from other ethnic backgrounds and cultures and an understanding of the learning style differences between people. (Many programs use tests like the Myers-Briggs Type Indicator (see Appendices) to help tutors realize how people differ in their learning preferences.)

In our program, tutors signed a training contract specifying the various staff-development activities in which they would participate. These included small-group meetings with a member of the senior staff or the counseling psychologist, case conferences, videotaping sessions, talks by outside speakers, and courses that were related to improving their skills. New tutors were expected to attend weekly seminars conducted by their supervisors.

One model for tutor training is described below. (Not all the topics suggested were taught in formal training sessions. However, most that were not taught arose informally during the course.)

The overall goal of the program was to assist tutors in developing their own flexible, comfortable tutoring style that will result in improved learning for the diverse students who use the learning center. Toward this end, the program had the following objectives: (1) increasing the tutor's knowledge and understanding of teaching, tutoring techniques, and his subject; (2) increasing the tutor's knowledge of and sensitivity to students' different learning/cognitive styles and the effects of different tutoring strategies on learning; (3) increasing the tutor's ability to become a facilitator of learning, not an answer machine; (4) improving the tutor's knowledge of the basic learning and study skills required for mastering the subject and methods of teaching study skills; (5) informing the tutor about the materials available to assist the student in learning the subject matter; and (6) increasing the tutor's knowledge of how to diagnose the student's difficulty and clarify the student's problem.

The program's activities fell into five categories: orientation, improving interpersonal effectiveness, improving intrapersonal skills, ethics and confidentiality, and evaluation as an ongoing process.

## ORIENTATION

The first step is to orient tutors to the mission and objectives of the center, its staff, organization, functions, and services, and how it fits into the administrative structure and the mission of the institution. (At Berkeley this was done through printed material and in a general orientation session for new tutors. The mission of our center was to assist students to become efficient, self-confident, and independent learners—a goal that was reinforced in all formal and informal training sessions.)

1.  **Description of center procedures and tutors' responsibilities**. Procedures and responsibilities of the tutors included keeping records on student contacts, scheduling appointments, not-

ing which groups were entitled to priority appointments, keeping a regular work schedule and adhering to other business policies, contacting faculty members during the first week of class to get course syllabuses and discuss course objectives, attending lectures and maintaining contacts with faculty members and teaching assistants. These points were briefly presented in the general orientation program, and a checklist of procedures was given to each new tutor. The checklist contained such items as getting employment forms signed, getting a mailbox, turning in schedules, getting one's picture taken, and turning in weekly student-contact sheets. It also listed the names and functions of our clerical and program staff members.

2. **Information on tutor backup materials**. New tutors were taken on a tour of the Library-Laboratory, shown instructional materials and the computer-assisted-instruction programs in their specialties, and given a list of resource materials. The Library-Laboratory contained textbooks, self-paced instructional materials, how-to-study books in different subjects, cassette recorders and tapes, computer terminals and CAI programs, reading machines, reference books, old exams, and tutor-training materials.

3. **Study skills training**. Learning specialists from science, mathematics, writing, and reading presented demonstration/ discussion sessions on the application of study skills techniques to particular courses and described techniques for analyzing a student's skills level and needs. The Library-Laboratory offered a diagnostic testing service to which tutors could refer students needing special help. There were a number of minicourses for students who want to improve exam skills, reading, general study skills, or math and science skills. Tutors were encouraged to

take the diagnostic tests themselves and to sit in on minicourses to learn techniques. (For additional information on skills training, see the chapters on study skills, test taking, reading, and writing.)

4. **Referrals**. Tutors were advised how and when to make referrals to faculty members, counseling and other student services, academic advisers, the ombudsperson, and others. Each tutor was given a copy of the student services handbook, which briefly described all the services on campus and gave their locations and phone numbers. The counseling-center liaison person participated in the general orientation, discussed how to make referrals to the counseling and psychiatric services, and indicated his willingness to work with individual tutors on general or special problems they might have with students. Speakers from other student-service units and academic departments were also invited to speak at regular staff-development meetings.

5. **Diagnosis and strategy development**. Tutors learned how to diagnose the student's learning difficulty, recognize different cognitive/learning styles, and develop appropriate strategies for tutoring. Through observing a videotape of an actual tutoring session by senior learning specialists (or, in some cases, a mock session), attending seminars, or reviewing videotapes of his own tutoring sessions with the supervisor, the novice tutor learned how to determine the appropriate level and material for the tutee.

6. **Insight into typical problems students bring to the center**. Typical problems were discussed at the general orientation session and modeled on videotaped modules, and tutors were given short journal summaries written by previous tutors and other reading materials, such as Jackie Goldsby's *Peer Tutoring in Basic Writing: A*

*Tutor's Journal* (1982), and Maxwell's *When Tutor Meets Student* (1994). The videotape modules illustrating tutee problems were discussed in the weekly training seminars where new tutors shared their experiences with one another and the supervisor. See also Appendix 3-2 for Mike Roses's *Difficult Tutoring Situations*.

Susan Kerwin of Champlain College, Quebec, uses several short (two- to five-minute) videotaped illustrations as a basis for discussion in her tutor-training program (called Tandem): (1) A smoothly running encounter between student and tutor. The tutor establishes rapport, reinforces the tutee's ideas, develops common objectives, and together they work out a study contract. (Discussion centers on how the tutor achieves this.) (2) An apathetic student who gives very brief answers to anything the tutor asks. (Discussion centers on how to mobilize the student's energies and reinforce commitment.) (3) A client who is extremely negativistic and claims he cannot handle college work, is too dumb, does not belong in college, and so on. (Discussion centers on how to respond to this kind of student.) (4) A situation in which the tutor/student relationship becomes a peer friendship and the tutor gets sidetracked from the major issues of tutoring. (Discussion centers on how to get the tutoring session back on base.) (5) A situation in which the tutor plays a very dominating role and lectures the student, asks "yes" and "no" questions, and generally controls the session. (Discussion centers on how this situation might be improved.)

Keeping a journal of one's tutoring experiences is an excellent way for tutors to track their reactions and experiences. Penelope Deakin of SUNY Fredonia lets tutors share insights and experiences by publishing a "reflective summary" of several tutoring journals each week which is circulated among all the tutors. She reports that this newsletter is eagerly awaited by the tutors and read thoroughly. Collecting tutorial experiences in this fashion is an excellent way to build your own tutor training materials.

Paul Treuer at the University of Minnesota-Duluth asks students in his tutoring-for-credit courses to prepare professional tutoring portfolios containing case studies, self-evaluation and reaction summaries, certificates earned, etc. Portfolios can be an invaluable aid for students applying for jobs or graduate school (Treuer, 1995).

## IMPROVING INTERPERSONAL EFFECTIVENESS

Some of the techniques used to improve tutors' interpersonal skills include modeling and imitating the supervisor's role playing, critiques of their own videotaped tutoring sessions, seminars and role playing, handouts, and lecture/discussion presentations by a counseling psychologist. The following skills were stressed:

1. Establishing rapport and a positive relationship with the student without encouraging dependency.

2. Jointly participating with the student in setting objectives for each session, starting and ending the session, and handling interruptions. Tutors are given ways of ensuring that the student accepts control of his own learning.

3. Improving listening skills and patience. Many tutoring programs have developed their own videotapes of tutoring situations and others use the UCLA videotapes (see Appendix 3-1) while some prefer using role playing instead.

4. Developing effective questioning skills. Through modeling and videotaping, tutors are

trained to establish a dialogue with the student and develop ways of helping the student ask relevant, important questions.

5. Avoiding lecturing and other nonfacilitative behaviors. Videotaping actual tutoring sessions and critiquing these with the tutor helps reduce the tutor's tendency toward such nonfacilitating behaviors as lecturing. For example, tutors were trained to wait a sufficient amount of time after asking a question; to avoid terminating thinking by saying "Right" to the first answer given, thus favoring the quick thinker and penalizing others in the class; to avoid the programmed answer, in which the teacher shoots a stream of questions that reveal the expected answer; to avoid asking vague feedback questions, such as "Do you all understand?"; or asking low level questions that yield one-word or yes/no answers. One goal of our training program is to help the tutor learn to recognize and avoid these behaviors.

6. Ways of assessing the student's progress using positive reinforcement. Tutors can find the appropriate cues in the material to convey what the student is to do to solve the problem or learn the material. Students who are too slow in responding in group situations can be rewarded for progress in individual tutoring sessions.

Hopefully, the tutoring situation lowers the tutee's anxiety, since it is private. Tutors need to learn what kinds of reinforcement different students need and how to continuously monitor students' responses so that they are accurate and appropriate. They can explore the reasoning behind the student's wrong answers, something which is useful diagnostically and which classroom instructors rarely have the time or interest to do. Tutors can repeat material in different ways and alter cues to fit individual learners' needs, cultural backgrounds, and experiences. They can help students actively participate. Tutors provide encouragement and support as the student struggles with a concept, and they honestly praise him when he has mastered it.

7. Techniques for dealing with special problems— i.e., the apathetic, passive student, the overly demanding student, the test-anxious student, and the procrastinator. Our counseling psychologist presented seminars on these topics and developed handouts with suggestions for new tutors.

8. Avoiding student manipulation—that is, not letting oneself be played off against the instructor and not "putting down" the instructor to gain rapport with students. A valuable article for tutors to read on this topic is by Karin Winnard (1991) titled Codependency: Teaching Tutors Not to Rescue, *Journal of College Reading and Learning*, XXIV(1), 32-40. Reprinted in M. Maxwell, Ed., *From Access to Success: A Book of Readings on College Developmental Education and Learning Assistance Programs*. Winnard compares the behavior of tutors that reflect co-dependent attitudes with those manifested by families of alcoholics—e.g., loyalty to the tutee, even when there is evidence that the loyalty is undeserved, yet the tutor is willing to bend the rules for the tutee—i.e., tutor more hours, meet with the student outside the center, etc. Tutors who judge themselves harshly if the student continues to do poorly and blame themselves, those who seem to need their tutees more that their tutees need them, those who feel compelled to take responsibility for the tutee's behavior or feels responsible for knowing the answer to every question the student asks, those are tutors reflecting co-dependent attitudes. She gives suggestions to the tutor director on how

to set limits (and help the tutor set limits), and on how to define the program's parameters, goals, and objectives so that they reflect empowerment. She stresses clearly articulating the responsibilities of each tutor's role and showing how each role supports the goals and objectives of the program.

9. Special role of the drop-in tutor—for example, tutors receive training to learn to serve as facilitator to maximize informal (student-to-student) learning and using the drop-in contact to screen students who need to be referred for more intensive one-to-one tutoring.

10. Techniques in working with groups. Sessions on group processes are provided by the counseling psychologist, and new tutors observe and critique group sessions run by senior tutors.

IMPROVING INTRAPERSONAL SKILLS

Intrapersonal skills are presented in the video-taped model sessions and through role playing and are discussed in seminars as problems arise. The counseling psychologist presents talks and handouts on the following topics:

A. Recognizing one's own fears and limitations.

B. Relaxing and concentrating, tolerating ambiguity, not taking hostility directed toward the tutor personally, and so forth. The counseling psychologist conducted a series of two relaxation/concentration workshops for the staff; relaxation tapes are also available in the Library-Laboratory. Helping the tutor resolve her own authority conflicts is often necessary, as the tutoring role requires that prospective tutors revise their perceptions of themselves as passive students or "good buddies."

Understanding the appropriate role of a tutor is often difficult for new tutors who experiment with different roles. Thom Hawkins describes five tutoring styles in his *Tutoring Typology* (Maxwell, 1993, p. A4-8): the expert, the guide, the scholar, the mentor, and the academic adjunct. There is another tutoring style that is even more effective and one that students expect—i.e., the tutor as coach or trainer whose job is to convince students that they can do it, give them support and encouragement, and help them hone their study and learning skills. The *Tutoring Typology* is a useful training device as it gives tutors a chance to look at different roles and their implications.

C. Understanding one's own learning style. Self-analysis of the tutor's own learning style and study techniques is an important part of the seminar training. A variety of techniques can be used for this. Administering the Myer-Briggs Type Indicator (see Appendix 2-1) to tutors and having them discuss the results is one way to help tutors understand that their preferred learning style may differ from their student's.

D. Learning to deal honestly with situations, feelings, and clients. How to respond honestly to students is a topic that comes up often in the informal training sessions and in critiquing videotaped tutoring sessions.

E. Figuring out what one does not know and articulating questions. This skill is related to the one just mentioned. Tutors need to know what to do when they do not know the answer. They need ways of saying, "I don't know; let's try to work the problem together," or of referring the student to an instructor.

## ETHICS AND CONFIDENTIALITY

Ethical principals for tutors, specifying the roles of tutors and their responsibilities toward their tutees, are discussed with new tutors. These include "Subject proficiency and knowledgeability have top priority in my task as tutor" and pledges to build motivation and self-confidence, not impose one's own value system on clients, and so on. Examples of situations which should be considered confidential are presented and discussed, as are avoiding and/or resolving conflicts between tutors and instructors. The "Recommended ethical standards and guidelines for writing tutors," developed by the New York College Learning Skills Association (NYCLSA) committee that appears in the Jan-Feb 1993 NYCLSA newsletter, are discussed with writing tutors.

**Other Tutor Training Programs**. The California Tutor Project, funded by the California Community College Fund for Instructional Improvement, is another effort to systematize and improve tutor training. This comprehensive project to develop, disseminate, and evaluate research-based tutor training includes a model tutor training program based on a socio-linguistic model of teaching as a linguistic process and is gaining converts nationwide. MacDonald (1991) states that over 100,000 students in California alone receive tutoring each year, but that tutor training (in two-year colleges) typically lasts less than eight hours. He proposes that colleges build a training program around a core curriculum of communication skills stressing these four parts:

1.  tutor roles (expectations and rights of tutors and tutees),

2.  tutoring cycles (a 12-step training lesson which takes the tutor through the main stages of a tutoring encounter and which emphasizes helping the tutee develop strategies for learning),

3.  tutoring patterns (asking and answering questions, and listening to and exchanging information), and

4.  tutor talk (coded as comprising five possible moves: initiation, reply, evaluation, addition, and marker, which along with doing nothing, constitutes the behavioral choices available to a tutor).

(See also, MacDonald, R. B. (1994). *The master tutor*. Williamsville, NY: Cambridge Stratford Study Skills Institute.)

## EVALUATION AS AN ONGOING PROCESS

1.  Supervisors continually evaluate tutors and provide feedback.

2.  New tutors evaluate the center's program and the training program through checklists and open discussions.

3.  As the semester goes on, tutors who work closely together evaluate each other. Kevin Davis of East Central University, OK, devised a questionnaire for tutors to rate each other that includes items on friendliness with coworkers, friendliness with clients, professional attitude toward job, knowledge of subject, ability to help others understand and improve, and diligence toward responsibility (Maxwell, 1993, p. A4-11).

4.  Tutors evaluate themselves and the supervisor writes an evaluation of each new tutor's progress at the end of the quarter and discusses the evaluation with the tutor. Tutors are also evaluated by their tutees through phone calls and questionnaires. Finally, the center has a complaint box where students may drop suggestions, complaints, or kudos.

For an extensive collection of the questionnaires and other instruments used in evaluating tutors and tutoring see Maxwell, M. (1993). *Evaluating academic skills programs: A sourcebook*. MM Associates: Kensington, MD.

## RESOURCE MATERIALS FOR TUTOR TRAINING

Many tutoring programs have developed their own training manuals and use videotapes, role playing, modeling, brainstorming, and handouts to train tutors through orientation programs and regular weekly/biweekly group or individual conferences with supervisors.

A resource library, well stocked with materials for student use and aids for tutors, is a necessary component of an effective tutoring program. Materials for student use should include self-paced instruction programs and audiovisual aids, including autotutorial systems, projectors with filmstrip programs, and audiotape cassettes with workbooks. Some tutorial services have computer-assisted instruction facilities. Videotaped lectures and reading programs can also be included. (Other specific tutor backup materials are discussed in the chapters on reading, writing, mathematics, and science.) You'll find more information on tutor training materials in Appendix 3-1.

## VARIATIONS IN TUTOR TRAINING PROGRAMS

As we pointed out previously, the amount of training offered tutors ranges from a brief orientation session to credit courses that last a year followed by regular training sessions for experienced tutors. Furthermore, many different techniques are used. Sometimes tutors are taught collaborative learning approaches to help students work in self-contained study groups, other programs focus on developing the tutor's interpersonal skills in one-to-one relationships, while others concentrate on teaching tutors how to conduct group sessions or become Supplemental Instruction (SI) leaders. Still others train tutors to improve students' study skills. Some focus on developing counseling skills, others emphasize how best to explain the course content, while still others concentrate on helping students overcome feelings of anxiety and improve their self-concepts. Communication and listening skills are usually included, and currently there is a great deal of emphasis on training tutors to help students improve their metacognitive skills.

## WHAT DOES METACOGNITIVE SKILL TRAINING FOR TUTORS INVOLVE?

Metacognitive skills usually refer to the thinking processes that students use to be aware of, to monitor, and to control their own learning. They include being aware of what we already know, reflecting on the learning task and what knowledge and skills it requires, formulating and testing hypotheses, realizing when one is confused and taking steps to clarify that confusion, strategic knowledge—knowing not only what information is relevant, but when and why to use it—and drawing conclusions (Gourgey, 1992). Tutors can greatly aid students in developing these skills by asking relevant questions which students will gradually internalize—especially, "why" questions.

Note: For more information on metacognitive training for tutors, you will want to read:

Gourgey, A. F. (1992). Tutoring developmental mathematics: Overcoming anxiety and fostering independent learning. *Journal of Developmental Education, 15*(3), 10-14.

Hartman, H. (1990). Factors affecting the tutoring process. *Journal of Developmental Education*, *14*(2), 2-7.

Rings, S., & Sheets, R. (1991). Student development and metacognition: Foundations for tutor training. *Journal of Developmental Education*, *15*(1), 30-32. ERIC EJ 431 649.

The usual training period is a short (half-day or one-day) orientation session for tutors followed by weekly or biweekly staff development meetings. In some programs, new tutors serve internships or are paired with senior tutors for training and supervision. If tutors are selected who are knowledgeable about their subjects, sensitive to students, and relatively mature and reliable, they do not need intensive training. However, they do need ongoing supportive supervision. On the other hand tutors for some groups need quite specialized training. For example, tutors for the deaf must master sign language and understand the special needs of deaf students and thus need intensive training. Tutors for the learning disabled also fall in this category.

## Example of a Brief Training Program

J. C. Condravy at Slippery Rock University (1993, 1995) uses an eclectic approach to interactive tutor training. She packs a tremendous amount of information and experiences into a nine-hour program. During the initial five hour orientation, she provides an opportunity for tutors to introduce themselves in self-selected dyads, to interview each other, and introduce each other to the larger group when it reassembles (getting acquainted activities). Then the policies and procedures and organization of the center are reviewed and the profile of the underprepared learner is discussed. The prospective tutors break up into small groups to list the tutor's responsibilities and tutee's responsibilities. She then asks them to brainstorm answers to two questions: 1) what information do tutors need to obtain from students during the first tutoring session, and 2) what information do tutors need to share with tutees to lay the ground work for a successful tutoring experience.

Sessions at a later date focus on verbal and non-verbal communication skills and active listening, stress management and difficult tutoring sessions. Study skills and learning skills are introduced briefly. These sessions involve sharing personal experiences, brainstorming, and solving problems together. Despite the minimal time and effort spent in training tutors in study skills and learning styles, she found that by the end of the year, her tutors possessed strong insights about learning and teaching which she feels were enhanced by their new responsibilities as tutors and their efforts to satisfy a diverse population of tutees. In other words, tutors, given an overall sketch, are able through their insights to fill in the blanks without necessarily being trained in each specific topic. Tutor training programs should encourage tutors to develop and express these insights.

## Incorporating Counseling Skills into Tutor Training

As tutoring components have been integrated with counseling and learning-skills services, there is greater recognition of the need to train tutors in interviewing and counseling techniques (Hancock and Gier, 1991).

The counseling philosophy of most tutor trainers might best be described as eclectic, with a heavy emphasis on cognitive counseling approaches such as Glasser's Reality Therapy (1965) or Ellis' Rational-Emotive Therapy (1973, 1977), usually coupled with behavior modification. For example, Susan Kerwin at Champlain College has tutors ask students to keep a log of their feelings as they study and to bring it in for discussion. The tutors are familiar with Albert Ellis' "common irrational beliefs," and when, for example, a student expresses negative self-perceptions or anxiety, the tutor may choose to refute the irrational belief that "I must be perfectly competent in everything I do," and "the idea that it is a dire necessity for an adult human being to be loved or approved by virtually every significant person in his/her community."

## GROUP TUTORING

Although more college programs are offering tutoring to a greater range of students, increasing costs and limited budgets have forced some institutions to restrict tutoring to entry-level courses or to special groups for whom extramural funding is available. In private colleges, tutoring may be offered to clients who can pay or for whom departments can be charged. Community colleges continue to offer tutoring to a wide spectrum of their students when there is state or federal funding, although as budgets decline, one-to-one tutoring is becoming a luxury, and group tutoring is replacing it in many schools.

### TRAINING TUTORS FOR GROUP TUTORING

Different skills are required to tutor small groups than to tutor individuals, and it has been my experience that graduate students who have taught large classes by the lecture method often have problems in making the transition to conducting small discussion-oriented tutoring groups.

Ross B. MacDonald (1993) suggests that five categories from the research in group dynamics are especially helpful in training tutors to work with small groups: roles and group cohesion, identifying students' needs, workable plan and time line, jumpstarting, and floor management. Based on interviews with 37 tutors from three colleges, MacDonald reports that groups sometimes founder when tutor and tutee roles are unclear or conflict—for example, when tutees play devil's advocate, skeptic, and/or sniper, group relations can break down. Some specialized roles can heighten tension, retard group development, and stall task completion. MacDonald suggests that if the leader articulates a common task and clarifies roles, group members will work well together and accomplish reasonable tasks.

In conducting group tutoring where students in the same class have differing needs, tutors often find their group polarized, and MacDonald suggests that, if possible, it would be best to split the group in two according to student needs rather than trying to deal with them as one group. The tutor then can move between groups.

Having a workable plan and time line is important because tutors are often frustrated when students demand more time or input from the tutor than is possible or want to accomplish more than is possible. Training group tutors to form a plan for how time is to be used, allocating time to different tasks, and having alternative procedures for group problem solving can ameliorate this difficulty.

Jumpstarting involves issues in getting a group started or redirected to the task. Often tutees drift away from the subject, and MacDonald suggests that understanding how group behavior can vary from dominant to submissive, friendly versus unfriendly, and task oriented versus emotionally expressive can help the tutor get the group back on task. He further gives a number of suggestions for getting the group back on track—i. e., assigning specific tasks to specific students, leading students to attend to these tasks rather than social concerns.

Floor management is another vital skill in group tutoring. This means facilitating each person's opportunity to speak and their corresponding obligation to listen and learn from each other. Again MacDonald suggests assigning specific tasks to tutees such as listening for supportive examples, or giving examples of transitions in themes, etc.

The group tutoring training module that MacDonald developed includes steps for getting a group started, tips for keeping a group functioning effectively when it is underway, and a group simulation card game involving prescribed needs and roles (MacDonald, 1993).

For more information on training tutors to run group sessions, you'll want to read:

MacDonald, R. B. (Winter 1993). Group tutoring techniques: From research to practice. *Journal of Developmental Education, 17*(2) 2-18.

## WHO SEEKS TUTORING?

As a director of a large voluntary tutoring program, I found that many at-risk students, as well as insecure, traditionally prepared students, seek tutoring when the curriculum includes required courses taught in large lecture sections, and students perceive the professors and teaching assistants as indifferent, punitive, and unavailable. In this setting, the tutoring program, if open to all students, acts as a barometer of the institution's undergraduate teaching. If a course goes awry and the professor sets unreasonable standards, assigns an excessive amount of work, or teaches poorly, many students seek tutoring services. There are courses in which students rarely, if ever, seek help. These tend to be well-planned and well-organized courses, self-paced courses, courses in which student tutors or monitors are available in the classroom, courses with Supplemental Instruction or Adjunct Skills classes attached, or courses involving team projects or individual contracts in which students play a major role in deciding on the work they will accomplish. The key to whether there will be a large demand for tutoring seems to be whether the professor and/or the teaching assistant is available and supportive and can convey this to students, not the nature or content of the course itself.

In difficult courses, almost every student may need individual assistance, and if help is not available from the instructor or teaching assistant, the more assertive students seek help from their friends, other students, or even their parents. Freshmen (particularly underprepared students) may feel too intimidated to ask the instructor, teaching assistants, or even other students for help and prefer to seek tutoring from a program in which they know the assistance they will get is nonjudgmental and will not have a negative effect on their course grades. They may feel that if they ask a question in class, they will be judged stupid. One goal for tutors working with these students is to improve their confidence and knowledge to a level at which they are comfortable enough to ask the professor or teaching assistant a question and informed enough to understand the answer.

As one minority student in our program said, "When I got into my classes at Berkeley, I found that in some subjects things were fuzzy and unclear. The classes and sections were too large to deal with individual questions adequately; there was just very little personal attention. Also, I was reluctant to ask questions in large classes. After coming to the center two or three times, I began to notice that those fuzzy areas were clearing up."

Note: The previous statement is an example of a tutee testimonial that might be part of your advertising—to let students know how they can benefit from tutoring.

## BUT WHAT IF YOU HAVE A TUTORING PROGRAM AND NOBODY COMES?

It takes awhile to get the word about your program around campus so don't be disappointed if demand is slow at first. Some coordinators have found that advertising can help get students in initially, especially if you include Will Rogers' statement, "Everybody is ignorant, but about different things."

To summarize, tutoring demands on a learning center are heavy when:

1. The material is difficult for the average student to learn or highly abstract in content, students lack the appropriate precollege preparation, the competition is strong, or classes are taught in large lectures. (Examples are chemistry, calculus, statistics, and economics.)

2. The professor stresses theory and expects students to be intellectually mature and have excellent reading and writing skills—skills that are higher than the average student possesses (for example, political-theory courses, anthropology). Student difficulties are manifested as problems in reading and comprehending the material or as problems in determining which topics to address in a term paper and how to organize the paper.

3. There is a group of students whose skills and background are lower than those of the institution's typical students.

4. There is little opportunity for individual conferences between instructor and students, or students perceive the instructor as distant, uninterested in them, and unapproachable.

On the other hand there is little need for tutoring in courses where:

1. Instruction includes supportive Supplemental Instruction or Adjunct Skills classes or is self-paced or when student aides work in the classroom.

2. The academic department maintains a well-staffed and well-equipped course center with audiovisual aids, teaching assistants, or paraprofessional aides.

3. The department provides its own tutors who work directly in the classroom.

4. The department has made special efforts to recruit minority TAs and train its TAs, and the TAs meet with students regularly.

5. The classes are small enough so that each student can meet regularly with his instructor or TA.

## SHOULD TUTORING BE REQUIRED OR VOLUNTARY?

Programs for high-risk students generally require that the high-risk students receive tutoring, at the same time offering tutoring to other students who volunteer to reduce the stigma. Since students who lack strong motivation toward school and have a weak high school background often become discouraged, they may not seek help voluntarily. Studies suggest that, generally, developmental programs with voluntary services are more successful than required programs. However, if the program's goal is to retain at-risk, disadvantaged, minority students, requiring them to attend tutoring and other services will result in higher retention rates.

The rationale for required tutoring programs is that underprepared students who regularly attend tutoring sessions make higher grades than those having the same background and ability who do not use tutoring, although there are very few studies to support this. In general, studies find that students who receive tutoring remain in college longer, which is a reflection of academic achievement, but grade changes in specific courses are much more difficult to show. For example, one study showed that it is not the number of hours or amount of tutoring that seems to makes the difference, rather it's whether the students come in for tutoring early in the term and attend consistently.

A major difficulty in trying to assess the effects of tutoring on grades is that the weakest students need the most tutoring and, even then, whatever tutoring they get may not be enough. For example, Rowe (1994) found that neither the amount of tutoring nor the number of courses high-risk students were tutored in related significantly to their first year GPAs. However, when she dropped the students who used no tutoring and those who were tutored more than 29 hours from her sample, she found that the amount of tutoring was positively correlated with GPA.

## TUTORING CONTRACTS

A contract arranged between the student, his counselor, and his tutors is a way of ameliorating the motivational problems that may reduce the effectiveness of required tutoring programs. A tutoring contract can be tailored to the individual needs of the student. Another advantage of contracts is that they can help bridge cultures, since contracting requires the student and the instructor to communicate their needs and expectations to each other.

The tutor should take part in developing the contract package, along with the instructor, counselor, and student, and the contract should specify not only the length and frequency of tutoring sessions but the specific objectives and skills relative to the course that the student will attain. Another approach is to have tutors working directly in the classroom or lab.

In conclusion, mandatory tutoring has advantages and disadvantages, and the choice depends on the institution's philosophy about accepting underprepared students. Unfortunately, the students who need tutoring the most are the least likely to volunteer for it. If the institution feels an obligation to see that these students succeed, it should provide "intensive care packages," including required tutoring. Even if tutoring is required, it is important to help students understand what tutoring can and can't do for them. Forcing unmotivated students to attend tutoring sessions is like the old required study hall —it probably provokes more student resistance and resentment than it does learning.

The most important factor in planning a successful peer tutoring program for high risk students is that tutoring should be part of a complete program of support services including advising, counseling, study skills, and developmental courses. In addition, it is most important that high risk students be identified and counseled early—preferably before they enter college courses. As part of the orientation, students should be told how each part of the program is designed to help them, what their responsibilities are in the program, and how the program has helped others. What doesn't work is sitting back and offering services and expecting that high risk students will seek them out. They won't. In many cases tutors and peer counselors find that they have to go after students and track them in the classroom, lounge, or dormitory—even when students are told that tutoring is required.

## EVALUATING TUTORING

Investigators usually agree that tutoring is an essential ingredient of a successful developmental skills course. However, because tutoring is only one part of the services provided for high risk students, and because it can take many forms—individual, group, drop-in, in-class, as an adjunct to programmed material, etc.—it is often impossible to show that one-to-one tutoring, by itself, leads to higher grades for developmental students (Maxwell, 1990). This may be due to the fact that studies rarely control on significant variables like the amount of experience, training, and supervision of the tutors nor the fact that the students who need the most tutoring are the academically weakest and the least likely to show significant grade improvement in one semester.

Some studies have found that students with relatively high ability, or those with more experience in college, improve their grades significantly as a result of receiving individual peer tutoring. For example, Irwin (1980) studied 150 students who requested tutoring in statistics, and divided them into three groups based on their academic records. One-half of each group was randomly assigned to tutoring and the other half got no tutoring. Students at all levels of achievement who received tutoring earned significantly higher final grades in statistics

than those receiving no tutoring. She replicated the study the following year and again found significant grade differences between students receiving tutoring and those who did not (Irwin, 1981).

Other studies suggest that the relation between tutoring and grades may be more complex and involve other variables. For instance, House and Wohlt (1990), in studying educationally disadvantaged freshmen, found that students who were tutored by a tutor of the same sex earned significantly higher grades than those tutored by a tutor of the opposite sex.

For more information on this topic, you'll want to read:

House, J. D., & Wohlt, V. (1990). The effect of tutoring program participation on the performance of academically underprepared college freshmen. *Journal of College Student Development, 31*, 365-370.

Maxwell, M. (1990). Does tutoring help: A look at the literature. *Research in Developmental Education*, 7(4). Reprinted in M. Maxwell, (Ed.). (1994). *From access to success: A book of readings on college developmental education and learning assistance programs*. Clearwater, FL: H&H Publishing Company.

Maxwell, M. (Fall 1991). The effects of expectations, sex, and ethnicity on peer tutoring. *Journal of Developmental Education*, (15), 14-16 . ERIC EJ 431 647.

Maxwell, M. (1993). *Evaluating academic skills programs: A sourcebook*. MM Associates, Box 2857, Kensington, MD. 20891. (Note: Chapter 4 concerns evaluating tutoring programs and contains an extensive selection of instruments used to evaluate tutors and tutoring.)

## Why it is Difficult to Show That Tutoring Improves Grades

Tabulating changes in GPA before and after tutoring and checking on retention rates for students who are tutored versus those who did not receive it are the most time-consuming, difficult and expensive measures to collect. Further, these measures may not be valid for the program if tutoring is given only to the weakest students. But because GPAs comprise hard data, "they provide more clout for the program if they are for it, but against it if they show no difference or are negative. Consequently, few tutorial programs use these measures and those that do usually base resultant decisions on an accumulation of data over an extended period of time" (Liberty, 1981, p.71).

Typical of the research showing that the amount of tutoring does not relate to grades is another study by Irwin (1981) where she randomly assigned students in a statistics course to tutoring and non-tutoring conditions. Irwin found no difference in achievement between tutored subjects who received different amounts of tutoring per week. In other words, those who had one to three tutoring sessions a week did as well as those who received four to six hours of tutoring per week. One can only speculate on the reasons for this. Perhaps those who came for tutoring more frequently were weaker students and/or became more dependent on the tutor.

## Peer Tutoring Does Affect College Persistence

Research does show that students who were tutored remain in college longer than those who were not tutored (for a review of these studies see Max-well, 1990). Perhaps tutors encourage students to persist in their education by serving as a mentor or role model. Or it may be that students who seek tutoring are more highly motivated to finish college than those who do not come in for tutoring. Note: Supplemental Instruction (SI), which uses peer leaders to conduct student groups, has consistently demonstrated that SI students improve their grades and grade-point-averages as well as retention and graduation rates when compared with students who don't attend SI. However, SI is a more structured course-related program than the typical peer tutoring service. (See Chapter 7 for more on SI.)

## Special Considerations in Managing Tutors

### On Matching Tutors and Tutees

Although it is inevitable that tutors will work better with some students, it is often impractical to try to match tutors and tutees. Logistically, it can be an impossibility, since tutors' and tutees' schedules may not mesh. Rather than try to match tutors and tutees, we staffed several tutors in each key subject, with flexible hours, so that students have a choice of tutors. We posted tutors' schedules and pictures (taken with a Polaroid camera in color) in the reception area to help students learn tutors' names and recognize tutors readily.

One disadvantage in allowing students free choice of tutors is that inevitably some tutors will be more popular than others and their schedules will fill rapidly. By offering different types of tutoring—small-group work as well as individual help—the more popular tutors can work with more students.

In addition to providing students with a choice of tutors, it is important that procedures permit students to change tutors if the relationship is not productive. The supervisor should be alert to problems that arise between tutors and tutees, so that students who need intensive tutoring do not become discouraged and give up. Students should understand that if they are dissatisfied with a tutor, they can talk to the tutor's supervisor to make other arrangements. In an open-choice tutoring arrangement, there will inevitably be students who are tutor-hoppers, shifting from one tutor to another until they have worked with all the tutors in the program. The supervisor should be aware of these students and help tutors coordinate their efforts so they can minimize the effects of students who play one tutor against another.

Sometimes it is surprising what tutor/tutee combinations work well. For instance, we once hired a paraplegic tutor who was very popular with student athletes, especially football players. However, some students are very concerned that the tutor be from their own ethnic background or of the same sex. We have found that many Chicano/Latino male students, as well as many male students from other countries, have difficulty working with female tutors. They can make the woman tutor feel very uncomfortable by denying that she knows her subject or by flirting with her instead of talking with her. These considerations are important to students and can be devastating, as well, to tutors. Supervisors should be alert to these problems and encourage the student (and the tutor) to permit, indeed encourage, the student to change tutors when necessary (House and Wohlt, 1990, Maxwell, 1990, 1991).

One cannot eliminate all complaints or fill all demands, particularly when the supply of tutors in some subjects is small. However, it is important that tutors represent, as far as possible, the ethnic and sex distribution of the students who seek help.

I believe that supervisors, at least in the beginning stages of training, should screen tutees and assign them to the newer, inexperienced tutors, for the benefit of both the tutors and the students. As new tutors gain experience, they can work with a wider range of student problems, but if their first tutee relationship is poor, it can be a devastating blow to their self-confidence, and it will require much effort and time for the supervisor to undo the damage.

## FLEXIBLE SCHEDULING

For a tutorial program to be most effective in reaching the students who need its service, the hours it is open must be compatible with students' schedules. In any institution, there are hours when most students will be in classes—for example, early morning hours—and this time can better be used by senior staff members in staff conferences or planning than in tutoring. Appointments at 8:00 A.M., like classes at 8:00 A.M., are not popular with students, and we found that students are not likely to keep early morning appointments, a discouraging situation for motivated tutors. In our program, noon and late afternoon were popular tutoring times but it depends on your clientele.

Some evening hours are a must if tutoring services are to assist employed students, those with heavy class schedules, and athletes for whom classes, coaching, and practice leave little free time during the day. In scheduling night tutoring, building security and the safety of staff members and students must be considered. Other constraints are the budget and the willingness of staff members to work nights. Tutors who are also students frequently prefer night hours. If the service is located in a library, there are fewer problems with safety and security, as other staff members and students are in the building, parking lots are well lit, and transportation service is usually available. Rather than attempt to keep our building open at night, we used rooms for evening tutoring in the undergraduate library, which was open until midnight. However, the program outgrew the space, and soon there were enough clients to open our building evenings. Another alternative might be to use dormitory meeting rooms for evening tutoring.

As we noted in the chapter on learning centers, it is also important to have adequate child care facilities near the tutoring center. Allotting a room at certain times for mothers to run their own babysitting program can help fill an important need.

In beginning an evening program, it is important that the service be well advertised through announcements in classes, in the campus newspaper, and on bulletin boards, and that sufficient time elapse for students to learn about the service. Drop-in and small-group tutoring services seem to work better than scheduled individual appointments in the evening so that tutors aren't left with empty schedules.

A major difficulty that tutoring programs encounter is staffing a separate night shift of tutors, particularly in schools with a large number of night classes. Since instructors in night classes tend to be hired on a part-time or per course basis and many are moonlighting from other teaching jobs, they tend to be minimally involved with the institution's support services and administrative programs and they don't have office hours. This makes it hard for tutors to contact and work with them. In addition, the night-shift tutors are not likely to have much contact with day-shift tutors and learning specialists, and unless special arrangements are made, they may get little support or supervision. One way to eliminate the morale and other difficulties generated by separate staffs is to systematically schedule regular meetings with both day and night staffs and faculty members (at the beginning and end of each term, at least), pay staff members to attend, and allow time for them to interact socially on an informal basis, as well as to discuss the program, its goals, and its effectiveness.

Staffing tutors on weekends can be expensive unless there is a regular and sustained demand for their services. The same problems of building security and safety that characterize evening tutoring sessions are encountered. However, adult part-time students who work full time and attend evening classes often need special help and are free only on weekends. A survey of students' needs for weekend tutoring, their willingness to use it, and their preferred hours can provide information on the feasibility of staffing a program on weekends and the most popular hours. For example, in our program we found that the most popular hours were from 10:00 to 3:00 on Saturdays and that some Sunday hours were desirable in the week preceding examinations.

In summary, tutoring hours should be flexible so that students who need the service can schedule it. Holding to a rigid eight-to-five or nine-to-five schedule and closing at the noon hour for lunch will restrict the number of students who can be tutored and will penalize those who work part-time or have heavy class schedules and may need tutoring the most.

## DROP-IN CENTERS

Drop-in Centers are a popular way to offer tutoring in math and science. The success of this arrangement depends on whether the tutors can work with more than one student at a time, with small groups, and/or move from student to student, spending just a few minutes with each. Our Drop-In Center had cafeteria tables, each labeled with a course name and number, larger tables for small groups, and carrels where tutors could work privately with one or two students at a time.

At the tables, the tutor's role was that of a learning facilitator, not an answer machine. The tutor helped students work together in groups of two to six and assisted them if they had difficulty. The objective was to create an informal, unpressured learning environment—a place where students could study with friends. (Libraries are too formal for many students, and librarians tend to frown on conversations. Besides, librarians usually cannot help students with their calculus problems.) One backup tutor at peak times can work individually with students who need more intensive help.

Students liked the Drop-In Center since they did not have to schedule formal appointments, and the idea of working with others with a tutor present proved very popular. Another aspect of the Drop-In Center is that it provided a comfortable place for commuter students to study who might lack facilities at home. At peak times—for example, before exams—the center was open longer hours on weekends including Sundays.

We found the Drop-In Center was a great way to encourage collaborative learning. Students who entered the Drop-In area alone, to sit and study, soon began working with another student or a tutor.

Studying in a group appealed to many students. It is hard for the freshman student who feels alone and alienated to make friends in a large lecture class. Some solve this problem by taking the same courses as their friends. Others spontaneously formed their own study groups in the Drop-In area and met regularly. Others showed up even when no tutor in their subject was scheduled. However, some complained, "I came here to get tutoring and ended up being the tutor." The problem of students who fail to keep appointments plagued us, as it has most tutoring centers. This problem is greatly reduced with a Drop-in Center, for if a student does not show for an individual appointment, the tutor can go to the Drop-In and work with another student or group of students. This improves the morale of the paid tutor or volunteer, since "no shows" are especially discouraging if tutors' pay or credit is determined by how many hours they work with students.

Drop-in services present special problems in evaluation because they lack clear criteria for student entrance and exit. Since students typically use drop-in services only occasionally, often just once or twice, it is not feasible to try to measure the effects of this kind of tutoring on grades. Student satisfaction with the service is the criterion most often used, although in a sense, evaluating a drop-in tutoring service is like evaluating an all night drugstore. If students (or customers) find what they are seeking, they are satisfied. If not, they are dissatisfied.

## OTHER PROBLEMS TUTORING PROGRAMS FACE

Tutoring services face problems that are similar to those of other student services, and some that are unique to tutoring. These include political problems, staff morale, logistical problems caused by a heavy student demand, and sometimes overt faculty hostility. Since tutoring programs typically serve special groups of students, especially disadvantaged minority students, they can get caught in battles between student groups. They may have less autonomy than other services when administrators are concerned about the institution's image with special groups. Sometimes friction between different ethnic groups about the administrator's ethnicity or the program's basic philosophy can doom a program to failure unless the college's administration can find ways to resolve these differences. It is sad, but true, that students may turn against the services that offer them the most personal and important help and, in a sense, bite the hands that feed them. It is the administrator's responsibility to see that the needs of different groups are adequately addressed.

## STAFF MORALE

In addition to pressure from minority student groups, staff members can suffer from morale problems and "burnout," just as others in the helping professions do. When the workload is heavy, the pace is frantic, future funding and positions are insecure, and tutors are continually being evaluated by anxious students, staff morale may fall. Faculty cynicism and criticism can have a devastating effect on a conscientious tutor. Moreover, a tutor loses enthusiasm when there is little or no improvement in his tutee's learning as the end of the term is approaching, when both tutor and tutee have worked hard. A tutor can become depressed when he fears the student will fail. Unrealistic expectations of what a student should be able to learn and commitment to help the tutee sometimes conflict, and under pressure the tutor tends to do the work for the tutee or becomes impatient or too strict. Tutors who expect gratitude from their tutees may be disappointed when

the tutee brags, "I got a B+ and I did it all myself." (But, then, isn't that the ultimate goal?) On the other hand, the tutor may be furious when the student brings in a paper with a low grade and says, "Look what we got."

Tutors need support in setting realistic objectives for tutees, and they need clear ways to evaluate learning gains. Usually peer tutors compensate for lack of knowledge through their enthusiasm and willingness to help; however, some have problems with the tutoring role and need help clarifying ways to become effective.

Other staff problems are those that affect a tutor's comfort and sanity: sheer physical exhaustion, lack of time, losing patience, handling the desperate tutee who comes in at the end of the tutor's scheduled work period and wants "just five minutes," having too many students to work with at once, having another tutor grab one's tutee, and not being able to help a student work a difficult problem. All these problems can be worked through if there is a regularly scheduled time for the tutor to sit down to talk with a supervisor and/or other tutors. Sometimes the answer is to "Just say NO. We can't take anymore students!"

We found that team-building and relaxation/concentration workshops given by our counselor were most productive when they were given to the staff, not the students. Boredom and anxiety may plague staff members too. To boost staff morale, experts recommend you try the following: (1) Members of the program staff must be given autonomy over the program. (2) Job descriptions should change within the program structure as often as possible. No person should work in one area more than three years. (3) Staff members should be trained to be people-oriented, not subject- or cash-oriented. (4) In-service training for all staff members should include consciousness raising, discussions of self-survival, and discussions of how to design effective strategies for low achievers.

## LOGISTICAL DIFFICULTIES

Tutoring programs often attract more students than they can serve, and even with tightly controlled caseloads, there are periods before exams when students want and need extra help. The logistics of bringing students and tutors together, finding enough space, and providing materials become formidable, particularly at the end of the term when students seek extra help and tutors themselves have to study. One can plan for these exigencies by limiting service and scheduling senior staff members for more time in group sessions. In one program, senior staff members were scheduled to cover all drop-in hours during the last two weeks of the term; we called them our "Band-Aid Brigade," realizing that helping students reduce their anxiety before exams was a useful service. I have not tried the "study table and panic clinic," in which facilities are open twenty-four hours a day during exam week, but some feel that it is worthwhile (Enright, 1976).

There are also differences in opinion concerning whether group review sessions and mock-exam practice sessions are beneficial to students. Certainly, if they are well advertised, many students will attend.

Some nagging questions haunt tutoring programs. Should there be a limit on the amount of help a student may receive or the length of time he or she may be tutored? (One way some writing centers are handling perennial tutees is to train them to be writing tutors.) Should ground rules for excluding students from tutoring be set, or should cases be decided individually? Each of these alternatives is used by some tutoring programs. Should students applying for tutoring be screened by a learning specialist? Should tutoring services be limited to students who sign up before a certain date (except for emergency referrals from administrators or faculty members)? Should advanced students, who may need an occasional boost to help them pass a difficult course, receive tutoring? Tutoring coordinators may have to decide where to draw the line on these questions if the program has limited funds.

## FACULTY NEGATIVISM

Some faculty members have negative attitudes about tutoring. They have either had direct experience with abuses of tutoring or heard horror stories about tutors who did students' homework, read their books for them, wrote their papers, and even took exams for them. It takes patience and effort to help professors overcome these prejudices and educate them to the quality and kind of tutoring that your program offers and how it can improve academic standards. Complaining about students' lack of skills seems to be an ingrained faculty position and one that new staff members may find most discouraging. A strong faculty advisory board can help strengthen the image of the tutoring service with other faculty members, as will the improved performance of students who are tutored, but it takes time and continual effort to build bridges of mutual trust between tutorial staff and faculty.

## RESEARCH ON TUTORING

Until quite recently, few studies on the effectiveness of college tutoring programs were done. Tutoring did not capture the interest of researchers, because historically, tutoring arrangements had generally been private and informal. If professors tutored, it was assumed that their students would learn. Similarly, if honor-society members tutored, they were considered qualified and their effectiveness was not questioned. The large tutoring programs developed in the 1960s to help minority and other disadvantaged students were not designed as educational experiments and tended to be informal and unstructured. As a result, their effectiveness, when judged by post-hoc investigators, could not be validated. As tutoring programs become more formal, structured, and costly, their effectiveness is being questioned, and college peer tutoring is beginning to attract greater interest from researchers.

It is interesting that researchers who evaluate college tutoring tend to attribute achievement gains to the enhancement of the student's self-concept resulting from the close personal relationship developed with the tutor, while those who study elementary students stress the structured aspects of the tutoring session as having the greatest impact on improving achievement (though not negating the improvement of self-confidence that comes from mastery of the material and from personal identification with a tutor). Although it is self-evident that tutors should relate to underprepared students in an empathetic and nonjudgmental manner, I question whether confidence in one's ability to achieve can improve unless one can see improvement in one's learning skills and understanding of the subject matter. A structured program enables students to measure their progress in these areas.

Another way to assess the effects of tutoring is to ask students whether they feel their achievement level has improved and what might have happened if they had not received tutoring.

A basic problem in studying the effects of tutoring is that most students who receive tutoring are weaker in the subject than those who do not, so that studies often reveal that the post test grades of students who were tutored are lower than those of students not receiving help.

Another factor that affects the results of research on tutoring is motivation to succeed in college. Studies generally show that those students whose grades are expected to be in the average range (based on high school background and entrance tests) participate in tutoring the most and profit the most from it. The predicted lowest achievers profit the least from tutoring or do not use it.

There is evidence, however, that underprepared college students receiving enough tutoring with enough regularity will get higher grades in the course, at least when tutoring is voluntary.

Motivated and better-prepared students use tutoring more regularly than the less well prepared, who may either get discouraged or deny their lack of background. If there is a large discrepancy between the tutee's background knowledge and skills and those of the typical student in the institution, one cannot expect tutoring alone, no matter how intensive, to improve the tutee's grades. Furthermore, the weakest students may not come in for regular tutoring. Mike Rose, when he was coordinating tutoring at UCLA, reported that students with GPAs below 2.3 often denied their need for tutorial support with the same reasons offered by those with GPAs of 3.5 or higher. They gave excuses like, "It doesn't seem necessary," or "I can't fit it into my schedule."

To improve this situation, the director must address the problem of how to identify those students who need tutoring early, find ways to encourage them to accept help, and make sure that the tutoring program is designed to meet their needs. For tutoring to be most effective with underprepared and academically weak students, tutors should be trained in teaching basic skills and using structured materials. Without this kind of preparation, tutors tend to emulate their professors, with the result that students who are motivated and closer to average in ability and background receive the most tutoring and profit the most from it. Tutors who have been selected for high achievement in a subject are not likely to use methods that differ from those used in their classes, and they are more likely to reward students who are motivated and can learn rapidly. Those tutees who do not fit this profile may soon become discouraged with the tutors' approach and stop attending tutoring sessions.

At-risk students who are achieving poorly and deny the need for help pose a special problem. Counseling and contracting may help if the student "doesn't know that he doesn't know," but if the student lacks motivation to study, it is hard indeed to help. It is important to understand that being tutored may have some negative psychological implications for the tutee, which may account for the reluctance of some to seek help. If tutoring is to reach more students who need it, ways must be found to avoid hurting their pride or making them feel inferior.

## IMPACT OF TUTORING ON THE TUTOR

I've always felt that tutoring is socialization for college teaching. Certainly, it provides an experience that differs from being a teaching assistant in a large class and reveals a different aspect of classroom learning—that of the individual student who may have misconceptions and misunderstandings about the subject even after listening to the best lecturer. Many tutor coordinators have observed that the tutoring experience affects tutors career plans too. For example, a study at University of Minnesota-Duluth showed that 39 percent of the tutors agreed that the tutoring experience had influenced their decision about their future profession and 69 percent said they planned to continue their schooling beyond the baccalaureate degree.

That tutoring benefits the tutor academically is amply documented in the studies of cross-age tutoring and peer tutoring in public schools, and there is increasing evidence that the same effects hold with the college-student tutors, whether they are tutoring mathematics, writing, or science courses. McKeachie (1990) in a review of the research in higher education concluded, "If you want to succeed in college, pay to be a tutor; don't pay a tutor." (This quotation is a great incentive to prospective tutors.)

Starting from the premise that one learns more by teaching or tutoring others than by being tutored, we got a small grant at Berkeley in the 70s to improve the retention of minorities and women in the sciences. Beginning freshmen who had some interest in science and at least average ability were apprenticed to senior tutors who taught them to tutor in the beginning college courses they were taking. Since they tutored in the same courses they were taking along with their tutees (a true peer-tutoring situation), they needed training and close supervision. The peer tutors attended group tutoring sessions where they observed the senior tutors' tutoring style, met in weekly seminars on how to tutor, and received intensive tutoring themselves. The results were very satisfying; most students from this group went on to finish graduate school or professional school programs in science, and they were excellent tutors throughout their undergraduate days.

Research on college tutoring, its programs, and its process is slowly increasing. The many studies of tutoring in public schools offer a framework for exploring more sophisticated questions about college tutoring, including whether structured tutoring is more conducive to producing learning gains in students than looser, more humanistic approaches, and how materials and interpersonal relationships interact to produce gains. Some studies suggest that the amount and regularity of tutoring correlates with college course grades (although this is often difficult to show), but generally, studies show that tutoring increases the retention of disadvantaged students.

Research findings reflect the experience of tutor coordinators—that tutors benefit from the experience perhaps even more than their tutees. The experience of being a tutor has many advantages. Not only do tutors improve their own knowledge and their achievement and performance on standardized graduate and professional exams, but it also helps them clarify their career plans, gives them experience and insights about teaching and learning, and provides them with valuable experience in participating in a multi-ethnic work situation that's difficult to get in predominantly white institutions. As Priscilla Fortier of the University of Illinois-Champaign's Office of Minority Affairs explains, "Providing a good experience for minority students can be a top priority, but how about the wonderful bonus to all students (especially majority) of learning to solve problems and accomplish meaningful work in a diverse environment? Actually, all of our campus upper level administrators should be concerned about whether or not we are training ALL OF OUR STUDENTS for the workplaces of the 21st century." We need more complex studies that include the many individual and intervention variables involved in tutoring and an adequate data base so that programs can be compared. At present, tutorial-program directors primarily assess student reactions to their services; this is a beginning, but additional studies on student outcomes are needed.

To summarize, individual peer-tutoring is probably the most frequently used academic support service. Students like tutoring and feel they gain from it. However, demonstrating that students who are tutored earn higher grades is difficult and rarely achieved. There is an increasing body of research that suggests that students who are tutored remain in college longer. This may be a result of the tutee's identification with the tutor, or the tutor's function as a role model, or something we don't know about. As studies become more sophisticated and begin to include tutor training and experience as variables, the effects of tutoring on academic success may be more clearly demonstrated.

Group tutoring appears to work best in courses with large lecture sections. It's more difficult to tutor students in groups when the class sections are taught by different professors. Given a choice between individual and group tutoring, most students will choose individual work, since it is hard to get any individual help on large college campuses unless one is persistent and assertive. However, some students prefer group tutoring. They feel less threatened in a group where others freely ask questions than in one-to-one tutoring, where they feel they are on the line to perform.

## THE FUTURE

Rapid changes in technology are affecting tutoring as they are other facets of higher education. In the 70's, when tutors were assigned to small groups of students reviewing professor's video-taped lectures so that they could stop the tape and question or discuss points, student learning was enhanced. Currently Videotaped Supplementary Instruction (VSI) groups have succeeded in developing needed skills for high-risk students enrolled in difficult courses at the University of Missouri-Kansas City. MIT has on-line tutors on the campus computer system to help students with problem-solving. These tutors are not paid, but rather tutor for the prestige of being an on-line tutor. For example, if a student is stuck on a problem in astro-physics, she can dial the computer to ask her question and the on-line tutor who feels most competent to discuss the topic with her replies. Purdue University has an on-line writing lab (OWL) that provides information on writing problems to anyone who seeks it, and community colleges are experimenting with using on-line tutors from four-year colleges.

Despite the tremendous growth and potential of Internet and related services, it is my personal opinion that live, one-to-one tutors will not disappear and will continue to be sought out by students. Those who need to talk out their problems will not adjust well to being lost in cyberspace when searching for answers, and even if someone gives them the answer, as we all know, it will be of little benefit unless they learn how to find answers for themselves.

# CHAPTER 4

## ESTABLISHING LEARNING CENTERS

"Why do you call your service a learning center? Isn't that the mission of the whole college?" This is the question faculty members and administrators most frequently ask learning-center directors. The usual answer is that learning centers assist students in basic skills and learning beyond that which faculty members have time for during their class sessions and office hours. Were it possible for colleges to offer small, homogeneous classes taught by professors deeply dedicated to and rewarded for teaching, perhaps learning centers would not be needed, and a skilled ombudsperson might suffice to negotiate and resolve problems that might arise between teacher and students. However, most public postsecondary institutions in the United States have become knowledge-dispensing factories. Mass production is as ingrained in American higher education as it is in automobile manufacturing, despite the lip service paid to the importance of working with individuals. Although students are permitted to choose colleges and their curriculums, they are subject to pervasive similarities in admission rituals, courses, credits, requirements, and teaching styles. In college one must adapt to the academic requirements in order to succeed, sometimes compromising one's own interests and needs with the demands and constraints set by faculty members and administrators. Learning centers exist to help our increasingly diverse students make this adjustment.

The majority of U.S. colleges and universities now have some sort of academic support service,

apart from regular academic courses, to help students improve their learning skills. In 1978, Sullivan undertook a comprehensive survey that identified 1,848 learning-center components in 1,433 independent colleges and universities in English-speaking North America (Sullivan, 1978). From Vassar to the Virgin Islands, from Georgia to Guam, colleges are offering special professional help to underprepared students. Learning center services proliferated in the 70s as colleges attempted to aid and retain underprepared students, with the number of learning centers doubling between 1974 and 1977. Four-year institutions showed the greatest increase (Sullivan, 1978).

### LEARNING CENTERS DEFINED

Learning centers are as varied as the institutions and the students they serve, yet, like other facets of academe, they share common functions, goals, and strategies. Sullivan (1978) defines learning center components as containing some or all of the following elements: instructional resources, instructional media, learning-skill development, tutoring, and instructional development. He reports that a number of institutions have more than one department or unit offering these components. Enright (1975, p. 81) defines a learning-assistance center as a "place concerned with learning environments functioning to enable students to learn more in less time and with greater ease, offering tutorial help, study aids in content fields, serving as a testing ground for innovative machines, materials and programs, and acting as a campus ombudsman." Peterson (1975, p. 9) offers a somewhat different description, "A learning center is an amalgamation of four services: library, audiovisual service, nontraditional learning activities (including tutoring), and instructional development service" (that is, the center assists faculty members in developing new teaching strategies, materials, and courses). The Committee on Learning Skills Centers (1976) explains that a learning center is a special location where students can come—or be sent—for special instruction not usually included in "regular" college classes. The committee notes that centers offer various services, from individualized instruction or special classes to tutoring, and work on self-help materials. The New England Association of Academic Support Personnel (1977, p. 1) describes learning centers as "places of various sizes, where students can find personnel (professionals or trained peers) and materials (of varying degrees of sophistication) to help them with specific problems. Classes are run from the center, drop-ins are encouraged, and much individual counseling takes place." Many learning centers offer students such multiple services as individual and group skills programs, tutoring, preparation for graduate and professional exams, and media and materials for self-paced instruction. Some concentrate their programs on special groups such as student athletes, the disadvantaged, the physically handicapped, or international students; others serve all students. Some offer credit for reading and other skills courses; others do not. Whatever the local title, learning centers are found in public and private colleges, two- and four-year institutions, universities, and graduate and professional schools. (See Chapter 1 for other definitions of learning assistance services and Figure 1-1 in Chapter 1 for a model of a comprehensive learning center for a community college.)

## HISTORICAL BACKGROUND

Campuswide learning centers that offer skills and tutorial services to all students are a relatively recent development. Enright (1975) notes that 57 percent of the learning centers in U.S. colleges became operational between 1970 and 1975 and that directors were considered mature practitioners after only four years in the field.

From an historical viewpoint, learning centers are merely the latest development in a long series of attempts to help students adjust to the academic demands of college. Study skills handbooks have been published since 1916, if not before, and "how to study" courses were required of underachieving applicants to the University of Buffalo as early as 1926.

During the 1930s reading-improvement courses became a part of college "how to study" courses. The tachistoscope and other devices developed and used in psychological research on vision and perception were adopted by college reading specialists, who attempted to apply the research findings of Javel's on eye movements, Buswell's on mature reading, and those of Huey and Tinker, among others.

During World War II groups of young men attended college for brief periods as part of their armed-services training, and courses were truncated. After the war, veterans flooded our colleges. Men from both rural and urban areas, who would not have considered going to college had it not been for the G. I. Bill, returned from service and tried their luck at getting a college degree. In many colleges the federal government funded vocational guidance centers, which later became campuswide counseling centers. Many of the veterans needed help with basic reading, writing, math, and study skills, so programs, usually located in counseling centers, were developed to help them.

By the late 1940s, college remedial and developmental reading and study skills courses were expanding rapidly. Many relied on the use of machines like bulky pacers (which required ripping books apart, since they held only one page at a time), tachistoscopes for increasing eye span (the number of words seen per fixation), films, and other devices. Reading specialists debated whether it was more effective to teach rapid reading with an instructor and a stopwatch or with a battery of machines. Spache (1955) wrote that college reading programs emerged from the laboratories of psychologists, traveled into the classrooms of education and English departments, and then moved into counseling services.

Required college orientation courses proliferated in the 1950s, including reading and study skills, career planning, and improving motivation. Orientation courses were usually offered for full or partial credit. As separate college reading-improvement courses became more common, they too were given for credit. Causey's nationwide survey in 1950 found that about half the colleges offering reading courses gave credit for them (Causey, 1955).

Although American public universities have historically been based on an egalitarian philosophy, by the 1930s most state universities required that entering students present at least a B average in college preparatory courses. Even with these standards, a large number of students were expected to drop out before the sophomore year. In the mid forties, a number of state universities were faced with a threat from state legislators who were proposing laws requiring them to admit all state high school graduates, as the University of Minnesota had been forced to do in the 1930s. Minnesota founded a General College, which accepted any state high school graduate who failed to meet normal admissions standards. The General College offered its students courses and

the opportunity to transfer to regular university courses if they earned high enough grades, or the option of remaining in the General College and getting a degree there. (The General College is still viewed with some opprobrium by Minnesota students, who call it Nicholson High School because its classes are held in Nicholson Hall.)

As a result of similar legislative pressure, Pennsylvania State University established a special Counseling College where students admitted on probation received counseling, reading and study skills help, and other services while they took regular courses. In 1947, the University of Maryland, facing the passage of similar laws, developed a "holding college" for students entering with below-C high school averages. Originally a part of the extension division, it later became a separate department. Students were required to take a study skills and college orientation program their first semester called "College Aims," for which credit was given. They received special academic advising, tutoring, and counseling and were permitted to take a light load of basic courses required for their intended majors. During their second semester, they were required to take a reading-improvement course, also for credit. They could transfer into a regular college if they earned an average of 2.5 (C+) their first semester or an overall 2.0 (C) for the year. Transfer students with poor academic records from community colleges were also required to participate in this program (originally called "Special and Continuation Studies"). By 1960 there were several thousand applicants for the program annually, and it was affecting dormitory spaces and departmental teaching schedules. To alleviate these pressures, all low-achieving applicants were required to take an intensive eight-week summer program consisting of counseling, reading, study skills, advisement, and two regular courses. (This program was named the Pre-college

Summer Session.) Students who attained a C average were eligible for regular enrollment in the fall. The required summer session greatly reduced the number of students applying and overloading facilities in the fall. Today we call such programs "summer bridge programs" but one should note that they started long before "Upward Bound programs" began.

Although the Maryland program included individual counseling, during most of the 1950s, group or class work was the major approach to teaching study skills and reading. Weigand and Blake's *College Orientation* (1955) typifies the techniques used, many of which were based on Robinson's earlier work, *Effective Study* (1946-1970), a rather pedantic, psychologically sophisticated work. By the mid fifties, the colleges and universities shifted their emphasis to identify and train the brightest students, and extramural funding for programs to help marginal students was practically nonexistent. With the launching of Sputnik, the pressure to develop the intellectually gifted increased.

By the late 1950s, programmed learning materials based on B. F. Skinner's ideas were being developed at a rapid rate. The new technology and philosophy made possible the development of individualized reading programs at the University of Florida (Spache and others, 1959), the University of Maryland (Maxwell and Magoon, 1962), and the University of Minnesota (Raygor, 1965). Other colleges soon adopted self-instructional programs.

The spread of open-admissions policies in the 1960s offered opportunities for disadvantaged minorities and underprepared students to attend college in large numbers. Even the most selective institutions increased the number of students who did not meet the school's regular admission standards.

Government funding enabled colleges to establish special minority tutoring, counseling, recruiting, and advising centers, independent of other services. Traditional reading and study skills programs also served these students, though in smaller numbers. The growth of educational technology, plus the admission of large numbers of underprepared students, led to the development of learning centers, often a product of the merger between minority tutorial programs and existing reading and study skills services. In 1966 I described plans for a campuswide multidisciplinary learning center (Maxwell, 1966a), and others expanded on this self-help, multi-skills model. Christ (1971) describes a "cybernetic, student-oriented" learning assistance center with diagnostic testing, specific objectives, and self-paced materials and machine programs geared to each student's needs. Christ's model operates with a small staff and does not offer credit programs. Many learning centers, particularly in the Western U.S., have patterned their programs after Christ's model. For example, Burns (1991) recently designed a comprehensive learning center model for the California community colleges, essentially based on Christ's program and includes developmental courses. You'll find a diagram of Burns' model in Chapter 1.

As a rule, learning centers in public universities provide diagnostic testing, individualized laboratory work, computer-assisted instruction, tutoring, and skills groups (usually noncredit minicourses). Two-year public colleges and open-admission colleges are more likely to offer courses with formal credit for their programs.

Centralized learning centers, like their predecessors, reading and study skills programs, are usually founded by administrative fiat, by pressure from academic departments, or, more rarely, by pressure from students. Some evolved from programs in counseling centers, where trained counselors found working with underprepared students' learning problems difficult and less satisfying than counseling clients with personal and/or vocational problems. Others started in colleges of education, an outgrowth of early reading clinics.

Improvements in educational technology and the resistance of many college librarians toward integrating media and self-paced instructional materials into their regular collections were other factors precipitating the development of learning centers. Some centers combine many functions, serving underprepared students and regular students as well as providing media resources for faculty members. For example, many colleges have a large learning-resources center that helps faculty members develop courses utilizing media as well as offering tutoring and skills help to students, under the assumption that through merging current learning theory with technology, classroom instruction could be improved.

Learning centers in large public universities continue to grow rapidly and offer a broad range of services. Today, most house undergraduate tutoring programs. However, some centers offer mainly reading and study skills programs and restrict their services to these general skills. Others have expanded their services and hired specialists in writing, sciences, mathematics, and other subjects and provide services for the learning disabled as well as physically challenged students.

## Organizing a Learning Center

The first step in organizing a learning center is that one or more faculty or staff members become interested and see the need for the service. They then must convince the administration of the value of implementing such a program. Many learning centers evolved casually—serendipity rather than careful planning characterizes their founding—usually "sponsored" by a single, dedicated faculty member. Today's emerging center is more likely to evolve as a result of the deliberations and recommendations of a task force set up by the administration and comprising faculty members, students, counselors, and administrators.

Note: Key questions that one who is setting up and/or applying for a position as director of a learning center should ask, as suggested by Karen Smith of Rutgers University, include:

"What were the motivating factors behind the decision to implement a learning center? Increased retention? Increased G.P.A.'s? Assistance for targeted groups? Other? Can I clearly define each factor to be addressed by the center?"

"What are the expectations (demands) of the administration? Can I identify the expectations of the supervising agency as well as all others who had input in the decision to implement the program? How can I balance the conflicting expectations which will arise in the development of the program? Can I respond to different divisions (athletes, faculty, dean, minority program director, etc.) without compromising the program's credibility with the students it will serve?"

## Administrative Location of a Center

Where should the learning center fit in the institution's organizational hierarchy? Existing centers vary in their location. Some are independent units, others are under academic departments or counseling centers or independent units under student affairs or attached to libraries or learning resource centers.

Ideally, the learning center belongs under the administrator who can provide maximum support and nurturance for its roles and functions and who will permit the director autonomy. The precise administrative structure in which these conditions are optimal varies from institution to institution, and historical precedence, power politics, and departmental feuds are important factors in choosing a structure. In large public universities, the present trend seems to be for learning centers to become separate units under the dean or vice president of instructional support services or teaching/learning center, a change from a decade ago when most programs, at least those in large universities, were in student services or, in some cases, libraries. While some programs today remain under counseling auspices, others are part of developmental skills departments or autonomous.

Perennial institutional reorganizations seem to insure that ancillary services such as learning centers will continue to shift positions in the administrative hierarchy. For example, the reading and study skills program at West Point was recently moved from the library to the Performance Enhancement Department, where students using modern technology (including Alpha Chamber Relaxation Machines) to improve their athletics performance, work along side others who are working to improve their academic performance. Certainly students and athletes share similar needs—improving self-image, concentration, and reducing stress—and perhaps that is the rationale for the change.

University programs nested in counseling centers often perform a function for counseling psychologists analogous to the services rendered by teaching assistants who instruct freshman classes for graduate professors. That is, by teaching the large undergraduate courses, TAs enable professors to teach small graduate seminars in their specialties. Similarly, the learning center, with its typically large number of student contacts and its lower paid staff, often enables the highly paid counselors to continue their traditional role of one-to-one counseling. The student contacts of the learning-center staff inflate the total use figures of the counseling center and are most helpful in justifying budgets. Some counseling-center directors provide a very comfortable, supportive environment for their learning centers, enabling them to develop large, strong programs and insulating them from bureaucratic problems and campus politics.

People in power, programs, and priorities change, and the present administrative organizations of learning centers as well as their functions will change, too. When enrollments in upper-division English, education, and humanities courses decline, there is increasing pressure for academic control of remedial programs in four-year colleges and for learning centers to be staffed by tenured faculty members, regardless of whether they have had experience in supervising learning assistance programs.

Although some studies, like the National Center for Developmental Education's EXXON Study, suggest that independent departments are more effective in preparing developmental students for college success, my feeling is that it depends on many factors, such as administrative support discussed above. (Note: The EXXON Study was directed by Hunter Boylan, Director of the National Center for Developmental Education at Appalachian State University, Boone, NC. Thus far there have been around 30 studies and papers resulting from the analysis of data in the study. Hunter Boylan has promised to put all of the information in a book. So I will refer to the EXXON Study and hope that by the time you read this, his book will be out. If not, write Hunter with your questions.)

## SETTING OBJECTIVES

The next step in organizing and developing a learning center is to determine its mission and specific objectives. The learning center's mission should be consistent with the mission of the institution within which it functions. It is important in accepting the position of learning center director that one understands what the administration sees as the center's mission and sometimes this can be difficult to learn. Asking the question directly may not even elicit the answer—an administrator may say something like, "Our students need tutoring and we want a learning center like our sister community colleges have." This would greatly restrict the center's functions. Or in a research university, the administration may feel that the Center's role is to help regularly admitted students primarily, and not work with developmental students or those with learning disabilities.

Functions will depend on institutional needs and funding. Specific objectives should be based on needs-assessment surveys of students and faculty members. The program's objectives should be clear enough to evaluate and to change when students' needs or curricular revisions dictate. Information describing the specific objectives of the learning center should be widely disseminated to students, faculty members, and administrators. The objectives should be developed with input from the center's staff and accepted by all staff members.

What are typical goals for learning centers? Reed's (1974) survey of seventy-eight college peer-tutoring programs for the educationally disadvantaged lists the following student service goals of the institutions responding in his sample. I believe that these goals are also applicable to learning centers.

1. To provide academic support for students who lack the educational background for college work. (This means underprepared students.)

2. To ensure student retention in college and subsequent graduation.

3. To help students improve their self-concepts as learners.

4. To help students develop self-confidence and reduce fear of failure.

5. To improve human relations and the sense of campus community among students.

6. To provide individualized help.

7. To provide help in developing study skills.

8. To improve academic performance. (This goal is "concerned with improving the academic performance of students who are performing at academically successful levels but who may be capable of doing better work"—Reed, 1974, p. 10.)

Other goals of learning centers include:

1. "To assist students in becoming more independent, self-confident, and efficient learners so that they will be better able to meet the university's academic standards and attain their own educational goals" (Student Learning Center, University of California at Berkeley). (Note: Some have defined the term "independent learner" even more narrowly, implying that the center somehow "fixes" students' problems once and for all so they should no longer need services. Others, particularly directors of writing centers, argue that students continue to need the advantages of peer support and collaborative learning that centers provide, and centers should plan how to incorporate former tutees into the program as tutors and continue to support their development as they move through college.)

Another viewpoint is that a desirable goal is to have learning programs assimilated by their institutions so that there will no longer be a need for them. As Enright states, "Learning centers will have succeeded when they have put themselves out of business, and less ideally, learning centers will continue to serve and to protect students as a group and to prod and push faculty as individuals, making slow headway toward renovation of the college. Under this construction, the learning center will be integrated into the educational system as a constructive critic."

2. To provide a place where faculty members can refer students in academic difficulty who need help in reading, writing, and study skills improvement or diagnosis of their learning problems.

3. To ". . . support each educational method of each instructor, meet the separate and individual learning and study needs of each student, and provide cultural and educational opportunities to the community" (Learning Center Unlimited, Cuesta College, San Luis Obispo, California). This last goal illustrates the wide scope of a center that combines tutoring, skills help, and a learning-resources center/library serving students, faculty members, and the community.

4. To enable students to professionalize their academic work with services that benefit high-achieving students as well as high-risk students and any student who wants to improve. The program also serves as a faculty/staff professional development resource for assessing teaching, learning, and working styles (The Learning Center, Lesley College, MA).

## OBJECTIVES AND CRITERIA OF SUCCESS

The objectives listed previously are mainly addressed to the student service functions of the learning center, and some seem quite easily measurable, like improving retention and graduation rate. However, one should be cautious in establishing objectives that are either too broad or too specific to be realistic. If the skills and knowledge of the population to be served are two or more years below those of the average student in the college, it is unrealistic to expect that the center's program will "save" most of these students. If, for example, 20 percent of the high-risk students survive to graduation (a not unusual rate), the program may be viewed as a failure by administrators and professors who expect more, yet may not be aware that the graduation rate of the average student in that college is only 25%. It is very important to put survival statistics in context. The national rate of persistence to graduation in four years among regularly admitted college students used to be around 50 percent, but today's students take longer to finish degrees and the percent graduating in four years varies greatly between institutions.

It is important to know the completion rate in your college and have background data on the success of high-risk students so that you can put the results of your program in proper perspective. Hinging the success of a learning-center program on unrealistic student retention goals or improvement in grade-point averages places the responsibility for underprepared students' success on the support service, not on academic departments and other enabling or deterring aspects of college life, so that the center risks being used to preserve the instructional status quo. Faculty members will resist making needed changes in their courses and curriculums if the center is considered solely responsible for survival of academically weak students.

Another caution in using client retention in college as the criterion for judging the effectiveness of a learning center is that dropping out of college may reflect a realistic and positive decision. For example, if students decide that they are better suited for a trade or technical career and leave college to enter on-the-job training, their decisions may indicate personal growth and maturity. Some way of accounting for such changes in student occupational goals should be a part of the center's evaluation plan. (For instance, learning-skills counselors could rate the degree to which a student's educational goal is appropriate or realistic.)

Currently many community colleges use as a criterion of success, not just whether students graduate or complete programs, but also whether they leave college in good standing (so that if they wish or have a need for more study, they can return without prejudice). This latter is important in an era when many students are adults, attending college on a part-time basis.

Another important goal might be to improve the academic performance of tutors or student aides, as well as that of the clients. Improving tutors' skills requires a more intensive training program and closer supervision if students selected as tutors are not highly skilled in their subjects.

## THE CENTER AS A CATALYST FOR CHANGE

I prefer to think of the academic support service as a catalyst for the improvement of undergraduate instruction in the institution as a whole. This means that the learning center assumes a preventive role and attempts to make the campus academic environment more conducive to student success, rather than limiting its functions to serving the victims of poor teaching, unrealistically difficult examinations, and unreasonable faculty expectations. It does not mean promoting lower academic standards or helping students find in curriculums the loopholes that will help them avoid learning. Serving a catalytic role requires that the center develop ways of working closely with instructors, not only to alert them to student difficulties and special needs, but also to encourage different ways of teaching. This is a difficult and sensitive area, but a great many instructors are concerned about how well students master their courses and welcome feedback about those who are having difficulty, especially since these students rarely complain.

The tutorial/skills program can be a barometer of the undergraduate climate, for when courses go awry, many students seek help. If data on student demand are systematically collected, they can be used to examine the causes of student problems and to explore ways to ameliorate them. In this way, students can be helped who do not volunteer for services. The center might be viewed as a large ameoba, reaching out to serve students in a particular subject, identifying needs and strategies for helping them, turning over the information to instructors, and then pulling back (or being pulled) into another area.

Heard (1976, p. 6) states that if we carefully define and intelligently limit the learning center's roles, "there should come a time when we don't measure our effectiveness by the numbers who walk in our doors. Rather we should observe the numbers whose needs are served comprehensively in a concerted effort throughout all departments on campus."

To summarize, learning centers need to clearly specify what their student services are and how those services are related to academic programs and the faculty. These goals should not be so broad in scope that they are unattainable and unmeasurable; however, they should describe the center's responsibility in improving instruction. If a center is to effectively help underprepared and low-achieving students, it must avoid assuming complete responsibility for redeeming failing students, but also it must work effectively with faculty and administrators to help students uphold high academic standards.

Note: In the mid 80s a set of standards and guidelines for learning assistance programs were developed and adopted by the Council for the Advancement of Standards (Materniak & Williams, 1987), an organization that currently is comprised of 28 associations in higher education. The Learning Assistance Program Standards have been reviewed and accepted by related professional organizations such as CRLA, NADE, ACPA (Commission XVI), and others, and address 13 topics: Mission, Program Leadership, Organization and Management, Human Resources, Financial Resources, Facilities and Equipment, Legal Responsibilities, Equal Opportunity, Access and Affirmative Action, Campus and Community Relations, Diversity, Ethics, and Assessment and Evaluation. In 1995, the original standards and guidelines were revised and are included in the Appendix of this book. Check the CAS S&G's Mission Statement #1 and other standards for more specific information about the topics discussed here. (See Appendix 4-1.)

## SELECTING THE DIRECTOR

To succeed, any academic support service needs the commitment of both administration and faculty to its goals. After defining the general goals of the program and the responsibilities of the director, the next crucial step in organizing a learning center is to select a strong director. The director should be knowledgeable about the social and political realities of academic communities, recognize the sources of power, be respected by faculty and students, and be sensitive to student needs. The director must also sell the program to the college community and have good business-management skills.

Directors of learning centers and tutorial programs come from many backgrounds and have been trained in a wide range of academic disciplines, including counseling, sociology, psychology, business, music, physics, and mathematics. However, most frequently they have teaching experience in English or social sciences and/or education.

What attributes are essential in a director? The director plays many roles—teacher, counselor, researcher, writer, public relations specialist, consultant, trainer of staff members and paraprofessionals, professional educator. In centers in small colleges, the director may be expected to perform all these functions. In centers where there is a large staff, the director may hire specialists to assume some of these duties. Successful directors must also function as catalysts for change within their institutions, as critical consumers of the emerging research and development literature in the field of college learning, and as administrators. They are expected to be excellent teachers, to be competent lecturers to groups of faculty members and students, and to be able to relate to both small groups and individual students. As administrators, they need the knowledge and skills necessary to plan, develop, and implement programs, supervise the staff, establish procedures, and make decisions. In this era of accountability, they must be able to evaluate and justify programs and justify their expenditures. (Accounting skills are useful.) The ability to develop good public relations is necessary, for the director must keep an ever-changing student body and peripatetic faculty informed of the center's services.

In our publish-or-perish academic society, directors—particularly those in larger four-year colleges and universities—are expected to do research and publish within their specialties. They must also prepare annual reports and descriptions of their programs for budget committees and the college administration, design and develop new programs to meet student and faculty needs, and obtain grants from outside funding sources.

Training staff members and paraprofessionals is a vital function, because few applicants for learning-specialist positions have either experience or formal training, and as budgets tighten, staffing must depend on paraprofessionals. Directors also serve as consultants and on campus committees, advising other faculty members within the institution as well as community and public school groups and other professional educators' associations.

Learning-center directors also need to be able to hold their own with other faculty members. Some directors maintain their identification with their own academic discipline—psychology, English, mathematics or whatever—as well as with reading, study skills, and educational professional associations.

Directors can function as catalysts for change within their institutions through serving on committees and working directly with faculty members in academic departments. In a sense, directors function as student advocates, and if they can contribute knowledge about student problems that are generated by rigid academic procedures, inappropriate instructional strategies, and unrealistic grading prac-tices, they can help make the academic environment more responsive to student needs and prevent their own programs from being overloaded with students.

As a critical consumer of research and development in the fields relevant to learning and basic skills, learning-center directors must keep abreast of current publications and other sources of information. They should be wary of the misleading advertising claims of some publishers and commercial companies that promise quick and easy solutions to student problems. For example, there are a number of high-priced rapid-reading programs designed for business and professional people that are inappropriate in content and method for college students, yet the salespeople insist these programs are suitable for the college market, with the result being that students who take them may find them a waste of money.

Directors need a broad background in reading and study skills at all grade levels—the theories, philosophies, controversies, methods, materials, and research. They also need to understand the principles of individual diagnosis and treatment, testing methods, and evaluation techniques. Knowledge of counseling theories and techniques is also important, as are the ability to, and interest in, continuing to learn and improve.

Directors must develop a thorough understanding of the academic procedures, customs, and rituals of their institutions in order to help students and train staff members. They need to understand faculty demands and expectations in different academic departments and be aware of instructional goals, teaching strategies, grading practices, and academic requirements. Directors must also know about the requirements and demands of professional and graduate schools if they are working in four-year colleges, where many students seek help in preparing for advanced work and in preparing for the admissions tests. In other words, directors must know how the system works and be alert to changes, particularly those that will affect the center. Ideally, directors of learning centers should participate in committees planning major changes in policies that affect undergraduates—changes in admission policies, degree requirements, departmental prerequisites for majors, and so on. But in reality, these decisions are usually made without input from the learning-center director, who is faced with revising his/her programs after the decisions are made. Directors also must know the other resources on campus for students so that they can refer students to appropriate units for help and develop cooperative rather than competitive programs.

In addition to being intelligent, knowledgeable, creative, and nice people, what other attributes are necessary for the successful learning-center director? Directors, particularly those running small programs who work directly with students' problems, should be able to relate well with students with diverse backgrounds—slow learners as well as fast learners, students with different learning styles and those from different socioeconomic backgrounds, members of ethnic minorities, foreign students, physically handicapped students, athletes, and many others. Directors must also be able to relate well to other administrators.

Directors should have broad intellectual interests. To develop strong programs in different disciplines, they need an understanding of the assumptions underlying different fields of knowledge and how knowledge is organized in different fields. Obviously one cannot be an expert in every field, but one should know how reading and study techniques can be applied to different subjects.

Perhaps the most important attribute the director of a small program needs is the ability to provide emotional support and encouragement to a student who has not learned how to learn but is now motivated to try. Directors of large programs must help their staff develop sensitivity and rapport with students, and it is the director who must provide the support for staff members and a favorable climate in which they can grow.

Flexibility and responsiveness to change, personal integrity, a high regard for intellectual goals and the individual, and a strong feeling of personal worth are other personal attributes that should be considered in selecting a director.

In summary, the center director serves many roles and needs much in the way of skills, knowledge, and personal attributes. Some of these skills can be learned, and knowledge can be acquired, but the personal attributes discussed may not be teachable. Those who select the director must, therefore, screen candidates for these characteristics. Since few of us can walk on water, it is highly unlikely that one individual will possess all the characteristics described, but they do represent areas that should be considered. Ideally, the director can then select specialists and other staff members to complement his/her abilities and fill in the gaps of his/her weaker areas.

Even if one were to possess all the abilities and skills described, it would help to have tenure in an academic department. With the vicissitudes of the current collegial Zeitgeist, one should not expect to grow old and retire as a learning-center director.

## STAFFING

Most learning centers have few full-time professional staff members. On the average, they employ a director and one or two learning specialists and rely on student help. In community college programs where remedial courses are given for credit, the usual pattern is to have several paid instructors and a learning laboratory staffed by paraprofessionals or work-study students. Often the courses are taught by part-time paraprofessionals as well.

College learning specialists, unlike college counselors and other college personnel workers, rarely have formal training or graduate study directly related to their positions. Coming from many backgrounds, including counseling, education, English, and psychology, they develop their skills in working with college students on the job. Few graduate programs in the country offer master's degrees in college reading and study skills. In the early 70s there was only one, offered by Dr. Alton Raygor at the University of Minnesota. However, in the past 15 years, a number of universities have started master's-level programs for community college reading and writing specialists, including Southwest Texas University, National Louis University (Chicago), and Appalachian State University. Grambling University (LA) is the only institution so far that offers a doctoral program specifically in developmental education. To be sure, there are many opportunities for direct experience with college students in other universities, where graduate students are usually offered teaching assistantships or internships in learning centers as part of their experience. Or they may take credit practicum courses that train them to work with students with special learning needs. Generally, applicants with a degree in reading curriculum, counseling, or English seek jobs that offer experience in establishing and managing reading and study skills programs or other support services. They learn by doing. Managerial training and experience are necessary for directors' positions in large institutions.

Professional associations provide institutes, special programs, and other in-service training, and local consortia of learning-center programs are forming all over the country to exchange information. For example, NADE (The National Association for Developmental Education), CRLA (College Reading and Learning Association), MCLCA (The Midwest College Learning Center Association) have regional and state affiliated groups.

Universities have often been criticized for neglecting training in remedial teaching for their students who are planning to be college instructors, yet the teachers themselves report that on-the-job experiences are more beneficial than their previous university courses. Learning specialists in mathematics and science tend to have degrees in these subjects but little training in remedial techniques or diagnosis; those who are motivated to work with student problems generally develop skills on the job. I have found that it is easier and faster to train a chemistry major to be a learning specialist in chemistry than to train a counselor to work with students with problems in chemistry. Currently, science departments in large research institutions are hiring Ph.D.'s in the subject (e.g., chemistry) to coordinate and improve instruction in basic lower division courses and to work with students, train tutors, etc. In other words, they are providing learning support services to both faculty and students. (For a description of the qualifications of a college reading specialist, see Brozo, W. G., & Stahl, N. A. (1985). The college reading specialist competency checklist. *Journal of Reading*, 28(4). A copy is included in Appendix 9-1 of this book.) For job descriptions and performance appraisal forms for College Reading Specialists, Learning Specialists (Levels 1 through 4), Center Library Assistants, Tutoring Directors, Administrative Associates, Administrative Assistants and Senior Office Assistants, see M. Maxwell's (1993), *Evaluating Academic Skills Programs: A Sourcebook.* MM Associates, Box 2854, Kensington, MD 20891.

## CLERICAL STAFF

Clerical staff positions are important too, but surveys suggest that learning centers have very few clerical positions unless they are federally funded. Large programs usually have an administrative assistant, a secretary-receptionist, and several clerical student aides. Some smaller programs have just one clerical worker, who functions as typist, receptionist, monitor of the self-help program, and recordkeeper. Others have only work-study student clerks and rely on other departments for typing reports or special work. The role of the secretary/receptionist is vital. In a personal communication, Sam Silas of William Paterson College (Wayne, New Jersey) says: "Whether the secretary/receptionist is a regular eight-hour-a-day staff member or a work-study worker, careful attention should go to this person's selection. It is normally the nature of the secretary/receptionist's job description that makes her/him the most visible person in the program. Hence, through the secretary/receptionist, the question of the program's public image becomes a critical issue. With the right person in this position, many glaring weaknesses can be skillfully covered up. With a slightly inept person in the secretary's chair, the possibility of negative misrepresentation forever hovers over the program. In brief, the secretaries of learning centers need to be sharp of mind and knowledgeable of office procedure and philosophy. Also, the secretary needs to be inordinately committed to the program's success and have a great deal of empathy for students."

The cost of staffing a learning center varies tremendously from college to college, depending on the kinds of services offered, the level and types of people employed, and the source of funding. Regardless of the size and complexity of the program, however, the costs of learning support services continue to increase as do college costs in general.

Grants for academic support programs are becoming harder to get, and the ever-increasing costs pose a special dilemma for programs that have been started or expanded with extramural funding. How will such programs survive when the soft money runs out? Campus administrators recognize that academic support services are and will continue to be essential to the many underprepared students they accept. Yet they are concerned about the financial feasibility of continuing the services. One solution is to employ a core staff (a director and several professionals) using permanent funding and supplement it with faculty rotated from teaching duties. Another is to make all positions 9-month appointments and pay anyone who works in summer programs from a special budget for summer school activities.

Computing projected costs for tutoring services is the most difficult aspect of budget planning. It is very difficult to predict with any degree of accuracy how much and what kind of tutoring students will need in a given year. Tutors who conduct groups are usually paid one or two dollars more per hour than are those who work individually with students, but group tutoring is appropriate for only some courses. To reduce tutoring costs, centers often give students credit for tutoring instead of paying and/or recruit volunteer tutors from the campus or the local community.

Certainly the number of staff members budgeted affects the number of individual student conferences the center can provide and the nature of the program. Some learning centers serve all students on a first-come, first-served basis, and when hours are filled, students must wait until the next term. Others provide free tutoring to special groups—athletes, EOP students, or students on financial aid, for example—but require other students to pay. Most study skills programs, particularly noncredit group programs, are open to any student without charge. Many private colleges charge extra tuition to students taking reading and study skills or remedial courses. Some centers charge a nominal fee to motivate students. For example, the Writing Clinic at the University of Southern California charges one dollar per visit. However, whether charging students additional fees is desirable is still a debatable question.

Learning centers often earn extra funds by providing services to faculty members and non students for a fee. Offering special summer programs for college-bound high school students and review sessions for students preparing for graduate and professional exams are other ways to get extra money.

## ATTRACTING STUDENTS AND DEVELOPING A POSITIVE IMAGE

A learning center's success depends on its image to students. A program can be carefully developed, staffed with excellent people, yet remain unknown and unused by students. One good indicator that a program is succeeding is when students refer their friends; however, in starting a new program or in informing an ever-changing pool of students, the services must be publicized. Academic advisers in small private colleges write personal letters to new students describing the special academic services that the college offers and counsel students into programs. Similarly, the counselors in most special programs for disadvantaged students or other target groups in larger institutions contact students individually by form letters and arrange conferences. In large public universities with many student services and complicated registration procedures, however, new students receive so many pieces of mail from the school that they ignore them. Many student services departments now produce student handbooks listing and describing all the services on campus (a way of reducing printing and mailing costs as well as coordinating services, although I'm not convinced that students are more likely to read them).

One must work to develop an image and to inform the campus community. This does not happen spontaneously. There are many ways to let students know about your services: movies, tape-and-slide presentations, talks at freshman orientation, brochures, bookmarks, articles and ads in the student newspaper, television "commercials" (between closed-circuit television classes), speeches to classes and student groups. To ensure that students will voluntarily use the program, it seems that they must learn about it from several sources. They may hear about the learning center in freshman orientation, but often they are too busy reacting to other students and the strangeness of the new experience they are in to recall services discussed in orientation. Of course, some students who fear that they are unprepared for college courses will sign up for programs immediately, but most need more than one exposure to the fact that the program exists. I find that many students hear about the center in orientation, see newspaper ads about minicourses, hear about it from their friends, and then see a small notice on a bulletin board that triggers their coming in for assistance. Others have heard about the program many times but do not come unless referred by a faculty member. In other words, students need to be reminded a number of times, and when they feel the need for the service, they will come. There may be a long incubation period between sending out publicity and seeing students arrive at the doorstep. I recall Henry, who carried an ad about our program in his wallet for two years before coming in; and more recently, a group of students came in with a brochure that was six years old asking about the old reading laboratory.

Our center had brochures and bookmarks placed in the library and the checkout stands at the student bookstore and, of course, announcements in the campus catalogue and student handbooks advertising group programs, tutoring for credit, and special services. We found that purchasing ads in the student newspaper was the quickest and best way to attract students. We also sent announcements to academic departments and other student services to post on their bulletin boards and put up posters at Sather Gate, where other student activities were advertised for students walking into the campus to see.

The effectiveness of our ads varied with the topic of the minicourse and the time of year. For example, an ad stating, "Wanted: Slow Readers . . . to help us test and evaluate a new self-help program in speed reading . . ." drew 150 students in the winter quarter but only 5 in the spring quarter. "Can you tune out the trivial and zero in on the important ideas in listening to lectures?" (an ad for the Xerox Listening Program), attracted fewer than 5 students each time it was placed. Speed-reading courses inevitably fill if they are scheduled at convenient hours, although during the first few years of our program, the groups tended to be fairly small. Currently, with a dynamic instructor, this program attracts more than 1,000 students a year. Study skills programs offered on a voluntary basis tend to attract fewer students

than speed-reading programs. We offered a minicourse titled "Academic Survival Skills: Coping with Berkeley's Course Demands," scheduled early in the fall, but few students signed up. Students apparently do not want to "survive"; they want to succeed. We changed the title to "The Academic Game: How to Play and Win" (from Hanau's 1972 book of a similar title), and about 20 showed up, but most dropped out by the third session. Undaunted, we scheduled informal one-hour sessions on particular skills; depending on the topics and when they were scheduled, they worked well. But watch the timing; do not schedule sessions on reducing test anxiety at the beginning of the fall term.

Usually it takes a few terms for a minicourse to "catch on." Two that I wish had been continued were "Improving Your Reading Skills—For Honor Students and Those Who Aspire to Be" and "How to Like Reading," an open-ended group dedicated to the proposition that reading can be fun, interesting, worthwhile, meaningful and that it need not be a bore or just a task. Only three students signed up for the latter course, and although they were enthusiastic about it, we did not offer it again.

Patricia Heard of the University of Texas-Austin suggests that the least popular programs (though they may be the most needed by students) be listed first in the center's publicity—such as groups in improving communication skills or improving reading comprehension. Students are usually highly motivated to take speed reading or attend review sessions for the Medical College Admissions Test and will spot these offerings, even if they have to turn the page or search a long list.

Some publicity strategies that learning-center staff members have developed to attract students are very creative. For example, Brenda Wright at the

University of Missouri Pharmacy School printed up colorful bookmarks in the form of prescriptions—Rx for academic success, listing the skills needed for textbook reading, test taking, notetaking, studying, and so on—and checked the box labeled "refill," typed each entering pharmacy student's name on top of a bookmark, and laminated them in plastic. Other programs print up paper placemats or napkins for the dining hall. Library displays also can be planned to illustrate services dramatically. I recall one we did years ago that featured an open book with a spider's web and a large rubber spider to illustrate the need for increasing one's reading speed. Announcements on the campus radio station, recorded or call-in programs, such as dial-a-study-tip, center hotlines, and just about everything else, with the possible exception of sky writing, have been used to inform students of services.

Occasionally, new center directors find that they have been hired to manage an ongoing program that has a negative image among students, administrators, and the faculty. Perhaps the previous director alienated a group of faculty members, or perhaps students found the programs rigid, boring, or simplistic. The first things I would do in this case would be to change the name of the center, develop and advertise new programs, and set about building bridges with the faculty and student clientele.

## WHAT'S IN A NAME?

Choosing a name for your learning center is an important step in establishing an image. Students inevitably use acronyms, so be alert. Academic Support Service may sound like a reasonable title, but do you really want your center to be known as ASS and your staff members called "asses"? Even the popular term Learning Assistance Center has its drawbacks. McHargue (1975) reports that the

Stanford program became known as "lack" and the staff members were dubbed "lackeys." The University of Texas Reading Improvement Program (RIP), called by some "rest in peace," was changed to RASSL (pronounced "wrassle"). After the service expanded to include tutoring, the director refused to change the name because 90 percent of the 40,000 students at the University of Texas at Austin knew about RASSL. Today, however, it is simply called The Learning Skills Center (LSC).

Titles for learning centers vary. If I were giving an award for the most appropriate title, it would go to OASIS, the support program for EOP students at the University of California, San Diego. Laura Symons, who directs the program at Sweet Briar College, calls her Academic Resource Center the ARC and her many student helpers, ARC-angels.

If you feel the need to rename your program, sponsor a contest and give a prize to the student who creates the best title. Not only will you get some clever entries, but this is an excellent way to publicize a new or revised program. Seminole Community College in Florida had a contest to name their program and the title that won the prize was "The Learning Center." Sounds pretty ordinary, doesn't it? But, think about the acronym. TLC stands for tender, loving care and has carried the Center's message to both students and staff. And it is not surprising that "The Learning Center" has become the title of choice in many colleges.

## BUDGET

Learning-center funds come from varied sources—departmental instructional budgets, student registration or activity fees, chancellor's discretionary funds, affirmative action monies, profits from vending machines on campus, direct charges to student users, etc. Some centers are funded from several of these sources, and often federal, state, or foundation grants make possible special services to underprepared or other target groups of students. Extramural funding, such as athletic funds or grants for veterans or the handicapped, may determine which students receive help. Some centers have no budget at all, and their staff and resource monies are contributed by different departments. For instance, one staff member may be paid by the counseling center and another from Department of English funds.

Budget size limits the number of staff members who can be hired, although in many colleges FTE (full-time equivalent) positions are harder to get than funds. Directors then must hire part-time or temporary staff members and live with high staff turnover. The best arrangement is to invest in a small permanent career staff (including both learning specialists and tutor supervisors) and hire part-time experienced tutors and/or paraprofessionals and train them to train others. Since few experienced, trained professionals are available for recruitment, most centers train their own staff. Undergraduate tutors-for-credit and volunteers, if trained and supervised, can enable the service to reach more students at minimum cost. We have found that a half-time tutor or study skills supervisor can train and supervise ten new, inexperienced student tutors. Currently, programs are forced by budget cuts and inflation to reduce their full-time staffs and place career employees, including clerical workers, on nine- or ten-month contracts, making it harder to develop programs and retain qualified staff members.

Some programs are funded on "soft money," so that staff contracts are negotiated on a year-by-year basis, with continued employment contingent on the renewal of the grant. Studies in the 70s showed that both directors of learning centers and those of tutoring programs felt they needed larger budgets, but in interviews with directors, researchers found that none had requested additional funds nor were they planning to do so.

In an era of tightening budgets, directors must often fight to hold onto existing funds and positions. Learning centers in private colleges are among the most vulnerable units for budget cuts, layoffs and elimination, unless the college is dependent for students on federally funded grants and scholarships. Even in public colleges where the need for learning centers is great, learning center directors may be constantly pressured to seek grants in order to keep their programs viable.

Besides salaries, discussed under "Staffing," what must a learning center budget include? Supplies and office expenses (including equipment maintenance) are essential items. Generally, these expenses make up 5 to 10 percent of the center's total budget, depending on the size and type of programs offered. In addition to supplies such as paper, and office expenses such as telephone and mailing, the learning center director should budget for replacement of instructional materials, tapes, and films. In centers with a large number of computers, audiovisual equipment, and other electronic aids, maintenance and rental costs may dictate that a larger percentage of the budget be spent on this item. Programs that serve large numbers of students find that advertising and handouts to students and other expendable materials can be costly but important. For example, the Learning Skills Center at the University of Texas-Austin gives out as many as 15,000 handouts on scheduling and time management in the fall term; fraternity scholarship officers and dorm counselors come in for armfuls.

I have observed that when new centers are formed from existing departments, the hardest funds to transfer are the supplies and equipment expenses, for they are often buried within the larger budget. For instance, while positions and the salaries attached are usually clearly spelled out on budgets, phone expenses, duplicating costs, equipment, and furniture are averaged per employee. In the case of a learning center that is formed from some of the staff of a counseling center, the learning center staff needs may be greater than those of the average counselor for duplicating, materials, and phones. Yet it may take years to acquire one's own xerox machine in the learning center while clerical staff are expected to run to another building for xeroxing needs.

Equipment is usually the costliest item in starting a new center. Tape recorders, audiovisual aids, software and computer terminals not only are very expensive but must be selected with care so flexible programs can be developed and maximal use obtained. And one must budget for maintenance and replacement costs. Different filmstrip machines use different kinds of film, different tape-recording devices may require different tapes, and computers may require different software. Machines wear out and educational equipment becomes obsolete quickly. For example, if you had a meeting and the speaker wanted to show a CD-ROM program, could you get the equipment quickly?

It is good to select equipment which has the software you need for your student clientele and which can also be used for other purposes, such as developing your own materials (if you have the staff, time, and talent).

In 1973 Karwin estimated that $53,000 would equip a center with forty-five study carrels wired for electronic equipment, twenty videocassette players, twenty color television receivers, five computer terminals, fifteen calculators, twelve electric typewriters, twenty microfiche viewers, fifty audiocassettes with headsets, and one cassette duplicator. I doubt that you could approach that amount of equipment for anything near that price today—nor would you necessarily want those items. With the rapid obsolescence of today's computers and other electronic equipment, it is wise to compute rental costs on an annual basis and compare them with purchase costs before making a decision to buy. I have visited many elaborately equipped learning laboratories where costly machines (including computers) are almost never used by students. Once the novelty wears off, the machines wait unused, quietly rusting unless heroic attempts are made to integrate the programs into the students' courses.

If you are outfitting a new lab, consider carefully what equipment is most needed. Think about what will happen when every student on campus has his or her own battery-operated computer, a condition that is rapidly approaching. What difference will this make to your program, especially if students can log in from their wireless lap tops at home and get your programs, or surf the Internet, or dial in class lectures they have missed? Will the Internet make your computer software obsolete? In fact, can your present computer stations handle CD-ROMS or Multi-media? (Note: As of 1994, less than 5% of college courses used these technologies but this is bound to change.) And there are other questions to ask as new technology is developed—if professors use pen-based automatic blackboards that convey written information directly to students' computers, will it change our notions of note-taking? Or will we find the old adage about notes going from the professor's notebook to the student's lap top without going through the heads of either still true? Perhaps we should begin thinking about the effect that the ever changing developments in computer capability and software will have on our programs. In other words, how soon will our present labs and equipment become obsolete?

## IMPORTANT CONSIDERATIONS IN PURCHASING HARDWARE AND SOFTWARE

There are other aspects of purchasing new hardware and software that should be considered to assure that the decision is a wise one. Robert Hahn and Gregory Jackson, in a recent article in the *Chronicle of Higher Education* (Point of View, May 24, 1995), warn that in purchasing technology, colleges often overlook some key elements of academic life such as institutional and individual resistance to change, and fail to realistically examine the ways that the new technology will improve learning or enhance teaching. (Note: Technology provides just another means of teaching or learning, and its effects are no more certain nor easily measured than traditional lectures, labs, or written assignments.) Furthermore, administrators often ignore the costs of providing security for the equipment, maintenance, depreciation and periodic replacement, much less the costs involved in training users and assisting them as problems and questions arise. To ensure that equipment becomes cost-effective by being used regularly, special programs must be offered to faculty and staff so that they will know how to make full use of the equipment in their daily activities.

Too often higher education administrators seem to believe certain myths about technology:
◊ that it saves time and money. This is usually not true. It does do some things faster and better like contacting students via e-mail, locating information in the library, and conducting research, but rarely do these save money or time.

◊ that investing in technology is a one-time event and/or that any continuing need for technology can be obtained through grants. In fact, budgeting money for technology upkeep and replacement must be a part of every annual budget or the advantages will soon disappear. Nothing gets obsolete faster than today's computer technology.

As mentioned earlier, it is important to keep up on ever changing software and we have included a section in Appendix 12-1 describing ways to keep abreast of new software for developmental education.

## BUDGETING FOR PROFESSIONAL AND INSERVICE TRAINING

Budgets should also include money for miscellaneous expenses, including travel costs (both for bringing in prospective employees for interviews and for sending staff members to professional conferences) and staff-training costs. Some educators recommend that 20 percent of the total budget should be allocated for evaluating the services, but learning centers rarely attain that goal unless funded by special grants under which evaluation costs have been allocated in advance. (Note that in the CAS Standards on Learning Assistance Programs in Appendix 4-1, we recommend that money for evaluation efforts be routinely included in the Center's budget.)

In preparing the center's asking budget, it is important to remember that asking budgets are created to be cut. Each administrator who reviews the budget may, depending on his conception of his role, slice items before it reaches final approval. (Years ago I headed a service where my supervisor inevitably red-penciled budget items. I requested a Reading Eye Camera, an expensive piece of equipment, each year for eight years, and since it was always at the bottom of the list of items arranged in order of priority, and was expensive, he always red-penciled it. Though I never got the camera, I was able to preserve staff positions and necessary materials and equipment by putting it on the end of my list each year.)

I like the model of the asking-budget process that some business executives advocate. They suggest thinking of the asking budget as a wheel with spokes and a hub. The hub represents the basic money you need to keep essential services operating. The spokes represent additional personnel or items that you would like and can prepare adequate justifications for. Ask for the wheel. You usually will not get the whole wheel, but you may get some of the spokes. If you request only the hub (the barebones budget), you are likely to have essential funds cut, with the result that you must either reduce your programs or overwork your staff.

When a center's budget for equipment and supplies is too small, the director may decide to write a grant proposal for money to equip the center or modernize its materials and media. It inevitably takes months to receive the funds, if the grant is approved at all. In the meantime, if you are offering services to students and need materials, try to find local sources that can provide money and/or services: student associations, research projects, community groups, local businesses, alumni associations, etc. Frank Christ at California State University at Long Beach sent letters to faculty members requesting donations of textbooks, self-paced programs, audiovisual equipment and other learning aids and collected a great deal of equipment and materials. You may get some useful items, and you can realize a few dollars from the junk by selling it at the flea market or a garage sale.

Many years ago it was possible to buy sets of used texts (older editions of those currently required) for five cents a copy. This was an inexpensive way to acquire realistic material for class instruction in study skills. However, today most labs use computer software for training. Nevertheless, maintaining a library of books as study aids is still desirable. For example, our center was given a library of some 300 calculus textbooks by the mathematics department because the department lacked storage space. The books were reviewed by our mathematics staff and catalogued. A math specialist wrote brief comments on the textbooks he rated as most valuable such as:

"Calculus by X—Covers concepts taught in our courses 1AB and 16AB. Nonrigorous, generally good reading. The author's explanations are often poor, but the book is full of comments inserted by the author's students, and these are quite illuminating. There is also a lot of excellent historical material. The examples and problems are very good and each chapter ends with six sample exams, four of which are one-hour length and two of which are longer.

Calculus by K—Covers concepts in our 16AB. Nonrigorous and very good reading. This book comes closest to reading like a novel of any calculus text I know, but long-windedness is its major fault. It has little historical material, but the author tries to make sure that the real-world need for each technique is apparent before it is introduced. This is the antithesis of the approach used in the current required texts where theoretical sections are followed by applications sections. There are two good summaries in the appendix which would be useful as reviews, not as introductions, to analytic geometry and trigonometry."

These reviews were useful for students who had trouble understanding their present text or just wanted to learn math from a different perspective.

We also rented a $4,000 cathode-ray-tube computer terminal from the local stock exchange for $1 a month during a lull in the stock market and obtained several teletype computer terminals free from professors who had completed their research projects or had bought newer models. (In those days computer hardware was much more expensive than today.) An incentive for professors to donate dollars, books, or equipment is the tax write-off benefit. If you estimate the fair market value of a donation of materials or equipment and write a "thank you" letter specifying the dollar value of the gift, the donor may use the letter to document the contribution for tax purposes. (Check with local Internal Revenue Service office for details.) Occasionally, professors have turned over the royalties from their books to our program. These modest amounts help pay tutoring costs. Some centers have established programs for regular faculty donations through payroll deductions. The alumni branch of the women's honor society often donates funds for the purchase of special pieces of equipment, and a number of smaller foundations have been generous in providing funds to start innovative programs. And we were able to purchase larger equipment, such as a computer multiplexer board and a videotape machine, through our regular budget channels by sharing the equipment and costs with other departments.

## LOCATION AND SPACE

Real estate is said to have value based on three factors: location, location, and location. The same thing can be said about the importance of location to a learning center. Experts seem to agree that the learning center should be centrally located on campus and easily available to students. But sometimes that can be difficult to arrange. For example, housing it in the library would seem to be an ideal spot, but if the library is located on the north end of campus and undergraduate classes are held one-half mile away on the southside, this may be a poor location. Of course there are certain spots that one should definitely avoid, such as being housed in the college's administration building, which can mean the kiss of death as far as students are concerned, or on the fifth floor of a busy office building with lots of workers heading out to lunch at the same time complaining about students tying up the elevators. One new director learned to her chagrin, that the space assigned to the learning center was an empty trailer located atop a hill on the perimeter of the campus. "The Loft" on the third floor of Old Main where the elevators don't work would be an undesirable spot for tutoring. I've been in one center that deserves to be named "The Dungeon." It is located in the bowels of the oldest building on campus where the only entry is through a narrow, winding tunnel.

The amount of space allocated can often be a problem too. Many learning centers have learned that their clientele expands much faster than the space they have. There are centers with a dozen staff members—both professional and clerical—operating the space of a small classroom. Sardines would feel at home there. When this occurs, there is usually a department head defending unused space for a smoking room for the staff or the class that meets one hour a week in the TV studio. But space and staff are the academic coin of the realm and academics fight to protect their turf.

For help in designing and furnishing a center, you'll want to read:

White, W. G., Jr., & others (1990). College learning assistance center design considerations. *The Educational Facility Planner*, 28(4), 22-26. (Reprinted in Maxwell, M. (Ed.). 1994. *From access to success.* H&H Publishing Co., Clearwater, FL.)

White, W. G., Jr., & others (1990). College learning assistance centers: Spaces for learning. In Hashway, R. M. (Ed.). *Handbook of developmental education.* Praeger, New York, 179-193.

White, W. G., Jr., & Schnuth, M. L. (1990). College learning assistance centers: Places for learning. In Hashway, R. M. (Ed.). *Handbook of developmental education.* Praeger, New York, 155-177.

Space and staff positions are the two territories over which academic power battles rage. It is the rare learning center that does not soon outgrow its allotted space—even when new buildings are designed especially for it. As staff and programs—especially tutoring—expand, the center is forced to schedule study skills groups in some far corner of the campus or to turn tutors loose to find empty classrooms, a corner of the library, or unused areas of the campus dining hall to meet their student clients. Part-time staff members are difficult to monitor when they are physically removed from the center's main facilities. As group programs draw more students, it requires the expertise of an experienced diplomat to find classrooms for minicourses or graduate-exam review sessions.

Learning-center directors sometimes find themselves involved in a continuous struggle to expand or hold onto their territory. They need some knowledge of architecture and facilities planning. Ideally the learning center should be located in an attractive building in the center of the campus. Occasionally this materializes, but on older campuses, centers tend to be housed in available space—for example, in "temporary" buildings on the wrong side of the tracks or in a corner basement office. When George Spache was director of the University of Florida's Reading and Study Skills Laboratory, he complained that students had to walk through his office to get to the reading laboratory. Winifred Cooke at Southeastern Community College (Whiteville, North Carolina) described the offices of her staff as located on a balcony high above and overlooking the basketball court in the college gym. The Learning Skills Program at the University of Texas-Austin has no enclosed space for tutors, and so they sit with their tutees at tables in the corridor, under the skylight and next to the railing lining the atrium on the fourth floor of Jester Hall.

The program's facilities ostensibly reflect the institution's commitment to the program. However, since older campuses have limited funds for capital improvements, newly emerging centers compete with expanding academic departments for space, and they are low on the priority list. Given the choice, I would select the facilities that are most conveniently located for students over a fancy suite of offices on the fifth floor of an office building on the periphery of the campus. In fact, we fought to retain our old World War II temporary building, rather than being moved to an upper floor of the student union building, by taking a traffic check of the number of students using our programs at noon and arguing that the move not only would restrict the number of students using our programs but would irritate other workers by tying up the two elevators during lunch hour, one of our peak demand times.

While fighting for additional space, one should also develop alternative plans for maximizing the utilization of existing space. I suspect that learning-center directors are already famous for the number of walls they have knocked down—I know I have ordered many walls removed to make room for learning labs, drop-in centers, and group programs. I learned long ago that it is better not to partition off space into small offices or carrels, for needs change. Movable furniture and dividers or screens are more practical and enable multipurpose use of space. If carpeting, drapes, and other sound-reducing materials are installed, the room can hold a number of staff members and students working individually or in small groups without the noise that seeps through plywood partitions. Although noise can never be totally eliminated, it is possible to reduce distracting noise by drop-in arrangements; the many conversations serve as white noise, masking individual voices. There are few activities that cannot be handled well in an open room, properly furnished and arranged. Even individual counseling on personal problems can be offered this way if student and counselor are in a movable cubicle so visual distractions are minimized. Foreign-language tutors can tutor in a drop-in center as well as math and science tutors. If you offer tutoring in speech, drama, or voice, however, a soundproofed room is necessary, not only for the speech clients but also for the protection of the eardrums of the rest of the staff. Similarly, typing rooms need to be soundproofed and shut off from other activities.

Some students find any noise distracting. The best solution I have found is to buy headsets like those worn by workers in jet airports for students to wear while working. Giving tests and exercises by tape recorder with a headset focuses the student's attention on the material and minimizes distraction from external sounds.

The building plans of new colleges usually include learning-center facilities, either as separate units or, more typically, as part of the library or academic departments. For example, the National Training Institute for the Deaf at Rochester Institute of Technology has a learning-resource center in each department, and Los Medanos College in Pittsburg, California, a one-building school, has learning centers on each floor.

White and others (1990) describe an idealized learning center based on the purposes and the nature of the instructional program that the service is designed to support. For example, they describe learning spaces, the learning/media laboratory, classrooms, technical support areas, counseling offices, tutorial rooms, administrative and staff offices, receptionist space and storage. Much of their articles are based on Karwin's (1973) recommendations of allotting twenty-five square feet per person for individual study areas, twenty per person for seminar rooms, forty per room for tutorial rooms (with space for five persons), and sixty per room for counseling offices. (It is interesting that we allow more space for a student talking about himself to a counselor in a one-to-one situation than for students working closely together on a math problem. Perhaps the need for personal space is related to the perceived intimacy of the subject discussed.) In Karwin's blueprint, a space of 2,500 square feet accommodates 100 students who are studying independently.

One way of using existing space more efficiently is to extend hours to evenings and weekends and adjust staff schedules accordingly. One space that often appears underused in voluntary learning centers is the individualized learning laboratory, where students work on self-help materials. Community college programs seem to have little trouble filling their laboratory stations to capacity when credit is given for modules completed or assignments require students to complete modules as part of their regular course work. However, the laboratories in university programs are seldom filled to capacity when students use them voluntarily and without course credit. Use of laboratory facilities varies with time of year. Depending on the materials and programs available, the laboratory may be crowded when students are preparing for graduate or professional exams, or for competency-based tests required for some course—or just before exams, when they use the laboratory as a place of study. Use of laboratory facilities also seems to depend on the people who staff the laboratory. If it is staffed with friendly, supportive people who can help students see the relation between the modules and their course work, more students will use it.

Since remodeling and redecorating costs at most institutions are exorbitant, it is important that directors plan ahead for future needs. Even routine repainting costs are high. Some centers brighten their walls with graphics or murals painted by students, rent or borrow paintings from the art department, and get leftover furniture from other units or the campus storehouse.

Furnishing a center is both costly and difficult unless special funds are available—that is, funds in addition to those allocated in your regular budget. One rule-of-thumb figure for furnishing a new center is 6 percent of the total cost of the building (Karwin, 1973, p. 17).

## OPERATING PROCEDURES AND RECORDKEEPING

Once funds and space are allocated, the director's next step is to establish procedures for the operation of the program and for compiling and maintaining student use records. One of the most complex aspects of a tutorial program is the logistics of getting students and part-time tutors together so that scheduling procedures are clear and consistent. One might have a message center where the receptionist places student schedules in the tutors' boxes; each tutor is then responsible for calling the tutee and arranging a session. (If you use this system, be sure to ask the prospective tutee what hours are best to phone him. Otherwise, it may take a long time for the two to get together.) Another arrangement is for the tutee to call the tutor; or tutor and tutee may exchange phone numbers.

Tutors should be scheduled for some regular hours each week so tutees may sign up for appointments on the tutor's schedule. If you have a drop-in service, the tutor can work with other students if the scheduled client fails to keep the appointment. However, missed appointments are very discouraging to tutors, and most tutoring programs strictly limit the number of times a tutee can miss an appointment and still continue to get help. We encourage tutors to call the student who missed as soon as possible and find out the reason for the absence. Tutors determine whether students who miss appointments should be dropped from the program. When there is a large student demand for a service, it may be too costly to try to punish tutees who do not keep their appointments. If the service is small and students negotiate tutoring contracts, then careful checks can be made. Generally, there are fewer "no shows" in appointments with learning-skills specialists than with tutors, but even this varies with the season of the year and type of service. (Note: there are a number of software programs to aid tutor/staff record keeping. See the Appendix 3-1 on Tutoring Resources and Technology for sources.)

Accurate records of student users' characteristics and student contacts are essential for budgetary justification and evaluation studies. Records should be as simple and short as possible and should be monitored regularly. The day has passed when tutoring programs saw their recordkeeping function as generating mountains of paperwork with lengthy weekly reports on each tutee which were unread and unnecessary. Complex data-collection systems and lengthy forms create resistance from both staff and students.

Minimal records should include a way of registering each student who uses the service and should include relevant demographic data and the subject and skill for which the student is seeking help. Usually college i.d. numbers or social security numbers are also obtained from each student. At a minimum, the student records should contain name, address, phone, campus registration number, sex, class, college, major, and ethnic background (optional) and the subject in which help is sought. The student also checks spaces for students given priority such as athletes or EOP status, etc. (See Fig. 4-1.) Our receptionist gave each student a small card that entitled them to use any of the center services for a year. Other programs use plastic cards like credit cards to record student visits.

**FIGURE 4-1 GENERAL RECORD CARD KEPT BY RECEPTIONIST**

SLC ID No.____________________
Reg. No. ____________________ Date__________
NAME ______________________________
Last First Middle
ADDRESS ______________________________
Street City Zip
PHONE _____ ______________ EOP_____ NON-EOP_____
Area Code Number
Athlete ____________ Ethnic Background ____________
Male _____ Female _____ Department _______ Major ______
CLASS: Fr. Soph. Jr. Sr. Grad. Other __________

Assigned to Subject Date

Keeping accurate records of how often students use the program is essential for payroll, budget, and accountability studies. We required staff members to fill out a weekly contact sheet on which they recorded the student's name and identification number for each individual appointment and the time they spent in other activities (drop-in, outreach, preparation, training, and so forth). They also attached student sign-in sheets from group sessions. In the drop-in program, students kept their own attendance records on sign-in sheets. These sign-in sheets and the tutor contact sheets were computerized so that the demand for help in different subjects and the tutor and staff workload could be readily retrieved.

Some programs adopt stricter procedures and require that tutees request tutoring help two weeks in advance. Others require that tutees be interviewed or tested before they can be scheduled for tutoring appointments, but I would estimate that the majority of programs have no entrance requirements for tutees except their willingness to sign up. Similarly, students seeking help in study skills, reading, etc., may be required to fill in lengthy questionnaires and complete test batteries. These are good ways to discourage students.

Periodically, supervisors prepare evaluations of staff members, including tutors. Supervisors base their evaluations on observations of the staff members' work with students, their reliability in recordkeeping and in keeping appointments, and their evaluations by students. At the same time, each staff member is rating himself or herself on each job function. The supervisor prepares a written report on each person, rates him or her as "more than satisfactory," "satisfactory," or "needs improvement" on each job function, and writes comments, including specific suggestions for improvement. Then the supervisor and staff person meet and discuss their ratings. These regular evaluations should come as no surprise to staff members, since the supervisor has been working directly and conferring regularly with them. Ideally, the staff members should participate in refining the job rating scales and writing explanations to clarify the ratings with examples.

Modern management strategies suggest that employees should set their own goals and objectives for the year and self-evaluations should be done concurrently with evaluations by supervisors and the results discussed and agreed upon in conferences. (See M. Maxwell's *Evaluating Academic Skills Programs* (1993) for examples of a staff evaluation plan and forms for describing jobs and evaluating learning assistance personnel, clerical staff, and tutor coordinators developed by Denise McGinty Swann and others at the University of Texas-Austin.)

## MANAGEMENT STYLES

"Management philosophies come in and go out of style over the years—managing by exception, managing by objectives, and the current front-runner, the manager as coach, part of the total-quality-management approach. The newer philosophies recognize that managing people is a complex task requiring the skills of a psychologist, a sociologist, a lawyer, and a rocket scientist, to say nothing of the technical skills of the specific industry involved," Judith C. Tingley, 1995.

In the 70s, management by objectives or a "systems approach" was widely adopted by academic administrators. Today you're more likely to find Total Quality Management (TQM) or Quality Control, Benchmarking, or the often incompatible Managing Diversity and Downsizing. "Reengineering" has become the latest buzzword referring to intentional or unintentional staff reductions when the emphasis is more on cost cutting than on creating revenue. Business advisers warn that reengineering concepts can backfire if not used properly when one tries to hack away at layers of management without determining which management functions add value to the customer. In reengineering, the customer's needs are the major concern and businesses are redesigning their operations to meet customers' needs. One of the problems faced is motivating employees to contribute who resist changes, are used to taking orders, and uncomfortable with being asked what they think. In colleges today the talk is of empowering students who are viewed as customers, and those students who are employed in learning assistance programs are increasingly treated like regular employees, participating in decision-making in all aspects of the program.

Industry has found that including employees in company decisions increases their performance 150-160 percent beyond that of employees who are not included in decision-making. Employees in some companies now decide on hiring, call up customers and ask questions about their satisfaction with the product, and even seek outside business and earn commissions. Similarly some learning centers are using student aides to make many of the routine management decisions including refurbishing space, scheduling, doing follow-up studies and offering outreach services to the faculty.

Total Quality Management is based on the work that W. Edwards Deming, called the father of quality management, did with American auto corporations in the 70s when U.S. manufacturers were losing out to Japanese car makers. Essentially, Deming's philosophy focuses on developing a better understanding of customer requirements and enlisting the support of every employee and supplier in improving the product's quality. Some aspects of quality can be easily measured, others are more elusive—pride of workmanship, pleasure in work—but these latter aspects are essential to a successful organization. In applying TQM to learning assistance programs, important issues include continuing education and inservice training of all staff, both professional and paraprofessional, keeping up to date in applications of technology, and developing effective evaluation procedures.

David Porter has applied TQM to courses and programs at the Air Force Academy and emphasizes that it involves encouraging teamwork and mutual support and trust. Thus, in conditions when colleges are downsizing programs, TQM is probably inappropriate. (Wondering who will be laid off next is not conducive to building trust in your fellow workers.)

Benchmarking (sometimes referred to as bettering the best) is defined as taking a long, hard look at how the competition produces a better product and then having the courage to make changes that at least match, if not surpass, the quality of that product. One way to apply this to learning centers is to send your staff out to visit other centers and carefully evaluate their procedures. The Quality Assurance Model (QAM), another management model, as applied to academic positions includes the input variables (previous training and experience required for entry into the profession), the standards, ethical principles and guidelines that impact on a profession, and assessment, recognition, and reward for quality performance leading to continuing professional education (staff development).

As a result of applications of these business quality systems, the "student as customer" has become a by-word in some colleges. It is important to recognize that college students differ from auto customers, and sometimes the analogy gets stretched too far, but it is a far cry from the traditional hostility and indifference that students faced in the past.

For more information on total quality management applied to learning centers, you'll want to read:

Milesko-Pytel, D. (Fall 1994). Total quality management in college learning centers. *Research & Teaching in Developmental Education, 11*(1), 115.

Porter, D. (1991). A perspective on college learning. *Journal of College Reading and Learning*, XXIV, 1-8.

Midwest College Learning Association. (1992). Quality management in college learning centers. Position paper for the MCLCA Conference, October 1992, Bettendorf, IA.

## A Management Information System

Developing an efficient management information system is important to the administrator, not only for evaluating and monitoring programs, but also for making routine decisions on such in-house operations as hiring, publicity, budget preparation, and budget management. I have used the model shown in Figure 4-2 to make decisions about when to hire additional tutors and other staff members and when to publicize the services. It was also invaluable in preparing the annual budget. Figure 4-2 shows how a set of procedures facilitates the collection, processing, and flow of information for administrative and staff decisions and actions. The information was compiled weekly from learning specialists' and tutors' student-contact sheets and reports from the receptionist, based on a count of the general record cards (see Figure 4-1), on the numbers of students requesting service, and on the waiting lists for the different programs. When the workload for particular components dropped, I sent out publicity to attract more students for those programs. Conversely, when the specialists' and tutors' schedules were filled, I canceled publicity and decided whether the waiting list merited hiring standby tutors.

### FIGURE 4-2. SLC COMMUNICATIONS SYSTEM

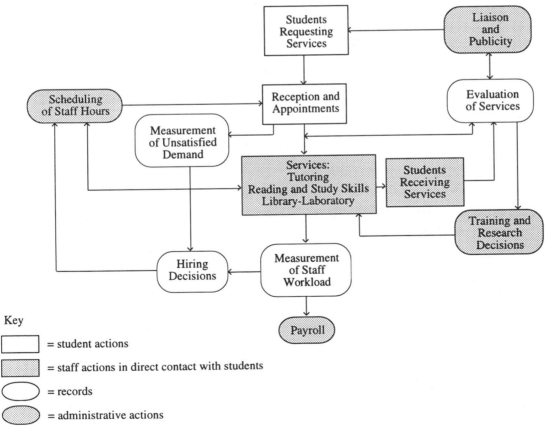

Key

☐ = student actions

▨ = staff actions in direct contact with students

⬭ = records

⬭ (shaded) = administrative actions

The following criteria for evaluating a learning center are based on a review of the literature and are subsumed under three headings: institutional commitment, implementation and administration of policies and procedures, and outreach and cooperation with the faculty. (See also the CAS Standards for Learning Assistance Programs in Appendix 4-1.)

## INSTITUTIONAL COMMITMENT

Institutional commitment is reflected in the objectives set for the program, the selection of a strong director, budget, facilities, space and resources allocated to the program, and support for decisions necessary to run the program effectively.

◊ The program should have clearly stated objectives, and these should be widely disseminated to the faculty and students.

◊ The program should be allocated adequate resources in money, staff, space and materials to support the objectives.

◊ A program director should be chosen who is skilled in program management, respected by the academic community, and committed to improving students' learning. The program director must be accountable to the institution but also must have the freedom and power and the administrative support to develop and maintain the standards of the program.

◊ The institution's commitment must be manifested not only through funding and resources but through acceptance by faculty members, counselors, academic advisers, and other members of the student personnel staff and by students.

◊ The program should be centrally located in an attractive facility with adequate space for services. (Decentralized services such as writing or math labs located in academic departments also need adequate space.)

◊ The program should be institutionalized so that services are offered to all students who need them.

## IMPLEMENTATION AND ADMINISTRATION OF POLICIES AND PROCEDURES

A simple, yet adequate data-collection system should be established and maintained for use in administrative decision making, evaluation studies, budget preparation, and so on. The director must also develop clear, efficient procedures for scheduling group sessions and appointments with staff members. Unnecessary paperwork and confusion that could alienate students should be eliminated. Simple recordkeeping procedures are needed to determine the hours worked by staff members for payroll purposes and for workload measures for administrative staff. Backup materials including textbooks and materials on teaching skills and tutoring techniques should reflect student needs and faculty expectations.

## OUTREACH AND COOPERATION WITH THE FACULTY

Acceptance by the faculty and its cooperation with the center's programs and goals are essential if the program is to be effective in assisting students.

Close working arrangements between center staff and faculty will enable members of the center staff to obtain information from the faculty that will help them in their work with students. Liaison also enables learning-skills specialists to disseminate successful techniques developed by center staff members. Successful programs usually have a full-time academic liaison person who expedites cooperation and resolves potential problems and conflicts.

For more information on this topic, you will want to read:

Van, B. (1992). College learning assistance programs: Ingredients for success. *Journal of College Reading and Learning, 24*(2), 27-39.

Materniak, G. (1980). Developing a learning center from A to Z: Guidelines for designing a comprehensive developmental education program in a postsecondary educational setting. Unpublished paper. Learning Center, University of Pittsburgh, Pittsburgh, PA.

Burns, M. (April 1991). A study to formulate a learning assistance model for the California community college. Ed. D. Dissertation Pepperdine University.

Casazza, M. E., & Silverman, S. L. (1996). *Learning assistance and developmental education: A guide for effective practice.* San Francisco: Jossey-Bass. (This book contains descriptions of learning centers in different types of colleges.)

# CHAPTER 5

## OVERCOMING PROBLEMS OF LEARNING SERVICES

Directors and staff of academic support services, whether large, comprehensive learning centers or small, departmental skills components, continually face problems in defining their roles in the campus community, in relating to faculty members and administrators, in clarifying and communicating their functions to students, and in forming their perceptions of themselves.

### RELATING WITH THE FACULTY

Of these problems, the most difficult concerns the service's role in relation to academic departments. To be effective, learning-skills components and skills courses must be accepted as a regular part of the college curriculum. Therefore, developing and maintaining the support of other faculty members is crucial. Each service should be clearly a prerequisite or support for sequences of beginning courses, and the programs of which they are a part should offer some services for advanced students. Both programs and courses should be open to any student who needs or feels he or she needs assistance. Despite the demonstrated need for special support services, some professors still harbor negative attitudes. They think that remedial instruction is not the proper province of colleges, and therefore, if such programs must be offered they should be temporary, as they are peripheral to the main mission of the institution.

Traditionally, remedial instruction has been viewed as the least prestigious work in academe, and the duties generally relegated to new instructors or graduate students. A common stereotype is that if we must accept underprepared students, they should be placed in special programs and the services restricted to them—as if the rest of the student body might be contaminated if it, too, were offered special academic support services.

In other words, many administrators and faculty members view the learning-assistance program as serving a practical, political function in the college— that is, as a token of "what we are doing for" minority students, the physically disabled, or some other special group. Heard (1976, p. 6) warns, "If the learning center does come to fulfill only the role of a microcosmic showplace college in isolation, then we have failed."

Underprepared college students want to be treated like everyone else, but at the same time they need and want intensive help. Providing an atmosphere that fits both needs poses a dilemma for learning services. Because intensive remedial programs are costly, administrators may order that special services be limited to the lowest achievers. Indeed, federal and other grant-funding agencies often mandate that services be restricted to targeted groups. This policy makes it difficult, if not impossible, for the program to avoid a remedial stigma. As a result, the students who need help the most may avoid the program. Colleges try to resolve this dilemma in several ways: some maintain separate but equal services for regular and disadvantaged students; some provide certain services, such as reading and study skills help, to any student, while restricting subject-area tutoring to students on financial aid; others provide free tutoring to EOP students but charge other students.

If a center becomes identified with the lowest achievers, professors who deny that remedial services are appropriate for college students may express negative attitudes toward students who use the services. If all students have access to the program, other professors may feel that the center threatens their roles and responsibilities. A needs-assessment survey of the faculty may help the learning-center director gauge these opinions and plan ameliorative strategies. However, this is an issue that must be addressed continuously as the learning center director interacts with college faculty.

Academic support services define their function as providing skills and tutorial services to students to support their academic work, but differentiating support services from regular classroom instruction may be difficult. Warnath's warning to counseling centers is also appropriate for learning skills centers. Warnath (1971, p. 65) points out that professional counselors do not occupy a precise and unambiguous role on campus because professors have difficulty discriminating what professional counselors do from the many other advising and counseling functions that teachers and other professionals perform. The learning-skills specialist's role is even more ambiguous. It is not easy to explain the difference between skills work and the content taught by instructors in their courses. Warnath's admonition

(1971, p. 41) that "the presence of a counseling center on campus (no matter how poorly staffed) may have the effect of increasing the depersonalization of contacts between students and faculty" is equally applicable to learning centers. "A busy faculty member, when faced with a student who wants to work through some personal feeling or vocational plans, can rid himself of the responsibility by referring him to the counseling center." How much easier it is for the same professor, when confronted with a student who has a series of questions about a homework assignment, to refer that student to a tutor or learning skills specialist!

Warnath cautions that if a student refuses to accept a referral from a faculty member, it may mean that the student is left with the problem that inspired the referral plus confirmation of his suspicion that faculty members do not care about individual students. However, students may find it less threatening or risky to seek help from a tutor or learning-skills specialist than to confront a faculty member with their questions about the course or the assignment. After all, faculty members grade students, and tutors do not.

There is also a danger that support services will attract students in greater numbers than do dedicated course assistants or instructors during their office hours. When students stop seeking help from their instructors, the instructors assume the students are not interested; the instructors, in turn, lose interest in trying to help. The result can be mutual distrust between students and faculty or between learning-skills staff and faculty. To avoid competing for students, the skills specialists must develop close working relationships with faculty members in academic departments and must work toward reciprocal referrals.

Sometimes students try to manipulate learning-skills staff members and play them off against instructors (or vice versa), and sometimes students develop dependent relationships with their skills specialists or tutors. Either of these activities will reduce the effectiveness of an academic support program. Steering between these extremes requires delicate balance and diplomacy. The learning-skills staff must constantly educate both students and faculty regarding the proper roles and functions of the support service.

If a learning center is to serve a preventive as well as a rehabilitative role, it must establish and maintain credibility with the faculty. Too often support-service staff members find themselves trapped in a situation in which they are so completely immersed in student problems that they lack time and energy for anything else. As Richard Berry, a Berkeley counselor, recently remarked, "I'm so busy trying to pull drowning students out of the stream one by one, I don't have time to look up and see who's throwing them in." Planning time for staff members to do more than pick up and try to resuscitate the student victims of academe is a major function of the learning-center director.

Direct person-to-person contact is the best way to build relations between the faculty and the learning-center staff, but it is also essential for the center to have a strong and supportive faculty/student advisory committee to aid in establishing and maintaining liaison with various academic departments and instructors. Learning centers can coordinate their efforts with faculty members' in other ways too, such as through jointly sponsored programs, team taught classes, split appointments (in which a staff member spends parts of his time in an academic department), cooperative research projects, presentations to faculty meetings, teaching-assistant training workshops, and faculty consulting services. Following are some of the strategies learning-center directors can use to gain the confidence and cooperation of their faculty colleagues.

## EXPLAINING YOUR PROGRAM TO FACULTY

Defining your center's role and functions and clarifying its image to faculty is probably the most difficult task facing the learning center director. Because a comprehensive center may serve many constituencies, from high-risk entering students to distressed undergraduates with special learning needs to high achieving undergraduate and graduate students who need to "professionalize their academic studies" (Lowenstein, 1993), its image may confuse faculty. Some will see its role limited to helping remedial students, providing academic first aid to those who need it before exams, or diagnosing and treating the learning disabled, but rarely do they have an accurate picture of the center's mission, services, and clients. Creating an appropriate image of the center for both faculty and students requires difficult, ongoing, time-consuming, complex but essential effort. (In the Appendix you'll find an article written for the Delta College faculty newsletter by an English professor who teaches developmental students as well as regular students. I feel that L. J. (Skip) Spiller has written an interesting and honest description of his role in teaching developmental students. Also there's a parable by Karen Martin who directs the Science Learning Center at Fisk University who expresses some of the frustrations of people in her role.) Other ways of communicating and involving faculty members include advisory boards, faculty sponsored tutoring-for-credit courses, split appointments, and so on.

## FACULTY/STUDENT ADVISORY BOARDS

Faculty/student advisory boards should be comprised of faculty members from different disciplines who reflect different points of view and students who are representative of the total student body. Do not select professors just because they support your program; include some conservatives as well as some liberals, and invite both student-oriented and research-oriented professors to sit on your board. Faculty/student boards will be most effective if regular meetings are scheduled at least once a term. Plan a specific agenda of issues and problems to discuss after the board has been thoroughly oriented to your program's aims and services. (A discussion of the services and a tour of the facilities are usually more effective in orienting faculty members than are lengthy, written reports, which few have time to read.) The meeting agenda could include asking members' advice on policies, new programs, and ways of improving relations with other faculty members. Professors are not happy attending meetings where little occurs—they want a chance to use their expertise and express their opinions.

It is advantageous for the center director to select a chairperson for the faculty board rather than try to chair the meetings herself. I found a strong board very helpful in supporting our center's efforts to develop new programs, to get grants, and to find ways to resolve problems with other departments. A strong board can help protect your service from problems with campus middle-management administrators and help mediate some of the inevitable conflicts that arise. Sometimes it is difficult to keep a board meeting regularly, for faculty members have heavy demands on their time which often make it hard to schedule meetings. So it is best to agree on the meeting schedule for the year well in advance—

preferably at the beginning of the fall term—and keep the same schedule throughout the academic year.

Between regularly scheduled board meetings, the center director can call on board members individually to ask for their advice or suggestions on particular problems or projects. It is important to recognize that board members have to work under pressure too and not to expect them to become involved in lengthy, time consuming projects—unless they volunteer. But despite the time constraints, boards can be very helpful. At one point our service was inundated with freshman chemistry students seeking tutoring help, and our board wrote to the dean of the College of Chemistry suggesting ways that our caseload might be reduced through faculty-group office hours, better scheduling of TAs' hours, TA training programs, and so on. The chemistry department implemented some of these ideas, and a number of chemistry faculty members were very supportive in helping us get grants so we could improve our services and develop learning aids for students.

There are those who suggest that the faculty members on the board be the most prestigious professors one can find. When the forerunner of the Upward Bound program was instituted at Berkeley in the early 60s, the director selected a prestigious faculty board that included several Nobel laureates. Subsequent directors have never regretted that decision, for the board has supported the program's efforts to raise funds from faculty contributions and has protected Upward Bound on many occasions from attacks by faculty members, administrators urging budget cuts, and other threats. In general, the board has ensured that the director retains sufficient autonomy for the program to function smoothly and survive.

Sharyn Lowenstein, Director of The Learning Center at Lesley University (MA), describes how to use a learning center advisory board—defining its mission of policy-setting versus advising, its role as an internal change advocate and agent to promote innovation, and as an interpreter of cultures within the institution. She explains how the advisory board can serve as center advocate in clarifying and projecting the image of the center. The selection of board members, defining their functions and responsibilities, planning meetings and providing formal and informal training for board members are also discussed. Her suggestions for training board members—both those who are experienced as well as new board members—will be particularly helpful. Last, but not least, she describes incentives for board members, including recognizing them at center events, sending birthday greetings, including their contributions in newsletters, and providing food at meetings (Lowenstein, 1993). I'd add that the most important thing you can do is send a letter thanking the board member, with copies also sent to the department chair, dean and/or provost.

For more information about advisory boards, you'll want to read:

Lowenstein, S. (1993). Using advisory boards for learning assistance programs. *Perspectives on Practice in Developmental Education*, New York College Learning Skills Association, 93-99.

# But What If Your Dean Does Not Permit You to Have a Faculty Advisory Board?

It is not at all unusual for college administrators, particularly those in student affairs, to veto suggestions that the Learning Assistance Center have a faculty advisory board. In those cases, it will be necessary for the director to find other ways to get faculty input, such as approaching them individually and asking their opinion on program proposals, etc. In other words, use individual faculty members as consultants.

## Faculty-Sponsored Tutoring-For-Credit Courses

Seeking out professors who will sponsor tutoring-for-credit or practicum courses is another way to involve faculty members in the center's work. We found professors generally supportive of these courses. For example, a professor of psycholinguistics was particularly interested in enrolling his upper-division majors in the tutoring-for-credit course so they could get first-hand experience with students who have dialect, bilingual, or second-language problems. Faculty members in a number of departments—mathematics, education, chemistry, languages, and English as a second language—sponsored tutoring-for-credit courses. Some professors prefer to offer such courses within their own departments as independent study courses; others agree to offer them through the education department or as fieldwork studies. Colleges vary in the amount of credit that a student can earn for tutoring-for-credit courses and in the number of hours a student must spend in this activity to earn credit. (For references describing tutoring-for-credit courses, see Truer, 1995, Maxwell, 1994).

## Split Appointments, Team Teaching, and Other Arrangements

Split appointments are an excellent way of coordinating skills programs and academic departments. If an English instructor teaches regular English courses and also serves as director of the writing center, the inevitable faculty criticisms of learning services will be reduced. Team teaching, unfortunately, is relatively rare in colleges today and may become even rarer as budgets decline. (See also the discussion of paired courses in Chapter 6.)

## OUTREACH ROLES

If the learning center is to function in a broader role on campus—as an ombuds-service or a catalyst for improving undergraduate instruction—then staff members must be trained and encouraged to view their responsibilities as extending beyond their work with individual students. Faculty members need help too, in coping with large classes of students from widely varying backgrounds. If I were starting another learning center, even one with a very small staff, I would spend most of my time—and see that my staff members spent more of their time—working to develop support programs with faculty members, rather than in individual conferences with students. If ways can be found to ease the burdens of faculty members and to help them develop more effective ways of helping students learn, many of the stresses that pressure students and create the large demand for learning assistance services might be eased.

Learning-center directors who view the learning-skills specialist as a resource person for the faculty report that skills specialists can effect positive changes in faculty teaching strategies, exams, lectures, and other areas (Heard, 1976; Martin and others, 1977, pp. 18-22). One way skills specialists can serve as resource persons is to lecture on how to study a subject as part of a regular course. For example, they can talk to a French class about how to study foreign languages. Another method is to offer adjunct, or supplementary skills courses that parallel regular classes. Adjunct skills courses re-

quire the skills specialist to attend the lectures of the regular class and work closely with the professor so the skills training sessions dovetail with course requirements. If the skills specialist attends lectures, she will be better able to help students and also interact with the instructor. "As the resource person presents the major student question/concerns for the purpose of seeking guidance, the instructor has the opportunity to evaluate the effectiveness of his last lesson. It is not uncommon for an instructor to say something like, 'Oh! If they are confused about this point, then obviously they haven't yet learned . . .' " (Martin and others, 1977, p. 20). Since instructors rarely pretest their classes in reading or other skills, they may assume that their students have knowledge and competencies that they, in fact, do not have. Hence, the skills specialist can alert the instructor to particular student needs and sometimes can make suggestions on what to do. As the New England Conference of Academic Support Services concluded (1977, p. 3), "Professors are often unaware of how helpful skills suggestions can be for some students in their classes. Other professors may recognize the needs of their students but not know how to deal with the work that is required."

Adjunct skills courses or SI can be quite costly in the amount of time and effort that a skills specialist must devote, and so the question of whether to offer them must be weighed carefully with the service's other priorities. One should select parent courses that have large enrollments, where many students have difficulty learning the content, where grading is tough—in short, courses where there is considerable evidence that students need help. In my experience, adjunct courses do not attract students when they are attached to courses where students' grades average B or higher, enrollment is small, the instructor is accessible or uses mastery learning or personalized self-instructional methods, or when teaching assistants or tutors are available to work with students in the classroom. Although many learning centers offer sessions or workshops to inform professors of their services, and many invite professors to speak to their staff members, some learning-center experts feel that learning-skills support services should not offer formal faculty-development programs.

"Faculty involvement should not be confused with faculty development; to do so is to jeopardize the integrity of the program. Learning centers exist to develop and/or augment the skills of students, not to tell faculty members how to improve their instructional techniques. Moreover, college teachers are not only required to teach but advise, publish, and continually advance themselves professionally. As highly sophisticated specialists, instructors must be allowed to select those areas in which they feel a need for assistance. [Unsolicited] suggestions from learning-center personnel that instructors should alter their instructional content or techniques could be viewed as academic infringement—an anathema to faculty support" (Martin and others, 1977, p. 13). Experts generally agree that faculty members often take a negative view of administrators' attempts to improve their teaching. If the learning center tries to implement a program to "teach professors to teach," it may engender wrath instead of cooperation.

A learning-skills program that is accessible to both students and instructors can, however, become the natural resource for instructors seeking assistance in designing instructional packets, constructing better test questions, reorganizing their presentation of material, and developing alternative instructional modes for special groups of students. The key is that the instructor, not the learning center, should initiate the request for services.

This is not to imply that the learning center director should avoid formal faculty development programs at all costs. Indeed, it is important that the learning center staff be involved in orienting new faculty and in most faculty development programs. But let them invite you; don't initiate the program. Faculty members must provide the leadership for faculty development programs with the instructional improvement office if the program is to be successful. Caveat: When I wrote the first version of this book in the 70s, I suffered a six months' writer's block. When I resumed writing the section on faculty development, I found that none of the learning center directors I had quoted were still employed in the same colleges. They were capable and enthusiastic people who, at the urging of a dean or a faculty member, had instituted their own faculty development programs—and had violated an area that faculty members considered their turf. It cost them their jobs.

## HELPING DEVELOP NEW TEACHING METHODS

Sometimes instructors or academic departments want to test new teaching ideas, techniques, or policies but hesitate to experiment in their regular classes. A learning center that attracts large numbers of students can provide a convenient testing ground for assessing the effects of new techniques on student learning and attitudes. Centers can help, for example, in selecting a new workbook in basic grammar, or in providing information on the readability level of proposed textbooks to assist selection committees in deciding on books that their students can read. Or centers can help in such policy decisions as whether to schedule TAs for evening hours in the library. (After we put tutors in the undergraduate library in the evenings and found that they did a brisk business with individual student requests, we were able to recommend this policy to the mathematics department.)

Many instructors are genuinely interested in developing new course materials, audiovisual aids, guides for their courses, and so forth but lack the time—and sometimes the skills—to do so. Implementing joint projects with instructors to develop and test study aids, materials and self-instructional programs, and even new courses that can be included in the regular curriculum are ways of enhancing a center's credibility. Some centers serve as "midwives" for new courses that other academic departments later adopt. New courses in precalculus (Berkeley and UCLA), credit reading improvement courses (University of South Carolina), writing programs (such as that developed by the Undergraduate Writing Program at Stanford) that were originally developed by support programs have been absorbed by academic departments. If the learning center is not concerned with improving instruction, it risks becoming the wastebasket for ever increasing numbers of victims of poor or inappropriate courses.

Helping faculty members develop new teaching approaches and materials is an area in which, I believe, the learning-center staff can have the most profound impact on student learning. In the 70s, Berkeley's Student Learning Center worked with instructors on a series of small grants to improve instructional materials for four years: developing a self-paced math course; selecting and designing self-paced and audiovisual aids for a chemistry resources center; conducting minicourses in prestatistics, prechemistry, and problem solving; building computer-assisted-instruction units in probability, organic-chemistry concepts, and trigonometry; and writing student guides for such courses as general chemistry, biochemistry, physiology, and mathematics.

## HELPING IN TEXT SELECTION

Locating materials that professors can review, and possibly adopt for their courses is another valuable function that learning centers can perform. Selecting appropriate textbooks, media, workbooks, and learning programs is a long and arduous task. Many commercial materials are available in every field. In some departments, committees select introductory texts and use such criteria as readability in determining which books they will adopt. Reading-skills specialists can offer information on ways to assess text readability and can help professors locate appropriate texts for underprepared students (see Chapter 9). Occasionally I have run contests inviting students to nominate "The Worst Textbook of the Year" and give their reasons. This takes some of the onus off the compulsive student who believes that textbooks are infallible and that he is to blame for not understanding. It also provides ammunition for professors to use in choosing textbooks. When one of our staff members was invited to testify before a departmental textbook-selection committee, he was able to persuade the professors to adopt a more readable, better-written introductory text, since their current text had recently won our "Worst Textbook of the Year" contest. But do be careful. This approach might antagonize some professors, especially if they are the textbook's author.

## OFFERING IN-CLASS DIAGNOSTIC SERVICES

Another valuable function learning centers can perform for professors is to offer in-class diagnostic services. In open admissions colleges, professors often face a wide range of students in their introductory courses and have no information on these students' skills. Juan Vazquez at the College of Alameda (Alameda, California) has developed a program in which professors can invite learning-center staff members to test their students for reading and other skills in their classrooms at the beginning of the term. Statistics on the range of abilities are given to the instructor, but not individual scores. Students are notified individually of their scores and needs and offered the services of the learning center.

## SHARING HANDOUTS

Sharing handouts on how to study particular subjects and asking faculty to evaluate them is another way learning centers can help faculty members. If learning-skills specialists develop handouts and offer them to professors to distribute in their courses, the professors may find the handouts helpful and/or suggest ways to improve them. (Some useful handouts are included in the Appendix.)

## OTHER WAYS TO INVOLVE FACULTY

There are many other ways to reach faculty members. During the first year of the Learning Assistance Center (LAC) at California State University at Long Beach, Frank Christ and Margaret Devirian had lunch each day with a different faculty member in the faculty dining commons. This greatly enhanced their image with many faculty members. (An interesting question is whether learning-center directors who habitually bring bag lunches and eat in solitude in their own offices have more difficulty retaining their positions or more problems with faculty members and administrators than those who eat out. Although I do not have enough data for statistical analyses, at this point the brown-baggers who eat alone appear to have more problems.)

Christ and Devirian also arranged "county fairs," inviting professors from different departments to a demonstration of materials, programs, and equipment appropriate for their students. As a result, professors made many direct referrals to the LAC. Some integrated skills modules into their courses and required students to use the LAC as part of their class assignments.

Planning an "open house" to which professors and administrators are invited to view the learning-center facilities and interact with the staff is a popular method for introducing your service. If you do plan an open house—and you should try one if you have not—it is best to hold it when students are using the center. Inevitably, professors recognize some of their own students among the tutors or tutees, and seeing students at work gives them a more realistic picture of your program.

Advertising for tutors, whether paid, for credit, or volunteer, is another way of alerting professors to your program, especially if professors are requested to write letters of recommendation for prospective tutors. In many centers, professors will volunteer to tutor.

Sandra Chadwick, Director of the Learning Assistance Program at Wake Forest University, sends out a brochure that includes the following services to faculty: 1) study skills presentations to classes; 2) consultations regarding students' learning needs; 3) assistance in providing accommodations to learning disabled students; 4) presentations at faculty meetings in areas such as learning disabilities, teaching strategies, etc.; 5) facilitation of faculty groups studying curriculum reform, continuous improvement of teaching, outcomes assessment, effective group communication, etc.; and 6) a small lending library of recent publications on teaching excellence, outcomes assessments, liberal arts issues, etc.

The best advertisement for a center is a satisfied clientele. If students who use the program regularly are enthusiastic and successful in their academic work, they become effective intermediaries with professors as well as referral sources for other students.

## SUMMARY

In this section I have discussed a number of ways learning centers can gain credibility with the faculty, including the following:

1. Developing a strong faculty advisory board (or identifying faculty members who will consult with your program individually).

2. Making direct person-to-person contacts with the faculty.

3. Holding open houses or faculty orientation programs.

4. Advertising the service through recruitment of tutors and soliciting recommendations for tutors from faculty members.

5. Requesting faculty members to sponsor tutoring-for-credit courses.

6. Team-teaching with faculty members in courses combining skills and content or other arrangements such as sequential teaching.

7. Offering to address classes on skills needed in the discipline.

8. Offering adjunct skills courses that parallel regular courses.

9. Providing an experimental laboratory for faculty members wishing to test new methods, materials, and procedures.

10. Cooperating with faculty members in research projects on the improvement of instruction.

11. Writing study guides for students.

12. Assisting faculty members in selecting appropriate textbooks and other materials.

13. Sharing handouts on "how to study" that faculty members may use in their classes.

14. Offering skills diagnostic services within the instructor's class time at the beginning of the term.

Although it is important to make friends with some faculty members, the larger task faced by learning-center directors is to build feelings of mutual acceptance, support, trust, and respect. This is a lengthy and continuous process. Do not expect to convert all faculty members to your viewpoint; in fact, do not try. There will always be some professors who feel that students who need any help with their academic work do not belong in college. Work with those professors who believe that students' learning can be improved. Develop a tolerance for those colleagues who greet you every time they meet you with comments like, "Still trying to save them?" or describe your efforts to help students as "love's labors lost."

Avoid the pitfalls that have resulted in the failure of many programs where the director and staff members are so busy seeing students that they isolate themselves from their colleagues and identify so strongly with students that they view professors as adversaries.

There are undoubtedly many other ways to build bridges of mutual trust and respect between skills specialists and academic faculty members, and some of these, such as serving on campus wide committees and performing other advisory services, are described in Chapter Four. But let us look at another area that greatly affects the quality of the undergraduate learning environment and in which learning centers, at least those in universities, are increasingly involved. That is the area of training graduate teaching assistants. The techniques described for TA training also have implications for programs that employ paraprofessionals and part-time instructors.

## TA TRAINING PROGRAMS

Many learning centers are providing (or helping others provide) training programs for departmental teaching assistants, who in large universities often carry the main responsibility for teaching and working directly with freshman and sophomore students. If I were to develop a program for training TAs in a large university or for orienting part-time paraprofessionals in a community college, I would focus the program on enhancing instructors' knowledge of peer-group processes and increasing their awareness of how to diagnose and work with problems that hamper students' learning, rather than attempting to improve their teaching skills directly. My rationale is that if TAs became cognizant of how to handle minor learning-skills problems and of their own nonproductive reactions to student difficulties, the number of students seeking help from costly tutoring, skills help, and counseling programs could be reduced, and students' satisfaction with their courses would increase. If students learned to work and study successfully with their peers in this course, they might be able to apply the same approach to other classes. Counselors and learning-skills specialists would train the TAs and assist them in helping students work together effectively.

Undergraduates have problems in learning when taught by research-oriented, specialized, and academically talented TAs who are inexperienced teachers. This is an old problem for public universities, where graduate TAs have been an integral part of American higher education for over 100 years (Trow, 1966).

Today, however, the problems are exacerbated as larger numbers of underprepared and nontraditional students enroll in university courses and larger numbers of TAs are foreign born. So today the disparity is greater between the knowledge and expectations of graduate TAs and the knowledge and skills of students. Also the increase of international students in graduate schools throughout the country and, concurrently, the number of TAs with limited English speaking skills worsens the situation.

Training TAs in departments where required courses with large freshman enrollments generate the heaviest demand for tutoring, skills help, and counseling help would seem a logical preventive measure. Such a training program might include group sessions with discussions and demonstrations of group processes, peer-learning techniques, and ways to create a supportive atmosphere for learning. Topics that might be presented are techniques for utilizing students enrolled in the course as peer tutors; ways to use dyads, as in a calculus course where students work together to solve problems; parcelled classroom arrangements, in which students are organized in groups, collaborative learning, peer-monitored assignments, reciprocal teaching, etc.

TA participants in this program could make videotapes of their regular classes, discussion sections, or laboratory groups and critique them with other TAs, faculty members, and skills specialists. Role-playing typical situations that new instructors face in teaching and conferring with students would also be an integral part of the training program. The training would be geared to the constraints and content of particular disciplines—chemistry TAs who supervise laboratory sections perform different roles than English TAs. The main emphasis of the program would be to develop and test peer-learning models and student-involvement techniques, but TAs would be cautioned that no student who prefers to study alone should be forced to participate in group problem solving or study groups.

In addition to the training sessions, an individual counseling/consulting service would be offered for new instructors and TAs. Here they could discuss their questions and problems in complete confidence with a counselor or learning specialist. Since TAs are students too, they often find themselves in a double bind: their own study obligations are highest in their list of priorities, and their teaching obligations secondary. Often there are personality clashes between supervising professors (who may also be major advisers) and TAs. Outside help may aid in resolving such conflicts, which if unresolved could place unneeded stress on the TAs' students. Counselors and learning-skills specialists might also assist TAs and faculty members in developing videotapes of particular teaching situations. Group and individual interactions that TAs typically encounter could be used in future TA-training groups. TA positions in many institutions turn over frequently, and each new group of TAs would profit from the training. These videotapes would reflect the course content peculiar to the department—math examples would be used with math TAs, writing examples with English TAs, and so on.

During the second year of the program, senior TAs and interested professors could run the TA orientation sessions. This would ensure that there would be residual effects from the first year and that the program could gradually become departmentally self-perpetuating. Each subsequent year, TAs who had been through the program the preceding year would be selected to conduct the program, and counselors and learning-skills specialists would serve as consultants to the trainers and work individually with staff members who requested special assistance.

The following criteria might be used to evaluate the program: (1) Reduction in the amount of tutoring, skills help, and counseling sought by students from classes of trained TAs, compared with students from untrained TAs' sections. (2) Students' greater satisfaction with their learning experience in trained TAs' classes than in control classes taught by untrained TAs, as shown in student evaluations. (3) Increased student retention and improved learning of students participating in the peer tutoring or other student-to-student learning situations. (4) Improved academic performance of low-achieving students in the experimental classes. Earlier studies found that low-achieving students who attended out-of-class review groups with other students significantly improved their course grades, compared with low-achieving students who studied alone. More recent studies on SI and collaborative learning also support this finding. (5) Improved TAs' satisfaction with the TA experience and improved self-evaluation of their effectiveness as teachers, compared with untrained TAs.

Specifically, students from experimental TAs' classes in which peer-teaching techniques were implemented could be matched with students from control classes for academic aptitude and relevant high school grades. The two groups of students could then be compared on the following measures, using an analysis of variance design: scores on a Likert scale or semantic differential measuring satisfaction with the course; academic performance in class (shown by grades on exams, projects, and so on); use of tutoring, skills, or counseling services (shown by number of students applying for service and number of contact hours); retention in college at the end of two terms and four terms; and number of students completing the course sequence (for example, those finishing a year of freshman chemistry). Three variables could be tested on the teaching assistants: satisfaction with own teaching experiences in the classes taught (shown by responses on a Likert scale); estimate of own effectiveness as a teacher (shown by responses on a Likert scale); and satisfaction with the training program (for TAs participating in the experiment only). It would also be interesting to ascertain whether the TAs in the training program shared ideas and techniques with TAs not in the program and whether a John Henry effect occurred —that is, did TAs who were not in the program try harder? If found, this would be delightful. (In the John Henry effect, the control-group teachers work harder.)

Learning-skills specialists could demonstrate how to identify students with skills problems or emotional problems using roleplaying or videotaped simulated scenarios. These training materials could be helpful to part-time instructors, as well as to TAs. Ways to refer students to support services could be demonstrated in a similar manner. It could be cost-effective for any institution that employs part-time instructors, and it also has implications for part-time students who work and therefore cannot make use of regular campus resources. Part-time students, especially adults, usually lack an appropriate study environment. If instructors encouraged students to gather in informal study groups and meet regularly outside class, the students could form their own study milieu. The learning-skills specialists and counselors who provided the initial training would revert to the role of consultants after training was completed, and the responsibility for implementing and continuing the training would pass back to the academic department. The resulting decrease in the need for tutoring and support services would permit learning-center staff members to have more time to consult and work with the faculty.

Innovations of this sort are especially hard to implement in large, well-established institutions; however, there are always some faculty members who are deeply concerned that TAs become effective teachers. A fringe benefit of the program described is that it would reduce the stress and time demands that teaching places on part-time TAs, whose graduate courses also drain their energy and time. If students complain less about grades and assignments and can work together cooperatively, TAs may be less pressured, and if peer-learning techniques are adopted, TAs can spend less time preparing for classes. This program might also provide an entree into faculty retraining in institutions that are hesitant about implementing new programs. (Note: The University of Minnesota at Duluth has implemented a combined TA and Tutor Training Program directed by Paul Treuer that is considered an important function in the institution. You might want to look at it as a model.)

A word of warning: before you plunge ahead on a formal TA training program, it is essential to have the full support of your institution's administration, the dean of the graduate school, the graduate student council, and some key faculty members. Despite the criticisms of college instructional methods by students and educators, TA programs are rare even today, and there is much resistance toward them. Avoid treading on what faculty members consider their turf, and be alert to the fact that the boundaries of their turf change rapidly.

If the campus lacks formal TA training programs, the learning center can still conduct informal training quite successfully. A concerned professor may bring over his TAs, as a mathematician did to our center, so that they can observe and learn techniques from tutors and skills specialists working with individuals, dyads, and small groups. Perhaps it is these informal, serendipitous arrangements that will produce the greatest change, for the larger, more formal programs are usually funded on soft money, and when the grants expire, so do the programs.

## TEACHING RESOURCES

A library of handbooks on college teaching is a useful resource for any learning center. These materials are valuable for tutor and staff training and as information sources for professors and teaching assistants. There are many current newsletters on teaching and learning. *The National Teaching and Learning Forum,* which is published bimonthly, contains descriptions of teaching strategies, an overview of current research, a TA Forum for TAs, and other salient articles on teaching and learning. (Order from The George Washington University, One Dupont Circle, Suite 630, Wash., D.C. 20036-1183.)

Some of the books we have found valuable are these:

Angelo, T. A., and Cross, P. K. (1993). *Classroom assessment techniques: A handbook for college teachers.* (2nd ed.). San Francisco: Jossey-Bass Publishers.

Brookfield, S. D. (1990). *The skillful teacher.* San Francisco: Jossey-Bass Publishers.

Davis, B. G. (1993). *Tools for teaching.* San Francisco: Jossey-Bass Publishers.

Eble, K. E. (1988). *The Craft of teaching: A guide to mastering the professor's art.* San Francisco: Jossey-Bass Publishers.

McKeachie, W. *Guidebook for the beginning college teacher.* Lexington, MA: DC Heath & Company. (First published in 1969 and now in its eighth edition, this is the classic guide to college teaching and is a must for any library.

## RELATIONS WITH CAMPUS ADMINISTRATORS

Directors of learning centers most frequently express concern about relations with the faculty, but concerns about gaining support from campus administrators run a close second in the hierarchy of problems centers face.

Studies of skills and tutoring programs have occasionally reported cases in which the director or the staff lacked commitment to helping students; however, lack of administrative support and restrictions on autonomy in directing the service are often cited as major problem areas (Reed, 1974). Since learning-center components usually assist underprepared students, especially those from ethnic minorities, their special services such as tutoring may become the focal point for political and social controversies between student groups, faculty members, and the external community. These quarrels create special problems for campus administrators because institutions have become increasingly sensitive to attacks on their affirmative action programs, and the learning service is viewed as a major part of the affirmative action effort. Student groups are more likely to attack the tutoring and skills services than criticize the faculty if they think the college is not providing appropriate programs for their ethnic groups.

A learning-center director's autonomy may be threatened in many ways—by pressure from administrators to perform certain functions or hire certain people, by interference in decision making, by lack of support for programs and budgets. Some of my experiences may illustrate the range of problems. During the learning center's first year, we were investigated by the Student Task Force Against Bureaucracy at the same time the student budget intern was evaluating our record keeping and workload measures, asking questions that generated more paperwork. Ethnic-studies divisions complained that they were not getting enough funding for their peer-tutoring programs and insisted that a centralized service could not meet the needs of their students. The Committee Against Racism, a student/faculty group, expressed concern that minority students were not receiving enough tutoring help, while student groups wrote angry letters demanding that tutors from their ethnic groups be hired in each and every subject.

Budget committees wanted our staff to conduct more group tutoring programs and spend less time in individual work with students, as an economy measure. At the same time, numerous students complained that they were being forced into groups when they wanted and needed more individual tutoring appointments. This issue took several quarters to resolve.

Student budget interns eliminated the salary of our part-time speech therapist, the only speech person on campus. They argued that speech assistance belonged under the health service, whose director rejected the idea flatly, citing a policy of not treating students for preexisting conditions. (We were able to collect contributions from an alumni group to retain the speech position for a few hours a week, but the position was not re-funded when the donations ceased.) Unfortunately, students with speech difficulties tend to be less vocal and assertive in their demands for special services than other student groups.

In addition to pressures from various campus constituencies whose demands and disputes affect the learning service, the expectations and misperceptions of the functions of the service by administrators may exacerbate the center's difficul-

ties. Some administrators, reflecting the views of their more conservative faculty constituency, may stereotype special assistance programs for students as remedial and feel that such programs are unnecessary. Other administrators may reluctantly concede the need for learning support services but insist that services be limited to open admissions or special-admit students. They justify this policy on the basis of budget limitations or lack of staff positions; however, restricting a service to those who need it most ensures that the program will be stigmatized by both students and faculty members as a salvage operation for academic misfits.

Current funding policies for many federal and state monies earmark them for the "disadvantaged student" or other special groups. Even in these specially funded programs, efforts must be made to provide comprehensive programs and to avoid the stigma of "tracking."

Centers in highly selective institutions may, of course, find that their administrations hold the opposite view. That is, administrators may view them as helping regularly admitted students and suggest that services for the lowest achievers be limited unless funded from extramural sources.

UNREALISTIC ADMINISTRATIVE EXPECTATIONS

Administrators may have unrealistic expectations about how much an academic support service can accomplish in improving students' skills and how long it will take. Some seem to expect that a student who is reading six years below grade level will be able to make up the deficiency in one semester while carrying other college courses.

If a learning center has the responsibility of assisting students who are accepted as "special admits" in a selective college, then it is vital that the director sit on the admissions committee and have input into the procedures for determining which applicants will have the regular admissions criteria waived. As Sam Silas of William Paterson College states (in a personal communication), "It is absolutely essential that the learning-center director and the admissions office share similar views on the admission of students. The admissions officer can make or break your special-admit program, and it certainly does not hurt if the director and the admissions officer are the best of friends."

Note: During the late seventies and early eighties, when colleges were admitting larger numbers of "new" students, faculty members often attacked their admissions officers, blaming them for admitting lower-ability students and demanding that the officers be fired. This was a modern version of "kill the messenger," for faculty often failed to realize that getting well qualified freshmen was a national problem, not one limited to their institution.

Among the many variables that affect the success of a special-admissions program is the recruiting process, the precollege counseling and advising services, the orientation program, and the involvement of the faculty. The college recruiters (or admissions counselors) must try to recruit students who, though they come from disadvantaged backgrounds, have the motivation and ability to learn quickly and have some chance of succeeding in the institution's academic programs. Counselors and academic advisers can help prospective students choose appropriate courses and plan majors, as well as aiding them in understanding how the skills services can help. There must be close coordination among the various components of the special-admissions program.

Misconceptions about the motivation of students with a history of low achievement also create difficulties for a learning service. Some administrators and professors expect the freshmen with poor college preparation to volunteer for special help and those with high achievement records not to. In reality, however, the reverse is true; weak students avoid the service, while stronger ones use it willingly. Often administrators are unaware of the shame, stigma, and despair that accompany poor achievement. So when administrators hear criticisms about their college's failure to uphold its commitment to disadvantaged minority students or other special groups, they investigate the learning center's services. If the center's services are not tightly coordinated with recruitment, admissions, counseling, advising, and faculty programs, the finger of blame points to the learning center. The dean may set up a faculty committee to investigate why so few special-admit students are completing degrees. The scenario that follows has been replayed in many institutions; the result is that learning services or reading and study skills services are eliminated or assimilated by other departments. The faculty committee interviews faculty members and other student services, and its final report may conclude with a statement like, "The director and staff of the present learning service do not hold as a priority instruction in basic skills for special problems, and they have had no systematic success in handling them. In our opinion, basic remedial service must take precedence over polishing and refining the skills of already prepared students."

Such conclusions sound the death knell for any hope of mainstreaming special-admit students and ensure the ghettoization of learning-support services. Since regular students are perceived as not needing reading and study skills help, those who do are considered different, dumb, and remedial. (A postscript:

Three years after the faculty committee's report quoted above, administrators in the same institution addressed strong letters to the chairperson of the developmental skills department, which had replaced the learning center, complaining about the heavy attrition rate of special-admit students, and the cycle began again.)

Faculty referrals of students in academic difficulty are another source of problems for learning services. To be sure, the service is the appropriate place for such referrals, but, as Felton and Biggs (1977) point out, administrators and professors often display a "tertiary responsiveness" to student problems. They are concerned about treating symptoms only when the symptoms have surfaced dramatically—that is, when the student is ready to drop out of school or is placed on academic probation. (Certainly, many aspects of our current system encourage this problem, since students rarely come to the attention of professors or administrators until they are at a crisis point.)

Therefore, an important goal for learning centers is to help professors and advisers identify students with learning difficulties early and make appropriate referrals. For instance, if a college has a policy that students who do not earn a C average at the end of two years be placed on junior-standing probation, and if advisers refer these probationary students to the learning center, it is difficult to help them. After an accumulation of 2 years of course credits with low grades, it is statistically impossible to get off probation unless they earn straight As—a highly unlikely event for students who, at best, may have earned a B or two, but never an A. If students with marginal grade-point averages were identified earlier, before earning low grades became habitual, it would be easier to help them. But preventive programs are usually considered too expensive or too intrusive by those who are convinced that young people can "grow out of their problems" if left alone. Students themselves often share this belief and express certainty that somehow their academic problems will disappear—next semester.

Faculty referrals can be the kiss of death if the students who are referred feel that the faculty member is just trying to get rid of them. They easily manage to get lost trying to find the learning program, even if it is in the next building. Suggesting that faculty refer students to a person, rather than an impersonal service is friendlier and easier for students to accept, particularly if they are told that the faculty person knows the person and feels that he or she is understanding and effective.

## PROBLEMS UNDER STUDENT SERVICE ADMINISTRATORS

Learning services that are supervised by student affairs administrators may face constraints resulting from the second-class citizenship conferred by academics on programs that they consider nonacademic. Warnath (1971) explains how the roles of student personnel administrators shifted in the 1960s from student concerns to budgets and facilities management. In effect, student affairs administrators have become business managers as their programs for students expanded and as radical, minority, and other student groups bypassed the dean of students, going directly to the college president with their complaints. Warnath (p. 103) describes the situation. "In increasing numbers, presidents seem to be coming to the conclusion that their student personnel deans are unable to give them assistance in working with important student problems. Even more distressing is that student personnel deans are ignored as sources of simple information about students and their concerns."

Hodgkinson's survey of college presidents' attitudes toward deans of students (1970, p. 49) lends further support to Warnath's position. Hodgkinson reports that top administrators frequently view student personnel administrators as an arm of the central administration, programmed to conduct messages down the chain of command. No longer are deans of students expected to synthesize information from students for interpretation up the organizational pipeline for action by the top-level administrators.

The gap between the ideal of student-centered functions (the focus of the professional counseling psychologist or student personnel specialist) and managerial functions has widened. Few people on campus take seriously the contention of student affairs deans and vice-chancellors that their first priority is concern for the welfare of students.

In sum, the political reality of the academic scene is that the learning service can count on little assistance from student personnel officers. "The amount of power the center draws from student personnel is usually zero. In fact, for the center staff to make effective contributions to the academic community and to the student body, they must frequently disclaim their connections with the student personnel structure. Unfortunately for the effectiveness of the total student personnel program, deans of students may feel threatened if members of the center become too closely identified with the academic. If the dean of students senses that he or she is viewed as having a low position in the campus community, a counselor who appears to identify with the academic community through teaching or research (or both) runs the danger of stirring up the resentments of the person on whose team he is supposed to be playing" (Warnath, 1971, pp. 43-44).

The staff members of learning centers may be hampered, then, by the credibility of the administrator to whom they report, and because they work closely with academic departments, they may pose a threat to student affairs deans or vice-chancellors. If these administrators are sensitive to the ambiguity of their own roles, they may overreact to faculty criticism of the learning center and block new projects, limit travel or general budget funds, and indeed appear quite punitive to the learning center.

Today's student affairs deans are quite well aware of the problems created by the artificial split between the academic needs (cognitive aspects of learning) and the affective needs (traditionally considered the sole province of student affairs). In fact, the American College Personnel Association has issued "The Student Learning Imperative," which delineates the duties and responsibilities of the learning-oriented student affairs division. Essentially this document spells out how student affairs organizations must support the intellectual and academic growth of students as well as their personal development.

Whether a learning service is under the aegis of academic or student affairs administrators, one of the most exasperating situations for a learning-center director occurs when her attempts to get grants for the program are thwarted by campus administrators before being transmitted to funding agencies. Administrators have discouraged grant seeking frequently enough in the past that the reasons for this action deserve mention. In some prestigious institutions, only tenured faculty members are eligible to become principal investigators on grants. This is a frustrating situation for the learning-center director who hopes to expand his/her program through outside funding, and who is concerned—and sometimes defensive—about the possible loss of autonomy in the program if someone else directs the grant project and controls the funds. One rationale for this policy is that funding agencies weigh heavily the academic experience and credentials of the principal investigator in making awards. Therefore, it is really to the center's advantage if a top academician or administrator can be convinced to sponsor a grant proposal, rather than for the learning-service director to attempt to fight for it through academic and administrative committees alone.

Some administrators are against grant seeking because federal programs entail much red tape and have strings attached or because they feel that placing a program on "soft money" will jeopardize the college's financial commitment to the program. These can be valid arguments. Less understandable, however, are the objections of administrators, particularly those in small public colleges, who argue that seeking special funds for learning-center services would tarnish the image of the institution because it constitutes an admission that the college accepts low-achieving students. It is sometimes possible to dispel this negativism by giving administrators information about learning-assistance programs in colleges with strong academic reputations.

## THE TENURE PROBLEM

After young learning-center directors have successfully established a service, they often seek academic tenure because it offers security and recognition. If they have taught undergraduate and graduate courses for a few years, they may feel they qualify and may ask for a tenure review. But in most colleges, getting tenure requires more than college teaching experience. Achieving tenure has never been easy, and it is particularly difficult in prestigious universities today. In the past, the proportion who gained tenure among those who aspired it had been

as few as one in thirty-five in some universities. Today, all colleges are more cautious in granting tenure, as financial problems and an aging faculty restrict the number of positions. Learning-skills professionals are often naive about the formalities of the tenure-review process. Indeed, in most colleges, the procedures are largely unwritten and rarely discussed. Although the tenure process varies from institution to institution, most universities require that a departmental committee review the candidate's qualifications in research, publications, teaching, and public and professional service.

The tenure committee tries to predict the candidate's future—to determine whether he or she will continue to be an active scholar/researcher with innovative ideas twenty or thirty years from now. The question addressed by the members is, "Will the candidate continue to grow and develop?" Since the committee members have no crystal ball, they must scan the candidate's previous publications, rate of productivity, growth, and scholarly qualifications, basing their final judgment of future potential on past performance.

In research universities, publications are judged very severely by tenure committees. The sheer number of publications by a candidate may mean little, while the quality and academic respectability of the journals in which they appear may be weighted heavily. Departments usually insist that publications appear in "refereed" journals—that is, journals where editorial boards of professional peers screen the articles to be published. Although most educational journals today are refereed, they differ in reputation. Both the quality of the journal and the range of readers are important and the criterion often used is whether the journal exposes one's ideas to other acknowledged experts in the field who can judge their worth. For example, a tenure committee might view one article in the *Harvard Educational Review* as roughly equivalent to ten articles in *The Journal of Adolescent and Adult Reading*. So it is important that the candidate find out from his faculty colleagues which journals they respect.

In some universities, textbooks are not considered in the candidate's publication dossier, because textbooks and articles in the popular press are considered remunerative and as part of one's teaching contribution, not as scholarly publications. Similarly, if one takes the time to rewrite one's doctoral dissertation into a book, one should not expect the review committee to be pleased. The committee may view this activity negatively, reasoning that the candidate is reworking old ground rather than advancing into new frontiers of knowledge.

Involvement with professional associations—serving on committees, holding offices, presenting papers, and so on—may be considered favorably by a review committee, but the committee members' attitude will depend on whether they recognize the organization as professional and scholarly. One can be nationally known in one's own field while one's work and qualifications remain unknown to one's peers on the faculty.

Another facet of the tenure evaluation is the collection of data on one's effectiveness as a teacher. Of course, having students evaluate your courses is one way. Another, and perhaps more important way, is to work directly with other faculty members—teaching classes jointly, working on projects with them, and generally becoming accepted as an integral part of the department. This is difficult to do if the candidate also has heavy administrative responsibilities or spends a great deal of time counseling students with learning problems.

If one manages to earn the committee's favorable recommendation, there still remain other hurdles in gaining tenure. Most colleges require that the approval of the department in which one teaches be unanimous and also that the approval of campuswide committees and administrators be secured. When departmental approval must be unanimous, one faculty member who feels the candidate's work is "not significant" or "too applied" can block the appointment.

Novice administrators often underestimate the length of time it takes to become tenured. Most universities allow seven or eight years for the candidate to go through the process, with a midcareer review in the fourth year, if requested. Some candidates who have been approved by departmental and campuswide committees are still denied tenure because of lack of available positions or money. In that case, they may have to reinstitute the whole process at a later date.

Because the role of the learning-skills specialist differs from that of the typical faculty member, it may be hard to convince one's faculty colleagues that one is an acceptable candidate for tenure. Even if the learning-skills specialist has excellent professional and teaching qualifications, her interests may be considered too specialized or too applied to be acceptable.

This is not to suggest that learning-center staff members and directors never attain tenure, but it is a difficult, lengthy process in universities. As a result, many who try become discouraged and give up. It is undoubtedly easier to gain tenure before becoming an administrator. Admittedly, few graduate students, when planning their future careers, consider becoming a learning-center director. Upon graduating, however, they find greater opportunities and higher salaries in learning center administration than in most teaching positions. Thus, they opt for administrative jobs without thinking about tenure. Other alternatives might be to find a new position in which tenure is included along with administrative duties (although such positions are difficult to find) or to return to full-time teaching and research. A final caveat is that even if the center director does have tenure, it will not immunize him from the other problems discussed in this chapter. Learning-service personnel often share with counselors characteristics that appear to foster low morale, and they often react to the inherent realities of their positions with what seems to be a persecution complex. In particular, they may react negatively to the slow pace of academic change and may tend to be naive about (and often uninterested in) the sources and uses of power. Warnath (1971, p. 43) describes the limitations of people who self-select counseling roles: "The counselor does not make a good politician. Those qualities which characterize the effective counselor—openness, a desire to encourage the optimum use of individual talents in others, and an opposition to arbitrary or imposed authority—unfit him to manipulate people or events to achieve some personal or organizational goal. To those familiar with the use of power, he appears naive in his direct use of confrontation or resistance. However, even if he has developed a political sense, a member of the counseling staff is in an extremely vulnerable position from which to become a political force on campus. Power resides in departments and schools in rough approximation to their status in that particular academic community. Since the counseling center is marginal to both academic and student personnel structures, what power or influence any one person in the center has may have to be drawn from an extremely small organizational supply."

The learning-skills specialist who lacks political acumen often asks, "Why do we have to continually justify our service to faculty members and administrators, explain our existence, and evaluate and document our effectiveness, when other departments do not?" "Why do they make our task so difficult by setting impossible goals and hurdles for students?" "Why must we be so careful to maintain a low profile?"

The answers lie in the institution's real, not professed, commitment to students, especially to the low-achieving and underprepared students whom it admits. Most colleges perceive support services as incidental to their main business of educating future scholars and leaders of society. We who help students cope with academe are endlessly confronted because we work where others, including professors, have failed, and if we succeed, our success calls attention to their failures.

Specialists who work with student learning problems rank low in academic prestige. For example, students and professors rank psychologists working with learning problems much lower in the hierarchy than psychologists working in clinics with patients' emotional and personality problems or those engaged in research. The complaints of learning specialists are related not only to the values of their colleagues in other disciplines but also to their own internalized acceptance of their low status. Some protest and confront faculty members, others side with students and become antagonists. Some revel in the positive evaluations they get from students and lose sight of other roles. For example, if a student says to a tutor, "I wish Professor Snodgrass could explain the problems as clearly as you do—you should be teaching the course!" it may be ego-building, but it gives one a false sense of importance. As Heard (1976) relates, compliments to the learning-center staff members may sidetrack them from performing functions as watchdogs, ombudsmen, and trendsetters.

## SEEKING THE SOURCES OF POWER

Finding and learning how to use the sources of power within the institution is a necessary task for a successful learning center director. We have mentioned the importance of having good working relations with the admissions director, but there are others who also can be of great assistance. For example, I encourage learning center directors to become good friends with the director of institutional research so that they can work together on research projects—such as adding questions about the center to questionnaires that are sent to students, faculty, parents, etc. Currently, directors are finding that they can strengthen their program and budget by identifying themselves with the person responsible for student retention or the retention committee.

## PREVENTING OUTREACH FROM BECOMING OVERREACH

Balancing the needs of individual clients against outreach activities designed to improve general student learning may, unfortunately, increase student demands for service in an already overloaded program. If learning-skills specialists speak to faculty or student groups one week, there are inevitably more referrals the next week. At least that may be the initial result. If the talk is structured as a general invitation to "come and let us help you, whatever your problems may be," the result will be an increase in clients. If, however, the skills specialist discusses ways students can help themselves and each other, then referrals may not increase.

Similarly, members of the skills staff can spend a lot of time preparing for presentations to classes. For example, the Reading and Study Skills Laboratory at the University of Texas at Austin received about a dozen requests for a staff member to address classes in the foreign-language department. The skills specialists decided that it was more efficient to develop a videotaped presentation on how to study foreign languages than to have staff members invest large amounts of time preparing for each class presentation. Another alternative is to consider developing adjunct skills or Supplemental Instruction classes in courses where there are frequent requests for help. Addressing a class with the professor present can introduce your services to both the students and the professor and can be the basis of more formalized arrangements.

When skills specialists are dispersed, as in a decentralized learning service, heavy student demand may not be a problem. However, difficulties arise when students who are not registered in a course or department with a learning-center component need assistance. For example, a mathematics laboratory may restrict its services to students enrolled in certain basic mathematics courses and not permit others, such as adults who need a quick review in algebra before enrolling in statistics, to use its services. Balancing out the amount of time and effort staff members spend in preventive activities and in direct work with students often poses difficulties for the learning-center director. In the final analysis, how this dilemma is resolved depends on whether the mission of the service is viewed by faculty members and administrators as serving a limited target population. The problems discussed in this chapter do not exhaust the difficulties faced by learning centers. There are many others that characterize any department, including staff relationships, expansion, and financial reengineering. However, too often directors believe that their problems are unique to themselves and their institutions. Rarely do they realize how ubiquitous these problems are throughout academe. Higher education has its rituals, and, although administrators and professors may vary from college to college, they hold similar values, goals, and beliefs and may enforce similar procedures. Perhaps if learning-center directors become aware of those conflict areas that are inescapable in academe, they will be able to cope more effectively with the problems inherent in academic positions.

# CHAPTER 6

## IMPLICATIONS OF MOTIVATION, LEARNING STYLES AND THE EXPERIENCE OF FAILURE

To provide effective instruction to individuals who need to improve their learning skills, teachers need to understand the effects on learning and performance caused by motivation, learning styles, and the developmental stages through which college students pass as they grow intellectually.

Motivation is often considered the prime factor in working with students, so much so that other difficulties may be overlooked. There is a mystique that if students are motivated, they can accomplish anything.

Unfortunately, it is not that simple. For college success, motivation is necessary but not sufficient. Certainly those who would succeed in college must be motivated to perform the tasks and assignments required, but they also need the skills and knowledge necessary to understand their courses, and they must be able to learn quickly, for colleges restrict the amount of time one has to complete learning tasks. Colleges have been criticized for dividing knowledge into semester or quarter segments and insisting that students complete their work during the term, but two mitigating factors should be considered: (1) students are permitted to retake most courses if they are unsuccessful in their first attempt; and (2) students usually expect to finish courses with their peers and are thus reluctant to recycle, or re-

peat, their classes. The number of students willing to repeat a course twice is very, very small—unless they have unlimited financial aid that they cannot lose.

Students who cannot read, write, or add may be highly motivated to become physicians or lawyers, yet they have no chance of passing freshman college courses. It is sad that the social and political pressures to redress historical grievances of disadvantaged minority groups resulted in the admission of some students, who lacked the most rudimentary learning skills, into our most selective institutions. Although this policy has been termed "equal opportunity," in reality it meant "guaranteed failure" when the student is neither prepared for nor understands the work required or doesn't feel capable of learning. It is not hard to understand why selective institutions are returning to more stringent admissions standards and phasing out programs for unprepared students.

In addition to background, aptitude, ability to learn quickly, and the desire to learn, students need persistence, flexibility, and a willingness to cooperate with instructors' demands and institutional policies if they are to succeed in college. They need the strength to avoid procrastination and to continue working even when conditions become stressful.

Adults whose school grades were not outstanding enter college with different expectations than those who are well prepared. Usually no one has encouraged them to go to college, in fact, even their parents may have been against the idea. Furthermore, although they have finished high school, they may be convinced of one thing—that they cannot learn academic subjects—or cannot improve in reading, writing or mathematics. To work effectively with these students, college skills instructors must find ways to enable them to change their attitudes toward themselves and develop strong feelings of self-efficacy before they can improve the skills that will make it possible to perform well in college. Wanting to do something and being motivated to work toward a goal are not necessarily synonymous.

## INTRINSIC AND EXTRINSIC MOTIVATION

Current motivational theory recognizes two kinds of motivation—intrinsic and extrinsic. Intrinsic motivation is the desire to perform a task because of the satisfaction directly derived from working on the task and the value associated with solving a problem or accomplishing an enterprise. On the other hand, extrinsic motivation is the desire to perform a task because success will lead to an external reward, such as money, grades, increased social status, or praise.

Some people have great pride in their ability to accomplish difficult tasks and seem to be motivated toward competency or mastery over their environment, not just toward external rewards. If people with high intrinsic motivation lack the background, skills, or aptitude to achieve a goal or solve a problem, they become frustrated and need to find ways to overcome their deficiencies or change their goals.

In the past, psychologists have argued that there is a negative relation between extrinsic and intrinsic motivation. If people act because of the promise of strong external rewards (or the fear of punishment), they are likely to assume that their motivation is wholly extrinsic. However, if external contingencies are not strong, people assume that their behavior is due to their own interest in the work. Therefore, if people are asked to perform an inherently interesting task but are lavishly rewarded for their efforts, they may infer that the task was really not very interesting or satisfying and that they were just working for the reward. As an illustration, a tight grading policy may turn what was an interesting learning task into dull work, and, in the future, students will refuse to perform the activity unless they receive clear rewards. Or students whose main reason for attending college is the financial aid they receive may develop little interest in continued learning. External rewards weaken students' general interest in learning and decrease their willingness to continue learning after they complete college. On the other hand, if most people perceive a task as dull, it may be necessary to provide an external reward to get them to do it.

Professors generally assume that students are intrinsically motivated—that is, they are in college because they chose to be and want to learn. Professors holding this viewpoint will be less concerned with administering grades as penalties and more likely to plan assignments that are varied and interesting. When intrinsic motivation operates, there is less need to monitor students' behavior, because the students feel responsible for their own work.

However, many students enroll in college for purely extrinsic reasons—family pressures, future social and economic opportunities, and sometimes because they can get grants to do so. These students view grades as what matters most, consider college courses mileposts to pass, and see their role as finding the easiest, least painful way to get through college. They may view all course work as dull and may take advantage of professors who try to make courses interesting and who do not administer grades in a punitive way.

Our present reward systems to lure disadvantaged students into college are based on the premise that if one provides extrinsic rewards for learning (adequate financial aid so that students need not work), students will eventually develop a preference for the learning activity itself, and external rewards will no longer be necessary. This rarely happens, whether learning is associated with M&Ms or dollars. Students will respond as long as the rewards are given, but there is no guarantee that they will continue learning on their own.

## How Motivational Differences Affect Course Selection

When I was an academic adviser, I observed that freshmen differed greatly in their expectations of what college offered and in their willingness to take required courses. One factor that seemed to be related to this diversity was the preparation and prior achievement of the student. The brightest, best-prepared students, committed to a particular major, were cautious about the number of courses they took as freshmen and were concerned about making high grades. They usually insisted on taking the required courses as soon as possible. I am convinced that although they might have grumbled a bit, they would willingly have taken a course labeled "Nongourmet Cooking: Eating Crow A, B, C" if it had been required for a pre-med or psych major that they coveted.

Average students without a clear educational goal, and those who had a career goal in mind but were vague about what it entailed, would reject required courses as "irrelevant" or "unnecessary" but take them within a reasonable time limit. There were exceptions like one young man who said he wanted to be a lawyer but fought taking the required political science course for two years (signing up and dropping it). Some years later, when he was in law school, he came back to tell me that now (at last) he saw the relevance of the political science course and appreciated its importance.

Academically weak students, particularly those whose interest in a major field was built largely on fantasy, demanded their right to take a course overload, wanted to take upper-division courses immediately, and did everything in their power to avoid required courses—even those that related to their professed majors. Some succeeded in avoiding them until their senior year, hoping the rules would change and they could graduate without them. Quite a few seniors were taking freshmen courses like library science—and hating them—during their final college semester.

I believe that many of these same observations hold today. The students weakest in writing still try to put off the required basic writing course as long as possible—even though it underlies success in other fields.

Underprepared students may see college only as a steppingstone to a better job and have difficulty understanding why they should have to take required breadth requirements or courses outside their field of interest. Helping them develop a broader perspective on how learning can contribute to one's satisfaction with life is a broad goal toward which both support staff and faculty must work.

## CHARACTERISTICS OF SUCCESSFUL HIGH-RISK STUDENTS

Although it is impossible to predict with much accuracy which underprepared, or high-risk students will succeed in college, a number of studies reveal some patterns of motivational characteristics that relate to college success. Potentially successful high-risk students seem to be distinguished by a general adaptive factor that involves goal aspiration, goal orientation, goal involvement, willingness to study hard, ability to solve personal problems, and a feeling of support from significant others, such as parents. Weigand (1949) gathered information about these characteristics through interviews with students who had entered college with high school grade-point averages below C. He found that potentially successful students had more favorable attitudes toward school and were less apathetic toward their previous school experiences. Successful students stated that they themselves had selected a goal or major and felt that their own interests had influenced the choices they had made. In contrast, unsuccessful students felt that their goals had been selected for them and gave more superficial reasons for wanting to attend college (for example, because their friends were going).

Successful students were convinced that college was important and, despite hardships, found ways of studying. They felt they studied harder than the average student did or "should." Although successful students reported having as many financial and personal problems as unsuccessful students, they seemed better able to cope with their problems and to take positive action to alleviate them. Unsuccessful students either took no action or took action that did not alleviate the stress. The parents of successful students were more consistently supportive and interested and offered a more democratic type of supervision than did unsuccessful students' parents, who did not encourage them even when they were not failing.

Even though Weigand's study was done at mid-century, long before Patricia Cross discovered the "new students," I have found nothing in my experience or the literature that would refute his findings; they are still applicable today. As researchers continue to probe for newer and more effective ways to describe the students who succeed, despite inadequate backgrounds and poor test scores, some factors have reemerged such as becoming involved with and identifying with the campus community. (See Tinto (1993), Astin (1977), Cross (1971).) For example, studies show that students who live off campus, and make no friends on the campus, are more likely to drop out.

Two new areas of emphasis by psychologists and epistemologists that promise to aid our understanding of young adults may help us understand the quandary about underprepared students. First is the work of William G. Perry, whose longitudinal study on the stages of intellectual and ethical development of college students extends the methodology and insights of developmental psychology into this crucial age group. Second is the extensive research on how learning styles and cognitive styles affect academic performance.

## PERRY'S SCHEME

Perry's work (1968) culminated in a scheme that lays out the stages of intellectual and ethical development of students during their four-year college experience. Interviews with Harvard and Radcliffe students through their college careers provided the data for the study. Interviewers asked students each year to reflect on their college experiences and recorded their conversations verbatim. Perry's analysis of these interviews involved a nine-position scale: In Position 1 the student sees the world in polar terms of we-right-good versus they-wrong-bad and feels that there is an ultimate truth, known by the instructor, and that there are right and wrong answers for every question, as on a spelling test. In Position 2 the student begins to perceive that differences of opinion and uncertainty exist but accounts for them on the basis that teachers are poorly qualified or that teachers know the answers but "want us to find them for ourselves." In Position 3 the student finds diversity and uncertainty pervasive but concludes that it is because we have not found the answer yet. In Position 4 the student accepts diversity and uncertainty as real and legitimate and accepts the belief that anyone has a right to his own opinion or sees the teacher's position as merely a special case of what the teacher wants rather than an authoritative viewpoint that has more validity than the views of others. By the time the student reaches Position 7, he is beginning to make an initial personal commitment to a viewpoint in a field of knowledge, and by Position 9 he "experiences the affirmation of identity among multiple responsibilities and realizes commitment as an ongoing, unfolding activity through which he expresses his life-style" (Perry, 1968, p. 10). Progress through these stages from dualism to commitment is not in smooth, automatic steps. Some students delay, deflect, and regress.

Perry concludes that the educational impact of diversity is best when it is intentional—that is, when it is deliberately planned to enable students to stand back and gain perspective. This can occur when individual professors are committed to different viewpoints and the student is exposed to this clash of ideas, provided that the diversity of views is based on disciplined independence of mind rather than the haphazard clash of dogmatic professors. There are challenges, one being that students may become cynical and gameplay, trying to throw the professor's views back at him and refusing to think on their own. On the other hand, one of the most frustrating kinds of learning experiences for students is when the instructor is completely neutral, presenting different viewpoints and theories but never expressing his own commitment. Perhaps this approach is necessary too, for it forces students to think for themselves rather than merely trying to please the professor.

Perry's scheme has been applied to both college teaching and student counseling in the belief that if instructors are knowledgeable about the stages of intellectual development, they might provide greater opportunities for student growth. The basic conditions for promoting growth are situations in which the student is both challenged and supported. Challenge is provided through presenting diverse viewpoints and experiential learning, while support is offered simultaneously through structured instruction and a personal atmosphere, including individual conferences between instructor and student. Furthermore, there is research that shows that students can advance from dualism as a result of a program providing challenge and support.

Kenneth A. Bruffee (1993) takes Perry to task for ignoring the ways that colleges could implement the social theories of knowledge and adhering to the traditional cognitive psychology approach, even though the accounts of the students he interviewed revealed the importance of interactions with peers in assimilating knowledge. Bruffee points out that although Perry accepts the theory that knowledge is contextual and relative, he resists the idea that creating communities of knowledgeable peers should be an important and deliberate function of a college education, preferring that such groups occur spontaneously. He claims Perry trivializes the social element of learning by calling it the need to keep friends rather than a central focus in student intellectual development.

Developmental skills courses are intended to enable students to move to a point where they can accept and learn intellectually demanding course material. Instructors often use many of the elements suggested by Perry, but often rigidly or haphazardly —that is, some instructors emphasize a supportive counseling/teaching strategy, and others restrict the course to a very structured set of experiences. Students need both. To implement these ideas in developmental skills courses, one might challenge students by planning diverse activities—having them share experiences and ideas with classmates, using a variety of materials and approaches to learning, varying practice to include discussion and written experiences, providing a large amount of direct experience. For instance, students might keep logs and interview older students about their reading and study experiences and techniques and the demands faced in advanced courses. They might also ask their instructors about their perceptions of how students should study and compare their own methods with one another. Students can be supported if the instructor structures the class carefully, adheres to due dates for work and lesson plans, and encourages work in collaborative groups.

For example, Kathy Steele and Jeanine Webb at the University of Florida use several questions concerning what they consider important criteria to assist interested professors in improving their course outlines. (1) Rationale: why should the student take this course? (2) Student outcomes: what do you expect students to achieve? (3) Topics: what are you going to teach? (4) Assignments: what must students do to complete the course? (5) Assessment procedures: how many and what kinds of tests, projects, and papers will you require? (6) Grading policy: how will you determine the grade? (7) Instructional materials: what materials are required—textbooks, lab manuals, and so on? (8) Policies: what are your rules about class attendance, class participation, office hours, use of facility, and so on? Today there are a number of programs to improve teaching including Bernice McCarthy's 4MAT Method for Lesson Plan Development, which includes teacher strategies/roles, overall goals and objectives, and aims at providing for student learning style differences. (Excel, Inc., 200 West Station St, Barrington, IL 60010, 1-800-822-4MAT.)

In the 90s we hear less about Perry's schema and more about concepts like "women's ways of knowing" which bear an interesting similarity to Perry's work. In the first stage, women are described as accepting uncritically what teachers or other authorities tell them (called received knowledge) and then move gradually up to "constructed knowledge" where they balance their own views with the knowledge they've acquired. Ursuline College (Cleveland, Ohio) has based its core curriculum on women's ways of knowing using freshman seminars, group discussions, and collaborative learning as the major teaching strategies. In the freshman seminars, there are no designated topics, but the instructors try to draw connections between the students' lives and the liberal arts. Many of the students are returning women, and some apparently find the jump from the personal knowledge emphasized in freshman seminars to more structured courses in mathematics and literature difficult. On the other hand, the students are said to develop a strong sense of self-assurance.

To learn more about sex-differences in learning, you'll want to read:

Belenky, M. F., Clinchy, B. M., Goldeberger, N. R., & Tartula, J. M. (1988). *Women's ways of knowing: The development of self, voice, and mind.* New York: Basic Books.

Pearson, C. S. (Winter 1992). Women as learners: Diversity and educational quality. *Journal of Developmental Education, 16*(2), 2-10.

## COGNITIVE STYLES

There are many ways to learn. Each person has consistent ways of organizing and processing information or preferred ways of organizing all he or she sees and thinks about. Psychologists call these ways "cognitive styles." Cognitive styles are conceptualized as stable attitudes, preferences, or habitual strategies that determine a person's typical mode of perceiving, remembering, thinking, and problem solving. Current research suggests that a person's cognitive style affects the way he or she learns in college and has implications for how students are affected by different teaching strategies. Psychologists currently believe that cognitive styles are not simple habits, but develop slowly and experientially, and are not easily changed by instruction. Cognitive styles differ from intellectual abilities, which concern content, or what is learned; cognitive styles concern how it is learned. Usually, cognitive styles are thought of as bipolar traits, either end of the scale representing appropriate adaptation in some situations, with individuals distributed along the points of the scale.

Early researchers such as Messick and Associates (1976) described nineteen dimensions of cognitive style; for example, scanning (differences in the extensiveness and intensity of attention deployment), reflection versus impulsivity, and risk taking versus cautiousness. These dimensions closely resemble what earlier psychologists called "learning style" or "learning set," found to be related to college learning. For example, Smith and others (1956) and Maxwell (1978) have reported that aspects of learning style (namely, impulsivity versus constriction and stability versus anxiety) relate to improvement in reading rate and scanning speed.

In the seventies, when the idea of learning styles was a new concept, a number of interesting but complex models were proposed—for instance, Hill's Cognitive-Style Mapping consisted of 28 elements leading to more than 3,260 different profiles for prescribing personalized programs that would maximize a student's academic success. Testing was time consuming and the plotting of cognitive maps difficult, and Hill assumed that the teacher's style should mesh with the student's. This implied that the cognitive maps of faculty members were available to the counselor, a most difficult thing to arrange. Although for a time, some colleges, including Oakland Community College (Michigan), used Hill's maps, the project was soon abandoned. Today, Phyllis Deutsch and Juelle Blankenburg at Oakland Community College use a simple questionnaire that asks students questions such as "How do you learn best? ___visual ___auditory ___tactile/kinesthetic ___individually ___in groups?" It includes 5 short open-ended items about what study techniques work best for that student and what that student feels are the characteristics of his/her best instructor. Not only are the questions brief and to the point, but students also enjoy taking the questionnaire and talking with a counselor about their answers, for no one has asked them these things before and they find the experience enlightening.

Currently there are many different approaches to examining learning styles. Verbal learning researchers have studied the characteristics of persons whose preferred way of learning is to master facts, in contrast to those who prefer to learn concepts. Siegel and Siegel (1965) developed a scale that measured educational set and tested a person's predisposition to learn facts without being driven to interrelate them into any contextual whole versus his predisposition to learn concepts. They compared scores of fact seekers with scores of those who preferred learning broader concepts. The fact-dominated students believed that a fact has an integrity all its own; the concept-oriented students rejected acquisition of facts except as units of information that are interrelated. Testing students in two biology classes, the Siegels found that concept-oriented students learned both facts and concepts better in the section where the instructor was more sensitive to conditions conducive to intrinsic motivation and attempted to interest and motivate students, than in the class where the students were motivated only to pass the course. In the extrinsically motivated class, concept-oriented and fact-oriented students performed equally well on exams.

## FIELD DEPENDENCE/INDEPENDENCE

In the 70s the dimension of cognitive style that seemed to have the greatest implication for educators was field dependence versus field independence. Field dependent people tend to be more sensitive to people and social situations, whereas field independent people respond well to situations that require them to use analytic and problem-solving abilities. Cross (1976) pointed out many similarities between field dependents and the "new students." New students spend their leisure time with people and report that their most important college learning experiences relate to getting along with others. Like field dependents, they are attracted to college majors and careers that emphasize interpersonal relations, are compliant with the wishes of others, are passive, and favor traditional women's roles. Field dependents tend to be poor at analytical problem solving, and new students scored low on instruments measuring preferences for analytic and critical thinking. Both groups tend to be guided by authority figures and extrinsically motivated.

Field dependence/independence also seems to influence selection of majors. In a recent longitudinal study, Witkin and others (1977) found that college students who persisted in college and graduate work either remained in majors consistent with their cognitive styles or transferred to them. A significantly greater proportion of field dependent (people-oriented) students majored in education than of field independents, who preferred majors in science and engineering. Most women are field dependent, and women are underrepresented in science and engineering fields. Although I find this an interesting study, I am concerned that findings such as these may be used to counsel freshmen into careers consistent with their cognitive styles, a premature application of the findings. Since most women are field-dependent, much more information is needed on the developmental stages that college women go through before concluding that "people who need people" (that is, field dependents) should not enter science, engineering, or mathematics. Rather than screening out applicants with the "wrong" cognitive style, I would like to see studies on the learning conditions and demands that attract different types of people to different majors. For example, in one of our programs, we trained women and minority freshmen as tutors in the sciences. They continued in these majors and stated that the tutoring experience and role gave them status with their friends and an opportunity to help others. (These are not the usual reasons science majors give for selecting their fields.)

There appears to be more field dependent than field independent people in college today, judging from the numbers who enroll in popular social science and education courses (even though the job market for social scientists and teachers is glutted). Perhaps, however, other factors account for the popularity of these courses, such as that they tend to be easier and less demanding than science and engineering courses.

## LOCUS OF CONTROL

Locus of control is another cognitive style that research suggests bears a real and consistent relationship to academic achievement and aspiration. According to Rotter's (1966) construct that individuals differ in their beliefs about whether external or internal factors affect rewards, individuals who are categorized as having a sense of internal control believe that rewards follow, or are contingent upon their own behavior. Conversely, those who have a sense of external control believe that rewards are controlled by forces outside of themselves and thus may occur independently of their own actions. Disadvantaged students are often said to have a sense of being controlled by external events; they feel powerless over their own lives. Since they feel unable to manage their environment and to obtain rewards by their own behavior, they may attribute their failing grades to teachers' discriminatory attitudes against them rather than to what they did or did not do. A number of programs have reported that counseling enables underprepared students to develop a realistic sense of both personal and collective power, which seems to be a necessary prerequisite for succeeding in academic courses (Klingelhofer and Hollander, 1973).

## SELF-EFFICACY

Another characteristic that has been shown to relate to academic success is Bandura's (1982) concept of self-efficacy (i.e., confidence in one's ability to learn). Sometimes considered a close relative to locus of control, researchers have found that high-risk students with low self-efficacy fail to learn even under the most optimal conditions (i.e., the best teachers) and have worked to develop strategies to enable students with low self-efficacy to change their self-perceptions. Perry & Penner (1990) were able to improve achievement in high-risk students by demonstrating that they were capable of improving test scores, by having the instructor describe how he had overcome difficulties as a student, and by other instructional strategies.

A number of different inventories have been developed to measure learning style; in fact, so many that Bonham and Boylan (1993) saw the need to describe an organizational framework to help practitioners understand learning style issues and instruments and their implications. Explaining that learning style instruments really measure different dimensions and characteristics of individuals, not just different "styles," they classify learning behaviors under three levels using Curry's model: 1) Cognitive personality style—the individual's approach to adapting and assimilating information; 2) Information processing styles—the intellectual procedures used by individuals in assimilating information; and 3) Instructional preference—the individual's preference for learning environments and activities. Curry graphed this model in the shape of an onion with different layers—the cognitive personality style being the most central, and the instructional preference as the outer layer.

Citing Witkin (1977) as the best known illustrations of cognitive personality style, they point out that field dependence/independence is a personality style that influences ways of learning. It is not a way of learning. The Myer-Briggs Type Indicator (1985) is another popular test of cognitive personality style, providing scores in 16 categories related to the ways an individual thinks vs feels, perceives vs senses, judges vs intuits, etc. It too is a personality test and requires a trained counselor to administer. However, it is often misused as a way of measuring students' attitudes toward the learning environment.

Information processing style, the second level in Curry's onion, refers to intellectual processes and procedures that are characteristically used by individuals to assimilate, organize, and make sense of information. Although partially determined by personality styles, they include learning strategies, metacognitive approaches, or critical thinking skills. Claire E. Weinstein, at the University of Texas–Austin, has demonstrated that learning strategies and metacognition can be taught, and students who learn these increase their performance. Tests such as the LASSI (Learning and Study Strategies Inventory), Watson-Glaser Critical Thinking Appraisal, and the Cornell Test of Critical Thinking Ability are instruments that measure information processing style. Study skills are also associated with information processing, thus tests like the Brown-Holtzman Survey of Study Habits and Attitudes and The Study Behavior Inventory reflect this factor also.

The outer layer represents student's preferences for different subjects, modes of instruction, and learning environments, as well as students' expectations of learning. These are said to be the least stable of all the learning style characteristics. Experts differ as to the implications of these for instruction. Some such as Canfield (1986) hold that students learn better when taught according to their instructional and environmental preferences. Others, such as McCarthy (1982), suggest that instructors should deliberately and systematically teach in a variety of modes to produce more flexible learners, rather than trying to fit the instruction to the student's preference. Examples of tests of instructional preference are Canfield's Learning Styles Inventory (1986) and Kolb's, The Learning Style Inventory (1986).

A new test, called PEEK, developed by Claire E. Weinstein and a team from the University of Texas, measures students' expectations of college learning—perceptions, expectations, emotions and knowledge about college, from three vantage points—the personal, social and academic. This test can also be used with instructors to compare their expectations with those of students.

For information and references about the various tests discussed in this chapter, see Appendix.

## CULTURAL STYLES

Bonham and Boylan (1993) also postulate that there may be a fourth set of learning styles and preferences related to one's specific cultural group and cite studies that suggest that some ethnic groups are more likely to prefer different learning experiences or to relate to learning in different ways than others. They point out that more research is needed to confirm whether these indeed are different than the three levels described above.

## SELF-CONCEPT

So much has been written about the negative effects of early school experiences on the psyches of disadvantaged students, who are now eagerly sought as college students, that the research on self-concept deserves mention. Concern about changing the negative self-concepts of underprepared students has become almost a cult among teachers and writers, with the result that the complexities of the relationship between confidence in one's ability and performance are often overlooked. Despite the eloquent and passionate writings of such authors as Holt (1964), Cross (1976), and Roueche and Snow (1977), there is little evidence to support the contention that underprepared college students consistently have lower self-concepts than their more able peers. In fact, there is compelling clinical and empirical evidence that just the opposite is often true. Intellectually capable and well-prepared students who lack confidence in their ability to succeed in college fill the caseloads of college counseling centers, while many underprepared students are very confident in their ability to succeed in college. When asked what grades they expect to earn in college, they will respond "A's," although they have never earned grades that high in school before. Perhaps this response reflects a sort of denial or bravado (although it is often dubbed unrealistic), but it is very hard to convince weak students with high expectations that they will need intensive assistance if they are to meet their goals.

At-risk students who are confident of their ability to study and learn tend to be those who earned high grades in academically weak high schools with very little effort. They consider themselves well prepared for college and reject help until they find that they are failing. As a result, we can expect to see many more students who are not prepared, despite good high school grades, entering our colleges.

Disadvantaged minority students (especially blacks, the group that has been studied most often) have much greater confidence in their ability to handle social situations than do white college students, and it may be this social confidence that leads them to be overconfident about their academic prospects. Certainly students who have been on the borderline of failure for years usually lack confidence in their ability to learn, but so do students who are high achievers. One consistent finding in studies of self-confidence is that women, as a group, have the most seriously damaged or lowest concepts of self. In reviewing a large number of studies of self-concept, Klingelhofer and Hollander (1973) conclude that at the college level, low self-concepts do not seem as typical of black women, but white women, lower-class women, white Southern women, and other minority women all contribute to a "morbid picture of low self-esteem, lack of self-confidence, and an unwillingness to take risks or be venturesome, which suggests the impact of cultural conditioning" (1973, p. 52). The women's movement faces a large task in raising the consciousness of women to recognize their own worth.

## IMPLICATIONS FOR PRACTICE

Although researchers may not have developed instruments for testing cognitive style that meet rigorous statistical tests for reliability and validity, one cannot conclude that differences in cognitive style do not exist. If schools had waited to teach reading until researchers had explained the process of reading and agreed on the best method of teaching it, you would not be reading this page today. Good teachers have always recognized that students differ in learning style and have tried to accommodate these differences. Some students prefer listening over reading, others learn better with pictures and graphs, and some even learn better with textbooks. Helping students discover what learning strategies work best for them is the essence of an effective skills program. Until instruments are perfected that will yield specific and valid scores, we may have to be content to use simple inventories and our best clinical judgment, tempered by experience and common sense, to improve students learning.

The studies on cognitive style reflect the changing nature of college instruction, particularly in basic skills. People who need people (field dependents, if you prefer) do not work well in a personally isolated situation, as in traditional reading labs. They do respond to the same materials when they can work with others—with tutors, in small groups, or in dyads—and these peer-teaching methods currently seem to be popular in every skills area. However, group learning does not fit every student or every subject. There are still no panaceas in instruction. However, the idea that learning styles or preferences can affect achievement is now generally accepted. More definitive research will surely follow, challenging some of our basic laws of learning. For example, a recent study by Mumford and others (1994) shows that learning preferences interact with massed vs distributed practice. In other words, those who prefer to cram will learn more with that strategy.

Short of revising their courses to be personalized, self-instructional programs, often a costly and difficult process, what can instructors do to more effectively teach students with different learning styles? There are some simple steps faculty members can take to make even a straight lecture course more palatable and effective. (1) Encourage students to work and study together. Group learning may take many forms. Students can work mathematics problems in dyads within the classroom, form study groups that meet outside class hours, or take turns serving as tutors. Instructors can facilitate work outside class by distributing names, addresses, and phone numbers of students who are interested. Obviously, students who do not want to be included should not be forced to study with others. (2) Intersperse lectures with small group discussions, giving students opportunities to quiz each other, and then give one minute tests. (3) Give assignments with suggestions on different ways the task may be completed. Instead of requiring all students to write papers, suggest that some may prefer to use other ways to show that they have mastered the information—for example, class presentations, tape and slide programs, individual appointment sessions, pictures, collections, or dramatizations. (4) Encourage students to determine the modality in which they learn most effectively, and then see that opportunities are provided to meet these needs. For example, see that the course content is available in the form of tape recordings, audiovisual aids, and so on. (5) Ask your learning resource service to locate computer software, audiotapes, filmstrips, and other aids for those students who learn best from them. With such materials, learning centers can offer flexible, personalized services that respond to individual students' unique learning styles and abilities.

## On the Nature and Etiology of Academic Failure

In this age of rampant grade inflation, when the average college grade is a "B" and D's and F's are infrequently given (except in science courses), it is difficult to see how many students can fail. But each term, a significant number of students manage to end up on academic probation.

In large public institutions, failure has always been an inherent part of academic life. Even before the days of open admissions, state universities admitted large numbers of freshmen each fall, many of whom failed or dropped out before the end of their first year. Colleges in those days were not termed "revolving doors"; a better metaphor might be "barb-wired-topped stone walls" over which few passed. Today, thanks to grade inflation, the failure rate should be much lower. However, many students fail because they don't know they should officially drop courses, or because they are bored, or feel that they don't fit in, or for myriad other reasons. Those who stay take longer to complete degrees so that follow-up studies of six-years or longer duration are needed to determine graduation rates.

## GRADE INFLATION

Grade inflation began in high schools in the 60s as they adopted automatic promotion and made other efforts to prevent students from dropping out of school. Students were given more choices of courses, and many colleges changed their entrance requirements; for example, students were no longer required to take four years of high school English or three years of laboratory science to qualify for college entrance.

Similarly, when the large group of disadvantaged students entered colleges under open admissions, these institutions made many concessions to accommodate them, including easing the grading system. As a result of open-admissions policies and the student protest movement, colleges dropped some requirements (such as foreign-language courses) and allowed students to substitute a wide range of electives for lower-division general-education courses. Some faculty members who were forced to teach large numbers of underprepared students were either unable or unwilling to modify their courses, and they instead lowered their grading standards. Faculty members who maintained their standards ran the risk of being attacked by students as "racist" and "elitist" and were considered nonsupportive of the efforts to help disadvantaged students get college degrees. Students from the ghetto brought with them survival skills that academics had never experienced—intimidation, threats, and emotional confrontations. In addition, to fail a student meant that the faculty member must justify his grading practices through a series of grievance hearings or conferences with administrators. Many felt that it was just not worth the time or effort. Finally, student groups published course evaluations in efforts to change professors' grading practices, and if one had the reputation of a tough grader, one's courses would attract fewer students.

Certainly college courses have not been equally affected by grade inflation. Social science courses have been the most susceptible to grade inflation while science grades have shown smaller increases. Social science courses, however, have been more popular with disadvantaged students than have science subjects. In addition, the students in the 1960s and early 1970s demanded that courses be relevant, and this led to new courses in current social issues and ethnic studies. Not only were the new courses different in content but also in method and assignments, often requiring that students discuss issues rather than write essays or take examinations. Grades in these new courses tended to be higher than those in traditional courses—after all, how can one fail "The Chicano Experience" course if one is a Chicano? In the minds of many students, relevant was equated with easy. As a result of these and other influences, more college students today are receiving A's than C's.

Even in the 90s, grade inflation remains an academic legacy that concerns many faculty members. Recent Doonesbury cartoons reflect the current reality—depicting a college student suing his professor for giving him a grade of B in a course, thus thwarting his ambition to enter law school. In the cartoon, the student won, and comments from faculty and the college president suggest that B grades have replaced D's.

The extent to which grade inflation has worsened is shown in a study by Arthur Levine of the Institute of Educational Management at Harvard, who reports that the percentage of students earning grade point averages of A minus or higher almost quadrupled between 1969 and 1993. In contrast, the number of students receiving grades of C or lower dropped by two-thirds in the same period, and since students' average ability has not risen since 1969, there must be another explanation. Levine suggests that college professors make up their own grading systems in whatever way seems most suitable, and many are grading undergraduates as they were graded in graduate school, where only A's and B's are passing.

Ironically, although today's students are receiving higher grades than their predecessors, Levine reports that they are not satisfied with their grades. What might the solution be? Levine suggests that the grading system be simplified to three categories: pass, fail, and honors, and that instructors be trained to set appropriate criteria for assigning these grades. This will not be easy since faculty members have increasingly abdicated their responsibility for setting high standards for grading.

There have been some suggestions that the grade inflation trend may be changing. Stanford faculty, who abolished the grade of F in 1970 and permitted students to retake courses without penalty until they made the grade they wanted, recently decided to institute a NP (not passed) grade. In 1994, 51 percent of the grades students earned at Stanford were A's. In fact, the grade of F in most colleges seems to be reserved for students who stop attending class

without officially withdrawing. Despite these changes, C remains the average grades in engineering and military colleges, where students whose academic performance is weak are still given D's and F's.

## CHARACTERISTICS OF UNSUCCESSFUL STUDENTS

Why do students fail? There have been many studies on the college failure that point to some of the reasons. For example, Pitcher and Blaushild (1970) list ten reasons for academic failure: lack of potential; inadequate conception of the work involved in succeeding; importance of other activities over study; interference from psychological problems; failure to assume responsibility for own learning; inhibition of language functions (poor reading, writing, and speaking skills); lack of understanding of standards for high-quality performance; selection of inappropriate major; vagueness about long-term goals; and selection of wrong college.

Pitcher and Blaushild (1970) analyzed data of 600 college failures from 250 colleges who attended the Berea, Ohio Educational Development Center for a ten-week educational rehabilitation program. They concluded that the problems of these underachievers had not started in college: they had been underachieving all their academic life. Other factors that exacerbated underachievement included upward-striving parents who considered anything less than full attainment of goals to be failure, the conflict between the developmental stages of late adolescence and college structure, and the disparity between most high school programs (where anti-intellectualism is rewarded) and college (where intellectual activities are valued). They found that the failure rate was highest in those state institutions which must, by law, take all graduates from accredited high schools and which solve the problem by dumping academically weak students quickly.

Studying the characteristics of the low-achieving college student was a popular research activity of counseling psychologists in the 1950s and early 1960s. Researchers were particularly interested in the "underachiever," defined as a student whose ability scores were high but whose grades were low. As research data accumulated, some studies showed that even students scoring poorly on standardized tests were "underachievers" too. Kornrich (1965) selected 51 articles from the more than 500 published studies for his book *Underachievement*. These papers range from research reports, case studies, and position papers to theoretical articles. For example, in an article "The Underachievement Syndrome," Roth and Meyersburg (1963) described the characteristics of the poor college achiever:

◊  The student's poor achievement does not arise from incapacity to achieve.
◊  Poor achievement is an expression of the student's choice.
◊  The student's choice for poor achievement operates in the preparation he makes for achievement.

Specifically, they found that the way a student studies, the subject areas he concentrates on or avoids, the amount of study time—reflects a decision that leads to low achievement. Poor achievers spend much of their study time with friends, relaxing, watching television, or fantasizing. They prepare only partially for exams and when they study, they are not sure what they are studying. I have known many students with these symptoms. For example, Peter, an engineering student I once worked with, complained that he studied over fifty hours for a physics examination but could not recall the topics covered in the textbook or lectures—or even the chapter titles. Studying for him seemed to mean staring at a book, trying to memorize each detail—a kind of penance serving.

◊  Low achievers have a history of poor achievement and poor or nonexistent study habits.
◊  Low achievement may be expressed as an overall limited achievement in all courses or as achievement in deviant channels.

When the student's overall achievement is low, Roth and Meyersburg conclude that the student's energies are directed toward maintaining the status quo. Some examples are 1) the student who resists learning new subjects "that I haven't had before" and refuses to take new subjects or 2) those who achieve in deviant channels, expending their effort in extracurricular activities (ie. Jim, a student who was too busy organizing the card section for the fall football games to study, or Kwami, who spent so much time and energy trying to organize his own alternative high school that he could not attend his graduate classes or write papers). Others show a strong resistance to authority, like Rondi, who read books avidly for her own pleasure and interest but refused to read any of the works assigned by her instructors—even those she had started on her own volition.

Roth and Meyersburg also postulate that the patterns for poor achievement are enduring and do not undergo spontaneous change. However, they postulate that counseling can serve as an impetus to change low-achievement patterns.

Others have reported that the low achiever tends to have family problems, is impulsively disparaging of self, is vulnerable to disparagement by others, tends to lack insight about self, lacks a clear set of personal goals and values, has frequent depressions, and is anxious. The psychodynamics of low achievement, as one might expect, are complex. Devalued by parents, these students learn early to get gratification from their peers, and they sometimes get attention from their parents for their embarrassingly low grades. And sometimes even students whose test scores are low can be underachievers.

## COUNSELING THE STUDENT WHO IS ON PROBATION

Students who are failing come in for counseling reluctantly, if at all, when sent by advisers or deans and reveal states of deep depression or denial. Poor achievers are not the college counselor's favorite clients, and the research on the efficacy of counseling in improving the academic achievement of failing students reveals a dismal picture. Barbara Kirk described the counselor's quandary in a book on underachievement written in 1965 as follows: "Universally in these cases [students on academic probation], the counselor reports that it was a matter of extreme difficulty to obtain any direct discussion of the problem with the counselee, however obvious and apparent the problem, and however voluntarily the counselee had sought counseling. Moreover, the recurrent report is that it was extremely difficult to obtain a description or discussion of any of the counselee's feelings, or even, in many cases, situations or vicissitudes which might be expected to occasion strong counselee reactions." She adds that the clients show no surprise when they learn they have done extremely well on ability tests and that their excuses for their poor grades are "unrealistic, superficial, and largely implausible." The counselor must work very hard with these students, and the prognosis is poor.

If students on academic probation who voluntarily seek help pose problems for counselors and others who would help them, think about the probationary students who don't come in for help. In a recent study, Sharon Silverman and Anne M. Juhasz (1993) examined an issue that has baffled counselors for ages—why students who are on academic probation reject help. Asking what factors contribute to the lack of responsiveness to offers of help to students on probation, they interviewed students who after being notified that they were placed on probation and offered help, failed to respond after three contacts. They found that help rejectors demonstrated unresolved conflict in the area of trust versus mistrust and were skeptical about offers of help; they had strong feelings of autonomy and were intensely independent.

The help rejector was characterized by lack of friends, companions, and family support, lack of self-confidence and a feeling of self-worth and presented a profile predominated by the need for safety, love/belonging, and esteem. None of the group studied had told their family or close friends about their academic failures. The researchers describe this (secrecy about their academic failure) as the best kept secret of all and probably the most devastating for the students since it interfered with their social and personal relationships and limited their opportunity for satisfactory experiences with those who might be supportive.

This study suggests that successful programs have to meet the help rejector's unmet needs of love and belonging and unresolved conflicts. Deans and others who inform students of services that can help them must do it in a very personalized way—not just by sending them a formal letter.

In other words, both referrals and programs must be personalized if the probationary student is to accept help. Personalization in programs can be enhanced if students are free to disclose their problems and conflicts to a group; to this end, students might make an oral as well as a written contract stating their commitment to the course and agreeing to maintain confidentiality about what other students reveal in discussions. Personalization can also be enhanced by encouraging small-group interactions, dyadic interactions, individual interviews with the instructor, and written and oral comments by the instructor about the student's log book, portfolio, or other work.

Colleges today, especially small colleges, strongly emphasize retention since the applicant pool is usually too small for them to afford the luxury of losing many students. As a result, there has been an increase in programs for students on academic probation. But as mentioned above, working with these students is not easy. As Sylvia Mioduski at the University of Arizona–Tucson points out, "Any time you require a student to do something because of 'less than stellar' performance, you need to be prepared for the possibilities of angry/passive-aggressive, whining behaviors, but you will also get those students who are eternally grateful that someone cared enough to help." She also stresses the importance of faculty support because students listen more carefully if their faculty actively support this kind of program.

Unfortunately, as a result of the budget cuts of the mid-90s, many colleges are closing these programs though the need for them is undeniable. Let's look at how some programs struggle to serve students while keeping costs down.

# EXAMPLES OF PROGRAMS FOR STUDENTS ON ACADEMIC PROBATION

## A PRIVATE TECHNICAL COLLEGE: ROCHESTER INSTITUTE OF TECHNOLOGY'S (RIT) COLLEGE RESTORATION PROGRAM

RIT's College Restoration Program (CRP) is a program that has been continuously offered since 1987 and has been a model for probation student programs in other institutions for many years.

Each term the program is offered to 25 students who have had academic difficulty and have been suspended from college. Students who are selected for the CRP are offered a program based on their needs. This program has been in operation for many years and demonstrated its success with students who are traditionally difficult to help—those who have tried college and failed (Payne & Smith, 1991).

Rochester Institute of Technology (RIT) is a private college and students who enter the College Restoration Program are charged the same fees as regularly enrolled students. Since CRP students have been suspended from RIT, they have special permission to enroll during the time they spend in the program as "Matriculated/Part-time Students," although they pay full tuition. After being accepted by the program, students pursue individual programs designed by the Learning Development Center staff for one term.

The CRP program can include individual and small group skills instruction, non-credit developmental courses and labs, credit content courses, and counseling. Each student is assigned a mentor from the Learning Development Center. Although successful completion of the CRP does not guarantee readmission to the college, students may request that a summary of their progress in CRP be sent to the readmission committee.

The College Restoration Program is based on the following constructs (from Payne and Smith, 1991):

1. The student must focus his/her attention upon the dilemma in which he/she has become involved. He/she must realize that underachievement is indeed, his/her problem. He/she may have rationalized otherwise, but, the fact remains, he/she simply has not functioned in the academic situation to the best of his/her ability.

2. The student must accept behavior modification as his/her personal responsibility. He/she must be willing to deal with his/her dilemma in a systematic, objective, and intensive manner, and he/she must be equally willing to motivate himself/herself through his/her own volition.

3. Goals are identified by each student which provide the specific program for change. He/she must see the relevance in the design of his/her course of study. He/she must also understand that the quality and quantity of his/her performance is to be a determining factor in significant behavior modification.

4. The realization of these criteria sets the stage for the active contribution of a fourth: implementation of a program of change. This is the focal point of the program. It involves an interplay of six distinct behavioral aspects that are stressed in the program:
   a. reconditioning of language inhibitions
   b. improvement of skills
   c. internalization of quality standards
   d. reduction of defensive mechanisms
   e. strengthening the self-concept

f. re-interpretation of the student's relation to his/her environment.

5. The final construct is a validation of the experience. This can be observed through the student's subsequent performance on returning to college, or, perhaps, in the successful fulfillment of an alternative goal.

After a student has been recommended for admission to the CRP, the Learning Development Center staff schedules him or her for an interview, a series of diagnostic evaluations, and a conference. If accepted by the CRP, the applicant is assigned a LDC mentor and scheduled in a block of seminars, classes, laboratory experiences, and one or two college courses. Other activities include:
   a. self-assessment—personal management seminar. (Note: Currently, the staff is considering substituting the self-assessment with a CRP Seminar required of all students and an additional, separate Career Course limited to students who are unsure about their major.)
   b. time management
   c. listening/note-taking

CRP students are assigned other activities depending on professional evaluation of their needs. These may include:
   a. efficient reading
   b. reading lab
   c. textbook reading
   d. writing skills
   e. writing lab
   f. proofreading
   g. persuasive presentations
   h. individualized math
   i. creative problem solving

Students with moderate skills improvement needs may enroll in two college credit classes.

One of the major strengths of this program is its emphasis on the affective needs of low-achieving students. They become involved in self-assessment and gain an understanding of the basic principles of human development. They must learn to reduce stress, improve their decision-making skills, their interpersonal relations, and their communication skills. Finally, they must learn how to build a feeling of competence, responsibility, and the ability to control their own lives.

## Evaluation Results

Irene Payne, who initiated the CRP, has kept records on the students since the programs' inception and has evaluated its success over time by comparing the percentage of students recommended for reinstatement, those who returned to RIT or transferred to another college—and by the number of terms they completed after finishing CRP. In a follow-up study of College Restoration Program students for 1984-86, it was found that 79% received positive program evaluations, and of those who immediately re-enrolled at RIT, 72% completed three quarters immediately following CRP.

A more recent follow-up study (Payne and Smith, 1990) shows that the overall student success rate has remained fairly constant since 1976. However, the investigators note that over the years there has been a gradual increase in the percentage of reinstated students who transferred to a different major after completing CRP. For example, 55% of the latest group changed majors. This they attribute to two factors: 1) the inclusion of a career exploration module in the Self-Assessment/Personal Management course in which students seriously examine their career/academic choices in relation to their abilities, interests, etc., and 2) the fact that each student sees a mentor regularly provides opportunities for personal counseling in career planning as well as academic matters.

## Cost-Effectiveness

An indication of the cost-effectiveness of the CRP is that since RIT students who fail are generally suspended for one year, students included in the study account for 374 full-time quarter registrations during a period when most of these students would NOT have been attending RIT. (Note: CRP students enroll as part-time students while they are in the program, but pay full tuition.)

The College Restoration Program is a unique concept; its focus is the student who has failed and, as a result, has been suspended. The CRP student, in most cases, is ready to make a commitment to explore reasons for failure and to follow through on a plan of action to remediate problem areas, develop needed skills, and work on attitudinal changes and habits that will lead to academic success. The results of the studies show that when good study methods are combined with satisfaction in an appropriate career/academic choice, students are generally successful.

## A Program for Probationary Students at a Major University (University of Minnesota)

As colleges have become increasingly concerned with retaining students, particularly minority students, many are offering special services for students on academic probation. For example, Joyce Weinsheimer, Director of the Learning & Academic Skills Center at the University of Minnesota, offers probationary students three choices: individual assistance, special workshops for students on probation, or a one-credit course called Choosing Academic Success. She recognizes that a letter from the dean informing students that their academic status is in jeopardy is no guarantee that they will take charge of the future and become academically successful so she encourages faculty, advisers, counselors and others to refer students to her program and advertises it widely. Her workshops focus on helping students deal with academic failure and make use of existing campus resources so they can 1) put failure in perspective; 2) determine what obstacles are interfering with their learning; and 3) gain the self-confidence and self-determination they need to succeed in college. The workshops use self-inventories, case studies and stories of other students who have been in similar positions and overcome the problem. She attempts to help students to reframe the negative experiences they've had and "resolve the dissonance between their expectations and the realities of the educational environment." One goal is to change the student from being a victim of failure to an agent of success.

Each of these approaches (individual appointments, the workshops, or the course) share similar strategies to help students. They determine the personal factors that interfere with student performance, decide whether the students are unhappy with the college they're attending, what specific course problems they have, why their approach to study does not bring good results, and whether they're really not sure that they belong in college. Then students are asked to make choices about what they will do to change things, devise a plan with do-able tasks, and determine how they can implement the plan effectively. A way of monitoring the plan through a schedule of activities that they agree to complete each week, called a "commitment monitor," ensures that the student is involved in accomplishing the small steps and gets across the idea that every day

makes a difference. Group interaction is encouraged in the workshops and class so that students learn to share their experiences.

Students use Weinsheimer's *Turning Point: Helping Students Get Off Probation and On With Their Education* (1993), Belmont, CA: Wadsworth Publishing Company as a text. It contains exercises, stories about students, suggestions and explanations about learning styles, study skills, career planning, setting up and carrying out their improvement plans, and so on. Grades are given on a pass/no-pass basis. However, students must earn 90% of the possible points on assignments and activities in order to pass. In order to raise their grades, students may arrange to complete extra credit assignments.

## A PROGRAM FOR STUDENTS ON ACADEMIC PROBATION AT A SMALL PRIVATE WOMAN'S COLLEGE (SWEET BRIAR COLLEGE, ENROLLMENT = 600 STUDENTS)

Students on academic probation at Sweet Briar College receive a letter from the dean encouraging them to make an appointment with the director of the ARC (Academic Resource Center, pronounced ark) who then assigns each of them to a peer mentor with whom they meet weekly throughout the semester. Peer mentors, known as Arc-Angels, are trained to work individually with probationary students on time management procedures, textbook reading and study skills, as well as identifying other problems that students might have and referring them to appropriate support services. The probational student must meet with a peer mentor at least once a week in the ARC office. The time management method used involves conceptualizing study time like a bank account—if you decide to take a break from studying, then you have to make it up at some other time during the week. Peer mentors report that it is often difficult to get their students to schedule sufficient time each day for exercise (1 hour) and meals (2 1/2 hours).

## A PROGRAM FOR STUDENTS ON ACADEMIC PROBATION AT A MEDIUM SIZED PUBLIC UNIVERSITY

Armand Policicchio directs a TRIO program at Slippery Rock State University for college students placed on academic probation. Most of these students qualified for regular admission but encountered academic difficulties, and most were first generation college students or otherwise eligible for TRIO funded programs. To enter the program, each student signs a contract that requires her or him to attend 10 meetings of a seminar on study skills and goal-setting, academic policies, etc., to complete a testing battery (Myers Briggs Type Indicator, LASSI, and other appropriate tests), and to attend 10 intensive individual counseling sessions per semester with their program advisor. Financial aid guidance, tutoring and SI programs are also available, and students are encouraged to seek help in selecting a major, career guidance, and looking at graduate programs, as appropriate. Once in the program, students can continue to get individual help for as long as three semesters. The two learning specialists in the program work with up to 150 students each semester.

Program results show that probationary students in this program raise their GPA about one half letter grade within four semesters and that they remain in college or graduate at about a 62% rate over seven semesters, compared with a rate of around 45% for typical Slippery Rock students.

Both the staff and students feel several factors enable students to pull themselves together and get out of their academic holes. First, the systematic and structured program is designed to help them learn to become more successful and effective students. Second, the program emphasizes affective concerns as well as traditional learning assistance help. Lastly, students are given a large amount of individual attention that is sustained through the semester. Students perceive the personal interviews as the most valuable part of the program, reporting that individual help is available nowhere else on campus. This is another example of how students sometimes say the learning assistance service is "an oasis of caring in a desert of institutional indifference."

## ACADEMIC SUPPORT FOR THE STUDENT WHO HAS FAILED

### THE ACADEMIC PROBATION INTERVENTION UNIT—TANANA VALLEY CAMPUS, UNIVERSITY OF ALASKA–FAIRBANKS (ENROLLMENT = 2000 FULL AND PART-TIME STUDENTS)

The Tanana Valley Campus, formerly a community college in Fairbanks, is now incorporated into the University of Alaska at Fairbanks. It has retained its community college mission and focus and has an open admissions policy. Tanana Valley Campus also readmits many students on academic suspension from University of Alaska baccalaureate degree programs and supports students on academic probation. The Tanana Valley Campus is located in Fairbanks, across town from the main University of Alaska campus.

Marjorie Illingworth (1995) reports that each semester a significant number of TVC's students are on probation and face the loss of financial aid, university housing, athletic participation, etc. Many of these students are adult women and minorities. But although the institution faces budget constraints, the problem is not one of lack of services but of linking students to existing services. Students on probation are offered the opportunity to participate in the Academic Probation Intervention Program but are not required to do so. Many of these students are on probation because they did not understand (or were not aware) of academic regulations such as the necessity of formally dropping courses, attending class regularly, etc.

What the program instructor does:
◊   reviews each student's academic record
◊   assesses basic skills
◊   places student in basic skills when needed
◊   limits course schedules (9-12 hours; some are advised to take even fewer hours)
◊   refers student to campus or community services as needed.

Students may be referred to tutoring, study skills classes or labs, and math or writing labs. Other services include study groups, guidelines for participation in classroom discussion, and learning how to communicate effectively with an instructor. Referral to other campus services may include intensive health, substance abuse, or personal counseling, and compensatory support for disabled students as appropriate. Also students might be referred to community services such as day care assistance, crisis counseling, respite care, AFDC (Aid for Families with Dependent Children), and transportation or housing assistance.

Financial aid is another major issue for these students. They may need help in appealing the loss of Pell Grants so their grants can be extended to cover the probationary semester, but in some cases students must raise their grades in order to requalify for financial aid. They need assistance in realistically assessing what they can take to raise their GPAs. Probationary students are also referred to career counseling services as appropriate.

Probationary students enroll in one section of an ongoing developmental studies course, College Success Skills, for one credit. This section is a "sheltered" class with controlled access and is limited to probational students. Taught by the program's academic advisor, it serves as a central hub between the support provided by the APIU and the rest of the college and provides a way for bonding between students as they are encouraged to help each other and as a way of strengthening their ties to the college.

Students are expected to meet regularly with the instructor, an advisor, or other developmental faculty members at least two or three times during the term, although often these meetings are informal.

This program, begun at a time when the state was considering curtailing funds for developmental programs, was designed to be as inexpensive as possible. Ideally, assigning students to the program can be done almost automatically as soon as grades are posted. Students are informed of the program as an option on their grade report, as a stipulation for continuation of financial aid, or a criteria for continuing at the university. The program is designed to be cost-effective because it coordinates the delivery of multiple services that already exist on campus and in the community, and the only additional costs are teaching one section of the developmental class and additional academic advising.

The Academic Probation Intervention Unit utilizes existing university courses and services and integrates them in such a way as to benefit each student. Formative evaluation is done through frequently administered, built-in student evaluation of instructors and the summative components involve a follow-up data bank so that students in the program can be compared with students on probation who do not choose to enter API. Currently supported by a grant, the program director hopes that it will eventually be absorbed by the university.

Class materials are based on:

Wlodowski, R. (1985). *Enhancing adult motivation to learn: A guide to improving instruction and increasing learner achievement.* San Francisco: Jossey Bass.

The advantages of the API program are that it is comprehensive, integrated, has a credit bearing option, is flexible, is easily prescribed and cost effective.

Although budget limitations are forcing colleges to cut back on many services for students, especially those on academic probation, the climate in academe continues to grow more stressful, increasing student demand for learning skills and counseling services. Attending college today may be placing greater numbers of students at risk, even those who are well prepared.

# CHAPTER 7

## SUCCESSFUL PROGRAMS AND STRATEGIES FOR TEACHING HIGH-RISK COLLEGE STUDENTS

In this chapter you will find brief descriptions of some of the strategies and programs that have been proved successful in teaching high-risk college students. Bear in mind as you read this that many of these strategies, such as collaborative learning, are even more effective with average and above average students. Others, like the programs listed, involve the structure that at-risk students need as they begin academic work and may not be necessary for the "college ready" student.

Earlier we explained that many of today's college students are not just academically underprepared, but are academically at-risk for many other reasons as well. They may be working full-time with family responsibilities, have minimal support from key family members, and not only have limited academic skills but often expect to fail college courses and have other personal difficulties that limit their success. Some are recovering from alcoholism or drug use or mental illness. These students differ from those we considered underprepared in the 70s in that their difficulties are greater. They often don't know that they don't know, nor do they understand what college professors expect. They need comprehensive services including effective counseling, advising, and mentoring, as well as academic skills development.

Since many of these students have dysfunctional academic adjustment, they tend to reject teaching methods, materials, and strategies that they have had in elementary and high school. They need counseling help and support to undo the negative attitudes, emotions, and fears they associate with their earlier school experiences.

## INSTITUTIONAL POLICIES THAT CAN PROMOTE LEARNING FOR HIGH-RISK STUDENTS

Before at-risk students can direct and monitor their own learning, they need models to demonstrate what's involved in good learning and an institutional policy that supports their needs. For example, policies that Miami-Dade Community College implemented to expedite learning include required testing and placement in skills courses as needed, restricted choices of courses until students have demonstrated achievement, strict enforcement of simple policies such as not permitting late registration—requiring that all students must be in class the first day, limiting the number of credits a students who is working 30 hours or more a week can carry, monitoring attendance, etc. (Roueche and Baker, 1987).

## CRITERIA FOR SUCCESSFUL BASIC SKILLS CLASSES
(Based on studies by Suanne Roueche, Roueche & Snow, 1977, Roueche & Kirk, 1973, Fullilove & Trieisman, 1990.)

**More time on task**. Weak students need more intensive courses involving extra time and credit for extra work. For example, Trieisman's intensive workshops for calculus students required nine hours per week for five credits compared with regular students who attended class three hours for three credits.

**Small classes and individualized directive teaching** (not just telling students to find the main idea but actually showing them what a main idea is and how it differs from specifics). They need opportunities for group interaction to help them overcome their passivity. New technology does not work well with these students unless it is incorporated into interactive activities with other students.

**At-risk students need to be identified early before they arrive at college**. For example, many science programs are sending tutors into elementary schools realizing that waiting until they are in high school may be too late to encourage them to enter college.

**The program for at-risk students needs strong support from the college's administration**. This includes strict enforcement of institutional policies—like not allowing students to register late, etc.

**Mandatory counseling and placement—including placement testing—characterize successful programs**. Two features involving the affective side of student success include 1) providing a focus on the personal development of each student, and 2) available counseling that is perceived as effective by both students and staff (Roueche and Kirk, 1973). For example, others stress the empathetic dimension as the most important of the counselor's skills and Chickering (1969) suggests that most college students are still developing their identity, for the psychic energies of late adolescents are directed toward developing a well-formed sense of self. The fact that the identity development of many college students is limited may make it more difficult to attain mastery of basic skills, i.e., the self may be fragile and vulnerable. Perry (1978) adds that learning has an ego dimension and may be ego-threatening under some conditions. For example, he says that if students are not able to integrate their new learning with their existing sense of self, they may either regress or retreat or escape. For the high-risk student this may mean dropping out of college.

**An interdisciplinary program curriculum** managed by a team of instructors, counselors, and administrators, enables students to progress step-by-step through a well planned program in which each member of the team contributes unique skills and creates a learning environment for professionals as well as students (Roueche and Snow, 1977).

Roueche and Snow (1977) found that without exception one variable separated the successful developmental program—that is, those with 80-90% persistence and high levels of achievement—from those with moderate success. **Instructors spent as much time on self-concept development as on better reading, writing, math and study skills**. The excellent developmental educator "understands that the content she is going to develop only makes sense if the students value themselves."

**Clear entrance and exit criteria** (institutions should have strict policies supporting attendance, registration rules; instructors should specify what exit criteria are).

**Structured courses with individual attention** to student progress and strict attendance requirements.

**Credit given.** At-risk students do not volunteer for courses or extra help. However, if they are given credit, they'll attend. This is true for basic reading, writing, and math courses, as well as adjunct classes and supplementary instruction. Many of these students need extrinsic rewards.

**Flexible completion strategies.** Students may need more than a semester to reach the criterion for passing the course.

**Monitoring of study behaviors.** Students need training in controlling and monitoring their own study skills.

**Interfacing with subsequent mainstream courses.** Developmental instructors must have a thorough understanding of the skills involved in the courses that follow.

**Motivated volunteer teachers.** It is very important that teachers volunteer to teach developmental students and not be coerced into teaching these classes.

**Providing multiple learning systems.** Students have different learning styles and may learn more effectively with the appropriate system. Instructors should present different ways to learn—i.e., media, discussion, etc.

**Using peer tutors.** Usually, at-risk students respond well to peer tutors—in fact, research shows that the incorporation of peer tutoring is a major factor in successful basic math courses and math labs.

**Contracts to monitor behavior.** It is important to spell out clearly and specifically what students are expected to do to succeed in the course. Contracts expedite this process and should be revised as needed.

**At-risk students with poor skills should not be permitted to take other courses until they have completed the appropriate skills courses** (Roueche & Roueche, 1993).

**Students should complete competency based individualized programs as part of their skills work.**

**Program evaluation.** Successful programs have regular evaluations so that the staff and students know how well goals are being met.

For a list of additional research validated strategies for teaching high-risk students, see Appendix 9-2. Also, in Appendix 1-1, an experienced developmental education professor describes what works in his classroom and what it takes to become a successful teacher in this field.

## RECOGNITION OF AFFECTIVE NEEDS AND MOTIVATIONAL TECHNIQUES

Hirsch (1994) describes the following motivational techniques for teaching developmental students.

### MOTIVATIONAL TECHNIQUES

**Goal Setting**

Building self-confidence—TEACH THEM THAT THEY MUST ASK FOR HELP.

Reinforcement—TELL THEM WHAT THEY'VE DONE SUCCESSFULLY.

Regular feedback—give them sense of control.

Provide choices—give them sense of control.

Positive mental imagery (creative visualization, spelling, design mapping). For example, imagine swimming in a round circle across a pool.

## Learning Contracts

1. Work at developing unconditional positive regard for each student, stating that teacher-student relationships based on warmth, acceptance, support, and praise are associated with increased test performance, more educational risk-taking during class, and decreased underachievement.

2. Address emotions and beliefs about learning as part of the learning process. Letting students talk about their perception of their abilities, emotions, and beliefs helps them begin to modify negative attitudes. Studies show that test anxious students who explored their feelings prior to or during the exam performed better than similar students who were not given a chance to express their feelings.

3. Help students develop success-oriented attributions about their learning. In other words, have them restate their difficulties in terms of things that they can control, such as the amount of effort they spend studying, and they will increase their motivation and their performance. One way to do this is to tell them things like, "Many students can do better in (reading, math, etc.) than they originally thought they could," and to show them specifically what effort they need to put into their studying.

4. Encourage students regularly to try new learning tasks since students with external locus of control tend to avoid new learning tasks.

5. Use successive approximations to emphasize student success. In other words, introduce material where students can experience success immediately and then add new material gradually. This will help students gradually overcome their expectations of failure.

6. Provide lots of verbal support for student effort. Verbal praise may provide the reinforcement students need to keep trying. However, there is a caveat here—one should understand the individual's culture because students from some cultures may feel uncomfortable when praised for their individual achievement.

7. Avoid negative motivators. Avoid judgments like saying *could* or *should* or criticism like, "You're not trying hard enough."

8. Model positive self-talk and encourage students to use it.

9. Teachers should feel free to disclose their own previous academic struggles to help motivate students. Admitting that you had a problem learning a course in college and discussing how you overcame it will help students view you as more human.

10. Take a personal interest in students.

11. Tailor learning experiences to individual student needs, taking into account individual learning styles. Students will do better in smaller classes where more attention can be given to each student and teachers can use a variety of teaching strategies to address learning style preferences.

12. Give students primary responsibility for learning. Research findings have documented that there is a positive relationship between the degree that students feel in control of their education and positive achievement. Help them believe that they can make learning happen for themselves despite the difficulty of the course, family problems, or other difficulties.

13. Support cooperation and personal improvement over intellectual competition and survival.

14. Help students respond successfully to failure. Emphasize whatever successes occur before the error, and help them shape the correct answer through prompting, if needed.

15. Focus on strengthening your own teacher efficacy—in other words, focus on your own successes.

16. Be familiar with other campus resources and refer students when appropriate.

You'll find more about how to implement these and other motivational strategies in Appendix 1-1.

## SPECIFIC TEACHING TECHNIQUES

During the past decade, college teachers have tried a number of non-traditional teaching methods such as collaborative learning, cooperative learning, reciprocal teaching, explicit teaching (Rosenshine) sometimes called direct teaching, and Smilkstein's "The Natural Learning Process." Also paired or team taught courses, Adjunct Skills classes, and/or Supplemental Instruction (SI) approaches to teaching course related skills have proved beneficial to at-risk students.

A recent survey of faculty attitudes by the UCLA Higher Education Research Institute, reported in the Chronicle of Higher Education (Sept. 13, 1996), shows that although more faculty than ever before are using innovative teaching strategies, extensive lecturing and class discussions still predominate. Collaborative learning is being used by 35% of the faculty and group projects by 23%. So they still involve a minority of courses. Interestingly, women faculty are less likely to do extensive lecturing in their classes and are more likely to use innovative techniques than are male professors.

The most important change in developmental courses has been the recognition of the importance of peers learning from each other and the variety of ways the teaching/learning responsibility can be shared with students. Peer-tutoring (as described in Chapter 3) is the most frequent method of using peers and there are many different ways to use tutors—in groups, drop-in, individual sessions with students, incorporating tutors into the classroom or lab, etc. Also students can be mentors, peer-counselors, classroom facilitators, discussion leaders, Supplementary Instruction (SI) leaders, and even sometimes "sheepdogs"—that is, students who are enrolled in a course encourage (or herd) their classmates to go to tutoring, attend SI classes, or use other academic support services.

Although there are many ways of using peers to help at-risk students, all implement some aspect of collaborative learning.

## COLLABORATIVE LEARNING

### WHAT'S THE DIFFERENCE BETWEEN COLLABORATIVE LEARNING AND COOPERATIVE LEARNING?

Kenneth Bruffee in 1995 observed that "College and university faculty members and administrators have been rediscovering recently that two or more students working together may learn more than individual students working alone: two heads are better than one. Some people call this rediscovery cooperative learning. Others call it collaborative learning," (Bruffee 1995).

Bruffee explains that although cooperative learning and collaborative learning are two versions of the same thing, they were developed for different kinds of people, and each of the methods tends to make different assumptions about the nature and authority of knowledge. Bruffee defines cooperative learning as a group of students working together on a project where all receive the same final grade, while collaborative learning refers to students helping each other learn but each receives a separate grade based on his/her own performance. Cooperative learning situations are used more often in elementary schools and in special field studies and practicum courses in college, while collaborative learning is being adopted widely in college classrooms.

Collaborative learning (or studying in mutually supportive groups) is not a new concept, although until very recently American professors frowned upon group study, insisting that students should study alone. One might trace this position back to the British system of higher education and the honor codes that still govern study behavior in military and other traditional college environments (although today, honor codes are directed mainly at examination behavior). Some professors argued that studying in groups would degenerate into bull sessions; others held that it was cheating.

However, back in pre-revolutionary America when higher educational opportunities were rare, Benjamin Franklin promoted learning groups as a way to increase his own informal education. In the 18th and 20th century America, autonomous peer groups were the only educational resource available to American women and most working men through Chattauqua and other groups. Peer-influence flourished in the 20s and 30s, then died out.

Graduate students taking difficult courses often set up their own self-contained study groups—at least they did when I was in grad school in the 40s. Stu-

dents living in the honors dormitories in the 50s were quick to set up networks so they could exchange notes and discuss assignments with others enrolled in the same classes. Asian students, as well as students from many other cultures, traditionally prefer group study.

In the past, these informal study groups tended to be surreptitious and not available to every student—in fact, professors and study skills counselors strongly discouraged group study. But things have changed today, as reflected by advertisements for residence hall counselors which encourage applicants who are experienced in setting up self-contained study groups.

Bruffee (1993) points out that collaborative learning (CL) is an underdeveloped, underused, and frequently misunderstood type of college learning. In CL students work on focused but open-ended tasks; they discuss issues in small consensus groups, plan and carry out long-term projects in research teams, tutor one another, analyze and work problems together, puzzle out difficult lab instructions together, read aloud to one another what they have written, and help one another edit and revise research reports and term papers (Bruffee, 1993, p. 1).

As students practice working together, they learn to depend on one another rather than relying exclusively on the authority of the teacher. They learn to construct knowledge as it is constructed in academic disciplines, and they learn interdependence. Proponents of this method see it as preparation for the real world where people work in groups.

It's difficult to pinpoint basic research that led to collaborative learning. (Although you might well also ask under what circumstances does basic research ever lead to a specific educational methodology?) For example, most writing professionals associate collaborative learning with Kenneth Bruffee, and cite his 1984 article, "Collaborative Learning and the 'Conversation of Mankind,'" *College English*, *46*, 635-52 or his 1986 article on writing, "Social Construction, Language, and the Authority of Knowledge: A Bibliographic Essay," *College English*, *48*, 773-90, where he traces the history and philosophical underpinnings of this strategy. He attributes the most recent version of collaborative learning to Edward Mason, whose book called *Collaborative Learning* was first published in London in 1970 and reprinted by Agathon, NY in 1971. Bruffee discovered the value of collaborative learning during the decade of the 70s when he taught writing to open-admissions students at Brooklyn College.

In his recent book, *Collaborative Learning: Higher Education, Interdependence, and the Authority of Knowledge* (Johns Hopkins Press, Baltimore, 1993), Kenneth Bruffee describes collaborative learning as based on the "Kuhnian" understanding of knowledge and explains that this model overturns traditional notions about the authority of knowledge, the authority of teachers, and the very nature and authority of colleges and universities, or as he puts it, "nonfoundational social constructionist thought changes our understanding of education." Thinking about learning as primarily a social interaction is a strange idea to most instructors even though the validity of scientific truths rests primarily on the consensus of other scientists. In other words, they were lectured to as students, and they expect to fulfill the same role as teachers, even though we've known for half a century that listening to lectures is a poor way for many students to learn.

Bruffee cites Thomas Kuhn's statement in *The Structure of Scientific Revolutions* that knowledge is "intrinsically the common property of a group or else nothing at all." University education, according to Bruffee, is a process by which students become members of the knowledge communities to which their teachers belong, and collaborative learning is part of that process. In addition to Kuhn, Bruffee considers Vygotsky's books, *Mind in Society* and *Thought and Action* as providing the rationale for constructivist theory and collaborative learning.

If Bruffee is the leading promoter of collaborative learning in writing and tutoring, then Uri Treisman is his counterpart in convincing mathematics and science teachers to use collaborative approaches. Treisman's work with calculus study groups began when he was working on his doctoral dissertation at UC Berkeley. He observed that Chinese-Americans excelled in calculus while 40% of Afro-Americans made D or lower in calculus. He discovered that Chinese-American students studied in informal, small study groups where they corrected each other's misperceptions and errors. In addition, the Chinese-American students spent from 10-14 hours each week studying calculus. They also spent a lot of time together—they ate together and hung out around campus together.

Using this group as a model, Treisman developed mathematics workshops for African-American and Latino students. He realized they needed to increase their study time and become more involved in the subject. His students spent 10-14 hours a week on their mathematics studies compared with non-workshop students who spent 6 to 8 hours. The time spent in the workshops was more productive and encouraged students to become committed to maintaining their success. The workshops also promoted a high level of academic performance—in fact, the students in the lowest triad of SAT-M scores persisted at a higher rate (58%) than did students whose SAT-M scores were in the top third of the distribution (49%), (Fullilove and Treisman, 1990). The title of the workshop was very important. Treisman said to call it intensive, call it interactive, call it honors, call it anything, but don't call it remedial.

By attending intensive workshops billed as an honors program, underprepared Afro-American students could identify themselves as high achievers and work conscientiously to achieve academic excellence. They overcame their disabilities and out performed students who entered college with better math backgrounds (Fullilove and Treisman, 1990). Although students help each other in problem solving, they are given a choice. There are no fixed rules as to how students must proceed. They may spend part of each session working alone, choosing the problems they want to work on, but must spend part of each session sharing their ideas with other students and critiquing their peers' work.

Currently Treisman is at the University of Texas-Austin and his program is now called the Emerging Scholar's Program. In the past, he has been hesitant about recommending workshops for developmental math students (Garland, 1993). However, graduate tutors at UC Berkeley's Learning Center were teaching collaborative learning classes in precalculus in the early 70s. They found it particularly effective with math-anxious, educationally disadvantaged adult students. They also trained other math TAs to use collaborative strategies in their classrooms.

For more information about the math workshops, you'll want to read:

Fullilove, R. E., & Treisman, P. U. (1990). Mathematics achievement among African-American undergraduates at the University of California-Berkeley: An evaluation of the mathematics workshop program. *Journal of Negro Education, 59*(3), 463-477.

Garland, M. (Spring 1993). The mathematics workshop model: An interview with Uri Treisman. *Journal of Developmental Education, 16*(3), 14-22.

## WHAT ARE THE LIMITATIONS OF COLLABORATIVE LEARNING?

One of the key features of collaborative learning in mathematics is that the teacher delegates considerable responsibility to the students and both teacher and students must adopt roles that are quite different from instruction to a whole class. The teacher's attitude must shift from being a transmitter of knowledge and center of attention and authority to being a manager of knowledge and facilitator of learning. Learning to tolerate a "noisy classroom" and consider it a reflection of a high level of thinking and learning instead of disruptive is an example of an attitude change that successful CL teachers must make. Teachers must also encourage students to take risks, make errors and view errors as a vital part of the process of becoming an effective problem solver (Hartman, 1995).

Hartman cites eight steps for teachers to follow for successful collaborative learning in the classroom.

1. Ensure a successful experience the first time.
2. Decide what to watch for.
3. Decide on a grouping strategy.
4. Prepare the materials.
5. Prepare yourself.
6. Explain the rules and expected behaviors.
7. Do it!
8. Debrief the class.

One fact that is often overlooked when teachers try to implement collaborative learning is that students need to learn to listen to other students. Few have had experience in working successfully in team efforts, and studies in the past have shown that college students pay little attention to what other students say in class—perhaps because they know it won't be on the exam. In order to have successful collaborative learning experiences, experts recommend that students be trained in observation methods, reasoning, asking key questions, being supportive and helpful to others, explaining clearly, understanding the problem, using the ideas of other students, among other processes. For example, Sue Hashway found that her math students at Grambling State University–LA misconstrued collaborative learning as dividing up the work—i.e., "Mary, you work the first three problems, Joe, you take the next three, and I'll do the others and we'll all get finished faster." They had to be shown how to work collaboratively on the same problems.

Some of the difficulties that arise in collaborative learning situations are students getting bored with each other, there may be inadequate leadership in the group, working on difficult problems may seem defeating while easier ones are boring, students may feel abandoned by the teacher, and students may need a change of pace or more praise. Teachers feel uncomfortable when they are not the center of the classroom, when they are not clear about what students have learned, and when they are unable to explain the collaborative task clearly enough to their students (Hartman, 1995).

Inevitably, teachers find that there are some students who do not and cannot work well in a cooperative setting. Participating in a cooperative or collaborative learning situation should be optional for them. For example, David Porter (1989-90, 1991), at the Air Force Academy, discovered that highly competitive cadets did not learn well in teams where they had to collaborate with others. Students who were mildly competitive or cooperative learned well.

This suggests that cooperative learning should probably be optional for students.

Another problem in implementing collaborative learning in mathematics is time. It is essential that what the group has accomplished is summarized by students at the end of the period. Summarizers can be appointed or the teacher can lead the summarizing. It is important to assess not only what is learned, but the group process itself. Hartman (1995) also cautions that there are many ways to use group problem-solving, and teachers should design an approach that best fits their subject and their class.

Gene Kerstiens in a personal communication points out collaborative learning is not used more frequently in college because teachers who are not willing to put themselves in a vulnerable position will find collaborative learning too threatening and, like any well executed delivery system, collaborative learning is difficult to sustain.

Adapting collaborative learning to college lecture courses, especially in the sciences, poses additional difficulties. A teacher's attempt to implement collaborative learning without prior preparation and planning can spell disaster. Developmental instructors who teach at-risk students who aren't willing to expend the effort may find that other teaching methods are more effective for them. Furthermore, when student attendance is sporadic and student motivation is low, study groups disintegrate.

Students, who expect to be lectured to, resist, complain, and give your class low ratings, something that is devastating to one's ego as well as to one's hope of tenure. Edward Nuhfer, an engineering professor at the University of Colorado at Denver, discusses the pitfalls in starting cooperative learning and suggests ten ways to ease the transition to group learning in a traditional science class:

*One criticism of cooperative learning workshops I have experienced in a number of presentations and short courses (is that they) hard-sell the benefits of structured group learning (cooperative/collaborative, etc.) without telling participants what will actually occur if they return from such a seminar to "spring" this onto their classes of students who have never experienced much other than the lecture method. In my experience with engineering students versus the other disciplines, I had more hard-core resistance to group learning from my classes of engineering students. I wondered why this was the case—whether it resulted from the kind of student attracted to engineering or the core philosophy of the profession itself which exerts strong influence on academic units in engineering. However, [although] I have attended many cooperative learning sessions [yet] ONLY one presenter I've witnessed honestly informed instructors that their evaluations could likely go down as they begin employing active learning methods for the first time. Knowing this, I did not get discouraged and give up when that very thing happened to me—my evals went down lower than they had ever been, and the negative comments that students wrote were exactly like those predicted by others. However, as I got less awkward with the non-lecture approach, my evaluations went back up, and two semesters later they were higher than they had ever been in my classes of engineering students.*

*Listed below are some suggestions that might help minimize the problem the first semester.*

1. *Don't come back from a conference in the middle of your term and "spring" these "new" techniques onto your ongoing class. Instead, wait until a new class begins, explain clearly in your syllabus the nature of what you are going to do that may differ greatly from their conditioned expectations of being lectured to.*

2. *Be prepared to explain briefly, but often, why you are adopting active learning techniques and how you expect these to benefit your students.*

3. *Be prepared to keep your finger continuously on the pulse of your class with frequent assessment techniques such as 1-minute or muddiest-point papers, or through an ongoing continuous dialogue with a student management team. Never wait to find out what's happening in your class through just an end-of-course student evaluation (good practice in any class actually, but critical when you're shifting through new gears).*

4. *Be prepared to teach the social skills to students that are required for successful team work in groups.*

5. *Start slowly and with simple techniques; don't switch from a 100% lecture class to 100% active learning just because an "expert" says the latter is always superior. Start by making active learning just a part of your delivery, and master those simple techniques well before trying more complex approaches. Remember that (a) cooperative learning isn't ALWAYS superior and (b) even the most accomplished users of cooperative learning still utilize a certain amount of lecture; they don't use active learning just for the sake of doing it. Rather they know when it's more appropriate to lecture and when to use a structured group experience.*

6. *Keep notes on rough spots that occur as they occur. Restructure your lessons and your syllabus for next class so that you don't have to re-live the uncomfortable experiences.*

7. *If your evaluations do go down after your first experience, don't give up and say, "Group learning doesn't work." It DOES work, but it takes time and practice to do it well. Those of us who*

*are very accomplished at lecturing are also prone to forget how bad our first attempts at lecturing actually were, and how much time and practice it took for us to lecture well.*

8. *If your evaluations are going to be critical to your tenure or rank, it is advisable to let your chair and possibly dean know of your plans to make a switch in your teaching style PRIOR to doing it. Inform them that there is an anticipated risk to such change that may include a temporary lowering of student evaluations and that you are taking that risk.*

9. *Purchase a good reference book, such as "Active Learning—Cooperation in the College Classroom" by Johnson, Johnson & Smith, to use when you design your lessons and review students' comments about their experiences with these lessons.*

10. *If you use a mid-term formative evaluation, be certain that it includes questions that apply to active learning formats. Although most offices of teaching effectiveness are encouraging employment of active learning techniques, some of these same offices are still trotting out the same old lecture based questions for formative evaluations. Formative evaluators now need to test for other things, particularly the presence of the "Five Basic Elements of Cooperative Learning" in group learning experiences. (See book by the Johnsons and Smith listed at right.)*

(From an e-mail letter from Ed Nuhfer, University of Denver. Reprinted by permission of the author.)

To learn more about collaborative learning, you'll want to read:

Artex, A. F., & Newman, N. (1990). *How to use cooperative learning in the mathematics class.* Reston, VA: National Council of Teachers of Mathematics.

Bosworth, K., & Hamilton, S. J. (Eds.). (1994). Collaborative learning: Underlying processes and effective techniques. *New Directions for Teaching and Learning #TL59.* San Francisco: Jossey-Bass.

Johnson, D. W., Johnson, R. T., & Smith, K. A. (1991). *Cooperative learning: Increasing college faculty productivity.* ASHE:ERIC, Higher Education Report #91-1. Washington, D.C. Association for the Study of Higher Education.

Sandberg, K. (1989). Affective and cognitive features of collaborative learning. *Review of Research in Developmental Education,* 6(4).

With careful planning by the teacher, projects that are relevant to "real life" can insure that group goals are more complex and more interesting than listening to lectures and can give students the emotional and academic support of peers while they solve problems. This support can enhance their self-esteem and give them opportunity to interact with each other and express their knowledge.

## Supplemental Instruction (SI)

Supplemental instruction (SI), also sometimes called Adjunct Skills, is a form of structured group tutoring requiring the SI leader, usually advanced undergraduates, to work closely with the instructor of the parent course. It is designed to assist students in mastering course concepts and, at the same time, to increase their competency in reading, reasoning, and study skills. In order to do this, the SI leaders attend course lectures where they take notes and complete assigned reading just as the enrolled students do. The SI leaders schedule and conduct three or four fifty-minute SI sessions each week at times convenient to the majority of the students in the course. Student attendance at SI sessions is voluntary (Blanc, DeBuhr and Martin, 1983, page 81).

An effective SI program also contains the main elements of collaborative learning.

The effectiveness of SI has been amply demonstrated by research that shows students who attend the program show significant improvement in their grades in the targeted course, their overall Grade Point Averages, remain in college longer, and graduate in significantly greater numbers than students who chose not to attend SI sessions. Typically the course grades of students taking SI are from one-half to one grade higher than those of comparable students who don't attend SI sessions, and fewer SI students withdraw from the class or earn D and F grades (Burmeister, 1994).

Although studies on program effectiveness using grades and persistence show that SI programs seem to work well, it is always difficult to define what factors in a program contribute to these positive results. Martin speculates that the following factors contribute substantially to the positive effects of SI:

1. The service is proactive rather than reactive.

2. The service is attached directly to specific courses.

3. The SI leader's attendance at each class meeting [of the targeted course] is considered essential to SI effectiveness.

4. SI is not viewed by students as a remedial program. (The goal of SI is to be viewed as an assistance program for students at all levels and that all students be assisted in the same groups to avoid the stigma usually associated with developmental/remedial services.)

5. SI sessions are designed to promote a high degree of student interaction and mutual support (Blanc, DeBuhr, & Martin, 1983, page 87).

Burmeister (1994) points out that wisely planned and carefully monitored SI programs not only improve student learning of the content of high-risk courses, but also create academic communities where small groups of students learn collaboratively. Consider this a working definition of collaborative learning:

*"In an atmosphere which is cooperative and safe for risk-taking, students generate ideas, evaluate and categorize these ideas, and teach one another as they work on common tasks. This 'cross-teaching technique' involves mutual contributions and mutual decisions regarding what to do and how to proceed. That kind of collaborative learning defines exactly what happens in well run SI sessions"* (Burmeister, 1994).

## VIDEOTAPED-SUPPLEMENTARY INSTRUCTION

In 1992 the staff at UM-KC tested the effects of using SI with a videotaped lecture course given to underprepared student athletes and found, to their surprise, that these underprepared students did as well as regular students who took the course in a normal lecture hall (Martin and Blanc, 1994). The course was presented in three stages where students had to 1) preview the vocabulary to be used and the main topics to be given in the lecture; 2) process the videotaped lecture, stopping wherever necessary to see that they understand the lecture, and; 3) review the lecture. Students in the VSI group took responsibility for their learning by conducting a preview, determining the pace of the lecture, assuring their mastery as the lecture progressed, selecting the key points for review, identifying their errors and misconceptions, and modifying their conceptions to achieve more complete understanding. The SI facilitators were described as experts in finessing answers from their groups.

Videotaped lectures, in general, have not been particularly conducive to improving learning. However, in this case the program incorporated the lecture and was not merely supplementary to the course. In other words, the videotaped SI sessions could be considered an alternative to the traditional course, strengthening the lecture by discussion.

Tutored videotaped instruction is cheaper than regular instruction or traditional paired courses since it uses tutors and does not require additional professors. It allows instruction to take place at students' convenience and is an efficient way to use available resources. Students who require a longer time to assimilate new ideas and information can be accommodated. Furthermore, the technique might be useful in equating the instruction that evening and day students receive.

## ADAPTING SI TO THE NEEDS OF DISADVANTAGED STUDENTS

The traditional SI model stresses voluntary participation and a program open to all students. There have been numerous questions about its applicability to disadvantaged students. A study by May Garland that appears regularly in *The SI Newsletter* reports that at-risk, minority students attending SI made significantly higher grades than their peers who did not attend SI, but the question has not been resolved. One of the problems is that high-risk minority students tend to prefer individual tutoring (when given an option) even though tutoring may not improve their grades.

There are some strategies that have been successful in attracting and retaining high-risk minority students in SI. Gen Ramirez (1993), Director of the Learning Assistance Center at California State University at Long Beach, describes how she introduced an SI program for TRIO students in 1985. Initially, five high-risk courses were targeted and outcomes were equivalent to those obtained by the SI Program at UM-KC (i.e., SI students improved about a half grade higher than those not attending SI). However, attendance was inconsistent and the progress of regular participants was disturbed by the temporary throng seeking only last minute assistance prior to exams. More importantly, TRIO student attendance was very sporadic, leading to problems about whether to pay SI leaders using TRIO funds when no project students were present.

These problems forced the program to adapt the SI model to local needs by making SI an adjunct course bearing one unit of nonbaccalaureate credit toward financial aid and other full-time enrollment obligations. Because disadvantaged students had failed to plan for regular SI attendance, their need to register for scheduled classes formalized their commitment to participate. SI classes are scheduled for three hours per week, either immediately before or immediately after the parent course. Although any student in the lecture class may enroll in SI, priority is given to participating academic assistance programs (TRIO, EOP, etc.) whose advisors identify and place students in SI. Classes have been taught by undergraduates (funded by categorical and state and federal funds) and TAs (funded by the University). Grades are based on a credit/no credit basis.

The criteria used to select high-risk courses include:
◊ large lectures minimizing faculty-student interaction;
◊ courses found difficult based on their technical nature (such as the sciences); or
◊ unfamiliarity of target population with those disciplines (e.g., economics, advanced math).

That a course is indeed high risk is confirmed by examining the final grades, which average "D."

## STAFFING

The California State University at Long Beach (CSULB) SI program uses no professional staff as leaders; their student leaders are recruited through a variety of networks including tutors, faculty, etc. Each applicant must have recommendations from three faculty members, GPAs of 3.0 or higher, and receive pre-semester training on learning skills and classroom techniques, as well as ongoing weekly inservice sessions. Each leader receives clinical supervision on the job. Their assignments include attending all target lectures, preparing for and conducting all scheduled SI class meetings, holding an office hour each week, meeting with supervisors as scheduled, reporting student attendance and performance (on target course exams), and administering mid-term programs and final university faculty evaluations to their class. They also assign Credit/No Credit grades to their SI students.

Currently, Ramirez says that the CSULB Learning Assistance Center offers 25 to 35 SI sections per semester with an enrollment of between 600 and 700 students, of whom 60% come from academic assistance programs.

Because the distribution of traditional and disadvantaged students vary between the parent course and the SI class, comparing final grades of the lecture course only with those of SI students masks real gains. Comparing performance of students with their own peer group reveals that underprepared students usually benefit more from SI than traditional students; gains for academic assistance program students often exceed the national average for SI. This is believed to reflect the stronger preparation of traditional students to do well without outside assistance, whereas entering disadvantaged students perform weakly in high risk courses without help. It may also be that the teaching style in SI is more beneficial to them than traditional lectures. For disadvantaged students, SI participation correlates with greater persistence rates.

The cost of the program is minimal—per student cost for a whole semester's instruction is $45 ($1 per hour), which would only pay for 7 or 8 hours of individual tutoring. The costs include the 10-hour week salary for each undergraduate or graduate leader, textbooks, training and supervision. The only remaining cost is the SI Coordinator's position. Ramirez adds that the SI program can service high-risk students more extensively than the tutoring program and do it more effectively.

To learn more about SI and VSI, you'll want to read:

Blanc, R. A., De Buhrm, L. E., & Martin, D. C. (1983). Breaking the attrition cycle: The effects of supplemental instruction on undergraduate performance and attrition. *The Journal of Higher Education*, *54*(1), 80-90.

Martin, D. C., & Arendale, D. R. (Eds.). (Winter 1994). Supplemental instruction: Increasing achievement and retention. *New directions for teaching and learning, No. 60.* San Francisco: Jossey-Bass Publishers.

# PAIRED COURSES

Team-taught core courses or team-taught interdisciplinary (paired) courses, plus counseling and tutoring, have long been regarded as successful ways to teach high-risk students, and better prepared students respond well to them too. Courses where reading and study skills or writing are paired with mainstream courses are most effective for students whose skills are marginal and are close to their college classmates. Offering combined or blocked courses reduces the stigma of taking a remedial course, increases student motivation, and reduces attrition. However, they are often difficult to schedule and may be more costly if both instructors are paid for attending each other's classes. Setting up registration procedures for enrolling students in block courses takes pre-planning, as does informing students accurately about the differences between paired versus individual courses. But studies show that pairing skills and content courses is a much more effective way of developing skills than are stand alone remedial skills courses.

There are ways to reduce the costs and professional time involved if the skills instructor observes classes, works closely with the mainstream instructor, and continues to teach the paired course so that materials and exercises can be reused in future paired classes. One way of doing this is to video-tape sample lectures from the parent course to use in lecture-note-taking sessions.

Writing Across the Curriculum Programs encourage departments to offer writing intensive courses in their subjects, and these courses may be taught by two instructors—one in writing and the other a subject area specialist. These writing intensive courses may account for the increase in team teaching reported in a national survey of faculty recently completed at UCLA. The survey found that 42 percent of the professors surveyed said they team taught a course during the past two years (from *The Chronicle of Higher Education*, Sept. 13, 1996).

## CORE COURSES FOR AT-RISK STUDENTS

Severely at-risk students may find mainstream college courses and correlated reading and study skills courses too difficult, particularly those whose skills are several years below college level. These students learn better in core courses where the same freshmen are enrolled in three team-taught courses such as reading, writing, and mathematics, as well as receiving tutoring and counseling. (Note: It is important that the students perceive the counseling and tutoring as being effective for these programs to work well.)

Core courses that are team taught allow academically at-risk students to bond, and can offer them simulated college material (i.e., teach them how to read sections of basic college social science textbooks and help them develop essential vocabulary acquisition skills). Another type of pairing involves combining reading and writing courses—a strategy that may be needed when students have very low reading skills which prohibit them from enrolling in mainstream courses.

For more information on paired courses, you'll want to read:

Gabelnick, F., and others. (1990). Learning communities: Creating connections among students, faculty, and disciplines. *New directions for teaching and learning*. San Francisco: Jossey-Bass.

Luvaas-Briggs, L. (1987, Winter). Integrating basic skills with college content instruction. *Journal of Developmental and Remedial Education, 7*(6-9, 31).

Resnick, J. (1993). A paired reading and sociology course. *Perspectives of practice in developmental education*. In P. Malinowski (Ed.). New York College Learning Association, Finger Lakes Community College, 62-64.

Smoke, T., & Hass, T. (1995, Winter). Ideas in practice: Linking classes to develop students' academic voices. *Journal of Developmental Education 19*(2), 28-32.

Note: You'll find additional information and references on paired courses in Chapter 8 (Writing) and Chapter 9 (Reading).

## Reciprocal Teaching

Singer (1993) points out that many developmental students lack strategies that allow them to process their reading assignments successfully, and give up or come to class without having read the assignment, hoping that the professor will explain the material.

The reciprocal teaching method is a procedure designed to help weak readers learn, master, and then integrate comprehension strategies that expert readers use naturally, and can aid students in understanding explicit text. The method calls for students to practice clarifying, predicting, and summarizing, and it recognizes that developmental students will need much practice in this. The aim is to teach students to engage in periodic self-review by observing the instructor modeling these dialogues, and then coached by the instructor, participate in trying these out, perhaps cued by questions. When the students demonstrate that they are familiar with the various strategies, they then take turns leading the dialogue and become discussion leaders. The instructor and other students provide scaffolding—a supportive context in which students can succeed in developing and demonstrating skills. When this is achieved the class may be divided into groups of four to six and the instructor moves around from group to group monitoring the discussions. Teachers are encouraged to be candid about their own difficulties, and teacher preparation is essential to the success of the technique. The instructor selects the reading passage, generates salient questions to be asked, makes predictions about what the students will predict, writes summaries for each section, and encircles difficult words. Hopefully the teacher can predict most of the students' responses to the material.

**Outcomes**—students begin to clarify concepts as well as words, gain confidence as they become discussion leaders, and gain appreciation for the demands of teaching.

To learn more about reciprocal teaching, you'll want to read:

Brown, A. L., & Palinscar, A. S. (1985). *Reciprocal teaching of comprehension strategies: A natural history of one program for enhancing learning.* Cambridge: Bolt, Beranek & Newman.

Hartman, H. J. (1994). Reciprocal teaching in reading and beyond. *Journal of Developmental Education. 18*(1), 2-8, 32.

Palinscar, A. S., & Brown, A. L. (1986). Interactive teaching to promote independent learning from text. *Reading Teacher, 39*(1), 771-777.

Palinscar, A. S., Ransom, K., & Derber, S. (1988-1989). Collaborative research and development of reciprocal teaching. *Educational Leadership, 46*(4), 37-40.

Singer, J. M. (1993). Strategic reading and structured dialogue: Their impact on reading comprehension. *Perspectives on Practice in Developmental Education.* Finger Lakes Community College, NY: New York College Learning Skills Association.

## Rosenshine's Teaching Functions

Rosenshine (1986) developed some simple steps for explicit or direct teaching that are being widely applied to developmental courses. Specifically, his list includes:

1. **Review**
   Review homework
   Review relevant previous learning
   Review prerequisite skills and knowledge
      for this lesson

2. **Presentation**

    State lesson goals and/or provide outline

    Teach in small steps

    Model procedures

    Provide concrete examples and negative examples

    Use clear language

    Check for student understanding

    Avoid digressions

3. **Guided Practice**

    High frequency of questions or guided practice

    All students respond and receive feedback

    High success rate

    Continue practice until students are fluent

4. **Correction and Feedback**

    Give process feedback when answer is correct but hesitant

    Give sustaining feedback, clues, or reteaching for correct answers

    Provide reteaching when necessary

5. **Independent Practice**

    Students receive help during initial steps or overview

    Practice continues until students' responses are automatic

    Teacher provides active supervision

    Routines are used to give help to slower student

6. **Weekly and Monthly Review**

To learn more about this method, you'll want to read:

Rosenshine, B. (1989). Direct instruction, Explicit teaching. *Educational Leadership, 43* (7), 60-69.

# THE NATURAL LEARNING PROCESS

Rita Smilkstein (1992) argues that all of our students—unless they are intellectually or emotionally impaired—are perfectly able to do abstract and critical thinking in all their classes. She points out that students have been operating at a high level of abstraction, speaking, using their critical and creative faculties since at least the age of nine. To learn language, one of the most complex skills, children have to learn abstract rules and structures. Smilkstein explains that the inability of college students to do abstract and critical thinking is not because they don't have the intellectual capacity, rather it is because they just can't use it in the classroom. To help students use their innate critical thinking capacity, she asks students to think of something they know how to do very well (e.g., swim, play the guitar, sing, run), making sure that everyone has a skill even if it's only driving a car. She then has them write down what they went through from the first encounter with this skill until they got to be really good at it. They write three to five minutes—just jotting down notes that will not be collected. Then they read their processes to each other in groups of three to four and compare whether there are any similarities in how they learned. Almost inevitably, following questioning and writing, they identify six stages of learning: 1. Motivation, 2. Beginning Practice (doing it, learning from mistakes), 3. Advanced Practice (increasing skill and confidence through more practice, more trial and error, getting comfortable, building the foundation), 4. Skillfulness (more practice, doing it one's own way, deviating from the norm, branching out; typically taking lessons and reading appear here for the first time), 5. Refinement (doing it automatically or becoming second nature, creativity, learning new methods, strong satisfaction), and 6. Mastery (increased creativity, broader application, teaching it, continuing improvement or dropping the activity). Sometimes the Mastery level may be telescoped into step 5.

Essentially Smilkstein observes that people learn by making and correcting (with helpful support from peers and teachers) their OWN mistakes. She points out that both students and teachers must see the importance of making mistakes by learners. Yet the fear of making mistakes is what holds students back from learning—in other words, because they are afraid to make mistakes, they fear the main thing essential for learning. She then proceeds to explain how learning increases dendrite formation in the brain. (Note: I don't feel that one has to bring dendrites into the discussion, but she reports that her students find thinking about what the dendrites in their brains are doing is highly motivating.)

For many years I tried to set up situations in study skills classes where students could discover the basic laws of learning for themselves rather than through my lecturing about them. However, my efforts were never effective because I was trying to have students analyze their efforts in acquiring new learning, and I suspect the material I chose was not very motivating. Furthermore, by not insisting that they had to make mistakes to learn, I inadvertently increased their resistance to learning something new. Smilkstein succeeded in getting students to describe basic learning concepts because she asked students to discuss how they had learned to master something in the past—in other words, she began with their successes.

## STUDENTS AS CLASSROOM FACILITATORS

One way to use students to help other students is as a teacher's aid or classroom facilitator. (Note: They may be called undergraduate teaching assistants.) Student facilitators, like tutors, are specially selected (usually from an instructor's previous class), carefully trained, unpaid volunteers who perform a variety of services for the instructor both during and outside the class. Students consider it an honor to be chosen as a class facilitator and, like tutors, facilitators are chosen, screened, and orientated before the class begins. Facilitators have job descriptions and sign contracts before they begin work. Training usually involves a semester-long seminar (including topics such as course content, ethics, confidentiality, public speaking, conflict management, crisis counseling, etc.) plus individual conferences with the instructor. In addition to being carefully selected and trained, facilitators are given regular evaluation and feedback.

## WHAT DOES THE STUDENT CLASSROOM FACILITATOR DO?

*"As classroom facilitators, students can teach, model, and demonstrate strategies appropriate to college success. They serve as role models, welcome students, initiate and contribute to class discussion by questioning, commenting and modeling appropriate student debate, make announcements about upcoming assignments, tests, and campus events, take roll and perform other clerical duties, lecture on specific topics, team teach topics with the instructor, engage in role playing with the instructor, refer students to campus resources and activities, and personalize the learning experience. Out*

of class, the facilitator can lead pre-examination review groups, answer questions about assignments, review student assignments, papers, and presentations, check for consistency in grading, and assist in the design of assignments and tests" (Hodges and others, p. 25).

The experience of being a class facilitator can sharpen the student's leadership and communication skills as well as improve her self-confidence and knowledge in the field.

For more about this topic, you'll want to read:

Hodges, R. B., Sellers, D. E., and White, W. G., Jr. (1994-95). Peer teaching: The use of facilitators in college classes. *Journal of College Reading and Learning, 26*(2), 23-29.

## JOURNAL KEEPING

Asking students to keep journals of their experiences in reading, writing, math, tutoring, and study skills classes, and/or use think aloud protocols are popular strategies in teaching developmental courses. Here are some suggestions to make these expressive activities effective.

◊ Give students clear journal assignments and provide them with examples of what you want.

For example, you might ask them to reflect on their previous experience in math, describe their math teachers, and/or describe their friends' experiences with math. Then you can ask them to reflect on their math homework, their grades, etc., emphasizing their feelings about the course. At the end of the course, ask them to summarize what happened in the course during the semester.

Math teachers who use journal writing feel that it relieves some of the anxiety in math anxious students as well as helping them develop reflective thinking and analyze their own behavior and progress in the course. In addition, it provides feedback to the instructor on how well his or her teaching is getting across to students. (Adapted from a letter from Joyce Hedrick, Math Instructor and Learning Center Director at Eastern Mennonite University, VA).

◊ Respond regularly to the students' journals.

To avoid students procrastinating in keeping their journals and postponing writing in them until the last five minutes before class starts, be sure you give them feedback regularly. Jim Force at Mt. Royal College, Alberta, describes his method of responding to students' journal entries.

*"I assign points to journals mostly to assist in assigning marks. I'm not convinced that points actually encourage students to do their best work. Rather, best work comes from the quality of your responses to their entries. I always tried to respond as reader-to-reader rather than teacher-to-student. Your entries need to be respectful of the student as a person first and a learner second, and to serve as a model. Criticism generally falls on deaf ears. Remember, the learning journal is a 'learning' experience more than an evaluation tool. With this in mind I assign points in the following manner.*

*1 point for each page to a max of 4 points (students can write as many pages as they please)*

*1 point for following prescribed format*

*2 points for addressing assigned topic or question*

*3 points for quality of answer*

*As you can see, just doing the journal as assigned gives the students 70% of their marks; only 30% is evaluated in terms of quality.*

*Selecting specific topics or questions for them to address may be helpful in getting specific responses. Students I have worked with tend to focus on generalities rather than on specifics. Student input regarding topics is also of value. Students need to have a personal commitment to learning journals. It might be helpful to begin with a discussion as to their purpose and to individual goals. It may help to do the first couple of entries in class and spend some class time discussing them.*

*In my responses to student entries, I often focus on one idea or comment and share my thoughts on it. Often I will ask questions, most of which are never responded to, but that's not the point. The question may or may not be important to them. What is important to me is that my response models the type of thinking and questioning that promotes learning.*

◊ *Encourage students to explore other ways, such as poetry, drawing, and mind mapping to express ideas in their journals.*" (From a letter from Jim Force.)

We could talk about other strategies and programs for underprepared students such as catch-up classes that work best with borderline or marginal students (those who have just one or two gaps in their knowledge), intensive review sessions at the beginning or end of the semester in math or writing for students who are near passing on cutoff criteria—or need a review in order to qualify for the next course. But the ones described are those that are getting the most attention at present. In the chapters on reading, writing, study skills, math, and science, more details on collaborative learning, Supplemental Instruction, paired courses, direct teaching, and journal keeping are explained.

# CHAPTER 8

## IMPROVING WRITING AND ENGLISH AS A SECOND LANGUAGE

In the 1978 edition of this book, I wrote, "No educational subject has engendered greater concern among faculty members and more national publicity in the past few years than the deteriorating writing skills of college students and college graduates. Indeed, the writing problem has long been viewed as a national crisis." "So," you may ask, "has student writing improved since the 70s?" Probably not. Despite many efforts, unceasing publicity, and heavy federal funding, the Nation's Report Card concludes that students' writing continues to be a problem. Students' scores on the National Assessment of Educational Progress in 1994 have not changed since 1984, (and writing scores of 17 year-olds have declined since 1984) while colleges continue to accept large numbers of students who are required to enroll in remedial writing courses. Why haven't things changed? The usual explanation is that most students don't do much reading, but I don't think they do much writing either.

In 1976, Lloyd-Jones criticized tests and other indicators of a decline in writing skills on the ground that they emphasize grammar and mechanics, which he considers superficial aspects of writing. He added that professors have secretaries and editors to make "silent changes" in their works, and politicians and movie stars hire ghostwriters, but "only in classroom exercises do Americans consider help with mere mechanics to be cheating" (p. 70).

The long history of writing problems among the nation's college students supports this position. In 1874, when 97 percent of the nation's high school graduates entered college, the Harvard faculty, distressed by the poor writing skills of upperclassmen, sought to remedy writing deficiencies by instituting freshman English. The original purpose given for the almost universal instituting of freshman English in colleges across the country, following the Harvard model, was to "make up" for what students "failed to learn" in high school. In essence, freshman English is and always has been considered a remedial course.

The first remedial writing course at the University of California at Berkeley, Subject A (a pre-freshman English course), began in 1898. At that time the university required high schools to certify each applicant's proficiency in "oral and written expression," and students not certified were required to take Subject A, a noncredit composition course. There have been many disputes about the course and its effectiveness, and students who took the course between 1922 and 1976 resented the extra fee they paid to take it, but it lived on, known to generations of Berkeley students as "bonehead English." In the 90s, the title was changed to College Writing, and students who failed the qualifying test took the course for two semesters, while those who passed the test took it for one semester. This change in title and organization removed much of the stigma of taking a remedial course, and fewer students failed, withdrew, or had to repeat it, and the morale of both instructors and students was greatly improved.

College professors seem to expect remedial writing courses to perform miracles, as shown by the goals they set for them. For example, a faculty-senate report (Turner, 1972, p. 19) described the role of the ten-week University of California remedial writing course stating that, "Subject A has been given the enormous burden of (1) preserving a high (that is, university) level of literacy in society; (2) preparing students to work at a high verbal level in other university courses; and (3) introducing students to the kind of communication in which university work is performed. These include both the 'complex competence required by society and the university' and the 'literacy level' which, at its minimum, will allow for communication in one mode of language, used at the university and elsewhere." Note carefully the assumptions in this statement, which speaks of both university-level communication and that of society in general and implies that one ten-week course will both solve the students' basic communication problems and introduce them to the complex discourse used by university professors. The differences between literal literacy and academic literacy create instructional dilemmas and sometimes confuse the issues. I will delve more deeply into this later. But first let us look further at the historical background of today's writing crisis.

How remedial writing is defined and the kinds of students required to take these courses vary greatly between institutions. Prior to 1990, the University of California at Berkeley, which draws its students from the top 12.5 percent of high school graduates, required 50 percent of its entering students to take remedial writing. This is the same percent that the

Bronx Community College, which draws 75 percent of its students from the lower half of New York City high school graduating classes, placed in required remedial writing.

Over the years many critics have argued that freshman composition fails to teach students to write, and an endless parade of professional educators urged that it be abolished, but the course remains a requirement in almost every postsecondary institution. But what is taught under the rubric of freshman composition varies widely. Kitzhaber (1963) surveyed composition courses in four-year colleges and concluded that their quality and content were exceedingly diverse. He described English courses as "meretricious" in content and philosophy, taught by unprepared graduate assistants and new faculty members, using a wide range of materials (from *Reader's Digest* to the classics) and approaches which reflected the idiosyncratic biases of the departments offering them. Although Kitzhaber's survey was made in 1960, he castigated composition instructors and their approaches with phrases that ring true today: "Teaching young people to write well has always proved so frustratingly difficult, and the methods used so time-consuming and laborious for teachers and students alike, [that] the problem has seemed to be a kind of standing affront to the American reputation for efficiency. Surely, they have thought, there must be some easy, quick, and fairly painless way to do the job; and they have looked eagerly, if often naively, for pat solutions" (Kitzhaber, 1963, pp. 73-74).

Indeed, instructors have tried many times to find panaceas for teaching writing. Among the solutions they have tried and found wanting were:

◊ Having students memorize "laws of discourse" to discipline their mental faculties so they could compose well with a minimum of practice (1880s and 1890s).

◊ Requiring that students write five themes a week, on the assumption that practice was everything (1890s).

◊ Emphasizing the writing of the paragraph as a miniature composition (1890s).

◊ Espousing the view that the only way to teach composition was to require students to read "good literature" (late 1890s).

◊ Emphasizing grammatical correctness as the supreme virtue in composition, so that writing was taught through exercises in grammar and sentence diagramming (1900 through 1940s).

◊ Teaching composition through general semantics (1940s).

◊ Combining speech, reading, writing, and listening into communications courses (1940s and 1950s). Communications courses had virtually disappeared from four-year colleges by 1960, although the courses remain in high schools and community colleges.

◊ Relying on the new educational technology—teaching machines, televised programs, overhead projectors, and computers—with the hope that it promised a way to teach more students with fewer teachers (1960 to present).

◊ Espousing the idea that writing is a process, not a subject, with the goal of preparing good writers, not good writing; through free writing, collaborative learning, peer tutoring, et al., (1970 to present).

No one approach has solved the problems, nor does it seem likely that any strategy or philosophy will provide the remedy. Each method helps some students and fails with others. Writing problems persist: students continue to need training and practice in writing if they are to develop effective academic writing skills.

As mentioned earlier, poor writing has been attributed to many causes—the deterioration of high school preparation, the decline in reading and increase in TV viewing, the ubiquitous nature of multiple-choice exams and the relative rarity of essay exams, the fact that students are given minimal opportunity to practice writing in public schools and provided minimal feedback (both essential to developing good writing skills), modern technology such as the telephone which has reduced the need to write, and the virtual disappearance of homework assignments. But most of all, poor writing has been attributed to the differences in the type of students seeking higher education today. Also, students who have received inflated grades in high school courses may enter college unaware of their inability to write well.

The rarefied atmosphere of colleges and universities, where faculties assume that students can write well, contrasts with the experiences students have had in high school, where many constraints restrict their development of confidence and skill in writing. Increasingly, college students are required to take remedial writing before they can undertake regular freshman composition courses. The percentage of entering students required to take remedial writing depends on the writing-quality standards of the particular institution and, as described above, these vary widely (from very few to 90 percent of the freshmen). Selective institutions view any as too many. Open admissions colleges are threatening to cut out basic writing courses, as they inevitably have more students than they can handle, by offering students "the opportunity to fail," a policy that the State of Colorado community colleges have recently adopted.

# BASIC WRITING PROBLEMS

The college student with minimal writing skills and little previous exposure to books and reading has been called the "Basic Writing Student." Shaughnessy (1977, p. 7) describes how these students view writing:

*For the Basic Writing (BW) student, academic writing is a trap, not a way of saying something to someone. The spoken language, looping back and forth between speakers, offering chances for groping and backing up and even hiding, leaving room for the language of hands and faces, of pitch and pauses, is generous and inviting. Next to this rich orchestration, writing is but a line that moves haltingly across the page, exposing as it goes all that the writer doesn't know, then passing into the hands of a stranger who reads it with a lawyer's eyes, searching for flaws.*

*By the time he reaches college, the BW student both resents and resists his vulnerability as a writer. He is aware that he leaves a trail of errors behind him when he writes. He can usually think of little else while he is writing. But he doesn't know what to do about it. Writing puts him on a line, and he doesn't want to be there. For every three hundred words he writes, he is likely to use from ten to thirty forms that the academic reader regards as serious errors. Some writers, inhibited by their fear of error, produce but a few lines an hour or keep trying to begin, crossing out one try after another until the sentence is hopelessly tangled.*

However, many students who do not have severe grammatical problems or other basic writing problems do have difficulty with academic writing assignments. Lamberg (1975) has identified the major problem areas in students' attempts at academic writing:

◊ They lack self-management skills. Symptoms include a history of incompletes in courses, turning in papers late, and not knowing specifics of assignments, such as due date or amount required.

◊ They lack a strategy for composing and have no set of procedures for working.

◊ They have difficulty in getting started and perform tasks at inappropriate times (for instance, reading references before deciding on a topic).

◊ They fail to understand and follow directions. They may write good papers, but not follow the instructor's assignment. For instance, they write a paper based on reading when the assignment calls for an original essay.

◊ They write poorly organized papers and sometimes fail to select a topic.

◊ They have many errors and patterns of errors; in other words, they lack a system for proofreading.

◊ They have problems in understanding and accepting the teacher's criticisms.

Unfortunately, these errors tend to persist, for they are seldom addressed in courses where writing is assigned. Thus writing instructors face a dual task—inculcating literal literacy into Basic Writing students and helping those who have some writing competency develop skills in writing more formal academic prose. Each of these tasks must be considered in relation to the expectations of faculty members who teach advanced courses.

However, there is another problem in teaching writing: even when instructors attempt to help students by writing comments on their papers, poor writers tend to ignore teachers' comments.

## Why Poor Writers Ignore Their Teachers' Written Feedback

That poor writers tend to pay no attention to their teachers' written comments and criticisms is a problem that has perplexed many instructors. MacDonald (1991), in reviewing the literature on teacher feedback, points out that compared to their more highly-skilled peers, less skilled writers are more likely to write poorly and receive negative feedback from their teachers. Therefore, less skilled writers may suffer the harshest consequences of the differences between teacher feedback and student understanding. In other words, the students who need to learn the most from the teachers may be learning the least as a result of this mutual misunderstanding.

When students receive a low grade on a paper, along with written comments, they are disappointed and often ignore the comments. Even when an instructor makes positive comments on an "F" paper, the student concludes they are just sugar coating on a bitter pill and doesn't pay attention to them. MacDonald suggests the communication between teachers and students in developmental writing courses can be strengthened in three ways: by reinforcing students' processing of written feedback in spite of their discouragement at receiving low grades, by examining the qualities of the teacher's comments, and by not giving grades and comments simultaneously (MacDonald, 1991). He points out the futility of correcting essays after they have been graded and recommends that English teachers change their practices and not write comments and give grades on the paper at the same time. If the grading is done separately after the feedback, then the student will not discredit the personalized instruction. Writing instructors can use at least three methods for separating formal evaluation and personalized instruction: conferencing prior to grading a paper, grading a portfolio of accumulated work rather than single finished essays, and peer-tutoring.

Peter Elbow in his 1986 book, *Embracing Contraries,* calls this dilemma the teaching paradox, where teachers struggle with the dual responsibilities of supporting students and grading them and have mutual but conflicting obligations to the intellectual community and to the students. Instructors' loyalty to students place them in the role of ally or friend, committed to bringing students to the academic community. This leads teachers to offer experiences which bring out the very best students have to offer—and this affects their exams, their papers, their projects, and their discussions.

However, their simultaneous commitment to maintaining high standards within the college, discipline, department, or society presents a conflict in responsibilities and places teachers in the role of guardians of knowledge who must "discriminate, evaluate, test, grade, certify that students can really understand and apply knowledge" (Elbow, p. 143).

Elbow describes how teachers typically resolve these role conflicts: they become hard teachers, strictly supporting knowledge, or soft teachers supporting students and being loyal to them. In reality, many take the middle road and become dispirited, not completely committed to either side. However, Elbow proposes a better solution which he calls a theory of paradox—where teachers commit themselves equally to students and to knowledge but not at the same time. Good teachers alternate between the two roles which are mutually reinforcing. That is, they clearly state course requirements and standards for grades and provide examples of excellence. Once standards are established and students understand them, the instructor can be an ally. The standards don't change but the instructor puts effort into helping the student, e.g., role playing the enemy by giving practice exams, or reading and commenting on early drafts of papers.

There is a negative side to being perceived by students as student-oriented. Strom, Hocevevar and Zimmer (1990), in a study of the relation between student satisfaction with the instructor and achievement, found that students were more satisfied with instructors who were perceived to be student oriented. However, a significant interaction involving student achievement indicated that students who prefer easy courses achieved less with instructors who were perceived to be student-oriented.

This study raises the question of when do students achieve well and rate their instructor highly and when are high instructor ratings antagonistic to achievement—in other words, when are students' ratings of instruction indices of instructional effectiveness and when are they not? So perhaps one should be cautious in implementing Elbow's suggestions and make sure that one tries both roles, not just one.

For more information on improving feedback to Basic Writing Students, you will want to read:

Elbow, P. (1986). *Embracing contraries*. Oxford: Oxford University Press.

MacDonald, R. (1991). Developmental students' processing of teacher feedback in composition instruction. *Review of Research in Developmental Education, 8*(5). Reprinted in M. Maxwell (Ed.). 1994. *From access to success: A book of readings on college developmental education and learning assistance programs*. Clearwater, FL: H&H Publishing Co.

McKoski, M. M., & Hahn, L. C. (November 1987). Basic forms, basic writers. *Journal of Developmental Education, 11*(2), 6-12.

## FACULTY EXPECTATIONS

It is not possible to understand students' writing problems without considering the expectations of college professors. Every professor, whether in a university or a community college, expects students to be literate. Many students have learned in high school to camouflage their lack of reading and writing skills, so that it is often difficult for professors to identify weaknesses until students turn in papers or take exams. Then the writing deficiencies are obvious. Depending on the perceived degree of inadequacy of the writing, professors may react by labeling the student dumb or by feeling that their own teaching efforts are wasted—or they may do both.

Shaughnessy (1977, p. 8-9) describes the faculty view of students' grammatical and spelling errors and how it colors professors' perceptions of students:

*So absolute is the importance of error in the minds of many writers that "good writing" to them means "correct writing," nothing more. "As long as I can remember," writes a student, "I wanted to be an English teacher. I know it is hard, keeping verbs in their right place, s's [where] they should be, etc., but one day I will make them part of me."*

*Much about the "remedial" situation encourages this obsession with error. First, there is the reality of academia, the fact that most college teachers have little tolerance for the kinds of errors BW students make, that teachers perceive certain types of errors as indicators of ineducability, and that they have the power of the F. Second, there is the urgency of the students to meet their teachers' criteria, even to request more of the prescriptive teaching they have had before in the hope that this time it might "take." Third, there is the awareness of the teacher and administrator that remedial programs are likely to be evaluated (and budgeted) according to the speed with which they produce correct writers, correctness being a highly measurable feature of acceptable writing.*

(See also the description of teaching basic writing students by L. J. Spiller at Delta College in Appendix 1-1.)

Professors in even the most selective colleges have traumatized students with hostile comments on their papers—like the Yale professor who wrote, "Where did you get these ideas? From *Sesame Street*? An illiterate high school teacher?" In former years, students learned to live with such criticism. Many of today's students will not.

Dedicated English professors who taught basic writing courses faced not only the negative attitudes of their professional peers but the misconceptions and expectations of students with severe language disabilities (Shaughnessy, 1973, 1976). As Gross (1978, p. 16) states: *"[We] strained so hard to be successful that we didn't have time to question the expectations imposed upon us by minorities and, more important, by ourselves. When our conservative colleagues screamed that the standards were failing, we answered by saying that the record wasn't in yet. When we failed to bring students up to the appropriate level of literacy, we blamed ourselves—we hadn't been adequately trained or we lacked patience or we'd set standards too high.*

*But in fact we had false expectations. Open-admission students came with a sense of fear and self-doubt confronting a standard language which was rendered even more complicated by their need to master, at the same time and in the same place, the separate language of biology or psychology. Their entire miseducation and bookless past rose to haunt them, and all the audiovisual aids and writing laboratories and simplified curricular materials we tried could not turn the trick.*

*The mistake was to think that this language training would be preparation for college education when what we were really instilling was a fundamental literacy that would allow social acculturation to occur. We were preparing our students to be the parents of college students, not to be students themselves. And the impossible burden that we assumed was one properly meant for the community colleges."*

English faculties in universities avoid teaching freshman composition, usually relegating those duties to teaching assistants. They argue that not every English professor is capable of doing a competent job in teaching freshman composition. Some English professors state flatly that they do not know how to teach students to write. Saul Bellow, in an interview following the awarding of his Nobel Prize, commented that he could not teach a student to write, he could only help the student realize that he was not crazy if he chose to write.

With the exception of a few composition and rhetoric faculty members, most professors seem to share the belief that good writing can be taught in a course, but "by somebody else, not me!" Besides this attitude, there are practical problems faced by those who want to teach writing but are constrained by large classes and other limits on their time. Consequently, support services in writing have mushroomed.

However, a few English professors take issue with the trend away from teaching writing. Miles (1975, p. 14) expressed the position that teaching writing is the responsibility of each faculty member: *"We know that good writing, like good thinking, cannot be taught 'once and for all.' It's not a simple skill like swimming; indeed, even a swimmer can be coached to get better and better. Thinking is one of the most complex abilities, and writing is evidence of it. So students need help with writing at many stages, from third grade to eighth, to tenth to high school, to college and beyond, and from subject to subject. Whenever a new stage of thought and a new subject matter comes along, the accumulated abilities of the student need conscious and thoroughgoing adapting to the new material and maturity. Therefore, the concept of 'remedial work' is misdirected; the teacher who sends a student back to brush up technical details is trivializing his own serious job of helping the young writer adapt his present active skill and latent knowledge to important new demands."*

Karliner (1974, p. 12) expresses a similar position in regard to the unrealistic results professors expect from remedial writing courses: *"Writing competency is a skill which needs continual reinforcement. It is impossible to expect that one or two quarters in the freshman year will make good writers out of students who have never written before and who will not be required to write again in their college careers. If professors require little or no writing, award A's to poor writers when they do require a paper, and provide no constructive feedback when writing is found to be inadequate, then it is foolish to expect that most undergraduates will further develop their writing skills from their freshman year to the time of graduation."* (Note: In the years since Karliner wrote this, composition teaching has gained much more respectability.)

## Faculty-Generated Writing Problems

As both Miles and Karliner view the writing problem, they reprimand professors who overlook the complexity of the writing/thinking process and the time and practice required for a student to develop mature, scholarly writing abilities. It is the rare undergraduate who can write a paper of the caliber acceptable for publication, and that should not be the criterion by which student work is judged.

(It is, however, a goal that prospective graduate students should work toward.) As Carkeet (1976) explains, often the dual role of the college English professor, as both a literary scholar and a teacher of writing, promotes the dangerous possibility that one will evaluate classroom writing style by what are ultimately bizarre and untenable criteria—the criteria for literary scholars. But English professors are not alone, for professors in other subjects sometimes apply professional standards to the writing their students produce.

The kinds of writing assignments that professors assign exacerbate writing difficulties for students, and at Berkeley as at other colleges, we found the most frequent problem expressed by students to writing tutors was their inability to understand assignments.

Connelly and Irving (1976, p. 670) state: *"Students who are given writing assignments they do not understand in disciplines they do not know tend in their uncertainty to write reports. Furthermore, these reports reveal the writer's uncertainty not only in poor organization, but also in more elementary compositional errors. We are convinced that the students' compositional incompetence is not the only cause of bad writing. The single most widespread external cause of bad writing is bad assignments."*

In a study that demonstrates how assignments affect writing, Miles (1967) studied the stylistic errors in students' writing and their relation to the type of assignment given. She found that the topics assigned tend to be subjects in the grammatical sense—"my summer vacation," "my home town," "the Vietnam War," and so on. She points out that a predicate increases or decreases the size of the subject, forcing students to give reasons and shape their ideas. For example, if a student is asked to write on the topic "What will happen to my home town if the drought continues for another year" instead of "My home town," or on "What I'd do to decorate my room if I had a thousand dollars" instead of "My room," the "if . . . then" predicate demands a cause-effect assertion. The appropriate predicate can also direct the students' writing to other organizational patterns, such as "either/or." This strategy has implications for all types of academic writing. I can remember well my own frustrations when faced with a doctoral prelim question that stated simply, "Discuss IQ": Where do I start? How much should be included? How can I narrow the topic? What does the professor expect?

The problems professors generate by their poor writing assignments and poor essay-exam questions are not new. (In fact, I sometimes wonder whether the professors who are most critical of student writing may have repressed their own writing struggles.) Few people can write well and fluently under time pressures and deadlines. For many of us, writing is an agonizing and time-consuming task that requires many revisions. Yet we expect students to produce several papers in a ten-week term. Students unskilled in writing but determined to survive have found ways to cope. Some hire the same secretaries who type and edit professors' papers during the day to type and edit theirs at night. Others ask a spouse, friend, or parent to edit their papers. Still others hire ghostwriters. Though research and paper-writing services are illegal, they are still available for students who can pay the price. There is even a theme collection on the Internet called "School Sucks." The increase in the number of institutions that now have Writing Centers also reflects recognition of the burgeoning writing help students need.

To counter some of these weaknesses, writing faculties are revising their curricula and their expec-

tations. An idea that is gradually being accepted is that reading and writing are modes of learning and should be taught together as processes, not as subjects or end products. In fact, under the new instructional standards for K-12 language arts developed by the Joint Task Force of National Council of Teachers of Writing, the International Reading Association, and the University of Illinois, literacy is redefined to include reading, writing, speaking, listening, technology and interpersonal communication skills. This new definition opens up new frontiers in teaching strategies as well as teacher evaluations, since the new products that will replace the essay can be much longer, more complex, take more time to produce, and may involve more than one student. Testing is aimed at providing "more authentic" tasks than traditional multiple-choice and short answer examinations. Furthermore, grades will reflect more than the teacher's opinion, involving instead all members of the educational community—parents, students, teachers, administrators, and the public. However, to change the way teachers perceive their role in grading will take a tremendous effort in inservice training.

## CURRENT SOLUTIONS

### WRITING ACROSS THE CURRICULUM

Periodically through the past century, colleges have tried Writing Across the Curriculum programs, only to have them disappear after a few years. However, today there is a wider thrust to the efforts. Since instructor-induced writing problems have long been part of academic life, it is not surprising that there have been many attempts in the past to improve the writing of both instructors and students. For example, in 1950 the Berkeley English department conducted an experimental program in "writing across the curriculum" among 1500 undergraduates who were taking courses in fifteen departments. Teaching assistants from the English department read and marked papers for professors in other departments, and the papers were also graded for content by departmental readers. Three methods of aiding poor writers were tried: (1) Requiring the student to rewrite his paper after a conference with the TA. (This proved effective but time-consuming.) (2) Setting up voluntary conferences between the instructor and students with low grades. (This was less effective because students participated less when they were not required to attend conferences.) (3) Having the English TA present a class lecture with the instructor or reader after each set of papers was graded; together they analyzed particular errors, indicated ways of clarifying answers, and stressed principles of organization. (This was the simplest procedure, and it was more effective than the other methods in improving students' writing. It was most effective when there was close cooperation between the instructor and the English TA.) Fifty percent of the students who earned grades of D or worse on their first exams and papers improved as a result of the program. The researchers stressed the importance of training readers in different disciplines to evaluate student composition and to aid and advise students in ways to improve their writing/thinking skills.

After a study with such positive results, one might expect that the program would be implemented on a wider scale and that student writing would continue to improve. This did not happen. A decade later, another committee on prose improvement reported on yet another experiment to remedy the fragmentary, impressionistic writing that they attributed to true/false questions and to a "serious weakening and diminishing of writing throughout the country."

In this study too, English TAs graded the essays of students in other courses and conferred with instructors and readers in an effort to improve writing. Although the final report does not describe the impact of the program on student writing, it does focus on how instructors were helped to understand how the intent of the question determines the structure of the answer.

Thus, at Berkeley—indeed, at most institutions—poor student writing seems to reappear each decade. Experiments and innovations are introduced with great enthusiasm, succeed briefly, and then die; in a few years, the writing problem emerges again and another innovative cycle begins.

Today, Writing Centers often serve as the hub in the resurgence of efforts to improve Writing Across the Curriculum (WAC). Bradley Hughes, Director of the Writing Center at the University of Wisconsin-Madison, has long been a proponent of the central role of the Writing Center in WAC (1994), and he is now director of the WAC program in which all liberal arts undergraduate departments are offering writing intensive courses. (Note: the UWM campus has not had a required freshman composition course for many years, but plans to implement one soon.) The UWM Writing Center serves all students except those enrolled in writing courses. The Writing Center attracts a diverse group of undergraduate and graduate students who are writing papers in a wide variety of subjects. Hughes views the Writing Center, not as a place where only failed writers go, but as a place for writers in all disciplines to improve their actual papers in progress. He also emphasizes the center's role in helping faculty improve student writing.

For example, he suggests that faculty:

◊ Front load your efforts—spend time in planning the writing assignment and make sure students understand what kind of paper you want.

◊ Integrate writing assignments into your course.

◊ Hold individual conferences to talk about student's first drafts of papers.

◊ Encourage students to take advantage of the Writing Center.

◊ Don't waste time responding extensively to minimal efforts.

◊ When you return papers, spend some class time sharing and discussing examples of successful papers.

◊ "Publish" some student papers—run them off in a copy shop and have them available for students to buy and read, for this will encourage them to do their best possible work.

◊ Encourage students to participate in peer review.

For more information on Writing Across the Curriculum, you'll want to read:

McLeod, S. H. (Ed.). (1992). *Strengthening programs for writing across the curriculum: New directions for teaching & learning. No. TL-36*. San Francisco: Jossey-Bass.

Griffin, C. W. (Ed.). (1992). *Teaching writing in all disciplines, new directions for teaching and learning, TL#12*. San Francisco: Jossey-Bass.

## WRITING CENTERS AND PEER TUTORING

Writing Centers, a service that has greatly expanded in the past two decades, help student writers but are not new. The University of Iowa started a Writing Center over sixty years ago. Today most colleges have Writing Centers that offer both individual and small group help to students. Depending on the institution, the writing laboratory may be staffed with professors, experienced graduate students, or advanced undergraduates as tutors. Increasingly, undergraduate tutors are providing individual work with students, although they are usually supervised by a teaching assistant or a faculty member. In addition, courses in tutoring for credit are widely offered. The virtues of a peer-tutoring program in a Writing Center are similar to those cited for tutoring in general—both the tutees and the peer tutors gain in knowledge of writing. Students relate better to peers, who are less threatening to students than professors and teaching assistants, and are more likely to say things like, "This part of your paper doesn't sound right; let's see if we can make it clearer," than to criticize them for too many dangling modifiers. Perhaps the major benefit of a Writing Center is that it offers students intelligent readers who respond to their writing.

English instructors are sometimes reluctant to have their students tutored, particularly those who think tutors are doing the students' work for them—and sometimes instructors are correct in thinking so. And other instructors who see themselves as adversaries of students will criticize tutors as unqualified and view students who receive tutoring as cheating. Smith (1975) points out that antagonism may be reduced if instructors are educated to the fact that tutors may save them many hours of individual work with students who have severe writing problems as well as serving other students whom instructors do not have time to see. He stresses the importance of each tutor's maintaining regular contact with the instructors to ensure coordination of efforts and reduce negative attitudes.

Jim Upton of Burlington High School, Burlington, Iowa, in the May 1995 *Writing Lab*

*Newsletter*, "A center sharing: A tutor's dozen" p 5. (vol. 19, No. 9), presents some of the beliefs about the function of writing instructors and writing tutors.

1. We are tutors of writers, not writers.

2. We tutor writers to help them become good thinkers, not to help them become great writers.

3. We must believe that a writer's work in progress is neither good nor bad; it is merely finished or unfinished.

4. Empathy is crucial. We must write ourselves, and we must seek response from others. As tutors, we must empathize with writers who have sought our assistance, and we must help writers empathize with the instructor who assigned the writing. Writers must clearly understand the intention, the audience, and the evaluation criteria for the assignment.

5. Possession is 90% of the law and 100% of the writing process. Our reaction to and suggestions for changes in a piece of reading are merely "possibilities" for the writer's consideration. We must help each writer understand that s/he is ultimately responsible for her/his own writing process and her/his final product.

6. We can respond and offer "possibilities" to the writing, the written, and/or the writer. We must be certain that the writer clearly understands the focus of our responses and "possibilities."

Upton urges tutors to be concise in their writing, their responses, and their discussion of possibilities which he insists should be meaningful options that don't overwhelm the writer. He sees the tutor's responsibility as helping each writer develop writing competence and confidence in their competence. Tutors are encouraged to be honest, but also supportive and encouraging. Tutors should constantly evaluate their methods of instruction, pay attention to correctness as the final act in writing, but also make sure that surface errors don't detract from the readability and authority of the writing. And last, the tutors must understand that the mark of their success is when their students no longer need them. For more information on the impact of tutoring on tutors, you'll want to read the stories of 51 writing tutors' experiences in M. Maxwell (ed.) *When Tutor Meets Student* (University of Michigan Press, 1994).

A Writing Center is often misconstrued as a place where students come to get their papers corrected or edited for grammatical errors. However, Writing Centers do many things to encourage students to become better writers besides tutoring them on writing assignments and implementing writing across the curriculum programs. Other Writing Center activities may include helping students who are writing job applications, resumes, and cover letters. Some even offer literary discussions for creative writers or set up self-contained study groups for graduate students writing theses.

To learn more about Writing Centers, you'll want to read:

Harris, Muriel (Ed.). (1982). *Tutoring writing: A sourcebook for writing labs*.

Harris, M. (1978). Individualized diagnosis: Searching for causes, not symptoms of writing deficiencies. *College English, 40,* 318-323.

Hawkins, T. (1980). Intimacy and audience: The relationship between revision and the social dimension of peer tutoring. *College English, 42,* 64-69.

North, S. M. (1984). The idea of a writing center. *College English, 46*(5), 433-446.

Seward, J. S., & Croft, M. K. (1982). *The writing laboratory*. Glenview, IL: Scott Foresman.

Descriptions of Writing Centers:

Jordan-Henley, J. (Sept. 1995). A snapshot: Community college writing centers in an age of transition. *The Writing Lab Newsletter, 20*(1), 1-4. (Describes the results of a survey of community college Writing Centers.)

Kinkead, J., & Harris, J. (Eds.). (1993). *Writing centers in context: Twelve case studies.* Urbana, IL: National Council of Teachers of English.

Wright, S. (1994). Mapping diversity: Writing center survey results. *Writing Lab Newsletter, 18*(10), 1-4. (Describes the results of a survey of Writing Centers mainly from four-year colleges and universities.)

Issues in Writing Centers:

Jacobson, B., & Meem, D. (1988). Image of writing center staff: Missionaries or misfits? In Weinger, L., & Caputo, E. (Eds.). (1989). *Issues in college learning centers. 9.* Brooklyn, NY: Long Island University, 21-26. (Describes issues raised in a forum at a 1987 Writing Center association conference—negative aspects include "second class" status in the university, a sense of displacement and dislocation, entrapment in part-time positions, etc. But it also points out the joys of the work: direct involvement in students' intellectual growth, empowerment of non-traditional students, a sense of "mission.")

# OTHER TRENDS AND IMPLICATIONS

Several major directions show promise in improving the current writing situation. None is really new or different except perhaps portfolios. We might say the others, such as interdisciplinary teaching, etc., have been rediscovered.

## PORTFOLIO ASSESSMENT

Having students keep writing portfolios is a relatively new approach to lessening the difficulties students have in accepting teacher feedback. In building a portfolio, the student produces a written project, it is corrected, but not graded by the teacher who adds suggestions and returns it to the student who rewrites it. This process continues until both the teacher and the student are satisfied with the product and at this point, it may be given a grade.

Since portfolios represent a new way of viewing writing assignments and require different skills of teachers, there are a number of questions teachers should ask themselves before adopting this technique. Susan Callahan of Kentucky State University has a list of questions you should ask yourself before trying portfolio assignments and some suggestions as to how to make the process easier that can be found in Appendix 8-1, 8-2, and 8-2.5.

## INTERDISCIPLINARY COURSES

Another way to implement writing across the curriculum is through paired classes or team-taught courses, also called interdisciplinary courses. Team taught reading/writing courses are increasing in developmental programs, but some writing faculty are teaming with instructors in other disciplines. For example, Gywn Enright of San Diego City College says that paired classes reflect the real connections across disciplines and are not just adjunct skills courses to support students in a content class. She taught in a paired Biology 100 (environmental science) and English 101 course. It was taught as a 7 unit City Blocks class, sharing a schedule of activities, a three hour time block, a classroom, and overlapping course topics and writing assignments. She reports that students in the blocked courses wrote more, both individually and cooperatively, were more likely to take additional English courses, were interested in tutoring future Biology/English City Blocks students, published letters in professional newsletters and college newspapers, volunteered for biology related civic causes, and stated on midterm and final evaluations that the combined classes were superior to the stand alone courses. Some of the difficulties in offering paired courses include scheduling paired courses, registering students in the courses, financing, and informing students accurately about paired versus individual courses.

For more information on paired courses, you'll want to read:

Gabelnick, F., and others. (1990). Learning communities: Creating connections among students, faculty, and disciplines. *New directions for teaching and learning.* San Francisco: Jossey-Bass.

Tinto, V., and others. *Building learning communities for new college students.* (Available from the National Center on Postsecondary Teaching, 403 South Allen St., Suite 104, University Park, PA 16801-5252.)

(See also references and descriptions of paired courses in Chapter 7 and Chapter 9, Reading.)

## What Is Needed?

To improve their composition skills, students need a supportive environment, a clear idea of what is expected, and information and ideas to write about. They desperately need adequate feedback from the instructor or from someone else, such as an aide or tutor. Underprepared students generally need highly structured programs in which they can be taught the grammatical and organizational skills that they have not learned in the context of a subject with which they are familiar. They need good, explicit teachers, not programmed texts that fractionate the skills and assume that they are capable of mastering prose writing on their own. They do not need sociological and psychological excuses for their poor composition skills or professors who cop out by stating, "It's not Joe's fault that he has no background in writing and was enrolled by mistake in my advanced Chaucer course when he should have taken remedial writing.

Even though he can't write a sentence, I won't fail him, since he's a victim of his poor background."

Instructors continue to need educating in more precise and reliable ways of judging and evaluating student prose, particularly in judging essays on complex topics and those that combine reading and writing.

## OTHER STRATEGIES TO IMPROVE COLLEGE WRITING

Of the many strategies for improving student writing currently used in colleges and universities, the ones that have the greatest potential for success are those that provide intensive inservice and pre-service training for high school teachers and college instructors.

### In-Service Training for High School Teachers

College professors usually blame high school and elementary school teachers for the sad state of student writing, rarely acknowledging that public school teachers are trained in college English departments. Articulation between high schools and college programs, although never strong, has weakened in the past decade. Realizing this and the futility of finger pointing, some universities are making greater efforts to provide effective in-service training to elementary and secondary school teachers.

In the 70s, programs such as The Bay Area Writing Project (BAWP), directed and developed by James Gray, attempted to improve university-public school articulation as a way of preventing college students' writing problems by training writing teachers to write better. Based on premises like (1) curriculum change cannot be accomplished by transient consultants who appear briefly, never to be seen again, or (2) by change agents who insist that everyone see the problem in the same way; the best teacher of teachers is another teacher who has had success in a similar situation and, teachers of writing must themselves write. The program expanded from the San Francisco Bay area to 36 sites across the U.S. English teachers responded to this project with an almost evangelistic enthusiasm. Perhaps one reason is that the program gives hope to the overworked and sometimes downtrodden classroom teacher, but it also involves teachers directly in solving a longstanding problem and does not submit them to the traditional ritual of educational reform—that is, call in the experts to tell the teachers what they are doing wrong. This project continues today as the National Writing Project.

## IN-SERVICE TRAINING FOR COLLEGE INSTRUCTORS

Universities are increasing their programs for present and future college teachers of composition. In the past, few university English departments offered formal training programs for teachers of composition at any level. The English department at the University of Iowa was reputedly the first to give graduate degrees in the teaching of composition, in a program developed by John Gerber when he was chairman of the department in 1953. For a number of years, the University of Northern Iowa and Florida State University have offered master's degree programs in teaching writing in community colleges. Currently, more institutions are offering courses and degree granting programs to train college instructors of basic writing and of English as a Second Language. (For example, there are master's degree programs in developmental writing at National Louis University in Chicago and in Southwestern Texas University.)

We can expect more emphasis on training new composition teachers and retreading old ones in the future. Some hand-wringing about the futility of trying to teach basic skills to college students will undoubtedly continue, and there will be setbacks similar to the Mellon Foundation's decision in the 1970s to stop funding projects to develop solutions to the writing crisis because they were unable to find experts who could agree on how it might be done. One thing is certain: for the foreseeable future, colleges will accept many students with poor writing skills. Faculty members must continue to learn how to teach them.

Today's most promising programs suggest directions and, although the ideas are not new, they are being tried with more vigor than was true in the recent past. These programs include writing across the curriculum, student-centered teaching approaches, writing labs, peer tutoring, structured programs combining reading and writing, redefining literacy to include oral language and educational technology, and interdisciplinary team-taught courses. Many of these are specific courses or intensive programs aimed directly at improving student writing. But they cannot succeed in a vacuum. All faculty members must be involved in the development and improvement of student writing skills.

## SPECIAL WORKSHOPS AND SMALL CLASSES

Placing students in special remedial writing courses, often without credit or with partial credit, has been and continues to be the traditional method of dealing with poor writers, and this approach has rarely been questioned. In the past, some attempts were made to modify these special writing classes.

For example, at the University of Maryland in 1964, probationary freshmen whose high school grades were below C were enrolled in special freshman composition classes during a summer session. They had regularly scheduled conferences with their English instructors and also received additional tutoring and skills help from writing and reading specialists. In addition, they were offered an optional four-hour workshop in organizational skills: differentiating among facts, opinions, and generalizations; limiting the topic and framing an adequate thesis statement; recognizing premise-conclusion and cause-effect relations; and outlining and organization. Students attending three or four hours of the workshop showed significant improvement in writing out-of-class themes (80 percent improved their grades, compared with 44 percent of the students not attending the workshop) and in-class themes (66 percent improved their grades, compared with 46 percent of those not attending the workshop). Interestingly, those attending the writing workshop averaged lower scores on the ACT English entrance examination than the control group and earned significantly higher final grades in freshman English (Maxwell and Zitterkopf, 1965).

If a four-hour workshop can significantly improve poorly prepared writers' composition performance, one wonders why more cannot be accomplished in the traditional semester composition course. Of course, in this instance, students who attended the workshop were motivated, but the study does suggest the possibility that traditional English courses waste a lot of time. Others who have tried offering short courses in lieu of semester writing courses to students whose scores were marginal have reported similar results, but rarely do these programs continue.

Catch-up classes are tried periodically and usually work well—at either the beginning or end of a term. Usually marginal students are selected for these special classes—those who might make the grade with a brief, intensive program.

Teaching writing subskills through modules and mastery learning, which was popular in the 70s and 80s, have largely disappeared now, except as aids to improving grammar and organizational skills. It has been replaced by teaching writing as a process, wholistic grading of writing samples, writing journals, portfolio development and assessment, computer approaches to writing including a variety of on-line tutoring and writing information services, and ways to incorporate collaborative learning techniques in the classroom.

(See Appendix 8-1, 8-2, and 8-2.5 for questions and suggestions on using writing portfolios.)

## STUDENT-CENTERED APPROACHES: INSTRUCTIONAL METHODS REFLECTING TODAY'S STUDENT-CENTERED EMPHASIS

In the 70s, Hawkins described the details of how to set up and implement a group-inquiry method for teaching freshman composition, calling his approach "the parceled classroom." In this method, the remedial writing class is divided into small working groups of four to six students. The aims of the program are to encourage students to take responsibility for their own learning in the classroom, to participate actively in the learning process through working in small groups, and to enable the teacher to function as a facilitator of learning during the small-group work by listening, questioning, and observing. The teacher circulates freely among groups, observing, asking questions, and troubleshooting. The groups select their own names (for example, the

Gerunds) and choose their own reading assignments, essay topics, and other work, such as grammar exercises, study of expository structure, and paraphrasing. During the typical fifty-minute work period, the first ten minutes are spent on passing out papers and making general announcements. Then the groups work on their writing tasks for twenty to thirty minutes, and during the last ten to twenty minutes they share their written work. Each student takes a turn in distributing his paper to the group and having it critiqued.

Hawkins states that this approach works best when there is a reasonably heterogeneous group and when students are willing to work and are motivated to improve their writing, and he reports that poorly prepared students often do very well in parceled groups. However, he cautions that students with skills below the eighth-grade level should not be placed in a group where other students are working on more advanced skills, but given individual tutoring if a group is not found that is closer to their needs. Most students seem to prefer this approach, although it does not work for all, Hawkins reports.

Among other student oriented approaches useful in reducing student apprehension about writing are free-writing and teacherless writing programs. Brown and Associates' *Free Writing: A Group Approach* (1977) and Peter Elbow's *Writing Without Teachers* (1973) provide many suggestions for implementing such programs in the writing classroom. The success of such student-centered methods depends on the capability and skills of the teacher, and not all instructors are able to work effectively with several small groups in the same classroom.

If you want to learn more about collaborative learning in writing programs and its philosophical basis, you'll want to read the following and see Chapter 7 in this book:

Bruffee, K. (1984). Collaborative learning and 'The conversation of mankind.' *College English, 46*, 635-52. ERIC EJ 306 541.

Bruffee, K. A. (1993). *Collaborative learning: Higher education, interdependence and the authority of knowledge.* Baltimore, MD: The Johns Hopkins Press.

Goodsell, A., Maher, M., & Tinto, V. (1992). *Collaborative learning: A sourcebook for higher education.* University College, PA.: National Center on Postsecondary Teaching, Learning & Assessment (NCTLA).

## WRITING APPREHENSION

Studies on the impact of self-efficacy and writing apprehension suggest that high and low scorers on writing apprehension report that apprehensive students have had less successful writing experiences in the past and feel that teachers will criticize their writing and give them lower grades. Studies show that there is a relationship between self-efficacy about writing and the amount of practice students have had in previous writing, students' perceptions of teachers' attitudes about their writing, and general frustration versus pleasure with their attempts at writing. Two scales to measure attitudes toward writing have been developed (the Daly Writing Apprehension Scale and The King Construct Scale) as researchers have become aware of how strongly affective factors influence people's ability to improve their writing.

If you are interested in learning more about writing apprehension and self-efficacy in writing, you'll want to read:

Daly, J. A. (1979). Apprehension in the classroom: Teacher expectancies of the apprehensive writer. *Research in the Teaching of English, 13*, 37-44.

Daly, J. A., & Miller, M. D. (1975). The empirical development of an instrument to measure writing apprehension. *Research in the Teaching of English*, *9*, 242-249.

Daly, J. A., & Wilson, D. A. (1983). Writing apprehension, self-esteem, and personality. *Research in the Teaching of English*, *17*, 327-341.

King, B. (1979). *Measuring attitude toward writing: The King construct scale.* Paper presented at the Conference on College Composition and Communication, Minneapolis, MN (ERIC Document Reproduction Service No. 172-258.)

McCarthy, P., Meier, A., & Rinderer, R. (1985). Self-efficacy and writing. *College Composition and Communication.* *38*, 465-471.

Minot, W. S., & Gamble, K. R. (1991). Self-esteem and writing apprehension of basic writers: Conflicting evidence. *Journal of Basic Writing*, *10*(2), 116-124.

Smith, M. W. (1984). *Reducing writing apprehension.* Urbana, IL: ERIC Clearinghouse.

(Some administrators never learn that educating students to become better writers is and always will be a labor-intensive job and that efforts to depersonalize teaching by relying exclusively on computers or programmed learning materials or books are doomed to fail. Furthermore, learning in college is so conditioned by attitudes about previous experiences and emotional attitudes about the subject that to depersonalize the teaching makes it even less effective. Someone has to convince students that they can learn to write effectively BEFORE they can profit from the best materials, teachers, and strategies.)

## LIMITATIONS OF USING STUDENTS AS WRITING TUTORS

Despite widespread enthusiasm about the use of students as writing tutors, tutoring programs do have limitations. Karliner (1974) describes with candor the problems of directing a remedial writing program serving 1,100 students a year with seventy undergraduate tutors and nineteen unenthusiastic teaching assistants, all of whom needed training themselves in the mechanics of English. She emphasizes that tutors and teaching assistants tend to focus solely on ideas and organization, "paying scant attention to gross mechanical errors and the more subtle problems of clarity, brevity, and precision which might be called style" (p. 12). Stating that it takes about two quarters to train a tutor or a teaching assistant, she begs for more experienced staff members to assist in the training and concludes that the use of untrained, inexperienced undergraduate and graduate students as the primary instructors is "a stopgap measure, which, while perhaps financially advantageous, is educationally bankrupt" (p. 12). Much has changed in the two decades that followed— Writing Centers and writing labs offer more sophisticated tutor training programs and have their own national and local organizations and journals (i.e., the *Writing Lab Newsletter* and the *Writing Center Journal*).

Today the trends in developmental writing include the exploration and availability of more online facilities for tutoring and helping students on the Internet, the merging of Writing Centers with Learning Centers as programs face budget cutbacks, and a revival of interest in grammar. Although grammar has not been neglected during the twenty years of teaching writing as a process, it has not been emphasized either. So many instructors are reexamining ways to emphasize grammar in student writing.

## COMBINING READING AND WRITING COURSES

Indeed, the dichotomy between the teaching of reading and writing is of long standing and was formalized by the establishment of separate professional organizations. NCTE (National Council for Teachers of English) was founded originally for *all* teachers of reading, writing, and English, but when it became dominated by college teachers of English groups, it began to splinter off. The 4C's (Conference on College Communication and Composition) was started in the late 40s, leaving several reading associations serving a large group of grammar school teachers that eventually formed the IRA (International Reading Association) in 1955. Also, teaching reading and writing as separate subjects was fostered by a belief that children must know how to read before they could learn to write.

There is evidence that this long-standing artificial dichotomy is breaking down as representatives of both NCTE and IRA have worked together to develop a set of Standards for Teaching Reading and Writing for Grades K through 12. These standards suggest that students be engaged in "a large pool of tasks lasting 3-5 days or longer, demonstrating the complex interaction between reading and writing." Obviously the assessment of this kind of performance does not lend itself to multiple-choice testing, and teachers must learn performance assessment strategies to evaluate products such as an assessment portfolio at the end of the line, or set up rooms that display examples of student performances, etc. These activities lead to problems of how to store information and how to display it.

## REDEFINING LITERACY

The new standards attempt to redefine literacy and expand it beyond print literacy with three significant additions: 1) oral and distanced oral communication (classroom discussions, the crossfire of television interviews, translation for a fellow student who is acquiring English for the first time); 2) visual texts (illustrations, photo-journalists film, videos, etc.); and 3) technological displays.

For example, one standard "elaboration" involves students participating as active and critical members of a community of readers and specifies that the teachers and the school must

◊ create environments in which collaboration is valued and students see its benefits,

◊ create environments that encourage students to collaborate in both large and small groups,

◊ help students learn how to debate and challenge one another with respect, and

◊ allow students to work with one another to develop, elaborate, and extend their responses to reading.

Students who meet the standards will

◊ construct meaning through conversation about text,

◊ read, talk, and write about what they are reading,

◊ voluntarily participate in activities,

◊ consider and evaluate the benefits of peer recommendations, and

◊ participate in cooperative learning activities.

Possible scenarios for classroom activities for meeting each standard are described for classes in the early school years, middle school years, and high school years.

Further information can be obtained from the National Council of Teachers of English. Ask for the Standards for the Assessment of Reading and Writing prepared by the IRA/NCTE Joint Task Force on Assessment.

These standards will redefine the roles of teachers and require extensive reeducation so that teachers can teach each student to reach the standards. Also, teachers can become sophisticated judges of students' reading and writing performance. Those who developed the standards have tried to redefine what literacy is and explain how these new ideas will lead to improved student knowledge and creativity. The teacher's role will be to help each student reach the standards.

Teachers must learn to write narratives and document reasons for judgments rather than give numerical ratings. There are some contradictions in the proposed system—although multiple pathways are encouraged, teachers are asked to determine comparability; obviously different paths mean variance and those involved won't be able to accept 100% agreement in judgments as essential.

This calls for accountability in portfolio grading practices. Rubrics are needed to score writing/reading performances, to delineate starting points, examples, and to score interpretative summaries. Teachers must be trained to develop and use these new instruments.

## INCLUDING REMEDIAL WRITERS IN REGULAR COURSES

Some institutions routinely enroll "remedial writers" in regular freshman composition courses. If students whose skills are not too far below others are offered intensive outside tutoring, they seem to fare as well in the regular courses as they do in special remedial courses and are less angry and apathetic about the experience. No one has yet shown unequivocally that assigning poor writers to remedial classes produces better writers than assigning them to regular courses and concurrently giving them

individual help in the basic skills they lack. Class size, instructor's acceptance, and the extent to which poor writers differ from others in the class seem to be crucial to the success of such a program. Obviously, in the best of all possible worlds, we'd only accept students whose skills are near enough to the typical student in our college so that they have a good change of success in mainstream courses with intense help. Also, we would be able to offer appropriate help at the crucial times it is needed.

## AN ALTERNATIVE TO PAIRED COURSES— SUPPLEMENTAL INSTRUCTION

Although Supplemental Instruction (SI) has been seldom reported in writing courses, Sandra Burmeister has been experimenting with offering SI in interdisciplinary (political science, economics) intensive writing classes at Hobart William Smith College (Geneva, NY). She reports that group brainstorming about clarifying the assignment and the approaches one can use seem to make a difference: students in the SI class wrote more interesting papers and were deeper in their analysis of the topic. One advantage of collaborative learning approaches in writing that Burmeister observed is that the group discussions help students clarify their assignments.

Although collaborative learning strategies have been used to good effect in basic writing classes for a long time, SI has rarely been attempted in writing. In this case, there was little class time devoted to the writing assignment which was the major basis of student grades. I'm sure that SI strategies can be used advantageously in other writing across the curriculum courses.

In fact, one idea being seriously discussed in writing lab circles is whether the writing lab approach can replace freshman composition. In other words, why have a writing course bereft of content—shouldn't writing tie in with a discipline to be most valuable to a college student?

## EDUCATIONAL TECHNOLOGY

The glowing promise of educational technology as a way to improve student writing skills is finally beginning to be realized. Although studies show that educational technology does not improve learning over traditional classroom methods, today's software has been greatly improved over what was available 15 years ago and students who use CAI (Computer Assisted Instruction) do develop more positive attitudes toward writing. Using the computer as word processor has made it much easier for students (particularly basic writing students) to revise their writing and spares them the drudgery of rewriting. Yet although computer programs can identify grammar and spelling errors, they cannot yet give students the feedback they need that a teacher or an audience can.

However, now that most colleges have on-line computer networks, writing tutoring can take place on the computer, using either local tutors or those from other colleges.

New writing programs are continuously being added to the Internet. For example, students and tutors can now access the Purdue University On-Line Writing Lab, where they can find a number of menus with brief discussions about many aspects of writing. This is easy to locate through Gopher. Topics range from a review of basic sentence structure and punctuation, an overview of writing from planning and organizing, to paraphrasing and proofreading, grammar errors, ESL, etc. These can be downloaded and used as handouts as long as the Purdue Writing Lab is given credit.

For example, the route to retrieve the handouts is as follows:

Academic Information
    Learning Center/Writing Lab
        Purdue Writing Lab
            Instructional Materials and Writing Help
                Helpful Definitions
                    General Writing Concerns
                        Specific Topics (as needed)

Recent research on computer assisted programs in writing suggests that students who needed a small amount of help improved; those who needed intensive help did not.

There are a number of sources to help you find suitable computer software for your students who need writing help. Project Synergy at Miami-Dade Community College is comprised of software reviews by developmental educators in reading, writing, and math. Reviews are regularly updated. (See Appendix 12-1 for more information on Project Synergy and other software sources.)

## ALTERNATIVES TO TRADITIONAL COMPOSITION

Some colleges are trying to de-emphasize writing skills, traditionally given high priority, by permitting students to create with other media in place of themes. Just as some students choose to submit videotapes of their accomplishments to college admissions officers in lieu of autobiographical essays, some courses give students options in completing assignments—for example, permitting them to substitute a video presentation for a paper. Courses in semiotics—defined as a special kind of literacy that requires students to compose with drawings, collages of photographs, and other elements with the goal of equipping students to cope with newer media of arts and communication—are increasing in popularity.

## Integrated Approach to Writing—Summary

College professors are still trying to develop preventive programs by coordinating new knowledge of teaching writing with teachers in the public schools. They recognize the necessity of improving the articulation between the two systems.

College professors in many disciplines are pitching in and teaching writing courses. The job is too large for English departments to handle alone. Writing across the curriculum programs have encouraged faculty in most undergraduate departments to offer writing intensive courses, not merely at the freshman level but as upper division courses as well.

There is an intensive search for methods and materials that will help students with minimal writing skills. There is a growing recognition that composition can be taught, and new strategies are being developed to teach students who have avoided writing in the past.

Finally, there is more emphasis on training writing instructors, including teaching assistants, at both two-year and four-year institutions, as well as helping faculty members in disciplines other than English teach and evaluate student writing.

Karliner (1974, p. 12) summarizes the current "state of the art." *"The teaching of composition is universally acknowledged to be difficult. There are no easy answers and no panaceas. What has been found to work is expensive: a low ratio of students to instructors and good, experienced instructors who have as their major commitment the teaching of com-* *position. Even a massive infusion of money intelligently used to attain these objectives, however, will not provide a miracle."*

We have not lacked the techniques to teach composition, but we have lacked the commitment. Although remedial composition has been an integral part of higher education for over a century, professors and administrators in many universities still seem to view it as temporary, allocating few resources to it and giving it low priority. The long-range solution is to recognize writing as a discipline, one that is essential for people at all levels from grade school students to graduate professors. Teachers must be trained to teach composition; faculty members must also assume some responsibility in ensuring that students improve their writing. The alternative can only be a continued deterioration of the writing skills of our media-oriented youths and adults and the hastening of the arrival of a postliterate society.

## English as a Second Language

Thus far in this chapter, I have discussed the writing problems of students for whom English is a first language and the programs that colleges have developed to help them. Students whose primary language or dialect is not standard English have even greater difficulty in reading and writing acceptable academic prose.

There have been many recent changes in college writing programs as the number of students whose native language is not English (or is not standard English) has increased. First, colleges are offering English as a second language (ESL) courses to disadvantaged U.S. students as well as foreign students. Colleges have long offered special courses in English as a foreign language to help international students; the realization that many students born and educated in the U.S. lack adequate communication skills in English is relatively recent. Current surveys show that one out of ten students in the U.S. comes from a home where English is not spoken. A second change is the application of linguistic research, especially contrastive language analysis, to ESL programs in an attempt to understand and ameliorate the problems non-English speakers have in learning to read and write English. A third, related change, following the research by linguists on the structure and grammar of Black English, is the recognition that for speakers of black dialect standard English is a second language. Fourth, there have been changes in the methods of teaching languages, including a trend away from using the audiolingual method exclusively and toward hiring more peer tutors and teacher's aides to work individually with students. Fifth, bilingual programs in the public schools, mandated by federal law, have proliferated in contrast to the situation thirty years ago, when teachers were forbidden to teach classes (other than foreign-language classes) in any language but English. However, currently there is a great deal of criticism about and political pressure to dismantle bilingual programs. Colleges have increased programs for adult students who come from bilingual backgrounds and need special help in learning to write effective essays in standard English.

## Tests for ESL Students

There are a number of standardized tests for measuring the English proficiency of non-English speakers, including the Michigan Test and Educational Testing Services Level of English Proficiency. However, ESL instructors usually find that they need more information than the standardized tests reveal. Ann Ludwig at the Intensive Language Program at the University of Nebraska-Omaha offers three levels of courses. Basic language skills comprise the

first level including tense, control, reading for main ideas, details, some inference, core vocabulary, listening for specific information, and functional conversational ability. The second level—advanced electives—includes skill-specific course work, second generation ideas, and academic conversation. Third is the university level including targeted writing, university support services, and computer literacy. In order to determine the appropriate starting level for an ESL student, in addition to the Michigan Test, she administers a dictation test where students write what she dictates, and she conducts an individual and a group interview. She finds these additional efforts lead to better student retention and make students more comfortable in her classes.

## Developing Cultural Competence as Well as Linguistic Competence

Communication anxiety is something many foreign students experience, and because it can be debilitating, the teacher should help students overcome their fear of speaking English by explaining the problems of culture shock and by using a variety of approaches to teach them interaction skills. Reducing their anxiety will enhance their learning.

Cultural competence should be taught as the student improves in linguistic areas. To survive academically, foreign students need more than fluency in English; they must understand the culture to avoid inevitable embarrassing situations or miscommunication.

Teaching students to create well-formed phrases and sentences in standard English is not the same as teaching students to use English in social interaction. Learning a language must include the rules for speaking in a given community, and these rules vary in different communities.

The effective ESL teacher must understand cross-cultural communication issues. For example, Russian speakers may be considered aggressive and rude by Americans because of their speech intonation. Many Asian and Pacific Rim students express politeness rather than real communication and offer themselves in non-verbal ways that Americans don't understand. African students are often viewed as naive and blunt, etc.

For more information on cross cultural communication, you will want to read:

Byrd, P. (Ed.). (1986). *Teaching across cultures in the university ESL program.* National Association of Foreign Student Affairs.

The Intercultural Communications Institute, 8835 Canyon Lane, Suite 238, Portland, OR 97225 (503) 297-4622, has a number of publications on communication styles of people from different language backgrounds and cultures and also offers summer institutes.

In teaching students who have problems in writing standard English, one must differentiate between those who have used English all their lives but whose families and friends habitually speak another language, such as Chinese, Spanish, or Black English, and those who have come to the United States within recent years as immigrants. Brooks (1978) reports that although these two groups can be taught in the same class, it must be done tactfully and with the understanding that students will apply the information they are given in different ways. Some will be meeting it for the first time, and others will be learning a different form from the speaking habits they have already acquired. Some will be acquiring new insights into why they write the way they do.

Students enrolled in basic ESL courses, whether native-born or immigrant, share certain traits. The little English they know has been acquired in listening and by talking. They have rarely had formal training in English grammar. The first step in helping these students is to listen to their speech and see whether they make the same errors in speaking as in writing. For example, find out whether they write "He would of gone" for "He would have gone."

Another factor that is important in understanding the language difficulties of students who were born in the U.S. is whether they were deprived of standard English models at a crucial time in their development of language skills. Students who as children spoke another language or were cared for by someone who did not speak Standard English tend to retain their confusion—and sometimes the syntactic structures of the other language for many years—in their writing and sometimes in their speech. Students who immigrated to this country before completing the equivalent of high school differ from the international students who are sent here by their countries to attend college. International students have usually mastered the formal writing and rhetorical skills and patterns of their native language. Students who come to the U.S. before completing high school have a double problem—learning a new language and at the same time developing formal writing skills in English.

Some international students have great difficulty learning English, and it is hard for an American instructor to determine whether a student has specific problems in learning English or general language deficiencies that affected her/his reading, writing, or even speech in her/his native tongue. In other words, students from other countries may have learning disabilities in their own languages.

## Contrastive Language Analysis

Having determined something about the linguistic background of the student, one will then find it useful to understand some of the differences between the student's mother tongue (whether a foreign language or a dialect) and standard English and to understand the cultural differences that affect writing and speech.

Knowledge of the lexical, syntactical, semantic, and rhetorical differences between English and other languages enables the ESL teacher to interpret student writing errors and to help the student recognize the systematic differences between his language and English. This understanding makes learning easier for the student. (For some examples of differences between English, Spanish, Asian languages, and Black English which cause confusion for the ESL student, see Appendix 8-3.)

## Cultural Influences on Student Writing

In addition to courses in the history, sociology, and literature of particular cultural groups, many ethnic studies departments have developed their own basic composition courses. As a result, colleges frequently offer special writing courses for Asian-American, Afro-American or Latino freshmen that are taught by professors in the respective ethnic studies departments, not the English department. These ethnic studies faculty members stress the importance of understanding the cultural influences that lead to writing problems as well as the structural differences between students' other languages and English. For example, Watanabe (1972, p. 1) explains that the appalling reading and composition problems of Asians and Asian-American students are symptoms of a much larger problem, "an antipathy toward articulation and an aversion for assertion."

Watanabe states that the Asian student needs more than a mechanical mastery of language skills—he needs both a thorough knowledge of the "unique cultural influences impinging on the Asian and an understanding of how the Asian experience in America has discouraged the development of a strong sense of self, which in turn has restricted the form and function of self-expression in English."

When asked to write an argumentative paper or take a position on a controversial issue, the Asian student tends to write a long, involved, convoluted essay, typically in the passive voice. The exasperated English instructor is likely to scrawl on the student's paper, "Why don't you get to the point?"—or make an even stronger comment.

Watanabe points out that it is difficult, if not impossible, to change the Asian student's preference for the passive voice in English unless one realizes that the preference stems from the student's wish to "suppress his individuality as Asian culture directs" (p. 1). Noting that the doctrine of filial piety shapes communication in the Asian home, Watanabe stresses that argument is almost unheard of in traditional families. Clearly defined roles of dominance and deference to one's elders virtually rule out argument and debate. By developing composition courses in Asian studies, ethnic instructors can connect the students' cultural identity to their expression in language and help them understand the reasons behind some of their difficulties in English composition.

## Grammatical Needs of the Asian-Language Speaker

In contrast to Watanabe, Brooks (1978) is convinced that the view of the passive Asian student who cannot be persuaded to make a firm statement in writing is in large part a myth. She thinks this view developed because the student selects the wrong verb, particularly in conditional clauses, thus conveying an impression of indecisiveness that can be corrected by giving him some clearer insights into how the English tense system works. She thinks that what linguistically inhibited or disadvantaged students need in order to improve their writing is to be taught English grammatical rules and shown some simple applications. No one has taught them, for instance, the conditions in which the definite article is used in English. Brooks recommends that they be given training in the use of the definite and indefinite articles, subject-verb agreement, and tenses, including specific instructions to stick to the present tense as much as possible, using other tenses only when a clear time indicator is present or when another tense is required by the sequence of tenses. She recommends exercises on the *-ed* ending on verbs; teaching students to check their papers for overuse of the conditionals *would*, *could*, and *might* and to omit these words or substitute *will*, *can*, or *may*; training in proper use of "if" and "when" clauses; and training in simple idioms (for example, providing lists of two-word verbs and be/have combinations).

If, after grammar lessons and correction of unconventional forms, the students are still having problems expressing themselves, then Brooks (1978) suggests that we start to probe the murky depths of cultural and psychological differences.

For additional information on Asian-American cultural differences and linguistic abilities, see Sue and Frank (1973) and Watanabe (1973).

## THE SPANISH-SPEAKING STUDENT

Spanish-speaking students come from homes representing a range of proficiency in English. In some families, no English is spoken. Other families speak dialects of American English such as Spanish-barriology or pochismo. Even if the student attended public school, s/he is likely to have difficulty reading and writing English, if her/his parents and friends do not speak English.

Native Spanish speakers have special difficulties in learning English as a second language. The fact that Spanish and English are written with the same alphabet is a major problem, in that a student may be able to pronounce English words and sentences but have no understanding of their meaning. The Latino student in the classroom often mimics the actions of other students and remains quiet, so the teacher does not realize that the student does not understand English.

English and Spanish differ in sound patterns, spelling, word order, stress, and intonation. These differences may interfere with the development of English speech, reading, and writing skills. (See Points of Interference in Learning English as a Second Language, Appendix 8-3.) An illustration of a student trying to translate English literally into Spanish occurred when a psychologist asked a Chicano during a test, "How many ears do you have?" When the student replied, "Eighteen," the psychologist referred him to a hearing specialist. One way to interpret the student's answer is that he was trying to translate the question literally and logically. In Spanish, ~Cuantos anos tiene Usted? (literally, "How many years do you have?") means, "How old are you?" One expects to be asked one's age more often than the number of ears on one's head.

## BLACK ENGLISH

Black Americans speak many dialects, not a single dialect, and usually their speech reflects the dialect spoken by white people in their geographic region. Because speakers of Black English are exposed to standard English through television, radio, movies, and daily life experiences, they usually understand it well, although they may not be able to produce it themselves. The greatest impediment to teaching black students standard English is the teacher's attitude. Regardless of their ethnicity, teachers tend to come from middle-class backgrounds and have strong attitudes about what is "correct" English. So teachers often punish students who speak and write in dialect for using poor or incorrect English, thus alienating them from attempting to learn standard English.

Studies have shown that black dialect does not interfere with reading comprehension; however, the major concern of college instructors is that Black English interferes with writing formal essays. Shaughnessy (1977) describes in detail how to help speakers of black dialect learn to write standard English prose.

## CAN WRITING ERRORS BE REDUCED?

Duffin and others (1977) analyzed the writing errors made by a group of ESL students enrolled in a basic writing skills course at the University of California at Davis. The classes were small (from four to six students). The students had very weak writing skills. Half were Latino, 14 percent Black, and 11 percent Chinese or Vietnamese. Errors made on entry essays were analyzed into nine major categories. During the course, the investigators found students made significant improvement in reducing errors in organization and focus (83 percent), omis-

sion of articles, diction, omission of inflections, and pronoun usage. The areas that were most resistant to change were those classified as mechanical conventions; spelling errors decreased by only one percent, and word choice, intrusion of articles, and some sentence-structure problems showed minimal improvement. Although all students made some of the same errors, the most frequent errors made by non-English speakers tended to be those predicted by contrastive language analysis. For example, Japanese and Korean speakers had problems with plural and possessive inflections and wrote "many homeworks" (Korean) or "much competitions at UCD" (Japanese). (Such noun countability errors decreased by only 22 percent during the term.) These findings support the theoretical inferences linguists have made about the types of grammatical difficulties that speakers of English as a second language and dialect speakers should have.

The investigators observed that most of the improvement occurred during the first three weeks of the quarter. After that, student interest and motivation lagged, and there was little improvement. Since the course was noncredit and required, the investigators believed that competition from other courses accounted for the decline in improvement and the dropoff in attendance. Most ESL courses stress pronunciation, writing, and conversation skills. Reading improvement and study skills are rarely included in college courses, although the students need them desperately. As a result, learning centers find that a number of students who have completed the ESL-required sequence of courses seek additional help because in reading and paper writing they still cannot compete with other students in their college courses. There is often a gap between what can be done for these students in ESL classes and the skills they need for the next-level course. Learning centers may be expected to help fill that gap.

## Impact of the Process Approach to Writing on ESL

Devine (1990) states that in the past decade an enormous amount of material has been published about writing instruction, almost all of it, unfortunately, from a single point of view: that of the writing process' approach (p.2). "Advocates of the process approach have been so persuasive and so vigorous in promotion that the bandwagon some of them started 30 years ago now appears to have almost everyone aboard. Yet," he adds, "no evidence supports the belief that the process approach leads to better writing."

Research does suggest that the process approach is particularly inappropriate for teaching writing to students for whom English is a Second Language, since it involves prewriting (i.e., pick a topic and think of things to write about. Write a Draft. Revise, Look for Ways to Improve the First Draft. Write the Final Draft).

Arthur Whimbey and others (1992) point out that picking a topic presents a problem for most students, but especially for ESL students, and although there are ways to help students find topics, this just takes time away from writing. He further suggests that two other methods for teaching writing to basic writers have proven highly effective in dozens of studies: Sentence Combining (SC), and Text Reconstruction (TR). In Sentence Combining students are presented with two sentences which can be combined with a preposition. SC enables students to write mature, informative sentences, reduces grammatical errors, as well as builds reading skills. It can be applied at any level. For example, if you have a group of Filipino nurses, with conjunctions you can use sentences from their nursing textbook and show them how to combine sentences. (There's a useful handout on sentence combining in Appendix 8-4.)

The second method, Text Reconstruction (TR), based on what professional writers use to improve their writing, requires that students rearrange sentences to form the best logical order, number them, and then check their results with a neighbor. When two students disagree, they try to explain why they arranged the sentences the way they did. Then they try to write the sentences in the order they numbered them but also to write them from memory as much as possible.

Each of these methods, Sentence Combining and Text Reconstruction, provide models of good writing and are especially valuable for those who have limited reading experience in English. The beauty of these approaches is that you can use material from any content area—nursing, engineering, literature, etc. In contrast, the process method emphasizes making sense, stating and developing a thesis statement and expressing ideas, and students are expected to be able to correct their own grammatical errors as they become more adept at free-writing and more confident about writing. However, this does not occur with students with limited reading and writing experience in English. They need models and scaffolding, such as SC and TR give them, to learn to write grammatically, rhetorically, and idiomatically correct English.

For more information on SC and TR, you'll want to read:

Whimbey, A., Johnson, M. H., Williams E., & Linden, M. J. (1991). *Blueprint for educational change: Improving reasoning, literacies, and science achievement with cooperative learning.* EBSCO Curriculum Materials, Box 486, Birmingham, LA 35201. 1-800-633-8623.

Whimbey, A., Johnson, M. H., Williams E., & Linden, M. J. (1991). *Keys to quick writing skills: Sentence combining and text reconstruction.* EBSCO Curriculum Materials, Box 486, Birmingham, LA 35201. 1-800-633-8623.

(Also see Appendix 8-4 for a useful handout on sentence combining.)

## CULTURAL RHETORIC

A second-language or dialect speaker who has thoroughly mastered English grammar, spelling, and sentence structure may still have problems in organizing his/her ideas and writing essays. Each culture has its own ways of organizing and perceiving speech and has its own rhetorical conventions. For example, Japanese discourse resembles a decreasing circle eventually arriving at a central point. Speakers of Semitic languages, such as Arabic, organize and perceive language in terms of parallels. They make Statement A and then rephrase it into a parallel Statement B. Spanish and Russian speakers use a digression pattern, roaming far from the point before returning to it. Dialect speakers also use rhetorical patterns that differ from those of standard English.

In teaching composition to non-English speakers, the instructor must help them see the maxistructure of formal English writing as well as understand the parts of sentences (ministructure). Unless students can see the broader rhetorical conventions of English and compare them with the conventions of their own language or dialect, they have difficulty organizing essays.

Sandberg (1976) experimented with training Malaysian ESL students in speed-reading techniques and mapping to teach them the structure of English prose. After the training, all the students were able to skim at 600 words a minute or faster, although their speeds before training had been 300 words a minute or slower. By reading selections rapidly, the students could read each essay three or four times, each time for a different purpose, move more quickly to writing tasks, and leave the instructor more time to spend on other skills during the class period.

## IDIOMS

Idioms give all non-English speakers problems, and deaf students have difficulty with them as well. ESL teachers usually emphasize idiomatic expressions and provide drill and practice using materials like McCallum's *Idiom Drills*. A dictionary of American idioms, such as Boatner's (1966) book for deaf students, can also be very helpful to ESL students.

Although most ESL courses involve class sessions and many instructors still use the audiolingual approach and require language-lab attendance, many programs rely on peer tutors and teacher's aides who work directly with individual students to help students practice English. As some experts have pointed out, peer tutors help create a healthy learning environment and reduce stress, whereas traditional classroom structure creates a ghettozation of non-English speakers and places the ESL teacher in an authoritarian role. It is vital to supplement the electronic learning devices and humanize the student's learning experiences.

# CHAPTER 9

## ENHANCING READING SKILLS

Today's college students continue to need reading courses and services. Students themselves are well aware of their needs, as shown by the fact that about half of today's freshmen say they believe that attending college will improve their reading and study skills. Whether reading test scores reflect declining skills or whether students are more anxious, or just indifferent to reading, the result is that colleges enroll many students in their reading courses and programs.

Many reasons have been postulated for the decline in reading abilities. Most often mentioned are the impact of television and other media, broader social changes including the increase in single-parent families, and the lowered expectations of high school teachers who assign little homework. Young people have been living social science, not reading about it. Both public school and college curriculums have been affected by new media, and there is evidence that the public may not view reading as essential in schoolwork or adult life as educators have led us to believe.

## POLITICAL AND SOCIAL FACTORS AFFECT STUDENT READING PREPARATION

Despite the billions of dollars invested in improving reading for disadvantaged children since the 60s, many students graduating from high school today have limited reading skills. Although there are hints from studies, like the recent Rand Corporation Report, that basic skills of students in elementary and secondary schools (especially the skills of disadvantaged minority students) have improved, these students have not yet entered college in substantial numbers; nor has the national press put much credence in these reports, for the headlines still stress the growing need for college remedial programs. In some areas of the country, especially in the sun-belt, 1995 marked the beginning of a surge in university applications from "college-ready" students. The University of Florida turned away many students it would normally have accepted and the University of Georgia reported that the freshman class was the best prepared in its history. Universities in other, less populous states, also managed to raise standards by cutting their budgets and restricting admissions. What's happening nationally is that states are relegating developmental courses to the two-year colleges who not only teach adult literacy classes, but also will be offering more college preparatory reading courses.

Unfortunately, the stigma associated with teaching skills in college colors the perceptions and exacerbates the difficulties. In the past, many government funded school programs assumed that if children got a good start in reading, they would continue to improve as they moved into higher grades. However, disadvantaged students' reading and other achievement scores traditionally drop off sharply when they leave elementary school. We shall soon see if this has changed if new groups of college students in the next few years are better prepared. Even if they are, the need for basic skills courses will not disappear because adults, many of whom have been away from school for years, are currently enrolling in college.

While politicians and college administrators try to cut back college skills programs, claiming that the taxpayer should not have to pay twice to teach the Three R's, they fail to recognize that reading is a developmental skill. Different levels of education demand different reading skills. In other words, the skills that make a child an outstanding third-grade reader will not get her through law school.

From a worldwide perspective, the U.S. is a leader in education with an expensive, compulsory education system. Yet U.S. adults read fewer books than adults in other English-speaking countries, and we do not begin to approach the literacy rate of little Iceland, which is reputed to be the only country in the world where all adults can read and write. However, Iceland has a homogeneous population with no immigrants, a sharp contrast to our large, ethnically diverse, and increasing immigrant population.

Certainly the growth of communications technology from television to the Internet makes information instantly accessible in many forms so that today's college students may ask themselves, "Why read college textbooks if you can get the information from other sources in less time and with less effort?" But college professors still expect students to be able to read well.

Since most colleges have well-equipped audio-visual centers and computer services, there are many opportunities for students with minimal reading skills to learn subjects without reading. Perhaps that is one reason that the correlation between reading-test scores and grades in community college courses has declined since 1970. Studies in the 70s showed that poor readers in community college courses did not think their textbooks were hard to read, even when the texts tested as very difficult on readability measures. Most students, both good and poor readers, reported that they found ways to get the information they needed to pass their courses other than reading textbooks. For example, they talked to their instructors either in class or during office hours, asked other students, and/or learned from audiovisual aids.

Another important influence on reading—the attitudes and values of students and parents about education—has recently been addressed in a 1996 book called *Beyond the Classroom* by L. Steinberg and others. Steinberg and his colleagues surveyed 20,000 high school students and reported that there is pervasive pressure for students to do the minimum—to get by—and that students face peer pressure to underachieve. About half the students reported they do no homework, few read for pleasure, and many say they go to school to hang out with their friends. Two thirds have jobs and most feel their parents are generally indifferent to what they do in school. We've always had some passive college students, but it looks like we can expect many more in the near future.

However, the present "reading problem" may become a bogus issue if students are able to function effectively in college courses without reading. Certainly students' grade-point averages, particularly in social sciences and humanities courses where grade inflation has been greatest, have improved while their reading scores have declined. So it's not surprising that college instructors are not able to detect poor readers in their classes. Reading disabilities are not obvious and students take great pains to hide them. You can easily identify poor writers or the student deficient in mathematics by the errors they make in written work, while poor readers have learned many ways to disguise their deficiency. Even when students perform poorly on tests, instructors can't determine whether they had trouble understanding the textbook or just did not read it at all.

Today's colleges support a wide variety of missions that are reflected in the wide diversity of students they attract. Selective colleges may restrict admission to students with high reading test scores, but even then, most selective institutions offer reading improvement programs for those who have problems with difficult and lengthy reading assignments. On the other hand, open-admission colleges accept any adult whose reading skills may range from functional illiteracy to high reading proficiency. These colleges may offer an array of reading services ranging from adult basic literacy to programs that prepare students for transferring to universities.

Therefore, when we talk about college reading programs, we need to differentiate between programs for the average student in a selective college who is relatively well prepared but still needs to improve her/his skills, those who are marginally prepared, and some of those who attend open-admissions colleges and are many years behind their peers in reading skills. Some college reading programs may serve all of these different students in voluntary programs. Other programs have a series of mandatory reading courses that students must complete before they can enroll in mainstream courses.

College reading assignments differ from those given in high school, as college instructors expect much more reading and homework preparations from students. Although high schools may offer reading programs, their services are usually limited to low-achieving students, and most students, including those planning to go to college, receive little attention. Rarely does the college-bound student get reading help except in the case of specially funded programs for the educationally disadvantaged or the physically challenged. Furthermore, special assistance is phased out as students with reading problems and special education students are mainstreamed, so that what early advantages and enthusiasms students may have acquired soon fade.

Discovering that there are poor readers in college is not a new phenomenon. As long as we have had colleges in the U.S., faculty members have complained about the reading abilities of their students.

## A BRIEF HISTORY OF COLLEGE
## READING PROGRAMS

As the field of psychology developed during the latter part of the nineteenth century, early psychologists—William James, Oscar Huey, and others—were fascinated with the process of reading. The development of high-speed photographic techniques intrigued the early psychophysicists, who performed many studies on the way adults perceive words, at first using crude observation and later using instruments like the tachistoscope. By the 1930s, remedial reading programs were an accepted part of the public school curriculum, and by the end of the 1930s many colleges and universities, including some of the most selective institutions, such as Harvard and Dartmouth, established reading programs for their students. Stella Center founded the Reading Laboratory at New York University's extension department in 1936, and Francis Triggs established a reading clinic at the University of Minnesota in 1938, while Harvard's program started that same year.

Much of the impetus for reading programs came from Ruth Strang's book, *Problems in the Improvement of Reading in High School and College* (1938), which alerted educators to the need to teach reading beyond elementary school. In 1941, Robert Bear of Dartmouth published a pamphlet called "How to Read Rapidly and Well," and college reading programs expanded rapidly from then on. (I suspect that one important factor helping create the need for reading services was the widespread adoption of general survey courses, such as "Survey of Western Civilization" or "History of Man," which covered the complete span of history in one year, and required that students read lengthy texts and long lists of original sources.)

Perhaps a look at the history of the Harvard reading course, which became the prototype for many university programs, will clarify the factors that led to the establishment of reading programs and the needs that those programs were designed to fill. In 1938, Harvard, as a result of faculty concerns with the reading disabilities of a few of its students, established an experimental "Remedial Reading Course." Each fall, freshmen were tested, and those who scored lowest were informed of their plight and allowed to volunteer for the course. Around thirty students regularly enrolled in the twenty-session class. In 1946 Harvard's counseling center, the Bureau of Student Counsel, took over the program, and when the bureau administered a standardized reading test to the remedial class, it found that every student scored higher than 85 percent of the college freshmen in the country. As a result, the program was revised, the term Remedial was dropped from the title of the course, which was renamed "The Reading Course," and 800 students and two law professors signed up (Perry, 1959).

To handle the multitudes of Harvard students who wanted to improve their reading, Perry devised a new kind of reading test to screen students most likely to benefit from the course, specifically those who "if they can be persuaded of their right to think, even though reading, can then develop a broader and more flexible attack on the different forms of study and put their skills to work on long assignments" (p. 195). The test consisted of thirty pages of detailed material, a chapter from a history book entitled *The Development of the English State—1066-1272*. Students were told to see what they could get from the text in twenty-two minutes of study. When tested with multiple-choice questions, they were able to answer "every sensible question we could ask concerning the details," Perry reports (p. 196). However, when 1,500 entering Harvard freshmen were asked to write a short statement on what the chapter was about, only one percent could do so, even though there was an excellent summary paragraph marked "Recapitulation" at the end of the chapter. Virtually all the freshmen read with what Perry calls an "obedient purposelessness" (p. 197) that would be most counterproductive in reading course textbooks. As a result, Perry devised an additional screening test in order to limit the number of students admitted to the course. This test consisted of a history exam question with two answers purportedly written by two students. One answer was a "chronological reiteration of the chapter by a student with an extraordinary memory for dates and kings and no concern for the question or any other intellectual interest" (p. 197). This answer might be graded a C- for effort. The other answer was shorter, contained no dates, and directly addressed the issues posed by the question. Probably this answer would be worth an A- or B+. Students were asked to judge which answer was better. One-third picked the C- answer, and these students were permitted to enroll in "The Reading Course."

Perry's article, "Students' Use and Misuse of Reading Skills: A Report to the Harvard Faculty" (1959), has become the document cited most frequently by college reading specialists to convince faculty members that a developmental reading program is needed and desirable in their institution. If Harvard students are not capable of reading college textbooks well and Harvard has a reading course, the implication is then that Winnemucca University students deserve one too. Faculty members in every institution, who see themselves as Harvard types regardless of their background or the students they teach, concede.

Periodically, the media calls our attention to college reading programs. In the 70s for example, a national magazine carried a story about Stanford University Learning Assistance Center enrolling 50 percent of Stanford freshmen in a reading and study skills course. This news item, like Perry's article, called the nation's attention to the fact that students in our most highly selective institutions were volunteering for help in reading and study skills. It seems that every generation of faculty members discovers that students cannot read as well as professors expect.

Not only have some of the most academically prestigious institutions had reading programs for many years, but remedial reading programs at public institutions have an even longer history. Some colleges were established for the primary purpose of teaching basic skills to disadvantaged, first-generation college students, and in the 50s, Oscar Causey founded the Southwest Reading Conference (which later became the National Reading Conference) and brought college remedial reading specialists together annually for a conference at Texas Christian University. From its inception, this conference has concerned itself with improving programs and practices

for the below-average college reader. In 1956, for example, Emory Bliesmer presented a paper describing materials and techniques for teaching college students whose reading skills were below the sixth-grade level.

So college reading programs were not a product of the 1960s. They have been with us for a very long time, but greater numbers of college students need reading improvement today and the demand for reading services is expected to continue for the foreseeable future.

For more information on the history of college reading, you'll want to read:

Cranney, A. G., & Miller J. S. (1987). History of reading: Status and sources of a growing field. *Journal of Reading*, 30 (5), 388-398.

Quinn, K. B. (Spring-Summer 1995). Toward reading and writing as modes of learning in college: A glance at the past: A view to the future. *Reading Research and Instruction*.

Wyatt, M. (September 1992). The past, present, and future needs for college reading courses in the U.S. *Journal of Reading*, 36(1), 10-20.

## SOME OF THE DIFFICULTIES REGULAR STUDENTS HAVE IN READING COLLEGE TEXTS

To reiterate, freshmen with poor reading skills continue to enter our colleges, and about 30 percent of today's freshmen are required to take remedial reading courses. To put the problems of underprepared students into perspective, one needs to be aware of the reading difficulties that college students experience in general and the situations that create these problems. Freshmen in selective colleges find that the amount of reading assigned exceeds anything they were exposed to in high school, and the difficulty level and the conceptual complexity of the assigned reading requires greater skills. So, on the one hand many students with limited reading ability are entering college and, on the other hand, even those who are "college-ready" may not be able to handle college reading assignments.

This means that the typical college reading specialist in four-year public institutions must work with a wide range of students—from those with the highest ability and excellent preparation to those who are considered poor college risks. Some clients are self-referred, others are sent by professors or advisers, and some are required to take the program because of low test scores. Whether students are very well prepared or unprepared for college, their skills problems are inextricably linked to fears about not succeeding academically. Those who volunteer for reading skills service complain about their inability to complete reading assignments (*and* their need to increase their reading speed) and their inability to understand and learn from their textbooks (*and* their need to increase their comprehension and memory). Their complaints of inadequate speed and comprehension may mask students' anxieties, conflicts, and anger at the expectations and demands of their professors.

Let us look first at the students served in voluntary programs and then we'll address the special problems of those taking mandatory, basic reading courses. Following are some of the kinds of reading needs that I encountered during my fifty years working in many different colleges and adult reading programs.

Early each fall, anxious new freshmen and transfer students voluntarily seek help from the reading service in large numbers or voluntarily enroll in reading courses. Although these clients tend to be very well-prepared, capable students, they fear that their backgrounds and skills are not adequate for the demands of their new environment. After a week or two, their symptoms often disappear as they discover their classes are not as hard as they expected. As their confidence increases, they may drop the reading program.

Another group of students who seek help early are bright and competitive people who are confident about their abilities but want to improve their reading efficiency so they will have more time for extracurricular activities or can earn higher grades with less effort. They are highly motivated and usually complete the program.

However, as the term passes, slow, very conscientious readers fill the schedules of reading specialists as the dreaded deadlines for examinations and term papers approach. For the slow, contemplative reader, attaining a liberal arts degree or completing a preprofessional program equals four years of nonstop reading. From the beginning, students are confronted each term with a veritable wall of books to consume each term. Reading lists, particularly in humanities and social science courses, range from lengthy to impossible. My surveys at the University of California at Berkeley suggest that reading assignments in undergraduate courses range from 300 pages a night in some history and political science courses to 10 pages a week in mathematics, although math students may spend twenty hours or more on those 10 pages. The sheer amount of reading staggers students who are unaccustomed to lengthy assignments, unsure of how to approach them, and unclear about what they are expected to learn from them.

For example, Gordon, an aspiring history major, failed an exam in a "History of American Diplomacy" course despite carefully reading Winston Churchill's five volumes of memoirs. He complained that the test asked only questions about the Yalta Conference and he had been unable to recall anything about it. While reading the five books, Gordon, rudderless and directionless, was adrift in a sea of words, doggedly consuming each page. The instructor's lectures on the theoretical framework of history, its mega- and metastructure, might as well have been delivered in Urdu as far as Gordon was concerned. He did not realize that he should concentrate on the international diplomatic issues and events in his reading, and he belatedly came to the reading program to try to salvage his grade.

Corinne, another slow reader, returned to college after spending a year in Japan. She was enchanted with Japanese customs and determined to major in Asian culture. When she enrolled in a Japanese history course, she soon found the reading list impossible. Thirty lengthy tomes, including translations of the diaries of Dutch missionaries, were assigned. She conscientiously asked the professor for suggestions on how to approach the reading assignments. The professor, assuming that her problem stemmed from her lack of background in the subject, assigned ten additional books to "prepare her" for the course. She came to the reading lab in tears, desperate to find ways to increase her reading speed. With the help of a librarian who recommended a short outline of Japanese history, we helped her plan a program around her assignments, emphasizing skimming and scanning skills. Had she enrolled in a speed-reading course that required additional reading, she probably would have withdrawn from college—or so she said.

The amount of reading expected in college courses may discourage students, who if they cannot find ways of coping, fall into deep despair, stop attending the class, and drop out of college. Some students, however, find ingenious ways to survive. They ask classmates (or the professor) which chapter is most important to read and what it says. Others use notetaking services, study guides, or outline series and ignore their texts and other reading assignments. The more gregarious form "reading conspiracies," divide up the reading assignments, and meet regularly to discuss the ideas they have read. The sheer amount of reading expected by faculty accounts for the popularity of speed-reading courses on campuses.

But are the long assignments really necessary? Some experts argue that professors and librarians are abusing books by assigning and displaying so many of them that students feel intimidated and ignorant. Thus professors, by giving lengthy reading assignments, may create an aversion to reading in students. (In analyzing the reading autobiographies of my graduate students over the years, I find that few retained their love of reading for pleasure after graduating from college. Many say they refuse to read anything unless it is required.) Spending four years compulsively reading dull, pedantic books and speeding through those that are most interesting may turn the most ardent bibliophiles into bibliophobes. Interviews with professors suggest that they, too, are not immune to reading aversion. As they age, professors admit that they read fewer professional articles outside their immediate areas of interest and become more selective in reading articles within their specialties, because of the poor quality of professional writing or the paucity of new ideas. Sometimes even professors admit that their pleasure reading tends toward the light and frivolous.

Why then, is so much reading assigned? Certainly the information explosion has affected every discipline, and academe's publish-or-perish economy requires that someone consume the products. Students are the designated, and often reluctant, consumers. Even professors who themselves are slow readers assign long reading lists, for they may forget the limitations of their students. But underlying these realities is something more basic: the veneration of academics for the printed page. Course committees evaluate courses on the basis of their reading lists. The longer the reading list, and the more prestigious the authors, the more likely the course committee is to rate the course as academically impeccable. Unfortunately this is an issue that the computer has not helped—in fact it has made the situation worse because it is now so easy for authors to paste everything they've ever wanted to quote in their books.

Unnecessary, lengthy assignments, when given without clarification of how to approach them, are the faculty-generated causes of the problems that many of our reading clients present. If you can suggest that instructors offer some simple suggestions about how to approach a long reading list, including the topics to emphasize and those that can be safely ignored, it will benefit many students. There are a few students, however, who have long-standing reading problems that are exacerbated by the stress of being in college.

## SPECIAL READING PROBLEMS

### RECIDIVISTS IN READING CLASSES

One group of reading clients consists of those I call recidivists in reading—that is, students who have had many years of remedial reading help. Some have had special reading assistance since first grade

and have grown dependent on reading teachers. They seek out the reading program as soon as they are admitted to college. Indeed, they may even select a college because it has a strong reading program. Although their reading skills may be quite adequate for college work, their confidence is low, and they attribute any prior academic success to their reading instructors' help. Weaning these students from their dependency on special help requires effort and tact. Sometimes they work out well as student aides in the reading program, if they can be convinced that they can help others, but often their attitudes and dependency symptoms preclude this solution. Then the reading specialist must slowly but persistently reduce the number and length of appointments and support the student in working on his/her own.

### THE LEARNING DISABLED

It is sometimes hard to discriminate between students who have a history of genuine dyslexia and those who develop the symptoms while in college, diagnose themselves, and come to the reading center for confirmation. This syndrome is most likely to occur when a student is under great stress, as when he/she is faced with a lengthy, difficult reading assignment or the intensive reading required when preparing for doctoral preliminary exams.

Paul's case is illustrative. Worried about his prelims in computer science, he described his early problems in learning to read. His mother, an elementary teacher, arranged for him to be tutored in phonics for three years, a failure experience that he recalled vividly.

When he was preparing for his doctoral exams, all those early fears and feelings of inadequacy returned, and he convinced himself that he was suffering from "word blindness." Students with this kind of problem take diagnostic tests willingly and respond to counseling and reassurance. However, it is sometimes hard to help them understand that although they had difficulties with reading in the past, their skills are adequate now, and they can cope with their present college requirements. If given sufficient support and encouragement, these students can discover ways to succeed in the tasks they currently face.

Other students who have had prior intensive reading help seem to cling to their classification as problem readers, and the thought of changing threatens them with losing their identity. For example, Jeff was diagnosed as dyslexic at age five and a half at a hospital clinic and has used this label ever since to manipulate his parents and teachers. The physician who called him dyslexic at such a tender age warned his parents not to frustrate him, and Jeff used this admonition to get his own way. His parents provided him with intensive help throughout his first twelve years in school, and his scores on a standardized reading test placed him in the 90th percentile in comparison with other freshmen in his college. However, once admitted to college, he announced to all his instructors that he was dyslexic and sat back while they reacted. They reacted indeed by holding meetings with the counseling staff and reading specialists to discuss what could be done for Jeff. Meanwhile, Jeff refused to work on spelling, the last vestige of his disability, refused to follow suggestions to dictate his themes and papers, and refused to attend classes or to accept tutoring help. He failed all of his courses.

Jeff differs from other dyslexic students who, despite their handicap, work very, very hard in college—far harder than their classmates. They may start reading the textbooks months before the term starts, and consistently come to class prepared—so much so, that other, lazier students ask them for answers and summaries of the reading assignments.

If these weak readers are bright, knowledgeable, and motivated, and learn quickly through listening, they can develop alternative ways of coping with reading assignments and written papers. I suggest that instructors treat these students as if they were blind, permitting them to hire someone to read their textbooks to them and to dictate their papers for someone to type. These strategies work quite well, take the pressure off the students, and sometimes even result in improvement in reading and writing. One freshman who used this approach made the honor roll at UC Berkeley, and other dyslexic students have completed doctoral dissertations despite their handicaps. However, it is very hard to convince instructors that a perfectly healthy young adult with normal eyesight has a reading/spelling handicap that cannot be cured. (For more information on dyslexia, see the Appendix.)

Other recidivists are intellectually capable, motivated students who, despite years of special help, enter college with very limited reading and writing skills. These clients are usually referred to reading specialists by writing instructors because they are poor spellers and exceedingly slow readers. Some were diagnosed as dyslexic in elementary school; others, usually from lower socioeconomic backgrounds, claim they did not learn to read until age nine or ten. If these students had good, intensive remedial programs before entering college, there is usually little more a reading specialist can do to help them. Condemning them to the treadmill of additional remedial courses does not help. Indeed, it may increase their frustration and require so much effort that they fail in other courses, such as science and mathematics, in which they have the skills and ability to succeed. They can be helped by allowing them to start reading assignments well in advance of the semester's start and by specially trained tutors and/or machines that read their textbooks to them. There are also a variety of special adaptive technology aids that help them learn more easily, such as computers that take oral dictation and machines that read materials aloud.

(See Appendix 9-3 for a description of the University of Pittsburgh's Adaptive Computing Training Laboratory, which offers special instruction for students with learning and physical disabilities—a program that grew out of an innovative collaboration between academic computing and the learning center.)

In 1987, 12 percent of college students were reported to have some physical or learning disability, and learning disabled students, whose numbers have been increasing dramatically, made up six to ten percent of freshmen in all colleges in 1990. Demographic studies suggest that the number of learning and physically disabled students who will seek to enter college will continue to increase in the foreseeable future. The Americans with Disabilities Act of 1990, although it does not directly affect education, does prohibit discrimination against persons with disabilities. Also, numerous lawsuits have encouraged colleges and universities to provide reasonable accommodations to disabled students. For example, there have been legal decisions that held a faculty member personally liable for failing to provide accommodations to a learning disabled student.

## Students Who Need Intensive Help

The adult student who has managed to avoid reading almost completely but wants to return to college may have many problems. Some can read but have not practiced, so that reading is a laborious, time-consuming activity—in short, sheer agony. Others have not learned to read and learned little through-out school. Perhaps they are members of the automatic pass generation. They may disguise their problems but they are not likely to volunteer for special help, and instructors may not discover their weaknesses until late in the term. Furthermore, you may find a few of these students even in selective universities, although you will meet many more of them if you work in an open-admission school.

Wanda's case illustrates the problems that students with minimal skills face when enrolled in a selective university through a special-admissions program. Although Wanda had graduated from high school, she could barely read, and she had great difficulty figuring out new words. During her first year in the university, she earned a C average, aided by tutors who read her textbooks for her and briefed her on their contents. However, she was unable to get tutoring in her sophomore courses and was left on her own to cope with reading assignments. She desperately came to the reading center for help, explaining that she had never had phonics and could not decode new words. However, she was able to recognize words at sight that she had learned before. Diagnostic tests confirmed that she had very poor decoding skills. She was given an intensive individual phonics and reading-enrichment program. In ten weeks she was reading material at the eighth-grade level independently and had decided to spend another term in intensive reading activities before resuming her college courses.

These are a few of the crises that motivate students to seek help in reading. Some are anxiously confronting new and higher academic demands; others have long-standing and very basic difficulties. In order to help them, reading-skills specialists must understand the student's problems and fears and work out a plan, if possible, to help the student reach the college's expectations.

## The Affective Basis of Some Reading Difficulties

As we've discussed in earlier chapters, students' attitudes, self-concepts, and emotional experiences affect their ability to use their skills effectively, as does their willingness to improve. Bandura (1987) hypothesized that students who had difficulties and unpleasant learning experiences in elementary school are likely to enter college feeling that "I probably cannot be successful at this task" (low self-efficacy) "and even if I do this task well there won't be a reward for doing so" (low task expectancy). Subsequent research supported these ideas, suggesting that developmental educators must convince students that they can learn and succeed academically before they teach them new skills. Hirsch (Winter 1994) summarized the research on affective variables that reduce college achievement including anxiety and fear, low self-esteem, external locus of control (believing that they have no control over what happens to them in the classroom), as well as low self-efficacy and low expectations. (See Hirsch's suggestions in Chapter 7 for additional information.)

While those who feel they can't learn won't volunteer, other slow readers don't seek help because they think that they cannot afford to spend the time on activities not directly related to their courses. If they do enter a voluntary program, they may get discouraged quickly and drop out, particularly when they observe that others are faster and better readers than they are. However, if identified early and required to enroll in a reading course, they can be helped. But success depends on the type of course. For instance, if very slow readers are placed in a completely self-help, machine-oriented speed-reading program, the experience can be demoralizing. Each question the student misses reaffirms his/her negative self-image. Such students cope, if they remain in school, by avoiding courses that require lengthy reading assignments and by majoring in subjects like art.

Clearly, reading instructors may spend more time dealing with students' problems of motivation and self-confidence than they do in teaching reading techniques, and certainly the two tasks must be done concurrently.

## Reading Assessment and Placement

College reading programs and courses vary greatly in format, content, methods, materials, and with the level of the students with whom they work. However, they have some characteristics in common. Virtually all use standardized reading tests for selection, placement, and/or evaluation (Wood, 1989). State-mandated reading programs such as those in Texas, Tennessee, Florida, and Georgia usually have their own standardized tests to determine who is held for remedial reading courses. Other college programs use tests like the Nelson-Denny Reading Test which measures speed, comprehension and vocabulary, and has grade-equivalent scores. But the Nelson-Denny is criticized because of its emphasis on speed, which may not be relevant in reading college textbooks but makes it easy to demonstrate that students can improve their performance on post-tests. Currently, many teachers are turning to computer-based tests like Educational Testing Service's "Computer Placement Test," which also provides packages of training materials to improve students' reading. (Note: You'll find information on different reading tests in the Appendix and in Chapter 2.)

However, standardized tests are beginning to reflect a more realistic picture of college reading, rather than the short paragraph comprehension items traditional tests give, and some programs are developing better ways of measuring college reading using textbook samples. For example, Simpson and Nist (1992) describe a comprehensive model for assessing reading with a variety of formal and informal instruments that sort, diagnose, and evaluate developmental students' reading. Then students are taught the strategies of good readers that focus on cognitive and metacognitive processes such as encoding, organizing, monitoring, planning and evaluating. Students are taught to take on the diagnosis of their skills themselves as they move through the course by answering questions like: Was the test what I expected? Did I follow my plan for studying?, etc. Students keep self-evaluation journals of their progress and their subsequent grades are recorded after they complete the reading course. Results indicate that they are quite competitive with regularly admitted students, for 70 percent of those who satisfactorily completed the reading courses made a C or better in their introductory social science courses.

Standardized tests can yield more information about the problems students have in reading than their scores and percentiles. For example, a committee reviewing New Jersey Basic Skills Placement Tests (NJBSPT) in reading and writing looked at the statistical analysis of each item and the statistical analysis of each form of the test and used their first-hand experiences judging the essays students wrote. They concluded:

◊ Many students appear to be skimming over reading passages that require careful reading—e.g., they respond to every question and finish the test early but miss questions that require thought and close reading.

◊ Students taking the reading comprehension test often have difficulty recognizing or selecting an appropriate paraphrase—e.g., they are able to recognize information questions when they are expressed in the exact words of the text, but have trouble when the information is restated or requires inference.

◊ Many students taking the test have limited information, a problem that manifests itself in poor reading skills.

◊ Students at all levels must be encouraged to do more reading and writing both at school and at home.

The NJBS Council recommendations for reading across the curriculum suggest that teachers:

◊ Include one or more essay questions in every test.

◊ Reinforce good reading habits by helping the student know the textbook. In other words, show them how the book is organized, how information is highlighted, what the glossary and index are, how to read charts and graphs, etc.

◊ Make students aware that finding the meaning of a word involves more than knowing what each word means. They need to understand tone and connotation and see implications and assumptions. They need to be questioned critically about what they read—i.e., author's attitude, validity, and logic of the argument.

◊ Teach students to deal with the more difficult words that they are required to read. They need to know how to preview a book and skim an essay by searching for the thesis statement. They need to identify the author's main idea, the evidence used to support it, and the methods used to present it. They should be encouraged to

reread to secure the information they need.
(New Jersey Basic Skills Council, 1984)

Note: These recommendations might be helpful for college teachers in other disciplines who are interested in helping their students improve in reading.

## Harmful Myths About the Reading Process

In their attempts to help college students improve reading skills, reading instructors may operate on a set of beliefs (myths) about reading development and may misinterpret research on the reading process. These attitudes lead to poor instructional strategies and the development of inappropriate materials.

1.   The view of reading skills as an absolute hierarchy with clearly defined steps, ranging from decoding to critical reading, affects both the materials chosen and the teaching strategies. College reading instructors holding this view may assume that poor readers must start at the first-grade level and recapitulate in sequence all the skills taught through elementary and high school. There is increasing evidence that students do not automatically read more difficult material as they improve their reading skills, nor do they read materials in different subjects. In fact, Hashway (1995) found that reading skills tend to be recursive rather than linear and the matrices of skills differ between adult readers from different cultures and between genders as well.

2.   Bloom's taxonomy (Bloom and others, 1971) is sometimes misinterpreted so that the various objectives are fractionated by students' levels; that is, poor readers are expected only to recognize specif-

ics and terms, while readers at the Grade 13 level are expected to analyze, synthesize, and evaluate materials. There are many examples of this error; for instance, some workbooks for the poor reader contain only questions on facts, while workbooks written at a higher level contain only interpretive and application questions.

The idea that one cannot teach students to read and think critically until they can function at a high school level is pernicious, yet it still persists in some school systems. Interpretive and application questions and statements can be written for students at any level. Similarly, Bloom's taxonomy can be applied to materials at any grade level and should not be used to restrict the teaching of principles and generalizations or universals and abstractions to advanced readers.

Good teaching and explicit guides are needed to help weaker readers develop these thinking/reading skills, but restricting questions to the most literal will not help them, nor will a series of questions tapping various intellectual abilities and skills at random—that is, an exercise that starts with difficult interpretive questions and intersperses factual questions. If the poor reader is to learn, exercises should begin with literal questions or statements and progress to interpretative and then to application questions. (See section on critical reading.)

An exception, of course, occurs when a student is weak in one particular skill, such as reading for main ideas, and needs extra practice in this skill. He may need intensive practice on materials that require main-idea identification, but he also should have the opportunity to transfer this training to regular textbook material and to develop critical reading skills.

3.    The misuse of diagnostic and prescriptive teaching is another reason many students fail to show gains, get discouraged, and drop out of college reading programs.  The problem here is that students are tested and found to be deficient in some basic skill (phonics or word-attack skills, for instance) and then are prescribed intensive training—in phonics, say—to remedy their weakness.  The teacher then requires college students to work on the very skills and exercises associated with their failure to learn to read adequately in elementary school.  Such exercises tend to be dull and meaningless, particularly if the student is expected to work alone on self-paced exercises.  An educationally more productive approach is for the instructor to analyze the student's strengths and interests and to offer materials and methods that capitalize on them.  When students cannot hear the differences between phonemes, teaching them to recognize whole words embedded in an interesting context yields faster results and fewer dropouts.  As students see that reading does not have to remain a painfully slow decoding process and begin to make progress, then special help in their weaker skills can be given.  Some experts have made this point more harshly.  For instance, Robert Samples recently commented that teaching phonics to dyslexics is analogous to treating anemia by bleeding the patient.

The rules of pronunciation and spelling that poor readers have learned in intensive phonics programs often hamper them in advanced reading and writing because they have not internalized English spelling patterns or learned to go beyond the rules.  Consequently, when faced with the many variations and exceptions inherent in English words that are not covered by rules, these students become very frustrated.

4.    The widespread use of standardized reading tests has limited college reading courses in two ways.  First, reading and writing are divorced and taught by different specialists, often in different departments.  Second, the majority of workbooks used in college reading courses resemble the reading tests—short passages followed by multiple-choice or true/false questions.  To be sure, some college courses still use multiple-choice examinations, but the reading selections on which course examinations are based are chapters in textbooks and lengthy lectures, not paragraphs.

5.    Materials used in reading courses, if not limited to short passages of several paragraphs, are articles from popular magazines.  They are rarely selected to challenge students intellectually; rather, they often appear to be the easiest, non-thought-provoking material that the author could find.  So deeply committed are some reading specialists to making the reading task easy and interesting that they seem unconcerned with helping the students grow intellectually or with relating the course material to other college subjects.  It is almost as if some reading specialists were determined to teach leisure reading, but at the same time to destroy the fun by giving tests, thus ensuring that reading would not replace television viewing for their students.  There is minimal evidence that students can transfer skills gained from practice with non-books and simple articles to reading the textbooks in their courses.  Textbooks and other assigned college reading materials pose problems for students because they often contain abstract concepts, copious information, and new terminology.  In introductory courses, textbooks are written to provide students with an overview of the structure of knowledge and of the specialties in a particular discipline.  Since the course content may be completely new to the student, understanding and mastering the concepts and terminology require great effort.

The myths presented include many beliefs that have held back college reading programs and probably contributed to some of the negative evaluation findings.

## Assessing the Results of College Reading Programs

### Administrators, Faculty, and Students Agree That Reading Programs Are Needed

Administrators generally agree that reading programs are necessary and helpful. Back in 1964, a national sample of college presidents were asked whether they felt their colleges' reading programs were necessary. The presidents were almost unanimous in agreeing that they were. To a further question on whether their reading programs helped students succeed in college, the majority replied yes but qualified that answer by saying that they had no definite figures to support their opinions. Similar surveys of faculty members suggest that they too are supportive of reading programs, particularly if they have known students who have been helped by the service.

It is clear that college administrators, most faculty members, and certainly college reading specialists believe strongly that their reading programs are necessary and that the programs help students who would not otherwise succeed in college. Students, too, expect colleges to offer reading-improvement assistance and have faith that the special programs will improve their skills.

### How Well Do Developmental Reading Courses Work?

On the other hand, there is little hard evidence to support reading program effectiveness. In the 70s, critics accused reading courses of being failures, pointing to the fact that although 80 percent of community college students in some states enrolled in remedial/developmental reading courses, only 20 percent of these same students went on to take further courses in English. The problem is, of course, that the weakest students are required to take reading, and if they aspire to traditional academic majors, they have little chance of succeeding even with several reading-improvement courses. It is particularly difficult when students who can't read are permitted to take mainstream courses competing with high achievers who have excellent reading skills. It is asking too much to expect developmental reading courses to remediate serious, long-standing linguistic deficiencies in a semester or two.

Some studies support this view. For example, John Losak (1972) performed one of the few true experiments on a developmental reading course at Miami-Dade Community College by randomly assigning underprepared students with low test scores to a remedial class or a control group. He found that the remedial program produced no significant difference in student attrition, but was effective in raising grade point averages during the semester the student was taking the remedial course (suggesting that the remedial course grade may have been inflated). Subsequent grade point averages between the groups were not different and students who took the remedial course did not score significantly higher on reading post-tests than did control students. This was one bit of evidence that developmental reading courses do not make a difference.

Gene Kerstiens warned of the dismal results of research on community college reading courses in 1979 when he pointed out that the objectives, as well as the methodologies applied in most developmental reading courses, hadn't changed in forty-eight years. His findings pointed out:

◊ the typical developmental reading program emphasizes comprehension, vocabulary, reading rate, and study skills;

◊ such courses characteristically ignore aural decoding or "phonics" as an instructional strategy;

◊ the training and competency of reading instructors are not sufficient for them to provide instruction in phonic analysis even were it deemed desirable;

◊ a high proportion of developmental reading students show slight to severe phonics disablement on tests; and

◊ college students' ability to recognize words and decode them orally is related to or prerequisite to reading comprehension.

But Kerstiens was concerned with the reading problems of open-admission community college students where you'd expect great variability in reading skills. What about selective college students? Do they share the same problems, and are their reading programs just as deficient?

Bohr (1994-1995) recently looked at general freshman courses that were associated with reading gains when initial ability was controlled in students enrolled in three different types of four-year colleges. Unfortunately, she reported that taking a developmental reading course did not improve students' reading scores. The courses that contributed most significantly to gains in reading ability were applied science and humanities courses, especially English literature and composition courses (as expected) but also freshman classes in engineering, music, and foreign language. Taking reading classes did not result in improved reading skills. This finding supports Astin's (1993) report that having been tutored and having taken developmental courses were negatively correlated with seniors' scores on advanced tests like the Graduate Record Exam and the National Teachers' Exam, suggesting that the effect of the stigma is long-lasting.

When Bohr examined which courses attract the best readers in different types of colleges, she found that the best readers were enrolled in college science courses, not the liberal arts. The poorest readers took courses in the soft applied sciences such as business math, child and family studies, etc. She concludes that 1) the best readers don't select fields that are traditionally associated with excellent reading—rather they are taking basic science courses; 2) students taking music, foreign language, and science courses, including calculus, show the greatest improvement in reading level; and 3) no significant association between developmental reading courses and reading improvement was found.

Bohr's results raise troubling questions about the effectiveness of college developmental reading courses beyond the broad questions about the validity of reading tests. Do students fail to improve in reading because they feel they are labeled unteachable by being placed in a developmental course, thus lowering their motivation and expectations? Do the reading instructors have low expectations and place minimal demands on their students? Or is failure to improve reading skills due to the nature of the courses (are they too easy, not challenging enough, don't require enough "time on task," or do they over stress methodology rather than empowering students to monitor and control their own reading efforts)?

Some might argue that music, foreign language and engineering courses are electives chosen by students who are interested in learning the material because they like it? Perhaps, but these freshman courses are required too, and although students may be more highly motivated to study, they rarely have a choice between these and other courses. Also, courses like music, foreign language, and engineering drawing are more rigorous than developmental reading and require not only regular class attendance, close attention, and effort, but also lots of homework.

As we have discussed, the traditional required remedial reading course has many short-comings. Students placed in it are stigmatized, they resent the work, and the courses are not designed to help weak students improve, but rather to teach skills that appear to be important in college learning. Very few courses are systematically evaluated and those that are often ignore important statistical concerns. For example, grade improvement tends to be temporary, and although many studies cite improvement in standardized reading post-tests, rarely do the authors take into account the phenomenon of regression toward the mean (i.e., students whose pre-test scores are low tend to make higher scores on a second test regardless of whether there is a course or any other intervention between the two test administrations). Other limitations of required developmental reading courses are that most textbook exercises and teaching methods have not changed for over 50 years. Even though researchers have a better understanding of the reading process and more effective ways to teach poor readers, most courses offer the same traditional skills (speed reading, comprehension, and vocabulary) taught in the same old, ineffective ways.

Certainly there are successful required developmental reading courses such as those offered at the University of Georgia and at Middle Tennessee State University, but they seem to be the exception rather than the rule. The problems of developmental reading courses stem from the course content, the strategies taught, the materials assigned, and the lack of training and assumptions of the instructors.

# Content of College Reading Courses

## Stressing Comprehension, Speed and Vocabulary

College reading courses generally focus on improving students' reading rate and comprehension skills. They may include intensive vocabulary work, paced practice on exercises with comprehension quizzes, and supplemental practice on reading machines. Traditionally, textbook reading skills like SQ3R were taught in study skills courses, but today's successful reading classes emphasize direct application of reading skills to textbooks.

Prior to the eighties, college reading specialists assumed that if college students were taught reading skills using SRA Cards or exercises in workbooks, they would be able to transfer the new skills to their college textbooks. We now know that this does not happen—i.e., that new reading skills are linked to specific content. So college reading teachers today don't use easy magazine and newspaper articles; they teach students the skills needed to read their textbooks in the other courses they are taking so they can immediately apply the new skills.

But what, you may ask, do you do if you are teaching a course for poor readers who are not permitted to take regular college courses until they complete the reading requirement? There are many intellectually honest ways to teach them by simulating college content (Stahl and others, 1991). For example, Ann Faulkner who teaches at Brookhaven College writes, "In Texas we've got a particular problem since most students who need remediation are NOT taking college level courses at the same time (a little-anticipated by-product of the Texas Academic Skills Program Law). Thus, my students don't believe that college texts are as demanding as they are—they have no reality base." I like the reading text by Jane L. McGrath, *Building Strategies for College Reading* (Prentice-Hall), because she includes a complete textbook chapter in each of four thematic units. However, we had to discontinue using it because our intermediate level reading students found it so difficult—they didn't learn well from it and their exit test scores dropped. It is better suited to developmental students who are almost ready for college mainstream courses. I also like McWhorter's texts which emphasize reading college textbooks:

McWhorter, K. T. (1994). *Academic reading.* (2nd ed.). NY: Harper-Collins.

McWhorter, K. T. (1996). *Efficient and flexible reading.* (4th ed.). NY: Harper-Collins.

McWhorter, K. T. (1996). *Study and critical thinkings skills in college.* (3rd ed.). NY: Harper-Collins.

(See Appendix 10-3 for a list of reading and study skills textbooks).

In teaching at-risk students who aren't ready to read college textbooks, you have a dual task—acculturating them to the real demands of college textbooks as well as helping them develop the vocabulary and comprehension skills they will need. Even ESL classes benefit by practicing on selections from basic psychology books and show better results than when assigned easy reading exercises from newspapers and magazines. This happens even when the students are not enrolled in psychology. Students find the class much more motivating than those where college text material is not used (Kasper, L. F., 1995-1996).

## What Should We Do About Stand-Alone Reading Courses?

I wish we could get college administrators, state legislators, and curriculum specialists to declare a moratorium on requiring stand-alone reading courses for poor readers. This is not to say that students don't need to improve their reading, nor does it mean that they shouldn't be required to take courses. But there are better ways to do it than by requiring them to take isolated reading courses, which is probably the most costly and least effective method. With marginal students (those who can also carry regular courses) there are many better options—pairing reading and content courses, adjunct skills classes, Supplemental Instruction, interdisciplinary core courses, team taught comprehensive programs, to name a few. In other words, for developmental reading courses to be effective they should be an integrated part of the academic curriculum.

On the other hand, students with very poor reading skills (i.e., below the 8th grade level) need team taught comprehensive programs that include reading, writing, and if appropriate, math skills. They also need counseling (that students perceive as being effective), tutoring, and content classes that will improve their background knowledge so they will be ready for mainstream courses. Richard Donovan (1976) called these programs for at-risk students "intensive care units." In other words, poor readers should not be concurrently enrolled in regular mainstream courses.

As mentioned before, successful programs for very poor readers use a "course simulation model" which replicates the tasks and tests of a regular academic course, but on a less complex level. For example, students read text selections and listen to (videotaped) lectures where notetaking is modeled. At the conclusion of the simulation, model students take an exam just like in a regular course. Students "take with them a physical product (marked text and class notes) and a cognitive product (greater prior knowledge and experience), and domain specific general and specific study strategies" (Stahl and others, 1991).

Required isolated reading courses may do more harm than good if they discourage students, lower student morale, and they don't improve reading. In addition, required reading courses also are difficult to teach, for students resent taking them and the courses suffer a high drop-out rate. A better strategy is to pair courses—i.e., a reading course can be paired with another course such as sociology, writing, biology, etc., where the same textbook is used for both the reading courses and sociology and students are taught skills in reading that they can immediately apply to the mainstream course. Adjunct skills courses or Supplemental Instruction (SI), where course related skills are taught separately from the regular course and enrollment is voluntary, have also proved successful in improving students course grades, grade-point averages, and graduation rates.

## What Characterizes Successful College Reading Programs for At-Risk Students?

Research suggests that counseling-oriented, multiple-skills, voluntary, individualized, and lengthy reading programs resulted in student grade improvement. For very weak students, interdisciplinary courses work well. For example, Brooklyn College (Obler and others, 1977) offered a special services program for underprepared minority students that functioned like a separate college. It involved interdisciplinary remediation in reading and implemented counseling and tutorial services directly in the classrooms. The program stressed close communication among instructors, counselors, tutors, and remedial personnel who met together three times a week. Average contact between students and staff through classes and individual appointments was eleven hours a week. In comparison with a control group who received the same services but whose counselors, remedial specialists, and instructors did not interact, the experimental group showed significantly more credits attempted and completed, higher grade-point averages, and a significantly higher rate of retention in college. Although there was considerable interest in the 80s in coordinating basic skills offerings with general studies requirements, paired courses have not been widely adopted. However, adjunct skills classes and supplemental instruction (SI) classes, which teach skills to students in specific high risk courses, have multiplied. Studies on these adjunct skills classes have consistently demonstrated improvement in student grades, grade-point averages, and persistence rates.

Core courses, where the same freshmen are enrolled in three team-taught courses such as reading, writing, and mathematics, as well as receiving tutoring and counseling that they perceive as being effective, are another way to integrate reading into the curriculum. In this setting, the instructors and counselor coordinate their activities (Clark, 1987). Combining reading and writing courses is another type of pairing. These combinations are needed when students have low reading skills which prohibit them from enrolling in mainstream courses.

## PAIRED COURSES

Typically, paired or team taught courses involve two different instructors who coordinate their teaching, attend each other's classes, and teach the same students who are co-registered in both classes. For example, an English 101 instructor might teach a paired course with a biology instructor. Although this approach has been tried for many years—usually with significant benefits to students—paired courses rarely last more than a semester or two because they are expensive and difficult to schedule. Department chairs frown at the costs of paying instructors to attend each other's courses—in other words, faculty who teach two courses are paid for teaching four. As a result, unless there is outside funding these courses rarely survive.

However, there are many ways to modify paired courses, thus reducing the expense and still providing advantages to students. For instance, Gretchen Starks-Martin teaches reading courses paired with a number of different courses including Contemporary Africa, Crime and Justice in America, and General Chemistry to general studies students at the University of Minnesota-St. Cloud. She does a task analysis of the target class's reading and homework assignments (such as exams, quizzes and or research papers, etc.), then teaches students how to set goals, manage their time and build sufficient time in their lives for study and review. For example, in the chemistry/reading course, she emphasizes problem solving, necessary mathematical skills, and learning the technical vocabulary. Students are reminded that they will need to commit two to three hours of study for each class hour. Her results show that developmental students—i.e., those whose reading skills are below the 12th grade level—who complete the paired courses have higher GPAs and pass the target course in significantly greater numbers than those who take separate reading courses.

Jacqueline Simon at Rider University pairs a reading and study skills course with courses like world history. She works closely with the faculty member, offers to sit in on regular lectures of the parent class, and gives faculty feedback on the course. By videotaping outstanding faculty who use effective study strategies in their teaching, and designing reading exercises around the traditional course content after they teach the course once, she reports that learning specialists can minimize the amount of time they spend in sitting in on the parent course. (If you try this, one thing to avoid is to sit in on the target course and take notes for the students, projecting them on a screen. It's far better to let students take their own notes and compare them with each other and/or the instructor's outline.)

At Widener University, Sam Noble teaches college reading and study skills paired with accounting and other courses that are traditionally difficult for freshmen. The reading and study skills instructors are paired with courses that they had not previously taken in college, thus creating a situation where the instructor provided a role model for less experienced learners as they both grapple with the course demands.

Judy Resnick (1993) paired reading and sociology courses at Manhattan Community College. About half of her class were students who had failed a reading course and were taking it for a second time. Of 11 repeaters, 9 passed reading and 10 passed sociology, which was equivalent to the success rates of the non-repeaters. Also, she has been offering reading courses paired with computer science for students with very poor reading skills who do not qualify for mainstream courses like sociology.

For further information on paired reading and content courses, you'll want to read:

Bullock, T., Madden, D., & Harter, J. (1987). Paired developmental reading and psychology courses. *Research & Teaching in Developmental Education*, 3(2), 22-29. (Describes the results of two years experience in pairing reading and psychology courses at the University of Cincinnati. "Students who took the paired reading course had better perception of their reading and study skills and performed significantly better on the Degrees of Reading Proficiency than their non-paired counterparts." Also discusses the obstacles to paired courses and suggestions for implementing and improving paired courses.)

Obler, M., and others. (1977). Combining of traditional counseling, instruction, and mentoring functions with academically deficient college freshmen. *Journal of Educational Research*, 5, 192-197.

Resnick, J. (1993). A paired reading and sociology course. *Perspectives of Practice in Developmental Education*. In P. Malinowski (Ed.). New York College Learning Association, Finger Lakes Community College, 62-64.

Luvaas-Briggs, L. (1987, Winter). Integrating basic skills with college content instruction. *Journal of Developmental and Remedial Education*, 7(6-9), 31.

## THE UNDERPREPARED COLLEGE READING INSTRUCTOR

Since there are very few graduate programs that specifically prepare college reading teachers, having a master's degree in reading and some teaching experience are the main qualifications for the job. As a result, new reading instructors have been trained and may have taught younger students in elementary and high school. They are rarely knowledgeable or experienced in working with adults. In addition, their perception of teaching reading is aimed at producing good general readers who can read newspapers, magazines, etc. Most have not had experience in teaching college courses and are not aware of academic reading demands and standards in different disciplines. Perhaps they understand assignments in education or English, but they don't know how to help students cope with difficult reading assignments in fields like science or economics.

Although graduate programs in reading have expanded in recent years, college reading specialists continue to be largely self-taught. As college reading specialists are expected to work with weaker and weaker students, they need training in remedial techniques. I know of few college reading specialists who can work with students who read below the sixth-grade level (and those who can are usually too busy with other students and other duties to spend the large amount of time necessary to help very weak students). Yet increasingly, inner city community colleges admit students who need adult basic education and English as a Second Language courses. Entering a community college seems to be more popular for adult non-readers than taking adult education programs in the public schools. Despite these services, some very poor readers manage to enter four-year college programs where a high degree of literacy is required. It would benefit both the institution and the individual student if students with very weak reading skills were not accepted by colleges whose faculty-designed curricula assume students can read well.

For more information on the differences between teaching reading courses in college and the earlier grades, you'll want to read:

Bohr, L. (1996). College and pre-college reading instruction: What are the real differences? *Learning Assistance Review*, 1(1), 14-28.

# What Skills Should Be Stressed in College Reading Courses?

Recent research has confirmed what reading specialists have long believed—vocabulary learning has a significant effect on a student's ability to comprehend a textbook. Certainly each discipline has its own technical words which one must know in order to understand the textbooks, and some fields put different meanings on the same words—for example, the word "void" has a different meaning to lawyers than it does to nurses. Furthermore, direct and systematic teaching of key vocabulary has been shown to improve subsequent reading comprehension. However, studies also show that teachers spend little time in vocabulary instruction. Simpson (1985) in reviewing the literature, came up with five characteristics of effective vocabulary instruction. 1) Using mixed methods to teach vocabulary. That is, using both definitional and contextual methods is superior to either method alone. 2) Students must be actively involved in their own vocabulary learning by imagining, finding examples and applications in new contexts, determining inter-relationships, and restating definitions in their own words. 3) Vocabulary should be taught in a unifying context, not as an isolated list of new words. 4) Student interest in learning vocabulary should be enhanced by encouraging them to seek out new words to study and learn and not limiting them to teacher-made lists. 5) Ensure that instruction is intense—characterized by multiple examples, repetition, review in differing contexts over a significant amount of time.

(Note: Researchers now call the above "generative" vocabulary activities, in contrast to older "additive," more passive activities where students memorized lists of new words and their definitions.)

# Building Your Own Glossary—An Old Fashioned Way to Build Your Vocabulary

I can remember our program in the early 60s where we encouraged students to keep their own glossaries of new words in the front of their textbooks and indicate the page numbers where each word appeared. After a word was used a few times, the student tried to guess the meaning and then checked the dictionary definition and used it in a sentence.

We made lists of the non-technical words (like implicit, explicit, etc.) that appeared in the sociology text. I began to appreciate the freshman's dilemma when I took the list to a photographer to make a film strip for our tachistoscopes and he said, "Hey, lady! What language is this?"

Certainly a good college reader needs to be highly skilled in learning new words.

## Limitations of Vocabulary Textbooks

In a content-analysis of 55 college vocabulary textbooks, Stahl and others (1987) found that most texts used additive approaches to teaching word knowledge (mainly by giving lists of words to memorize). Twenty-two percent of the workbooks taught words exclusively from lists followed by tests and used memory-oriented, multiple-choice, matching, or completion tasks. Rarely did they ask students to demonstrate their understanding of the word by writing a sentence using it.

Few vocabulary workbooks examined used lengthy samples from actual textbooks as the practice material, nor did they use mnemonic guidelines or rehearsal strategies. The investigators urge authors to incorporate research findings in building more appropriate vocabulary exercises.

This study demonstrated that we need materials that encourage students to develop their vocabularies independently, select their own words, generate novel contexts or definitions for the words studied, put definitions in their own words, write original sentences, create categories for words in lists, and answer thought-provoking questions about targeted words. In other words, workbooks and lessons with generative exercises are sorely needed if students are to learn vocabulary.

For more information on teaching vocabulary, you will want to read:

Simpson, M. L., & Dwyer, E. J. (1991). Vocabulary acquisition for the college student. In R. A. Flippo & D. C. Caverly (Eds.). *Teaching reading and study skills strategies at the college level* (pp. 1-41). Newark, DE: International Reading Association.

Simpson, M. L., Nist, S. I., and Kirby, L. (November, 1987). Ideas in practice: Vocabulary strategies design for college students. *Journal of Developmental Education. 11*, (2), 20-24.

Stahl, N. A., Brozo, W. G., & others. (1991). Effects of teaching generative vocabulary strategies in the college developmental reading program. *Journal of Research and Development in Education, 24*(4), 24-32.

Note: New software based on research-based techniques for more effectively increasing vocabulary is being developed. For example, Bruce A. Gamble of the University of Toledo has designed a computer software program where students identify words they don't know, or find difficult from their reading, and are then plugged into a handout that goes with Vocab biLLder 5.4 (which contains 5,600 words). They work with their words a few weeks and then take computer-built quizzes to ensure they've mastered the words.

## THE READABILITY OF COLLEGE TEXTBOOKS

How readable textbooks are is another important factor in college reading that also relates to the individual's vocabulary. In recent years there have been concerted efforts to make college textbooks simpler and more readable, and as a result, many of today's college texts are easier to read than those of two decades ago. But making books more readable can be a two-edged sword. Some books are still written in an unnecessarily pedantic style; but an attempt to simplify complex ideas and technical information and reduce them to a very low level may be a disservice to both the student and the subject.

College reading specialists frequently are asked to conduct readability analyses on textbooks and inform instructors of those that are too difficult for their average students. There has been a recent resurgence of interest in the readability of textbooks, particularly in community colleges where the students' reading abilities range widely.

Early ways of quantifying readability included lists of the most frequently used words in the English language, sentence length and the number of polysyllabic words in a passage. Also the number of personal pronouns and personal references in a passage was considered a measure of its interest (Flesch, 1943, 1958). Drama and fiction scored as highly interesting, science reading was considered very dull on this measure. Other readability measures such as the Dale-Chall Formula (1948) counted sentence length and the number of words not appearing on a list of 3,000 common words, validated against measures of reading comprehension. (Note: A computer version of the Dale-Chall Formula is available.)

Although all the various readability and reading-interest measures can be applied objectively to written material, they consider neither the semantics nor the syntax of the passage, and they have other serious limitations. However, they are useful as quick and easy ways of judging a book's difficulty level and its appeal to students, provided that their limitations are recognized.

Reading experts often attack science and mathematics textbooks as too difficult for students, but the simplistic readability formulas they use are not designed for specialized fields with technical vocabulary. Each field has its own terminology, whether it is physics, horse racing, or helicopter maintenance. Readers must master the vocabulary to understand the concepts in the discipline. Books that are judged difficult according to readability measures usually become easy if the student understands the terms. Wouldn't it be more rational to teach students the specialized vocabulary they need than to simplify the book? Shouldn't reading specialists take the responsibility to help other faculty members teach the terminology of their subjects more effectively rather than throwing up their hands in horror at the vocabulary load of mathematics, biology, or physics?

(Note: For information on some of the special problems in reading science, see Chapter 12.)

Reading instructors often assign light fiction or easy magazine articles to their remedial classes. However, in my experience, very poor readers, when given the choice, prefer to read to solve problems or learn something rather than reading novels or even short vignettes (such as tales of the ghetto), which many of them could write themselves. In other words, when you find reading difficult and painful, you don't read for fun. Perhaps the reading teachers' obsession with readability and our confinement of reading instruction for "poor readers" to a narrow niche of high-interest, easily read materials (or watered-down literature), contributed to the decline of thirteen- and seventeen-year-olds' inferential reading skills. The National Assessment of Educational Progress (1976) reported: "All ages are doing exceptionally well on items that are straightforward, basic, literal; they are doing very well on minimal levels of reading tasks. But as soon as the tasks start to get harder (that is, as soon as the passages become longer or the questions require more manipulation), the results seem to drop off rather quickly." And twenty years later, we hear the same complaints—students can't read critically or understand complex material.

Unfortunately, the environmental, social, economic, and political issues which our country faces and on which our citizens vote, are not literal, straightforward, and basic. Students must be taught how to think critically about complex problems, weigh evidence, use logical processes, and problem solve—and must be expected to do so. Rather than crusading, as some reading associations have done, to simplify all textbooks, reading specialists might better serve their students by teaching them how to read more difficult, intellectually challenging works, including mathematics and science materials.

## READING MATERIALS

There are many self-help books and computer programs designed to identify reading problems and provide training in eliminating them by practicing reading modules on different skills. The Appendix contains a list of reading and study skills books and descriptions of some computer programs.

I feel that a more personalized approach to teaching poor readers directly is preferable. For example,

Sherrie L. Nist and Cynthia Hynd (1995) describe a college reading lab for students taking a basic reading course at the University of Georgia. This program is based on the conviction that reading should be taught using a holistic, content-based approach, in contrast to the usual individualized program where students work independently on self-paced exercises. Focusing on students who needed to pass a state-mandated reading skills test and those whose SATs or GPAs were significantly lower than other students, the instructors stressed test-taking techniques and practice on sample tests. Half of the students had severe difficulty with word recognition, all had problems with oral language and comprehension, and many had poor reading habits—less than half had ever read magazines and some had never read a book. The lab work emphasized text comprehension and word mastery using materials from their regular reading course, using sustained silent reading (where they read their regular reading course assignment), using reading and study strategies, brainstorming terms from their reading and categorizing them, and getting direct instruction in comprehension and pre-reading. That the program was successful was attributed to the qualified staff who were attuned to providing direct instruction to very weak students.

## CRITICAL READING

Some experts feel that teaching students how to read and think critically improves students performance more than any other element. And, although we have talked about how to do this for years and years, it is increasingly a concern in teaching at-risk students. One problem is the variety of topics subsumed under "critical thinking." For example, Chaffee lists the following critical thinking skills:

◊ solving problems and making informed decisions;

◊ generating, organizing, and evaluating ideas;

◊ reasoning analytically with concepts and abstract properties;

◊ exploring issues from multiple perspectives;

◊ applying knowledge to various contexts and new circumstances;

◊ critically evaluating the logic and validity of information;

◊ developing evidence and arguments to support views;

◊ carefully analyzing situations with appropriate questions;

◊ discussing subjects in an organized way; and

◊ becoming aware of one's own thinking process in order to monitor and direct it.

Brookfield (1987, p. 44) proposes four other components:

◊ identifying and challenging assumptions;

◊ developing awareness of context;

◊ imagining and exploring alternatives; and

◊ engaging in reflective skepticism.

Although critical thinking is widely regarded as a necessary skill in college courses, it has rarely been taught systematically at any level. Most questions asked by teachers in elementary and high school classes require yes/no answers or involve facts. Teachers rarely ask questions that require application, analysis, synthesis, and evaluation, and there is evidence that college students don't change much over their four years of college. Developmental students especially need critical thinking skills when they encounter rigorous mainstream college courses.

Today's students must be able to deal with the information explosion which increases each year. Even without Internet, 50,000 books are allegedly published annually in the U.S., more than 1,500 daily newspapers circulated, and literally thousands of general journals and magazines published. In addition, students are bombarded with information from other media, and today's Internet sources provide an overwhelming amount of information. Because of the inevitable information overload, librarians are shifting their emphasis from demonstrating procedures on how to locate information to teaching students that it is necessary to evaluate information, not just find it.

As Clair (1994-95) points out, students are often unaware of the importance of challenging what they read, are particularly reluctant to challenge academic material, and lack the skills to do so. She sees her objective as instructor of library science as developing assignments that require students to reflect upon, analyze, synthesize, and thereby internalize research strategies for future applications. Also, she sees her role as teaching students strategies that enable them to challenge scholarly discourse.

## Getting Students to Challenge Scholarly Writing

Clair bases her beginning library research course on the assumption that if students are given assignments that require them to reflect upon, analyze, synthesize and thereby, internalize research strategies and learn to challenge scholarly discourse, they will write better papers. She says that a student's ability to gather relevant information, evaluate it and communicate what is learned makes the difference between a composition that meets minimum requirements and one that exemplifies a well thought out and executed product. Using collaborative learning strategies and active learning, as well as assignments that require students to reflect upon the content, she teaches a combination of critical thinking, library research, and writing.

Clair starts by having students evaluate topics by looking them up in different encyclopedias. For example, she assigned the topic "Wounded Knee" and students found marked differences in the "facts" (i.e., dates, number of soldiers, guns, etc.) between the two encyclopedias. Furthermore, the same event was described in different language; one called it an "engagement" and another "a massacre." This led to interesting class discussions about how the author's frame of reference impacts writing.

John Chaffee (1992) takes issue with the belief of most teachers that although critical reading is important, developmental students need the basics first. In fact, most people still believe the myth that youngsters cannot be taught to think critically. I like to reply by citing Aiken's (1995) description of how she gave her adult basic education students three illustrated versions of the story of the three little pigs—one version was the original story, the second was the Disney version with a happy ending, and the third was told from the wolf's viewpoint. Since they had been exposed to the tale as children, they enjoyed analyzing and critically discussing the three versions. (Note: Children also could compare and criticize these three stories.)

Unfortunately the teaching of critical reading and thinking has too long been reserved for advanced students. Yet Chaffee offers a large critical reading program at LaGuardia Community College where over 80 percent of the entering students are held for remedial skills courses and also have large gaps in their knowledge. Chaffee's course focuses on developing critical thinking abilities as well as reading and language skills. He reports that students enrolled in the key program have doubled the college-wide pass rate on standardized exit exams in reading and writing.

In Chaffee's program, students analyze substantive writing assignments as they explore various critical thinking topics using Chaffee's book, *Thinking Critically,* as the text: solving problems, perceiving, belief and knowing, using language, constructing arguments and reasoning critically through an integrated approach to reading, writing, speaking and critical thinking. Attempts to infuse critical thinking across the curriculum start with the basic course, which is paired with another, selected from courses in English, reading, mathematics, social science, etc. Faculty members who teach the two courses meet weekly to redesign their courses and refine their teaching methodology to foster critical thinking. The program met the criteria of the National Endowment for the Humanities in three of it's objectives: literacy, reasoning and problem solving, and critical attitudes. (Among the factors related to critical attitudes are affective effects like being more attentive, less likely to be absent, quicker to follow instructions, more serious about course work, better at asking questions and verbalizing, less afraid of thinking and expressing themselves, and showing increased self-confidence.) Students in the course assume the role of analytical thinkers who are willing to tax their brains. Critical thinking goals are built into the course structure. Active learning is stimulated, reasoning and well supported conclusions encouraged, as is perspective seeking. The course is designed to stimulate thinking and language use at all levels, building from the student's experience and expanding it into more abstract, formal situations.

Chaffee cites the example of a student named Diego, who had been placed on probation for robbery and was naive about academic experiences.

When, during the second week of class, he analyzed critical and uncritical thinking about the period that he and others were robbing delivery boys, he discovered ideas are important. Diego wrote an essay about his failure to think correctly and critically. Although Chaffee admits Diego's writing efforts were not a passing paper, it marked his transformation toward self-discovery and helped him develop the commitment needed to work energetically to pass the course. Chaffee says that Diego spent more time in the Writing Center than any other student and moved in 10 weeks time from a state of functional illiteracy to one of relative fluency (Chaffee, p. 39).

## SOURCES OF INFORMATION ON CRITICAL READING

The *Journal of Developmental Education* has a regular column on how-to-teach critical thinking and critical reading. For many years this column was written by Curtis Miles. Currently, Linda Elder and Richard Paul are authoring the column.

Two workbooks on critical reading that you will want to examine are:

Chaffee, J. (1985). *Thinking critically.* (3rd ed.). Boston, MA: Houghton Mifflin.

Miles, C., & Rauton, J. (1985). *Thinking tools.* (2nd ed.). Clearwater, FL: H&H Publishing.

## SPEED READING

Speed-reading courses continue to be popular and will undoubtedly always attract students as long as publishers print endless numbers of books, professors assign long reading lists, and teachers insist that one must read every word to comprehend the message. Many people seem convinced that the measure of one's intellect is the number of books one has swept one's eyes through. As early as the 1940s, articles about speed-reading courses reported astronomical reading rates when the students' final grades were based on how fast they read. Experts in the reading profession, including myself, have verbally battled commercial speed-reading courses since the 1950s, but these programs continue unabated. Our criticisms of the commercial programs were directed against their exorbitant claims and guarantees to teach people to read at speeds as high as 20,000 words per minute. (Note: There are many articles in the reading journals of the 50s and 60s on this problem, but experts today have not identified people who can read faster than 1000 words per minute. More than that is skimming.)

My personal concern about commercial speed-reading courses was that they did not screen their students, so that the weaker students who took the courses ended up in my office feeling even more inadequate and insecure about their reading and intellectual abilities. The very anxieties that had led them to take the courses in the first place were heightened rather than reduced. Another problem was that some students entered speed-reading courses with poor comprehension and finished with higher speeds but even lower comprehension—they apparently had learned only to turn pages faster. Other students were convinced that they must read everything "dynamically" or they would lose the skill they had paid so dearly to acquire. This attitude was fatal for students with weak high school backgrounds who compulsively speed read their chemistry textbooks and later wondered why they failed chemistry.

But there are many people who can be helped by a speed-reading course if it gives them the freedom to read rapidly and helps them to trust their own judgment of which ideas are worth reading slowly and which are trivial and can be ignored.

The information explosion, which I have long considered diarrhea of the presses, is the raison d'etre for speed reading. With so much to read in every field, mature readers must read selectively and skim. Reading specialists have maintained that an important goal of reading improvement courses is to train students to read flexibly—that is, to vary their speed and depth of comprehension with their purpose. Improvement in flexibility has been hard to demonstrate, however. Kershner (1964) discovered that adults who read rapidly do not vary their speed with the difficulty of the reading matter. Slow readers display more flexibility in that they read difficult material more slowly than easy material. A problem in teaching students to vary their speed with their purpose is that they may not understand the purposes that mature readers have. After all, the freshman is reading textbooks mainly to learn the material that the instructor thinks is important enough to include on examinations. Novices in any field lack the background to make the sophisticated judgments of experts on what is important (and should therefore be read carefully) and what can be skimmed or skipped. So speed reading—although I prefer the term skimming—represents a mature reading skill involving making critical judgments about the material one reads.

Today's college speed-reading courses differ little from the commercial programs. Both use standardized reading tests at the beginning and end of the course, paced practice, and easy materials. The major difference is that the commercial programs are far more expensive for students. Today's speed reading is more likely to be taught on computers than by traditional reading technology such as the tachistoscope or the Controlled Reader (a paced projector). Both the reading machines and the computer software have limitations, and learners often have difficulty transferring skills learned on them to regular textbook reading. Those who use reading improvement software, just as students who formerly used reading machines, need careful explanations about the advantages and limitations of the computerized program and should have frequent conferences with an instructor to avoid the discouragement that often accompanies mechanized self-paced instruction. Some students need to be reassured that each item missed does NOT equal failure. (For more information on Computer Software see Appendix 12-1.)

## What Does Research Say About Speed-Reading Courses?

We know that if students in speed-reading courses are offered information on the nature of the reading process and current theories of memory and retention, not just paced practice, they will show greater improvement. For example, Cox (1977) taught students information-processing theory in a speed-reading course and showed them how to apply it to difficult books. These students varied their speed and purpose according to the difficulty of the material and the amount of information they needed in order to identify, understand, analyze, and outline key ideas from an advanced political science book. In other words, students were taught to develop their own advance organizers for keying into major concepts. Cox's control group, taught with a diagnostic-prescriptive approach using the same reading materials, but without receiving training in information processing, scored significantly lower on tests of reading flexibility at the end of the course.

Hansen (1977) taught speed reading to a class of honor students and matched them with a control honors section who did not receive speed-reading training. She found both quantitative and qualitative differences between the experimental and control classes. Analyzing the college-textbook materials used for the pre- and post-test measures, she found that slower readers were more likely to recall temporal relations (that is, they were able to follow the chronological sequence of events) than speed readers, but that speed readers excelled on recalling concepts involving reasoning, coordination, relationships, comparison, and contrast. She found no evidence that her speed-reading group was just skimming for main ideas. They were reading the post-test material two or more times for different purposes and recalling more units.

Sandberg (1976) taught speed reading to Malaysian students in an ESL class and found that it enhanced their ability to see the overall organizational patterns of English prose by permitting them to read the passage more than once for different purposes. He states that the ability to read rapidly with good comprehension requires skill in selecting the important concepts carefully and rejecting those that are insignificant.

Slower readers, particularly those with poor comprehension and vocabulary skills, spend a great deal of time decoding individual words and struggling with the syntax. Although some poor readers can remember details, many cannot synthesize the information they read into principles and concepts. It is unfortunate that more efforts are not being made to introduce younger students to skimming and scanning, not as a substitute for careful, slow reading, but as a tool they will surely need in determining for themselves what should be read slowly and carefully. Students need to have a variety of reading skills in their repertoire when confronted with material that they consider difficult and dull. I once asked a high school group how many students read material that they considered dull and difficult more slowly than material they found interesting. Ninety percent replied that they read difficult material slowly and procrastinated a long while before tackling it.

So, the belief persists that one should read dull and difficult material very slowly, despite Mortimer Adler's (1940) suggestion that the more difficult one finds a selection, the faster one should read it, at least the first time through. Too many students equate reading with serving penance. They feel that if they sit staring at the book hard enough, the facts and ideas will rise and come into their heads, but by approaching reading slowly and negatively, they recall little.

Sometimes college reading programs capitalize on the fact that there is no stigma attached to taking a speed-reading course and call both their developmental and basic reading sections "speed reading." Because virtually no one is completely satisfied with his reading rate, these courses attract a wide variety of students. One method is to enroll students in a speed-reading course and then test them and divide them into sections on the basis of their comprehension scores. In the 1970s, students in the lowest speed-reading section at California State University-Hayward had to meet clear standards in order to pass the course. They had to read selections from each of fourteen disciplines, pass a criterion referenced reading test on each, and write a summary of each selection that someone who has not read the selection could understand. Although the reading materials were simpler than the average college textbook, students were exposed to the differences between the skills required in reading and understanding different subjects which they certainly would not have selected voluntarily.

## SUMMARY AND CONCLUSION

Many of the skills that can be taught successfully at the college level could be implemented in earlier grades and should be offered more widely in public schools. Such skills as selective reading, skimming and scanning, speed reading, and critical reading are necessary for college success. Since a larger proportion of our population is attending college, high schools have a responsibility to prepare a far larger percentage of their students for continuing education than they currently are. It is reported that 30% of students entering college today have not taken college preparatory courses.

Without concerted effort from both college instructors and public school teachers, the inevitable result will be a continuing deemphasis on reading as a tool for learning, and, in their desperation, professors and students will turn increasingly to nonprint media as substitutes for reading.

How many students a college enrolls in its reading program is determined more by the budget and facilities available than by student need. As in other skills areas, reading programs are most successful with students of average or near-average ability in relation to the typical student in the institution. Highly anxious, well-prepared students, and those who have had reading help in the past, are the most frequent volunteers for reading programs. Academically sophisticated students are often painfully aware of their reading limitations and worry that they cannot complete the lengthy reading lists assigned. They may have unrealistic ideas about the level of performance professors expect or may set impossibly high standards for themselves. But professors contribute to such students' problems by requiring long reading lists without specifying their purpose or describing how they should be approached. Some critics suggest that needlessly long reading assignments lead to apathy and laziness in today's college students, result in superficial reading habits, and may create an aversion to reading.

The weakest college readers rarely volunteer for reading help unless they are identified early, counseled about their skills deficiencies, and shown that they can improve. Most community colleges require poor readers to take developmental reading courses. These courses traditionally relied heavily on self-help materials, reading machines, and workbooks. Today's reading courses are more likely to emphasize individual teaching, sustained silent reading, transfer of skills to regular college courses, and use more difficult materials than was typical of courses 15 years ago. Again, students who show the greatest improvement are those with average or borderline skills relative to the other students in the class. In these reading courses, class sizes tend to be large and students' skills very weak. Reading instructors usually carry a heavier course load than instructors in other subjects, despite the fact that their students need more intense personal attention and direct teaching. Unless poor readers are highly motivated, can sustain their motivation, and can work relatively independently on self-paced materials, their chances of improving their skills significantly so that they can advance to higher-level courses are minimal. The weakest students who are barely literate need individual one-to-one tutoring with a carefully trained tutor and closely supervised practice. They also need programs that last longer than one semester. Current research on motivation, cognitive psychology, and brain physiology suggests that we can do a better job with students whom we have failed in the past by using new teaching strategies in smaller classes that focus on improving affective factors such as self-esteem, self-efficacy, and reversing expectations of failure.

In conclusion, reading programs succeed when the skills taught directly relate to the content of mainstream courses in which students are concurrently enrolled or are most relevant to their career goals. Also, success depends on the reading program being an integral part of the regular curriculum and involving effective counseling, tutoring, and instructing services.

# CHAPTER 10

## BUILDING STUDY SKILLS

Colleges have offered programs to orient new students to the rituals of college study since the 1920s, and today's programs differ little in content from those of the past. Typically they teach students time management skills (setting priorities, scheduling one's time), taking lecture notes (and sometimes improving listening skills), textbook-study methods, preparing for and taking examinations, and improving memory and concentration. Depending on the course's length, units on research-paper writing, career planning, adapting to academic regulations (and learning them), and improving personal and social adjustment may also be included. Study skills courses are usually offered separately from reading and writing courses, and in universities they may be presented as noncredit minicourses, supplemented by individual appointments with learning-skills counselors. Although community college programs mainly concentrate on improving students' skills in basic reading, writing, and mathematics, they too may offer courses in reading and study skills improvement for students who plan to transfer to senior colleges.

One might question why textbook reading methods are taught under study skills or, as a visiting dean from Sweden once asked me, "Why do you Americans call it reading and study skills? How can you separate the two?" "A good question," I answered, "but I guess it's just our tradition." Perhaps it's the result of the American need to divide knowledge into separate departments and different courses. I really don't know, but I firmly agree that it's time we stopped thinking of them as separate subjects.

## HOW CAN YOU DETERMINE WHETHER A STUDENT HAS POOR STUDY SKILLS?

If a student earns poor grades in college, parents and professors often conclude that he has "poor study habits"—a euphemism for not studying or investing minimal time and effort in study. Before assuming that the student needs a study skills program, the learning-skills counselor should find out whether the student has studied at all. It is currently fashionable to label college students with poor grades "learning-disabled" (see Chapter 9 and Appendix 9-4). However, I found that many of the students referred to me as potential learning disability cases shared one characteristic—they managed to avoid studying, reading, and writing in high school and do not study in college. They are quite capable of improving, once they can be convinced that intensive studying and practice are necessary. Should you meet students who insist that they are learning disabled but have not been certified, you can refer them to community resources for testing to resolve the question and to determine whether they are eligible for special accommodations. (You can find local resources by calling vocational rehabilitation offices and/or local universities. Remember that the student bears the cost of testing.)

As you are probably aware, increasing numbers of students today are entering college who were diagnosed as learning disabled in high school, have been in programs where they received special help, and expect to find similar services in college. Inevitably, they will find their way to the learning center if there are no learning disabilities offices on campus. It is important that you and your staff develop some expertise in understanding their needs, the legal implications of the college in providing accommodations, and where to refer them. If, indeed, your program has the responsibility of offering services to learning disabled students, it is essential that you have a specially trained staff person in charge of the program to liaison between your staff, faculty, and community resources. To attempt to work with L.D. students without a liaison person inevitably results in overworking your staff, low morale, and unending problems. See Appendix 9-3 for a description of the Adaptive Computing Training Laboratory, at Georgine Materniak's University of Pittsburgh Learning Center, which offers special instruction for students with learning and physical disabilities—a program that grew out of an innovative collaboration between academic computing and the learning center.

The reduction of homework assigned in high school courses over the past two decades has widened the gap between high school and college courses because many students entering college simply have not been required to study in the past. That college instructors expect them to devote much time to study may come as a great shock to them.

On the other hand, there are a few students who devote endless hours to studying in college but get little payoff in either learning or grades. Discriminating between students who know how to study but do not and those who need to develop more effective study methods is crucial but sometimes difficult.

## LIMITATIONS OF STUDY SKILLS TESTS

Unfortunately, standardized study-habits inventories rarely help the skills specialist make this determination because they are attitude tests, and most students know what answers are expected. (See Chapter 2 and the List of Tests in Appendix 3-1 for descriptions of study-habits inventories.) Students taking study skills tests are instructed to answer the questions honestly, and those who are worried about their study skills problems usually do, but those who are uninterested may not.

If students are given the same inventory twice with different instructions such as, "Answer the questions as you think a straight-A student would," they make surprisingly high scores. Indeed, if they do not score in the 90th percentile, there is reason to suspect that they really do not know how to study. Accordingly, study-habits inventories are not effective for determining who should be required to take a study skills program, although they may be useful in counseling students who are motivated to seek help voluntarily and as one measure of attitude changes before and after taking a course. (Note: Another way to assess change in a study skills course is to have students prepare portfolios of how they apply principles to their course work, as Gretchen Starks-Martin at the University of Minnesota-St. Cloud does.)

I first realized the limitations of attitude tests in the 50s when the Brown-Holtzman Study Habits and Attitudes Inventory (BHSSA) was new. Attempting to develop local norms on our students in study skills courses at the University of Maryland, I analyzed the test results from my classes along with those of another instructor. To my surprise, I found that my classes' average scores were deciles below those of my friend's classes and asked him what instructions he gave his students before they took the test. He insisted that he had read them the instructions printed on the test. So I went back to the drawing board, reanalyzed the data hunting for errors, but got the same results. Finally I asked him what he had told his students BEFORE he read the test instructions to his classes, and he said, "I told them to do your very best on the test for the results will go on your permanent record." Obviously, they answered the questions to make themselves look good.

So the basic question is whether students know what effective study skills are but do not use them, or whether they really do not know how to study. Robyak and Patton (1977, p. 200) state that "prior research has supported neither the notion that students do not know efficient study skills and must be taught them, nor the notion that the content of a study skills course accounts for the effectiveness of the course. On closer inspection, the gradepoint average that usually follows the completion of a study skills course may be a more accurate reflection of the degree to which students learn to use effective study skills rather than the degree to which students acquire knowledge of them. Thus, a student's increased use of study skills may be more closely related to improved academic performance than their increased knowledge of study skills." In their research, Robyak and Patton found that students' personality types seem to determine whether they will increase their use of the study skills taught in a course.

For example, they state that students rated as "judgers" on the Myers-Briggs Type Indicator used significantly more study skills after taking a course than students rated as "perceivers." (Judgers are characterized by a propensity to come to a conclusion and reach a verdict; perceivers tend to expect new developments to occur and to await new evidence before doing anything they fear is irrevocable.)

As a result, counseling may be important in helping perceivers understand their resistance to studying and their tendency to procrastinate, while judgers respond well to a structured study skills course. (See Appendix 3-1 for more on the Myers-Briggs Type Indicator.)

## THE INSTRUCTOR'S ASSUMPTIONS MAKE A DIFFERENCE

Some instructors still teach study skills courses as if they were formal academic subjects, lecturing on methods and topics and assigning routine projects without first determining whether students already know the skills. Unfortunately, these kinds of courses usually waste the instructor's time, the students' time, and the institution's resources. Inevitably students who know or think they know how to study will find the course boring and irrelevant, particularly if the exercises are based on information that is not directly applicable to the mainstream courses that they are currently taking. If students know the skills but do not use them, then counseling and practice on strategies that they can directly apply to their courses are necessary. Discussing study skills strategies in pairs and in small groups can also help students find ways to learn and apply new techniques. But an unsupplemented lecture on improving study skills is a poor way to change attitudes.

To identify students who need the course, successful programs use screening interviews and do not rely exclusively on study-habits inventories. In summary, study skills courses tend to be most successful in improving student achievement when they blend counseling, structured presentations, intensive practice on course-related materials, and involve peer discussion and/or techniques like reciprocal teaching. (See Chapter 7 for more on teaching strategies.)

But what about the content of these study skills courses? Traditionally instructors have stressed "desirable" strategies for managing time, taking notes, and so forth. Unfortunately, some of these suggestions are based neither on research nor on common sense. For example, we used to warn students that they must spend two hours studying for each class hour in order to pass—a time-honored axiom, but one that has no basis in fact. Students soon recognize that some classes demand much more study time; others require less. In other words, the amount of study time needed depends on the subject and on the student's background and ability. For example, studies show that students average 9-10 hours a week studying calculus, and those taking statistics study an average of 10 hours a week.

As researchers begin to investigate how students really study, other old-fashioned rules that have gone by the boards include 1) don't study with friends, 2) don't read the same passage twice, 3) read with your mind not your mouth! Even cramming, which was strictly forbidden, has been found to be useful under some conditions when it is compatible with the student's preferred learning style. So although freshmen continue to have study problems, some of the solutions offered by skills specialists have changed over the years.

## Time Management

Some college situations that bother freshmen never seem to change. Today's students have problems managing their time just as college freshmen students always have. Whether they are entering Harvard or an open-admission community college, they share the same problem—finding enough time to study. Evidence that managing time is a major adjustment problem is suggested by the huge num-

bers of time management tips and schedules requested from learning centers. One example—the Learning Skills Center at the University of Texas-Austin reports that it distributes an average of 5,000 time schedules and time management instructions each semester. (Note: Fraternity and sorority scholarship chairpersons carry off armfuls.) Furthermore, a survey shows that the majority of midshipmen at the US Naval Academy (where practically every minute of every day is scheduled for students) report that they consider the biggest hurdle to academic achievement is "time"—if they only had more time, everything could be accomplished. What they need, of course, is to be able to use their time more efficiently. (For an example of a time-management handout see Appendix 10-2.)

Study skills programs and college orientation programs routinely include skills in time management, but their suggestions are usually based on principles adopted from business management, such as Lakein's (1973) *How to Get Control of Your Time and Your Life*. Books on time management generally agree that one should identify needs and wants, rank them in regard to their importance or priority, and then allocate time and resources appropriately. Other time-honored tips include delegating work, handling each piece of paper only once, and continually asking yourself, "What is the best use of my time right now?"

Richard Light (1992), using Harvard students and faculty in his assessment about teaching/learning, points out that for some Harvard freshmen the inability to manage their time will spell failure. As an ice breaker in student conferences, he encourages advisors to question students about whether they have enough time to study, and to point out that how they allocate their energies and plan their study time is crucial to success. He describes a study by K. W.

Light, in which a group of Harvard freshmen were trained to track how they actually spent their time, and then debriefed each student with questions like, "How was your time actually spent?" "Are you pleased with the way you spend each day?" "Are there changes you might like to make?" among others. He found it helpful to ask students to divide the day into three parts, Morning, Afternoon, and Evening, and encourage them to choose the extracurricular activities they'd like to do, as well as plan for uninterrupted study time. Light reported that having students log their time enables the advisor and student to get together with an agenda to discuss, providing a better chance for an advisor to genuinely advise.

## WHAT RESEARCH SUGGESTS ABOUT TIME MANAGEMENT

Despite the pervasiveness of the problem, there has been surprisingly little research on time management for college students until very recently. Skills counselors continue to use the same strategies that were developed for business situations. What little research has been done mainly concerned how training in time management can change behavior, and although a number of studies have reported behavior changes, few studies have shown that time management training reduces stress or improves students' overall performance. The research prior to 1990 deals with time management training aimed at teaching what was assumed to be a single, simple construct of good time management. Not only were there no tests to assess conventional college time management behaviors, but little was known about naturally occurring time management and its correlations with personality, stress and performance.

More recent studies are beginning to examine these questions. Macan et al. (1990) developed a time management questionnaire, administered it to college students, and then checked it against time management behaviors, attitudes, stress and self-perceptions of performance, and grade point average. They concluded that time management is comprised of four independent factors.

**Factor 1.** Setting short-term goals and priorities.

**Factor 2.** Mechanics—scheduling, planning, etc.— time management behaviors taught in seminars like "I carry an appointment book with me, I make a list of things to do each day and check off each task as it is accomplished," etc.

**Factor 3.** The student's perceived control of time includes items like "I feel in control of my time," and "I feel overwhelmed by trivial and unimportant tasks."

**Factor 4.** Preference for disorganization consisted of items like, "I can find the things I need more readily when my workplace is messy," and "I have some of my most creative ideas when I am disorganized." (Note: As might be expected, those students with a high preference for disorganization felt more ambiguity about their roles as students, had higher somatic tensions, and made lower GPA's.)

Of the four factors revealed by the questionnaire, perceived control of time was found to be the best predictor of GPA. Students who felt they were able to control their own time reported significantly better performance, greater satisfaction with work and life, less role ambiguity, less role overload, fewer job-induced and somatic tensions, and higher GPA's.

Overall scores on the time management questionnaire were found to be positively correlated with age and sex. Older students were more likely to engage in traditional time management activities, while women made significantly higher overall scores on the time management questionnaire, but were significantly lower on one factor—they did not feel that they were in control of their time. In other words, women better understood how to manage their time than men but were less likely to feel that they could control their own time.

## MANAGING TIME AS A PREDICTOR OF COLLEGE GRADUATION

In another recent study on time management, Britton and Tesser (1991) gave 90 freshmen a time-management questionnaire and compared their responses with their cumulative grade-point averages four years later. Two time management components were found to be related to overall grades.

1. A time attitudes factor—consistent with Bandura's 1986 concept of self-efficacy and the findings of the Macan and others study. Students with positive time attitudes seem to be able to control their time, say "No" to people, and stop unprofitable activities or routines. Feelings of self-efficacy, according to Bandura (1986), allow and support more efficient cognitive processing, more positive affective responses, and more persevering behavior.

2. Strong short-term planning skills.

(Note 1: This study did not use the same questionnaire used in the Macan study, but both studies agreed on these two factors.)

(Note 2: One standardized computerized study skills instrument, The Study Behavior Inventory, includes a score on perception of one's academic ability, security about one's ability to learn, and factors related to self-efficacy. See List of Tests in Appendix. 2-1.)

Interestingly, long-term planning skills were not related to final GPA, and the researchers postulate that, in a college environment, short-term planning may be more important than long-term planning due to changes in expectations and demands that are relatively rapid and frequent. *"Different parts of the course may unpredictably vary in difficulty; the overlapping of demand from different courses is often unpredictable; instructors may change their minds about the due date on papers or the date an exam will be scheduled; on occasion, they give out no syllabus and sometimes when there is a syllabus, they often deviate from it. In this type of ever changing environment, if one's goal is to maximize grades, the ability to change one's plans quickly is optimal; long range planning may be more important in a less volatile, more stable environment"* (Britton & Tesser, 1991).

The fact that long-range planning was negatively correlated with SAT scores is more difficult to explain. The investigators suggest that several of the items on the long-range planning scale may reflect an inability to tolerate complexity; i.e., keeping a clean desk. *"To the extent that these items indicate a low tolerance for ambiguity, people who score high on this factor may be unable to cope with other kinds of complexity such as the complexity involved in taking the SAT. These remain unanswered questions for further research."*

**Implications**. Although a limitation of the Macan et al. study is that it was based on self-reported information, the finding that time management is made up of multiple factors suggests that managing one's time is a more complex activity than was previously thought, and that attitudes about one's ability to manage time are more important than the strategies one uses.

That four independent factors were found in one study and two in the other give additional support to the idea that time management is complex. The most important factor in predicting achievement (whether it is current GPA or GPA at graduation) seems to be whether students feel that they are in control of their own time, not the mechanics nor the time-planning activities they engage in. Both studies agreed on a second independent time-management factor—short-term goal setting. That people who are long-term planners are at a disadvantage in college and don't do as well as those who plan only for the short-term is intriguing. Perhaps we should stop pushing our students to decide on long-term goals and encourage them to be more responsive and adaptable to the inevitable changes they will face in college and in later life.

## NOTE-TAKING

As long as lectures remain the prevailing way to present information in college courses, taking good lecture notes is a necessary survival skill. Regardless of the fact that lectures are generally considered a poor way to present vast amounts of new information, most college classes are still taught by lecture. An hour's lecture on new information presents far more information than anyone can possibly store in one's memory, as Paul Hettich's pyramid in Figure 10-1 dramatically shows.

### FIGURE 10-1  THE PYRAMID OF SELECTIVE LEARNING

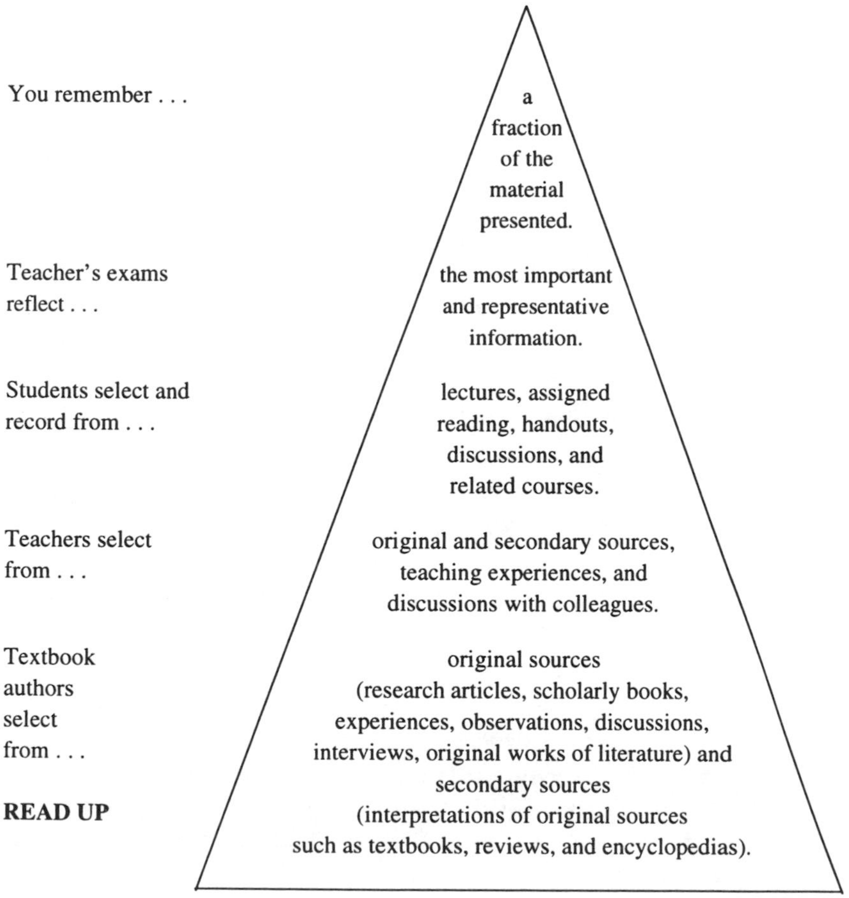

You remember . . .

    a fraction of the material presented.

Teacher's exams reflect . . .

    the most important and representative information.

Students select and record from . . .

    lectures, assigned reading, handouts, discussions, and related courses.

Teachers select from . . .

    original and secondary sources, teaching experiences, and discussions with colleagues.

Textbook authors select from . . .

**READ UP**

    original sources (research articles, scholarly books, experiences, observations, discussions, interviews, original works of literature) and secondary sources (interpretations of original sources such as textbooks, reviews, and encyclopedias).

From Paul Hettich, *Learning Skills for College and Career,* Pacific Grove, CA: Brooks/Cole Publishers, 1992.

(Hettich also describes ways lectures can be improved to enhance student learning by attacking both from the top down and the bottom up.)

In fact, researchers have found that it's not taking notes, but what you do with them after you take them that determines what you retain.

The most popular notetaking system taught is the Cornell Notetaking System developed by Walter Pauk (1989). In this method, students take lecture notes on one side (or one half) of the notebook page and then correct and add clarification from reading the textbook or reviewing the material on the other side of the page.

A study by Stahl et al. (1991) suggests that good notetaking is not solely the responsibility of the learner, but instructors need ongoing training in how to present a considerate lecture. Before students can engage in efficient study practices they must have good notes that provide the focus of studying. One technique is NOTE, a notetaking observation with training and evaluation scales involving a four stage instructional sequence of modeling, practicing, evaluating and reinforcing activities for helping students take better notes. It is comprised of two parts—first, taking the notes and then reviewing them. Stahl et al. point out that traditional notetaking systems such as the Cornell method are based on time honored practices, but require a degree of effort that most students, especially those at risk, are not willing to expend. In their NOTE System, modeling and practice notetaking doesn't differ much from traditional approaches. However, combining these with evaluation and reinforcement appears to motivate students and also provides guidance for ongoing practice. In other words, the instructor demonstrates notetaking on an overhead while a lecture proceeds on audio or videotape and thinks aloud. This is repeated for several weeks while the students take their own notes—observed by an instructor walking around. Thus, NOTE involves students engaged in long-term monitored practice, evaluated by

a formal document review progress (p 618).

(Note: A number of Stahl's studies emphasize that the skills textbooks currently published don't reflect research on the most effective ways of improving learning, study strategies, vocabulary, reading, etc. One cannot assume that if authors of textbooks don't include appropriate exercises, that teachers will make up their own, since this would assume that teachers read the research and don't teach from the texts.)

## USING NOTES FOR REVIEW

Haenggi & Perfiti (1992) examined the roles of basic reading processes and prior knowledge in processing expository text by asking average and above-average college readers to either review their notes, reread notes, or reread their textbook in a course on human decision-making. Results showed that the three strategies were equally effective in improving comprehension for test-explicit and text-implicit information, and reading ability and prior knowledge were more predictive of comprehension than was the type of reproductive activity. Rereading the text might help average readers compensate for their lower performance in answering test-implicit questions, whereas above-average readers seem better able to combine more text information with their previous knowledge. Working memory played the major role in comprehending text-implicit information, whereas knowledge was relatively more important for explicit and script-implicit information.

These results tend to support studies from the early 1940s that reported that a rereading strategy improved comprehension on immediate and delayed tests better than note-taking, summarizing, or outlining. In fact, Anderson (1980), in a review of research on study strategies, found that only two studies reported a rereading strategy was inferior to either notetaking or underlining, while several studies showed no difference. Subsequent studies tend to show that rereading is superior when processing time is constant.

Yet how many of us still warn students that rereading is less effective than SQ3R or notetaking? And do we still discourage them from rereading their textbook chapters? Some students may need to do ALL of these things to learn (i.e., read, take notes, reread, underline, annotate, etc.).

In another study, Kiewra & others (1991) investigated three notetaking functions: taking notes/no review, taking notes/review, and absent self from lecture and review somebody else's notes. (Note: This third condition is similar to students renting notetaking services.) The results indicated that taking notes and reviewing them was superior to taking notes and not reviewing them, to reviewing borrowed notes for performance on a recall test, and superior to not reviewing notes on a test of synthesis. That is, those who borrowed someone else's notes and reviewed them scored higher on a synthesis test than those who took their own notes, but didn't review them. The researchers also reported that taking notes in a matrix fashion (i.e., mapping) was superior to linear notetaking. Current study skills manuals often include exercises in mapping (drawing diagrams rather than taking notes in outline form) which has been found to improve writing ability as well as memory.

## What Instructors Can Do To Aid Students In Recalling Class Lectures/Discussions

Some ways to help instructors aid students to recall information from class lectures and discussions are described in *Classroom Assessment Techniques* (Angelo and Cross, 1993). Among these is RSQC$^2$ (Recall, Summarize, Question, Connect, and Comment). This is described as a five step protocol that classroom instructors can use to guide students through simple recall, summary, analysis, evaluation and synthesis exercises focusing on a previous class session. This strategy provides students with a comprehensive framework for recalling and reviewing class sessions and can be used in a variety of courses from remedial math to conversational German. The steps include:

1. Recall – Make a list of most meaningful important points from previous class–1 to 2 minutes.

2. Summarize – Try to summarize these important points in one sentence.

3. Question – Jot down one or two questions that remain unanswered from the class.

4. Connect – Explain in one or two sentences the connections between the main points and the major goals of the course.

5. Comment – Comment on what you enjoyed most/least, what was most/least useful, how you felt about the subject.

6. Collect – Collect papers and tell students when they will get feedback.

(Angelo & Cross, 1993, p. 344-348)

RSQC$^2$ is especially helpful for students who are underprepared in the subject.

## Textbook Reading Skills

Study skills texts describe many ways to improve textbook reading and each of them is usually identified by an acronym. Each represents someone's interpretation of the basic laws of learning, expressed in a formula.

## SQ3R

The textbook-reading method taught most widely in study skills programs over the years has been the SQ3R method, developed by Frank Robinson of Ohio State University during WWII. Almost every study skills book published since the 1940s suggests (with or without credit to Robinson) that students should use SQ3R or some modification of this strategy. The acronym SQ3R represents the four steps in the method: **S** for Survey (read topic headings and summary), **Q** for Question (turn topic headings into questions), **R** for Read to answer the questions, **R** for Recite (try to recall the answers to the questions without looking back at the text), and **R** for Review (check back in the text to clarify the answers you may have missed or are confused about). Smith (1961) added a fourth R: 'Riting (take notes on your answers to the questions).

The SQ3R method has often been criticized by skills experts because it has not been systematically researched as a total method, although there is research to support each of the separate steps. But the critics miss the point. For the fearful student, faced with a long, difficult text to read, the SQ3R method provides a technique for getting started. Moreover, it makes explicit the steps that a skilled learner automatically follows. So even if students grumble that it takes too long or that underlining passages in their textbooks is quicker and easier, they will find that, when all else fails, using SQ3R will help them gain a better understanding from their reading. I have found that many students modify the method in their routine studying, but when they are desperate—that is, when faced with an examination that will determine whether they pass or fail a course, or when in a situation in which they must make a high grade— using the original SQ3R without modification pays off.

Other criticisms of SQ3R are that it is taught inflexibly, and it is not easily applied to required reading that isn't written in a traditional textbook format. Furthermore, teachers rarely make an effort to show students how to modify it for different purposes.

However, newer reading methods based on more recent research are beginning to replace SQ3R, such as PORPE, a system that integrates reading and writing, places more stress on metacognitive skills and relating what one reads to prior knowledge, as well as being more flexible.

## PORPE

After reviewing the research on summarization and the analytic essay, Simpson & others (1988) concluded that a more comprehensive study strategy, based on the metacognitive processes needed to regulate and oversee learning, is needed; a process in which the students are more involved in encoding and manipulating their own learning. The method they developed, PORPE, involves five steps: **Pre**dicting potential essay questions to guide subsequent study; **O**rganizing key ideas using their own words, structure, and methods; **R**ehearsing the key ideas; **P**racticing the recall of the key ideas in self-assigned writing tasks that require analytical thinking; and **E**valuating the completeness, accuracy, and appropriateness of their written product in terms of the original task, the self-predicted essay questions. These five steps build on each other and guide students through the processes necessary to read, study, and learn content area material.

In a study to determine the effectiveness of PORPE in a realistic college setting, the performance of students using PORPE was compared with a similar group of students who used writing in a more traditional and restrictive manner. It was hypothesized that PORPE students would make higher scores on both multiple-choice and essay exam questions and that the active involvement of the PORPE students would be reflected in measures of content, organization, and cohesion in their essays, and finally, that PORPE would increase delayed recognition and recall measures. The subjects were college freshmen enrolled in developmental reading/study strategy courses in two state universities, and the reading material was selected from an introductory psychology textbook. The control group received a series of short answer questions similar in style and format to those teachers frequently ask in classroom discussions and authors typically include at the end of each chapter. The experimental group was taught the PORPE method. The results showed that students trained in PORPE scored significantly better than those given questions to answer on both recall and recognition measures, and that their essay answers were better organized and more cohesive than students trained in answering questions.

For more information on PORPE, you'll want to read:

Simpson, M. L., Hayes, C. G., Stahl, N., Connor, R. T., & Weaver, D. (1988). An initial validation of a study strategy system. *Journal of Reading Behavior*, *XX*(2), 149-180.

Simpson, M. (1986). PORPE: A writing strategy for study and learning in the content areas. *Journal of Reading*, *29*(5), 407-414.

You might want to look at some other reading methods such as SMART and PLAN before deciding what's best for your class.

SMART encourages active reading by having students read a selection silently and then take turns being the instructor—asking each other questions. The instructor closes the book, asks students to ask each other questions, then another section is read and the roles reverse. When students can predict what the remaining text will be about, they finish on their own.

SMART—Estes, T., & Vaugh, J., Jr. (1985). *Reading and learning in the content classroom*. Boston: Allyn and Bacon.

The PLAN steps involve 1) PREDICT the content and structure of the text by making a map or diagram showing how the ideas relate to the reader's purpose. 2) LOCATE known and unknown information on the map by putting a check mark or a question mark by each point. This enables students to assess their prior knowledge. 3) ADD. This means that the reader adds words or phrases to the map to explain the concepts marked with question marks. 4) NOTE is the last step completed after the student has read the material and completes the map now that s/he has a better understanding of the content and how well it serves the reader's purpose.

Caverly, D.C., Mandeville, T., Nicholson, S. (1995). PLAN: A study-reading strategy for informational text. *Journal of Adolescent and Adult Literacy, 39* (3), 190-199.
(Note: There's a home page where developmental students can find out more about PLAN located at: http://www.schooledu.swt.edu/Dev.ed/PLAN/PLAN.teach

## ANNOTATING AND UNDERLINING TEXT

After looking at six study variables (annotating/underlining, recitation strategies, vocabulary, planning for tests, and lecture note format), Nist (1987) observed that the variable that was consistently correlated with test performance was annotating/underlining. Hypothesizing that the ability to mark a text well leads to a deeper understanding of the material, Nist investigated ways to teach students to improve their underlining skills. She found it easy to motivate students to work on this skill, as they normally underlined, and realized that it was something that they could apply quickly to their textbooks.

She found that weak students underline too much or fail to recognize key words and concepts. She taught them to activate prior knowledge, assess potentially important ideas by surveying, review class lectures, break learning into manageable chunks, monitor understanding, and formulate questions to guide reading. As all of these skills are involved in successful underlining, it is clear that it takes time, patience, an abundance of practice, and feedback from the teacher to improve. Nist recommends that students 1) throw away the yellow highlighters and use a pen so they can write in the margins, 2) think in terms of test preparation, 3) annotate during reading, 4) underline after reading and annotating, and 5) review annotations regularly. She emphasizes that underlining should be the last step, not the first step that students usually take.

Nist recommends that teachers should model the desired annotating behaviors for students. Explain why it's necessary to underline more than single words, allow time for practice with lengthy text, and give students feedback. In this way students can be trained to be selective and distinguish between important concepts and extraneous information.

## Reading/Study Methods for Specialized Textbooks (Medical and Legal Courses)

Hanau's Statement PIE (1972), a method for reading medical texts, requires readers to identify the Statement in a text or lecture and separate it from the PIE, which means classifying ideas into **P**roof, **I**nformation, and **E**xamples. Mayfield's FAIR (1977), a strategy for reading law cases, involves four steps: FAIR—**F** stands for Facts, **A** for Action taken in the case as well as action taken in the lower court, **I** for Issues the court is deciding and the court's holdings on these issues, and **R** for the court's Reasons for its decision. Students are instructed to write the appropriate letter in the margin as they are reading a law case and underline the appropriate word or phrase for a quick review later. I have known law students who discovered this technique for themselves and sailed through law school with minimal study, much to the consternation of their classmates, so I am delighted that it has been written down and is being taught to others who may not discover it unaided.

To help students master these methods, peers are often used as study skills counselors. Study skills programs have historically accepted student aides and trained them as peer counselors because of the large number of students who need skills help, the shortage of trained professionals, and the budgetary limitations that afflict most programs. Students respond well to peer helpers, and those who have completed the skills program themselves provide a convenient and motivated pool of applicants for peer-counseling training programs and part-time positions.

## Test-Taking Skills

To do well on an objective examination, students need good reading ability and vocabulary skills so that they can interpret the questions and recognize information and concepts stated differently than the way they are presented in textbooks and lectures. Essay examinations, in contrast, require that students recall information from reading and lectures, integrate, synthesize, and organize it, and express one's ideas well in writing. Although performance on the two kinds of examinations is correlated, some students excel on one kind and do poorly on the other. One way to help such a student is to review his/her completed examination paper (after it is graded by the instructor) and analyze the types of errors he/she makes (Maxwell, 1967).

Probably the best strategy for strengthening students' test taking skills is to simulate the test situation. In our center, students felt these practice test sessions were the most helpful part of the course that we offered to students preparing for graduate and professional school admissions tests.

Exercises that increase test-wiseness also improve test performance. Research suggests that the examinee's capacity to utilize the characteristics and format of the test or the test-taking situation to receive a high score is independent of his knowledge of the subject matter that the items purport to measure. Moore (1971) found that thirty to forty minutes of practice on different kinds of analogy questions significantly increased a group's performance over the performance of a group that did not practice. If it is possible to improve one's performance on analogy items through practice, it should be possible to improve one's scores on other types of items. (Note: If you still have old SRA Reading Cards around, they are excellent practice materials for preparing for standardized exams, whether for nursing boards or GRE exams.)

Some of the time-honored strategies that good students usually discover for themselves in preparing for exams have been supported by recent research. For example, when you begin an essay exam, taking time to plan your answer before you start writing improves grades. (Note: You can find other strategies in the study skills books listed in Appendix 10-3. One book that is particularly recommended is Gregory Galica's *The Blue Book*, New York: Harcourt Brace, 1991. Galica's book summarizes his experience in presenting workshops at the University of Wisconsin-Madison on how to write better essay exams.)

## How Do You Identify Students With Test Anxiety?

Students seem to have few qualms about discussing their test anxiety. If a program to alleviate test anxiety is advertised, students will volunteer, just as they frequently discuss their test fears with instructors, counselors, skills specialists, friends, or anyone who will listen. Instructors can identify exam-panic victims easily, even in large classes, for they turn in blank bluebooks. Learning-skills centers that administer checklists for students using their service find that a number of students will check test anxiety as a problem. In addition, there are a number of scales that purport to measure the degree to which test anxiety affects student performance, such as Alpert and Haber (1960), Liebert and Morris (1976), Mandler and Sarason (1952), Spielberger and others (1970), and Suinn (1969).

The two test-anxiety scales most often used in learning centers are Alpert and Haber's Achievement Anxiety Questionnaire (1960) and the STABS (Suinn Test Anxiety Behavior Scale, 1969). Alpert and Haber's questionnaire yields two measures of test anxiety—facilitating anxiety and debilitating anxiety—and is based on the hypothesis that anxiety is debilitating only to students who have learned a habitual class of interfering responses. Without these interfering responses, the authors believe, test anxiety leads to task-relevant responses and good performance. For example, the test contains items like "Anxiety helps me do a better job on an exam." (For more information about these tests, see Appendix 2-1.)

Exam anxiety can camouflage other problems, and academically weak students are just as susceptible to it as those with strong skills. In diagnosis, it is important to consider the paradigm presented in Figure 2-2 (Chapter Two), for the skills specialist needs to determine whether the student's anxiety is due to lack of study skills or basic reading inabilities or is a learned way of responding to evaluative situations or a condition precipitated by poor instruction. In my experience, the most pernicious cases of exam panic occur in students whose anxiety masks a deficiency in reading for inference, a deficiency in logical thinking, or a refusal to read material carefully. Controlled, intensive practice on the skills these students have avoided is necessary, for neither deep relaxation, desensitization, intensive therapy, nor tranquilizers will result in improved performance, though these treatments may reduce the anxiety felt about tests.

## Test Preparation Programs for Graduate and Professional Examinations

So intense is the competition among students applying for advanced training that most learning centers in senior colleges offer review courses to prepare for graduate and professional admissions exams. Review courses help students overcome anxiety, orient them to the types of problems on the test, and instruct them on how to use the answer sheet and how to break down difficult problems and solve them. Information on how the test will be scored and the meaning of standardized scores is also given, and students take a mock version of the test under timed conditions. Colleges offer their own review courses for two reasons: they reduce students' anxieties about the test, and they save students money, for the commercial test preparation programs are very expensive and of variable quality.

Because acceptance by graduate and professional schools is contingent on a student's passing admis-

sions examinations, and because competition for entrance is keen, many students enroll in special programs to prepare themselves for these tests. The claim by some test publishers that a preparatory course cannot significantly raise one's score has not discouraged applicants from enrolling in prep courses. Each student who has done poorly on the Law School Aptitude Test (LSAT) and plans to take it again, is convinced that he or she can beat the odds and become that one person out of 300 who will improve by 150 points. Also, there are an increasing number of studies that show that intensive, lengthy test preparation programs can result in higher scores (e.g., Whimbey and Whimbey's *Intelligence Can Be Taught*, 1975). Special programs to help students who have previously failed professional examinations, such as the national medical boards, are sometimes offered by learning centers like that at the University of Missouri-Kansas City. These may involve intensive review, self-concept improvement, and group therapy.

## Characteristics of High-Achieving Low Testers

The most pernicious and hardest-to-treat problems of test anxiety are found in those few students who have exceptionally high course grades but tend to fall apart when taking a standardized test.

Clark (1977) studied thirty-seven University of Maryland students who scored low on the LSAT, although they had distinguished academic, employment, and extracurricular records. The group included four Phi Beta Kappas, one Fulbright scholar, one candidate for Rhodes scholar, six officers of the student government, and others with high academic standing. Their mean LSAT score was at the 23rd percentile, and their mean SAT verbal and mathematical scores were also undistinguished (32nd and

34th percentiles); however, their GPAs were in the 89th percentile on the university's norms. Ten were women. The twenty-nine who were accepted into law school are performing well in a preliminary follow-up study.

Clark differentiates these academically superior "low testers" from "overachievers," students whose grades represent extreme painstaking struggle and who may be said to be performing academically above their potential. She (1977, pp. 18-19) lists a cluster of traits that describe the "genuine low tester."

1. He is academically superior but has consistently done poorly on standardized ability tests.

2. The motivation to study law amounts to an all-exclusive, long-lived passion. The student almost always feels there is no other career for him. Although he may have laid alternate plans, as the author [Clark] always tries to advise him to do, pursuing the alternate would be like going from first choice to last choice. He has always "known" he was going to be a lawyer since he first became aware he had a choice in the adult world.

3. He is usually rendered desperately anxious at the prospect of having to take the LSAT, often dreading it for his entire college career because of his shockingly bad performance on the PSAT and the SAT.

4. He has very rarely suffered any abnormal anxiety about his performance on tests in academic subjects. If there is something that can be studied and mastered, he can count on himself for superior performance, regardless of how difficult or how much preparation is required. Before the LSAT, however, there is nothing he can study; therefore, he feels the situation is out of control.

5. He is extremely competitive and has been so all his academic life, as far back sometimes as elementary school. He is a perfectionist with often impossible standards for his own performance. The fact that others do better than he on standardized ability tests sometimes "proves" to him not that there is something unrealistic about his attitude toward the test, but that the test is telling the truth: it is exposing him for what he really is; he really does not have the ability he needs; his superiority is a sham. The student is apt to react to all this self-generated pressure, in addition to the genuine pressure of the testing situation, with paralyzing anxiety and rigidity, which sometimes progresses to a kind of petrification in which no conscious anxiety is experienced, and the complaint is that concentration on that kind of problem is impossible or that the test is boring.

6. The "gamesmanship" aspect of the test, which is a very important component in high scores, eludes him. For instance, the same perfectionism which drives him academically and which may help make him into a top law student and lawyer, militates against his being able to choose the "right" answer to a mildly ambiguous question of the kind [the Educational Testing Service] (ETS) is so fond of asking in the rigid framework of multiple-choice. [Clark believes] that ETS is also testing for tolerance of ambiguity and unreality. This student cannot tolerate either in this situation. The test is very real to him. He is forced to guess the answer to a question that his less brilliant neighbor has answered "correctly" without even detecting the ambiguities involved. He wants to write "but on the other hand" in the margin on an answer sheet that is being graded by machine, and for him this is a genuine dilemma. Another important aspect of "gamesmanship" is being able to

abandon a question and go on to the next, since the score depends entirely on the number of correct answers. This student perseveres. He cannot abandon a question. In law school and in life, this same quality may be part of what makes him superior.

7. Most of these students, with one or two notable extroverted exceptions, are guarded and private people, well defended, socially adept (indeed, delightful), and helplessly ashamed of their performance on such tests. It is singularly difficult—in fact, has proved impossible—for this author to refer such a person to psychological counseling, which might help mitigate some of the unrealistic anxiety he experiences. He would not know what to say when he got there that he has not already said to himself, and he is completely, though in this area unrealistically, self-reliant. These "low testers" are at a classic and painful competitive disadvantage in the applications process, because all the low scores are permanently on their records. ETS describes them as one kind of "discrepant predictor." Since all the ETS "discrepant predictor" studies show that the low-score, high-grade group does not significantly break the pattern of LSAT validity on law school campuses, most admissions officers feel that no special attention need be paid to these students. In addition, the committee that admits a "low tester" has inevitably displaced one who had a better test score—sometimes with unpleasant consequences for the committee.

When confronted with a student with problems like those described above, learning-skills specialists should write a strong letter of recommendation to the professional school's admissions committee explaining the student's problem with tests. A former dean of admissions counseled admissions officers late in 1973 that such brilliant "low testers" are likely to add an important dimension to a law school and later to the legal profession itself, and added that if the LSAT score is the only negative factor in the admissions folder, "the probability of success may be high enough to mandate admission." Yet admissions committees cannot easily feel justified in reserving spaces for "low testers" when the pressure from other applicants is so great.

## WHAT CAN BE DONE ABOUT TEST ANXIETY?

Should exams, which cause students so much anguish, anxiety, and frustration, be abolished? Should all knowledge be arranged in small pieces and fed to students so success is assured if they complete enough steps and branches of a program? Are ease of learning and security in one's knowledge essential concomitants of successful learning? Or are there satisfactions and values to be gained from the struggles and uncertainties of the present examination system?

Ideally, testing should be a positive learning experience, one in which students recognize their goals, are assured of their knowledge, and feel competent. However, students rarely feel satisfied after taking final examinations or standardized tests. In fact, exams are dreaded and feared—or, at best, tolerated as an inevitable part of a college education. A few students, however, do view examinations as a challenge and a way to express their knowledge or pit their skills against the examiner. There are even students who write to the Educational Testing Service and describe what an ecstatic experience it was to take the Scholastic Assessment Test. Naturally, these are the people who do well on tests.

Many of us as students, however, have had the experience of suffering a bout of amnesia in the middle of an examination. This is a most frustrating experience indeed, especially when an hour or two after we turn in our bluebooks, the ideas we were struggling so hard to recall pop back into our heads.

Always endemic among college students, exam panic currently seems to be reaching epidemic proportions, judging from the number of programs offered by counseling and learning centers. It is therefore essential that anyone who works with college students be aware of its dynamics. First, it is important to realize that many students are genuinely afraid of failing, in fact paralyzed by anticipated failure. Not just underprepared college students who have failed in the past, but those who have excelled in school can also fear failure. Of course, our school system encourages this fear from the first grade on by reinforcing the idea that to be a worthwhile person, one must succeed in school. Unconsciously or consciously accepting society's values, thus equating one's worth with being bright and getting A's, sets the stage for continued frustrations as one ascends the educational ladder.

Students may rank in the top 5 percent of their high school graduating classes, yet find themselves in the middle ranks in college, earning B's and an occasional C. In graduate or professional schools, former straight-A students find themselves in competition with the top students from other colleges and may earn lower grades despite intensive study. A "B" average, to a former "A" student, can be more humiliating than an "F" to an average student, but such is the selective sieve we push our students through. As public colleges and professional schools implement affirmative action regulations and accept large numbers of educationally disadvantaged students, the struggle to maintain prior academic standards and, at the same time, prepare these students for high-level careers, places great stress on both the faculty and the disadvantaged students. Ironically, as undergraduates become accustomed to grade inflation, business concerns still pick the top students and put them through a highly competitive intensive training program where some fail and many drop out.

If students feel that grades reflect their self-worth and attach great significance to them—that is, equate failure with letting down family, friends, former teachers, or other significant persons—they will be susceptible to exam panic. Individuals handle this tendency in different ways. Some become superstrivers and fiercely compete, others suffer deepest despair, and some avoid situations in which they will be tested. Sometimes fear of failure is genuine, as in a student who has not prepared for the exam; sometimes it represents an overreaction, or what might be termed a neurotic anxiety. Freud stated that anxiety occurs in three forms. One is a free-floating general apprehensiveness, ready to attach itself for the time being to any new possibility that may arise—a condition he termed "expectant dread." Students with this type of apprehensiveness will undoubtedly be anxious about reading, homework, exams—anything that they feel represents a threat.

A second kind of anxiety is firmly attached to certain ideas. These ideas may have some connection with danger, but the anxiety felt toward them is greatly exaggerated. This Freud terms a phobia, and there are some students with exam phobias. Each time such students are faced with taking an exam, they have an anxiety attack. By developing a phobia, they protect themselves from the anxiety and either feel very uncomfortable during the exam or find an excuse to avoid taking it. Thus exam phobias externalize neurotic anxiety and protect the person's ego. If students panic each time they take a test by blanking out, then they will either avoid courses requiring exams and write reports instead, or drop out of school, thereby preserving their feelings of intellectual adequacy, since no one can discover their real intelligence or ability (or self-worth) if they suffer from text anxiety.

A third, more severe neurotic anxiety, similar to that which occurs in hysteria, may manifest itself as an attack or a condition that persists for some time, but always without any visible external danger sufficient to justify it.

Treatment for severe cases of text anxiety can be very difficult and can take a long time. Like some of Freud's anxious patients, the afflicted students express their subconscious sense of guilt in a negative reaction to therapy. If one gives a person a solution to a problem or symptom, one expects at least the temporary disappearance of the symptom, but this does not happen in these cases—the client gets worse! Even a few words of hope and encouragement may aggravate the condition. Thus one might conjecture that some students do not want to be "cured" of their exam phobia despite its painfulness and the handicap it creates for them. This observation leads to the diagnostic question, "What benefits or advantages accrue to students with exam panic? What do they gain from being helpless victims rather than masters of the test?"

College students who are secretly afraid that they do not have the intelligence ascribed to them by teachers and parents may refuse to put their full efforts into studying. Not studying gives them an excuse if they fail; if they had invested time and effort in studying, then failing would confirm that they were not really very bright. They protect themselves from this exigency by procrastinating, study-

ing too little and too late, developing myriad excuses for failing, or—if, despite all, they do pass—dismissing responsibility for their grade by saying that the test was easy. I once asked Peter, a Berkeley junior in physics who claimed that he had not had to study in college, whether he had ever failed a course. "Yes, once," he replied, "when I lost my math textbook the first week of the course. I looked for it the night before the final, and I'm sure that if I could have found it, I would have passed the course." Since Peter had lost his textbook, he had a convenient excuse for not studying and therefore did not lose face for failing.

Research findings on test anxiety provide some additional clues to the dynamics of test anxiety. Highly anxious test takers divide their attention between themselves (their own internal cues) and the task; they spend time doing things that are not related to the test. For example, they worry about how well they are doing, reread the same questions, ruminate over choices, notice where others are on the test, and observe that their peers are finishing faster. These superfluous activities guarantee poor performance on tests that require one's full attention.

Studies also suggest that test anxiety can be either facilitating or debilitating. It is facilitating when it results in students paying close attention to the test, but debilitating when students have learned responses that interfere with the task.

Supporting the idea that anxiety may have different effects on different individuals' performance is a study by Clark (1977), who asked students who had taken the LSAT, "What degree of anxiety did you consciously experience during the test? (1) very little; (2) noticeable; (3) considerable; (4) severe; (5) incapacitating." Students who made the highest scores described themselves as having been noticeably anxious, while those who made the lowest scores stated that they had been severely anxious, had been incapacitated by anxiety, or had felt very little anxiety. This last response suggests that some students with low scores felt numb during the test, suggesting a hysterical repression of anxiety. Or perhaps it means that they could relax because they knew they were flunking. If people who are anxious in the face of uncertainty ask themselves, "Will I pass the test or will I fail it?" then students who realize that they are doing poorly while they are taking the test will no longer be anxious because they know what the outcome will be.

When extremely test-anxious students are taking a test, they tend to spend so much time worrying about how well they are doing that they have trouble concentrating. They reprimand themselves with negative thoughts like, "I should have spent more time studying." Studies have also shown that they develop a kind of tunnel vision, a narrower attention to test cues, which leads them to overlook the important clues and misread key words. For example, a student recently failed an exam despite writing an excellent answer describing the ecological factors in the social development of certain animals. Unfortunately, the question asked for the evolutionary factors. Perhaps my poem will help those who have never experienced exam panic understand:

> *Test panic's a worm that erases the blackboard*
> *of my mind and writes, "Worry!"*
> *So I worry about those I'll let down.*
> *What will they say? What will they think?*
> *What will I do if I fail?*
> *Panic's now a python crushing my chest, gnawing my gut, turning my adam's apple to stone.*
> *While my bluebook waits, time runs.*

## TREATMENT METHODS

If your diagnostic attempts have eliminated inadequate study skills and poor reading as possible causes of exam panic, and you find that the student can perform adequately in the subject as long as tests are not involved, you may wish to consider using relaxation therapies.

Behavior therapists have tired of personally administering the relaxation instructions to each student and have tape-recorded relaxation suggestions. One can buy these tapes commercially or record one's own. If you make your own tape, find someone with a relaxing, soothing voice to make the recording. We used tapes for a number of years in our program and found that relaxation exercises were very helpful to some students, enabling them to relax enough to study or read. However, one should warn students not to fall asleep while listening to the tapes; otherwise some of them will. (Note: You'll find other suggestions for handling stress and anxiety in Girdano & Everly, (1979), Schirldi, (1988), and other study skills books in Appendix 10-3.)

Most published accounts of treating test-anxious subjects describe various systematic desensitization techniques and report reduction in self-reported measures of text anxiety. Sometimes practicing in a similar environment helps greatly. Like the occasional student who goes into an empty auditorium to practice delivering a speech in the real setting, we often administered practice tests to anxious students prior to their real exams and most Supplemental Instruction (SI) classes also use this technique.

Exam panic is a complex problem, and there have been many attempts to reduce its effects—individual and group counseling, lecturing, explaining the causes, behavior modification, relaxation therapy, and even Zen meditation. Students in group sessions often suggest activities they find relaxing—exercise (including swimming or other sports), drinking alcohol, sexual activity, smoking marijuana, and other stress-reducing activities not mentioned in study skills books.

Learning centers can take other steps to ameliorate the test anxiety problem, in addition to providing a strong study skills and test-taking skills program, by working with professors in improving examinations, and by encouraging professors to experiment with anxiety-reducing ways of administering tests. For example, administering exams on the computer where the student responds by indicating the letter of his answer on the keyboard and also his degree of certainty. If the student misses the item, she/he receives additional information about the concept on a projector, and gets a chance to try another question on the same material. This enables students to take the test whenever they feel ready and saves the professor valuable class time that would otherwise be spent giving the exam. Besides, the students receive their test results immediately after the test.

Another stress reducing technique is to train peer counselors to administer test-anxiety scales and help students use self-administered relaxation tapes or to establish a study table and panic clinic during exam week where commuter students can receive tutoring, study, snacks, and health care twenty-four hours a day, as Enright tried when she was directing a program at California State University-Northridge. Other programs rely on handouts on test taking skills with suggestions on how to avoid panic. (See Appendix 10-1 for an example of a Test-taking Handout.)

A word of warning: Few members of a campus community see their role as correcting the conditions that impose the stresses which result in test anxiety. However, there are a number of professionals who view test-anxiety reduction as their special province. These vary from campus to campus. Sometimes physicians in the student health service offer group relaxation training as a way of reducing the number of stress-generated illnesses they treat. Elsewhere, it is the counseling or psychiatric service that maintains that only it can offer test-anxiety help to students. On some campuses, test-anxiety reduction is assigned to learning-skills specialists, or student peer counselors may be briefly trained to work directly with test-anxious students. In initiating any program in test anxiety, it is vital for learning-skills staff members to determine which campus department or service claims this role, and if none does, then to take steps to gain the cooperation of counselors and other relevant professionals as the program is developed.

## CRAMMING

No discussion of exam panic is complete without mentioning cramming and the institutional procedures that create and perpetuate it. Cramming has been almost totally ignored by psychological researchers studying the learning process, and study skills manuals invariably admonish students that it is a poor way to study, citing research showing that lower retention results more from "massed practice" than from "distributed practice." Cramming is usually considered a cause of exam panic; yet it remains a student ritual engaged in by 97 percent of the students attending our most selective colleges (Sommer, 1968). Despite the discomfort associated with cramming, many students report that it is helpful and that they remember information better if they study intensely just before an examination.

Faculty members tend to view cramming as a natural result of student procrastination and the pressure students feel about earning grades. Students, however, report that cramming is most useful in courses that require considerable memorizing, particularly "Mickey Mouse" courses with multiple-choice examinations. Other reasons that students give for cramming include boring courses with poor teachers who give disorganized lectures, courses that require extensive outside reading, courses with no daily assignments and long intervals between tests, and courses in which the student has fallen behind in his work. (Note: Only one of these reasons involves the student's work habits; the others are a function of the course and the academic system.) Students report that cramming is least useful in courses that require thought, problem solving, or creativity or are very difficult (Sommer, 1968).

Exam week is a stressful period for college students, as evidenced both by self-reports and by observations. Men students wear old clothes and appear unkempt and unshaven; women take less care in their dress and appearance. Men students tend to eat less and lose weight; women report weight gains and delayed menstrual periods. Both sexes report sleep loss or problems in sleeping, worry more, are fatigued and nervous, and spend less time socializing. High-achieving students report less stress and fewer somatic disturbances, although they may cram too, but lower-achieving students more frequently have both stress symptoms and health problems during the exam period (Sommer, 1968).

The many "how to study" manuals that cajole, threaten, and lecture against cramming have not decreased the practice. Recent writers are starting to admit that cramming is an inevitable study strategy, are discussing it openly, and are even providing suggestions on "If you must cram, then . . ." (Wood, 1977). Some researchers, like Mumford & others

(1994), conclude that whether one's performance is enhanced by distributed versus massed practice depends on one's learning preference. This adds support to the arguments that students use to justify cramming.

High achievers usually have crammed for high school examinations and developed skills for doing it effectively. Underprepared students, particularly those who have studied rarely or not at all, have not mastered the art of cramming, and if they cram, they are more likely to develop symptoms—either physical or nervous—and do poorly on the exams.

If today's colleges demand anything of students, it is the ability to work under time pressure and against deadlines. Unfortunately, if academically weak students who have not developed regular study habits try to emulate students who are skilled at working under pressure and do well in courses when they cram, they will fail.

## SUMMARY

Some anxiety seems to be an essential precursor of learning. Freud suggests that even the more traumatic anxieties associated with examinations may serve a useful function in later life. In *The Interpretation of Dreams* he discusses at some length his recurring "examination dream" and notes that it occurred at times when he was anticipating performing a responsible task the next day, failure at which would bring him disgrace. He observed that he always dreamed about exams that he had passed brilliantly, never about ones he had failed. Hence, he interpreted the "examination dream" as a way of consoling himself that things would work out well. In effect, his preconscious mind was saying, "Don't be afraid of tomorrow; think of the anxiety you felt before your exam in history (for instance). Yet nothing happened to justify it, for now you are a doctor."

Perhaps the role of the learning-skills specialist can best be described as supporting students who are experiencing anxiety, reassuring them that it is normal to feel anxious about examinations, and helping them focus their attention on the test questions and the tasks entailed in preparing for the test. Further, one can help students avoid slipping so deeply into the quicksand of their own anxiety that they cannot function. We should not present them with an unrealistic model of the supercool, nonanxious genius. Surely, the force feeding of facts leads to boredom, indigestion, and regurgitation. There is no challenge or feeling of accomplishment unless one struggles to attain a goal, and struggling involves uncertainty and anxiety. Students show their contempt when courses are made too easy for them.

As for preventing cramming, students' suggestions are as valid as any I have heard from professionals. "Cramming doesn't work," they say, "when the course demands thought, problem solving, and creativity." Instructors take heed.

## REVERSING THE EXPECTATION OF FAILING

On the other side of the exam panic coin is the student who expects to fail and apparently is unwilling to do anything to change that expectation. For a long time educators believed that if marginal, at-risk students were exposed to the best teaching a college has to offer, they would do well. But experiments on control theory shows that this does not happen, for unless students feel that they have some control and can influence their environment, their capacity to learn from good instruction is limited. Students feel they lack control if they believe they cannot learn the subject or if there are unannounced tests, poorly organized lectures, unclear assignments, and other situations that they find difficult. However, research suggests that giving students with low perceived control feedback on individual aptitude items before a lecture temporarily altered their perceptions of control and improved their performance (Whimbey and Whimbey, 1977, Perry and Penner, 1990). Perry and Penner also studied the effects of attributional retraining, a therapeutic method for reinstating psychological control, which involved showing the class an 8-minute videotape of the professor recounting an instance when he was in college, and despite repeated failure, persisted because a friend urged him on. He eventually went on to complete his studies through graduate school. He encouraged students to attribute poor performance to lack of effort and good performance to ability and proper effort. Also the students were given a chance to improve aptitude scores with feedback. As a result of these brief interventions, students with external locus of control (i.e., those who place the blame for their failures on outside factors—teachers or exams) improved their performance on a test following a lecture, a test a week later, and on homework performance.

As I have said frequently, these studies give us clues about how to work with students who manage to fail despite our best efforts. Whether we are teaching courses or counseling students on skills, it is clear that it's not what we teach, but the way that we teach it—and the way students feel about their ability to learn it—that makes the difference in whether they learn.

## Materials and Books to Improve Study Skills

There are hundreds of study skills books and materials on the market, ranging from scholarly tomes to multimedia, activity based, self-instructional programs and computerized programs. For example, Walter Pauk's *How to Study in College* (1989) has remained one of the most popular manuals for decades. There are books to meet almost any need and learning style, and a quick glimpse at some of the titles suggests how styles have changed over the years. Whipple's *How to Study Effectively* was published in 1916, and before her work, books on increasing one's will power or developing self-control and on improving one's memory were popular. Some books stressed making studying easier; others tried to convince students that studying is difficult but able to be mastered. Among the books that were popular in the past were Smith's *Learning to Learn* (1961), Gilbert's *Study in Depth* (1966), *Use Your Head* (1974) and *Use Both Sides of Your Brain* (1976) written by Tony Buzan, a teacher of study skills courses on British television for open university students. One book that has maintained its popularity over many years and through many editions is Voeks' *On Becoming an Educated Person* (1970), a series of sensitive essays on adjusting to college.

Currently books range from shaping up one's instructors to explicit directions for reading different types of textbooks, preparing speeches and term papers with precise illustrations as to how one should approach these tasks, such as Wood's (1977) *College Reading and Study Skills* (I prefer the original title, *Some Ways to A's*). The book has a readability level of about ninth grade and should be helpful for community college students who are beginning academic programs.

## Customized Study Skills Books

Directors of study skills programs, especially those with high achieving students, sometimes find that books for the general student are not suitable and write their own manuals. An excellent example is *Academic Effectiveness: A Manual for Scholastic Success* at the United States Naval Academy by Eric D. Bowman (Kendall-Hunt Publishing Company, 1994). Bowman's book addresses the special needs of midshipmen and the high-stress culture of the Naval Academy and contains information and exercises about academics at the Naval Academy, personal goals and motivation, time management, note-taking, reading effectiveness, test taking, stress management, and a description of Academy student services. It also includes a chapter on how to avoid plagiarism including a definition and history of the concept, its relation to the honor code, and specific examples. Students will enjoy discussing the story of a Princeton University coed who was accused of plagiarism, judged guilty and prevented from graduating. She had quoted a number of passages verbatim from one source in her senior thesis without footnoting, although she had cited the reference.

(Note: You'll find a list of current study skills books and software sources on study skills in the Appendix.)

Exam panic and cheating (which is rampant, although we haven't mentioned it before) and the stressors which underlie them seem to be inevitable consequences of traditional lecture/exam teaching strategies. Whether the trend toward collaborative learning, shorter lectures with opportunity for feedback and discussion, using computers in the classroom, and other new teaching strategies will make these problems obsolete remains to be seen. But there is hope that exam panic and cheating will eventually become historical artifacts of an archaic college environment rather than daily issues to be confronted.

# CHAPTER 11

## DEVELOPING MATHEMATICAL SKILLS

The increasing need for college remedial courses in mathematics, prompted by the continuing decline in entering college students' mathematical ability, has been attributed to many factors. First, since the 60s colleges have offered calculus (traditionally a sophomore-level course) as the first general math course for liberal arts freshmen. Second, this curriculum change was followed by the recruitment of lower-ability minority and economically disadvantaged groups, many of whom lacked traditional college preparatory mathematics courses with a concomitant lowering of admission standards and prerequisite requirements. Thus, four-year colleges and universities accepted a different pool of students and lowered their entrance standards, but kept general calculus as their required freshman math courses. Third, the expansion of theoretical knowledge in mathematics and its rapid application to many academic disciplines and professions created a need for a larger proportion of college students to take mathematics and statistics courses. Fourth, the technological advances in computers and the resulting proliferation of data processing in all fields make it essential that college students have a more sophisticated understanding of mathematics. In addition, it is obvious that the reforms implemented in public schools over the past forty years have failed to improve the mathematics knowledge of high school graduates.

Hackworth (1994) points out that, traditionally, mathematics instructors have believed that if they provided better delivery systems, students would improve their learning of mathematics. But improved delivery systems are often ignored by the students who most need them. Regardless of what they have tried, students ignored better explanations and reverted to memorization and continued to fail. Professional associations in mathematics (both the Mathematical Association of America, and the National Council for the Teaching of Mathematics) have tried to change current teaching practices and encourage instructors to rely less on lectures and encourage more student involvement by trying alternative techniques, like cooperative learning or organized study groups, but these are not universal practices. In addition, it is most important that the perception of the public—that math learning requires memorization of rules and procedures without understanding—must change.

We'll discuss the latest standards for mathematics instruction a bit later in this chapter. However, even if the current proposed reforms are implemented successfully, it will take years for their effects to be noticed at the college level. There are too many generations of adults who don't understand how to learn mathematics and too few well-prepared students for most colleges to reject the weak. So experts predict that colleges will continue to need remedial courses in mathematics for years to come. In the meantime, more students are held for remedial mathematics than for poor reading or writing skills.

## Math Placement

Despite the fact that mathematics is considered to be an hierarchical subject (one must master the basics before one can advance to the advanced courses), and most experts agree that the consequences of "misplacement can be devastating to the student" (Akst and Hirsch, 1991), the standards for math placement seem to be vague indeed. In a review of the literature on mathematics placement, Akst and Hirsch describe four strategies colleges use in placing students in mathematics courses: 1) self-assessment—where students give themselves a take-home test and then decide what course to enroll in, 2) advisement—counselors make recommendations to the students, 3) mandatory placement—where the placement is binding based on test scores, and 4) modified mandatory placement—where students may obtain a waiver from a designated advisor. There is evidence that when the placement tests are appropriate and valid, mandatory placement results in remedial students attaining comparable persistence, math grades, and grade point averages to non-remedial students (New Jersey Basic Skills Council, 1988). In general, the authors conclude that whether mandatory placement should be considered in math courses depends on the validity of the test, the quality of advising, and the nature of the student population. (Some studies show that substantial numbers of students are misdiagnosed as underprepared and that other students who skipped the remedial course performed adequately in mainstream courses.)

Other factors that affect math placement include:
◊ math placements vary significantly from college to college—and there is no general consensus as to what skills are needed for which courses nor where cut scores should be drawn.

◊ most in-class math tests feature open-ended questions, while most math placement tests are multiple choice format. Hopefully, the College Entrance Exam Board's recently changed format, stressing both multiple-choice and open-ended questions, will open up new avenues for math placement testing.

◊ test administration—how the tests are administered also affects student scores and test validity. Speediness has received less attention in mathematics testing than in reading; however, it may be important. Using computer administered tests has the advantage of short test time, briefer tests, and more rapid scoring. Whether calculators should be used on placement tests is another issue (it appears to depend on how much computation is required on the test).

Akst and Hirsch (1991) conclude that mandatory testing and placement in mathematics is most common in colleges with large minority populations. Certainly the majority of states with mandatory college placement testing and required remedial courses for those who fail are in the South, although having difficulty mastering math is not just a problem facing minority students, for the majority of students enrolled in developmental college courses are white (Boylan and Bonham , 1992).

## Changes in Mathematics Education

The decline in mathematical ability is particularly interesting because, since the launching of Sputnik in the 1950s, mathematics has held an unprecedented favorable position in the public schools as a result of the technological competition between the United States and Russia. The National Science Foundation, other federal agencies, and private foundations have invested heavily in innovative mathematics programs, particularly in the elementary grades. Many large-scale efforts were made to reform the teaching of mathematics, reconstructing its scope and sequence through the introduction of set theory, the application of learning theories (particularly those of Bruner and Piaget), and a heavy emphasis on teacher training and the development of new classroom materials. Yet today, almost forty years later, mathematics teaching continues to be a focus of intense criticism as U.S. students at all levels continually score lower on tests of mathematics proficiency than their peers in other developed countries. Mathematics teaching continues to be described as excessively formal, deductively structured, and too theoretical. The diversity of textbooks, approaches, and teaching strategies that were called the new mathematics have been referred to as a vast array of patchwork programs, and the strategies that replaced them have not worked well either.

Inexpensive hand-held calculators, while not rendering computational skills completely obsolete, still require that students understand the logic and processes involved in making appropriate applications of mathematics and the ability to estimate. Despite the monies spent on innovative programs, surveys suggest that the way most elementary teachers teach mathematics has changed little, if at all, for over thirty years.

## Calculus as the Beginning Math Course

In the early 60s, many high schools revised their college preparatory programs, and students soon began entering college having completed more advanced math courses than their predecessors. State universities and selective colleges were able to drop their traditional remedial math courses and also abandon the college algebra, trigonometry, and analytic geometry sequence, which had been the freshman series. There were many well-qualified applicants, and those who were not prepared could easily be diverted to the junior colleges and state colleges that were changing from teachers' colleges to liberal arts institutions. Most state universities made general calculus the beginning freshman math course in the early 1960s, and it remains so today.

## Changing College Population

Toward the end of the 1960s, the same institutions that had changed their freshman math courses were admitting increasing numbers of educationally disadvantaged students, minority applicants, and women. These students not only lacked the intensive, theoretical college preparatory math courses, but generally came from high schools with very weak mathematics programs, and most had not been exposed to the new math. Entrance requirements were eased so that students could enter with only two years of high school math.

Minority students, with the exception of Asian-Americans, tend to perform poorly on mathematics tests and are less likely than white males to complete the full four years of college preparatory mathematics. Black students score lower on mathematics aptitude tests at both the elementary and secondary levels than on verbal tests. Puerto Rican students score lower on mathematics tests than on reasoning tests (Lesser, 1976, Stodolsky and Lesser, 1967). Black students and others from low socioeconomic backgrounds average 100 points lower on the SAT math section than white males and others from higher socioeconomic levels (Wirtz and others, 1977).

Women students share some of the same problems in math with ethnic minority students. Women have always averaged lower scores on college-level aptitude and achievement tests in mathematics than men. Although in elementary school there is little difference between boys' and girls' mathematics scores, in junior high girls' scores begin to drop, and by the time women enter college, their mathematical SAT scores average 50 points lower than men's.

Whatever the reason—social pressure, counselor's advice, or something else—women take fewer mathematics courses in high school than men. By not having taken enough mathematics in high school, women students are disqualified from fifteen out of twenty majors (or if they choose a major requiring mathematics, they have to take remedial mathematics). Lack of mathematics training and skills thus excludes women from entering many professions.

Many reasons have been given for the poor mathematics skills of girls, including early conditioning to believe that being good in math is unfeminine. High school counselors, who themselves are insecure about math, often discourage girls from taking math courses—so claim the feminists. (However, as a former counselor, I recall how very difficult it was to persuade young women to take math courses.) Teachers who do not care about math, dislike teaching it, and communicate passive attitudes toward it are part of the problem. The tendency to teach math, at least at the high school level, in rulebook form rather than presenting concepts and reasons is also listed as a cause.

Recent efforts to encourage women to take high school mathematics courses and elementary school math programs for girls may be having some effects, for 40 percent of the freshmen women entering college in 1976 had four years or more of high school mathematics, compared with 61 percent of the freshmen men (Admissions Testing Program of the College Entrance Examination Board, 1976, p. 13). However, even in national tests administered in the 90s, women's average mathematical SAT scores remain significantly lower than men's.

The reasons given to explain women's poor performance in mathematics tend to be psychological, while the poor performance of minority students in mathematics is attributed to weak schools, and it is clear that poor elementary and high schools continue to contribute to the need for affirmative action programs in colleges.

Women and minority students (whether men or women) share interests in social science majors and biology (if they have a scientific bent), and both these areas now generally require some training in mathematics or statistics. Many of the special fields that traditionally attract women and minority students have become mathematicized.

The rapid development of computers and of their applications in almost every field has created a greater need for mathematical skills. In fact, some experts claim that knowledge of computer algorithms has become the fourth basic "literacy" skill needed by college graduates. Mathematics will continue to be increasingly important as computer technology advances and its applications broaden.

So the problem is complex.

## SHOULD PRECALCULUS BE CLASSIFIED AS REMEDIAL?

As large numbers of students with minimal high school mathematics backgrounds continue to be accepted into college, the need for precalculus and prestatistics courses increased. I fail to see the logic of mathematicians who term these courses "remedial" when students are legitimately accepted into college without precalculus. How can one remediate students in a subject they have not studied before? If colleges and universities admit students without adequate preparation, it seems only reasonable that they should provide the necessary skills courses to prepare students for their courses. Indeed, this is what must be done, since few institutions today can restrict admission to well-prepared students. As the number of young, well-prepared high school graduates who choose to enter college declines, colleges will be compelled to accept a larger number of students with weak high school math preparation and offer remedial programs if the colleges themselves are to survive.

## How the Nature and Teaching of Mathematics Create Learning Problems

For most people, mathematics is a difficult, complex subject to learn. It requires the ability to think abstractly and analytically, to reason logically and deductively, to translate words into mathematical symbols, to manipulate these symbols to solve word problems, and to integrate this information and apply it to practical situations. To solve math problems, one must use disciplined and structured thought patterns, develop flexibility in translating between words, symbols, and pictures, understand their relations, and develop a conceptual framework of the processes involved.

Researchers who have reviewed studies based on Piaget's theory of intellectual development conclude that about 75 percent of the seventeen-year-olds and over half the college freshmen in this country have not reached the level of formal operations which is necessary to understand the abstract concepts required for modern college preparatory and college mathematics. One prerequisite for college mathematics is the ability to think precisely and logically, an ability many people apparently have not developed.

Another prerequisite is the ability to learn mathematical language. Learning the symbols and terminology of mathematics is one of the major problem areas students meet in trying to master mathematics. Richard Good of the University of Maryland summarized the problem well in a personal communication many years ago: "Much of the difficulty experienced by students in mathematics courses is not really mathematical in nature, but rather due to poor acquaintance with the language in general. We use language to communicate ideas. However well expressed the input of a student may be, it is futile if he is unwilling to realize the precision of the words he hears or reads. Vice versa, when he expresses himself, either orally or in writing, his careless or disorganized output will not convey his meaning satisfactorily."

Others question whether it is even possible to communicate mathematical ideas to the general public, since mathematics relies on terms with such precise, technical meanings and on such clearly defined concepts, while English and other languages owe their expressiveness to the ambiguity and changing meaning of their words and phrases. Translating mathematics into English has been described as being more difficult than translating Chinese poetry. Yet young children can learn both Chinese and mathematics.

Leonard Henkin in 1975, describing the linguistic factors that influence one's understanding of mathematics, agrees that there is extensive naming in mathematics, but notes that the basis of the logical operations in mathematics is the use of connective words—not, or, if, . . ., then, etc.—and that it is the concepts these words represent on which mathematics is based. Elementary school children do use these words in their speech normally but must be taught to think about their special implications for mathematics.

Critics of mathematics teachers have been strident and harsh. In 1968, in a statement at the conference of the Mathematical Association of America, Johntz said: "The reason there are so few mathematicians in the U.S. is that only a few people have been able to withstand from six to fourteen years of miserable mathematical education and come out of it with any interest at all. There is a prevalent myth which says that mathematical talent belongs to only a small percentage of the population. The truth is that it is extremely widespread among young children before they are corrupted. One source of corruption is rote learning promoted by textbooks which rigidify concepts based on one set of assumptions and teachers who suffer from ego—and are afraid of children's intellectual curiosity."

So elementary teachers have been attacked for being generalists who are intimidated by mathematics, and high school math teachers have been criticized for being weak in knowledge, rigid, and dull. In the 1950s and 1960s, it was hard to keep highly trained math teachers in public schools because there were excellent opportunities in industry, business, and government for people with mathematics training. Even though the economic situation has changed, I do not see that conditions will improve, because schools are facing reduced funding, classes are larger, and there is less opportunity for new, younger people to enter the field. Nor is there much incentive for teachers who are secure to change their teaching methods.

The negative effects of the current stagnation of math teachers are made worse by confusion about how mathematics should be taught. For two decades, math teachers have faced political and administrative pressures to make what the Conference Board of the Mathematical Sciences (1975) considers false choices between the old and the new in mathematics, skills and concepts, the concrete and the abstract, intuition and formalism, structure and problem solving, and induction and deduction. The board recommended that every mathematics program needs both, the balance between the two being determined by the goals of the program and by the nature, capabilities, and circumstances of the students and teachers in the program (Conference Board of the Mathematical Sciences, 1975, p. 137). Teachers would then be freed from the constraints of one method, approach, or book, and enabled to work directly with students, adapting to their special needs.

The board also recommended that mathematics curriculums include as essential features the maintenance of logical structure, the use of concrete experiences as an integral part of the acquisition of abstract ideas, the opportunity for students to apply mathematics in as wide a realm as possible, the development of familiarity with the use, formalities, and limitations of mathematical symbols, and the wider use of hand-held calculators and computers in secondary schools (1975, p. 138).

Although there have been many attempts to implement these ideas, the pressure for teachers to go "back to basics" probably constrains teachers even more than they have been in the past. Thus, we still have the same problems despite years of efforts to develop and implement teaching standards.

College mathematics professors have had their share of criticism also, but teaching is ignored in graduate training in mathematics, as it is in many other fields, and mathematicians have acquired a widespread reputation as casual teachers, which may be undeserved. In contrast to other disciplines, mathematicians do not usually specialize at the undergraduate level; therefore any well-trained mathematics instructor can teach any undergraduate course. This makes it easier to assemble a team of mathematics instructors to experiment in different ways of teaching. As a result, there were many innovative mathematics programs in the 1960s and 1970s; however, despite apparent initial successes, most have disappeared. What has happened is that instructors evolve back to traditional prototypes—good teaching and hard work.

## THE ISSUE OF PART-TIME INSTRUCTORS

Surveys of college developmental education programs show that the majority of courses in developmental mathematics are taught by part-time instructors. Part-time instructors usually have even less background in how to teach and need orientation, particularly if they are teaching at-risk college students. Although there are some published materials to help them such as the Mathematical Association of America's (1979) *College Mathematics: How to Teach It* and B. A. Resnick's (1985) *Chalking It Up: Advice to a New TA* (Random House, Cambridge), used frequently by adjunct instructor training programs, such programs are not universal. Studies that have been done on the differential success between full-time and part-time math instructors in community colleges show that although students earn higher grades from part-time instructors who teach remedial courses, they do less well in mainstream math courses than those who complete remedial courses taught by full-time math teachers. Since

most colleges are dependent on part-time instructors to teach remedial courses, and the need for inservice training is obvious, some have tried two-day workshops to orient new adjunct skills instructors.

For example, Kaiden and others (1992) describe a two-day workshop for new math instructors at Ramapo College (NJ). They were introduced to the college's philosophy and goals, provided with content area workshops, informed about the college's grading practices and instructional procedures, shown new instructional techniques including collaborative learning, the use of writing and vocabulary, and the use of technology in teaching math, and familiarized with the college's facilities and academic support services. It is obvious that colleges will not be able to dispense with part-time math instructors in the forseeable future, especially community colleges. The only solution seems to be to increase the inservice training they need. Finding adequate funding to do this poses a challenge to those who direct programs.

## IMPLICATIONS OF COGNITIVE PSYCHOLOGY FOR THE TEACHING OF MATH

As the psychology of learning and thinking has impacted on literacy teaching it has encouraged math, writing, and reading to be viewed as processes, not as a skill made up of logically arranged subskills that can be spoon fed to students in small doses to prepare them for rigorous college courses, as was often claimed in the 70s.

Claire E. Weinstein, professor of educational psychology at the University of Texas, stresses that instruction in any field must address the following three facets.

1. Skill – the language, techniques, facts, etc., of a subject.

2. Will – the attitudes and motivations which drive efforts to learn.

3. Management – the ability to make appropriate decisions for engaging in learning activities.

In addition, Weinstein outlines four areas that she claims are necessary and sufficient conditions for learning:

1. Create quality learning environments.
   (Hackworth points out that instructors teaching in colleges that were designed in the same architectural style as prisons have their work cut out for them.)

2. Process information correctly. Students need to know when to memorize (definitions, symbols, occasionally a rule) and when to reason (procedures, rules, problems).

3. Retain an active mind (or in other words, think).

4. Monitor comprehension. Self-evaluation is crucial in effective learning. (To encourage students to engage in metacognition, Hackworth suggests telling them that all learning of mathematics comprises two components: first, learning the subject and second, learning to what degree the subject has been learned.

Every aspect of the teaching of mathematics has been, or is being, subject to scrutiny, and what seems to be emerging is that many of our traditional ways of teaching, logical as they may have seemed in the past, are wrong. For example, Blais (1995) argues that the only really effective way to carry out remediation in mathematics is to get mathematically weak students to use their minds the way mathematical experts do. Researchers have identified how capable mathematics students think and the subtle abilities that underlie successful performance in mathematics. For example, failure to excel at mathematics may be due to the inability of the brain to develop appropriate selectivity. Blais argues that expert mathematical thinking depends on acquiring and using a variety of techniques to escape from or reduce the complexity of mathematical material so as not to exceed the brain's limitations for receiving and processing information. Excellent mathematics teaching, then, would involve teaching students to pay attention to the appropriate things and ignore the irrelevant. Rote memorizers who pay attention to the steps to follow because they believe that these are what leads to good grades and ignore the rationale behind the steps must be helped to attend to the relevant things.

Good mathematical thinkers are described as never getting involved with trivia and details and always being able to single out what is primary or basic. They can see common elements, look for the simplest way to reach a goal, and don't flounder on the exhausting struggle with detail that characterizes the incapable student.

What the most common approach to teaching math stresses is the opposite of good mathematical thinking; instead of teaching students to find the simplest way to approach a problem, teachers load poor learners with masses of details in their examples and explanations. Blais calls this throwing up a blizzard of information presented in an alien language while not showing them how to ignore most of the snow. Furthermore, to ensure that students think for themselves, teachers believe that the students should construct knowledge without help from the teacher—to be sure this may stop them from memorizing, but it does not promote good use of the mind. To improve weak students' mathematical thinking, one must help them change mathematics language into a more familiar language or material. This will minimize the burden placed on working memory (which is limited even in the most brilliant minds), and promote simplicity and clarity of thought. By telling what is involved in the art of knowing, and describing the conditions under which the mind works smoothly and efficiently, even very weak students can process mathematical material expertly.

Blais (1995) feels that much of the problem results from the fact that teachers generally do not understand what good mathematical thinking is.

## FEAR OF MATH

Whether it's because of poor teaching or something else, it is clear that many students learn to be afraid of math. This fear of math, rather than lack of ability, prevents them from pursuing careers that require math courses. Also students will go to great lengths to avoid studying math in college, even when it is essential to their career goals. I can recall students forty years ago who desperately majored in journalism, not because they were the least bit interested in writing but rather because journalism was the only major in the business college that did not require mathematics. Fears and anxieties about math have existed for generations, but today there is more concern and greater effort to reduce these negative attitudes.

Jacobs (1977) describes the approaches being tried to increase women's participation in the study of mathematics as reducing "math anxiety" and "math avoidance." In the math anxiety approach, self-selected individuals work through their negative attitudes toward mathematics in a group therapy setting, sharing their negative feelings. After the group session, the leaders (usually a counselor and a math instructor) help the participants use intuitive approaches to solving mathematical problems and feel more at ease with mathematics. For example, the Math Anxiety Clinic at Wesleyan College (Stent, 1977) offers supportive workshops, classes, a psychology lab, and individual counseling. Students enrolled in the program keep logs describing how they feel about homework and the class. Many of the students do not use the psychological services, but are interested in the course because they want to improve their grades on the Law School Admissions Test and the Graduate Record Examination.

Another example of programs to reduce anxiety is a private group therapy program, Mind Over Math, based in New York City. Two thirds of the clients were women with blocks about mathematics, and the techniques used were similar to those in the Wesleyan program—group therapy, efforts to demystify math, and practice.

A third approach—that is, treating the problem as math avoidance—is exemplified by the Wellesley College program, which does not include psychotherapy and is described as experimental rather than remedial (Stent, 1977). Students who have average mathematics ability are encouraged to take the course, which stresses instruction by supportive faculty members. The goal is to help women broaden their career options by learning math and to show them how mathematics is applied to other disciplines.

Recent studies on the affective factors in learning show that the tests used to measure mathematics anxiety and mathematics efficacy (confidence in one's ability to learn math) are highly correlated (Goolsby & others, 1988).

Self-efficacy or confidence in one's ability to learn a subject affects mathematics performance as it does in other disciplines. In a study of both male and female high school seniors, Ranhawa & others (March 1992) found that math self-efficacy is a mediator between math attitudes and math achievement. Goolsby & others (1988) looked at the attitudinal variables of mathematics anxiety, confidence in learning mathematics, teacher's perception of student as a learner of mathematics, and locus of control as predictors of math achievement in a college developmental course. They found that confidence in one's ability to learn mathematics was a better predictor of grades in developmental math than were high school grades and SAT-Q scores. Since, by definition, most college students taking developmental math in college have done poorly in high school, this leaves the developmental teacher with a quandary—how can one enable students to develop confidence in their ability to learn math when they have done poorly in the past. Goolsby and others suggest that these students can benefit from a less threatening class environment and a commitment to teaching excellence. Specifically, using individual tutoring, requiring that students keep a mathematics journal to teach study skills and analyze student progress, and seeing a counselor to reduce their anxiety toward mathematics through systematic desensitization and/or cognitive restructuring seem to work. Also, students are taught to be more assertive in asking for clarification or extra help.

Whether one calls it math anxiety, math avoidance, low self-efficacy, or just fear of math, it is a widespread problem that every tutoring or skills program will encounter and a major deterrent to completing self improvement programs in mathematics, even when good programs are available and the student knows she/he needs the skills. Providing a supportive environment as the student works on improving mathematics skills is essential, whether in a tutoring situation or a class.

Some books that address this problem are 1) Sally Wilding & Elizabeth Shearn's *Building Self-Confidence in Math: A Student Workbook, 2nd Ed.*, Kendall-Hunt Publishing Co., 2460 Kerper Blvd., Box 539, Dubuque, Iowa, 52004-0539, 2) Robert Hackworth's *Math Anxiety Reduction, 2nd Ed.*, H&H Publishing Co., 1231 Kapp Drive, Clearwater, FL 33765. Phone 800-366-4079, and 3) Sheila Tobias's *Overcoming Math Anxiety*. Boston, MA. Houghton Mifflin. (Note: A new edition of this book is in press from W.W. Norton and Co., Inc., NY.)

## MATHEMATICS IS DIFFICULT TO READ

Virtually all the college math courses offered in the U.S. today use textbooks where students find that not only the abstract symbols but the syntax and style of mathematical writing make them hard to read, particularly for the student who is a poor reader. Mathematicians themselves describe the books as being unreadable to the uninitiated, with concepts buried in such a complex context that students do not understand the context and cannot find the concepts. Such a textbook can be disastrous for a previously unsuccessful reader (Jason and others, 1977). Reading specialists, who are also concerned about the readability level of math textbooks, find that they often test four to six grades higher in difficulty than the students are able to understand. Although the traditional readability yardsticks (such as Flesch and Dale and Chall) are less relevant to mathematics texts than to those in other subjects, most reading experts agree that the nonredundant writing style and density of the abstract concepts in mathematics are difficult for students to grasp. There is an ongoing debate about whether it would be more desirable to rewrite the textbooks at an easier reading level or to try to improve students' abilities to read so that they can understand the texts. Or perhaps we need to do both.

## MATERIALS AND SOFTWARE

There are many textbooks, workbooks, and other learning aids to help students master mathematics—too many to try to list. Internet discussion groups are a good way to find out about what books and programs other instructors recommend, and there is also a computer-based program that contains reviews of developmental mathematics software (Project Synergy). See the Appendix for more information on this and suggestions on how to keep up to date.

For information on how to help students study mathematics, you'll want to read:

Hudspeth, M. C., and Hirsch, L. R. (1982). *Studying mathematics*. DuBuque, Iowa: Kendall/Hunt Publishing Company. (A brief booklet that outlines how to study math.)

Smith, R. M. (1991). *Mastering mathematics: How to be a great math student.* Wadsworth Publishing Company.

## TEACHING MATHEMATICS

Instructions in most mathematics books assume that the student knows what to look for in the problem and how to follow directions. Herber (1978) uses a somewhat different approach to teach students to solve mathematical word problems. He recommends that the student be given a reading guide rather than just being told to read to see what the problem asks him to find. Herber's reading guides are developed by the teacher to help the student comprehend at three levels: the literal level (what is actually stated—the facts), the interpretive level (what is meant—the mathematical concepts underlying the problem), and the applied level (the numbers involved in solving the problem and any previous knowledge or experience related to the task). The guide consists of a series of statements, not questions, at each level. The student shifts back and forth between the problem and the statements to determine which guide statements are facts that will help, which guide statements are ideas that are related to the problem, and which of the guide statements illustrate mathematical formulas that will lead to the answer. After the teacher has demonstrated how to use a guide with a related problem, students use the guide in small-group discussion sessions. Although this approach requires more work by the teacher in preparing the guides, it can be very effective in enhancing students' interest and learning. It shows them precisely how to do the problems, as well as how not to do them (for incorrect or irrelevant "facts" and concepts can be deliberately written into the guide).

Another problem-solving strategy is to think aloud. Reading experts have long observed that adults, when reading very difficult prose, read slowly and vocalize. However, talking to oneself may be viewed as strange behavior by teachers who scold pupils, "Read with your eyes, not your mouth," or tell them to "do the problem in your head." Ferguson (1974) found that encouraging disadvantaged students to participate orally in interpreting mathematical relations was an excellent technique for getting them to understand highly symbolic mathematical language. Similarly, Bloom and Broder, as early as 1950, found that one could produce better problem-solvers by having low achieving students solve problems aloud, explaining to them the ideal problem-solving approach and ensuring they recognized the difference between their approach and the ideal.

## Problem Solving

In analyzing the differences between good and poor problem solvers, Arthur Whimbey in the 70s found that poor problem solvers work too hastily, skip steps, lack the motivation to persist in analyzing the problem, reason carelessly, and fail to check their solutions. Good problem solvers are more active than poor ones: they visualize the idea, draw diagrams and scribble, talk to themselves, count on their fingers, and so on. Whimbey then developed materials and began to test students working in pairs. One student serves as listener and the other as problem solver who must solve the problem orally. The listener's role is to work actively with the problem solver and to check each step as the problem solver verbalizes it for accuracy and sense. The listener and the problem solver alternate roles as they work through Whimbey's exercises. When they agree that they have the solution to a problem, they look on the back of the page, which contains a description of each step and an explanation. If they have trouble with a problem, they can ask the teacher or a tutor for help.

Whimbey's materials are designed to help students develop the basic logic and problem-solving skills needed to learn basic courses in science and mathematics. His materials contain word problems, figures and verbal analogies, and problems in other formats traditionally used in intelligence tests. By going through the exercises step by step with a partner, students learn to solve word problems and other types of problems. Whimbey's materials are being widely used in courses in problem solving for academically weak students, but I have found that other students profit from them as well. Students thoroughly enjoy vocalizing their thoughts and working with a partner. Whimbey claims that students who complete these exercises show improvement on tests of scholastic aptitude as well as developing the analytic thinking skills needed for studying mathematics and science. For current references, see:

Whimbey, A., and Lochhead, J. (1990). *Problem solving & comprehension: A short course in analytical reasoning.* (2nd ed.). Hillsdale, NJ: Lawrence Erlbaum Associates, 365 Broadway, 07642. (800) 9BOOKS9.

Whimbey, A., and Lochhead, J. (1984). *Beyond problem solving & comprehension: An exploration of quantitative reasoning.* Hillsdale, NJ: Lawrence Erlbaum Associates, 365 Broadway, 07642. (800) 9BOOKS9.

Whimbey, A., and Lochhead, J. (1981). *Developing math skills: Computations, problem solving and basics for algebra.* New York: McGraw-Hill.

Jack Lochhead and Art Whimbey have also developed *MATH TRAC: Solution Reconstruction*, a form of text reconstruction to help students understand and write problem solutions in math and science. (For details, contact the Institute for TRAC Research, 3920 Avalon Rd., NW, Albuquerque, NM 87105 (505) 831-2654.)

Text reconstruction is described as helping students overcome two obstacles in learning math and science.

1. Many students do not accurately follow the reasoning (logical steps) or worked examples in textbooks.

2. Research by the National Assessment of Educational Progress indicates that many students have difficulty writing out the steps they use in solving problems. In the TRAC Model, students are presented with a problem and the steps to solve it are jumbled. Students copy the steps in logical order. Text reconstruction helps students become consciously and verbally aware of the steps used in solving sample problems,

and it engages them in actively pinpointing the operations involved in each step. Furthermore, the TRAC method can be applied to problems in physics, chemistry, etc., as well as mathematics.

Another very useful book describing ways to improve mathematics reasoning with cooperative learning, as well as other literacies, is by Arthur Whimbey, Mary H. Johnson, Eugene Williams, Sr., and Myra J. Linden called *Blueprint for Educational Change: Improving Reasoning, Literacies, and Science Achievement with Cooperative Learning* and is published by EBSCO Curriculum Materials, Box 486, Birmingham, AL 35201 (phone 800-633-8623).

The approaches of both Herber and Whimbey are consistent with current research and theory on the development of cognitive skills, in that they make explicit the steps a skilled learner uses in the process of solving problems. High achievers can make the inferential leaps from vague directions to the answer, but the weak student cannot. Both methods maximize learning for students whose preferred learning style is to talk and socialize. With these approaches they can do both and learn to think analytically.

## Using Writing in Math Courses

One of the ideas that has emerged out of metacognitive research is the idea of writing as discovery. It is based on the belief that students can discover their own thinking about topics, see relationships, and consider the validity of their own statements when they write them down. In other words, writing becomes the means for translating the strange into the familiar or the incomprehensible to understanding. According to Grossman & others (1993), this forms the rationale for applying writing as a way to learn mathematics; thus writing becomes a way of expressing what one knows, as well as a fundamental way to learn. The 1990 Mathematical Association of America's yearbook, *Using Writing to Teach Mathematics*, contains 31 articles describing how to use writing in mathematics courses ranging from algebra to calculus and statistics. As a result, having mathematics students keep journals or write up experiments is becoming a common teaching technique. Grossman & others (1993) experimented with 70 developmental math students taking an algebra course and found that the group who wrote about mathematical concepts were significantly better at solving mathematical problems. Writing about mathematics also correlated significantly with overall ability in math as shown by course grades.

To learn more about incorporating writing into math teaching you'll want to read:

Grossman, F. J., & others. (Fall 1993). Did you say "write" in mathematics class? *Journal of Developmental Education, 17*(1), 2-6, 35.

Mathematical Association of America. (1990). *Using writing to teach mathematics*. Washington, D.C.: The Mathematical Association of America.

Powell, A. B., Pierre, E., & Ramos, C. (1993). Researching, reading, and writing about writing to learn mathematics: Pedagogy and product. *Research & Teaching in Developmental Education, 10*(1) 95-110. (Note: This is an annotated bibliography developed by a mathematics professor and two of his developmental students who managed to demonstrate his thesis since both of the students are now in graduate school.)

## Other Approaches to Teaching Mathematics

Traditionally, lecture-discussion has been the most frequently used approach to teaching college mathematics. However, in the 70s, 40 percent of university mathematics departments also used large lectures and still do today. Individual tutoring is provided by most institutions but is more common in two-year colleges than in universities. Two-year colleges are more likely to use modularized delivery systems, mathematics labs, and mathematics teaching centers than four-year colleges and universities. Four-year colleges are more likely to offer mathematics courses as independent study programs than other types of colleges. Computer-assisted instruction and closed circuit television courses are also offered, but not extensively.

Math professors in two-year colleges tend to use the most varied materials. They use computer-assisted programs, slides, audiotapes, self-contained modules, demonstration models, and programmed materials more than math professors in four-year colleges and universities. In the past, a major difficulty of programmed learning for teaching underprepared students was that most of the students were weak in the reading skills that the programs required. When they cannot understand a problem or a set of instructions, they soon become frustrated and give up. However, when the materials are readable, are written at an appropriate level, and the students are tutored regularly or work in collaborative learning groups, disadvantaged students persist in mathematics courses longer than those enrolled in traditional or in completely self-paced courses (Carman, 1975, Treisman, 1985).

## Collaborative Learning Approaches

Collaborative learning approaches are an outgrowth of the self-paced calculus and pre-calculus courses that used the Personalized Self Improvement (PSI) model introduced in the 70s. The chance to work problems and discuss them with peers seems to be the most effective way for many students to learn mathematics, as many studies have confirmed. One should be warned, however, that collaborative learning techniques do not work well with all students—in fact, studies at the Air Force Academy have shown that highly competitive students do not like and do not do well in cooperative learning situations.

## Group Workshops in Learning Calculus

The person most responsible for the dissemination of ideas about group workshops (collaborative learning) in mathematics is Urie Treisman, whose doctoral dissertation involved why minorities flunked calculus at UC Berkeley. He learned that Asian students studied calculus in informal study groups, and decided to apply this same approach to Black and Chicano students who tended to study in isolation. In 1977 he created the Berkeley Mathematics Workshop, a kind of "honors program" for Blacks and other students to work on interesting and challenging calculus problems together. The result was that the grades of Black students studying in groups were dramatically higher than those who had previously studied alone (Garland, 1993). The keys to success of the group program include providing students with extraordinarily rich mathematical materials, a supportive community of other students, and good coaching. He cautions that another important factor in the program is mainstreaming the faculty (not relying on part-time instructors) and in re-creating the curriculum. Students enrolled in the "intensified" math sections do get extra credit. In the present Emerging Scholars Program (ESP) that he directs at the University of Texas Austin, students attend three hours of calculus lecture per week and 6 hours of group ESP work, for which they get two additional hours. Counseling, advising, and student support are integrated with the academic courses themselves, not off in some other part of the campus.

Treisman recommends that programs start with small groups of students and programs be customized to the needs of the institution. Although he concedes that similar programs have been adapted for biology and other science subjects, he emphasizes the importance of getting faculty support and involvement and the importance of rethinking and sometimes redesigning present curriculum.

At the University of Texas-Austin, over 85% of the minority ESP students enrolled in the ESP earn A's or B's in calculus, compared with fewer than one-third of minority students who received A's or B's in calculus historically. Also, the percentage of math majors who are ethnic minorities increased significantly from 2% to 25% in ten years. Treisman recommends that developmental educators forge partnerships with academic departments in the educational restructuring that is ahead (Garland, 1993). (See Chapter 7 for more information on collaborative learning.)

## Pre-Calculus Strategies

Although Urie Treisman has begun to apply group workshop procedures to pre-calculus courses, collaborative learning goes back a long way in math courses. Traditionally, graduate students have formed study groups in statistics where they worked together on problems (at least we did when I was in graduate school in the 40s). Furthermore, I know of at least one instance where the statistics professor died in the middle of the semester, but the graduate class continued meeting sans professor until the end of the term.

## Self-Paced Pre-Calculus

In the 1978 edition of this book I described the self-paced pre-calculus course at the University of California at Berkeley, which was helpful to students with very weak mathematical skills and those who were fearful of math. When instructors were well trained and committed to individualizing instruction, both students and teachers enjoyed the program. The Cummings Publishing Company's Series of Mathematical Modules were used, and students were encouraged to work on the problems in pairs and/or small groups; or if they preferred, they could work alone. Instructors appreciated the time it saved them in preparing for the class and gave them the opportunity to work individually with students. Before the self-paced course was offered, the learning center had a large demand for tutoring from students enrolled in precalculus. The self-paced course virtually eliminated the need for tutoring in precalculus, because the stronger students took the regular lecture-discussion courses, while those with weaker skills enrolled in the self-paced sections. Students who need very intensive help in basic math, particularly special-admissions students, may have difficulty with the self-paced course, but if they can get help from a tutor during class or can work with the instructor, they rarely need additional tutoring. Evaluations of the course showed that the weaker students performed better in the self-paced course and remained in the mathematics course sequence longer than equally weak students who take the regular lecture-discussion course. In addition, students with the poorest preparation in math were more likely to choose to enroll in the self-paced course.

For another description of a classic self-paced mathematics course at a community college, see:

Stine, C. W., Eugenie M., Trow, E. M., and Brown, B. (1979). Math X: Variable for student progress. *Journal of Developmental Education, 3*(1), 12-13.

## EVALUATING DEVELOPMENTAL MATH COURSES

Akst (1986) reported on a survey of 500 two- and four-year colleges having remedial math courses and found that about half had evaluated their programs, although there was great diversity in the approaches and strategies they used. Most of the colleges used locally built tests, and the most frequent evaluation measure was pre- and post-test score differences. Forty percent of the group used subsequent grades in mainstream math courses, comparing students who were remediated with those who had not been held for remedial courses.

Wepner (1987) used the latter method to study students enrolled in a remedial mathematics course. She found that not only did students' math skills improve on the post-test in both computational and algebraic concepts, but students completing the remedial course were as successful in passing mainstream courses as those who were not required to take remedial math. She admitted that although it was hard to pinpoint the specific elements that contributed to the course's success, it was probably a combination of

a.  appropriate placement of students in math classes,

b.  integration of peer tutoring into the instructional process,

c.  the use of Piagetian oriented instructional philosophy, and

d.  the instructors' commitment to the success of the remedial program.

Wepner's study used the New Jersey Basic Skills Placement Tests in basic arithmetic and algebra and was typical of the results reported by other colleges during the period when mandatory testing and placement was required at public colleges and universities in New Jersey.

## CURRENT TRENDS IN MAINSTREAM MATH TEACHING

Although some instructors were experimenting with teaching mathematics to underprepared engineering students in the 70s by combining counseling, traditional lectures, workshop sessions, and even cooperative learning, such efforts were relatively rare. Today, mathematics teaching is changing, and the newer strategies (combining technology, small group learning and other teaching techniques) are proving not only more effective in improving achievement, but also less expensive for mainstream courses as well as developmental ones. For example, Rensselaer Polytechnic Institute restructured its large introductory courses (including calculus) in 1993 by instituting an integrated introductory "studio" course format in place of large lectures. The studio format permits students to pursue many different paths to the same knowledge. The studio approach involves 50 or 60 students taught by one faculty member, with assistance from a graduate student and several undergraduates. Freshmen are linked through multimedia workstations and perform hands-on experiments in a cooperative learning environment. Faculty members circulate among students, leading discussions and responding to students' questions. The results are reported to be far better than were anticipated: not only has student attendance in introductory courses increased to an unprecedented 90 percent, but the university is projecting a savings of from $12,000 to $250,000 per course. Students satisfaction with the courses has also greatly increased.

## OTHER PROGRAMS USING TECHNOLOGY IN TEACHING MATH

Because mathematics instructors probably have greater access to computers than instructors in other disciplines, one would expect that computer-assisted instruction (CAI) would be popular in teaching basic mathematics. Certainly many CAI programs have been developed, tested, and disseminated. However, in 1976 a survey showed that only about 10 percent of the institutions used CAI to teach mathematics. Of the 424 mathematics modules listed in the Undergraduate Mathematics Applications Project Directory, only 3 were developed for CAI use. Thus, using the computer as a teaching device was not widespread.

However, the situation is changing and instructors have discovered other ways to help students learn with computers. For example, some instructors found a novel use for the computer to help students and instructors (who might get irritated or bored correcting the same errors by the same student over and over). One method was to design a diagnostic program that students can use when they cannot solve a problem or when they make an error. The computer retraces the student's work and helps him or her explore the methods used and locate the error, but it does not work the problem. Thus the computer functions as a diagnostic aid, not a teaching device, saving the student embarrassment and time.

The University of Arizona mathematics department's award-winning efforts to use computers to improve instruction, incorporating them into cooperative learning, group work, team teaching, and faculty support, is a recent example. Based on Dr. David Lovelock's statement, "Talking isn't teaching. Listening isn't learning," the department provides Special Purpose Computer Aided classrooms and an open-access lab which encourages one-to-one student-instructor interaction. The program has produced a twenty percent increase in the retention of math students, a significant increase in the number of students completing the math sequence in four semesters, and a doubling of the number of math majors, including a huge increase in Hispanic and female math majors.

H&H Publishing Company has also come up with an innovative combination of texts and the Internet. Using Hackworth's self-paced texts, ranging from basic arithmetic to trignometry, they offer students one-on-one mentoring using e-mail. When students encounter difficulty, they contact a math mentor and are instructed individually over the Internet.

The caveat regarding computer instruction seems to be that most students apparently learn better with a combination of teacher-student interaction, hands-on experience, collaborative learning or group discussion focused on real-life problems with computers as an aid. It seems that it's not what's on the computer that matters most, but rather using the computer as a tool rather than a teacher.

## INTERACTIVE VIDEO-BASED AND CD ROM PROGRAMS

Audio-tutorial or CD-ROM programs can also help the poor reader learn math by providing reinforcement through hearing.

Interactive video math programs are rapidly appearing on the market. Whereas in 1993 costs were quite high, this situation is changing as textbook companies publish textbooks and course materials on CD-ROM. For example, D.C. Heath (1-800-235-3565) recently released an Interactive Calculus program that contains a complete calculus textbook plus sound, graphics, supplementary articles, 200 animations and 20 videos for $74—*Calculus, Fifth Edition* by Roland E. Larsen, a mathematics professor at Pennsylvania State University—to mention just one.

A much more expensive program for basic arithmetic and algebra is the Videodisc Software called Interactive Mathematics I & II, *Arithmetic & Basic Algebra* which is published by Ferranti International Educational Systems Division, Suite 200, PO Box 4428, 3725 Electronics Way, Lancaster, PA 17604-4428. Phone: (717) 285-7151; FAX (717) 285-2721.

This program has helped students who are rusty or have gaps in their recall of math, or are math anxious, to review the subject and overcome their difficulties. Students like it because it puts math in real-life settings with each lesson presenting a scenario (like workers in a pizza factory figuring out a recipe), so it's useful for on-the-job math review for workers too. It doesn't talk down to students like some multi-media programs do, and those who use it say students stick with it.

One caution is that students who use this software need careful supervision, and it is recommended that they also work on improving math confidence and reducing math anxiety by using materials like the Wilding and Shearn or Hackworth books mentioned previously under math anxiety. There is also a description of sources for finding out about other math software in the Appendix.

## PAIRED COURSES

Pairing courses is another teaching strategy that deserves mention, although it is not often tried in developmental mathematics courses—at least not as often as in combining writing and reading with other subjects. Sometimes called team-taught courses, these are courses in which the same students are enrolled in both courses and the instructors coordinate their presentations. This is a very effective method if the instruction is well planned. It takes the onus off the skills course since the math work, for example, is integrated into and supports the chemistry course or other content course. I'd predict that we'll see more team taught or paired courses in the future.

## 1994 STANDARDS FOR INTRODUCTORY COLLEGE MATHEMATICS

The American Mathematical Association of Two-year Colleges released new standards for Introductory College Mathematics in 1994, setting new instructional guidelines for a course that serves the needs of more than half of college mathematics students. Starting from the premise that learning mathematics should be a joyous experience, the standards stress the need for mathematics to be meaningful, for students to actively participate in learning, the importance of using technology, and the need for increased participation by all students in mathematics—to increase their options in educational and career choices. Also emphasized is the importance of incorporating writing into mathematics teaching—through journals, portfolios, and lab reports—so that students are forced to think before they write, crystallizing in their minds the concepts studied and providing another way for students to communicate with others about mathematics. Some of the goals are impressive. For example, 1) to pass on to students the mathematical mind without the drill and manipulations, 2) to design the mathematics classroom as a mathematical community, where students and teachers are actively involved in creating their learning experience, and 3) to give students responsibility for their own learning by creating a new kind of classroom leadership that truly guides, encourages, and enlightens.

The authors of the new standards are realistic about the effects of these new challenges on teachers, whom they recognize must be helped to overcome the anxieties and frustrations associated with changing their roles and their teaching strategies, as well as the curriculum. For instance, collaborative learning, peer tutoring, and computer assisted instruction as supplements to traditional teaching will be encouraged. Hopefully instructors will recognize that these new strategies require preparation and professional judgment—not just letting students do their own thing. Since many of the college mathematics instructors are part-time or adjuncts, these changes will not come easily or quickly.

The Standards address some interesting issues in teaching college developmental mathematics. Specifically they state:

> *Remedial courses must be restructured for success, not simply as replicas of the high school experiences. Noting that there is a subtle, but critical difference between building a curriculum around students' needs and building it around their deficiencies, the authors recognize that implementing these strategies will require a fundamental change in teaching attitudes.*

## SUMMARY

The most frequent approach to teaching developmental mathematics seems to be well-designed modules and/or computer programs used with peer tutors or small collaborative learning groups. There is a trend toward smaller classes, asking students to keep writing journals and portfolios of their math experiences, more hands-on practice on realistic problems, as well as collaborative learning experiences. Paired or team taught courses are also breaking down some of the barriers between disciplines. Although some developmental instructors are using these techniques, they are still trends, and not universally accepted. Furthermore, although software is widely available, recent surveys suggest that less than 6 percent of college classrooms have the technological capability to offer the newest computerized interactive CD-ROM multimedia programs. Currently, experts are stressing the use of manipulatives in teaching basic math—an apparent revival of techniques that were popular in elementary school math classes in the 60s. More important, however, is the widespread acceptance that changing students' attitudes toward mathematics and making them more comfortable in the learning experience are vitally important in learning mathematics, as evidenced in the 1994 standards for teaching introductory college mathematics.

# CHAPTER 12

## INCREASING SCIENCE SKILLS

College students have always found science courses difficult and demanding, but today, learning science must be viewed in the context of the growing demand for scientific literacy, the rapid expansion of scientific knowledge, its increasing application to other disciplines, and a growing public disenchantment and disinterest in science. Although students are showing an increased interest in some science majors, particularly those focused on environmental issues and health-related fields, the dire prophecies of the National Science Foundation in the 80s that our country would soon face a shortage of scientists have not come to pass. Indeed, there is currently an oversupply of Ph.D.'s in physical science, as job openings have declined in academe, in research, and in industry. Recent defense cutbacks have further reduced grant funding that traditionally supported graduate students and beginning researchers. As a result, some research universities are restricting the number of students admitted to their graduate physics programs, smaller colleges are phasing out physics departments, while graduate programs on many campuses are increasingly filled by international students, and U.S. students pursue more lucrative non-science careers.

However, large enrollments remain the norm in freshman science courses, particularly in the physical sciences—a direct result of the expanding application of physical science to the "softer sciences," including biology and psychology. The creation of new fields like molecular biology, medical physics, and genetic counseling typifies this trend. Even mental-health majors may be required to take biochemistry courses. Moreover, the information explosion, which has virtually doubled scientific knowledge each decade, shows little sign of abating. As a result, freshman science courses require a higher degree of abstract thinking and problem-solving ability, the ability to synthesize and apply large amounts of information, and to perform more complex laboratory experiments than were typical in the past.

In addition, affirmative action efforts to attract minority and women students to physical science careers continue to bring underprepared students into science courses. Despite strong affirmative action efforts for over a decade, women and minority groups continue to be underrepresented in physical science and engineering majors, although both graduate and undergraduate programs aggressively recruit them.

Although scholarships are readily available for disadvantaged students who are interested in science, these students often lack the college preparatory courses in mathematics and science that college courses demand. Women and minority students (with the exception of Asian-Americans) still tend to get lower grades in high school science courses, take fewer science courses, and score lower on science achievement and mathematics tests at college entrance than do white males.

That this situation has not changed much since the 60s is shown in a 1994 study that reported that three-fourths of the college scholarships from the

National Academic for Science, Space and Technology were awarded to males. Receiving a scholarship was contingent on high school students' performance on the American College Testing Program Assessment, and this has caused the National Center for Fair and Open Testing to object to using test scores as the single criterion for awarding the scholarships as Congress had mandated.

## PROBLEMS IN LEARNING SCIENCE

How does learning science differ from learning other subjects? Perhaps Huxley's definition of science will clarify the difference between science learning and learning in other disciplines. Huxley wrote, *"Science is the reduction of the bewildering diversity of unique events to manageable uniformity with one of a number of symbol systems so as to control and organize unique events. Scientific observation is always a viewing of things through the refracting medium of a symbol system, and technological praxis is always the handling of things in ways that some symbol system has dictated. Education in science and technology is essentially education on the symbolic level"* (Huxley, 1962, p. 281).

To succeed in college science courses, students must be motivated to master the precise definitions of symbols and terms and the systematic problem-solving and laboratory procedures demanded by the professor. They must also think analytically, conceive abstractions, visualize the invisible, and understand and apply principles. For many students, science learning demands a much heavier investment of time and mental effort than is required in other courses. Students who have not had strong high school science courses must have persistence and a dogged determination to master college science courses. Unfortunately, our rigid college academic terms set time constraints on learning, which work against part-time students or those who learn more slowly. Often they become discouraged and drop the courses. Students from academically weak high schools and students returning to college after years of working find science courses especially difficult to learn. Others, who have expelled science and its tool, mathematics, from their personal universes, often find that they must take science courses to qualify for their chosen careers. They both need and demand intensive support services as they study basic college science courses.

## THE INFORMATION EXPLOSION

The information explosion in science has had major effects on college science courses. The sheer amount of information poses problems for textbook authors, instructors, and students. An organic-chemistry textbook in 1900 contained about 200 pages; in 1976 the same text required 1,500 pages (Haight, 1976). Wending one's way laboriously through such a lengthy and difficult text is a challenge for even the best-prepared and most highly motivated student.

Another illustration of the way scientific information has proliferated is that over two million organic compounds have been identified in the past 200 years, and the number of possible compounds is virtually infinite. Although there are systems for organizing this vast knowledge, mastering these systems requires both dedication, effort, and much time for the uninitiated.

## MASTERING TERMINOLOGY

Learning the symbol system and terminology accepted by scientists is analogous to learning a new language. The vocabulary in courses like biology is immense and requires a skilled memory. When students must learn a large number of terms, memorizing the glossary is not effective. Research suggests that students learn terms more readily from a chart that shows the relations among the terms. Providing such a chart is sometimes called "mapping" (Hanf, 1971) or presenting a "structured overview" (Ferguson, 1969). Although instructors sometimes present, or authors include, structured overviews that show the relations among terms in a discipline, students sometimes merely memorize the chart without understanding it. Research continues to suggest that students who draw their own maps after reading science material perform better on recall tests than students who are given the structured overview prepared by the teacher or the textbook author.

However, when there is a large amount of material for students to assimilate, it is very tempting for a teacher to organize and present a graphic model showing the relations among facts and terms. For instance, one of our chemistry tutors filled three chalkboards with small figures illustrating the interrelations among all of the major, and most of the minor, concepts in freshman chemistry. It was an impressive display of her ability to organize the material, but I doubt that it helped those students who felt that they had to memorize all of it. It may even have caused them to feel inadequate, since they were nearing the final exam and were unable to synthesize and relate the course information as successfully as she did. How much better it would have been for the group to fill in the map.

## VISUALIZATION SKILLS

The manuals written to improve students' study skills suggest that students should try to draw their own charts and graphs as well as studying those in their science texts. For example, physiology students are told to draw their own "visuals" of diagrams and anatomical charts. Researchers are confirming that the ability to visualize abstractions, such as molecules and atoms, and their relations is an important skill in learning science. Visualization skills are particularly needed in effective problem solving (Whimbey, 1976).

Historically, chemists have used three-dimensional models to help them visualize molecules. In the 1890s, the German chemist Baeyer stuck toothpicks into bread crumbs as he tried to visualize the shapes of sugar molecules. Today's chemistry instructors are more likely to use color-coded styrofoam balls weighted with buckshot. Prelog won a Nobel Prize for his system of assigning descriptors for specifying asymmetrical organic molecules. He devised a two-dimensional notation system for describing, assigning, and deciphering molecules as a substitute for the classical bulky, three-dimensional, tetrahedral figures (Prelog, 1976). To understand this choreography of molecules requires talent in visualizing from the two-dimensional sketches.

Besides the ability to visualize abstractions, college science increasingly requires sophisticated motor skills as equipment in laboratories becomes more complex. Programs have been developed to teach students to use compound optical microscopes and computer graphics, as well as other necessary technology.

## READING SKILLS

Students need strong reading skills to succeed in science. They need to be able to read flexibly (that is, to vary their rate and approach according to the relevance and difficulty of the material), to learn from graphic aids including charts, tables, and diagrams, to interpret and formulate questions, to read directions accurately, to evaluate scientific writing and draw conclusions, and, finally, to apply information from their reading to practical problems.

Reading experts generally agree that students have difficulty reading science because of the high density of facts and ideas. Science textbooks differ greatly from texts in subjects like social science and literature, where the writing style is more redundant and repetitious and fewer concepts are presented. For many years experts have been aware that poor reading habits are a major reason why students who are otherwise capable fail to understand science. They have attempted to teach them to use the study aids built into their textbooks, such as topic headings and glossaries, and to read less superficially. Science instructors should, but sometimes do not, analyze the steps of the scientific method to determine which reading skills are needed and then teach them. For instance, they should show students how to define a problem and how to determine its limits, how to collect evidence that bears on a problem, how to locate information that is appropriate to the problem, and how to integrate skills in order to construct hypotheses, test them, draw conclusions, and apply solutions. These skills are crucial to understanding science, but are rarely addressed in beginning science courses or in college developmental reading courses.

The readability level of college science textbooks has been a topic of great concern among college reading specialists, for the methods they use to determine the readability level of a book are designed in such a way that science books score as dull and difficult (and to students they usually are!). In addition, since most standardized reading tests do not reveal whether or, how well, students comprehend material in the sciences, other techniques must be devised to determine whether a given textbook is suitable for a class or for an individual student. Skills specialists (or the instructor) can construct simple, informal comprehension tests based on the text material. An even quicker and easier method is to construct a "cloze" test based on a passage from the text. To construct a cloze test, select a passage of about 200 words from the text, leave the first and last sentences intact, and delete every fifth word from the rest of the text. Give the passage to students with instructions to fill in the blanks. Students who supply the exact words in 50 to 70 percent of the blanks are able to learn from the text independently. When a student scores between 30 and 50 percent, the instructor should check to see whether the words supplied are synonyms of the deleted words; if they are not, the text may prove frustrating to the student. Under these circumstances, it would be best to assign an easier text or to provide intensive help with the concepts and terms. Students with scores under 30 percent should not take the course.

But it is not just the readability and the terminology of science textbooks that causes difficulty for students. Recent studies suggest that the way science concepts are organized in textbooks exacerbates the problem.

## HOW THE ORGANIZATION OF SCIENCE TEXTBOOKS INFLUENCES COMPREHENSION

DeLucas and Larkin (1990), in a study aptly sub-titled "Consider the particle p. . .," compared the rhetorical structure common to many mathematics and science texts (a proof-first structure) with an alternative organization that is more typical of expository writing—i.e., where the principle is stated first. For example, in science texts, the author may start a chapter by describing an atom and work up to a theory or principle. The researchers found that readers were more likely to recall the gist of the principle after a delay when they had read the principle-first texts. Furthermore, the amount of information recalled was greater, and more readers recalled the core-principle sentence after reading the principle-first rather than the proof-first texts. The investigators posited two main reasons for this: the serial position effect—i.e., more new information is presented at the beginning of the text in the proof-first structure—and the habitual perceptions of readers who expect the most important information to be presented first.

In other words, readers had more difficulty determining what was important when they read proof-first texts. When they summarized them, they reorganized proof-first texts into principle-first texts. Students who read the proof-first text also had more problems recalling the principle.

One implication of this study is that the traditional way of writing science texts (where the proof is given first) may penalize the novice reader who is uncertain about the importance of the information given in this sequence. Using the principle as a conceptual framework is typical of the thinking in many disciplines. Support for this as a reason for students' science reading is found in other research. For example, Sheila Tobias (1990) studied a group of liberal arts graduate students whom she asked to enroll in a basic freshman chemistry course and keep logs describing their experiences. They reported that a major frustration for them in reading chemistry texts was that the basic principles were not presented first and, unlike the way that material was organized rhetorically in their liberal arts reading materials, the chemistry text required them to infer the principle.

These studies suggest that we must either train students how to read proof-first materials, training them to reorganize to find the principle first (see DeLucas & Larkin (1988) for a description of strategies for comprehending scientific texts), or encourage science textbook authors to organize material with the principle stated first, especially when writing to a general audience of beginning students.

## TO READ SCIENCE YOU NEED STRONG VOCABULARY ACQUISITION SKILLS

Reading-skills specialists often see students who have been referred by their science instructors for help in vocabulary development, only to find that the vocabulary that the students lack is the specific terminology for the science course they are taking. In this situation, reading-skills specialists feel ill equipped for teaching the physics or biology terms which they think should be the instructor's task. The skills specialist must work both with the student, on general techniques for learning new terms, and with instructors, to help them learn effective ways to teach technical vocabulary.

The sequence of problem sets can make learning more difficult. In science, as in mathematics, many students have difficulty recognizing and applying the principles underlying the problems they are asked to solve. If a problem is stated in different words, or if the syntax is rearranged, students may not recognize it even if they have solved a half dozen similar problems successfully. The arrangement of problems in a chemistry text, for example, may make solving them harder. If the problems are arranged in random fashion, with easy items interspersed among difficult ones and with problems involving different principles mixed together, some students will have difficulty working them. Although Haight (1976) spoke contemptuously of programmed learning materials in chemistry, stating that chemists have taught with similar problem exercises in workbooks for over 200 years, an element of "let the student find his own way through the maze" is still implicit in the arrangement of problem sets in chemistry textbooks. Editors have told me that one of their most difficult tasks is to try to extract from authors an answer to the question, "Which of the problem sets are the most crucial for a student to master?" Authors usually answer, "All of them." Gradually, however, some authors of chemistry textbooks are adopting more cognitively appropriate principles in developing new teaching materials, such as the interactive computerized CD-ROM chemistry courses that also include a traditional textbook and audiovisual material.

Because so many students have difficulty with the underlying mathematical concepts and logic necessary for mastering college-level science courses, academic departments and learning centers sometimes offer special problem-solving pre-science courses and math review courses aimed specifically at the math skills needed to understand college chemistry and physics. In addition, many community colleges and some four-year colleges offer basic high school chemistry courses. Although chemistry review courses help a few students, I have found little evidence that these courses by themselves aid large numbers of students. The dropout rate in college science courses remains high, and fewer students complete the chemistry courses in proportion to the numbers who aspire to careers like medicine, where organic chemistry is the prerequisite of many required courses.

## SCIENCE ANXIETY

In addition to the cognitive reading and vocabulary difficulties inherent in science courses, attitudes and fear about taking science exacerbate students' difficulties. Some community colleges offer pre-science courses to help students reduce their anxiety and learn the basic academic skills science courses require. For example, Lansing Community College (MI) offers a natural science course to meet the science needs of the non-science major who plans to transfer to a four-year college, but found that 33% of the students failed to complete the course (Brown, 1995). In an effort to improve the student success rate, a Science Discovery Course was developed to teach the basics of the scientific method and to introduce students to scientific reasoning through hands-on experiences, as well as to teach them the study skills involved in learning science. The faculty developed a Science Inventory comprised of (a) items measuring the degree to which performing certain activities, like solving a mathematical story problem or interpreting a graph, was seen as stressful; (b) attitudes and fears about learning science; (c) a reading test based on passages from different sciences, a mathematics test, and some items on geography (needed in an earth science course). Students making low scores on the test were encouraged to take the Science Discovery Course. As a result of using the Science Inventory and referring students with low scores to the Science Discovery Course, follow-up studies showed significantly increased retention rates in the mainstream science course. For further information on science anxiety tests, you'll want to read:

Brown, M. H. (1995). Intervening for success with the underprepared college science student. *Research & Teaching in Developmental Education*, *11*(2), 71-78.

Mallow, J. (1986). *Science anxiety.* Clearwater, FL: H&H Publishing Company.

## CRITICISMS OF SCIENCE TEACHING

Chemistry remains the most difficult science course taken by a large number of students. Typically taught in large lecture sections that rely on television monitors so all can see, it is considered the main hurdle by prospective science majors and by students planning to enter health-related professions. In the 70s, Purdue University enrolled over 5,300 students in freshman chemistry each fall—probably the largest number of students enrolled in freshman chemistry of any U.S. college. The intrinsic difficulty of the course and the fact that, unlike many college courses, it has not been subject to grade inflation, explain why so many students have trouble with chemistry. If you picture the largest lecture hall on campus, packed with students listening to chemistry lectures, you can imagine how traumatic this course can be for the student who *feels* and/or *is* underprepared.

Instructors face a dilemma in planning and teaching large lecture courses in introductory science. Although most of the students enrolled have no intention of becoming research scientists, some will go on to graduate school as majors. Those in the former group will probably never perform a scientific experiment again. Instructors must acknowledge their needs as well as those of students who will become scientists. Most colleges have not completely resolved the question of whether there should be separate courses for nurses, dietitians, poetry majors, engineers, pre-meds, and others who do not plan to become chemistry majors. In many universities all students are required to take the same course, but some colleges offer chemistry courses without concepts from mathematics or physics. Other colleges consider these courses watered-down and inferior and refuse to accept them for transfer credit.

## INSTRUCTIONAL PROBLEMS

Science instructors have often been criticized for their emphasis on having students memorize predesigned experiments, which violates the authentic discovery process a scientist must endure in practice, when hours or even years of tedious work precede a discovery and breakthroughs come very rarely (Skinner, 1968). In short, scientific methods are rarely applied to teaching science, and the laboratory experiments required of students bear little relation to the work of the professional scientist. Hurd states it another way: "To teach only the findings of science is to teach an illusion of scientific knowledge." Yet these arguments are somewhat specious unless our objective is for everyone to become a research scientist, an idea that may have seemed the ideal goal in the 1950s and 1960s, when scientific opportunities were expanding and research funds seemed unlimited. Today, young scientists, like many other college graduates, are facing problems in finding appropriate employment, and science literacy among the general public seems to be declining.

What the critics do not acknowledge is that teaching the findings of science is a worthy and difficult objective in itself. Furthermore, it is a crucial need in an era when scientific issues have entered the political arena and citizens must weigh the differing opinions of scientific experts and vote on scientific issues.

As a result of the unending criticism, there have been many efforts to reform science teaching over the past three decades, but most reforms have been failures. They have not had any lasting effect on the problems. However, there are some signs that science instructors are moving away from the traditional descriptive approach in teaching, with its concomitant rote memorization, and they are placing greater emphasis on conceptualizing and on application of the scientific process—requiring students to generate hypotheses and view problems from more than one perspective. The difficulty they face is how to teach students these strategies—that is, how to get students from concrete operations to an understanding of the abstractions involved in scientific methods. Some educators proclaim that the majority of adults and adolescents have not attained the level of formal operations described by Piaget as essential to understanding the abstractions of scientific thought.

Others argue that thinking at the formal-operational level develops at different rates for people exposed to different disciplines, and that lack of exposure to scientific terminology and modes of thinking is an important factor in the problems students have in learning college science. Still others, who are not scientists, suggest that students' difficulties may be due not to inability to think in abstractions, but rather to lack of flexibility in shifting from the abstract to the concrete. This rigidity of thinking would make it difficult for the student to master chemistry and other sciences, in which shifts in thinking from abstract to concrete must be done frequently and quickly.

## Efforts to Change Science Teaching

Tobias (1992) points out that although over 300 studies aimed at reforming science education have been published over the past decade, there has been little lasting change in the way college sciences are taught. Undergraduates typically find "introductory physics and chemistry courses less than positive experiences for those who come to college with some talent and taste for science" (Tobias 1990).

In her latest book, she examines programs and courses that appear successful in terms of faculty accomplishments, students graduating and entering advanced study or the professional workplace, and where morale is high among both faculty and students. Using case studies, she describes what successful programs are doing in institutions ranging from the University of Wisconsin-Eau Claire, California State University at Los Angeles, Trinity College in San Antonio, and some of the nation's great research institutions including Harvard and the University of Michigan (Tobias, 1992).

Tobias concludes that the common elements in successful innovative programs include abandoning an exclusive emphasis on problem solving and modifying the lecture format to permit teaching of underlying concepts. Other important factors are persuading students to major in science, bringing more minority students into the field, or combining physics and different subfields of chemistry in different ways to promote better understanding.

What is clear from these descriptions is that improving science teaching is far from easy—too many earlier reforms were merely "quick fixes." In no institution did Tobias find that an outside idea—nor even an outside expert—was as vital in achieving high quality instruction as local initiative and control. Most of the changes that succeed and last are internally generated and internally paid for by the college itself, not by outside funding. This calls for rethinking the traditional reform model of external funding and, as Tobias insists, finding new ways to nurture departments and faculty who are committed to lasting change.

That institutional inertia is the most potent factor standing in the way of change—that is, new ideas and new teaching techniques are initially greeted enthusiastically but inevitably dissipate in a few years—reminds me of a book two sociologists wrote about UC Berkeley in the 60s aptly titled *Berkeley: Always Innovating, Never Changing*—a title equally appropriate for science teaching. Yet the search for an educational panacea continues as reformers suggest new curricular devices, course materials, and teaching enhancements as they have tried in the past, but these are minor variables in the factors that make science difficult to learn. What Tobias says hinders students in learning science are the pace, the conflicting purposes of the course (to weed out students, provide an introduction, lay a foundation for a research career, etc.), the exam design and grading practices, class size, unexplained assumptions and conventions, attitudes of their professors and fellow students, the almost exclusive presentation of information via the lecture, and the absence of a feeling of a learning community. These are factors that are rarely addressed by curriculum reformers.

There are successful innovations in teaching science, but new programs seem to involve only a small proportion of professors and students in any institution, and when the soft money dries up or the dedicated professor leaves the program ends. Some innovations that work are so time consuming and enervating for the professor that no one else cares to replicate them. On the other hand, some new approaches seem to be spreading, like jointly taught chemistry/math courses or physics/mathematics, but they involve relatively few students and few professors.

The most successful programs are designed by those whom Tobias calls first generation intellectuals (professors who were trained under the GI Bill or other scholarship programs and who are described as passionate teachers dedicated to encouraging students to become science majors). State and private four-year colleges without graduate programs tend to have more innovative programs that last. Also what works best is described as a process model rather than a research model.

Here are some examples of what exemplary programs are doing:

◊ Mathematics majors currently comprise about 10% of SUNY Potsdam's graduating seniors, compared with the national average of 2%, and more than half the freshmen at Potsdam elect to take calculus. What makes the difference is that the faculty is committed, students are warmly welcomed, and the department encourages effective teaching and provides a warm, caring environment for both students and faculty. Although instructors are free to chose their own teaching method, most stress process rather than content.

◊ The University of California at San Diego recruits and nurtures prospective chemistry majors from non-science students through a one year general chemistry course. It is taught by an outstanding lecturer who combines lectures and demonstrations with frequent reviews and labels the course parts with intriguing titles—The Periodic Table (1st quarter), Molecules and Reactions (2nd quarter), and The Chemistry of Life (3rd quarter). Another innovator is Case Western Reserve's Professor Robert Brown, who communicates daily and individually with each of 120 students in his physics class through e-mail.

◊ Undergraduates working as partners with professors on research projects is another way to produce more and better science majors, although this generally works better with chemistry undergraduates than with physics. In physics it is important that professors set up equivalent experiments rather than use students in "real" experiments.

◊   Professor Eric Mazur at Harvard encourages collaborative learning in a physics course where he gives several 15 minute lectures, each followed by a brief concept test which each student takes and then discusses with a small group of other students. Students retake the test after discussing it and indicate their level of certainty about the answer. This approach gives both the students and the professor information about how well students are learning.

◊   At Yakima Community College (WA) a biology teacher uses groups for informal review sessions, though each person works on assignments alone. Each member of the group may be called on for questions and the answer determines the grade for the whole group, thus ensuring that students see to it that all of the students in their group learn—an attempt to use cooperative learning in biology. In addition, half the course grade depends on students' scores on individual quizzes.

Undoubtedly, some of these innovations will last only as long as the motivated professors who started them continue to teach, for they take too much time and effort for most teachers to replicate (e.g., it takes a lot of time and effort to keep in touch with 160 students daily by e-mail). It will be interesting to see which strategies last.

Kenneth A. Bruffee (1993) argues that Tobias did not get to the heart of the problem—in other words, fine-tuning teaching is not enough. He explains that college students should be learning collaboratively how scientists confront the uncertainties and ambiguities of science, by collaboratively constructing, interpreting, manipulating, and calibrating scientific models and symbol systems. In other words, science students should be learning how to talk science with one another and write science to one another (p. 145). Bruffee attributes the decline in undergraduates who choose to major in science to the changing needs and hopes of intellectually talented students and proposes that the solution is not to make science courses more user-friendly, but to design courses that will hold the interest of intellectually more adventurous students. He insists that it's not the difficulty of science concepts that discourages bright students, but rather the rigidity of scientific orthodoxy and the beliefs one has to accept—e.g., facts are facts, and there is only one correct answer.

However, there is another indicator that science teaching may change, i.e., the proposed standards for science teaching for grades K-12. These standards stress inquiry-oriented classes filled with hands-on activities rather than lectures. They emphasize teaching more concepts, not just fact. Teacher training will also emphasize major structural changes such as stressing that teachers themselves must learn and continue to learn science through active investigation. Some high schools recognize the importance of teachers and researchers working together as partners and have already implemented cooperative research projects. The voluntary standards also specified the content to be achieved by all students.

The National Academy of Sciences, after many revisions, released a preliminary draft of its voluntary National Science Standards in December 1994. Focusing on concepts, not terms, the standards contain recommendations on the content of science courses from kindergarten through high school. Emphasizing that all of the understandings and abilities described in the standards should be achieved by all students, the document specifies, for example, that kindergartners to 4th graders should understand the life cycles of organisms—including birth, developing into adults, reproducing, and eventually dying.

5th to 8th graders should understand reproduction and heredity (i.e., the fact that reproduction is a characteristic of all living systems, that a new individual that develops from an egg and a sperm has an equal contribution of information from its mother and father, etc.) while 9th to 12th graders should understand the molecular basis of heredity (DNA, chromosomes, etc.). Similar goals are set for teaching other concepts such as geochemical cycles, causes of wind and weather, etc. The draft also addresses testing, saying that many different types of measures—even multiple-choice questions—may be appropriate but encourages teachers to develop exercises that involve students in real world experiences and require resourcefulness.

Gradually the barriers between subjects are beginning to break down as team taught courses bridging disciplines increase. High schools are now recognizing earth science as equivalent in importance to chemistry, biology and physics and are offering courses in earth systems that involve all four sciences. College courses seem slower to adapt to this new paradigm.

## PROGRAMS FOR IMPROVING SCIENCE SKILLS

Most learning-skills specialists, except those working in reading and study skills programs within engineering, medical, nursing, or other science-related professional schools, do not emphasize skills in science. They have instead focused on improving general study skills and reading in the social sciences and humanities. Perhaps they trusted students to transfer these skills to science, or, more likely, they felt unprepared to teach science skills, since few had formal training in science.

Recently, however, the number of learning centers offering assistance to science students has increased dramatically at both the undergraduate and graduate levels. Programs, particularly in large universities, are hiring science specialists or graduate students to supplement the standard instructional services provided by instructors and teaching assistants. Particularly in institutions where minority tutoring programs merged with reading and study skills services to become learning centers, services have expanded to include help in basic science courses and preparation for admissions examinations for medical school and other health-science professional schools. Increasingly, science tutoring and skills work are being offered by academic departments, who hire skills specialists to work with students and communicate directly with faculty members. Some, like the University of California at San Diego's chemistry department, have hired tenured lecturers to coordinate general chemistry courses, develop new ones, train TAs, and generally be an "instructional trouble shooter." In other departments, these lecturers may work directly with students, train tutors and SI leaders, and perform many of the functions of learning assistance specialists.

## EFFECTIVENESS OF STUDY SKILLS PROGRAMS IN SCIENCE

Although many researchers have tried to evaluate the effectiveness of general study skills programs on science achievement in the past, most have failed to find positive results. The paucity of results may spring from the problems in designing appropriate experiments and also from the assumptions underlying the studies. For instance, if one assumes that a program of a few weeks' duration will yield significant grade improvement, one is ignoring the fact that students need time to practice and to internalize new skills. If students are concurrently enrolled in a demanding science course, they must master a large amount of information in the same short period when they are changing their learning skills. The criteria used in some studies militate against obtaining positive results, especially when the dependent variable is change in overall GPA or in course grades during the same term.

Another factor that makes it difficult to show results is that a large percentage of the grades given in a science class are C's, and if grade improvement is used as the criterion, it is hard to demonstrate statistically that improvement has occurred as a result of a brief study skills program. For instance, the spread of points between a low C and a high C is greater than that between a high C and a B, so that students could conceivably improve substantially during the course but still receive a grade of C.

The earlier studies focused on the skills that seem logical, such as textbook reading and notetaking, and used materials that were related to the students' texts but easier. Current studies are focusing on the specific cognitive skills necessary to learn the actual course material and devising ways to explain and demonstrate these skills explicitly. As a result, these studies more often demonstrate that students show significant learning gains.

## RESULTS OF RECENT STUDIES ON SCIENCE LEARNING

More recent studies, especially in physics, are focusing on the cognitive processes involved in learning science.

## PHYSICS

Larkin and Reif (1976) trained students in a general physics course to understand various relations in physics, including interpreting without confusion the symbols in the relation and identifying the situations in which the relation could be applied. (A very simple example of such a relation is summarized by the equation $d = st$, which describes the distance $d$ traveled during a time $t$ by a particle moving with constant speed $s$ along a straight path.) The students studied textbook descriptions and answered questions requiring them to demonstrate the specific abilities necessary to apply the relations. They were asked to state the relation, give an example of its application, list the properties of the quantities in the relation, interpret the relation by using information in various symbolic representations, make discriminations and comparisons, and use the relation to form other relations. Larkin and Reif found that the explicit description of a learning skill—in this case, understanding quantitative relations—is useful even without associated training in the skill, since the description can be used as a goal toward which both instructors and students can work. Further, they conclude that providing direct instruction in a quantitative skill is a reliable way to help students become independent learners. Students taught with Larkin and Reif's system learned more from their textbooks than students in an intensive self-paced physics course. In addition, students taught to understand and apply relations in physics were able to transfer this skill to concepts in a completely different field (inventory turnover in cost accounting). Larkin and Reif achieved their goal of training students to understand text material as well as an experienced reader does—one who reads with selective attention and remembers essential information. Basic learning skills of this type, which would have direct application to the improvement of students' learning and instructors' strategies, must be identified in other disciplines. (See also Whimbey and Barbarena, 1977, on physics skills.)

## ADJUNCT SKILLS CLASSES

Two early attempts to integrate reading and study skills programs directly into the content of college classes were those by Tomlinson and Green (1976) and Tomlinson and others (1974). In these studies, the reading skills students need to understand basic college biology were analyzed. The investigators then offered an adjunct skills course designed to follow the course content and to teach the skills as they were needed. The subjects were volunteers who scored low on the biology midterm examination and enrolled in the adjunct course for the rest of the term, remaining in the biology class as well. The skills taught included surveying, mapping biology concepts, analyzing text material for comprehension, systematic vocabulary study including using context clues and analyzing Latin and Greek roots, understanding graphs and diagrams, and developing self-questioning strategies at the literal, interpretive, and integrative levels. (See Figure 12-1 for an overview of the skills taught and their relation

## FIGURE 12-1. ANALYSIS OF THE SCIENCE READING TASK
Outline of the task analysis done while planning this unit on science reading.
Roman numerals represent the lessons in which the basic teaching of the various skills took place.

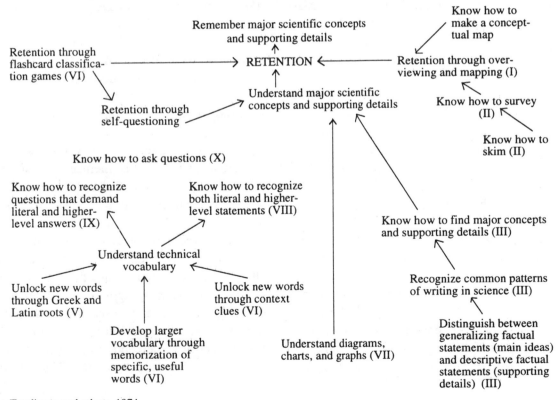

*Source*: Tomlinson and others, 1974.

to the sequence of lessons). Study skills specialists attended the biology lectures and worked closely with the professor. Students taking the experimental adjunct skills course made significant improvement in their biology exams, including the final. They also retained their gains over the next quarter's course in biology, and they persisted in the freshman biology sequence longer than control subjects.

We have long known that it is more effective, particularly for the academically weak student, to learn the skills needed for a particular science course in an adjunct skills course or to have the instructor integrate the skills directly into the course than to take a general "how to study" course, which assumes that students can adapt and transfer the skills learned to their mainstream classes. However, recent studies lend even stronger support to the idea that course related skills programs are superior. Mary Dimon (1981) in describing the results of six years experience with adjunct skills courses states that ". . . adjunct courses work because they have a definable purpose, function as a support group, challenge students, promote participation, are flexible, and do what they say they do. . ." Although some problems still remain in this fairly new form of supplemental instruction, it holds promise for today's college students because it helps them to succeed.

## Supplemental Instruction

The most widely used teaching approach to adjunct skills courses in the sciences is Supplemental Instruction (SI), a structured course-related skills program developed by Deanna Martin at the University of Missouri-Kansas City in the mid-70s. Representatives of more than 300 colleges have attended the UM-KC certified SI training sessions, and follow-up data on the effects of SI programs on students' grades have been collected systematically in each college implementing the program.

Essentially, the SI program involves training SI Supervisors who, in turn, select and train student SI Leaders to conduct skills classes paralleling the parent course. The SI Leader attends class with the students, modeling and demonstrating ways to learn the material and leading discussions on the topics. Thus SI is a form of collaborative learning. The parent courses are selected from high risk courses— that is, where the grading policy is tough and many students earn D's and F's. Obviously, science courses often fit this model and have been connected with SI since its inception.

The founders of SI argue that the SI model is a politically sound model for higher education because it does not compromise academic standards, but instead supports the fair, yet challenging teaching of professors in rigorous disciplines. Faculty support is integral to the success of the SI model and methods of securing and acknowledging faculty support are emphasized throughout the three-day training workshop used to disseminate the UM-KC SI model to professionals who wish to implement the model. After all, an SI Leader is hired only with the endorsement of the faculty member who teaches the targeted course, and the SI Leader attends class sessions with the approval of that faculty member.

Furthermore, the SI Leader and the SI Supervisor ask the faculty member to encourage students to attend SI sessions and ask for the faculty member's assistance in planning appropriate SI sessions. Interestingly, for cooperating faculty, the SI model both improves student learning and also raises the student's positive perception of the faculty member who helped offer the SI support (Blanc, DeBuhr & Martin, 1983).

The latest change in SI is Videotaped Supplementary Instruction in which regular lectures are videotaped by a professor, and the videotape is shown in an SI session where the leader and students can stop the tape at any time or rewind it and discuss it. This technique has been found to be particularly effective with underprepared students who are weak in note-taking and test taking skills, but has also been used successfully in the past with engineering extension courses. (For more details on SI, see Chapter 6.)

## COLLABORATIVE LEARNING

Certainly SI and Adjunct Skills classes encourage students to learn and study with one another in groups, an effective teaching strategy in many subjects. However, collaborative learning and group discussions are not effective ways to communicate large amounts of information to naive students, as those who have tried to completely abolish lectures in science courses have found. Even Harvard students enrolled in a combination physics/chemistry course that had no lectures but only group discussions had much difficulty mastering the course material (Tobias 1992). However, incorporating collaborative learning strategies into class lecture sections, or as additions to the course, can be extremely valuable to students. (See Chapter 6 for more information on collaborative learning.)

## COMPUTER-ASSISTED INSTRUCTION

Although there are some excellent science programs written in the CAI format, the computer as an instructional tool is still not used as widely as the early enthusiasts predicted. However, now the increased availability of hardware at modest prices, the rapid growth of Internet, and the development of multimedia software at a more rapid pace is bringing computer services into many college classrooms.

Faculty acceptance is increasing, although we have a long way to go to convince the more reluctant faculty members, who may be computer-phobes themselves, of the advantages of using computers. In the 70s, experimental CAI programs tended to be abandoned as soon as the grant funding that supported them ran out, and as a result, it became increasingly hard to obtain grant funding to install CAI programs. However, in the 90s, as more students bring their own PC's to college and most faculty have access to computers, the situation is different, and new developments in multimedia and CD-ROM programs promise the radical changes in instruction for which we have waited so long. Hopefully, the needed software will be developed and include incentives for students to interact with one another about the material they are learning.

However, even with the most expensive and elaborate CAI programs (such as the PLATO Chemistry Program developed by Stanley Smith of the University of Illinois), which were ingeniously designed to make learning chemistry exciting and fun, evaluations showed that students who worked on computer programs had more favorable attitudes toward chemistry but did not learn more than students in traditional chemistry classes. The differences in achievement between the two groups were no greater than those usually found between classes taught by different instructors. We've yet to find studies that show that learning via computer is superior to learning in traditional classrooms. I suspect that we won't until software is developed that includes group interactive activities.

## Computer-Managed Instruction (CMI)

Another way the computer helps students learn science is CMI, in which the computer keeps a record of the student's progress, test results, and work completed. For instance, Purdue University's Chemistry Resources Center uses CMI to individualize instruction for the more than 5,000 students who enroll in freshman chemistry. After students are tested each week, the computer analyzes their scores and prints a detailed program sheet for each student, delineating the concepts they need to work on. This gives the tutors and teaching assistants information on which to base their work with the student. With so many students and with a large collection of materials and media for students to use, the center finds that the computer is a necessary tool for arranging for students to find and use the appropriate materials.

## Tutoring

Tutoring is probably the most frequently used method for aiding low-achieving students in science courses. When getting tutoring is easy, tutoring attracts large numbers of students. Drop-in tutoring and group tutoring seem to be the most popular arrangement for working with underprepared students, particularly in the physical sciences. But as we discussed in Chapter 3, tutors need training and careful supervision.

In addition to providing encouragement and support to struggling students, science tutors clarify concepts and problems. Their major function, I believe, is to help students determine which facts and concepts are not important to learn in the vast amount of material presented in lectures, laboratories, and textbooks.

If student tutors are carefully selected and well trained, they help underachieving students remain in college longer. (See Chapter 3 for more detailed information on tutor selection and training.) Tutoring also improves the tutors' knowledge in science. However, demonstrating that tutees improve their grades is more difficult.

## What Does a Successful Science Program for Minority Students Require?

The studies of the 70s on the retention of minority students in engineering have implications for programs for other low-achieving students as well, and they reflect the importance of designing programs that have both cognitive and affective components. The Retention Task Force found that the lower graduation rate for minority students in engineering (54.8% compared with 77.8% for non-minority students) was caused by:

◊ insufficient preparation in mathematics and the physical sciences.

◊ inadequate motivation toward engineering as a career.

◊ lack of adequate financial resources.

◊ absence of self-confidence, which is closely tied to poor preparation in math and science.

◊ personal or family problems, which often interfere with the academic performance of minority students.

◊ excessive occupation with social and nonacademic activities, which demand so much of a student's time that studies are neglected. (However, organizations of minority engineering students appear to affect retention rate positively and offer students an opportunity to gain professional identity and peer support.)

Certain characteristics of engineering programs were found to stimulate higher retention rates among minority students, and many of these are equally important today:

◊ The programs have well-integrated and coordinated components and provide a variety of services to better serve the needs of a diverse student body.

◊ Although most programs do not change radically from one year to the next, the most successful ones evolve constantly by identifying the successes and failures of previous years and integrating them into future planning.

◊ Programs operating within the engineering college are generally more effective than university-based programs in providing career guidance, academic counseling, tutoring, and similar services.

◊ Effective personal counseling is an important component of minority retention programs. The need for such counseling appears to be greater at predominantly white private colleges than at black colleges.

◊ Tutoring by minority upperclassmen has proved an effective means of encouraging freshmen and sophomores at many colleges.

◊ Most predominantly black engineering colleges have a critical need for larger staffs. Increasing the number of staff members in administration, tutoring, and counseling almost always improves the quality of the academic services.

◊ Many colleges in the Southwest need more Hispanic staff and faculty members to serve as role models for their large concentrations of Hispanic students.

◊ Personal interactions of students with instructors and staff members should be encouraged. The more time that minority students spend with college representatives, and the richer the quality of their interactions, the more successful the students have been in the engineering programs.

◊ Retention programs should be flexible enough to meet the needs of individual students. The broadly varying needs and abilities of minority engineering students will demand correspondingly varying degrees and forms of assistance.

Among the variables that account for retention, and that institutions can control, most critics agree that admission criteria and the quality of support services are the most important.

A final finding was that a part-time job, unless directly related to coursework, may adversely affect a student's performance, depending on the student's academic ability and dedication.

If minority students are admitted whose academic preparation is weaker than is typical of the general student body, effective, comprehensive support programs are needed. The number of minority students needed in each entering class to achieve "critical mass" for providing enough intra- and interclass support should be determined. The Retention Task Force report also stresses the importance of demonstrating sincere institutional commitment if retention rates are to be improved. In particular, the faculty should be flexible with regard to course scheduling and placement during the freshman year to allow for the possibility of inadequate academic preparation. Furthermore, if the instructors overemphasize theoretical concepts, they will present "notorious" problems for engineering students and provide added difficulties for unprepared minority students.

## ABILITY TO COPE WITH RACISM IMPORTANT SURVIVAL ATTRIBUTE

Recent research suggests that the ability to cope with racism characterizes successful black students who enroll in institutions where the student body is predominantly white. An excellent illustration of this is Yvonne S. Thornton's 1995 book, *The Ditchdigger's Daughters* (Carol Publishing Co.), the story of a Black New Jersey family. The father worked as a ditchdigger and the mother, a maid, as they raised six daughters determined that they would become doctors. Two of them overcame the odds of racism and sexism and became doctors, attesting to the importance of the family's single-minded devotion, support, and insistence that their children learn to confront the harsh realities of life in the 50s.

Today there are many comprehensive programs that encourage and support minority students planning careers in science, mathematics, and engineering. Most select students in the eighth grade or sooner and provide meetings, field trips, summer courses and work experience, tutoring, and counseling. Programs like MESA offer strong social support systems for minority disadvantaged students from their junior high school years through college, through graduate school, and into their professional careers. At each stage, students become role models and helpers for younger people entering the program. In addition, the students themselves monitor one another's progress as they advance. The various student services are integrated, and the program elicits strong faculty support.

## IMPORTANCE OF COUNSELING, GUIDANCE AND MENTORING

A recent analysis of NIH and NSF programs to increase minority enrollment in the sciences sug-gested that a major problem in attracting minority students, especially black students to science programs in majority institutions, was in counseling, guidance, and mentoring during their freshman and sophomore years, when they are making career decisions. In fact, many college educators believe that successful retention practices must begin as early as elementary school. Precollege preparation (retention of requisite skills) is being addressed in science minority retention programs, as are exposure to college life, the integration of social and academic life, and the development of coping strategies and study skills. For some examples of what programs are currently doing to improve minority retention, you'll want to read:

Fiedler, P. P., & Godwin, M. A. (Spring 1994). Retaining African-American students through the freshman seminar. *Journal of Developmental Education, 17*(3), 34-40. Tells how the University of South Carolina's Freshman Seminar Program has been adapted to address the needs of African-American students and its success over a decade.

Kluepfel, G. A., Parelius, R. J., & Roberts, G. (Spring 1994). Involving faculty in retention. *Journal of Developmental Education, 17*(3), 26-27. Describes the Rutgers University Gateway Program that gives incentives to academic departments to develop their own retention programs and developmental courses that satisfy the departmental criteria for regular, credited coursework and has resulted in large increases in graduation rates for minority students in engineering and other areas.

Robert, E. R., & Thompson, G. (Spring 1994). Learning assistance and the success of underprepared students at Berkeley. *Journal of Developmental Education, 17*(3), 4-15. Focuses on the contributions of the Summer Bridge program and the Student Learning Center services offered to students enrolled under affirmative action goals to increase minority student graduation rates at UC Berkeley.

Roueche, J. E., & Roueche, S. D. (1993). *Between a rock and a hard place: The at risk student in the open-door college.* Washington, D.C.: Community College Press (American Association of Community Colleges). Presents a thorough review of the issues, problems, and programs of open-admissions policies and courses for high-risk students.

Simmons, R. (Spring 1994). Precollege programs: A contributing factor to university student retention. *Journal of Developmental Education, 17*(3), 42-45. Describes the University of Virginia's programs to provide academic and social integration and hands-on experience to entering minority students in engineering through the Research Assistantship Program, the Summer Transition Program, and the Introduction to Engineering Program.

## Materials for Improving Science Skills

In contrast to the number of publications on improving general college reading and study skills, the number of books on how to study science are limited (although some study skills manuals include a chapter on science). Often staff create their own programs such as the handbook Watanabe and Gordon (1977) designed for students in freshman chemistry at Berkeley. (The Appendix reproduces excerpts from this booklet which contains a do-it-yourself diagnostic test to evaluate a student's readiness for freshman chemistry, suggestions on how to prepare for each lecture, how to listen and take notes, how to read the text, how to use the laboratory, and a list of places around the campus where students can get additional help.)

If you are interested in improving students' reading, writing, and critical thinking skills in science through cooperative learning, you'll want to read this how-to teach handbook:

Whimbey, A., Johnson, M. H., Williams E., & Linden, M. J. (1991). *Blueprint for educational change: Improving reasoning, literacies, and science achievement with cooperative learning*. EBSCO Curriculum Materials, Box 486, Birmingham, LA 35201. 1-800-633-8623.

## Caveats in Selecting Materials

There are a vast number of modules and special programs to help students learn virtually every basic concept in lower-division science courses. These aids come in many forms—from programmed learning, tape-and-slide presentations, audiotutorials, and videotapes, to CD-ROMS, interactive video programs, films, and workbooks. One has a wide choice of materials since they are written on many levels, ranging from chemistry programs that do not even assume that students know how to divide, to those that are most rigorous and assume that students have a strong high school background in chemistry and mathematics.

In selecting supplementary materials, one must consider the level of the course and the background of the students. Science courses vary greatly from institution to institution, although all cover the same general concepts. An aspiring beauty operator, enrolled in a community college course to review chemistry in order to pass the state licensing examination in cosmetology, is working at a different level than the anxious pre-med in a university chemistry course, although each may find learning chemistry difficult. The audiovisual aids and other materials that are useful for the community college student struggling with chemistry for cosmetology are usually far too simple for the pre-med student. Science courses vary also in the way the topics are sequenced, in their scope and depth, and in their philosophy. These features depend on the professor and the textbook. For example, if Professor Snodgrass does not lecture on Concept A until the fifth week of the term but does introduce Process C in the third week, a videotaped explanation containing both Concept A and Process C may confuse students, unless they are alerted to the difference between the tape and the professor's lectures. In selecting computer software, try to make sure that the program does more than a photographed book or a videotaped lecture. To be maximally useful to students, it should be interactive. Test out the product with students and/or consult with other programs who are using it.

Indeed, selecting from the many supplementary materials published for college science courses that would be most appropriate for students in a given course can be a lengthy process. David Caverly and Bill Broderick write a regular column in the *Journal of Developmental Education* that will help you keep up to date on sources for current computer software. For example, in the Fall of 1993, they discussed how to find the best programs in these categories: interactive tutorial, simulation, drill-and-practice, or customizing courseware. (See Appendix for the sources they suggest.) Reading their column is a good way to keep up in an ever changing field.

### USE INTERNET GROUPS TO EXCHANGE IDEAS ABOUT MATERIALS

Let me also add that getting on an e-mail discussion group like LRNASST or a science group is another excellent way to exchange ideas about materials, find out about what others use and what works best with their students.

The learning assistance center may help instructors select and/or evaluate media and materials, and/or it may function as a place where students use the aids. If learning center staff members have the responsibility for purchasing materials in science, they need input from science instructors on what should be included in their collection.

(Note: Faculty members have very strong viewpoints on what will help their students, as I once learned when an instructor threatened to come over to the center and burn some workbooks I thought would benefit students.)

## COMPREHENSIVE PROGRAMS

As I have stated in other chapters, the success of an academic support service in aiding underprepared or underachieving students does not depend on the quality of the individual services alone, whether they be outstanding instructional programs, tutoring, counseling, or skills help. What it does depend on is the extent to which the various support programs are well coordinated with one another and with instruction. Science is not an exception. The programs that work best are comprehensive, coordinated, integrated, and involve the student in many services.

Nevertheless, I have found no compelling evidence in the research to suggest that science instructors should abolish their traditional lecture-laboratory teaching approach. However, there are many ways to improve the delivery of science information through lectures and laboratory sessions—including classroom assessment techniques, collaborative learning sessions, etc., but the programs and strategies described to help underprepared students succeed in science courses are designed to supplement, not replace, the lecture-lab teaching paradigm.

## SUMMARY

The intrinsic difficulty of college science courses, which use abstract concepts, unfamiliar symbol systems, and technical vocabulary, poses special problems for the motivated but underprepared college student. The situation is exacerbated by the pace at which these courses are taught, the amount of information covered in traditional semester or quarter courses, and the over reliance on lecture/ laboratory methods used. Currently, many colleges offer a variety of programs ranging from computers to audiovisual aids to help students learn science. These are usually accompanied by tutoring from carefully selected and trained peers. But the adjunct skills/Supplemental Instruction paradigm is the one type of program that has been able to consistently demonstrate its value in improving science learning. As is true for other skills, the science skills programs that are most effective are comprehensive, coordinated programs in which tutoring, skills assistance, counseling, and social support groups are integrated into the course instruction, and the instructor encourages and motivates students.

# CHAPTER 13

## EVALUATING LEARNING SERVICES AND COURSES

Over the past three decades, a voluminous literature on educational evaluation procedures has been published, and in this era of educational accountability there is great pressure on new programs to provide evidence of their value and long-range effects. Yet the truth is that colleges and universities rarely undertake systematic evaluation programs that are not mandated by government grants, outside funding sources, or regional or national accreditation boards, and even these sometimes are very cursory. In 1975 Ball and Anderson stated that most government departments and private industrial and commercial enterprises were receiving some sort of evaluation, but that colleges rarely indulged in formal program evaluation, and that continues to be true today. Indeed, instructional programs rated as innovative in colleges and universities rarely use rigorous, analytical evaluation procedures even when evaluation is required as a condition for program funding. The most frequent problems encountered in using evaluation results have been evaluating the effectiveness of new programs, developing cost effective evaluation measures, and interpreting the results of the assessments. Recent national surveys such as the EXXON Study (Boylan and Bonham, 1992) and the USOE Study (Black and others, 1991) show that systematic evaluation is still rare in developmental skills programs today.

Traditionally, evaluation has not been an integral part of academic decision making in colleges and universities. However, in times of budget cutbacks and re-engineering efforts, it is helpful to have the results of a comprehensive evaluation to defend your program, although by then, it is too late to start an evaluation. When campus-wide budget cuts are pending, having evidence of your program's value to students may not save it, but not having information about evaluation will certainly be in your detriment.

Institution-wide accreditation reviews occur every ten years, and these usually require intensive self-studies by each department and follow-up visits by teams of external evaluators who write reports and make recommendations. Developmental skills and learning assistance programs are not exempt from these efforts. The professional standards developed by the Council for the Advancement of Standards (CAS), *Standards and Guidelines for Learning Assistance Programs* (see Appendix), and the *NADE Self-Evaluation Guides* for Adjunct Skills Programs, Tutoring Services, Developmental Courses, and Teaching and Learning (published by H&H Publishing, 1994) should be particularly useful to learning assistance and developmental education programs struggling in this process. The questions and guidelines are custom-designed for learning assistance programs.

Many people fear evaluation, especially when it is imposed from the outside. Before undertaking an evaluation, it is important to get commitment from the people involved in the program. They should agree that evaluation and improvement of the service should be a regular, ongoing part of its operation. To do this, focus on the positive—the gains that can accrue, the recognition of successful programs and individuals, the opportunity to strengthen the weaker aspects of the program. And be sure to develop a way to use the results in making decisions, solving problems, continuing and strengthening strong services. The goal of the evaluation should be to promote academic excellence by focusing on student outcomes, performance and positive improvement. Then the evaluation process itself should undergo evaluation so that it can be improved in future years (McClure, 1988).

In other words, the purpose of evaluation should be to help people and programs improve, and it is a necessary tool for managerial decision-making. Evaluation requires the involvement of everyone who is concerned with and contributes to the program.

## Planning an Evaluation Study

In planning an evaluation study for a skills program, one should be very clear about why it is being done. Certainly evaluation studies can yield information used to make more effective in-house decisions and improve a program, but often the evaluation questions are asked by the campus administration or faculty. Ball states that evaluation studies have six basic functions: 1) to contribute to decisions about installing programs, 2) to contribute to decisions about program continuation, expansion or contraction, and accreditation, 3) to contribute to decisions about program modification, 4) to obtain evidence favoring a program to rally support, 5) to obtain evidence against a program to rally opposition, and 6) to contribute to new knowledge. Ball cautions that one should first consider the appropriateness of the program to be evaluated before planning studies that may contribute to new knowledge. In other words, studies that might be acceptable as

doctoral dissertations may not be appropriate program evaluations. For example, one might design a study to identify the differences in body language between Black and Chicano clients; such a study might contribute to new knowledge but have little direct application to the program under investigation. If however, one studied the ways clients from different ethnic groups viewed the program's registration procedures, the results might both suggest ways to improve the program and contribute to new knowledge. The reason for the evaluation dictates the most effective design and the kinds of data to be collected. See the Appendix for Ball's model. I think this model will be very useful in helping learning-center directors recognize the often hidden agenda in requests for evaluation information, as well as helping them design more effective studies.

Although there are many ways to evaluate, the two basic strategies are professional standards and outcomes. Professional standards, guidelines, and ethics statements represent a consensus of experts as to the minimum requirements of a successful program. Making sure that you have the necessary elements in place should be the first step in evaluating a program. The second step is to collect data—the goal being to determine whether your program is producing the desired outcomes in terms of student success (sometimes called summative evaluation). Obviously, summative evaluation generally takes several years and is not something you can do in one semester. However, it is important that you initiate a good data collection system and monitor the results periodically before you can implement a summative evaluation.

### Set Up a Data Base

Regardless of the purpose of the evaluation or whether it is done by outside evaluators or internal staff members, it is essential that records be set up, maintained, monitored for accuracy, and ready for inspection before an evaluation can begin. In other words, one of the first things that a new program director should do is set up a data base.

In developing a data base you will want to compile the following information:

◊ a written statement of the program's mission, goals and objectives, and a history of the program.

◊ systematically collected, accurate records of students' use of your program, broken down by the appropriate categories corresponding to the services used to develop an adequate, operational data base for administrative decision-making. Keep components separate—i.e., individual appointments with skills counselors versus tutoring appointments versus drop-in tutoring contacts versus hours spent in lab or classroom, etc.

◊ an accounting system for 1) publishing catalogues of materials used in matching learner needs with resources; 2) keeping track of purchases and other expenditures; 3) cataloguing and measuring students' use of program materials, computer software, product announcements, research articles, and reports; 4) recording program outreach activities and publicity; and 5) faculty contacts and referrals. There are a number of computer software programs that simplify this record keeping and analysis, e.g., a barcode reader, etc.

Here are some items that should be included in your data base:

◊ number of student contacts per type of service

◊ number of students served (individuals)

◊ student satisfaction from questionnaires, etc.

◊ present grades and GPA's of students using the program

◊ end of term grades of students completing the course (or parent course in the case of Supplemental Instruction or Adjunct Skills courses)

◊ grades (or GPA's) in subsequent mainstream courses

◊ entrance test scores or other test scores

◊ faculty contacts and contributions

## QUESTIONNAIRES AND STUDENT'S SATISFACTION WITH THE PROGRAM

Be sure to includes items about:

◊ students' reports of increased skills after attending program or using the materials

◊ students' statements of satisfaction with the program

◊ students referred by their peers (or willing to refer friends)

◊ retention and success in subsequent mainstream courses

◊ grades of students who complete your program in subsequent mainstream courses

◊ whether students return next semester/next year (or complete freshman year, re-enroll as sophomores, etc.)

◊ graduation or program completion

◊ improvement in course grades, or GPA's pre-post test gain scores of student users

◊ faculty attitudes toward the program

◊ impact of the program on campus as a whole (i.e., improvement in retention, participation in developing new courses or curriculum, etc.)

◊ "serendipitous" benefits—like the number of users who refer friends and siblings to the institution, the number of faculty members who volunteer to spend time in the learning center, the institution's decision to build a new tutoring center (as the University of Minnesota-Duluth has recently done), or the fact that students who complete your developmental courses tend to remain in and work in the area after graduation.

## STUDENT USE OF THE SERVICE

The number of students who use a service (or enroll in a skills course) and the number and kind of student/staff interactions are essential basic data for any evaluation study. If the program provides different kinds of services, such as tutoring, group study skills programs, and counseling, the record keeping system should reflect student contacts in each type of service. Records should be kept on the student's name, college, sex, major, type of problem, type of service used, and number and kinds of contacts—group meetings, self-paced instruction, individual appointments, and so on.

Because there are many ways to count student contacts, it is impossible to compare figures on student use from learning centers in different colleges. Some programs base their figures on compilations from student sign-in sheets and total the number of contacts, while others count the number of different (unduplicated) students seen and record hours for each. Some compile records of the total number of unduplicated students seen each term, while others report totals for the year. Thus, Program A may report that it serves 900 different students a year (that is, 300 per quarter) while Program B reports serving 600 students per year (based on the annual total). However, it is possible that both programs serve the same number of different students per year

(if, for instance, one third of Program A's students receive help for more than one quarter). Some learning centers count a talk given at orientation to 500 students as 500 student-contact hours and add them to the number of students seen by their staffs in individual appointments. Others count this presentation as one staff hour of outreach and do not include it in their tally of student-contact hours. Ideally, someday it will be possible to standardize these kinds of data so that programs can be compared, but meanwhile it is very important for the program director to decide on a simple, workable system for compiling student-use data and stick to it.

The number of students who seek help in a voluntary program and the amount of time they spend in the program are important criteria. The argument is that attendance be used as the criterion for evaluating voluntary, noncredit reading programs because if students persist in a program voluntarily, they must be gaining something from it.

Demand for the service can be reflected in several ways. For instance, a positive sign is whether courses or programs fill each term and if students must wait to enroll in the course or program. Then the numbers on the waiting list reflects student interest and perceived need. Attendance is a useful criterion in assessing a required course, as is the percentage of students dropping out of the course.

## STUDENT SATISFACTION

Most academic support services and remedial courses collect information on student satisfaction, and in some institutions collecting data on client satisfaction is mandated for budget-review procedures. Students' evaluations of the service can be obtained by handing out or mailing questionnaires or by telephone or personal interviews. It is preferable to have someone not directly connected with the program conduct the mailed survey or interview clients. If outsiders conduct the survey, students may respond more freely, and the service is less likely to be criticized for being too subjective. Sometimes staff in another department such as the counseling center are willing to interview clients of the learning center. Or students taking a sociology or psychology class may conduct and analyze a survey by mail or interview student clients as a project for credit.

Generally, learning center clients rate the services they received as beneficial. How positive their reactions are depends not only on the specific service they used but on how the questions on the survey are worded. For instance, most students will check favorable responses to questions like "How much did the reading program help you?" or "To what extent were you able to apply the study skills taught in the course to your regular course work?" Questions like "How do you feel the program might be improved?" will yield more-critical comments. In surveys of this sort, it is best to ask for an overall rating of the program and then ask specific questions aimed at finding out whether the student was able to use the skills—not whether he liked the instructor, the tutor, or the course. Questions like "What do you think you might have done if you had not been tutored?" with alternatives like "Done the same things," "Seriously considered dropping the course," and "Definitely would have dropped the course" yield useful information.

A less obtrusive indicator of student satisfaction is whether students encourage their friends to use the program. This information can be obtained easily by asking clients to indicate how they heard about the service when they sign into the program and/or by asking them on the post-questionnaire whether they would refer their friends to the program. Too often student evaluations of courses and programs are limited to assessing whether students enjoyed the experience and liked the instructor. It is more important to find out whether students learned new skills and were able to apply them to other courses. One way to elicit specific information about transfer of skills is to use the critical-incident method (Flanagan, 1954). In this technique, students are asked to respond to questions about how frequently they use skills and to describe specific examples of how they applied them. For example, if one asks, "To what extent have you used speed-reading techniques in your other courses?" the student might reply, "Very frequently." Then one could say, "Give an example of how you used this skill most recently."

When college learning-skills specialists think of evaluation measures, they usually consider questionnaires, statistical analyses of grades, and other measurable outcomes, but they rarely think of case studies. Yet a well-written, realistic case study gives administrators and faculty members an understanding of the problems of students and the processes used to resolve them that they cannot get from lengthy statistical reports (assuming that they even read the latter).

Testimonials from students who have been helped by the program are also useful, both for publicizing the program among potential clients and for conveying the message of how valuable students view the service to faculty members and administrators. (And don't neglect to include testimonials from faculty members whose students have improved as a result of your efforts.)

Inviting faculty members and administrators to a symposium where students who are using the program discuss it can be an effective way to give faculty information about the program and how students view it. And this can be far more effective than a written summary of the results of a survey of student users.

## GRADES AND GRADE-POINT AVERAGES

Evidence that students improve their grades, their grade-point averages, or both as a result of a skills-improvement program is the kind of hard data that administrators like to see. However, demonstrating grade improvement may be difficult if one's program is limited to the weakest students or students attend your program for only a few hours. (See the discussion on evaluating tutoring in Chapter 3.)

In this age of grade inflation, it is essential to have a comparison group if grades or GPA's are used as criteria. In assessing a tutoring program, for example, the tutored group may attain C averages, which may seem to represent adequate progress, but the nontutored students may average B. Finding a comparison group may be difficult even in a voluntary program, for those who volunteer for tutoring may be more highly motivated than those who do not. If the program or course is required, then one cannot match tutored students with a comparable group. There are ways, however, to handle this problem statistically by calculating predicted grade-point averages based on students' high school background and test scores at entrance.

Note: Although students still manage to make D's and F's in courses, the average grade in most non-science courses today is B, while the standards for academic probation remain the same (usually a GPA below C). If your follow-up results on students who complete developmental courses indicate that they earn C's in mainstream courses, recognize that although they may be persisting in college, they are still performing below average.

A further difficulty in using grades as a criterion is that the skills program the student has taken may not be related to his work in other courses. One would not expect that a reading-improvement course would necessarily help students enrolled in mathematics and chemistry, or that a student tutored in chemistry would improve his grades in English. On the other hand, significant grade improvement is usually reported when the grades of students enrolled in a voluntary adjunct skills or Supplementary Instruction program that is directly integrated into a mainstream course are compared with those of students who do not volunteer for the adjunct skills course. (For more information on adjunct skills courses, see Chapter 12.)

Changes in the qualifications of students recruited and accepted by the college from year to year can influence the apparent effectiveness of a skills program. If a better-prepared group enters one year, their grades may be higher than the grades earned by weaker students in a previous year, regardless of the skills program. Or if academically weaker students are accepted by the program, they may earn poorer grades, affecting both the programs existence and depleting staff morale. Changes in academic policy and instructors' grading patterns can also affect the overall grades students get, regardless of how successful they are in improving their skills.

Another caveat in using grades as a criterion is that often the grades used for evaluation are limited to those earned by students in the same term that they are taking developmental courses. It is important to follow up students after they have completed the skills program and examine their subsequent grades and grade-point averages. In other words, give the students an opportunity to internalize and apply the techniques that they have been taught, and their skills gains should be reflected in their future grades in relevant courses.

In assessing the effects of brief, noncredit minicourses that teach one skill among the many required in a regular course, it is wiser to examine the students' performance on that aspect of the course, rather than final grades. For example, one might use course quizzes or the items on the final exam that relate to the skill taught.

RETENTION IN COLLEGE

Another criterion for assessing skills programs is whether their students persist in college longer than comparable groups who do not take skills work. Retention studies require careful and long-term follow-up of students. Usually data are collected on a term-by-term basis, or, for students enrolled in a sequence of courses such as chemistry, mathematics, or English, persistence in the sequence is examined. Since many college courses are subject to grade inflation, and since academically weak students typically complete fewer credits, it is generally best to examine group differences after a two-year period; this allows students time to complete a number of courses and to advance through the sequence.

These days students take longer to graduate— perhaps even 6 years or more—so it's better not to confine your analysis to a shorter period, particularly if you are evaluating students who are taking developmental skills courses that do not count toward graduation.

An illustration of a cost-effective program is the Academic Restoration Program at Rochester Institute of Technology, a private institution. Program directors systematically demonstrate the cost-effectiveness of the program by reporting the number of students who return and successfully complete college, as well as how the cost of the program is covered by the student tuition while they are taking the program. (See Chapter 7 for more details on this program.)

There is considerable evidence to show that effective services do increase student retention, whether it's the result of tutoring or counseling or skills programs. However, if the students selected for the program have much weaker backgrounds than other students, don't expect retention rates to be high.

Using graduation rates as the criterion for success in a freshman skills program is risky at best, particularly if you are working with high-risk students. It implies that what they learn in your program will be sufficient to carry them through the entire curriculum. A successful minority retention program, for example, involves the entire college faculty and staff, not just the developmental skills program. One service cannot carry the burden alone. In the instances where learning centers have received credit for improving minority retention, such as the UC Berkeley program (Robert & Thompson, 1994), there were major changes in admission policies and many additional services provided—plus institution-wide commitment toward making the minority program successful.

TEST SCORES

Using differences between students' pre- and post-test scores on standardized tests to assess a program requires a knowledge of the limitations of these instruments:

1. They rarely reflect the objectives of a specific skills program because the skills they test are more general.

2. Standardized tests are reliable, which means that they have been designed to be relatively impervious to change, particularly over a brief period.

3. It is hard to evaluate change on standardized tests when the scores of the group tested are not normally distributed. If only the bottom 25 percent of students are required to take a reading or mathematics course, then one can expect the students' scores to improve as a result of chance regression effects alone. In situations like this, control groups are needed. Similarly, if students are sectioned into high and low groups on the basis of a pre-test, the high group's scores may decline on the post-test if pre-test scores cluster near the test ceiling.

4. The raw scores on alternate forms of a test are rarely equivalent. For instance, when we developed local norms in the Nelson-Denny Reading Test, we found that Form B was easier than Form A. To use these tests as pre- and post-tests, it is necessary either to compute standard scores for the group and use statistical analyses, or to counterbalance the forms of the test (that is, give Form A to half the group for the pretest and Form B to the other half, and then on the post-test give Form B to the first half and Form A to the second).

5. Standardized tests have very limited application in assessing individualized skills programs. If students work on different skills, at different levels, and at different rates—for example, some on spelling, others on vocabulary, reading rate, or critical-reading exercises—one test, unless it is a lengthy battery, will not reflect their gains. One can use criterion-referenced tests to determine improvement on particular skills, or one can use units completed, but then one must report results in percentages—for example, 70 percent of those working on spelling completed exercises at the eighth-grade level.

Despite these limitations, standardized tests are often mandated as a condition for evaluating federally funded programs and for state-mandated basic skills courses. When they are used as post-tests, one should use other criteria as well in judging the effectiveness of a skills program, for the tests may give just one piece of the picture—that is, how students' scores compare with those of a norm group or whether they meet the minimum standards.

Simpson and Nist (1992) urge that instructors adopt a multi-dimensional, comprehensive model of assessment in reading so that the information gleaned is viewed as an integral part of the instructional process. Thus instruction and assessment become recursive and continuous, and through regular feedback students are empowered to become informed about and responsible for their own learning. Thus, testing sorts students, diagnoses them, and evaluates them. As more varied, complex testing is used (replicating real-life situations rather than standardized test scores that delineate subskills or specific objectives), the teaching-learning process is supported and students can attain more realistic short-term and long-term goals.

## FACULTY ATTITUDES TOWARD THE PROGRAM

Assessing faculty attitudes toward the skills program is another way of evaluating its effectiveness. Instructors can be sent short questionnaires, but they should only be sent to those who know about the program—unless you are doing a needs assessment, in which case you might contact all instructors who teach courses at the appropriate level of your program or send questionnaires to a random sample of faculty. Faculty members also might be interviewed by phone or in person and queried about their suggestions for the program.

A more objective criterion of faculty members' interest and involvement is the number of students they refer to the service. This information can be gathered from the faculty member (and is easier to obtain if one has referral forms) or from the students when they arrive at the service.

## STAFF ATTITUDES ABOUT THE PROGRAM

Another important source of information for making decisions about a program is evaluations by staff members, including skills instructors, tutors, learning specialists, receptionists, and clerical workers. The director or chairperson might hold postmortem group sessions at the end of each term and have the staff members discuss their experiences and their suggestions for improving the program. In addition, I would suggest that a questionnaire be sent to each staff member to fill out privately—one that included items about each of the program's objectives with questions like, "How well are we meeting this objective?" and, "What should we be doing?" Staff members should also be asked to rate their in-service training experiences, their supervision, and other aspects of their work, including scheduling and receptionist activities. Providing one's staff members with sufficient time to think about the problems they have in working with students, and to identify the most frequent problems students present, can result in useful ideas for developing better in-service training programs and for generating new programs or improving old ones.

## IMPACT OF THE PROGRAM ON THE CAMPUS AS A WHOLE

If one of the program's objectives is to serve as a catalyst for improving undergraduate experiences, then a criterion must be found to reflect this. For a learning center, one indicator of success might be

that courses or programs developed by the center staff are accepted by an academic department and become institutionalized—for example, a trigonometry review course or a unit on reading for ESL students. For a developmental course, a criterion might be higher retention rates in appropriate mainstream courses.

A less obtrusive indicator of the impact of the program would be that the director is invited to sit on campus committees, particularly those that make policy decisions concerning curriculum or textbooks or regulations that affect students' academic progress, or that administrators or faculty members solicit the director's advice.

The image of the program held by the student body may also reflect the impact of the program. We always attempted to add a question or two about our learning services to any survey being sent to student groups, whether seniors or sophomores or prospective freshmen. (It helps to learn that 90 percent of seniors in your college know about your program and that 70 percent have used it and regard it favorably—or conversely, that they do not know about it. In the latter case, you may be hiding your light under a bushel. We also found that after a few years, prospective freshmen knew about the program and were looking forward to participating in it.)

## UNEXPECTED INDICATORS ATTESTING TO A PROGRAM'S SUCCESS AND WHY THEY HAPPEN

Occasionally good things happen that are unpredictable and unexpected. For example, a wealthy Texas family endowed a learning center building in memory of their son who died in an accident. The

University of Minnesota-Duluth is building a new tutor center. Why? The mission of the University is to "Provide students with opportunities . . . to attain personal goals through a supportive learning environment." Certainly, the tutoring program under Paul Treuer, who also supervises TA training, has long been regarded as a vital part of the supportive learning environment.

When her university was faced with massive budget cuts, Carol Bader, Director of the Developmental Skills Department at the Middle Tennessee State University, offered to return $100,000 of her program's funding, but the president refused to accept the money saying that her program was too valuable to cut. What does she do to convince her administrator that her program is indispensable? Well, she does all of the things suggested plus more. For example, each year she documents the increase in the percentage of the graduating class who started as developmental students. Of the current MTSU students receiving bachelor's degrees, 38% started as developmental education students and 6% of those earning graduate degrees began as developmental students. Bader makes sure the president has these figures. She disseminates data about her studies—including the cost analysis of losing students—to her staff, all deans, vice presidents and other directors, the retention task force, departmental historian, etc. Her goal is to change the image of developmental-studies teachers as retention specialists to assets, not liabilities, and she makes special efforts to see that they are perceived as scholars and full partners in the university. She encourages her staff to publish in-house and through professional journals, texts, and in books by other faculty. She urges them to work toward advanced degrees and perform university service by serving on committees. For example, the staff served on nine faculty committees last year, as well as with other university groups.

By volunteering to chair committees, attending faculty social events, advising student organizations, and aggressively pursuing grants, awards, and certifications, her programs presence is felt and respected. Her staff is also expected to perform community service. Members of her staff have won campus awards as outstanding teachers, outstanding graduate assistant and research awards, as well as state and national awards. Her program recently won the NADE Award for Outstanding Developmental Program.

The University of Minnesota-Duluth and the Middle Tennessee State University exemplify programs that ensure that their administrators and faculty colleagues are continually reminded of their successes. Program directors in very large institutions may have to do more than submit annual reports and self-evaluation studies to convince their administrators of their worth. Many routinely call in outside evaluators to study their programs, as well as doing in-house evaluations.

## Outside Evaluators

Hiring an outside expert (or a team of evaluators) not directly connected with one's program adds credibility to the evaluation report submitted. Administrators may accept the expert's recommendations a bit more readily than those of the program director. Also, a person not directly involved with a program may observe aspects of the service that should be improved which the staff might overlook.

Outside evaluators proceed in different ways. Some prefer to review the program's objectives and data before they visit. Others use Scriven's goal-free methods (1974)—that is, they prefer not to know the objectives of the program in advance, but rather to come in and observe what is actually happening in the program, claiming that this is a more objective way of proceeding. Regardless of their philosophy, evaluators usually talk to staff members, the director, students in the program, and administrators in the college, as well as observing the program in action.

## EVALUATORS PERFORM DIFFERENT SERVICES

Some evaluators will aid the program director in planning an evaluation study, and most are requested to write a report. Evaluators also can help troubleshoot in the event of staff problems and can recommend ways that innovations can be implemented.

If program directors are interested in improving the efficiency of their programs but cannot afford an outside evaluator, they may be able to get management assistance from the college's business unit or school of business administration. Sometimes this assistance is called a management audit or a system analysis. A management audit can be particularly helpful in a time of crisis. For example, Haase and others (1977) describe how a management audit of a college reading program helped the program's administrator resolve staff morale problems resulting from the denial of university credit for reading program courses and recent budget cuts.

Another source of knowledgeable outside evaluators are people from your network in professional associations who direct learning assistance programs in nearby colleges. If money is a problem, you might arrange to evaluate each other's program.

(Note: In revising CAS Standards for Learning Assistance Programs, we included a statement that evaluation efforts should be routinely included in program budgets. See Appendix.)

## EVALUATION REPORTS

After conducting an evaluation study, the next step is to prepare and write the report. How the report is written depends on the purpose of the evaluation. That is, if the report is designed to answer questions about one's program raised by administrators, it should be written in a format that administrators will read. Too often evaluation reports are so comprehensive, detailed, statistical, and lengthy that they confuse issues rather than clarify them. Some directors feel that preparing lengthy statistical reports will impress faculty members and administrators. My experience has been that one will arouse interest and get a response more quickly if one prepares a clear, readable, concise summary of the findings and recommendations, not longer than four pages. Save your means, multiple regression analyses, and covariance for your dissertation or the papers you submit to professional journals. Write a summary in plain English of the work you have done. Percentages may be far more effective in presenting your results to an administrator than means and standard deviations. For example, if you have studied three groups of EOP students—those who came in regularly for tutoring in biology, those who came in occasionally for tutoring, and those who received no tutoring—it is better to state your findings as, "90 percent of the students who were tutored regularly attained grades of C or higher in Biology 1, compared with 40 percent of those tutored occasionally and 60 percent of those who received no tutoring" than as, "The mean for the regularly tutored group was 2.697 (S.D. = 0.2435), compared with the occasionally tutored group mean of 1.883 (S.D. = 0.2276) and the nontutored (control) group mean of 2.483 (S.D. = 0.3354)." Which statement conveys more useful information?

## Additional Tips for Annual Reports

Don't be anonymous. Take credit for your work. In my files I have dozens of annual reports written by authors who did not give their names, and some don't even identify their college. Always include the names and titles of your staff members—after ten years, it's hard to remember who worked for you when.

Always send a copy of your annual report to the campus archivist (if you don't know who that is, ask your librarian). Someday, someone will want to know what students were like in 1995-96 and what services they were offered. Also, if you are like most learning center directors, your administrator often asks you to write proposals, studies, and special reports. Make sure they too are sent to the archives.

Popham (1975) suggests using bar graphs and dancing girls to highlight evaluation results in presenting them to administrators. I have not tried the dancing girls, but I have been tempted on occasion to hire violinists and weeping mourners to provide melancholy background music for our lengthy budget hearings.

## Summary

Here are some basic principles to keep in mind when you implement systematic evaluation:

◊ In designing evaluation studies, always use multiple methods and multiple criteria. The behavior and outcomes that concern learning assistance programs are far too complex and the instruments are far too primitive to produce valid results from a single method or a single instrument.

◊ There are many ways to evaluate a program, but there is no best way to do it.

◊ Qualitative, as well as quantitative, methods should both be used.

◊ In planning evaluations using long-term criteria such as student retention or graduation, be sure to define your terms operationally—that is, how much of what kind of program equates with using a service. Also use comparative information about typical students on your campus. For example, if 20% of students in your developmental program graduate in five years, be sure you include the percent of typical students who graduate also. Always put your figures in context.

◊ In planning studies on retention, other units on campus should work with the skills program in setting up a multi-program data base so that the individual efforts of each program can be assessed, as well as the combined efforts of all.

Evaluation, then, should be an ongoing process to inform the central administration about your program, and to aid you as program director in making effective day-to-day management decisions as well as helping you and your staff improve your program.

For more information on evaluation designs for outcomes of developmental skills courses, you'll want to read:

Akst, G., & Hecht, M. (1980). Program evaluation. In A. Trilling (Ed.). *Teaching basic skills in college*. San Francisco: Jossey-Bass.

Akst, G. (1986). Reflections on evaluating remedial mathematics programs. *Journal of Developmental Education*, *10*(1), 12-15.

Boylan, H., George, A., & Bonham, B. (1991). Program evaluation. In R. Flippo & D. Caverly (Eds.). *College reading and study strategy programs*. Newark, DE: International Reading Association.

Clowes, D. A. (1984). The evaluation of remedial/developmental programs: A stage model. *Journal of Developmental Education*, 8(1), 14-15, 27-30.

Maxwell, M. (1993). *Evaluating academic skills programs: A sourcebook*. Kensington, MD: MM Associates (Box 2857, Kensington, MD 20891; phone 201-530-5078).

Morante, E. A. (1986). The effectiveness of developmental programs. A two-year followup. *Journal of Developmental Education*, 9(3), 13-15.

New Jersey Basic Skills Council (1991). Effectiveness of remedial programs in public colleges and universities. Trenton, NJ: New Jersey Board of Higher Education, 27-30.

# CONCLUSION

## ACCEPTING REALITIES AND TAKING ACTION

The problems colleges face in maintaining effective academic support programs for their regular students, as well as those for poorly prepared students, must be viewed in the context of the changes that are occurring in higher education today, the individual institution's standards and goals, the diverse expectations and characteristics of the students themselves, and the attitudes, teaching strategies, and expectations of the faculty. Most institutions, both public and private, are facing financial problems, although the gap is widening between the "haves" and "have-nots," with those who have the highest academic reputations able to attract both students and grants for their faculty, while less prestigious schools suffer from low enrollment and declining public and private support. Colleges in some sections of the country find that the pool of highly qualified recent high school graduates has declined, while endless numbers of unprepared adults and displaced workers who find they need college to remain employable seek admission. However, overriding student demand are the fiscal problems besieging most colleges and a political climate that is forcing four-year institutions to retrench their developmental programs or banish them to community colleges. Thus, the gap between selective colleges and open-admission colleges is growing wider in many ways.

The numbers of traditionally prepared college freshmen in some geographical areas are declining, while in other places, public universities are flooded with applications from "college-ready" high school graduates. In their haste to abandon needed skills programs, colleges may be acting prematurely. The open-admissions policies of the 1960s, based on social and political pressures to provide higher education to students from widely divergent and historically isolated backgrounds, have given way to admissions policies and financial aid based on academic merit. These policies are adversely affecting college opportunities for low income students, as well as adults who seek degrees needed to maintain an adequate income in an ever changing economic environment and to compete effectively in a job market where specialized skills can become obsolete as fast as computers.

While faculty members still complain about the lower skills of entering students and the disintegration of academic standards (as always blaming the latter on the students and the high schools), grade inflation continues, confusing able students and robbing lower-ability students of their incentive to learn. The failproof course has improved neither motivation nor learning. Interestingly, while both students and faculty are unhappy with grade inflation, it has not diminished. Grading policies are being addressed by some colleges and this may signal an impending change, but grade inflation is still omnipresent.

Out of the experiences of open admissions programs to help disadvantaged students enter the country's mainstream through attaining college degrees have emerged some principles and programs that suggest effective ways to help underprepared college students succeed in college. In addition, the failures of this period suggest paths to be avoided. The heritage of college remedial instruction has recorded many failures, and this fact has perpetuated negative attitudes among faculty members. However, recent studies are encouraging; for example, successful course-related services like Supplementary Instruction (SI) are fast becoming institutionalized, and we now have better understanding of what's required for reading and writing courses to be successful—albeit, these policies are not always implemented. Furthermore, while affirmative action policies are under attack, there is clear evidence that attending open-admission colleges has provided economic gains for thousands of disadvantaged minority students. For example, a CUNY study released in 1996 shows that more of the needy students graduated with degrees than earlier expected and that thousands have gone on to earn graduate degrees.

## What Are the Trends?

Since today's trends suggest tomorrow's conventions, a glimpse at present trends may help us understand what lies ahead. Professors at many institutions (including our most prestigious universities) are rediscovering lower division undergraduates and their problems. Perhaps the reduction of graduate programs gives the faculty time and opportunity to turn their attention to beginning college students as they recognize the importance of retaining students and their obligations to see that they learn. In addition, rising costs makes student retention necessary for institutional survival. As a result, selective institutions are reaffirming standards and reintroducing required courses dropped during the permissive 1960s. For example, foreign language courses are currently reappearing as freshman requirements in liberal arts colleges. Tests that require sophomores and graduating seniors to demonstrate their proficiency in reading, writing, and mathematics are mandated, even by prestigious colleges where faculty are not concerned about declining admissions. Other colleges, which a few years ago admitted anyone, regardless of background, without testing, are now requiring that entering freshmen take tests, hoping that proper placement will increase student retention.

Universities are reviving articulation programs with high schools in an effort to improve college preparatory courses and ensure better skills preparation of future college students. However, there seems to be a persistent belief in high schools that only a few graduates will go on to college, and in some geographical areas there are few opportunities for high school students to take all of the necessary college prep courses. Even in counties where the majority of students go on to college, there are problems. For example, in Montgomery County, Maryland, where 86 percent of students go on to college, the local community college complains that 70 percent of the local students need remedial math, and nearly half fail the reading and writing tests. Nationally, about one-third of those attending college have not taken college prep courses in high school.

Colleges throughout the country are devoting more of their resources and staff time to basic skills courses. Higher education institutions are offering credit for basic skills courses in greater numbers than ever before—even though the credits students earn may not count toward graduation. However, credits seem to be offered more as a sop to students (in an effort to encourage them to work harder) and to ensure that students maintain their financial aid packages than as evidence of greater academic recognition of the value of skills courses.

Along with the increase in basic skills courses, academic support services for students have expanded, especially through learning assistance centers. The recent growth has been greatest in four-year colleges, particularly in private colleges that rarely offered such services before.

However, budget restrictions in many colleges mean significant cuts in student services, including academic support programs. Services, including dining halls, computer services, dormitories, health services, etc., have been privatized. There is even pressure to privatize academic support services; however, there is also pressure to keep those as part of the campus and as a way to improve faculty understanding of their teaching roles.

## The Professionalization of Developmental Educators

Large numbers of people are employed in college developmental education and learning assistance work today, and there are signs that college learning specialists/skills instructors are beginning to view themselves as professionals in their special functions (rather than as English teachers or mathematicians or general educators). A number of journals devoted to improving college remedial/ developmental skills programs are published, and new professional organizations have been established. Although more skills program directors have doctoral degrees today, there are few graduate schools that offer specific courses and training for college learning specialists. Many people still enter the field from teaching jobs in the public schools.

The role of learning center staff members and their impact on other facets of the academic commu-

nity seems to be gradually improving, although they still are among the least powerful and least persuasive groups in academe. In the past, college administrators and faculty committees have largely ignored the input of learning skills specialists in decisions about academic policies and curricula, but there are signs that this is changing.

Efforts are being made to revise courses and curricula to make them more appropriate for college students with limited skills. More curricular changes are needed if students are to be taught effectively, and it is important that course planners avoid the mistakes made by college remedial teachers in the past. That is, the new courses should not be watered down versions of traditional college courses; rather, they should involve the preparatory knowledge and skills needed for mainstream courses, but shifted to a lower gear. This metaphor implies that students who have attained speed in a lower gear can shift to a higher gear (that is, an advanced course), whereas those who consume a watered down course cannot easily advance to more sophisticated courses.

Students still complain that courses based solely on educational technology are dull. Technological programs do not work well as complete courses because weaker students rarely complete "do-it-yourself, by yourself" courses. Self-paced instruction, with its goal of mastery learning, is most effective when it is used as an adjunct to other teaching methods, when there are good instructors and sensitive and competent aides, and when the program is truly individualized—that is, when not all students have to complete all parts. However, the most effective methods are those that combine technology and tutoring, such as Video Supplementary Instruction (VSI). Interactive software, multi-media and CD Rom make it possible to design course materials that are more interesting and challenging and that will appeal to students with different learning styles. But even these exciting new products won't replace the need for supportive teachers and tutors and the opportunity to discuss ideas with other students.

There are also signs that professors are beginning to accept their new roles and their changing students. Some of the old myths and stereotypes are beginning to break down. However, I am not sure that most professors will agree with Kenneth Bruffee who writes eloquently of the profound scholarly opportunity that teaching underprepared students provides.

## MYTHS THAT HAMPER EFFORTS TO HELP STUDENTS IMPROVE THEIR SKILLS

College skills programs have long been hampered by some enduring faculty beliefs that can be termed myths or partial truths. These ideas concern the characteristics of college students and the best types of treatment programs for those with low skills. As myths, they ignore the complexity of the problem, the motivations and expectations of students, and the kinds of resources it takes to improve students' skills. Some examples include:

*"If students have been properly taught and have properly learned the three R's in elementary school, they should need no further help."* A corollary belief is that if students have passed freshman composition courses, they should need no additional help in writing, even when they write their doctoral dissertations. This belief ignores the developmental stages that all students must go through as they move up the educational ladder. Skills are not mastered once and for all. Each subject area and each level of college requires somewhat different skills, or the refining and polishing of skills already learned, and

different disciplines do not share the same rhetorical principles—i.e., compare science and literature. Writing skills cannot be separated from the topics one writes about. Freshmen should not be expected to write papers on theoretical topics at the same level of sophistication that one expects of seniors. As this idea is gradually being accepted, writing across the curriculum (WAC) efforts are increasing, though funding cuts still threaten these.

*"Underprepared students will learn more if taught in separate classes and removed from the main body of students."* The tenacious belief in the superiority of homogeneous grouping seems to affect teachers at every level, but fifty years of research refutes it. Ability grouping has consistently been found to reduce the achievement of low-ability students and to impair their motivation and attitudes toward education, while inflating the self-esteem of high-ability students. Yet the practice persists. To be sure, at the college level there are limits on the range of skills and abilities that an instructor can teach in one classroom. However, there should be flexibility in placing students, so that those who have mastered the subject matter can move on to advanced courses, for there is nothing more devastating educationally than requiring students who know a subject to repeat it; nor can most students pass an advanced course if they lack the prerequisite knowledge. Therefore, placement in college courses should be based on knowledge of the subject, not on skills. If a student has the knowledge, he or she can be helped to develop the necessary skills through intensive skills work related to the course content.

*"Students who need remedial programs will volunteer for them, and average students will not."* College programs find the reverse is true. Those most in need of academic support services will not volunteer; in fact, they will avoid services planned to help

them, while students who have stronger skills are often motivated to improve. The academically weakest students need to be identified early, held for skills courses before they enter advanced classes, and strongly encouraged to use support services.

*"Illiteracy is a disease that should be stamped out (or cured)."* A corollary is that students who have limited writing and reading skills should be excluded from college. The perception of illiteracy as a pathological condition, rather than the natural state of the uneducated, protects faculty members who prefer to teach students whom they consider their intellectual peers and reject students who need to grow and develop knowledge.

There are also beliefs about the arrangement of courses and methods for underprepared students that have little basis in fact. For example, the assumption that slow learners learn best in small classes taught with group-discussion methods has not been verified by research. In fact, some studies show that high-ability students profit most from small discussion classes, while low-ability college students achieve better in larger classes taught by a well-organized instructor in an authoritarian manner. However, classroom strategies are changing as college instructors experiment with new methods such as collaborative learning, reciprocal teaching, and small group workshops. And this will lead to changes in students' expectations.

The belief that slower learners can learn any subject if given enough time, espoused by many progressive educators, may be theoretically valid. But in practice, few students are motivated to continue working indefinitely on a skill unless, like kids whose rich parents endlessly support them as long as they stay in college, they are continuously rewarded by generous grants. Most underprepared

students expect to be able to keep up with their peers and advance to graduation at the same pace. Rarely are they motivated to repeat a course more than twice. Furthermore, underprepared students are not expecting to major in reading, writing, or math, and if they are required to complete long sequences of skills courses before being permitted to enroll in mainstream courses, drop-out rates will soar.

One other pernicious assumption held by some faculty members deserves mention. That is the belief that there is only one way to learn in college—that is, the way I myself learned, by studying alone in my room or the library without help from anyone. In truth there are many ways to learn, and students have different learning styles and different ways of studying. As faculty in many disciplines are recognizing, students have different learning styles, and new teaching methods and technology are more effective than traditional lectures in producing better students.

In the past, innovations in college teaching have benefited the best and brightest students and been of little benefit to those who are less well prepared. Indeed, externally funded research to improve instruction has had little lasting effect. Also, ideas about what works best have changed. For example, mastery learning and personalized self-instruction, heralded as ideal methods in the 70s, have yielded more failures than successes and have been substantially changed or abandoned.

Immediate knowledge of results, a feature of mastery learning, is purported to enhance learning. This assumption is being questioned by psychologists who, in recent studies, have found that under some circumstances and with some students, immediate feedback may have negative effects on learning (McKeachie, 1976). For example, low-ability students may not be able to think of alternative ways to solve a problem. If they learn through feedback that their first attempt is wrong, they lose motivation quickly and give up. What they need is support from the instructor until they can accept feedback without giving up.

High-ability students, in contrast, do not need feedback because they usually know whether their answers are correct. Immediate feedback is most effective in facilitating learning for students of average ability who can think of alternative ways to solve a problem and who are uncertain whether their answers are correct.

## Peer Learning

Peer learning through tutoring or specially structured groups is the most popular technique for aiding the underprepared student in both skills and subject matter areas. Sought most often from the array of services provided by learning centers and other support agencies, and rated most helpful by academically weak students, peer learning also includes peer tutoring, peer teaching, dyads and self-contained study groups in which students study regularly together, and classroom grouping procedures, such as the parceled-classroom and group-inquiry methods.

Techniques such as collaborative learning, cooperative learning, and reciprocal teaching have been widely adopted in skills courses but are more successful and easier to implement with average and above-average students.

Good peer tutoring programs improve the retention of tutees, and also help the student tutors improve their understanding and grades. Tutoring-for-credit courses, in which tutors are trained in study skills, counseling, and teaching techniques, provide an inexpensive way to help tutors and students. Studies suggest that most freshmen are more comfortable with, and willing to meet with peer tutors than they are with graduate assistants or instructors. Younger peer tutors can compensate with enthusiasm and patience for what they lack in experience. Research suggests that peer tutoring is most effective when structured materials are available for the tutors to use with students and when tutors are trained and supported as they work with students.

There are caveats to peer tutoring programs and peer learning approaches. They are not panaceas—some students respond poorly to working with others. Peer tutors need strong support and the opportunity to talk their problems over with a trainer. Teaching is hard work, and tutoring a student with learning difficulties can be frustrating and discouraging. It takes patience, fortitude, and ingenuity. So tutors themselves need encouragement if they are to be effective with their tutees. Careful screening and selection of peer tutors is a necessary part of a successful program. The fact that a person has struggled from the ghetto to graduate school does not guarantee that he or she will be a good tutor. Incorporating peer learning methods effectively in a classroom or group situation also requires special skills of the instructor or group leader. Not all the personal characteristics that good group leadership requires are teachable, but if instructors are interested in learning how to work with groups, their skills can be improved.

In very difficult courses, adjunct skills or Supplemental Instruction are more effective than tutoring with at-risk students as well as regular students, for they have been shown consistently to improve students' grades, their GPAs, graduation rates, and reduce attrition. We're also discovering better ways to motivate students to volunteer for this intensive work, such as giving partial credit and making attendance an expected part of the course.

## WHAT NEEDS TO BE DONE?

Most of the government funding available to higher education institutions to enable them to accept underprepared students has been directed toward establishing programs that provide academic support services to students. Very little money has been allocated for developing pre-service or in-service training programs for staff members, nor for conducting basic or applied research, nor for conducting evaluation studies. These, then, remain the greatest needs in the field.

### SKILLS SPECIALISTS NEED MORE PROFESSIONAL TRAINING

Graduate programs to train college learning-skills specialists, administrators, and remedial instructors are sorely needed. Surprisingly few universities offer courses, and even fewer offer programs leading to degrees for those who plan to teach college reading, writing, basic mathematics, or basic science courses. Because most colleges offer basic skills courses, learning-center services, or both, there are many job opportunities for college skills specialists, but there is only a very small pool of trained, qualified, and experienced people to fill these jobs. Usually interested faculty are appointed who learn on the job. Without special incentives, including outside funding, graduate schools of education are not likely to start new programs for college skills teachers. On the other hand, directors of learning centers are increasingly earning doctorates from their local

institution, so perhaps they may be having an effect on graduate programs. Nevertheless, it is wasteful and tragic that so many people enter the field with minimal preparation.

More and better in-service training programs to help those who are newly hired by college skills programs are also needed. Although there are a number of professional organizations who hold regional conferences and special institutes, these do not begin to serve the needs of the large number employed in entry level positions. Job turnover tends to be high, and as new people enter college skills from more traditional teaching positions in elementary and high schools, they create a continuing need for professional training programs.

### NEW ROLES FOR STUDY SKILLS SPECIALISTS

Research is needed to find the most effective ways to implement academic support programs within different types of institutions. For example, placing learning-skills specialists in academic departments, where they serve as resource persons for other faculty members, seems an excellent way to help the faculty increase their repertory of teaching skills, and thus improve its work with underprepared students. Skills specialists can also be part of a team to help faculty plan more effective courses. As academic departments begin to create courses that will provide both skills and knowledge in the discipline for underprepared students, the skills personnel can be invaluable. In addition, learning-skills specialists are an important source of information about student learning for those who make decisions about academic policies and those who plan curriculums. Since learning-skills specialists are rarely consulted about such decisions, they represent a neglected resource. Investigations of how learning-skills specialists' talents and information might be effectively used in academic decisions and what kinds of decision models might be tried could yield valuable information for the selection and training of skills-staff members.

## Need for More Basic Research

There is a great need for more basic research to illuminate the processes involved in teaching basic skills in college and the nature of mature learning and thinking. The research funded by the National Institute for Education has been largely limited to elementary school learning. Few studies have been done on the basic reading processes of academically underprepared adult students and the strategies that can be used to teach them. Also, what little work that has been done is rarely disseminated and does not reach those who need it most.

I hope that in our present desperation to find ways of meeting the needs of all students, we will not forget that a college education should involve more than an accretion of facts and skills force-fed to students in small amounts. A college education is not complete unless students are exposed to great minds and great ideas and have opportunities to test their thoughts in dialogues with those more learned than themselves so that their views can be questioned and expanded. Passively watching eminent professors on television in living color does not fulfill this need unless students have a chance to talk with mentors about the ideas they have heard. There are great thinkers in every field—from auto mechanics to cosmetology to philosophy. Students should be exposed to them and given the opportunity to discuss and debate their ideas.

## What Lies Ahead?

Although the Internet promises to put all the world's information at the fingertips of a person with a lap-top computer, we still have a ways to go to reach underprepared students. Although higher education may be finally on the verge of radical change, the technical basis for change has been available for years while faculties and institutions have been slow to accept technology. Now fiscal realities may force institutions to adopt teaching strategies from distance education and use the teaching promise of the Internet. Students may need classrooms, but they do not need to be on a traditional campus to learn. As smaller colleges in remote areas face bankruptcy, perhaps they can be converted into the kinds of live-in institutions that our current society seems to have more need for than colleges—i.e., nursing homes and prisons.

The information highway is already beginning to change the way some college courses are taught; we have on-line writing centers, on-line tutors, and even courses taught on the Internet. If and when all students have their own laptop computers with batteries and can tap into cyberspace from any place on earth, what will happen to today's learning assistance programs? Will they become virtual learning laboratories? Will learning center directors serve as intellectual disc jockeys describing the benefits of new CD-ROM learning software and suggesting sources to help students on the Internet? Will we still need the physical space we currently use and our extensive electronic gear? Perhaps not, but inevitably what we will always need are people to work with students who feel intellectually insecure. Cyberspace tutoring may work well for exceptionally bright and able students, but I predict it will not be enough for those high risk students we currently see. They will continue to need a friendly person to support them as they struggle to learn—perhaps a learning coach and a few cheerleaders too, to encourage them to keep trying.

At this point, the future for developmental education in four-year colleges grows dimmer as universities implement the cutbacks they have threatened to carry out since 1980, when they first realized that the pool of college applicants was shrinking fast. The pressure to relegate all developmental courses to the community college, primarily as an effort to save money and raise academic standards, may cause hardship for those who want college but are the most economically disadvantaged.

Certainly this decision does not stem from the evidence—which points to consistently greater success of developmental programs in research universities than those in two-year institutions, albeit universities accept fewer students with remedial needs. Our society needs more educated people not fewer, something that would be restricted by the cutbacks, and community colleges would find their ability to serve missions other than developmental education would be reduced.

Raising tuition and restricting developmental courses will adversely affect the more than 1.6 million students who are currently enrolled in remedial college courses. Many are economically disadvantaged. Can we afford not to educate these people?

The trend to privatize student services can be questioned, just like the trend to turn over public schools to private entrepreneurs. Also called contracting or outsourcing, it is driven by the desire to save money by hiring a private company at a lower cost, or to make money by sharing the profits with a commercial outfit. Currently, bookstores and food-services are the most popular services going to private vendors, but also campus health, computing, custodial, printing, security, etc., are fast changing. Will student services and instruction be next? In the past, smaller colleges sometimes contracted out their reading and study skills services and indeed, they may have to do this with learning centers also. My main objection to this is that when private groups offer skills services, they may help the students they work with, but there are no residual benefits. Regardless of whether these private services last or not, neither the faculty nor the college as a whole gains.

In our enthusiasm for new technology and teaching strategies such as collaborative learning, it is important to remember that there is no such thing as "one size fits all teaching." Lecturing was never a panacea, although we assumed that it worked for all. In our efforts to improve instruction and reduce some of the many learning problems that afflict students, we should not forget Snow's law (1976): "No matter how you try to make an instructional treatment better for someone, you will make it worse for someone else." In other words, there are no panaceas in higher education. Good teaching is, and always will be, a labor-intensive, time-consuming, and highly personalized activity.

# APPENDIX 1-1

## TEACHING DEVELOPMENTAL STUDENTS: WHAT WORKS?

L. J. Spiller, Delta College

(Reprinted by permission of the author from *Academic Forum: Faculty Center for Teaching Excellence Newsletter*, Delta College, February 1993, p. 3.)

When I was asked to present my thoughts about teaching developmental (underprepared) students, I was both flattered and intimidated, especially when the tag line, "What Works," was added. There are some days when I am convinced that nothing works. On those days, I long for a teaching schedule of upper division courses or classes filled with Honors students. But I usually rebound quickly after I remind myself of the following concepts:

1. Each of us is a developmental learner. Each of us is "underprepared" to learn some things.

2. Our students, who have been identified as developmental or underprepared learners in one or more academic areas, are proficient, even masterful, in other areas or activities—endeavors in which we may be grossly incompetent.

3. We can be better teachers of all students and especially underprepared students if we remember the preceding points.

4. We may be even better teachers if we periodically attempt to learn things that are difficult for us, perhaps even things we do not want to learn but that someone else recommends or requires that we learn. These situations are inevitable, of course, but the key is that we monitor our experience by paying attention to our uncertainties and our awkwardness, our frustrations and our confusion.

5. We can be effective teachers of underprepared students if we employ our most effective instructional approaches with our least prepared as well as our best prepared students.

6. We have to teach in ways which are compatible with our personalities.

7. We need each other. We have to share frustrations and successes. We need our colleagues' creative ideas as well as their encouragement. We have to reciprocate and provide encouragement and inspiration for our colleagues.

8. We need to listen to our students, especially the least co-operative or the most obnoxious or the terribly sullen individual. That person is telling us something important about him or herself, our teaching, etc.

9. Most of us probably should not teach developmental courses exclusively. Burnout is inevitable; we don't need to accelerate the process.

10. We should understand, though this will not protect us from the pain, that some situations will be heartbreaking. Some of our students' lives are too chaotic for them to focus on their studies. In addition, some of our students are used to creating problems for themselves; they are not used to experiencing academic success.

When these concepts help me to bounce back from my disappointments and feelings of inadequacy, I am confident enough to believe that some things actually do work when teaching underprepared students.

◊ diagnosing strengths and weaknesses early in the course
◊ keeping things "simple" but not simple-minded
◊ requiring tutoring and/or group study sessions
◊ being patient
◊ slowing things down
◊ requiring conferences
◊ providing specific, timely feedback
◊ laughing with them
◊ using some form of competency learning
◊ keeping tabs on people, calling them when they aren't in class, not letting them disappear
◊ teaching academic survival skills
◊ listening to their stories of success and failure
◊ requiring students to work in small groups, to teach one another, and so on
◊ teaching to different learning styles
◊ having them do their papers on a word processor during class time when I can coach and instruct them as they work
◊ encouraging all students while being honest about strengths and weaknesses
◊ expecting the best from each person

These things work some of the time because they show respect for the students and they reflect my optimistic belief in the students and their desire to learn.

I think of Liz (not her real name) who is a divorced, single parent. She is trying to reconcile with her ex-husband (whom she depends on for her transportation to campus), parent three children, and earn an associate's degree as a medical assistant. Liz is both at risk because she lacks the experience and the confidence of working independently on academic tasks and because she lacks reading and writing skills necessary to succeed in college and on the job. But she is making progress: she has told her ex-husband and children that she will stay on campus to work on her assignments rather than leaving immediately after class, she is working hard to find the main ideas in material we read and discuss in class, and she is struggling to write an autobiographical sketch of her "Life as a Reader."

Liz is in a developmental course, English 208: Effective Reading One and Vocabulary Development, where she is learning about the nature of the reading process while practicing various strategies that will make her a more proficient reader. But when she finishes the courses, I doubt that she will be ready to succeed in the Intro to American Government Course or Intro to Psychology. Liz, and others like her, has too much ground to make up. She will need several semesters of developmental work. But like most such students, Liz will probably move on to other courses—perhaps an American history course—before she becomes proficient enough as a reader and writer to begin to struggle with the challenges she will have in that two hundred level course. Furthermore, she will still lack the extensive background knowledge so crucial to success in college. For instance, Liz and her classmates could not name the seven continents nor draw a flat map of the earth when we dealt with these subjects a few weeks ago.

Liz and other developmental students are usually keenly aware of their "deficiencies"—the gaps in their knowledge and skills. In general, they do not expect me to "coddle" them as Jerry fears many of us at Delta do. Nor do they want me to patronize them. (They may not yet know this vocabulary word, but they recognize the behavior.) Nor will they tolerate disrespect or insulting comments or behavior from me. They expect, and I try to provide, useful and accurate instruction, appropriate and timely feedback, plus individualized coaching and encouragement.

In short, I do not make excuses for their lack of knowledge or skills because they may have spent several years of their lives in an alcoholic haze, nor do I ignore their relatively poor writing and reading skills caused by learning disabilities or lack of practice. They expect me to teach them how to overcome these problems and to help them succeed at Delta and on the job. (I have yet to work with a developmental student who wanted to "put in time" so he or she could avoid work, stay on welfare, or in some other way avoid improving his or her life and that of his or her family.) But I do acknowledge that such problems exist. I relate some of my developmental experiences and some of the behaviors and choices which have put me at risk at times. I see students nodding in agreement and recognition. I am "human," a flawed person like themselves. I also share some of my successes and I encourage them to share theirs. We read and discuss up-lifting aphorisms such as Martin Luther King's statement that "We must accept finite disappointment, but we must never lose infinite hope."

While not making excuses or ignoring deficiencies, I try not to rush the process of learning new information and consolidating new skills. This means I am almost always behind in my syllabus—actually I only do a two-week syllabus because I have to make my schedule fit the needs and progress of the students. I also provide a lot of coaching in private conferences—the time when I do my best teaching, I think, and initially, a very intimidating experience for most students. I encourage, and sometimes require, the students to use the Math Lab and the Learning Center. And I encourage participation in the P.A.L. programs and regular contact with Peer Listeners, the Campus Minister, and their counselors. With varying degrees of success, I try to set up study groups and encourage good study habits.

Much of what I am doing in my developmental courses such as English 101 and 108, I carry over to my general ed courses such as English 111: College Composition One and English 271: Survey of American Literature. I encourage study groups, I require individual conferences, I teach note-taking, I provide study guides, and so on. At times I get frustrated. I wonder, "Why can't I just teach the course? After all, this is college, not high school!" When these frustrations occur, I have to remind myself that developmental education, as a recognized part of the college experience, started at Harvard over a hundred years ago, that George Washington Carver, the son of slaves, was an at-risk student, and that Delta, like all of America's colleges to some degree, is in business to provide opportunities to all citizens who want to learn more about themselves and the world, while preparing for an active and productive career in the world.

Because I believe these things and because I have seen at-risk and developmental students make amazing progress in spite of heavy odds against them, I will continue to tolerate the uneasiness that comes when I wonder if I am being "too soft," whether my courses are "too easy," and whether I am being too lenient. It seems to me that this unease must be part of my professional life as long as I choose to teach at a community college.

# APPENDIX 1-2

## A FABLE FOR DEVELOPMENTAL EDUCATORS

By Karen Martin, Director, Hughes Science Learning Center, Fisk University
(Reprinted by permission of the author.)

Once upon a time, Developmental Educators sailed upon the ark known as Traditional Psychology and Education. Each educator and psychologist was allowed two hypotheses or two theories of his/her choice aboard. And they sailed the seven seas in search of students upon which they could use their theories. In time, the hypotheses became theories, and the theories multiplied exponentially, and the educators and psychologists were very happy.

The Developmental Educators—an off-shoot group composed of both disciplines—were uneasy. They attributed their uneasiness with the status quo to being seasick, but when they could find no physiological reason for their distress, they began to look around. They peered over the side of the ark, and were shocked at what they found. At once, they noticed two things. The sea was full of struggling students who were trying to stay afloat in an education system that threw them out to sea and blamed them when they were not successful. Also, to their horror, the ark upon which they were sailing, overburdened with theories and new hypotheses, was sinking. The Developmental Educators tried to sound the alarm, but to no avail. They could not get permission from the Captain's five secretaries to see him about the problem, and the secretaries could not agree on where the alarm was located.

So the Developmental Educators gathered up a few theories they thought would be useful— Maslow, Glasser, Piaget—and they jumped overboard into the sea of struggling students. They found every type of student imaginable, every race, ethnic background, learning problem, age group, and both genders. They quickly learned that if they were to stay afloat, they would have to jettison all unnecessary traditions and theories, and respond accordingly to the unpredictable sea and climate. And for their trouble, they were given the scraps of food thrown away by people from the ark.

One by one, they began to reestablish contact with each other, and soon decided to build their own boat, and many Developmental Educators advocated bringing students instead of theories aboard. It remains to be seen what will happen with the space on the boat, but it could be that the best use of it will be for teaching—that is, teaching students how to build boats.

# APPENDIX 2-1

## LIST OF FREQUENTLY USED TESTS

Note: Many of the test publishers have web pages on the Internet. Check the ads in the *Journal of Developmental Education*.

### BASIC SKILLS PLACEMENT BATTERIES

The following tests are examples of those colleges currently use to place students in basic skills courses and for assessing their progress in skills programs. Some states like Georgia, Texas, and Tennessee have their own mandated testing program and use their own instruments. These state tests may be available for purchase in the year after they are used by the state.

*Computerized Placement Tests* measure basic skills in reading comprehension, sentence skills, arithmetic, and elementary algebra. Tests are administered by computer and average 15 to 20 minutes each. *ACCUPLACER*, computerized placement management software, is available. Publisher: The College Board, 45 Columbus Avenue, NY, NY 10023-6992 (Attn: L. J. Abernathy). Can be scored with desktop scanners or scantron and includes:

    Tests of verbal assessment:
        Levels of English Proficiency (for low
            proficiency English speakers and
            English-as-a-second language (ESL) students)
        Reading Comprehension
        Sentence Skills
    Tests of Mathematics Assessment
        Supplemental Skills
        Arithmetic
        Elementary Algebra
        College level mathematics
(Note: *COMPANION* is the College Board's paper and pencil version of CPT Assessments and is available in large print, audio, and Braille.)

For information about the accuracy and development of computerized adaptive tests, call the College Board for a copy of COMPUTERIZED PLACEMENT TESTS: BACKGROUND READINGS, which includes descriptions and validation studies from different colleges (212) 713-8082.

*COMPASS* is the American Council of Testing's (ACT) computerized adaptive placement, assessment, and diagnostic test for underprepared students. The companion paper and pencil test is called ASSET. For more information, contact the ACT Education Services Division–11, P.O. Box 168, Iowa City, IA 52243-0168 FAX (319) 233-3021.

*ABLE (Adult Basic Learning Examination* 2nd Edition, Form E, Level 3) measures vocabulary, reading comprehension, spelling, language, number operations and problem solving. Publisher: Psychological Corporation c/o Harcourt Brace Jovanovich, 7500 Old Oak Blvd., Cleveland, OH 44130.

*Tests of Adult Basic Education (TABE)* Form 5, Level D. Estimated level: Grades 6.6-8.9. Measures vocabulary, reading comprehension, mathematics computation, mathematics concepts and applications, language mechanics, language expression and spelling. Publisher: CTB/McGraw-Hill, Del Monte Research Park, Monterey, CA.

*Tests of Adult Basic Education (TABE)* Form 5, Level A. Level: Grades 8.6-12.9. Measures same skills as TABE Level D. Publisher: CTB/McGraw-Hill, Del Monte Research Park, Monterey, CA.

*TASK—Stanford Test of Academic Skills*: Basic Battery Level 2, For E. Level:  Grades 9-14.  Measures reading vocabulary, reading comprehension, mathematics, spelling, English.  Publisher: Psychological Corporation c/o Harcourt Brace Jovanovich, 7500 Old Oak Blvd., Cleveland, OH  44130.

The College Board's *Guides to Learning and Instruction* is a microcomputer program of assessment and instruction with modules in writing, reading and study skills designed specifically for students placed in developmental studies programs.  Interactive programs offer individualized diagnosis and instruction with built-in special assistance for ESL students.  Can be used individually or in classes or in tutoring situations.  Comprised of ten units of reading and study skills and ten units of written communication skills.

*Degrees of Reading Power (DRP)* measures a single, holistic objective of reading comprehension. Three levels (Grades 7-9, 9-12, 12-14). Publisher: DRP Services, Dept. WA7, The College Board, 45 Columbus Ave., New York, New York  10023-6917.

*Maintaining Reading Efficiency Tests*. College Level. Measures reading rate, comprehension, efficiency—Five forms: History of Brazil, Japan, India, New Zealand, and Switzerland. Publisher: Developmental Reading Distributors, 1944 Sheridan Ave., Laramie, WY 82070.

*Metropolitan Achievement Tests*: MAT6 (Grades 7-9.9) Measures vocabulary, rate, skimming and scanning, and reading comprehension. Publisher: Psychological Corporation c/o Harcourt Brace Jovanovich, 7500 Old Oak Blvd., Cleveland, OH 44130.

*Metropolitan Achievement Tests*: MAT6 Reading Survey Tests-Advanced 2, Form L (Grades 10.0-12.9) Measures vocabulary, grammar, reading comprehension skills. Publisher: Psychological Corporation c/o Harcourt Brace Jovanovich, 7500 Old Oak Blvd., Cleveland, OH 44130.

*Nelson Denny Reading Test:* Form F. (Grades 9-16). Measures vocabulary, reading rate and comprehension skills. Publisher: The Riverside Publishing Company.

*The Reading Progress Scale*: Form 2c. Level: College.  Gives a holistic measure of reading level. Publisher: Revrac Publications, Kansas City, Missouri.

*Stanford Diagnostic Reading Test*: Third Ed. Level G. Grades 9-12 and Community College. Measures reading comprehension, vocabulary, word parts, phonetic analysis, structural analysis, scanning and skimming, fast reading. Publisher: Psychological Corporation c/o Harcourt Brace Jovanovich, 7500 Old Oak Blvd., Cleveland, OH 44130.

Reference:
Wood, N. V. (1989). Reading tests and reading assessment. *Journal of Developmental Education*, *13*, 14-18.

# STUDY SKILLS HABITS AND ATTITUDES TESTS

* Indicates these tests are also available on computer program software.

*Brown-Holtzman Survey of Study Habits and Attitudes*. (Level Gr. 7-16). Sub-scores: delay avoidance, work methods, study habits, teacher approval, education acceptance, study attitudes, study orientation.  Publisher: Psychological Corporation c/o Harcourt Brace Jovanovich, 7500 Old Oak Blvd., Cleveland, OH  44130.

*\*Learning and Study Strategies Inventory (LASSI)*. Level: College (A high school version is also available called *LASSI-HS*). Measures attitude, motivation, time management, anxiety, concentration, information processing, selecting main ideas, study aids, self-testing, and test strategies. Weinstein, C.E., Palmer, D.R., & Schulte, A. (1987). Publisher: H&H Publishing Co. Inc., 1231 Kapp Drive, Clearwater, FL  33765.  (800) 366-4079.

*Survey of Reading/Study Efficiency II* Level: College (diagnostic and prescriptive test). Measures time management, study environment, personal aspects, study reading, listening/note-taking, exam strategies, writing, library research, math, memory, reading, vocabulary, concentration, health and vision, attitudes, campus involvement. (Note: This survey is designed to be used in counseling sessions. When the test is scored by Scantron, the student and counselor receive the test results and a prescription listing materials to use in improving skills in each area.) Publisher: Personal Efficiency Programs, PO Box 249, Sierra Vista, AZ 85636-0249.

*The Study Behavior Inventory.* (Revised computer version dx.) 15 minute computer-administered test, which immediately analyzes, reports, and explains a student's scores and proficiencies and prints scores in 12 areas related to academic success. A paper and pencil version is also available. Publisher: Andragogy Associations, 5947-0 Armage Spring Rd., Rancho Palos Verdes, CA 90275.

Data management software retrieves, collates, sorts, analyzes, prints, and performs statistical treatment on scored test data. Measures three factors: 1) students' perceptions of their academic abilities and feelings of security, 2) preparation for day-to-day routine academic tasks, and 3) preparation for special academic tasks such as term papers and examinations. It is assumed that feelings of competence as shown by scores on the first factor mediate study behaviors in factors 2 and 3.

*PEEK (Perceptions, Expectations, Emotions and Knowledge about College).* Self-report instrument designed to assess thoughts about possible personal, social, and academic changes that may occur in college. Helps compare student and faculty expectations about college, (20 minute test—academic experiences, personal experiences, and social experiences in college.) H&H Publishing Company, 1231 Kapp Drive, Clearwater, FL 33765. (800) 366-4079.

*The High-Risk Student Profile.* Jeanne L. Higbee and Patricia L. Dwinelle. *Research & Teaching in Developmental Education,* 7(1) (Fall 1990), 55-64.

The authors assert that some measures of affective variables are more potent predictors of academic success among high-risk students than are high school grade point average or scores on standardized tests. Inventory format helps instructors understand the individualized needs of high-risk students. Includes a goals checklist where students check their reasons for coming to college and for attending the specific institution they chose (in this case the University of Georgia); Meyers Briggs Type Indicator and the James and Galbraith Learning Style Inventory; Career Exploration (The Holland Self-Directed Search, measures of stress and academic anxiety—test anxiety, math anxiety, etc.); The Student Developmental Task and Life Style Inventory assesses whether the student has made progress in completing the developmental tasks of the traditional age college student and includes such dimensions as educational involvement, life management, academic autonomy, emotional autonomy, etc.

*James and Gailbraith Learning Styles Inventory.* James, W. B., & Galbraith, M. W. (1985). Perceptual learning styles: Implications and techniques for the practitioner. *Lifelong Learning,* 8(4) 20-23.

*Canfield's Learning Style Inventory,* Humanics Media, Liberty Drawer 7970, Ann Arbor, MI 48107. Conditions: Concerns for the dynamics of the situation in which learning occurs. Subscores include:
A.  Affiliation: Relations with others
    P-Working with peers
    T-Knowing the teacher personally
B.  Structure: Logical, well-defined, and clear study plans
    O-Organization: Course work logically and clearly organized, meaningful assignments, and a logical sequence of activities
    D-Detail: Specific information on assignments, requirements, rules, and so on
C.  Achievement: Independence of action, pursuit of own interests, and so on
    G-Goal Setting: Setting one's own objectives, pursuing one's own interests and objectives
    I-Independence: Working alone and independently

D.  Eminence: Comparing self with others
E.  Competition: Desiring competition with others
F.  Authority: Desiring classroom discipline and order; desiring informed and knowledgeable teachers
G.  Content: Major area of interest
    N-Numeric: Working with numbers and logic, computing, and so on
    Q-Qualitative: Working with words or language, writing, editing, talking, and so on
    I-Inanimate: Working with things, designing, constructing
    P-People: Working with people, interviewing, counseling, selling, helping
H.  Mode: General modality through which learning is preferred
    L-Listening
    R-Reading
    I-Iconics: Viewing illustrations, graphs and movies
    D-Direct experience: Handling or performing (as in shop, laboratory, field trips, practice exercises)

*Kolb's Learning Style Inventory.* Smith, D. M., & Kolb, D. (1986). *User's guide for the Learning Style Inventory: A manual for teachers and trainers.* Boston: McBer & Company.

*Myers-Briggs Type Indicator* measures four thinking styles:
    Extraversion/introversion
    sensing/intuition
    thinking/feeling
    judging/perceiving

References:

Briggs, K. C., & Myers, I. B. (1943). *Myers-Briggs type indicator.* Palo Alto, CA: Consulting Psychologists Press.

Myers, I. B. (1980). *Gifts differing*, Palo Alto, CA: Consulting Psychologists Press.

Myers, I. B., & McCaulley, M. H. (1985). *Manual: A guide to the development and use of the Myers-Briggs type indicator.* (2nd ed.). Palo Alto, CA: Consulting Psychologists Press.

# SELF-CONCEPT MEASURES

Reynolds, W., Ramirez, M., Magrina, A., & Allen, J. (1990). Initial development and validation of the academic self-concept scale. *Educational and Psychological Measurement, 40*, 1013-1016.

*Test of Reactions and Adaptation in College (TRAC):* A New Measure of Learning Propensity for College Students by S. Larose and R. Roy. *Journal of Educational Psychology, 87*(2), 293-306. Consists of 50 items addressing beliefs, emotional and behavioral factors that intervene in typical college learning situations. Factor analysis suggests that these are three independent factors and the test has been shown to improve the prediction of first semester college grades over high school grade factors. Measures disposition toward subject, teachers, and peers. (Items are included with article.)

James, W. B., & Galbraith, M. W. (1985). Perceptual learning styles: Implications and techniques for the professional. *Lifelong Learning, 8*, 20-23.

# MEASURES OF MATHEMATICS ANXIETY

Fennema, E., & Sherman, J. S. (1976). Fennema-Sherman mathematics attitude scales. *JSAS Catalog of Selected Documents in Psychology, 6*, 31. (Includes a math anxiety scale.)

Richardson, F. C., & Suinn, R. M. (1972). The mathematics anxiety rating scale: Psychometric data. *Journal of Counseling Psychology, 19*, 551-554.

Suinn, R. M. (1972). *Mathematics anxiety rating scale (MARS).* Fort Collins, CO: Rocky Mountain Behavior Sciences Institute.

## Test Anxiety Scales

Speilberger, C. D. (1977). *The test attitude inventory.* Palo Alto, CA: Consulting Psychologists Press.

## Tests of Critical Thinking

*Watson-Glaser Critical Thinking Test Appraisal.* Measures ability and logic in defining a problem, selecting information for solution, recognizing stated and unstated hypotheses, and drawing valid conclusions. Publisher: Harcourt Brace Jovanovich, 757 Third Ave., New York, N.Y. 10017.

*The Academic Profile.* Level: College. Measures college-level reading, college-level writing, critical thinking, and using mathematical data in 3 disciplines: humanities, social sciences, and natural sciences. Publisher: Educational Testing Service, College and University Programs, Princeton, NJ 08541-0001.

*Cornell Critical Thinking Test.* Level 2. Level: advanced high school students and college students. Measures induction, deduction, observation, credibility, defining, and assumption identification. Publisher: Midwest Publications, P.O. Box 448, Pacific Grove, CA 93950.

*Ennis Weir Critical Thinking Essay Test.* Level: Grades 7-through college. Students are given 40 minutes to write a letter to the editor that takes a particular position. Students critique the thinking in the letter. Measures getting to the point, seeing reasons and assumptions, stating one's point, offering some good reasons, responding appropriately. Publisher: Midwest Publications, P.O. Box 448, Pacific Grove, CA 93950.

*California Critical Thinking Dispositions Inventory* (7 scales) and the *California Holistic Critical Thinking Scoring Rubric* that can be applied to essays. Source: Peter A. Facion, Noreen C. Facion, California Academic Press, 1994.

## Teaching Goals and Classroom Assessment Techniques (CATS)

*Teaching Goals Inventory and Self-Scorable Worksheet.* In Angelo, T. A., & Cross, K. P. (1993). *Classroom Assessment Techniques: A Handbook for College Teachers*, Second Edition. San Francisco: Jossey-Bass. A self-assessment of 52 instructional goals with three purposes: 1) to help college teachers become more aware of what they want to accomplish in individual courses; 2) to help faculty locate classroom assessment techniques they can adapt and use to assess how well they are achieving their teaching and learning goals; and 3) to provide a starting point for discussion of teaching and learning goals among educators.

## Multicultural Attitude Tests

Kelley, C., & Meyers, J. *The Cross-Cultural Adaptability Inventory.* This is a self-assessment instrument designed to measure how well an individual can adapt to any culture. It measures 5 needs: 1) to understand the qualities which can enhance cross-cultural effectiveness; 2) to become self-aware of one's strengths and the areas one needs to improve; 3) to aid in decisions about working in a cross-cultural company or situation or whether to live abroad; 4) to prepare to enter another culture through customized, individualized training, and 5) to improve one's skills in interacting with people from other cultures in a work or social situation. This test has been used widely by trainers in helping people adapt to culturally diverse work environments and those planning to work or travel abroad. Publisher: Intercultural Press, P.O. Box 700, Yarmouth, ME 04096. (207) 846-5168.

Anderson & Harrington. *Multi-Cultural Awareness Scale.* In Judy Stanos Harrington. (Spring, 1991). Multicultural awareness training for learning assistance staff, *Journal of College Reading and Learning*, XXIII (2).

References:

Wittmer, J., & Associates. (1992). *Valuing diversity and similarity: Bridging the gap through interpersonal skills*. Minneapolis, MNL Educational Media Corporation.

Taylor, K. E. (1990). *The dilemma of difference: The relationship of the intellectual development, racial identity, and self-esteem of black and white students to their tolerance for diversity*. Dissertation. Univ. of Maryland-College Park. Ann Arbor, MI: Dissertation Abstracts #9121439.

Ottsen, C. C. (1994). *L.A. stories: The voices of cultural diversity*. Yarmouth, ME: Intercultural Press, Inc. Adult students from diverse cultural backgrounds who are enrolled in remedial writing at an L.A. college write about their lives, giving the reader a deeper understanding of what multiculturalism in America is all about. Also the book reflects the efforts of a mainstream teacher who helps her students translate their feelings into acceptable English prose.

# APPENDIX 2-2

## TYPICAL EVALUATION QUESTIONS AND METHODS

(Adapted from Anderson & Ball, 1980)

The following is a list of evaluation questions, followed by some of the evaluation methods that are appropriate to answer them.

1. **Program Objectives.**
   How valid are they, how useful in meeting student needs?
   EVALUATION METHODS: expert judgment surveys of other learning centers.

   A. Are your objectives consistent with best practices in your profession?
   EVALUATION METHODS: survey of other learning centers, CAS Standards and Guidelines, observation/testimonials, expert judgment.

   B. Are your objectives consistent with those of your college?
   EVALUATION METHOD: expert judgment.

   C. Do students accept your objectives?
   EVALUATION METHOD: student survey, observations, testimonials.

   D. Do faculty accept your objectives?
   EVALUATION METHODS: faculty survey, expert judgment, testimonial.

2. **Program Curriculum Content.**
   Is curriculum relevant to your objectives?

   A. Are your objectives covered in the curriculum?

B. Is the material technically accurate?

C. Is the structure appropriate?
EVALUATION METHODS: expert judgment.

D. Is curriculum relevant to background of students? Is curriculum relevant to the advanced courses the students will take later?
EVALUATION METHODS: student survey, expert judgment.

E. Are the components and sequencing of components effective?
EVALUATION METHODS: Experimental study, quasi-experimental study, expert judgment.

F. Is the difficulty level appropriate?
EVALUATION METHODS: student surveys.

3. **Instructional Methods.**

   A. Are presentation methods effective? Pacing, length, grading?

   B. How effective is the instruction?

   C. Are students actually learning the skills and are they able to apply them?
   EVALUATION METHODS: experimental study, quasi-experimental study.

4. **Program Context.**

   Administrative support, administrative procedures (i.e. staff roles and relations, public relations, facilities, budget sources and stability, budget procedures).

   EVALUATION METHODS: survey of other learning centers, expert judgment, case study, observation/testimonials, CAS Standards and Guidelines. (See Appendix 4-1.)

5. **Policies and Practices.**

   Is the student recruitment policy working well? Are students well informed about the program? EVALUATION METHODS: correlational study, student survey, student assessment, expert judgment.

6. **Student selection and placement.**

   Are the placement procedures adequate? Are cut-off scores accurate in determining who needs the program? Are counseling/advising services working well as a part of placement? EVALUATION METHODS: experimental study, quasi-experimental study, correlational study.

7. **Impact on Student Retention.**

   For example: Does a comprehensive learning assistance program increase the retention of high risk students? EVALUATION METHODS: correlational study, student assessment. One example is a study by Helm and Chand (1983), who evaluated their program's goal of improving persistence and completion rates of high-risk students.

Focusing on the low completion rate of the math courses, which had the highest enrollment but where only 40-50% of the students completed the course, they set up development activities for mathematics faculty and staff. As a result of the staff training program, they were able to increase the student completion rate of these courses by around 24%. By identifying very high-risk students early and putting forth team effort to help them, they were able to increase the retention rate to 60%.

8. **Cost Benefits in Relation to Other Strategies.**

   A. Can the same amount of learning be provided at lower cost or in a shorter time?

   B. Can more learning be acquired at the same cost?

   C. Do students who receive group tutoring in science benefit as much as those receiving more expensive individual tutoring?

   D. Should scarce resources be allocated to developmental skills programs which help underprepared students or should they be allocated to other departments that are more cost-effective? (Note: This is a loaded question, but one that administrators often ask.)

   EVALUATION METHODS: quasi-experimental study, correlational study, experimental study (if there's a way to randomly assign students/tutees to each condition).

# APPENDIX 3-1

## TUTORING RESOURCES

### MANUALS

Clark, B. L. (1988). *Talking about writing: A guide for tutor and teacher conference*. Ann Arbor: University of Michigan Press.

Myer, E., & Smith, L. Z. (1987). *The practical tutor*. New York: Oxford University Press.

(The Clark and Meyer & Smith books are primarily for writing tutors.)

Myers, L. (1990). *Becoming an effective tutor*. Los Altos, CA: Crisp.

MacDonald, R. (1994). *The master tutor*. Cambridge Stratford Study Skills Institute, 8560 Main St., Williamsville, NY 14221 (800) 466-2232. (For tutoring in any subject.)

### GENERAL INFORMATION FOR TUTOR TRAINING

Gier, T., & Hancock, K. (Eds.) (1993). *Tutor certification registry & tutor resources*. College Reading & Learning Association (CRLA). For information contact: Ms. Gladys Shaw, Coordinator CRLA International Tutor Certification Program, Tutoring & Learning Center, 300 Library, University of Texas-El Paso, TX 79968-0611. Phone (915) 747-5366.

*The tutoring exchange*. Published by CRLA. Address: Karan Hancock, 8102 Harvest Circle. Anchorage, Alaska 99502.

Maxwell, M. (Ed.). (1994). *When tutor meets student*. Ann Arbor: University of Michigan Press. (Stories by 51 writing tutors about their tutoring experiences, plus a complete description of a tutoring writing-for-credit course that's been offered for over 20 years.)

Silberman, M. (1990). *Active training: A handbook of techniques, designs, case examples and tips*. New York, Lexington Books.

Treuer, P. (1995). *Credit-based peer tutor: A centralized peer tutoring program*. Send a check for $20.00 made out to the University of Minnesota-Duluth to Paul Treuer, Campus Center 40, University of Minnesota-Duluth, 10 University Drive, Duluth, Minnesota 55812-2496.

Those who are planning tutor-for-credit courses will find lots of information to justify their proposals, including figures that indicate cost-effectiveness (current budget and student use figures) and arguments for justifying the course to faculty committees. The syllabi for the course and practicum contain excellent suggestions for improving existing courses, as well as criteria for evaluating and grading students and grading contracts for students delineating what is required for grades A through F. Also assignments including specifics for developing a professional tutoring portfolio, reflective papers on the tutoring experience, developing one's personal philosophy of tutoring, tutoring ethics, and examples of students' work.

In addition to the course information and an overview and history of the UM-D tutoring program, the book has sections on Tutor Center Management and Internet Tutoring Applications (the Homework Hotline, OWL, etc.), evaluation, etc.

*The tutor's guide*. 14 fifteen-minute video programs for training tutors, plus a handbook. Produced by the UCLA Office of Instructional Development. Order from: GPN, P.O. Box 80669, Lincoln NE 68501-0669. (800)-228-4630.

(Topics include: Introduction to tutoring—helping students help themselves; three strategies for initiating the first session, developing a tutorial plan, diagnosis and the Socratic method, diagnosis through observation, tutoring learning skills, managing group tutorials, the tutor as counselor, bridging cultural gaps, tutoring physical science, tutoring social sciences, tutoring humanities, tutoring the writing process, and tutoring ESL.)

# Tutoring the Disabled

Order the following from: AHEAD—Association on Higher Education and Disability, P.O. Box 21192, Columbus, OH 43221-0192  Phone (614) 488-4972.

*Assisting College Students with Disabilities: A Tutor's Manual* by Pamela Adelman and Debbie Olufs.  For tutors who work with students with learning disabilities.

*Peer Mentoring: A Support Group Model for College Students with Disabilities* by Roberta Gimblett.

# Newsletters

*The Writing Lab Newsletter.* Muriel Harris, Editor, Department of English, Heavilon Hall, Purdue University, West Lafayette, IN 47907.

*The Dangling Modifier*, a newsletter by and for writing tutors. Penn State Writing Center, 219 Boucke Bldg., University Park, PA 16802  FAX (814) 863-8704.

*National Tutoring Association Newsletter.*  For membership, contact Diana Williams, Student Resource Center, Mail Stop 526, Medical College of PA and Hahnemann University,  201 North 15th Street, Philadelphia, PA 19102-1192.  Phone (215) 762-7682.

# Evaluating Tutoring

Maxwell, M. (1993). *Evaluating academic skills programs: A sourcebook.*  Chapter 4 concerns evaluating tutoring and contains information, references, plus 30 pages of instruments that programs use to evaluate their tutors and tutoring programs.  ($40 plus $6 S&H) Order from MM Associates, Box 2857, Kensington, MD 20891.

Maxwell, M. (Ed.) (1994) *From Access to Success: A Book of Readings in Developmental Learning and Learning Assistance.* Has seven articles on tutoring including one on evaluating tutoring programs.  H&H Publishing Co., 1231 Kapp Drive, Clearwater, FL 33765  (800) 366-4079.

NADE's *Self-Evaluation Guides* for Developmental Skills and Learning Assistance Programs (1994). Published by H&H Publishing Co., 1231 Kapp Drive, Clearwater, FL 33765  (800) 366-4079.  Has a complete guide for evaluating a tutoring program.

*TESAT–Tutor Evaluation and Self-Assessment Test* (1996). Cambridge Stratford Study Skills Institute, 8560 Main St., Williamsville, NY  14221 (800) 466-2232.  A new self-assessment scale for tutors that can be used before and after training to show their improvement in interacting with students in any subject.  Measures tutor's performance in a single session.  Although it is based on Ross MacDonald's twelve step cycle for tutoring, it can be used by any tutor to improve tutoring and/or as a basis for discussion with their supervisor.

(Also see Maxwell's *When Tutor Meets Student* and Treuer's *Credit-Based Peer Tutor: A Centralized Peer Tutoring Program* for ideas about qualitative indicators of tutoring effectiveness.)

# Learning Center Standards

Materniak G., & Williams, A. (September 1987). CAS standards and guidelines for learning assistance programs. *Journal of Developmental Education*, *11*(1), 12-18. (Copies of the CAS Standards and Guidelines for Learning Assistance Programs and The Learning Assistance Programs Self-Assessment Guide can be obtained from the Council for the Advancement of Standards, Douglas K. Large, Dean of Student Affairs, South Dakota School of Mines and Technology, Rapid City, SD  57701.  Note: These standards are being revised and updated. The current draft is included in Appendix 4-1.

# General References on Evaluation

Herman, J. L. (Ed.). Center for Evaluation at UCLA. *Program Evaluation Kit.*  Sage Publications, Inc. 2111 West Hillcrest Dr., Newbury Park, CA  91320. The kit contains nine books on different aspects of evaluation.

# APPENDIX 3-2

## DIFFICULT TUTORING SITUATIONS

MIKE ROSE (UCLA)

The interpersonal dimension of the tutoring process is as important as the tutor's subject competence. And while most tutorial sessions offer no significant interpersonal problems, the difficult, ineffective encounter is always possible. The following discussions might be of help if such an encounter should occur. This material is reprinted by permission of Mike Rose (1976), Tutor Coordinator, University of California, Los Angeles.

## DYSFUNCTIONAL TUTEE STYLES

The majority of contacts between a tutor and a tutee go rather smoothly—both parties honestly and effectively engaging in the learning process. However, there are some tutorial encounters that do not go smoothly because of a disruptive affect or attitude presented by the tutee. Indeed, the student may even assume an entire "style" in relating to the tutor. The following taxonomy offers seven such disruptive styles, common identifying characteristics, and suggested approaches to aid in establishing an effective learning relationship.

Two cautions:

1. Do not see these as mutually exclusive or as rigid postures evident from the first day. Under the various pressures of the quarter, a previously efficient student may drift into or assume one or more of these styles. The suggested approaches, however, would remain the same, with the additional suggestion of appealing to history—for example, "Well, three weeks ago, this was going fairly smoothly. Let's figure out when it was that things got confusing."

2. Though much of what a tutor does involves academic "counseling" (for example, tips on classes, study suggestions, warnings about specific professors), a tutor should not slip into the role of psychological counselor. The tutor should be extremely cautious about probing into any issues that seem to be highly emotionally charged, deeply defended, or significantly volatile. Doing this can either trigger disruptive emotional material or foster an inappropriate dependency, or both. If you have reason to suspect that your tutee is experiencing emotional difficulties, please consult with the tutorial coordinator and the tutee's AAP counselor. With this in mind, the taxonomy on the following page is to be used to establish an effective learning relationship, a relationship that allows a tutee to grow intellectually, and allows a tutor to avoid frustration and grow as a learning facilitator.

| STYLE | CHARACTERIZED BY | APPROACH |
|---|---|---|
| 1. Blocking | ◊ low frustration tolerance<br>◊ immobilization/hopelessness<br>◊ freezing up/blocking<br>◊ "It's beyond me."<br>◊ "I'll never get it."<br>◊ "I'm stuck." | ◊ determine what the tutee does know and discuss that—show him that he has some foundation<br>◊ begin from what he knows and build, in simple steps, toward increasingly complex material<br>◊ offer continual support<br>◊ reinforce success consistently |
| 2. Contusion (a blocking) | ◊ bafflement/disorientation/ disorganization<br>◊ helpless feeling about the class<br>◊ "I just don't know what to do."<br>◊ "I don't know what the prof wants."<br>◊ "I studied for the test and got a D."<br>◊ "I'm not sure where we're going." | ◊ utilize the above four approaches<br><br>◊ give structure and order to the tutee's tutorial sessions, to his notes, to papers |
| 3. Miracle Seeking | ◊ global interest or concern but with little specificity<br>◊ enthusiasm about being with tutor, but fairly passive in actual tutoring process<br>◊ high (often inappropriate) level of expectation<br>◊ evasion or inability to concentrate on concrete tasks | ◊ downplay your role (for example, "Look, I've simply had more exposure to this stuff, that's all.")<br>◊ focus again and again to specific task<br>◊ involve student continually with questions, problems<br>◊ explain significance of active participation in learning process |
| 4. Overenthusiasm (somewhat a variation of Miracle Seeking) | ◊ high expectations/demands of self<br>◊ talk of limited time, long range goals versus immediate tasks<br>◊ global interest/enthusiasm<br>◊ often found with older students (for example, "Look I'm thirty years old; I don't have the time these kids have.") | ◊ explain counterproductiue nature of this eagerness<br>◊ be understanding, yet assure the student that he has time<br>◊ utilize numbers 2, 3, and 4 under Miracle Seeking as listed above |

| STYLE | CHARACTERIZED BY | APPROACH |
|---|---|---|
| 5. Resisting | ◊ variations of sullenness/hostility/ passivity/boredom<br>◊ disinterest in class/work/tutor *or*<br>◊ defensive posture toward class/ work/tutor<br>◊ easily triggered anger | ◊ allow student to ventilate<br>◊ spend first session—possibly even second—on building relationship<br>◊ be pragmatic, yet understanding (for example, "Look, I know this class is a bore, but you need it to graduate—let's make the best of it.")<br>◊ establish your credibility/indicate past successes in similar situations<br>◊ if it comes up, assure student that his complaints about a class are confidential |
| 6. Passivity (often a variant of Resisting) | ◊ noninvolvement/inattention/ low affect<br>◊ boredom<br>◊ little discussion initiated/ few questions | ◊ empathize (for example, "You're not crazy about asking a lot of questions in class, are you?" or "It's pretty much of a drag to sit here, isn't it?")<br>◊ attempt to build a relationship and mobilize the student<br>◊ utilize as many mobilizing techniques as possible—questions, problems, minitasks to be accomplished by next session (even checking a book out of the library)<br>◊ reinforce all activities and successes |
| 7. Evasion | ◊ manipulation<br>◊ verbal ability/glibness versus focused writing or problem solving skills<br>◊ global/nonspecific praise of tutor's skill, course content, and so on. | ◊ as with 2 under Miracle Seeking, downplay your role<br>◊ focus the student on specific tasks; involve him continually with questions, problems<br>◊ If evasion continues, you should ask, in a nonthreatening way, why the student has come for tutoring and what he expects from you (for example, "You know, we've met several times already, but we haven't gotten much done—do you think we should plan for future sessions?" or "My biggest concern is your success in this class; how, specifically, can I help you with that?") |

# Difficulties with an
# Older Student

Some tutoring considerations derived from a case study: Susan Williams is thirty-seven years old. Except for a few scattered adult school or junior college classes, she hasn't been in school for over fifteen years. Two years ago she divorced her husband and, as part of her movement toward autonomy, began a curriculum at a community college; now she is in her second quarter at UCLA: a junior sociology major. Her tutor is Betty, a twenty-one-year-old senior who is bright, enthusiastic, and very friendly. In almost a year of tutoring, Betty has had nothing but positive experiences.

After four sessions with Susan, however, Betty reported that she was unhappy about her work with this student. She wasn't sure about the roots of her disappointment, but she did say, "We get off the track; there's some material that doesn't get covered." Several consultations later, the following picture emerged:

---

*Susan was:*

( 1 ) given to mood swings—one session she would appear collected and fairly calm, another session she would be confused, pushy, irritated, and irritating.

(2) given to talking—in her anxious times more than others—about tangential, even unrelated, topics. Often these topics were related to life experiences that her years had afforded her.

(3) at times extremely friendly, almost motherly. (She even called Betty several times "just to talk.") This would sharply contrast with the pushy, abrasive side of her personality.

(4) given to requesting a change in the topic Betty had planned to discuss in a session. Something else, in Susan's eyes, seemed to be more important or, at least, more interesting.

*Betty would:*

go with the mood. She had good sessions when Susan was composed, but when Susan was scattered and aggressive the sessions would quickly lose direction. Betty felt "time was wasted."

be reluctant to pull Susan back to the specific subject, having learned that a "good teacher" should give a student "freedom to be and explore." Betty also "felt my youth" here versus the "experience" of Susan.

feel quite good about the warmth and feel hurt by the abrasiveness.

feel frustrated ("wasting time") about the request, but did want to keep Susan interested in the material, and, also, accepted the idea that learning should be "student centered."

---

By the fifth week, Betty was angry, frustrated, and felt manipulated. To make matters worse, Susan got a D on the midterm. Going back to the previous (admittedly simplified) representation of their relationship, the causes of ill feelings and poor grades are obvious:

◊ Susan was anxious and unsure at UCLA and a bit troubled, perhaps, in other areas of her life. She would bring both her needing and her abrasive side to the sessions.

◊ Furthermore, she not only felt insecure about the material but probably felt a loss of esteem since the "expert" was young enough to be her daughter.

◊ Finally, she was a classic avoider and manipulator—dodging the challenge of the material by raising more secure interests from her own life and defending against the humiliation of having a young tutor by making a little girl of Betty.

Simply stated, Susan was a troublesome tutee even for the experienced Betty; Betty obviously needed some advice. After the consultations, Betty was able to conduct effective sessions and feel rewarded. The best news, however, was that Susan got a B on the final exam.

What happened?

What Betty came to understand was that tutoring is not the same as a peer relationship (though many new tutors find this hard to admit). Therefore, though in many areas of life experience Susan was more knowledgeable than Betty, when it came to academic sociology Betty did know what was best and, therefore, should guide the direction of the sessions. (The same point could be made here substituting a father, a veteran, an ex-convict, an athlete, and so on, in place of Susan.)

A helping relationship like tutoring exposes one to the disparate but strangely connected possibilities of dependency or inappropriate hostility. If you (like Betty) feel that a student is getting a little too needy or, on the other hand, is treating you harshly, you should consult with your supervising tutor or the center coordinator to get another perspective on the situation. Are you inviting dependency? (I suspect, for example, that Betty occasionally liked being Susan's "daughter.") Do you know how to gently but firmly put limits on your time and energy? (It's surprising how often we will not say "no" when we really should—dependency results on one end and anger results on ours.) Conversely, are you too harsh because a student reminds you of someone else or "is not your kind of person?"

Anxiety can express itself through a variety of behaviors, not just "the jitters." Confusion, digressing, abrasiveness can all indicate that a student hasn't prepared, doesn't understand the material, is apprehensive about an exam, etc. If you suspect that this is the case, gently raise the possibility. For example, "I wonder if that test next week has got you jumpy?" "Maybe not getting that material read last night has thrown you today." Once the basis of the anxiety is uncovered and briefly discussed, you can get down to some productive work.

Very valuable processes like student-centered learning, inquiry learning, "education for relevance," etc., should not be confused with the tangential, avoidance-laden reminiscences and curiosities of a student like Susan. This is definitely not to say that Susan couldn't profit from relevant discovery and self directed inquiry in an unlimited variety of educational situations. But in the encounters with Betty, the digressions always seemed to occur when Susan was confused about specific material; furthermore, they occurred continually. This should be sufficient indication that the student is avoiding, and therefore, the tutor should gently but assertively refocus the discussion, consistently backtracking to known material to engender security, then moving progressively ahead into the troublesome areas. Yes, the student might get angry, but face the anger and be honest. Say: "This is important material that I'm sure will appear on a test. I realize it's difficult, but if we take it slowly, we can master it. Understand, I'm going to keep us on this stuff until you get it. And you can get it."

Admittedly, the interaction between Susan and Betty was not representative of most tutorial encounters. Yet our examination brought into focus some considerations that are critical in any tutoring contact: issues of role-definition, dependence, guidance, and assertiveness. And these issues, as you saw, are as important as one's knowledge of the material being tutored.

## THE STUDENT WHO GLIDES INTO FAILURE

Some implications from a pilot study (with thanks to Phil Volland for doing the research described [next]): We are all familiar with the student who is anxious, irritable, and on edge because he is doing poorly in school. A lot more puzzling, however, is the student who seems calm, in control, even confident and yet ends up on probation. In some cases, he may flunk out of the university. This kind of student is especially problematic for the tutor who must monitor progress and who must often do so through the verbal reports of the tutee.

Recent preliminary research conducted by the AAP tutorial center adds another dimension to this puzzle. Brief reports received through a series of telephone interviews indicate that students with a GPA below 2.3 often explain away their need of tutorial support with the same reasons offered by students with GPAs of 3.5 and above. To put it simply, many students with low GPAs say that tutorial support "seems unnecessary," "can't be fit into a busy schedule," "isn't needed yet," etc. These comments are not unlike those offered by high achievers and, if taken at face value, can be enough to mislead or at least confuse a tutor. Many new tutors often will agree to skip an appointment, abbreviate a session, or skim material because of the apparent self-confidence of a tutee. Inevitably, however, harsh reality comes crashing down in the form of a D or an F on a quiz, test, or paper. Yet it is still not uncommon for this type of student to quickly regain composure, after the initial shock, and continue to "assure" himself and the tutor.

## WHAT'S GOING ON HERE?

Well, one possibility is that the student simply has a very poor ability to assess his own skills and the requirements of the university. Another, perhaps more likely, explanation is that the student is quite aware, on some level, that he is in serious difficulty. His entire perception of his intelligence might be very bleak. Underneath the patina of assurance and self-reliance (superficially like that of the successful student) might well be a kind of despair. His defense, to self and others, becomes a variation of denial, a whistling by the academic graveyard.

## WHAT TO DO?

Whether we're dealing here with poor self-assessment or with elaborate defensiveness, it's not a tutor's job to probe psychologically. The roots of inadequate self-assessment might go quite deep, and as for defenses, it takes a great deal of skill and time to alter them. However, a combination of reality, focusing, and assertiveness could be of great and unthreatening assistance.

1.  First of all, you should never take a student's word on progress for more than several sessions. Quiz informally, ask to see exam results, confer with TAs or instructors.

2.  If your evidence indicates that the student is doing poorly but he denies it in some way, gently but firmly raise the facts to him. For example: "Well, this D doesn't seem to go along with what you're telling me. How would you explain it?" "You know, I've tutored a lot of people in French, and the ones who are where you're at now usually don't do well on the midterm. What can we do?" "Gee, you're pretty confident, yet you've got all this to read and the exam is only three days away. How are you going to swing it?"

3.  Raise what may well be the misconception at the base of the student's denial, but do it cautiously and indirectly. For example, "You know, it's clear to me that you're good at working equations, but word problems seem to throw you." "I've worked with lots of people who think they're just terrible at understanding literature, yet usually it's just a few authors that give them trouble." "It amazes me how folks seem to think that because they can't read music, they'll have an impossible time with ethnomusicology."

What these kinds of questions hopefully tap safely into is the student's global attitude toward his own intelligence. Rather than being able to focus on single difficulties, many students quickly generalize about their overall abilities. (That is: "I'm not just unskilled in mathematics; I'm unskilled period.") Sometimes this is deeply rooted. Focus on specifics; guide the student into seeing what he does and doesn't know. This kind of reality testing might be the first step in his moving away from discouragement and toward a realistic understanding of his strengths and weaknesses.

4.  Though I've stressed being gentle when dealing with the psychological side of all this, the tutor should be fairly assertive when it comes to scheduling tasks, receiving assignments, etc. Don't get caught up in the student's cavalier front. Set firm schedules; keep focused on tasks; show the student how to study ahead; review material with him. You need to become very directive, even to the point of sitting alongside him and guiding his study. For example, "I know this is a drag, but I want us to work one more hour. It's no fun, but it's absolutely necessary if you're going to make it through this course."

Babysitting? Yes, to a degree. But the hope is that all the avoidance and denial is rooted in insecurity and that insecurity can be slowly remedied through mastery. As the student begins to see that he can understand material, he should become at least a little more curious and self-directing. Then you can begin to slowly decrease the intensity of your guidance. A truer, more lasting assurance will have been generated.

# APPENDIX 4-1

## STANDARDS AND GUIDELINES FOR LEARNING ASSISTANCE PROGRAMS

(Submitted for approval to the Council for the Advancement of Standards, Sept. 1996 by
Georgine Materniak and Martha Maxwell.)

## I. Mission

The learning assistance program must develop, record, disseminate, implement and regularly review its mission and goals. The learning assistance mission statement must be consistent with the mission and goals of the institution and with the standards of this document. The mission statement must address the purpose of the learning assistance program, the population it serves, the programs and services it provides, and the goals the program is to accomplish.

The learning assistance program must teach the skills and strategies to help students become independent and active learners and to achieve academic success.

The learning assistance program must be a partner with faculty, staff, and administrators in addressing the learning needs, academic performance, and retention of students.

Models of learning assistance programs vary but should share the following common goals:

1.   to make students the central focus of the program;

2.   to assist any member of the campus community in achieving his/her personal potential for learning;

3.   to provide instruction and services that address the cognitive, affective, and socio-cultural dimensions of learning;

4.   to introduce students to the learning expectations of the faculty and the culture of higher education;

5.   to help students develop a positive attitude towards learning and confidence in their ability to learn;

6.   to foster personal responsibility and accountability for learning through the ability to plan, monitor, and evaluate one's own learning;

7.   to provide a variety of instructional approaches that are appropriate for the level of skills and learning styles of the student population;

8.   to assist students in transferring skills and strategies they have learned to academic work across the curriculum;

9.   to provide services and resources to faculty, staff, and administrators that enhance and support classroom instruction and professional development; and

10.  to support the academic standards and requirements of the institution.

## II. PROGRAM

The formal education of students is purposeful, holistic, and consists of the curriculum and co-curriculum.

Learning assistance programs must be (a) intentional; (b) coherent; (c) based on theories and knowledge of learning and human development; (d) reflective of developmental and demographic profiles of the student population; and (e) responsive to the special needs of individuals.

Learning assistance programs must promote learning and development in students through assessing and teaching the cognitive and affective skills and strategies necessary for achieving academic and personal learning goals.

Learning assistance programs must encourage outcomes such as intellectual growth, ability to communicate effectively, realistic self-appraisal, enhanced self-esteem, learning style awareness, self-monitoring strategies, and the ability to work and learn independently and collaboratively. Students must assess their learning, set goals and identify strategies to accomplish the task, monitor their progress and adjust their strategies to produce successful learning outcomes. The program must promote, either directly or by referral, the affective skills that influence learning such as stress management, test anxiety reduction, assertiveness training, concentration improvement, motivation improvement, clarification of values, appropriate career choices, leadership development, physical fitness, meaningful interpersonal relations, social responsibility, satisfying and productive lifestyles, appreciation of aesthetic and cultural diversity, and achievement of personal goals.

Learning assistance programs must refer students to appropriate campus and community resources for assistance with personal problems, learning disabilities, financial difficulties, and other areas of need outside the purview of the learning assistance program.

The scope of the learning assistance program should be determined by the type and level of skills students require and the format utilized for strengthening academic skills, which may include mandatory credit-bearing developmental courses or non-credit elective workshops.

The scope of programs and services should also be determined by the needs of the student populations the learning assistance program is charged to serve, which can range from special populations, such as culturally and ethnically diverse students, international and English-as-a-second-language students, student athletes, returning students, and students with physical and learning disabilities, to the entire student population at all academic and developmental levels.

Formal and informal diagnostic procedures should be conducted to identify skills and strategies which the student should further develop to achieve the level of proficiency prescribed or required by the institution or known to be necessary for college learning. Assessment results should be shared with the student to formulate recommendations and a plan of instruction.

Learning assistance programs should provide instruction and services for the development of reading, mathematics and quantitative reasoning, writing, critical thinking, problem solving, and study skills. Subject-matter tutoring, adjunct instructional programs and Supplemental Instruction groups, time management programs, freshman seminars, and preparation for graduate and professional school admissions tests and for professional certification tests may also be offered.

Modes of delivering learning assistance programs should include individual and group instruction and instructional media such as print, video, audio, computers, and skills laboratories. Instruction and programs can be delivered on-site or through distance education services.

Learning assistance programs should give systematic feedback to students concerning their progress in reaching cognitive and affective goals, teach self-feedback methods utilizing the metacognitive and self-monitoring strategies students have learned, and give students practice in applying and transferring skills and strategies learned in the program to academic tasks across the curriculum.

Learning assistance programs should promote an understanding of the learning needs of the student population. The program should be a resource to educate other members of the campus community about the skill needs of students and how to help students achieve their learning goals. Some of the ways in which learning assistance programs should educate the campus community include:

◊ establishing advisory boards consisting of members from key segments of the campus community;

◊ holding periodic informational meetings with staff, faculty, and administrators;

◊ extending consultation services to staff, faculty, and administrators concerning the recognition of, understanding of, and response to the learning needs of students;

◊ participating in staff and faculty development and in-service programs on curriculum and instructional approaches that address the development of learning skills, attitudes and behaviors;

◊ encouraging the use of learning assistance program resources, materials, instruction and services as integral or adjunct classroom activities;

◊ conducting in-class workshops that demonstrate the application of learning strategies to the course content;

◊ disseminating information that describes the programs and services, hours of operation, procedures for registering or scheduling appointments through publications, campus and local media announcements, and informational presentations;

◊ training and supervising paraprofessionals and preprofessionals to work in such capacities as tutors, peer mentors, and advisors; and

◊ providing jobs, practica, courses, internships, and assistantships for graduate students interested in learning assistance and related careers.

## III. LEADERSHIP

Effective and ethical leadership is essential to the success of learning assistance programs. Institutions must appoint, position, and empower learning assistance program administrators within the administrative structure to accomplish stated missions.

Learning assistance program administrators must be selected on the basis of formal education and training, relevant work experience, personal attributes and other professional credentials. Institutions must determine expectations of accountability for learning assistance program administrators and fairly assess their performance.

Learning assistance program administrators must exercise authority over resources for which they are responsible to achieve their respective missions; must articulate a vision for their organization; establish the program mission, policies, and procedures; set goals and objectives; prescribe and practice ethical behavior; recruit, select, supervise and develop others in the learning assistance program; manage, plan, budget and evaluate; communicate effectively; and marshal cooperative action from colleagues, employees, other institutional constituencies, and persons outside the organization. Learning assistance program administrators must address individual, organizational, or environmental conditions that inhibit goal achievement. Learning assistance program administrators must improve programs and services continuously in response to changing needs of students and institutional priorities.

The learning assistance program administrator should:

◊ participate in institutional planning, policy, procedural, and fiscal decisions that affect learning support for students;

◊ be informed about issues, trends, theories, and methodologies related to student learning and retention;

◊ represent the learning assistance program and its students on institutional committees;

◊ collaborate with leaders of academic departments and support services in addressing the learning needs and retention of students;

◊ be involved in research, publication, presentations, consultation, and the activities of professional organizations; and

◊ communicate with professional constituents of the learning assistance field and related professions.

## IV. ORGANIZATION AND MANAGEMENT

Learning assistance programs and services must be structured purposefully and managed effectively to achieve stated goals. Evidence of appropriate learning assistance program structure must include current and accessible policies and procedures, written job descriptions and performance expectations for all employees, functional work flow graphics or organizational charts, and service delivery expectations. Evidence of effective learning assistance program management must include clear sources and channels of authority, effective communication practices, decision-making and conflict resolution procedures, responsiveness to changing conditions, accountability systems and recognition and reward processes. Learning assistance programs must provide channels within the organization for regular review of administrative policies and procedures.

The administrator of the learning assistance program should report directly to the executive administrator of the division to which the program reports.

The mission and goals of the learning assistance program, the needs and demographics of its clients, and its institutional role should determine where the unit is located in the organizational structure of the institution. Learning assistance programs are frequently organized as units in the academic affairs or the student affairs division. Regardless of where the learning assistance program is organized, it should communicate and collaborate with a network of key units across the institution to assure the coordination of related functions, programs, services, policies, procedures, and to expedite client referrals.

The learning assistance program should have a broadly constituted advisory board to make suggestions, provide information, and give guidance.

The learning assistance program should provide written goals, objectives, and anticipated outcomes for each program and service. Written procedures should exist for collecting, processing, and reporting student assessment and program data.

Regularly scheduled staff meetings should be held to share information; to coordinate the planning, scheduling, and delivery of programs and services; to identify and discuss potential and actual problems and concerns; and to collaborate on making decisions and solving problems.

## V. HUMAN RESOURCES

Each learning assistance program must be staffed adequately by individuals qualified to accomplish its mission and goals. Learning assistance programs must establish procedures for staff selection, training, and evaluation; set expectations for supervision, and provide appropriate professional development opportunities.

Adequate time and financial support should be allocated to encourage learning assistance program staff to conduct research, to publish professional papers, to present at local, regional, and national conferences, and to participate in work of committees, task forces, and special interest groups.

Staff and faculty who hold joint appointments with the learning assistance program must be committed to the mission, philosophy, goals, and priorities of the program and must possess the necessary expertise for assigned responsibilities.

Professional staff members must hold an earned graduate degree in a field relevant to the learning assistance position description or must possess an

appropriate combination of education and experience.

The director should have an earned graduate degree in a relevant discipline and professional experience in learning assistance program design, instruction, evaluation, and administration.

Professional staff should have earned degrees from relevant disciplines such as reading, English, mathematics, student personnel and student development, guidance and counseling, psychology, or education. Learning assistance professionals should be knowledgeable in learning theory and in the instruction, assessment, theory, and the professional standards of practice for their area of specialization and responsibility. In addition, they should understand the unique characteristics and needs of the populations they assist and teach. Learning assistance program professional staff should vary and adjust pedagogical approaches according to the learning needs and styles of their students, to the nature of the learning task, and to the content of academic disciplines across the curriculum.

The functions and roles of learning assistance program professional staff are multi-disciplinary combining the expertise and practices of various fields. Learning assistance professionals should be knowledgeable and appreciative of learning assistance practices beyond their own personal area of specialization.

Learning assistance program professional staff should be competent and experienced in:

◊   teaching, advising, and counseling students at the college level;

◊   written and oral communication skills;

◊   working in a culturally and academically diverse environment;

◊ consulting, collaborating, and negotiating with staff, faculty, and administrators of academic and student affairs units;

◊ designing and implementing instructional strategies and materials and utilizing instructional technologies;

◊ training, supervising, and mentoring paraprofessionals and preprofessionals; and

◊ identifying and establishing lines of communication for student referral to other institutional and student support units.

Degree or credential seeking interns or others in training must be qualified by enrollment in an appropriate field of study and relevant experience. These individuals must be trained and supervised adequately by professional staff members.

The learning assistance program should be informed of the policies and procedures to be followed for internships and practica as required by the students' academic departments. The roles and responsibilities of the learning assistance program and those of the academic department should be clearly defined and understood by all involved.

Learning assistance program student employees and volunteers must be carefully selected, trained, supervised, and evaluated. When their knowledge and skills are not adequate for particular situations, they must refer students and others in need of assistance to qualified professional staff.

Professional organizations should be consulted for information on learning assistance paraprofessional programs such as the National Association for Developmental Education (NADE) *Self-Evaluation Guides* for Tutoring Services and for Adjunct Instructional Programs and the Tutor Certification Program Guidelines of the College Reading and Learning Association (CRLA).

The learning assistance program must have secretarial and technical staff adequate to accomplish its mission. Such staff must be technologically proficient to perform activities including reception duties, office equipment operation, records maintenance, and mail handling.

Secretarial and technical staff should be updated on changes in programs, services, policies and procedures in order to expedite smooth and efficient assistance to clients. Staff development workshops in assertiveness, effective communication, conflict resolution, and confidentiality should be available.

Appropriate salary levels and fringe benefits for all staff members must be commensurate with those for comparable positions within the institution, in similar institutions, and in the relevant geographic area.

To reflect the diversity of the student population, to ensure the existence of readily identifiable role models for students, and to enrich the campus community, the learning assistance program must intentionally employ a diverse staff.

Affirmative action must occur in hiring and promotion practices as required to ensure diverse staffing profiles.

## VI. FINANCIAL RESOURCES

The learning assistance program must have adequate funding to accomplish its mission and goals. Priorities, whether set periodically or as a result of extraordinary conditions, must be determined within the context of the stated mission, goals, and resources.

Prior to implementing a new program or service or significantly expanding an existing program component, a financial analysis must be performed to determine the financial resources required to support the addition or expansion and the appropriate funds must be made available.

The learning assistance program budget should support its instructional and student support service functions. Adequate funds should be provided for the following budget categories: staff and student salaries, general office functions, student assessment and instructional activities, data management and program evaluation processes, staff training and professional development activities, instructional materials and media, and instructional and office computing.

## VII. FACILITIES AND EQUIPMENT

A learning assistance program must have adequate, suitably located facilities and equipment to support its mission and goals. Facilities for the learning assistance program must be convenient and accessible to students, faculty, and other clients.

Facilities and equipment must be in compliance with relevant federal, state, provincial, and local requirements to provide for access, health, and safety.

Facilities and equipment should support the instructional, support services, and office functions of the learning assistance program. Facility considerations should include flexible space that can be adapted to changes in the delivery of programs, services, and instructional modes; classrooms, labs, resource rooms, media and computer centers, group and one-to-one tutorial space to support instruction; private, sound-proofed areas to support testing, coun-

seling, and other activities that require confidentiality or concentration; adequate and secure storage for equipment, supplies, instructional and testing materials, and confidential records. Attention should be given to environmental conditions that influence learning such as appropriate acoustics, lighting, ventilation, heating and air-conditioning.

The learning assistance programs and services should accommodate students with physical and learning disabilities as required by the Americans with Disabilities Act (ADA) and other federal regulations.

## VIII. LEGAL RESPONSIBILITIES

Learning assistance program staff members must be knowledgeable about and responsive to laws and regulations that relate to their respective program or service. Sources for legal obligations and limitations are: constitutional, federal, and statutory, regulatory, and case law, mandatory laws and orders emanating from federal, state, provincial, and local governments, and the institution through its policies.

Learning assistance program staff members must use reasonable and informed practices to limit the liability exposure of the institution, its officers, employees, and agents. Staff members must be informed about institutional policies regarding personal liability and related insurance coverage options.

The institution must inform learning assistance program staff and students, in a timely and systematic fashion, about extraordinary or changing legal obligations and potential liabilities. Staff development programs must be available to educate learning assistance program staff of these changes.

## IX. EQUAL OPPORTUNITY, ACCESS AND AFFIRMATIVE ACTION

Learning assistance program staff members must ensure that services and programs are provided on a fair and equitable basis. Each learning assistance program and service must be accessible. Hours of operation must be responsive to the needs of all students. Each learning assistance program and service must adhere to the spirit and intent of equal opportunity laws.

Learning assistance programs must not be discriminatory on the basis of age, color, disability, gender, national origin, race, religious creed, sexual orientation, and/or veteran status. Exceptions are appropriate only where provided by relevant law and institutional policy.

Consistent with their mission and goals, learning assistance programs must take affirmative action to remedy significant imbalances in student participation and staffing patterns.

## X. CAMPUS AND COMMUNITY RELATIONS

Learning assistance programs must establish, maintain, and promote effective relations with relevant campus offices and external agencies.

The learning assistance program should:

◊ be an integral part of the academic offerings of the institution;

◊ establish communication with academic and student services units;

◊ encourage the exchange of ideas, knowledge, and expertise;

◊ provide mutual consultation, as needed, on student cases;

◊ expedite student referrals to and from the learning assistance program;

◊ collaborate on programs and services that efficiently and effectively address the needs of students;

◊ comply with pertinent academic and other institutional policies and procedures;

◊ disseminate information about the services;

◊ inform the campus community about the learning characteristics and needs of students;

◊ have representation on institutional committees relevant to the mission and goals of the program such as committees on retention, orientation, basic skills, learning communities, freshman seminars, probation review, academic standards and requirements, curriculum design, assessment and placement, and faculty development;

◊ solicit volunteers from the local community to contribute their skills and talents to the services of the learning assistance program; and

◊ provide training and consultation to community-based organizations, e.g., literacy associations, corporate training, and school district-based tutorial services.

## XI. DIVERSITY

Within the context of each institution's unique mission, multi-dimensional diversity enriches the community and enhances the college experience for all; therefore, learning assistance programs must nurture environments where similarities and differences among people are recognized and honored.

Learning assistance programs must promote cultural educational experiences that are characterized by open and continuous communication, that deepen understanding of one's own culture and heritage, and that respect and educate about similarities, differences and histories of cultures.

Learning assistance programs must address the characteristics and needs of a diverse population when establishing and implementing policies and procedures.

The learning assistance program should facilitate student adjustment to the academic culture of the institution by orienting students to the practices, resources, responsibilities, and behaviors that contribute to academic success.

The instructional content, materials, and activities of learning assistance programs should provide opportunities to increase awareness and appreciation of the individual and cultural differences of students.

## XII. ETHICS

All persons involved in the delivery of learning assistance programs and services to students must adhere to the highest standards of ethical behavior. Learning assistance programs and services must develop or adopt and implement statements of ethical practice addressing the issues unique to each program and service. Learning assistance programs and services must publish these statements and insure their periodic review by all concerned.

All learning assistance program staff members must ensure that confidentiality is maintained with respect to all communications and records considered confidential unless exempted by law. All staff must receive training in what constitutes confidential information and in proper procedures for obtaining, processing and recording confidential information relevant to their role within the learning assistance program.

Information disclosed in individual learning assistance sessions must remain confidential unless written permission to disclose the information is given by the student. However, all learning assistance program staff members must divulge to the appropriate authorities information judged to be of an emergency nature, especially where the safety of the individual or others is involved. Information contained in students' educational records must not be disclosed to non-institutional third parties without appropriate consent, unless classified as "directory" information or when the information is subpoenaed by law.

Learning assistance programs must apply a similar dedication to privacy and confidentiality to research data concerning individuals. All learning assistance program staff members must be aware of and comply with the provisions contained in the institution's human subjects research policy and in other relevant institutional policies addressing ethical practices.

All learning assistance program staff members must recognize and avoid personal conflict of interest or the appearance thereof in their transactions with students and others. Information and training must be made available regarding conflict of interest policies.

Because learning assistance program staff work with students' academic coursework, they must be knowledgeable of policies related to academic integrity, plagiarism, student code of conduct and other similar policies. All staff must be cognizant of the implication of these policies for their specific work with students to avoid circumstances that could be construed as contributing to or participating in violations of these policies.

Learning assistance program staff members must strive to insure the fair, objective and impartial treatment of all persons with whom they deal.

Statements or claims made about outcomes that can be achieved from participating in learning assistance programs and services must be truthful and realistic.

Learning assistance program staff members must not participate in any form of harassment that demeans persons or creates an intimidating, hostile or offensive campus environment.

All learning assistance program staff members must perform their duties within the limits of their training, expertise, and competence. When these limits are exceeded, individuals in need of further assistance must be referred to persons possessing appropriate qualifications.

All learning assistance program staff members must use suitable means to confront and otherwise hold accountable other staff members who exhibit unethical behavior.

When handling institutional funds, all learning assistance program staff members must ensure that such funds are managed in accordance with established and responsible accounting procedures. Learning assistance program funds acquired through grants and other non-institutional resources must be managed according to the regulations and guidelines of the funding source.

Various means of assessment should be conducted for the purpose of identifying the learning needs of the students and guiding them to appropriate programs and services. Assessment results should be communicated to the student confidentially, honestly, and with sensitivity. Students should be advised into appropriate, alternative educational opportunities when there is reasonable cause to believe that students will not be able to meet required guidelines for academic success or when the students' level of need exceeds the purpose and function of the learning assistance program.

With the prevalence of student paraprofessional and tutorial staff within learning assistance programs, specific attention should be given to properly orienting and advising student staff about matters of confidentiality. Clear statements should be distributed and reviewed with student staff as to what information is and is not appropriate for student staff to access or to communicate.

The central learning assistance goal, meeting the needs of students, is paramount and evident in research projects. The privacy, protection, and interest of the student should supersede that which is important, significant and beneficial for research purposes.

# XIII. Assessment and Evaluation

Learning assistance programs must undergo regular and systematic qualitative and quantitative evaluations to determine to what degree the stated mission and goals are being met. The learning assistance program must have the ability to collect and analyze data through its own resources and through access to appropriate data generated by the institution.

Although methods of assessment vary, learning assistance programs must employ a sufficient range of qualitative and quantitative measures to insure objectivity and comprehensiveness.

Data collected must include responses from students, staff, faculty, and administrators or any other affected constituencies. Results of these evaluations must be used in revising and improving programs and services and in recognizing performance of the learning assistance program and its staff.

Qualitative methods should include standard evaluation forms, questionnaires, interviews, observations, or case studies.

Quantitative measurements should range from data on an individual student's performance to the impact on the campus' retention rate. Quantitative methods may include follow-up studies on students' grades in mainstream courses, GPA's, graduation, re-enrollment and retention figures. Comparative data of learning assistance program participants and non-participants is also a measure of program effectiveness. Quantitative measures can include data on the size of the user population, numbers utilizing particular services, number of contact hours, the sources of student referrals to the program, numbers of students who are on the waiting list or who have requested services not provided by the learning assistance program. Quantitative data should be collected within specific time periods and longitudinally to reveal trends.

Learning assistance programs should conduct periodic self-assessments, utilizing self-study and certification processes endorsed by professional organizations.

Periodic evaluations of the learning assistance program and services should be performed by on-campus experts and outside consultants and disseminated to appropriate administrators.

The learning assistance program should periodically review and revise its goals and services based on evaluation outcomes and based on changes in institutional goals, priorities, and plans. Data that reveals trends or changes in student demographics, characteristics, and needs should be utilized for learning assistance program short- and long-term planning.

# Appendix 4-2

## Professional Associations

For current information on addresses, call or write the National Center for Developmental Education, Reich College of Education, Appalachian State University, Boone, North Carolina  28608  (704) 262-3057

### Learning Assistance/Developmental Education

College Reading and Learning Association (CRLA)

Midwest College Learning Center Association (MCLCA)

National Association for Developmental Education (NADE)

National Tutor Association

National Council of Educational Opportunity Association

National Resource Center for the Freshman Year Experience and Students in Transition

New York College Learning Skills Association

### Selected Journals

*Journal of Adolescent and Adult Literacy*

*Journal of College Reading and Learning*

*Journal of Developmental Education*

*Learning Assistance Review*

*Perspectives on Practice in Developmental Education*

*Research & Teaching in Developmental Education*

### Mathematics

Mathematics Association of America

National Council of Teachers of Mathematics

American Mathematics Association of Two-Year Colleges

## Other Professional Associations

Association on Higher Education and Disability (AHEAD)

American Assoc. of Community and Junior Colleges (AACJC)

American Educational Research Association (AERA), (DEV. ED. SiG)

American College Personnel Association (ACPA-Div. 16)

American Personnel & Guidance Association (APGA)

Association for the Development of Computer-Based Instructional Systems (ADCIS)

Association of Black Women in Higher Education (ABWHE)

Association on Handicapped Student Service Programs in Post Secondary Education (AHSSPPE)

College Reading Association (CRA)

Conference on College Composition & Communications (CCCC)

Intellectual Skills Developmental Association

International Reading Association (IRA)

League for Innovation in the Community College

National Academic Advising Association (NACADA)

National Association of Academic Advisors for Athletes (N4A)

National Reading Conference (NRC)

National Council of Teachers of English (NCTE)

National Orientation Director's Association (NODA)

Orton Dyslexia Society

# APPPENDIX 8-1

## PLANNING QUESTIONS YOU SHOULD CONSIDER BEFORE YOU USE WRITING PORTFOLIOS IN YOUR CLASSROOM

(From a paper by Susan Callahan of Kentucky State University presented at the KADE Meeting, Frankfort, KY 1993.  Reprinted by permission of Susan Callahan.)

Once you have decided why you want to use portfolios, you will need to answer the following questions:

1.  What will go into the portfolios?  Who will decide this?

    Possible contents might include published products (with or without cover sheets); evidence of process; certain genres or strategies; self-evaluation; a timed writing to a single prompt.

    Decision maker could be you, you and colleagues, you and students, students, outside authority, or colleagues.

2.  Who will select what goes into the portfolio and why?
    ◊ you                    ◊ you and colleagues
    ◊ you and students       ◊ students

3.  How many pieces will go into the portfolio and why? (Should be at least two pieces; 3-5 on avg.)

4.  Who will decide how the portfolio will be evaluated?
    ◊ you                    ◊ you and colleagues
    ◊ you and students       ◊ students
    ◊ external authority

5.  Who will evaluate the portfolio?
    ◊ you                    ◊ you and colleagues
    ◊ you and student        ◊ outside reader

6.  What criteria will be used to evaluate the portfolio?  Why?

7.  How will evaluation criteria be structured?
    ◊ open-ended comment sheet
       (e.g., "strengths" and "weaknesses")
    ◊ descriptive rubric based on over-all quality
    ◊ analytical score sheet for whole portfolio
    ◊ analytical score sheet for individual pieces

8.  How will evaluation criteria be communicated to students?

9.  How will Writing Center or other personnel be involved?

10. How will evaluation be communicated to student?
    ◊ written comments       ◊ conference
    ◊ check-off sheet        ◊ descriptive label
                                or number

11. What will you do with the portfolio after it is evaluated?

12. What procedure will you use for students (or faculty) who question a portfolio grade?

13. Will you want a trial run at midterm?

# APPENDIX 8-2

## SOME PORTFOLIO SUGGESTIONS

(From a paper by Susan Callahan of Kentucky State University presented at the KADE Meeting, Frankfort, KY 1993. Reprinted by permission of Susan Callahan.)

1.  Talk with other teachers, look at lots of portfolios, read, and be willing to "tinker" with your decisions. No portfolio system is ever perfect.

2.  Let the portfolios drive your assignments and class structure. Portfolios won't work as an "add on" or in classes where students are required to write one example of several types of writing or organizational patterns. Class time will also have to be spent differently than in non-portfolio classes. It takes time and practice for students to learn how to articulate writing standards, set personal goals, and reflect on their writing.

3.  Set high standards. If at all possible, involve students in articulating the standards of "good" writing as it is understood in your class. These standards can grow in complexity as the semester progresses and the students' understanding increases.

4.  Give students lots of practice applying the criteria of good writing to models—anonymous pieces, work by peers, and their own drafts.

5.  Be flexible. Students often can help us grow as teachers if we are open to new ideas.

6.  Create your own portfolio or portfolios. Learn how they work from the inside.

7.  Turn as much responsibility as possible over to your students. The more ownership they feel, the more of themselves they will invest, and ultimately the more they will grow.

8.  Use portfolios as a way to help students see the connection between the time and effort they put into writing and the amount of confidence and competency they gain. Require a cover letter or written self-evaluation that forces students to look honestly at the effort they have put in their work.

9.  Encourage typing or word processing for polished portfolios. Word processing has almost become a necessary skill for college students, and most campuses provide basic instruction if you cannot work it into your class structure. Students are usually proud of the way their papers look when they are word processed, and they are much, much easier for you to read.

10. Avoid writing on students' finished portfolio pieces. Use a comment sheet or post-it notes. Most of your comments will address the improvement you have observed over the semester or passages that you particularly like. This is not the place to offer suggestions for further editing.

# Appendix 8-2.5

## Should I Use Portfolios in My Classroom?

(From a paper by Susan Callahan of Kentucky State University presented at the KADE Meeting, Frankfort, KY 1993. Reprinted by permission of Susan Callahan.)

1. How much control do I feel I need over these aspects of course content and why do I need this control?

   ◊ number of writing assignments attempted
   ◊ number of writing assignments completed satisfactorily
   ◊ length of individual assignments
   ◊ topics for writing assignments
   ◊ due dates
   ◊ number of revisions
   ◊ organizational patterns or genres used
   ◊ level of editing
   ◊ establishing criteria for grades
   ◊ choice of required readings
   ◊ guiding class discussions
   ◊ providing revision suggestions
   ◊ instruction in grammar, mechanics, rhetorical forms

2. What aspect of my course will portfolio assessment not cover?

3. Will "my" kind of classroom portfolio assessment fit within departments or institutional requirements?

4. How will I have to change my course materials, structure, and teaching style in order to use the kind of portfolio system I am imagining?

5. Am I comfortable with the idea of continuing to "tinker" with my system once I've tried it?

# APPENDIX 8-3

## POINTS OF INTERFERENCE IN LEARNING ENGLISH AS A SECOND LANGUAGE

Note: This material is adapted from California State Board of Education (1973), Johnson (1975), Labov (1972), Tucker (1969).

### TONE

*Spanish*: In both English and Spanish there are four tone levels, but Spanish speakers use only the three lower-pitch tones, except when they express extreme anger or alarm. Then the fourth, upper-pitch tone is used.

### STRESS

*Spanish*: Most Spanish words are stressed on the last or next-to-last syllable; most English words are stressed on the first or second syllable. In English a word may have two or three stresses; Spanish generally uses only one stress except for a few adverbs.

### PRONUNCIATION

*Asian Languages*: Chinese use a tone system for distinguishing word meanings. Words having the same pronunciation may have four or more different tones to represent different meanings. These meanings would be represented by four written forms.

*Black Dialect:* In words where /r/ and /l/ appear in medial or final position, dialect speakers often drop these sounds.

Dialect speakers often change the pronunciation of English words with a medial or final *th*, saying "wit" or "wif" for "with" and "muver" for "mother."

### VOWELS

*Spanish*: Spanish does not have short vowel sounds for *a, i, o,* and *u*, as English does, although there are five vowel sounds in Spanish with corresponding sounds in English: *a* as in *father, e* as in *step, i* as in *machine, o* as in *over,* and *u* as in *ooze.*

### CONSONANTS

*Spanish*: Consonant sounds *v, b, d, t, g, h, j, l, r, w, v,* and *z* are not the same in Spanish as in English, and students must be taught the point of articulation to produce these sounds in order to become aware of the differences. *Asian Languages*: The schwa sound that is used in English does not exist in Chinese, Japanese, or Korean. Chinese speakers usually cannot distinguish the English sounds /v/ and /b/ or /l/ and /r/. Cantonese speakers use /l/ and /n/ interchangeably.

## CONSONANT CLUSTERS

*Spanish*: Spanish words never begin with the following consonant clusters: *sp*eak, *st*ay, *sc*are, *sc*hool, *st*reet, *sp*ring, *sc*ratch, *sp*here, *sl*ow, *sm*all, *sv*elte. Spanish speakers will add an initial vowel when pronouncing such words: *e*street, *e*speak. Spanish speakers often have problems with the 371 consonant-cluster endings used in English.

Spanish speakers are often confused by the use of English *s* endings to indicate a plural noun but a singular verb.

There is a strong carryover from the Spanish /ch/ to the English /sh/, and the student may say "share" for "chair" and "shoes" for "choose."

The /b/ and /v/ sounds in Spanish are exactly alike phonetically in that each has two sounds. Which sound is used is determined by the surrounding sounds.

*Asian Languages*: Cantonese has no consonant clusters, and as a result Cantonese speakers usually hear and pronounce just one of the sounds in an English cluster. Since there are so many consonant clusters in English, this creates severe problems. Many English clusters are formed or augmented by important syntactical elements, as in the expression *What's this?* The addition of /'s/ forms a cluster that gives an important clue to the meaning of the sentence, but the Cantonese student can neither hear nor say it.

Explicit plural markers are not used in Chinese or Japanese. The spoken language does not contain the sibilant /s/ sound. Plurals are formed by placing auxiliaries before the noun. An example (translated literally into English) is "*three* boy."

*Black Dialect:* When two or more consonant sounds appear at the end of words, they tend to be reduced by dialect speakers: /tes/ for "test" and /des/ for "desk." This reduction in consonant clusters affects words ending in /s/, third-person singular forms, and possessives.

## WORD ENDINGS

*Spanish*: Spanish words can end in any of the five vowels (*a, e, i, o,* or *u*) or any of the following consonants: /l/, /d/, /r/, /z/, /j/, /y/, /n/, or /s/. Spanish speakers often have difficulty with words ending in /m/, /p/, /k/, /c/, /b/, /d/, /f/, /g/, /l/, /y/, /v/, and /x/ (when voiced as /z/).

*Asian Languages*: Chinese, Japanese, and Korean speakers tend to drop, glottalize, or add a vowel to the English word endings /t/, /d/, /s/, /l/, /p/, /b/, /k/, /f/, /g/, /r/, and /v/. For instance, they may pronounce "college" as "collegi" and "church" as "churchi."

## GRAMMAR

### VERBS

*Spanish*: Spanish speakers often have problems distinguishing between the uses of the simple past ("he worked") and present perfect ("he has worked") because the rules for their use are different in Spanish. Spanish speakers are also confused by the double meaning of the *-ed* ending, which is in part comparable to the Spanish *-ado*, which signifies the past participle, and in part comparable to the endings for the simple past.

*Asian Languages*: The Chinese verb has only one form and is not conjugated to indicate tense.

Tenses are formed by placing auxilaries before or after the stable verb form.

*Black Dialect*: The use of the verb *to be* is different in black dialect. Often it will be absent in situations in which a contraction is used in standard English, especially in the present tense. For example, dialect speakers say "I here" and "We going."

Dialect speakers drop the *-ed* endings on the past tense in both speech and writing.

## NEGATIVE

*Black Dialect*: The use of more than one negative form is acceptable in black dialect sentences like "I don't take no stuff from nobody."

## WORD ORDER

*Spanish*: Spanish speakers need to cultivate the idea that English relies heavily on word order to indicate grammatical relations where Spanish relies on morphological change. Word order is sometimes flexible in Spanish, but never in English. This difference leads to confusion when Spanish speakers translate direct and indirect questions literally. For example, the question "What are you doing?" may be stated in Spanish as "I do not know what you are doing." The distinction in Spanish lies in the form of "what"—/que/ versus /lo que/, in this example, rather than word order.

In Spanish the adjective usually follows the noun and must agree with it in gender and number. In English the adjective usually precedes the noun.

In Spanish the adverb usually follows the verb, rather than following the direct object—for example, *Yo Jose vi inmediatamente . . .* ("I saw Jose immediately . . .").

*Asian Languages*: Chinese do not manipulate word order to change meaning. For example, it is impossible in Chinese to reposition *is* to convert a statement to a question, as in "He is a teacher" and "Is he a teacher?"

## ARTICLES

*Spanish*: In Spanish, articles are placed in some positions where English does not require them—for example, *Veo al doctor Brown* ("I see *the* Doctor Brown").

*Asian Languages*: The article *a* is used in Chinese for a very specific reason, as a unit of measure rather than a general article as in English. Korean and Japanese use only function words or function particles that follow content words, unlike English, which uses a combination of function words (articles and auxiliary verbs) as well as word endings to show grammatical distinctions.

## COMPARATIVE AND SUPERLATIVE

*Spanish:* Spanish speakers tend to express comparative and superlative by using *more* and *most,* where English uses *-er* and *-est*; thus expressions like, "He is more big" or "He is the most tall student" reflect Spanish structure.

## PRONOUNS

*Asian Languages*: In both Mandarin and Cantonese, a single sound represents the pronouns *he* and *she*; however, the written forms for these and the other third-person singular forms are very distinct. Often Chinese students use the spoken "he" for both "he" and "she."

## IT-THERE

*Spanish*: In Spanish one word (*es*) is used for *it is*, *there is*, and *there are*.

*Asian Languages*: Words like *there* and *it* in expressions like "It is cold" and "There are many clouds" do not exist.

*Black Dialect:* Dialect speakers use *it* for *there*. For example, instead of "There's a rug on the floor," they say, "It's a rug on the floor."

## SPELLING

*Spanish*: Although both Spanish and English have words of Latin origin, Spanish spelling does not use the following doubled or combined consonants: /bb/, /dd/, /ff/, /gg/, /mm/, /pp/, /ss/, /th/, /zz/, /gh/, /ph/, or /hn/. As a result, English spelling patterns using these forms are confusing for the Spanish speaker.

There are similar words in Spanish and English which create false analogies and confusion. For example, *lectura* means "reading," while the Spanish equivalent of "lecture" is *conferencia.*

*Asian Languages*: Dictionary skills must be taught Asian students, for the Chinese dictionary does not list words in alphabetical order, but by the traditional word-radical groups and the number of strokes each character has. Both Japanese and Koreans share the Chinese ideographic writing system, but Japanese uses a supplementary syllabic system and Korean uses a supplementary alphabetic system.

*Black Dialect*: Dialect speakers have difficulty spelling word endings and vowel sounds in syllables they do not pronounce or hear.

Dialect speakers attach meanings to words that are different from the meanings in standard English and are based on different experiences. For example, the words *bad* and *poor* may be used to mean "good."

# APPENDIX 8-4

## SENTENCE COMBINING

(Beverly Davis and Jan Nemes, Elizabethtown Community College (KY), from a paper presented at the KADE Conference, Frankfort, KY 11/12/93. Reprinted by permission of Beverly Davis and Jan Nemes.)

OPTION 1:    USES COORDINATING CONJUNCTIONS AND COMMAS
CREATES A COMPOUND SENTENCE

| , and | , so | , nor |
|-------|------|-------|
| , but | , yet | , or |
| , for | | |

We're going to the movies, and we have just enough money for admission and popcorn.

OPTION 2:    USES A SEMICOLON (;)
CREATES A COMPOUND SENTENCE

We're going to the movies; we have just enough money for admission and popcorn.

OPTION 3:    USES A SEMICOLON AND CONJUNCTIVE ADVERB
CREATES A COMPOUND SENTENCE

| ; moreover, | ; of course, | ; thus, |
|-------------|--------------|---------|
| ; besides, | ; for example, | ; still, |
| ; furthermore, | ; for instance, | ; then, |
| ; indeed, | ; meanwhile, | |
| ; in fact, | ; accordingly, | |
| ; likewise, | ; also, | |
| ; however, | ; anyway, | |
| ; nevertheless, | ; finally, | |
| ; otherwise, | ; incidentally, | |
| ; therefore, | ; instead, | |
| ; consequently, | ; similarly, | |

We're going to the movies; incidentally, we have just enough money for admission and popcorn.

OPTION 4:   USES SUBORDINATING CONJUNCTIONS AND RELATIVE PRONOUNS
            CREATES A COMPLEX SENTENCE, SOMETIMES WITH A COMMA

| | | |
|---|---|---|
| although | because | that |
| since | when | what |
| while | after | which |
| as | as if | who |
| before | if | whose |
| unless | until | whatever |
| whether | whenever | whichever |
| whereas | as long as | whoever |
| even if | so that | whom |
| though | as though | whomever |
| as soon as | just | |
| in order that | considering | |

Although we don't have enough money for popcorn, we do have enough for admission.

We have enough money for admission to the movies although we don't have enough to buy popcorn.

*A League of Their Own*, which was filmed in part in Indiana, starred Madonna. Any movie which is filmed in Indiana is unusual for the film industry.

# APPENDIX 9-1

## THE COLLEGE READING SPECIALIST COMPETENCY CHECKLIST

(William Brozo and Norman Stahl, 1985)

Directions: Indicate the degree to which the candidate possesses each competency.

|  | COMPETENCE/ATTITUDE LEVEL | | |
|---|---|---|---|
|  | LOW | MEDIUM | HIGH |

### UNDERGRADUATE TRAINING

SKILLS:

| | LOW | MEDIUM | HIGH |
|---|---|---|---|
| Reads well with a command of all basic skills to be taught to college readers | ____ | ____ | ____ |

ADDITIONAL COMPETENCIES:

KNOWLEDGE:

| | LOW | MEDIUM | HIGH |
|---|---|---|---|
| Has a broad academic background | ____ | ____ | ____ |
| Knows the sciences | ____ | ____ | ____ |
| Knows the social sciences | ____ | ____ | ____ |
| Knows reading methods | ____ | ____ | ____ |

ADDITIONAL COMPETENCIES:

### INSTRUCTION

SKILLS:

| | LOW | MEDIUM | HIGH |
|---|---|---|---|
| Individualizes instruction | ____ | ____ | ____ |
| Groups for instruction | ____ | ____ | ____ |
| Uses a variety of techniques for teaching college reading and study skills | ____ | ____ | ____ |

|  | COMPETENCE/ATTITUDE LEVEL | | |
| --- | --- | --- | --- |
|  | LOW | MEDIUM | HIGH |

Specific Components:

| | LOW | MEDIUM | HIGH |
| --- | --- | --- | --- |
| comprehension | ____ | ____ | ____ |
| critical reading | ____ | ____ | ____ |
| rate and flexibility | ____ | ____ | ____ |
| reference skills | ____ | ____ | ____ |
| retention/memory skills | ____ | ____ | ____ |
| spelling | ____ | ____ | ____ |
| study reading | ____ | ____ | ____ |
| test taking skills | ____ | ____ | ____ |
| time management | ____ | ____ | ____ |
| vocabulary development | ____ | ____ | ____ |

| | LOW | MEDIUM | HIGH |
| --- | --- | --- | --- |
| Integrates language arts into the instructional program | ____ | ____ | ____ |
| Devises original materials | ____ | ____ | ____ |

KNOWLEDGE:

| | LOW | MEDIUM | HIGH |
| --- | --- | --- | --- |
| Knows the literature on effective teaching and learning in higher education | ____ | ____ | ____ |
| Knows current studies on developmental, late adolescent, and adult psychology | ____ | ____ | ____ |
| Knows statistics and research design | ____ | ____ | ____ |

ADDITIONAL COMPETENCIES:

## ADMINISTRATIVE AND COUNSELING SKILLS

SKILLS:

| | LOW | MEDIUM | HIGH |
| --- | --- | --- | --- |
| Supervises professionals | ____ | ____ | ____ |
| Provides appropriate training for staff | ____ | ____ | ____ |
| Serves as a college reading consultant on and off campus | ____ | ____ | ____ |
| Interacts with and trains content area teachers | ____ | ____ | ____ |
| Sets goals and objectives | ____ | ____ | ____ |
| Develops learning programs | ____ | ____ | ____ |
| Budgets programs | ____ | ____ | ____ |
| Engages in public relations and conducts advertising programs | ____ | ____ | ____ |

Checklist Continued Next Page.

| | COMPETENCE/ATTITUDE LEVEL | | |
|---|---|---|---|
| | LOW | MEDIUM | HIGH |
| Publishes in-house program evaluation data in the form of annual reports | ____ | ____ | ____ |
| Develops and maintains relationships with other departments | ____ | ____ | ____ |
| Serves on campus-wide committees | ____ | ____ | ____ |
| Refers and directs students to appropriate campus agencies | ____ | ____ | ____ |

ADDITIONAL COMPETENCIES:

KNOWLEDGE:

| | LOW | MEDIUM | HIGH |
|---|---|---|---|
| Knows institutional traditions and requirements | ____ | ____ | ____ |
| Knows the organization of curricula and courses within academic units | ____ | ____ | ____ |
| Knows the courses with high failure rates | ____ | ____ | ____ |
| Knows the history and role of the college reading program on campus | ____ | ____ | ____ |
| Knows scheduling procedures, campus regulations, transfer and graduation requirements | ____ | ____ | ____ |

ADDITIONAL COMPETENCIES:

## PERSONAL CHARACTERISTICS

ATTITUDES:

| | LOW | MEDIUM | HIGH |
|---|---|---|---|
| Positive regard for students from varied socioeconomic and academic backgrounds | ____ | ____ | ____ |
| Desire to assist young adults to meet their career objectives | ____ | ____ | ____ |
| Empathy towards the problems students encounter in their coursework | ____ | ____ | ____ |
| Flexibility and willingness to carry out program procedures and instruction to meet students' needs | ____ | ____ | ____ |
| Creativity in developing student-centered learning programs | ____ | ____ | ____ |
| Perseverance in the face of adversity | ____ | ____ | ____ |
| Feeling of self-worth | ____ | ____ | ____ |
| Commitment to the college reading program and profession | ____ | ____ | ____ |

ADDITIONAL COMPETENCIES:

# APPENDIX 9-2

## TEN RECOMMENDATIONS FROM RESEARCH FOR TEACHING HIGH-RISK STUDENTS

(Adapted from: Stahl, N. A., Simpson, M. L., & Hayes, C. G. (1992). "Ten Recommendations from Research for Teaching High-Risk College Students." *Journal of Developmental Education*, *16*:1, pp. 2-8)

The ten ideas include:

1. adopt a cognitive-based philosophy (as opposed to a deficit view in which the goal for the students becomes increasing their scores on the Nelson-Denny or some similar test). The cognitive viewpoint assumes that students are active participants and in control of their own learning—capable of becoming effective, independent learners;

2. use a course model that stresses transfer of skills learned to "real" college courses;

3. use reliable, process-oriented assessment procedures rather than an over-reliance on standardized tests;

4. broaden the students' conceptual background knowledge since many developmental students lack the reading experience and have misconceptions about reading and college courses;

5. reconceptualize vocabulary development by helping students realize that "the fundamental avenue to college success is the ability to quickly expand their vocabulary, and that students must immerse themselves totally in the *language of the academy*";

6. use learning strategies that have been research-validated and insure that students know how to use them and how to choose among them;

7. systematically train students to employ strategies through self-control training and other validated training approaches and insure that instruction is direct, informed, and explanatory;

8. promote strategy control and regulation by teaching students to plan, monitor, and evaluate their own learning;

9. teach high utility strategies to maximize immediate acceptance and reduce the negative attitudes students have about taking developmental courses; and

10. incorporate writing into the curriculum to insure that students become co-creators of the texts they read, and create their own understanding of content material, and can develop a way to monitor and revise their understanding.

**Implications**: These ideas should be very valuable in training novice developmental instructors in math and writing as well as college reading.

# APPENDIX 9-3

## A COMPUTER LAB FOR THE DISABLED

### COMPUTER LABS AT THE UNIVERSITY OF PITTSBURGH LEARNING SKILLS CENTER

*"The Learning Skills Center Computing Labs at the University of Pittsburgh are a good example of a "win-win" situation that comes with collaboration between a learning center and an academic computing unit. But the biggest winners of this deal are the students,"* (Georgine Materniak, Director, Learning Skills Center, University of Pittsburgh, 1995).

In 1994, the Academic Computing division of the University's Computing and Information Services provided start-up funds to convert two rooms in the student union, where the Learning Skills Center (LSC) is located, into two computing labs. These labs consist of the Computer-Assisted Learning Lab and the Adaptive Computing Training Lab, together referred to as the LSC Computer Learning Labs. Academic Computing financed electrical upgrades, connections to the University network, carpeting and furnishings, and the purchase of hardware and software. The division of Public and Student Affairs provided the site to house the labs and the staff to develop, manage, and support the programs and services for students in the labs.

The learning center staff is responsible for data collection, student assessment, program evaluation and reports, dissemination of information and promotional materials, and fostering communication and collaboration among the various academic and student support units that are interested in the functions of the labs. In addition to the start-up costs, Academic Computing provides annual capital budgets for each lab and makes the technical expertise of its computing and adaptive technology staff available for support and maintenance of the hardware and software. This technical backing allows the learning center computing staff the time and freedom to focus on students and how to best meet their needs, knowing that troubleshooters and technical consultation are just a phone call away. An added advantage of this arrangement is that Academic Computing support provides the opportunity to upgrade hardware and software as needed, so that the problem of technology obsolescence is eliminated. It also gives the LSC flexibility to exchange equipment with other public computing labs. So if needs evolve or shift requiring the current mixed platform of DOS and MAC units to become predominently one or the other, units can be traded within the University public lab system.

The labs enable the LSC to incorporate computer-assisted approaches into a repertoire of learning support services for the general student population and for students with disabilities. As a campus-wide resource for skills development, the LSC is involved in collaborative programs with academic and other student support units. The labs enable the Center to foster new collaborative projects by functioning as a location where faculty and student support staff can team together for planning and implementing computer-assisted learning projects. The labs are also a potential site for demonstration projects and research involving computer-assisted learning and for hosting practica and internships for future professionals.

## COMPUTER-ASSISTED LEARNING LAB

This lab provides the resources to enhance current LSC services through computer-assisted assessment, instruction, drill and practice in developing math, reading, and study skills.

In the area of mathematics, the LSC is identifying math software to supplement the LSC math tutoring program, which currently provides over 2400 hours of individual and group tutoring for students enrolled in introductory math courses. In addition to enhancing current tutorial support, the labs will enable the LSC to address the math needs of students who are not simultaneously enrolled in a math course. One population of students who have been identified are those who need instruction, drill, and practice in applying specific basic math concepts to the sciences and non-math courses. Discussions are underway with the faculty in Biology and in the History and Philosophy of Science who are concerned about the inability of some students to apply general math to discipline-specific problems. Another population not currently served by the LSC but who need assistance are students who want to build math skills prior to enrolling in a credit-bearing math course, i.e., adults returning to higher education. An additional group of potential clients are students who need to refresh their math in preparation for taking graduate school entrance exams.

In addition to math, projects are underway to incorporate computer-assisted assessment and instruction for study skills. The LSC is currently piloting a computer version of the LSC Study Skills Survey, an instrument developed by the LSC and used over the past 16 years, to provide students with an individualized and detailed assessment and analysis of their learning strategies. The Study Skills Survey is not only used within the LSC but it is also administered to all students in the College of Arts and Sciences Freshman Studies classes, Nursing Freshmen, and Freshman Engineering Seminars.

Application software is being identified that can be readily adapted to strategies taught in the study skills component. For example, an outlining and cognitive mapping package will be used for practicing applications of organizing lecture note material and information extracted from texts as part of the Study Skills Workshops. Calendar and scheduling programs are available for students to develop personal time management plans. Hypercard stacks will be taught to students to demonstrate how to organize and categorize information for memory and understanding. These are some of the initial projects for the upcoming year to actualize the lab from the concept phase into reality.

## THE ADAPTIVE COMPUTING TRAINING LAB

This lab provides adaptive computing training and learning skills instruction for students with physical and learning disabilities. It contains $70,000 worth of state-of-the-art adaptive hardware and software that enable students with disabilities to access, manipulate, and process information and to do tasks that would otherwise be significantly difficult or impossible for them to do. The technology also promotes greater independence for students with disabilities, gives students greater control over their learning process and, in many cases, increases learning efficiency while reducing the time spent on tasks.

Students are individually assessed to determine their requirements for adaptive computing. They are then oriented to and trained in the use of the hardware and software that most appropriately accommodates their needs and which best suits the nature of the learning tasks they encounter in their academic courses. Students also receive guidance in how to incorporate adaptive computing into effective learning strategies.

The Adaptive Computing Training Lab works closely with the Office of Disabilities Resources and Services and the adaptive technology staff of Academic Computing to integrate support and accommodation services. In addition to providing training to students, the lab is a site for pilot testing new adaptive hardware and software under review for acquisition. It also has the potential to become a practicum site for students interested in adaptive computing and learning assistance for students with disabilities.

The devices available range from simple enlarged-print display software (i.e., the Large Print DOS which uses any DOS-based PC) for the visually challenged student who may need more time to read assignments to the more complicated voice-activated PC. A wheel-chair accessible station is available. (Note: Any student may use these facilities provided they vacate if a disabled student requests to use the equipment.) The goal is to enable a person with any disability, whether physical or learning, to improve their learning skills including test taking, note taking, and so on. Other technology includes text scanners that can read text aloud, a Braille interpreter and printer, and a personal computer that can respond to voice commands. Printing equipment includes both a laser printer and a Bookmaker Braille printer capable of printing 40 characters a line on both sides of the paper. (As Tim Fitzgerald, the communications expert points out, this is a signficant advantage to blind students since the paper stock used for Braille is heavier than standard paper and a term's worth of notes might require a wheelbarrow if only one side of the page were used.)

One PC is equipped with a Master Touch tablet, a touch-sensitive palette with 25 rows and 3 columns set off by raised lines. The rows represent the 25 lines of the screen of a personal computer, and when a student presses down on any of the 25 cells, the voice synthesizer will speak the text on that line. Another interesting device is the voice-activated PC that can recognize individual voice commands and execute them. The software works by recording the harmonics on an individual's speech and then attempting to match patterns with words or commands in the file. In that way, the user trains the software to recognize voice commands and then builds a file of commands for future use. Also PCs are equipped with track balls that are more amenable to users who have physical disabilities than is a mouse.

These are some immediate goals for the new and emerging Computer-Assisted Learning Lab. In the future, the LSC would like to collaborate with faculty and campus organizations in the development of software that incorporates reading, math, or learning strategies. The lab is envisioned as a site for faculty to pilot-test educational software and courseware that are relevant to the mission and goals of the LSC. The possibilities for advancing technology as a tool for learning at the University of Pittsburgh LSC are just beginning.

References:

Brown, C. (1987). *Computer access in higher education for students with disabilities: A practical guide to the selection and use of adaptive computer technology.* San Francisco: George Lithograph Company.

Fitzgerald, T. (October, 1994). CIS/LSC project expands adaptive computing services with state of the art technology. *Connections!* A newsletter about computing and information services at the University of Pittsburgh, pp. 1-5.

Hart, P. (May 1995). Expanding access. *Ventures.* The College of Arts and Sciences, University of Pittsburgh, Vol. 5, Issue 2, pp.8-9.

# APPENDIX 9-4

## WHAT ARE LEARNING DISABILITIES?

(Adapted from Patricia C. Grove's "Learning Disabilities and Attention Disorders: A User-Friendly Guide for Faculty,"
Cook/Douglas Campus, Rutgers University, 1995.)

Learning disability is a general term that describes a heterogeneous group of disorders manifested by significant difficulties in the acquisition and use of learning, speaking, reading, writing, reasoning, or mathematical abilities. These disorders are intrinsic to the individual, presumed to be due to central nervous system dysfunction, and may occur across the life span.

Problems with self-regulatory behavior, social perception, and social interaction may exist with learning disabilities but do not by themselves constitute a learning disability.

Although learning disability may occur concomitantly with other handicapping conditions (for example, sensory impairment or serious emotional disturbance) or with extrinsic influences (such as cultural differences, insufficient or inappropriate instruction), they are not the results of these conditions or influences. (Adapted from a report from the Joint National Committee on Learning Disabilities.)

Learning disability (LD) occurs in persons of average or above average ability, manifests itself irregularly, and shows a pattern of uneven abilities. It is presumed to be due to dysfunction of the central nervous system and is manifested in one or more of the following areas: reading, oral expression, listening comprehension, writing expression, reasoning, social skills, mathematical abilities. Learning disability (LD) is not a form of mental retardation nor the result of poor schooling, emotional disturbance, lack of motivation, or visual or auditory acuity problems. Nor is it a homogeneous group of disorders.

### DYSLEXIA

The term dyslexia is considered a "minimal brain dysfunction" disorder and is generally diagnosed from school histories and other "soft signs."

Recently however, using functional MRI (Magnetic Resonance) brain scans, investigators have found physiological markers that differentiate the brains of dyslexics from those of normal readers. Specifically, in dyslexics the visual-motor area of the brain fails to activate. (Articles by C. Frith & U. Frith in *Nature*, vol. 38, July 4, 1996, & Wake Roueh in *Science* 31 March, 1995.) Furthermore, the *Science* article shows that more than 50% of school children were diagnosed as learning disabled (LD) in 1992-93, compared with around 25% eighteen years ago. This may be an overestimate but we can rest assured that we can look forward to many more LD students attending college in the future.

Specifically, dyslexic children (who make up 80% of LD groups) have problems matching the letters in written words with the sounds and, in general, are characterized by having "high intelligence that leads their teachers to expect high achievement."

A study by G. F. Eden and others in the same issue of *Nature* found that dyslexics show abnormal processing of visual motion as well as a lack of phonological awareness. They have difficulty reading the Times Square ads with moving letters that seem to slide across flashing light bulbs. They also tend to have poor temporal judgment, visual instability, and a higher coherent motion threshold.

So it looks like we'll have better ways to diagnose these problems in the future (albeit brain scans are expensive and difficult to interpret). We are also developing better ways to train these students. When a student has had excellent reading training, the only residuals of the problem at the college level are slow reading speed and spelling problems. I worked with college students in the 50s who had been diagnosed as dyslexic at 5 years old (which is pretty early). Their reading comprehension scores were above average but their reading speed was slow and, despite many years of help, their spelling was atrocious.

The current explanation of why some people's brains make reading so difficult is interesting. It hypothesizes that these brain differences have always existed in some people but were invisible until highly complex writing systems evolved. In other words, these folks could get along very, very well in a preliterate society, but they are not easily educated in our highly literate society.

## ATTENTION DEFICIT DISORDERS (ADD)

Diagnosing Attention Deficit Disorders is even more difficult. For many years, doctors believed that attention disorders were behavior problems of children and that they disappeared as one aged. More recently, they have discovered that attention deficits can persist into adulthood and can significantly disrupt and interfere with adult life.

Attention Deficit Disorders (ADD) is a neurobiological disorder that interferes with a person's ability to sustain attention or focus on a task and to delay impulsive behavior. The condition may or may not be impacted by the ability to control motor activity level (hyperactivity-ADHD). Increased anxiety or stress can exacerbate the manifestations and lead to extremely low levels of concentration and attentiveness. Attention disorders are now considered to be a broad class of neurobiologically based conditions affecting between 2 and 5 million U.S. adults, accompanied by symptoms that are usually manifested before the age of 7 and last throughout life. They are considered hereditary and since they often place an individual at risk for cognitive and behavioral difficulties at school, they often require psychopharmaceutical intervention to enable satisfactory performance in school. Not all of the core symptoms (inattention/concentration, impulsivity, and hyperactivity) need be present in those affected.

On the other hand, attention disorders are not classified as forms of mental retardation, are not considered learning disabilities (although they can have a negative effect on learning), and cannot be cured. Nor are they outgrown by adolescents and do not occur exclusively during the course of a psychotic disorder. However, attention disorders are disabilities and therefore, they are covered under the Americans with Disabilities Act (ADA), the Individuals with Disabilities Education Act, and Section 504 of the 1973 Rehabilitation Act.

Associated Symptoms of Attention Disorders in Adults:
1. Poor Academic/Vocational Performance
   ◊ Does not complete required paperwork
   ◊ Easily bored by tedious materials
   ◊ Demonstrates poor organization and planning
   ◊ Procrastination in completing assignments
   ◊ Makes impulsive decisions
   ◊ Difficulty in working independently

◊ Confuses directions and/or instructions
◊ Frequently late for class and appointments
◊ Frequently misplaces things
◊ Demonstrates poor self-discipline

2. Interpersonal Difficulties
◊ Frequent mood swings
◊ Lack of tact in comments to others
◊ Frequent temper outbursts—"short fuse"
◊ Verbally abusive to others
◊ Lack of follow-through on commitments
◊ Appears immature and/or selfish
◊ Trouble in keeping friends or relationships going
◊ Failure to see others needs or points of view as important

3. Anti-Social Behavior
◊ Alcohol and substance use/abuse
◊ Frequent lying/stealing
◊ Tending toward verbal/physical aggression
◊ Full anti-social personality disorder
◊ Others

The Impact of ADHD upon the Adult Personality:
◊ Feelings of helplessness (Most ADHD adults are aware of the inadequacies but feel helpless to do anything about them.)
◊ Sense of grief and loss: Inability to live up to their potential.
◊ Low self-esteem (History of failures, unfinished projects, difficulties with others. )
◊ Explosive temper—quick tempered, fast to anger, set off by trivial incidents, low frustration tolerance, angry at being misunderstood, uses denial as a defense.
◊ Emotional liability—over-reactive, difficulty in filtering things out, frequently becomes emotionally flooded.

(Adapted from Barkeley, R. A. *Attention-Deficit Hyperactive-Disorder: A Handbook for Diagnosis and Treatment.* New York: Guilford Press.)

# LEGAL ASPECTS OF LEARNING DISABILITIES

The two Acts which are most relevant to students with disabilities in post-secondary settings are Section 504 of the Rehabilitation Act of 1973 and the Americans with Disabilities Act (ADA) of 1990. However, before we discuss these laws, there are three important issues that must be noted:

1. Faculty will only be notified that a student has a disability if the student gives his/her consent to do so in writing to the student's campus coordinator.

2. The coordinator may only apprise the faculty member of the fact that the student has a disability and the accommodations the student requires. The coordinator may not divulge the nature of the disability or any other particulars.

3. Faculty are prohibited by law from disclosing to anyone information s/he has been made privileged to by the coordinator/student. In other words, a faculty member may not mention to another faculty member that Susie Smith has a learning disability/attention disorder, needs accommodations, or whatever.

A brief summary of Section 504 of the Rehabilitation Act of 1979:

1. Section 504 provides that: no otherwise qualified individual with a disability in the United States . . . shall solely by reason of . . . disability be excluded from the participation in, be denied the benefits of, or be subjected to discrimination under any program or activity receiving federal financial assistance.

2. The coverage of Section 504 extends to:
   ◊ persons who have a disability
   ◊ persons who have a history of a disability
   ◊ persons perceived by others to have a disability

3. A person with a disability is "anyone with a physical or mental impairment that substantially impairs or restricts one or more major life activities: caring for one's self, performing manual tasks, walking, seeing, hearing, breathing, learning and working, etc."

4. The term physical or mental impairment includes, but is not limited to, speech, hearing, visual and orthopedic impairments, cerebral palsy, epilepsy, muscular dystrophy, multiple sclerosis, cancer, diabetes, mental retardation, emotional illness, specific learning disabilities, brain injury, minimal brain dysfunction (today this is known as Attention Deficit Disorder and may occur with or without Hyperactivity), and developmental aphasia alcoholism and drug addition.

5. Under the procedural requirements of Section 504, each institution that receives federal funds should:
   ◊ appoint a Section 504 coordinator;
   ◊ adopt a grievance procedure for handling discrimination complaints;
   ◊ complete an institutional self-evaluation and develop a transition plan;
   ◊ provide for notification of policy of Section 504; and
   ◊ submit assurance of compliance form to the OCR.

6. Section 504 mandates that reasonable accommodations be made for students, faculty, and staff with disabilities. Program accessibility means that all programs and activities "when viewed in their entirety" be accessible.

7. Preadmission inquiries about an applicant's disability are strictly prohibited, except when institutions are taking steps to cover past discrimination or to correct conditions which may have led to limited participation of persons with disabilities.

8. Programs and activities which must be operated in a non-discriminatory manner include (but are not limited to): recruitment, admissions, academic programs, research, occupation training, housing, health insurance, counseling, financial, and physical education, athletic, recreation, and transportation.

9. Students with impaired sensory, manual or speaking skills must be provided with auxiliary aids such as taped texts, interpreters, readers, and classroom equipment adapted for persons with manual impairments. The institution has flexibility in choosing the effective methods by which the aids will be supplied.

10. Academic requirements must be modified on a case by case basis to afford qualified handicapped students and applicants an equal educational opportunity. However, academic requirements that the institution can demonstrate are essential will not be regarded as discriminatory.

(Adapted from: Section 504 of the Rehabilitation Act of 1973: Handicapped Persons Rights Under Federal Law. U.S. Department of Education Office for Civil Rights, Washington, DC, September, 1984.)

## The Americans with Disabilities Act

The passage of the Americans with Disabilities Act (ADA) in 1990 focused the attention of faculty on students with disabilities and many have concerns about their rights and responsibilities under the law when it comes to teaching and accommodating the needs of disabled students who take their classes.

Issues concerning physically disabled students are easier to understand than those issues involved with learning disabilities, often called the "invisible disabilities" which are not as easily understood or accepted. Nonetheless, students with invisible disabilities are protected by the same law as those with physical disabilities, and their rights under those laws must be adhered to by institutions and individuals alike.

Criteria for providing accommodations:
◊ It is the responsibility of the individual with the disability to identify himself or herself and to provide documentation. If the individual has not been evaluated and diagnosed previously and wishes to be considered for accommodations, the cost of evaluation must be assumed by the individual, not the institution.
◊ Delivery of services and arrangements of accommodations are to be arranged by a designated ADA coordinator and the ADA requires that accommodations do not pose an "undue hardship" to those providing the accommodations.

Note: Public institutions are covered under Title II and private institutions are included under Title III of the ADA.

(Adapted from: The Americans with Disabilities Act: the Law and its Impact on Postsecondary Education. Wash. D.C.: Health Resource Center, American Council on Education, 1992.)

## What Are Reasonable Accommodations?

Sally Scott, Virginia State Coordinator of Higher Education, says "an accommodation is reasonable if it is based on documented individual needs; allows the most integrative experience possible; does not compromise the essential requirements of a course, or programs; does not pose a threat to personal or public safety; does not impose undue financial or administrative burden and is not of a personal nature."

List of frequently used accommodations:
◊ extended time and separate exam site (Note: some learning centers have testing rooms and offer this service.)
◊ readers
◊ note takers
◊ administer tests in alternate formats (essay, multiple choice, short answer, oral, tape, computer)
◊ alternate demonstration of mastery (paper/oral presentation /project)
◊ use of calculator
◊ use of talking calculator/computer program
◊ use of speller or dictionary during class exams
◊ tape recording lectures
◊ proofreader
◊ adjusted classroom seating
◊ extended time to complete a program or degree
◊ adapted methods of instruction
◊ course substitution (i.e., perhaps a logic or problem-solving course could be substituted for a math course if student has a certified math disability; a speech class for a required composition course if student has dyslexia). It may be more difficult to find a substitute for the language requirement. We used to use pictorial languages like Chinese as substitutes for French or German. However, in some cases it may be

necessary to exempt a dyslexic student from a language requirement.

◊ part-time rather than full-time registration.

(Adapted from Scott, S. (In press). Determining reasonable academic adjustment for college students with learning disabilities. *Journal of Learning Disabilities.*)

## TEACHING STRATEGIES

Here are some teaching strategies that are especially helpful for LD and ADD students, but will help other students as well.

1. Provide a detailed syllabus.
2. Include in the syllabus a brief statement regarding services available at your institution for students with disabilities and your willingness to accommodate documented needs.
3. Choose textbooks carefully—a well-written and well-organized text can make independent reading a more powerful learning tool.
4. Explain how to use textbook aids.
5. Provide a list of outside readings in advance of the first day of class.
6. Develop a positive student-teacher relationship.
7. Use a multisensory approach to instruction.
8. "Model" the way you want papers, assignments, and projects done.
9. Use "attention grabbing" techniques.
10. Asks questions in a clear and concise manner.
11. Personalize information as much as possible.
12. Give frequent quizzes. Speedy and regular feedback can provide very positive results.
13. Teach mnemonics.
14. Provide lecture outlines.
15. Help students follow lectures by summarizing and using "cueing words/phrases."
16. Encourage student groups and small discussions.
17. Present lecture information in a logical order.
18. Use concrete presentations to explain abstract ideas.
19. Be open to alternative ways of demonstrating learning.
20. Before each lecture, recap what was discussed in the previous lecture.
21. Don't change policies and procedures in midstream. Because students with learning disabilities can't depend on themselves for consistency, they look for it in others.
22. Keep a sense of humor.

(Adapted from: C. T. Mangrum and S. S. Strichart. *College and the Learning Disabled Student.* New York: Grune and Stratton.)

# Appendix 10-1

## Student Tips: A Checklist for Discussion Questions

(By Carolyn Hopper, Middle Tennessee State University. Reprinted by permission of the author.)

Students often have difficulty transferring what they know about writing effective essays to answering discussion or essay questions in other courses. I have found the following checklist helpful to students when they are answering discussion questions. Instructors may also find it helpful in grading such questions.

1. Do I really understand what the questions asks me to do?

2. Does the first sentence of my answer repeat the question and clearly show the reader how I will develop my answer?

3. Have I done preliminary planning of my major points?

4. Do major points stand out?

5. Are my major points supported with examples and facts?

6. Are there clear transitions between major points?

7. Would someone who had not taken this class be able to understand the concept the way I discussed it?

8. Have I completely covered all major points needed to answer the question?

9. Did I stick to the question?

10. Did I proofread for misspelled words, sentence fragments, run-on sentences, comma splices, subject verb or pronoun antecedent agreement errors, and other errors which might cause the reader not to understand what I have written?

# APPENDIX 10-2

## STUDENT TIPS: CLASS SCHEDULING & TIME MANAGEMENT

(By Laurie Witherow, Middle Tennessee State University. Reprinted by permission of the author and the Learning Assistance Association of New England.)

1.  Do not schedule all your classes so that they are crowded into one part of the week. The days "off" may look good to you now, but the days you have class become very long. What about when you have several tests and assignments due at the same time?

2.  Schedule classes that are harder for you or classes that involve practice (math, language) as widely as possible across the week. It's tempting to take a subject you don't care for in two days rather than three, but resist. You need the extra days of practice and preparation.

3.  Schedule more difficult classes earlier in the day before you get physically and mentally fatigued.

4.  Be realistic about your personal habits and energy level. If you never get started until 10 a.m., don't schedule 7 a.m. classes.

5.  Schedule breaks between classes. Resist the temptation to "get them over and out of here." You need to have time to gather your thoughts, study for tests/quizzes, prepare for your next class, and to go over your notes from earlier classes.

6.  Schedule classes involving similar assignments (reading, papers, working problems) on different days. Doing this will help you avoid having to read too many chapters to prepare for classes or write too many papers due at the same time.

7.  Schedule a course load you can handle. Be realistic about what you can pass successfully. The number of credits you take will vary depending on many factors, including what classes you need. Anything between 12 and 18 hours is full-time.

Note: All suggestions are on a "when possible" basis. Sometimes obligations like work, practice, meetings, etc., will determine when you can take classes.

# APPENDIX 10-3

## READING AND STUDY SKILLS BOOKS

This list represents a small sample of the many current books used in reading and study skills programs. They differ widely in orientation, topics, and the level of student for whom they are most appropriate. Although college reading instructors today emphasize skills that students can directly apply to mainstream courses, many still use reading textbooks. Certainly, you will want to select a book that is appropriate for the reading ability of your students, but also one that stresses academic preparation skills rather than one that teaches general reading skills or recreational reading. Some entries have comments by various reviewers, others don't.

Bogue, C. (1993). *Studying in the content areas: The sciences*. Clearwater, FL: H&H Publishing Co.

Bogue, C. (1993). *Studying in the content areas: The social sciences*. Clearwater, FL: H&H Publishing Co.

Campbell, W. (1989). *The power to learn: Helping yourself to college success*. Belmont, CA: Wadsworth Publishing Co. (In addition to assuming that the student has found a college that matches his/her ambitions and level of preparations *and* that the student is committed to succeed, the book will show the student how to succeed. Among the strategies explained are collaborative learning (how to learn with a partner, and exercises including how to invent a study group for one of your courses). Also there are four chapters of paired anecdotes about male and female students, including one on the funseekers.)

Ellis, D. (1991). *Becoming a master student*. College Survival Press. (A text that's popular in community college courses.)

Flippo, R. F. (1988). *Test/Wise: Strategies for success in taking tests*. Belmont, CA: David S. Kale.

Galica, G. (1991). *The blue book*. New York: Harcourt Brace.

Gardener, J., & Jewler, A. J. (1992). *Your college experience: Strategies for success*. Belmont, CA: Wadsworth.

Gates, J. K. (1988). *Guide to the use of libraries and information services*. (6th ed.). New York: McGraw-Hill.

Girdano, D., & Everly, G. (1979). *Controlling stress and tension*. Englewood Cliffs, NJ: Prentice Hall.

Gross, R. (1991). *Peak learning*. Los Angeles: Jeremy R. Tarcher.

Hyatt, C., & Gottlieb, L. (1987). *When smart people fail*. New York: Simon & Shuster.

Kahn, N. (1989). *More learning in less time: A guide for students and professionals*. (3rd ed.). Berkeley, CA: Ten Speed Press. (May be useful for returning adults.)

Kaner, C. C. (1991). *The confident student*. Boston: Houghton-Mifflin. (Has a self-test on locus of control.)

Kining, M. L., & Rose, M. (1992). *Critical strategies for academic thinking and writing*. (2nd ed.). New York: Harper Collins.

Lakein, A. (1973). *How to get control of your time and your life*. New York: Peter W. Wyden, Inc.

Lewis, L. M. (1992). *Academic literacy: Reading and strategies handbook for academic literacy*. Lexington, MA: D.C. Heath & Co. (This has been described as a unique collection of reading and study strategies concentrating on both general and discipline-specific reading skills.)

McWhorter, K. T. (1994). *Academic reading* (2nd ed.). NY: Harper Collins.

McWhorter, K. T. (1996). *Efficient and flexible reading*. (4th ed.). NY: Harper-Collins.

McWhorter, K. T. (1996). *Study and critical thinking skills in college*. (3rd ed.). NY: Harper-Collins.

Mullen, J. (1987). *College reading and learning skills*. Englewood Cliffs, NJ: Prentice-Hall. (This book has eight major parts: the whole person, study skills, comprehension, vocabulary, memory, the paper, the examination and technology.)

Nist, S., & Simpson, M. (1996). *Developing textbook fluency: Active reading and studying in the content areas*. Lexington, MA: D.C. Heath & Co. (1-800-235-3565).

Phillips, A. D., & Sotiriou, P. E. (1992). *Steps to reading proficiency*. Belmont, CA: Wadsworth.

Schirldi, G. R. (1988). *Stress management strategies*. Dubuque, IA: Kendall-Hunt.

Schmelzer, R. V., & Christen, W. L. (1992). *Study skills systems for studying*. Dubuque, IA: Kendall-Hunt.

Sotirious, P. E. (1989). *Integrating college study skills reasoning in reading*. Belmont CA: Wadsworth.

VanBlerkom, D. L. (1994). *College study skills: Becoming a strategic learner*. Belmont, CA: Wadsworth Publishing Co.

Weinsheimer, J. (1993). *Turning point: How to get off probation and on with your life*. Belmont, CA: Wadsworth Publishing Co.

Wood, N. V. (1992). *College reading and study skills: Learning, thinking: Making connections*. (5th ed.). Fort Worth, Texas: Harcourt Brace. (Stresses skills that can be applied to regular college classes. However, I'm not sure that all developmental students are ready for it.)

Vacca, R. T., & Vacca, J. L. (1993). *Content area reading*. (4th ed.). Glenview, Il: Scott, Foresman, & Co.

## Reading/Writing Relationships

Collins C. (1984). *Read, reflect, write: The elements of flexible reading, fluent writing, independent learning*. Englewood Cliffs, New Jersey: Prentice Hall, Inc.

# APPENDIX 12-1

## SOURCES OF COMPUTER SOFTWARE

*Project Synergy*
Miami-Dade Community College
Product Development & Distribution
1011 S.W. 104th St.
Miami, FL 33176-3393
(305) 237-2158

Project Synergy Software Selector is a software database of more than 170 IBM and IBM-compatible software programs for developmental education courses in reading, writing, and /or mathematics that have been reviewed by developmental faculty. The information includes discipline, level of content matching (whole program, topics, individual objectives), computer environment—stand alone/networked, instructional mode—drill & practice/tutorial/simulation/game, objectives and attributes scores—percentages implemented satisfactorily, etc. Reviews and ratings are updated as new software becomes available and reviews for study skills, critical thinking, and ESL software are planned.

Software for keeping a data base:
*IBM/Clone*        *DBASE*
*MacIntosh*        *File Maker Pro*

## OTHER SOURCES OF COMPUTER SOFTWARE

To find appropriate computer software for your students, you'll want to order the following publications that are free to higher education personnel—from Broderick & Caverly (Fall, 1993). Techtalk: Choosing and purchasing software. *Journal of Developmental Education, 17*(1), 40-41.

*T.H.E. Journal* (150 El Camino Real, Suite 112, Tustin, CA 92680-9883).

*Campus Tech* (P.O. Box 52180, Pacific Grove, CA 93950-9935).

*Higher Education Product Companion* (1307 S. Mary Ave., Suite 218, Sunnyvale, CA 94087).

*New Media* (P.O. Box 1771, Riverton, NJ 08077-7331).

*Syllabus: The Definitive Technology Magazine for Colleges, Universities and High Schools.* Syllabus Press. 1307 S. Mary Ave., Suite 211, Sunnyvale, CA 94087 (408) 746-2000. FAX (408) 746-2700.

Subscriptions to each of these magazines are free and each contains articles that are written for postsecondary education. Each also contains descriptions and reviews of various software products appropriate for higher education. Higher Education Product Companion is especially useful in that it supplies manufacturer's addresses, prices, and the target audience.

A second source to consult is a catalog. It should be from an educational software distributor rather than from an individual company. Probably the most comprehensive is the E.I.S.I. (Educational-Interactive Software Institute) Computer Courseware Catalog (225 Grant Road, Los Altos, CA 94024). Courseware is organized according to subject matter with separate categories for Reading, Language Arts, Mathematics, ESL, and Study Skills. Within each subject product, titles are listed and the following information provided:

1. hardware requirements;
2. name of publisher;
3. suggested grade level, including identification of courseware appropriate for special populations such as adults and "at-risk" students;
4. courseware descriptions in a clear, concise manner;
5. special designations noting "Exemplary" or "Desirable" courseware that has been identified by the California Technology in Curriculum Project as high quality, and courseware that has received special awards from panels of educators throughout the country;
6. products that have been reviewed by an independent source are given a Review Grade (i.e., a letter grade of A, B, etc.); and
7. cost, including a price for lab packs, and networked versions (E.I.S.I. provides a discount for orders over $500).

## How Computers May Change Higher Education

What changes are expected in higher education as computer technology becomes mainstream? Alan Collins wrote in the Phi Delta Kappan in 1991 that we may expect the following changes based on what has happened in K-12 classes:

1. a shift from whole class instruction to small group instruction where teachers have a more realistic picture of what their students know;
2. a shift from teachers' working with better students to working with weaker students as teachers are drawn to students who need help;
3. a shift from lecture and recitation to coaching;
4. a shift toward more engaged students, as students who find traditional classes boring will see technology to be encouraging and supportive of their long-term effort and will increase their personal investment in learning;
5. a shift from a policy of assessment based on test performance to assessment based on products, progress, and effort, once teachers have been introduced to ways of using different assessment techniques;
6. a shift from a competitive to a cooperative social structure, as some software requires students to work together on assignments;
7. a shift from all students learning the same things to different students learning different things, as students work on different pieces of a problem and bring the pieces together for the solution; and
8. a shift from the primacy of verbal thinking to the integration of visual and verbal thinking.

# APPENDIX 12-2

## HOW TO STUDY CHEMISTRY

This material is abridged and adapted from Colin Watanabe and Friedel Gordon, *How to Study Chemistry*, rev. ed. (Berkeley: Student Learning Center, University of California, 1977).

### AN OVERALL STUDY STRATEGY

For an introductory science course such as Chemistry 1A, lectures usually provide the best guide to the study of the subject. The instructor presents and explains important material in lectures. Examinations are based primarily on lecture material. The text is often used only to explain more fully material covered in lectures and as a source for homework problems.

For these reasons, this study guide focuses on taking good lecture notes and suggests the following strategy: (1) prepare yourself *before* each lecture by reading relevant portions of your text; (2) do your best to take complete, accurate, and organized notes; (3) review your notes as soon as possible after each lecture; and (4) use your text to clarify and complete your notes.

For maximum effectiveness, you should preread and review within twenty-four hours of the lecture. If you decide to use this strategy, you will find yourself studying regularly, reading and/or reviewing a little each night. Many surveys have shown that regular study produces best results—both in understanding and in grades.

You can also integrate homework, lab work, and additional indepth reading into this regular cycle of prereading, notetaking, and review. In addition to the regular review of your lecture notes, you may find that a weekly or biweekly review will help you gain a clearer picture of the entire course and will help you prepare for quizzes and exams. Frequent review results in better retention than does a single, intensive review.

Whether you use the suggested strategy or decide to devise one of your own, you should keep in mind the advice given by last year's chemistry students: don't get behind; keep up with the reading assignments; don't miss any lectures; do all assigned problems; use your TA (or someone else's); get help quickly if you find yourself in trouble.

### LECTURES AND NOTETAKING

A. *Preread the assigned reading before class.* At this point, don't try to understand everything; just get a general idea of what the lecture will cover and become familiar with new terms. Look at *chapter headings*, *subtitles*, and *diagrams* and their *captions*, and scan the text briefly. This procedure does not take very long, but it will be of great help in following the lecture.

B. *Come early to the lectures and leave late.* Often instructors give helpful hints in the first and last minutes of their lecture—just when most people aren't listening. Frequently they give an outline of the lecture, or they at least *imply* their organization in the beginning, for example: "Today we will get into 'Metal Ions,' but before we start with the topic we'll talk a little about . . ." Your notes and, what's more important, your understanding will be clearer if you are able to fit the pieces together by paying attention to such verbal outlines.

C. *Take good notes*. The harder you work during one hour of lecture, the less studying you will have to do at home. Your notes should be complete, though not to the point of looking like a transcript; little words, repetitions, and digressions can and should be eliminated. Some students feel that all they have to write down is the information on the blackboard; but what is on the board is frequently not sufficient for understanding. It is very important to listen carefully to the verbal elaborations and to take notes on them.

Following are some specific suggestions for notetaking.

◊ Write on one side of the page only, leaving the back of each sheet empty. Use the empty side to rewrite messy or unclear sections, to add information when studying the book at home, or to write down related material from the discussion group. This way you can create one convenient source for study and review.

◊ Use *abbreviations* to cut down on writing time. Apply symbols like → (leads to); ↑ (increase); ↓, (decrease) in regular sentences as well as in formulas.

◊ *Identify unclear areas*. If you miss part of a section or don't understand what's being presented in a part of the lecture, write down as much as you *can* catch, especially key words;

skip several lines in your notes; make a big question mark in the margin of your notes. Later you will be aware that there is something you must clear up and complete.

◊ *Indicate experiments and demonstrations in your notes*. Watch carefully and listen for an explanation of the concept being exemplified.

◊ *Look and listen for relationships*. Each lecture will have a main topic (for example, "Metal Ions") and about three to six subtopics. If these topics are stated by the professor in the form of an outline, very good; but if they are not stated directly, they are nevertheless implied, and you should try to discover them when studying your notes at home. Make it a habit to think about and write down a brief outline for each lecture, and you will gain a much better sense of how the whole course hangs together, how the details fit into the total framework, and what the relationships are between the different parts. This is also one of the best techniques to *improve memory*, because things are remembered better when they are seen in relationship.

◊ Look for categories of information. A student might have a list of facts in her notes without knowing what they belong to. This happens a lot when students just copy what is on the board. Example:
1. Methyl alcohol $CH_3OH$
2. Hardening fats, margarine, and so on.
3. $NH_3$—ammonia
4. Filling balloons

Without a categorizing label these facts are almost meaningless. In this case, the title would be "Uses of Hydrogen."

◊ *Add explanations and labels to diagrams, charts, and formulas*. Beware of simply copying what is on the board and spending too much time on the artwork. Diagrams and pictures can often be found in your text; so sketch them quickly and concentrate on the lecturer's comments.

Comments and labels will (1) provide connections to preceding and subsequent material and (2) provide more complete notes, which will facilitate review.

D. *Review your notes as soon as possible after class.* Many studies have shown that longterm memory increases dramatically if this is done. If you review your notes, even just briefly, on the day of the lecture, it will save you a great deal of study time.

Some students have found it helpful to stay right in their seats after class and immediately go over their notes. Or, while walking to the next lecture, try repeating in your mind what you have just heard, asking yourself questions: What was covered today? What was it all supposed to mean? What were the topics? What did I not understand?

That same night, study your notes carefully and use your text to clarify confusing points.

## READING THE TEXT

A. *Read selectively.* Not all parts of the text should be studied with equal care. Reading assignments are often vague (for example, "Read chapters 9 and 10 this week"), and you must decide for yourself how to organize your reading. Here are three tools to guide you:
1. Use your lecture notes and assigned prob-

lems to determine reading priorities, that is, important points (topics extensively covered in lecture on which problems have been assigned), digressions (examples or special cases of important points), and background information (topics not emphasized in lecture).
2. Preread before studying a section in detail. Quickly scan the text to get an overview of the material and how it is organized. Look at the table of contents; titles and subtitles; diagrams, illustrations, and their captions; and introductions and summaries. Prereading is very effective in improving concentration, comprehension, and longterm memory.
3. Use problems to guide you to important material. Before reading your text, look at the example problems and the problems listed at the end of the section or chapter. Note the variables (for example, temperature, pressure, concentration, volume) which appear in the problems. Look for definitions and concepts involving these variables when reading the text.

B. *Read actively and ask questions.*
1. Before reading a section or chapter, formulate questions by extracting questions implied in the problems and turning titles and headings into questions. Title: "Some Chemical Systems at Equilibrium." A student's questions: "What is a chemical system?" "What conditions define equilibrium?" "Why is 'equilibrium' important?" Look for answers to your questions as you read.
2. During the actual reading, continue to question. You needn't question so much the detail as the organization and the importance of what you are reading. Ask: "Why was this

section placed here?" or "Can I skip this section?" or "How does this new concept relate to previous concepts?"

C. *Find connections and relationships in the material.* In order to understand and better remember the overwhelming quantity of information contained in your notes and text, you will need to construct an organizing framework:

◊ Bring together all material on each topic. Create a single study source by integrating your lecture and lab notes with textbook material.

◊ Outline the reading assignment. Make a list of section titles. A pattern should emerge. This is especially important if the lecture and text follow different organizational schemes.

◊ Use introductions and summaries in your text and lab manual to gain an overview of a topic.

◊ Create your own summaries of the assigned reading. Try to condense each chapter into a single page of notes.

D. *Underline and mark the text with care.* Your goal in marking should be to create a visual summary which will be meaningful when reviewing the text days or weeks later. Here are some general guidelines. (1) Read a paragraph or section *before* underlining. Then go back and mark selectively. (An effective form of instant review.) (2) Use your hi-liter sparingly; avoid indiscriminate underlining. Circle or underline key words or the topic of a paragraph. Underline summarizing sentences. (3) Write comments in the margin which will reorganize the text to meet your needs.

E. *Use the index.* The index can transform your text into a private instructor ready to answer your questions, clarify your notes, point out relationships. For example, a student might find in his

lecture notes a complicated diagram, copied from the board without clarifying labels, and remember only that the instructor mentioned "hydrogen atom." Looking in the index under this heading, he is referred to "H atom," where he sees the following:

> H atom boundary conditions, 487
> > energy level diagram, 488
> > energy levels of, 472, 484, 487
> > line spectrum of, 469, 472
> > orbitals, 483, 487 . . .

He is not sure where to look next, but he does notice that most of the entries cluster around page 480. He turns to this page and begins to scan nearby pages. On page 488, he sees something resembling the diagram in his notes.

Another index may organize the same topic differently:

> Atomic structure
> > Bohr model, 470
> > hydrogen atom, 476, 487 . . .

Try looking under each word, for example, hydrogen and atom.

If you cannot find your subject, think of a larger category that may include your subject as a subcategory.

Notice the other entries under your subject. You may find additional information and begin to see relationships more clearly.

## PROBLEM SOLVING

Chemistry is a problem-oriented course. In studying chemistry, you should keep in mind that your knowledge will eventually be used to solve problems. You may understand chemical concepts, definitions, formulas, and so on, but this knowledge will be of little value unless you can use it to solve problems. You should organize your studying accordingly:

◊ *Study the example problems.* Even though you may understand the concepts, working through an example problem will often disclose mathematical techniques, "tricks," or shortcuts you need to know in order to apply your conceptual understanding.

◊ *Do all assigned problems*, even if they are not to be turned in. Many instructors give similar (sometimes identical!) problems on exams.

◊ Practice problem solving. One of the best ways to prepare for an exam is to practice solving the kinds of problems you think will be covered. Look at assigned problems for clues. The more practice you have in problem solving, the less likely you are to make those obvious mistakes that cost valuable points.

A. *Understanding the problem.* Most problems, both on homework and exams, are "word" problems. You will almost never be asked just to solve an equation; instead you must sort through a lot of words to get the information needed to set up an equation. *The most important step in solving any problem is to establish clearly WHAT IS GIVEN and WHAT IS WANTED.* Here are some techniques helpful in sorting out the information given in word problems:

1. *Find out what is WANTED.* Set it off clearly from everything else in the problem by circling, underlining, etc. Reread what you have marked, and don't jump to conclusions because your problem is similar to another problem you remember. Take time to make sure you understand what you are to do. There are few things more frustrating than getting the right answer to the wrong problem.

2. *Examine the data you have been GIVEN.* Set off the important information by underlining or some other means (but use a different mark to distinguish the GIVEN from the WANTED). On long word problems especially, some students find it helpful to summarize both the GIVEN and the WANTED before starting to solve the problem.

   ◊ *Too little information.* Some problems will omit "obvious" information (such as the value of the gas constant R or relevant thermodynamic data). You are expected either to know or to be able to look up such data. On tests many instructors will give you this information on the first sheet of the exam; in textbook problems such information is usually tabulated in the text or is given in an appendix at the back of the book.

   ◊ *Too much information.* In multipart problems, you must select from all of the given data that which is needed to solve each part of the problem.

B. *Doing it.* Although you may clearly understand what is wanted and what is given, the connection between the two may not be clear. Here are some ways to clarify the connection:

   ◊ Draw a picture or a diagram.
   ◊ Summarize a chemical process by writing a reaction.
   ◊ Analyze definitions. Important relationships are sometimes hidden in definitions. For example, density is defined as the ratio of mass to volume. Pressure is defined as force per area. Molarity is defined as moles of solute per liter of solution.
   ◊ Look for similar example problems in the text.

◊ Set subgoals. Ask yourself, "What do I need to know to be able to solve the problem?" Set as your subgoal the task of finding any missing pieces of information.

◊ Use your imagination. Pretend you are looking into a very powerful microscope and can actually see atoms and molecules. How do they interact with one another?

◊ Reread the problem for word clues. Important information is often given in short phrases which are easily overlooked: "at constant pressure," "for an ideal gas," "for complete combustion," "in an acidic solution."

◊ Brainstorm. Write down everything you know about the kind of situation described in your problem. Assemble all your fragments of knowledge and see whether you can piece together a way to solve your problem.

## C. *Checking your answers.*

◊ Is there a type of mistake you tend to make? Do you often make errors when working with scientific notation or when dividing fractions? Recheck these steps.

◊ Question your calculator. It will always give an answer, but only you can tell whether it is the right answer.

◊ Always ask yourself whether your answer makes sense: If you were asked to calculate the molecular weight of compound X, your calculated weight cannot be less than 1 gm/mole. (No element or compound is lighter than hydrogen.) If you were asked to calculate the pH of a 0.1 M aqueous solution of a weak acid using its dissociation constant, your calculated pH cannot be greater than 7. (The solution cannot be basic.)

◊ Use units to check your answer: Given 3 liters of 0.5 M NaOH, how many moles of NaOH do you have? Your answer should be in *moles*.

## Exams

Some chemistry instructors prefer frequent short quizzes, others give only a midterm and a final. Quizzes require keeping up with course work because some instructors will announce a quiz only a few days before it is to be given, leaving you little time to prepare. Midterms and finals, on the other hand, require carefully planned selective review.

## A. *Preparing for an Exam.*

1. *Predicting the exam.* Find out as much as you can about format and content of the impending exam. Ask fellow students, your TA, the professor, and try to obtain copies of old exams from the library or other sources.

*Preliminaries.* When and where will the exam be given? (Exams are sometimes not given in the regular classroom.) What is the grading policy? (Is partial credit given? Will you be penalized for guessing?) Will the exam be open- or closed-book? Can you use your calculator? Should you bring a bluebook?

*Format:* Will the exam contain problems requiring calculation, short-answer questions, multiple-choice questions, essay questions? How many of each type? How will the points be distributed?

*Content.*
◊ Will the exam be cumulative (that is, will it cover all material to date), or will it cover only material introduced since the last exam? Will lab material be included?

◊ Listen carefully. Has the instructor raised questions and problems in recent lectures without giving answers? Has s/he mentioned topics covered in earlier lectures?

Has s/he suggested that the class "think about" certain concepts?

◊ Make a list of assigned readings. Include not only page numbers but also chapter titles and/or section headings. Note sections and chapters not to be covered by the exam.

◊ Make a list of assigned problems, noting what you were given and what you were asked to find.

◊ Look at your lecture notes, your list of assigned readings, your list of assigned problems. Which topics seem to have received the most emphasis? What kinds of questions have you been asked about these topics; what kinds of questions would you ask if you were trying to design an exam to cover these topics?

2. *Scheduling your time.* Make a long-range schedule. This should be done about three weeks prior to the exam. Note all commitments (deadlines for papers, exams in other classes, etc.) to get an overview of what you must do and how much time you can allot to each demand. Many students make such a schedule for the entire quarter.

Make a detailed schedule. Some students set deadlines by which they will have covered a certain portion of the material. Others schedule study time each day and use the time flexibly. Some combine both methods. Choose whichever method seems to work for you.

Reassess your progress every few days. Are you falling behind? Can you take time from other activities; can you make your review more selective? Beware of cutting down on sleep—this usually reduces efficiency.

3. *Setting priorities.* Apply this rule: If you can't study everything, or if you must cram, concentrate on a few topics and review them thoroughly. Understand basic information first. The most difficult topics are not always the most important. In introductory courses, difficult material is sometimes presented to preview more advanced classes. You will often not be responsible for such material.

4. *Taking a practice test.* This is an important strategy suggested by many learning specialists to counteract test anxiety. You can "desensitize" yourself by simulating an actual test situation and applying your knowledge under realistic conditions. The method:

◊ Make a list of problems and questions, using old exam questions, homework problems, and your own questions.

◊ Set a time limit, one which will force you to work at top efficiency.

◊ Work without interruption; try to finish your "exam." Stop when time has expired.

◊ Evaluate your performance, give yourself a "grade." Determine your strengths and weaknesses. Decide where you need more review.

B. *Test-taking strategies.*

1. *Assessing the quiz or exam.* Before starting to write, glance over the whole exam quickly, assessing questions as to their level of difficulty and point value.

Get a sense of how much time to spend on each question.

Begin to work on those questions with which you are most comfortable and/or those worth the most points. In general, in problem solving exams, as in essay exams, it is better to do the easiest questions first. In multiple-choice exams, on the other hand, it is probably better to work through from beginning to end (again, however, skipping very difficult questions). Never leave a question completely blank. Write down everything that seems to apply—you may receive partial credit.

2. *Analyzing the question.* Read each question carefully.

   Underline or circle key words (see "Problem Solving").

   Jot comments and ideas in the margin as you think about the question.

   Ask yourself: What is this question asking? How is it related to what I've been studying? Have I seen a similar question?

   Clarify confusing questions. Add comments, clarifying remarks.

3. *Writing down the answer.* Show all work clearly. You may lose points for incomplete or messy answers.

   Write in pencil—not ink—so you can erase.

   If you write on the back of a page, make a note so that the reader will not overlook it.

   Evaluate your answer. Does it make sense? See "Problem Solving" for techniques.

## LABORATORY

Your lab work will account for about 30 percent of your total grade. In addition, many exams and quizzes will contain questions pertaining to laboratory material.

◊ *Be prepared.* You should read the current experiment twice *before* coming to lab. On the first reading, read the introduction and skim the text to get a general picture of the experiment (that is, procedures, amount of time required, objectives) and its relationship to previous experiments and/or the lecture. Look at the problems and questions for clues to procedures and concepts. Go through the procedure in detail during the second reading. Some students write outlines or draw detailed flow charts complete with pictures of test tubes, beakers, and so on, labeled with experimental conditions such as temperature, molarity, volume, weight.

◊ *Get help before you make a mistake.* Ask your TA about confusing points before you proceed. Rely on the advice of your TA rather than that of fellow students, who may also be confused.

◊ *Analyze your data as soon as possible after completing an experiment.* If you complete your lab work early, you may want to stay and analyze your data. This will give you a chance to confer with other students or your TA if you have difficulty with calculations or the interpretation of your data.

*Notebook policy varies from TA to TA.* Listen carefully to your TA's instructions. Ask questions if you are not sure about notebook policy. Here are some commonly followed notebook policies:

Use a bound notebook with numbered pages (not a spiralbound notebook).

Save the first few pages for a table of contents.

Record all observations and primary data (temperature, weights, volumes, the date, and so on) directly into your notebook.

Do not record data on scratch paper for later transfer to your notebook.

Do not remove pages from your notebook.

Draw a line through incorrect data; do not erase or obliterate.

Show all calculations; do not give just the answer.

Write answers to all questions and problems.

# APPENDIX 12-3

## HOW TO STUDY PHYSICS

### PROBLEM SOLVING IN PHYSICS

Two things are important to remember in solving physics problems. First, a physicist seeks those problems which can be modeled or represented pictorially or schematically. This means that *almost any problem you encounter in a physics course can be described with a drawing.* Moreover, such a drawing usually contains or suggests the solution to the problem. Second, *a physicist seeks to find unifying principles* which can be expressed mathematically and applied to the broad classes of physical situations. While your physics textbook contains many specific formulas, the broader "laws of nature" must be understood in order to grasp the general overview of physics. This broad conceptualizing is vital if you are to solve those problems which embody several different principles. Virtually all specific formulas in physics are combinations of "the basic laws."

The following is a general outline of how to approach a physics problem:

1. *Read the problem* and make sure that you understand all the terminology used. Look up the meanings of any terms that you do not know.

2. *Make a drawing of the problem.* In your drawing, you should identify the quantity you are seeking; identify the given values of the parameters (variables) on which the solution depends; identify unknown parameters which must be calculated from other information in order to find the solution; and make sure that all quantities in the problem are expressed in [consistent units of measure].

3. *Establish which general principle relates the given parameters to the quantity you are seeking.* Usually your picture will suggest the correct formulas. However, at times, further information will have to be generated before the proper formulas can be chosen. This is especially true of problems in which the solution you seek must be calculated indirectly from the given information.

4. *Calculate the solution* (a) by calculating the values of any parameters which were obtained from the given information (if any such parameters were necessary), then (b) by putting the values of all the parameters, both given and calculated, into the main question.

5. *Criticize your solution to see if it makes sense.* Compare your solution to any available examples. Many times an error in a calculation will result in a solution that will be obviously wrong. Check the units of your solution to be sure that they are appropriate. *Examining your solutions will develop your intuition about the correctness of solutions—an intuition immensely valuable to use with problems that you will later encounter on an exam.*

When you have completed a problem, you should be able (at some later time) to read the solution and understand it without referring to the text. This means that you should include necessary notation as to which principle you have applied. If, when you read a solution, you come to a step that you do not understand, then you have either omitted a step that is necessary to the logical development of the solution, or you need to write notes in your solution to remind you of the reasons for each step.

While it may take more time to write careful and complete solutions to homework problems, you will find that this will be "paid back" by the help in problem solving, as you are prevented from overlooking essential information; it will also provide excellent review material for exam preparation.

## EFFECTIVE TEST PREPARATION

If you have followed an active approach to study, similar to the one suggested below, your preparation for exams will not be overly difficult. Let us repeat that *physics courses, and therefore physics exams, involve problem solving.* Therefore your approach to studying for exams should stress problem solving.

Here are some principles:

1. In the week prior to the exam, completing steps (a), (b), and (c) should give you a reasonably good idea of what has been stressed and on what you can expect to be tested. (a) Quickly review your notes and recheck the syllabus. (Your goal at this point is to ascertain what has been emphasized.) (b) Reread quickly your solutions to the homework problems. (Remember that these solutions, if complete, will note underlying principles of laws.) (c) Quickly review the assigned chapters. (Once again, your purpose in this early stage of exam preparation is to ascertain what topics or principles have been emphasized.)

2. From this rapid overview, generate a list of themes, principles, and types of problems that you expect to be covered.

3. *Review Actively.* Don't mistake recognition of a principle when you see it for actual knowledge that will be available for recall in a test situation. *Try to look at all the possible ways that a principle can be applied.* For example: If velocity and acceleration principles have been stressed, look over all your homework problems to see if they, in any way, illustrate these principles. Then, if you also can anticipate an emphasis on friction and inertia, once again review *all* your homework problems, checking to see if they illustrate, in any way, those principles.

Effective examination preparation involves your developing an interaction between homework problems, the lecture, and the text. If you review actively and "self-test," including creating on your own problems which involve a combination of principles, you are not likely to look back on an exam and say, "I knew how to do friction problems, it's just that they were asked in a weird way, so I didn't recognize them."

## A WEEKLY FLOW CHART FOR STUDYING PHYSICS

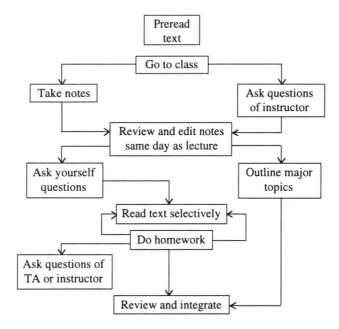

# REFERENCES

ACE Report Provides Data on Students in Developmental Courses. (1996, January 22). *Higher education & national affairs* (American Council on Education), 45, ii, pp. 3 & 6.

Adler, M. J. (1940). *How to read a book.* New York: Simon & Schuster.

Aikman, C. C. (1995, Fall). Ideas in practice: Picture books and developmental students. *Journal of Developmental Education, 19*(1), 28-32.

Akst, G. (1986). Reflections on evaluating remedial mathematics programs. *Journal of Developmental Education, 10*(1), 12-15.

Akst, G., & Hirsch, L. (1991). Selected studies on math placement. *Review of Research in Developmental Education, 8*(4), 1-4.

Aldridge, M. (1989). Student questioning: A case for freshman academic empowerment. *Research & Teaching in Developmental Education, 5*(2), 17-24.

Alpert, R., & Haber, R. N. (1960). Anxiety in academic achievement situations. *Journal of Abnormal and Social Psychology, 61*, 207-215.

American Mathematical Association of Two-Year Colleges. (1994). *Standards for introductory college mathematics.* Memphis, TN: American Mathematical Association of Two-Year Colleges.

Anderson, T. H. (1980). In Spiro, R. J. & others (Eds.). *Theoretical issues in comprehension: Perspectives from cognitive psychology, artificial intelligence, linguistics and education.* Hillsdale, NJ: Erlbaum, pp. 483-502.

Angelo, T. A., & Cross, K. P. (1993). *Classroom assessment techniques: A handbook for college teachers.* (2nd ed.). San Francisco: Jossey-Bass.

Argyris, C. (1983). *Reasoning, learning and action: Individual and organization.* San Francisco: Jossey-Bass.

Astin, A. (1977). *Four critical years: Effects of college on beliefs, attitudes and knowledge.* San Francisco: Jossey-Bass.

Astin, A. (1993). *What matters in college: Four critical years revisited.* San Francisco: Jossey-Bass.

Ball, S., & Anderson, S. B. (1975). *Practices in program evaluation: A survey and some case studies.* Princeton, NJ: Educational Testing Service.

Bandura, A. (1982). Self efficacy mechanism in human agency. *American Psychologist, 37*, 122-147.

Bandura, A. (1986). *Social foundations of thought: Social cognitive theory.* Englewood Cliffs, NJ: Prentice Hall.

Beery, R. G. (1975). Fear of failure in the student experience. *Personnel and Guidance Journal, 54*, 191-202.

Belenky, M. F., & others. (1988). *Women's ways of knowing: The development of self, voice and mind.* New York: Basic Books, Inc.

Black, M., Mansfield, W., & Farrin, E. (1991, May). *College level remedial education in the fall of 1989, survey report.* Washington, DC: U.S. Department of Education.

Blais, D. M. (1988). Constructivism: A theoretical revolution in teaching. *Journal of Developmental Education, 11*, 2-7.

Blais, D. M. (1995). Elemental psychology and the teaching of mathematics. *Journal of Developmental Education, 18*(3), 2-8.

Blanc, R. A., De Buhr, L. E., & Martin, D. C. (1983). Breaking the attrition cycle: The effects of supplemental instruction on undergraduate performance and attrition. *The Journal of Higher Education, 54*(1), 80-90.

Blanton, W. E., & Bullock. (1973). Cognitive style and reading behavior. *Reading World, 12*, 276-287.

Bloom, B. S., & Broder, L. (1950). *Problem solving abilities of college sudents*. Chicago: University of Chicago Press.

Bloom B. S., & others. (1971). *Handbook of formative and summative evaluation of student learning*. New York: McGraw-Hill.

Boatner, M. T. (1966). *A dictionary of idioms for the deaf*. West Hartford, CT: American School for the Deaf.

Bohr, L. (1994-95). College courses which attract and generate good readers. *Journal of College Reading and Learning, 26*(2) 30-44.

Bohr, L. (1996, Spring-Summer). College and precollege reading instruction: What are the real differences. *The Learning Assistance Review 1*,(1), 14 -28.

Bonham, B. S. (1989). *An investigation into the effect of learning style preferences and various instructional strategies on achievement and course completion rate of college freshmen in a developmental mathematics course*. Unpublished doctoral dissertation, Pennsylvania State University.

Bonham, B., & Boylan, H. R. (1993). A new look at learning styles. *Research in Developmental Education, 10*(4).

Bosworth, K., & Hamilton, S. J. (Eds.). 1994. *Collaborative learning: Underlying processes and effective techniques. New directions for teaching and learning #TL59*. San Francisco: Jossey-Bass.

Boylan, H. R. (1995). Making the case for developmental education. *Research in Developmental Education, 12*(2).

Boylan, H. R. (1995). The scope of developmental education: Some basic information on the field. *Research in Developmental Education, 12*(4).

Boylan, H. R., & White, W., Jr. (1987) Educating all the nation's poeple: the historical roots of developmental education. *Research in Developmental Education, 5*(1-4).

Boylan, H. R., & Bonham, B. S. (1992). *Research project on developmental education*. National Center for Developmental Education, Appalachian State University, Boone, NC.

Boylan, H. R., & Bonham, B. S. (1992). The impact of developmental education programs. *Research in Developmental Education, 9*(2).

Boylan, H. R., Bliss, L., & Bonham, B. S. (1993). The performance of minority students in developmental education. *Research in Developmental Education, 10*(2).

Boylan, H. R., Bonham, B. S., & Bliss, L . B. (1993). Characteristic components of developmental education. *Research in Developmental Education, 10*(2).

Boylan, H. R., Bonham, B. S., & Bliss, L. B. (1994). Characteristic components of developmental programs. *Research in Developmental Education, 11*(1).

Boylan, H. R., Bonham, B. S., Jackson, J., & Saxon, P. (1994). Staffing pattterns in developmental education programs: Full-time, part-time, credentials and program placement. *Research in Developmental Education, 11*(5).

Boylan, H. R., Bonham, B. S., Bliss, L. B., & Saxon, P. (1995). What we know about tutoring: Findings from the National Study of Developmental Education. *Research in Developmental Education, 12*(2).

Britten, B. K., & Tesser, A. (1991). Effects of time-management practice on college grades. *Journal of Educational Psychology, 83*(3), 415-422.

Brookfield, S. D. (1987). *Developing critical thinkers: Challenging adults to explore alternative ways of thinking and acting*. San Francisco: Jossey-Bass.

Brookfield, S. D. (1990). *The skillful teacher*. San Francisco: Jossey-Bass.

Brookfield, S. D. (1995). *Becoming a critically reflective teacher*. San Francisco: Jossey-Bass.

Brooks, P. (1978). [When the bilingual student goes to college]. Unpublished paper, Subject A Department. University of California-Berkeley.

Brooks, P., & Hawkins T. (Eds.). 1981. *Improving writing skills, New directions for college learning assistance, No. 3*. San Francisco: Jossey-Bass.

Brown, A. L., & Palinscar, A. S. (1985). *Reciprocal teaching of comprehension strategies: A natural history of one program for enhancing learning*. Cambridge, MA: Bolt, Beranek & Newman.

Brown, J. & Associates. (1977). *Free writing, a group approach*. Rochelle Park, NJ: Hayden.

Brown, M. H. (1995). Intervening for success with the underprepared college science student. *Research & Teaching in Developmental Education, 11*(2), 71-78.

Brown, W. C. (1987). [Measuring tutoring effectiveness using interaction analysis.] Unpublished doctoral dissertation. University of California-Berkeley.

Brubacher, J. S., & Willis, R. (1976). *Higher education in transition: A history of American colleges and universities, 1636-1976.* (3rd ed.). New York: Harper & Row.

Bruffee, K. (1984). Collaborative learning and 'The Conversation of Mankind.' *College English, 46,* 635-52. ERIC EJ 306 541.

Bruffee, K. (1986). Social construction, language, and the authority of knowledge: A bibliographic essay. *College English, 48,* 773-90.

Bruffee, K. (1993). *Collaborative learning: Higher education, interdependence, and the authority of knowledge.* Baltimore, MD: Johns Hopkins Press.

Bruffee, K. A. (1995). Sharing our toys: Cooperative learning vs collaborative learning. *Change,* 12- .

Bullock, T., Madden, D., & Harter, J. (1987). Paired developmental reading and psychology courses. *Research & Teaching in Developmental Education, 3*(2), 22-29.

Burmeister, S. (1994). The challenge of Supplemental Instruction (SI): Improving student grades and retention. In Maxwell, M. (Ed.). 1994. *From access to success.* Clearwater, FL: H&H Publishing Company.

Burns, M. E. (1991, April). *A study to formulate a learning assistance model for the California community college.* EdD dissertation, Pepperdine University.

Canfield, A. (1976). *The learning style inventory.* Ann Arbor, MI: Humanics Press.

Canfield, A. (1986). Revised edition. *The learning style inventory.* Ann Arbor, MI: Humanics Press.

Carkeet, D. (1976). How critics write and how students write. *College English, 37,* 599-604.

Carman, R. A. (1975). *A long term study of the effects of students tutored in developmental mathematics.* Santa Barbara, CA: Santa Barbara Community College. ERIC Document Reproduction Service: No. ED 112 983 [746].

Casazza, M. E., & Silverman, S. L. (1996). *Learning assistance and developmental education: A guide for effective practice.* San Francisco: Jossey Bass.

Causey, O. S. (1955). A report on college reading programs in the nation. In Causey, O. S. (Ed.). *Evaluating college reading programs.* 4th Yearbook of the Southwest College Reading Conference for Colleges and Universities. Fort Worth, TX: Texas Christian University Press.

Caverly, D. C., & Broderick, B. (1988-present). Tech talk. *Journal of Developmental Education.*

Chaffee, J. (1992, Spring). Critical thinking skills: The cornerstone of developmental education. *Journal of Developmental Education, 15*(3), 2-8, 39.

Chichering, A. W. (1969). *Education and identity.* San Francisco: Jossey-Bass.

Christ, F. L. (1971). Systems for learning assistance: Learning facilitators and learning centers. In Christ, F. L. (Ed.). *Interdisciplinary aspects of reading instruction.* Proceedings of the 4th Annual Conference of the Western College Reading Association.

Christ, F. L. (1972). Preparing practitioners, counselors, and directors of college learning assistance centers: An intensive graduate workshop. In Greene, F. P. (Ed.). *College reading: Problems and programs of junior and senior colleges.* Twenty-first yearbook of the National Reading Conference Vol. II, 179-188.

Christ, F. L. (1978, November). Management is evaluation. *Audiovisual Instructor,* 26-62.

Christ, F. L. (1984). Learning assistance at California State University-Long Beach, (1972-1984). *Journal of Developmental Education, 8*(2), 2-5.

Clair, L. H. (1994-95). Teaching students to think using library research and writing assignments to develop critical thinking. *Journal of College Reading and Learning, 26*(2), 65-74.

Clark, C. S. (1987). *An evaluation of two types of developmental education programs as they affect student's cognitive and affective domains.* Unpublished doctoral dissertation, University of Pittsburgh.

Clark, D. R. (1977). *The law school admissions workshop.* College Park, MD: The Reading and Study Skills Laboratory, University of Maryland.

Clark, I. (1985). *Writing in the center*. Dubuque, IA: Kendall/Hunt.

Clark, I. L. (1988). Collaboration and ethics in writing center pedagogy. *The Writing Center Journal, 9*(1), 3-13.

Claxton, C. S. (1989). Fostering student learning and development through effective teaching. In Hashway, R. M. (Ed.). *Handbook of developmental education*. NY: Praeger Publishers, 84-108.

Claxton, C. S., & Muriel, P. H. (1987). *Learning styles: Implications for improving educational practices. ASHE-ERIC higher education report #87*. ASHE-ERIC George Washington University: Wash., DC.

Clowes, D. A. (1980). More than a definitional problem: Remedial, compensatory, and developmental education. *Journal of Developmental Education, 4*(1), 8-10.

Clowes, D. (1994). Research, respectability, and legitimacy of post-secondary remedial education. In Smart, J. (Ed.). *Higher education handbook of theory and practive, vol. viii*, 464-468. Bronx, NY: Agatha Press.

Clowes, D. (1994). Remediation in American higher education. In Smart, J. (Ed.). *Higher education handbook of theory and practive, vol. viii*, 460-493. Bronx, NY: Agatha Press.

Cohen, J. S., & Quinn, K. B. (1995). *Faculty views of college students literacy: The missing factor in the retention equation*. Paper presented at the College Reading and Learning Association Conference, Tempe, AZ.

Condravy, J. (1993). Learning together: An interactive approach. In Malinowski, P. A. (Ed.). *Perspectives on Practices in Developmental Education*. A 1992 Monograph of the New York College Learning Skills Association, 68-71. (Reprinted in Maxwell, M. (Ed.). 1994. *From access to success*. Clearwater FL: H&H Publishing Company.)

Condravy, J. (1995). Tutors learning about learning: An assessment. *Research & Teaching in Developmental Education, 11*(2), 43-56.

Connelly P. J., & Irving, D. C. (1976). Composition in the liberal arts: A shared responsibility. *College English, 37*, 668-670.

Cooke, W. B. (1977). *Resources for student learning resources report: 1977, National project II. Alternatives to the revolving door*. Whiteville, NC: Southeast Community College.

Cox, G. I. (1977). *Different effects of instructional strategies on reading rate flexibility and comprehension*. Paper read at the American Psychological Association Meeting, San Francisco, CA.

Cross, K. P. (1971). *Beyond the open door*. San Francisco: Jossey-Bass.

Cross, K. P. (1976). *Accent on learning: Improving instruction and reshaping the curriculum*. San Francisco: Jossey-Bass.

DeLucas, D., & Larkin, J. H. (1988). Novice strategies for comprehending a scientific text. *Journal of Memory & Language, 27*, 298-308.

DeLucas, D., & Larkin, J. H. (1990). Organization and comprehensibility in scientific proofs: Or "consider a particle p." *Journal of Educational Psychology, 83*(4), 701-714.

DeVerien, M. (1973). Data collection: A cybernetic aspect of a learning assistance center. In Kerstiens, G. (Ed.). *Technological alternatives in learning*. Sixth Annual Proceedings of the Western College Reading Association, vi, 51-58.

Devine, T. G. (1990, Fall). Caveat emptor: The writing process approach to college writing. *Journal of Developmental Education, 14*(1), 2-4.

Dimon, M. (1981). Why adjunct courses work. *Journal of College Reading and Learning, xxi*, 33-40. (Reprinted in Maxwell, M. (Ed.). 1994. *From access to success*. Clearwater FL: H&H Publishing Company.)

DiPardo, A. (1993). *A kind of passport: A basic writing adjunct program and the challenge of student diversity* (NCTE Research Report # 24). Urbana, IL: National Congress of Teachers of English (NCTE).

Donovan, R. A. (1976). The Southwest institution of national project II. *Alternatives to the Revolving Door Newsletter #2*, 1-6. New York: Bronx Community College.

Duffin, B., & others. (1977). *A study of writing problems in a remedial writing program for EOP students*. Davis, CA: English Department, University of California-Davis.

Ede, L. (1990). Writing as a social process. *The Writing Center Journal, 9*:2, 3-15.

Elbow, P. (1973). *Writing without teachers*. New York: Oxford University Press.

Elbow, P. (1981). *Writing with power*. New York: Oxford University Press.

Elbow, P. (1986). *Embracing contraries*. Oxford: Oxford University Press.

Enright, G. (1975) College learning skills: Frontierland origins of the learning assistance center. In Sugimoto, R. (Ed.). *College Learning Skills: Today and Tomorrowland*. Proceedings of the 8th Annual Conference of the Western College Reading Association.

Enright, G. (1976). The study table and panic clinic. In Sugimoto, R. (Ed.). *The spirit of '76: Revolutionizing college learning skills*. Proceedings of the 9th Annual Conference of the Western College Reading Association.

Enright, G., & Kerstiens, G. (1980). The learning center: Toward an expanded role. In Lenning, O. T., & Nayman, R. (Eds.). *New roles for learning assistance*, 1-24. Western College Reading Association.

Felton, C. S., & Biggs, B. E. (1977). *Up from underachievement*. Springfield, IL: Thomas.

Ferguson, D. A. (1974). A structure for unstructured lectures. *American Mathematical Monthly, 81*, 512-514.

Ferguson, J. (1969). Teaching the reading of biology. In Robinson, H. A., & Thomas E. L. (Eds.). *Fusing reading skills and content*. Newark, NJ: International Reading Association.

Fidler & Godwin. (1994). *Journal of Developmental Education, 17*(3).

Flanagan, J. C. (1954). The critical incident technique. *Psychological Bulletin, 51*, 327-358.

Flesch, R. (1943). *Marks of readable style: A study in adult education*. New York: Bureau of Publications, Columbia University.

Flesch, R. (1948). A new readability yardstick. *Journal of Applied Psychology, 23*, 221-223.

Flesch, R. (1958). *A new way to better English*. Garden City, NY: Dolphin.

Flippo, R. A., & Caverly, D. C. (1991). *Teaching reading and study strategies at the college level*. Newark, DE: International Reading Association.

Flower, L. (1979). Writer based prose: A cognitive basis for problems in writing. *College English, 41*, 19-37.

Fullilove, R. E., & Treisman, P. U. (1990). Mathematics achievement among African-American undergraduates at the University of California-Berkeley: An evaluation of the mathematics workshop program. *Journal of Negro Education, 59*(3), 463-477.

Galica, G. (1991). *The blue book*. New York: Harcourt Brace.

Garland, M. (1993, Spring). The mathematics workshop model: An interview with Uri Treisman. *Journal of Developmental Education, 16*(3), 14-22.

Gier, T. (1993). College Reading & Learning Association's tutor certification program. *Journal of Developmental Education*. (Reprinted in Maxwell, M. (Ed.) 1994. *From access to success*. Clearwater FL: H&H Publishing Company.)

Girdano, D., & Everly, G. (1979). *Controlling stress and tension*. Englewood Cliffs, NJ: Prentice Hall.

Goodsell, M., Maherm, M., & Tinto, V. (1992). *Collaborative learning: A sourcebook for higher education, Vol. 1*. University Park, PA: NCTLA, 19.

Goolsby, C. B., Dwinell, P. L., Higbee, J. L., & Bretscher, A. S. (1988). Factors affecting mathematics achievement in high-risk students. *Research & Teaching in Developmental Education, 4*(2), 18-27.

Gourgey, A. (1992). Tutoring developmental mathematics: Overcoming anxiety and fostering independent learning. *Journal of Developmental Education, 14*(2), 2-6.

Gourgey, A. (1992). Tutoring practices that promote cognitive and affective development. In Malinowski, P. A. (Ed.). *Perspectives on Practices in Developmental Education*. A 1992 Monograph of the New York College Learning Skills Association, 66-67. (Reprinted in Maxwell, M. (Ed.). 1994. *From access to success*. Clearwater FL: H&H Publishing Company.)

Grant, M. K., & Hoeber, D. C. (1978). *Basic skills programs: Are they working?* AAHE/ERIC/Higher Education Research Report, No.1.

Griffin, C. W. (Ed.). 1992. *Teaching writing in all disciplines, new directions for teaching and learning.* San Francisco: Jossey-Bass.

Gross, T. L. (1978). How to kill a college: The private papers of a campus dean. *Saturday Review*, February 8, 1978, 12-20.

Grossman, F. J., & others. (1993, Fall). Did you say "write" in mathematics class? *Journal of Developmental Education, 17*(1), 2-6, 35.

Haase, A. M. B., & others. (1977). Evaluating the college reading program: A management audit. In Pearson, P. D. & Hansen, J. (Eds.). 1977. *Reading theory, research and practice.* 26th Yearbook of the National Reading Conference.

Hackworth, R. (1992). *Math anxiety reduction.* (2nd ed.). Clearwater, FL: H&H Publishing Co.

Hackworth, R. (1994). Teaching mathematics effectively. In Maxwell, M. (Ed.). 1994. *From access to success.* Clearwater FL: H&H Publishing Company.

Haengi, D., & Perfitti, C. A. (1992). Individual differences in reprocessing of text. *Journal of Educational Psychology, 84*(2), 182-192.

Haight, G. P. (1976). Balancing chemistry's priorities. *Change: Report on Teaching #1*, 4-5.

Hanau, L. (1972). *The study game: How to play and win.* New York: Barnes & Noble.

Hancock, K., & Gier, T. (1991). Counseling skills: An important part of tutor training. *Journal of College Reading and Learning, XXIII*(2),55-59. (Reprinted in Maxwell, M. (Ed.). 1994. *From access to success.* Clearwater FL: H&H Publishing Company.)

Hanf, M. B. (1971). Mapping: A technique for turning reading into thinking. *Journal of Reading,14*, 225-230, 270.

Hansen, D. M. (1977). A discourse structural analysis of the comprehension of rapid readers. In Pearson, P. D., & Harris, J. (Eds.). *Reading theory, research and programs*, 26th Yearbook of the National Reading Conference, Clemson, SC.

Hardin, C. J. (1988, Fall). Access to higher education: Who belongs? *Journal of Developmental Education, 12*(1), 2-6. (Reprinted in Maxwell, M. (Ed.). 1994. *From access to success.* Clearwater FL: H&H Publishing Company.)

Harris, M. (1978). Individualized diagnosis: Searching for causes, not symptoms of writing deficiencies. *College English, 40*, 318-323.

Harris, M. (Ed.). (1982). *Tutoring writing: A sourcebook for writing labs.*

Hartman, H. (1990, Winter). Factors affecting the tutoring process. *Journal of Developmental Education, 14*:2, 2-7.

Hartman, H. (1994). From reciprocal teaching to reciprocal education. *Journal of Developmental Education, 18*(1), 2-8, 32.

Hartman, H. J. (1995). Cooperative learning approaches to mathematics problem solving. In Postamentier (Ed.). *The art of problem solving: A resource for the mathematics teacher.* NY: Kraus International Publications.

Hashway, R. M. (1989, Spring). Developmental learning center designs. *Research & Teaching in Developmental Education, 5*(2), 25-38.

Hashway, R. M., & Hashway, S. E. (1991-1992). Solving mathematical word problems, integrating two different world models. *Innovative Learning Strategies.* Tenth Yearbook. 3-7.

Hashway, S. E. (1995). *The validity of a hierarchy of reading comprehension skills for young adults.* Unpublished Doctoral Dissertation, Grambling State University, Grambling, LA.

Hawkins, T. (1980). Intimacy and audience: The relationship between revision and the social dimension of peer tutoring. *College English, 42*, 64-69.

Hayes, John R. (1989). *The complete problem solver.* (2nd ed.). Hillsdale, NJ: Erlbaum Associates.

Heard, P. (1976). College learning specialists: A profession coming of age. In Sugimoto, R. (Ed.). *The spirit of '76: Revolutionizing college learning skills*. Procedures of the 9th Annual Conference of the Western College Reading Association.

Herber, H. L. (1978). *Teaching reading in the content areas*. Englewood Cliffs, NJ: Prentice Hall.

Higbee, J. L., & Dwinell, P. L. (1990, Fall). The high-risk student profile. *Research & Teaching in Developmental Education, 7*(1), 55-64.

Hirsch, G. (1994, Winter). Helping students overcome the effects of difficult learning histories. *Journal of Developmental Education, 18*(2), 10-14, 16.

Hodges, R. B., Sellers, D. E., & White, W. G., Jr. (1994-95). Peer teaching: The use of facilitators in college classes. *Journal of College Reading and Learning, 26*(2), 23-29.

Hodgkinson, H. L. (1970). How deans of students are seen by others—and why. *National Association of Student Personnel Administrators' Journal, 8*, 49-54.

Hodgkinson, H. L. (1985). *All one system: Demographics of education, kindergarten through graduate school*. Wash., D.C.: Institute for Educational Leadership.

Holt, J. (1964). *How children fail*. New York: Dell.

House, J. D., & Wohlt, V. (1990). The effect of tutoring program participation on the performance of academically underprepared college freshmen. *Journal of College Student Development, 31*, 365-370.

Hudspeth, M. C., & Hirsch, L. R. (1982). *Studying mathematics*. Dubuque, Iowa: Kendall-Hunt.

Hughes, B. (1994). Reaching across the curriculum with a writing center. (Reprinted in Maxwell, M. (Ed.). 1994. *From access to success*. Clearwater FL: H&H Publishing Company.)

Huxley, A. (1962). Education on the non-verbal level. *Daedelus, 91*, 279-294.

Illingworth, M. L. (1995). *An integrated approach to academic probation intervention: A route to college success*. Paper presented at the National Association for Developmental Education, Chicago, IL.

Irwin, D. E. (1980). Effects of peer tutoring on academic achievement and affective adjustment. In Enright, G. (Ed.). *Proceedings of the Thirteenth Annual Conference of the Western College Reading Association, XIII*, 42-45.

Irwin, D. E. (1981). Final statistics grades as a function of the amount of tutoring received. In Enright, G. (Ed.). *Proceedings of the Fourteenth Annual Conference of the Western College Reading Association, XIV*, 55-62.

Jacobs, J. E. (September-October 1977). Focus: Women and mathematics. Must they be at odds? *Pi Lambda Theta Newsletter*, 10.

Jason, J. E., & others. (1977). Introduction to an accelerated program in science and technology for the disadvantaged. *Journal of the Society of Ethnic and Special Studies*, 36-39.

Johnson, D. W., Johnson, R. T., & Smith, K. A. (1991). *Cooperative learning: Increasing college faculty productivity. ASHE:ERIC, Higher education report #91-1*. Washington, D.C. Association for the Study of Higher Education.

Kadel, S., & Keehner, J. A. *Collaborative learning: A sourcebook for higher education, Vol. 2*. University Park, PA: NCTLA.

Kaiden, E., & others. (1992). Developmental adjunct faculty orientation and training program. In Malinowski, P. (Ed.). *Perspectives on Practice in Developmental Education*. Finger Lakes Community College: New York College Learning Skills Association, 79-82.

Karliner, A. (1974). *A report on problems of subject A/composition program*. San Diego, CA: University of California.

Karwin, T. J. (1973). Flying a learning center: *Design and costs of an off-campus space for learning*. Berkeley, CA: Carnegie Commission of Higher Education.

Kasper, L. F. (1995-1996). Using discipline-based texts to boost college ESL reading instruction. *Journal of Adolescent & Adult Literacy, 385*(4), 290-296.

Keimig, R. T. (1983). *Raising academic standards: A guide to learning improvement*. Washington, DC: ASHE-ERIC. Clearing House for Higher Education/Association for the Study of Higher Education.

Kershner, A. M. (1964). Speed of reading in an adult population under different conditions. *Journal of Applied Psychology, 48*, 25-28.

Kerstiens, G. (1979). Yet another look at developmental reading courses. In Enright, G. (Ed.). *Proceedings of the Twelfth Annual Conference of the College Reading Association, 12,* 12-18.

Kerstiens, G. (1995) *Five models of learning assistance.* Torrance, CA: Andragogy Associates.

Kiewra, K. A. (1988). Notetaking and review strategies: Theoretical orientations, empirical findings in instructional practices. *Research & Teaching in Developmental Education, 42,* 5-17.

Kiewra, K. A., & others. (1991). Effects of repetition, recall and note-taking strategies for learning from lecture. *Journal of Educational Psychology, 83,* 120-123.

Kinkead, J., & Harris, J. (Eds.). 1993. *Writing centers in context: Twelve case studies.* Urbana, IL: National Council of Teachers of English.

Kirby, K., Nist, S. L., & Simpson, M. L. (1986). The reading journal: A bridge between reading and writing. *Forum for Reading, 19,* 13-19.

Kitzhaber, A. R. (1963). *Themes, theories, and therapy: The teaching of writing in college.* New York: McGraw-Hill.

Klingelhofer, E. L., & Hollander, L. (1973). *Educational characteristics and needs of new students: A review of the literature.* Berkeley, CA: Center for Research and Development in Higher Education.

Kluepful, G. A., Parilius, R. J., & Roberts, G. (1994). Involving faculty in retention. *Journal of Developmental Education, 17*(3), 16-26.

Kolb, D. A. (1981). Learning styles and disciplinary differences. In Chickering, A. (Ed.). 1985. *The modern American college.* (232-254). San Francisco: Jossey-Bass.

Kolb, D. A. (1985). *Learning style inventory.* Boston: McBer and Co.

Kolb, D. A. (1986). *Users guide for the learning style inventory: A manual for teachers and trainers.* Boston: McBer & Co.

Kornrich, M. (Ed.). 1965. *Underachievement.* Springfield, IL: Thomas.

Kulik, J. A., & Kulik, C. C. (Summer, 1991). *Developmental instruction: An analysis of research. Research Report #1.* Boone, NC: National Center for Developmental Education and the Exxon Research Foundation.

Lakein, A. (1973). *How to get control of your time and your life.* New York: Peter W. Wyden.

Lamberg, W. J. (1975). Major problems in doing academic writing. *College Composition and Communication, 26,* 26-29.

Larkin, J. H., & Reif, F. (1976). Analysis and teaching of a general skill for studying science texts. *Journal of Educational Psychology, 68,* 431-440.

Lesser, G. S. (1976). Cultural differences in learning and thinking styles. In S. Messick & Associates, *Individuality in learning: Implications of cognitive style and creativity for human development.* San Francisco: Jossey-Bass.

Levin, M., & Levin, J. (1991). A critical examination of academic retention programs for at-risk minority college students. *Journal of College Student Development, 32*(4), 323-334.

Liberty, S. (1981). Learning by tutoring in two-year colleges. In Christ, F. L. and Coda-Messerle, M. (Eds.). Staff Development for College Learning Support Services, No. 4, (64-73). *New Directions for Learning Assistance.* San Francisco: Jossey-Bass.

Liebert, R., & Morris, L. (1976). Cognitive and emotional components of test anxiety: A distinction and some initial data. *Psychological Reports, 20,* 975-978.

Light, R. J. (1992). *The Harvard assessment seminar: Second report.* Cambridge, MA: Harvard University.

Losak, J. (1972). Do remedial programs really work? *Personnel and Guidance Journal, 50*(2), 383-386.

Losak, J., & Miles, C. (1991). A history of developmental education. [Unpublished paper.] Piedmont Techical College (SC) and Nova University (FL).

Lowenstein, S. (1993). Using advisory boards for learning assistance programs. *Perspectives on Practice in Developmental Education,* New York College Learning Skills Association.

Macan, T. H., & others. (1990). College students' time management: Correlation with academic performance and stress. *Journal of Educational Psychology, 82*:4, 760-768.

MacDonald, R. (1991). Developmental students' processing of teacher feedback in composition instruction. *Review of Research in Developmental Education, 8*(5). (Reprinted in Maxwell, M. (Ed.). 1994. *From access to success.* Clearwater, FL: H&H Publishing Company.)

MacDonald, R. (1993). Group tutoring techniques: From research to practice. *Journal of Developmental Education, 17*(2), 2-18.

Mandler, G., & Sarason, S. (1952). A study of anxiety and learning. *Journal of Abnormal and Social Psychology, 47*, 228-229.

Marshall, S. (1994, Winter). Faculty development through Supplemental Instruction. In Martin, D. C., & Arendale, D. R. (Eds.). 1994. *Supplemental instruction: Increasing achievement and retention. New directions for teaching and learning, No. 60.* San Francisco: Jossey-Bass Publishers, 31-40.

Martin, D. C., & others. (1977). *The learning center: A comprehensive model for colleges and universities.* Grand Rapids, MI: Aquinas College.

Martin, D. C., Arendale, D., & Associates. (1992). *Supplemental instruction: Improving first-year student success in high-risk college courses.* Columbia, SC: National Resources Center for the Freshman Year Experience.

Martin, D. C., & Arendale, D. R. (Eds.). 1994, Winter. *Supplemental instruction: Increasing achievement and retention. New directions for teaching and learning, No. 60.* San Francisco: Jossey-Bass Publishers.

Martin, D. C., Blanc, R., & Arendale, D. (1994-95). Mentorship in the classroom: Making the implicit explicit. *Teaching Excellence, 6*(1), 1, 2.

Materniak, G., & Williams, A. (1987, September). Standards and guidelines for learning assistance programs. *Journal of Developmental Education, 11*(1), 12-18.

Mathematical Association of America. (1990). *Using writing to teach mathematics.* Washington, DC: The Mathematical Association of America.

Matthews, J. M. (1981). Becoming professional in college level learning assistance. In Christ, F. L., & Coda-Messerle, M. (Eds.). 1981. *Staff development for learning support services, new directions for college learning assistance, No. 4.* San Francisco: Jossey-Bass, 1-18.

Maxwell, M. (1966). An individualized college learning laboratory. *Reading Improvement, 4*, 5-6.

Maxwell, M. (1967). Integrating the college reading program with science and mathematics. In Figurel, J. (Ed.). *Vistas in reading, Part 1.* Proceedings of the 11th Annual Convention of International Reading Association. Newark, DE: International Reading Association.

Maxwell, M. (1978). Learning style and other correlates of gains in skimming speed. *Journal of Reading Behavior, 10*, 49-56.

Maxwell, M. (1978). *Improving student learning skills.* San Francisco: Jossey-Bass.

Maxwell, M. (1990). Does tutoring help?: A look at the literature. *Review of Research in Developmental Education, 7*(4). (Reprinted in Maxwell, M. (Ed.). 1994. *From access to success.* Clearwater FL: H&H Publishing Company.)

Maxwell, M. (Fall 1991). The effects of expectations, sex, and ethnicity on peer tutoring. *Journal of Developmental Education, (15)*, 14-16.

Maxwell, M. (1993). *Evaluating academic skills programs: A sourcebook.* Kensington, MD: MM Associates.

Maxwell, M. (Ed.). 1994. *From access to success: Readings in learning assistance and developmental education.* Clearwater, FL: H&H Publishing Co.

Maxwell, M. (Ed.). 1994. *When tutor meets student.* Ann Arbor, MI: University of Michigan Press.

Maxwell, M., & Magoon, T. M. (1962). Self-directed vs traditional study skills programs: A descriptive and comparative evaluation. *Journal of College Student Personnel, 3*, 385-387.

Maxwell, M. J., & Zitterkopf, D. (1965). Evaluation of the writing workshops offered PCSS during the summer of 1964. *Reading and Study Skills Lab, Research Report #65-01.* College Park, MD: University of Maryland Counseling Center.

Mayfield, C. K. (1977). Establishing a reading and study skills course for law students. *Journal of Reading, 20*, 285-287.

McCarthy, B. (1982). *The 4 MAT system*. Oak Brook, IL: EX-CEL, Inc.

McClure, M. (1988). *Designing your own system of assessing developmental education*. Paper presented at the Sixth Annual Conference of the South Carolina Association of Developmental Educators, Hilton Head, SC, November 4, 1988.

McGrath, J. L. (1989). *Building strategies for college reading*. Englewood Cliffs, NJ: Prentice-Hall.

McHargue, M. (1975). *Learning assistance center, autumn 1975*. Palo Alto, CA: Learning Assistance Center, Stanford University.

McKeachie, W. J. (1969). *A guidebook for the beginning college teacher*. Lexington, MA: Heath.

McKeachie, W. J. (1976). Psychology in America's bicentennial year. *American Psychologist, 31*, 834-842.

McKeachie, W. J. (1990). Research in college teaching: The historical background. *Journal of Educational Psychology, 82*(2), 199-200.

McLeod, S. H. (Ed.). 1992. *Strengthening programs for writing across the curriculum: New drections for teaching and learning*. San Francisco: Jossey-Bass.

McWhorter, K. T. (1994). *Academic reading* (2nd ed.). NY: Harper Collins.

McWhorter, K. T. (1996). *Efficient and flexible reading* (4th ed.). NY: Harper-Collins.

McWhorter, K. T. (1996). *Study and critical thinking skills in college*. (3rd ed.). NY: Harper-Collins.

Messick, S., & Associates. (1976). *Individuality in learning: Implications of cognitive styles and creativity for human development*. San Francisco: Jossey-Bass.

Miles, J. (1967). *Style and proportion: The language of prose and poetry*. New York: Little Brown.

Miles, J. (1975). What we already know about composition and what we need to know. *California English, 11*, 14-15.

Moore, J. C. (1971). Test-wiseness and analogy test performance. *Measurement and Evaluation in Guidance, 3*, 198-202.

Mumford, M. D., Costanza, D. P., Baughman, W. A., Thirflfall, V., & Fleischman, E. A. (1994). Influence of abilities on performance during practice: Effects of massed and distributed practice. *Journal of Educational Psychology, 86*(1) 133-144.

National Association for Developmental Education. (1994). *NADE self-evaluation guides: Models for assessing learning assistance/Developmental education programs*. Clearwater, FL: H&H Publishing Company.

New Jersey Basic Skills Council. (1991). *Effectiveness of remedial programs in public colleges and universities. Fall 1977-Spring 1989*. Trenton, NJ: New Jersey Board of Higher Education.

Nist, S. L. (1987). Teaching students to annotate and underline text effectively: Guidelines and procedures. *Georgia Journal of Reading, 12*(2), 16-22.

Nist, S. L., & Hynd, C. R. (1985). The college reading lab: An old story with a new twist. *Journal of Reading, 18*(3), 305-309.

North, S. M. (1984). The idea of a writing center. *College English, 46*(5), 433-446. Reprinted in Murphy, C., & Sherwood, S. (Eds.). 1995. *The St. Martin's sourcebook for writing tutors.*

Obler, M., & others. (1977). Combining of traditional counseling, instruction, and mentoring functions with academically deficient college freshmen. *Journal of Educational Research, 5*, 192-.

Palinscar, A. S., & Brown, A. L. (1984). Reciprocal teaching of comprehension-fostering and comprehension-monitoring activities. *Cognition & Instruction, 1*(2), 117-175.

Palinscar, A. S., & Brown, A. L. (1986). Interactive teaching to promote independent learning from text. *Reading Teacher, 39*(1), 771-777.

Palinscar, A. S., Ransom, K., & Derber, S. (1988-1989). Collaborative research and development of reciprocal teaching. *Educational Leadership, 46*(4), 37-40.

Pauk, W. (1974). *How to study in college*. (2nd ed.). Boston: Houghton-Mifflin.

Pauk, W. (1989). *How to study in college.* (7th ed.). Boston: Houghton-Mifflin.

Payne, I. M., & Smith, W. (1990). *Retention study for RIT development center college restoration program students enrolled Fall 1986-Winter 1990.* In-house Report, Rochester Institute of Technology, PO Box 9887, Rochester, NY 14623-0887.

Perkinson, H. (1984). *Learning from our mistakes: A reinterpretation of twentieth-century education.* Westport, CT: Greenwood Press.

Perry, R. P., & Penner, K. S. (1990). Enhancing academic achievement in college students through attributional retraining and instruction. *Journal of Educational Psychology, 92*:2, 262-271.

Perry, W. G., Jr. (1959). Student's use and misuse of reading skills: A report to the Harvard faculty. *Harvard Educational Review, 29,* 193-200.

Perry, W. G. (1968). *Forms of intellectual and ethical development in the college years: A scheme.* New York: Holt, Rinehart and Winston.

Perry, W. G. (1981). Cognitve and ethical growth: The making of meaning. In Chickering, A. (Ed.). *The modern American college.* San Francisco: Jossey-Bass, 76-116.

Peterson, G. T. (1975). *The learning center.* Hampton, CN: Shoestring Press.

Peterson, G. T., & others. (1978). *West Valley College comprehensive plan for special education. 1978-1979.* Saratoga, CA: West Valley College.

Pitcher, R. W., & Blauschild, B. (1970). *Why college sudents fail.* New York: Funk & Wagnalls.

Popham, W. J. (1975). *Educational evaluation.* Englewood Cliffs, NJ: Prentice-Hall.

Porter, D. B. (1989). Educating from a group perspective: What, why and how. *Proceedings of the Human Factors Society* 33rd Annual Meeting, pp. 507-511.

Porter, D. B. (1991). A perspective on college learning. *Journal of College Reading and Learning, XXIV*:1.

Porter, D. B., Bird, M. E., & Wunder, A. (1990-1991, Winter). Competition, cooperation, satisfaction, and the performance of complex tasks among Air Force cadets. *Current Psychology Research & Reviews, 9*:4, 347-354.

Powell, A. B., Pierre, E., & Ramos, C. (1993). Researching, reading, and writing about writing to learn mathematics: Pedagogy and product. *Research & Teaching in Developmental Education, 10*(1) 95-110.

Prelog, V. (1976). Chirality in chemistry. *Science, 193,* 17-24.

Quinn, K. B. (Spring-Summer 1995). Teaching reading and writing as modes of learning in college: A glance at the past; a view to the future. *Reading Research & Instruction.*

Rabinski-Caroulo, N. (1989). An interview with Edmund W. Gordon. *Journal of Developmental Education, 13*(1), 18-22.

Ramirez, G. M. (1993). Supplemental instruction. In Miodoski, S. and Enright, G. (Eds.). *Proceedings of the 13th and 14th annual institutes for learning assistance professionals—Winter institute, 1992 and 1993.* Tuscon, AZ: The University Learning Center, University of Arizona, 29-31.

Ranhawa, B. S., Beamer, J. E., & Lundberg, I. (1992). Role of mathematical self-efficacy in the structural model of mathematics achievement. *Journal of Educational Psychology, 85*(1), 41-48.

Raygor, A. L. (1965). Individualizing college reading programs. In Figural, J. A. (Ed.). *Reading and Inquiry, Part 1.* Proceeding of the International Reading Association. Newark, DE: International Reading Association.

Reed, R. (1974). *Peer-tutoring programs for the academically deficient student in higher education.* Berkeley, CA: Center for Research and Development in Higher Education, University of California.

Resnick, J. (1993). A paired reading and sociology course. *Perspectives on Practice in Developmental Education.* Finger Lakes Community College, Canandaigua, NY: New York College Learning Association.

Richardson, R. C., Jr., & Martens, K. J. (1982). *A report on literacy development in community colleges.* Washington, DC: National Institute of Education.

Richardson, R. C., Fisk, E. C., & Okun, M. A. (1983). *Literacy in the Open-Access College.* San Francisco: Jossey-Bass.

Robert, E. R., & Thompson, G. (1994, Spring). Learning assistance and the success of underprepared students at Berkeley. *Journal of Developmental Education, 17*(3), 4-15.

Robinson, F. P. (1946). *Effective study.* New York: Harper and Row.

Robyak, J. B., & Patton, M. J. (1977). The effectiveness of a study skills course for students of different personality types. *Journal of Counseling Psychology, 24,* 200-207.

Rodriguez, R. (1983). *Hunger of memory: The education of Richard Rodriguez.* South Holland, IL: Bantam Books.

Rose, M. (1983). Remedial writing courses: A critique and a proposal. *College English, 45,* 109-28.

Rose, M. (1988). *Lives on the boundary: The struggles and achievement of America's underprepared.* New York: The Free Press.

Rosenshine, B. (1986). Synthesis of research on explicit teaching. *Educational Leadership, 43*(7), 60-69.

Roth, R. M., & Meyersburg, A. (1963). The non-achievement syndrome. *Personnel and Guidance Journal, 41,* 535-539.

Rotter, J. B. (1966). Generalized expectancies for internal versus external control of reinforcement. *Psychological Measurements, 80,* 1-28.

Roueche J. E., & Kirk, R. W. (1973). *Catching up: Remedial education.* San Francisco: Jossey-Bass.

Roueche, J. E., & Snow, J. J. (1977). *Overcoming learning problems.* San Francisco: Jossey-Bass.

Roueche, J. E., & Baker, G. A. (1987). *From access to excellence: The open-door college.* San Francisco: Jossey-Bass.

Roueche, J. E., and Roueche, S .D. (1993). *Between a rock and a hard place: The at-risk student in the open-door college.* Washington, DC: The American Association of Community Colleges.

Roueche, S. D., & Comstock, V. N. (1981). A report on theory and method for the study of literacy development in community colleges. *Techical Report NIE-406-786-0600.* Austin, TX: Austin Program in Community College Education, University of Texas.

Rowe, (1994). Unpublished dissertation.

Rubin, M. (1991, Spring). A glossary of developmental education terms compiled by the College Reading and Learning Association Task Force on Professional Language for College Reading and Learning. *Journal of College Reading and Learning, XXIII*(2), 1-13.

Sandberg, K. C. (1976). *Discussion of a general education, critical reading requirement for all freshman students: What, why, how?* Paper presented at the annual meeting of the National Reading Conference, Atlanta.

Sandberg, K. C. (1989). Affective and cognitive features of collaborative learning. *Review of Research in Developmental Education, 6*(4).

Schirldi, G. R. (1988). *Stress management strategies.* Dubuque, IA: Kendall-Hunt.

Schmelzer, R. V., Brozo, W. G., & Stahl, N. A. (1985). Using a learning model to integrate study skills into a peer tutoring program. *Journal of Developmental Education, 8*(3), 2-5. (Reprinted in Maxwell, M. (Ed.). 1994. *From access to success.* Clearwater FL: H&H Publishing Company.)

Schon, D. A. (1990). *Educating the reflective practitioner.* San Francisco: Jossey-Bass.

Scriven, M. (1974). Evaluation perspectives and procedures. In Popham, J. (Ed.). *Evaluation in education: Course applications.* Berkeley, CA: McCutcheon.

Seward, J. S., & Croft, M. K. (1982). *The writing laboratory.* Glenview, IL: Scott Foresman.

Shaughnessy, M. (1973). Open admissions and the disadvantaged teacher. *College Composition and Communication, 24,* 401.

Shaughnessy, M. (1976). Diving in: An introduction to basic writing. *College Composition and Communication, 27,* 234-239.

Shaughnessy, M. (1977). *Errors and expectations.* New York: Oxford University Press.

Sheets, R. A. (1994, August). The effects of training and experience on adult peer tutors in community colleges. [Unpublished doctoral dissertation]. Arizona State University.

Siegel, L., & Siegel, L. C. (1965). Educational set: A determinant of acquisition. *Journal of Educational Psychology, 56,* 1-12.

Silverman, S., & Juhasz. (1993). A developmental interpretation of help rejection. *Journal of Developmental Education, 17*(2), 24-26, 28, 30-31.

Simmons, R. (1994). Precollege programs: A contributing factor to university student retention. *Journal of Developmental Education, 17*(3),42-45.

Simpson, M. L. (1985, Fall). The characteristics of effective vocabulary instruction. *Georgia Journal of Reading, 11*(1), 4-9.

Simpson, M. L., Nist, S. L., & Kirby, L. (1987). Ideas in practice: Vocabulary strategies design for college students. *Journal of Developmental Education, 11*(2), 20 24.

Simpson, M. L., & Nist, S. L. (1992). Toward defining a comprehensive assessment model for college reading. *Journal of Reading, 35,* 452-458.

Singer, J. M. (1993). Strategic reading and structured dialogue: Their impact on reading comprehension. *Perspectives on Practice in Developmental Education.* Finger Lakes Community College, NY: New York College Learning Skills Association.

Skinner, B. F. (1968). Teaching science in high school: What is wrong. *Science, 159,* 704-710.

Smilkstein, R. (1992). *The natural learning process.* Paper presented at the Research in Developmental Education Conference, Charlotte, NC, Nov. 11-14, 1992.

Smith, D. E. P. (1961). *Learning to learn.* New York: Harcourt Brace, Jovanovich.

Smith, D. E. P., & others. (1956). Reading improvement as a function of student personality and teaching method. *Journal of Educational Psychology, 47,* 47-59.

Smith, D. M., & Kolb, D. (1986). *User's guide for the learning style inventory: A manual for teachers and trainers.* Boston: McBer and Company.

Smith, G. D., & others. (1975). A national survey of learning and study skills programs. In McNinch, G. B. and Miller, W. B. (Eds.). *Reading convention and inquiry,* Twenty-fourth Yearbook of the National Reading Conference. Clemson, SC: National Reading Conference.

Snow, R. E. (1976). Aptitude-treatment interactions and individualized alternative in education. In Messick, S. & Associates (Eds.). *Individuality in learning: Implications of cognitive style and creativity for human development.* San Francisco: Jossey-Bass.

Snyder, W. C. (1987, September). Ideas in practice: A sentence-revising format for basic writers. *Journal of Developmental Education, 11*(1), 20-22.

Sommer, R. (1968). The social psychology of cramming. *Personnel and Guidance Journal, 47,* 104-109.

Sommers, N. (1980). Revision strategies of student writers and experienced adult writers. *College Composition and Communication, 31,* 378-88.

Sowell, T. (1974). The plight of black students in the United States. *Daedelus, 103,* 179-196.

Spache, G. (1955). Trends in college reading. In Causey, O. S. (Ed.). *4th yearbook of the Southwest Reading Conference for Colleges and Universities.* Fort Worth, TX: Texas Christian University Press.

Spache, G., & others. (1959). College reading programs. *Journal of Developmental Reading, 2,* 35-46.

Spann, M., Jr., & Boylan, H. R. (1981). Developing basic education specialists and program directors. In Christ, F. L., & Coda-Messerle, M. (Eds.). *Staff development for leaning support systems: New directions for college learning assistance, No. 4.* San Francisco: Jossey-Bass.

Spann M. G., & McCrimmon. (1994, In press). Remedial/developmental education: Past, present, future. In Baker, G. (Ed.). *Handbook on community colleges in America.* Westport, CT: Greenwood Press.

Spielberger, C. D., & others. (1970). *Manual for the State-Trait Anxiety Inventory.* Palo Alto, CA: Consulting Psychologists Press.

Stahl, N. A., Brozo, W. G., & Gordon, B. (1984). The professional preparation of college reading and study-skills specialists. In McNinch, G. (Ed.). *Reading teacher education: Yearbook of the 4th annual conference of the American Reading Forum.* Carrollton, GA: West Georgia College. ERIC #248-761.

Stahl, N. A., Brozo, W. G., & Simpson, M. L. (1987). Developing college vocabulary: A content analysis of instructional materials. *Reading Research & Instruction, 26*(3) 203-221.

Stahl, N. A., Simpson, M. L., & Brozo, W. G. (1988). The materials of college reading instruction: A critical and historical perspective from 50 years of content analysis research. *Reading Research and Instruction, 27*(3), 16-34.

Stahl, N. A., Hynd, C. R., & Brozo, W. G. (1990). The development and validation of a comprehensive list of primary sources in college reading instruction. *Reading Horizons, 31*, 22-41.

Stahl, N. A., King, J. R., & Henks, W. (1991). Enhancing students' notetaking through training and evaluation. *Journal of Reading, 34*, 618-622.

Stahl, N. A., Simpson, M. L., & Hayes, C. G. (1992). Ten recommendations from research for teaching high-risk college students. *Journal of Developmental Education, 16*(1), 2-8.

Steinberg, L., & others. (1996). *Beyond the classroom.* NY: Simon & Schuster.

Stent, A. (1977, January). Can math anxiety be conquered? *Change: Report on Teaching #3*, 40-43.

Stine, C. W., Trow, E. M., & Brown, B. (1979). Math X: Variable for student progress. *Journal of Developmental Education, 3*(1), 12-13.

Stodolsky, S. S., & Lesser, G. (1967). Learning patterns in the disadvantaged. *Harvard Educational Review, 37*, 546-593.

Strom, B., Hocevevar, D., & Zimmer, J. (1990). Satisfaction and achievement: Antagonist in ATI research on student-oriented instruction. *Educational Research Quarterly, 14*(4), 15-21.

Sue, D. W., & Kirk, B. A. (1972). Psychological characteristics of Chinese-American students. *Journal of Counseling Psychology, 61*, 471-476.

Sue, D. W., & Frank, A. C. (1973). A typological approach to the psychological study of Chinese and Japanese-American college students. *Journal of Social Issues, 29*, 129-144.

Suinn, R. M. (1969). The STABS: A measure of test anxiety for behavioral therapy-Normative data. *Behavior Research and Therapy, 7*, 335-339.

Sullivan, L. I. (1978). *A guide to higher education learning centers in the United States and Canada.* Portsmouth, NH: Entelek.

Teitel, L. (1994). *The advisory committee advantage: Creating an effective srategy for programmatic improvement.* ASHE-ERIC Higher Education Report 94-1. Washington, DC: The George Washington University ASHE-ERIC Higher Education Reports.

Thornton, Y. S., & Coudert, J. (1994). *The ditch digger's daughters.* Bruce Lane Press.

Tinto, V. (1993). *Leaving college: Rethinking the causes and cures of student attrition.* (2nd ed.). Chicago: University of Chicago Press.

Tinto, V., & others. (1991). *Building learning communities for new college students.* (Research Papers.) University Park, PA.: NCTLA.

Tobias, S. (1980). *Overcoming math anxiety.* Boston, MA: Houghton Mifflin. (Note: a new edition of this book is in production.) Also listed as NY: W. W. Norton and Co., Tobias, S. (1993). *Overcoming Math Anxiety.* New York: Norton.

Tobias, S. (1990). *They're not dumb, they're different: Stalking the second tier.* Tucson, AZ: Research Corporation.

Tobias, S. (1992). *Revitalizing undergraduate science: Why some things work and most don't.* Tucson, AZ: Research Corporation.

Tobias, S., & Tomizuka, C. T. (1992). *Breaking the science barrier.* New York: The College Board.

Tomlinson, B., & others. (1974). *A preliminary report on a project integrating the teaching of reading and studying in science with biology*. Unpublished paper, University of California: Riverside.

Tomlinson, B. M., & Green, T. (1976). Integrating adjunct reading and study skills classes with the content area. In Sugimoto, R. (Ed.). *The spirit of '76: Revolutionizing college learning skills*. Procedures of the 9th annual conference of the Western College Reading Association.

Treuer, P. (1995). *Credit-based peer tutoring*. Duluth, MN: University of Minnesota-Duluth.

Treisman, P. U. (1985). *A study of the mathematics achievement of black students at the University of California-Berkeley*. Unpublished doctoral dissertation. University of California-Berkeley: Professional Development Program.

Triesman, P. U. (1992). Studying students studying calculus: A look at the lives of minority mathematics students in college. *College Mathematics Journal, 23*, 362-372.

Tripodi, L. (1978). *Ingredients for tutoring services.* Paper presented at the New York College Learning Association Conference.

Trow, M. (1966). The undergraduate dilemma in large universities. *University Quarterly, 21*, 17-43.

Turner, R. (1972). *Report to the academic senate on Subject A*. Berkeley, CA: Academic Senate, University of California.

Visor, J. J., Johnson, J. J., & Cole, L. N. (1992, Winter). The relationship of supplemental instruction to affect. *Journal of Developmental Education, 16*(2), 12-18. (Reprinted in Maxwell, M. (Ed.). 1994. *From access to success*. Clearwater FL: H&H Publishing Company.)

Waits, B., & Leitzel, J. (1984, Fall). Early university placement testing of high school juniors. *Mathematics in college*.

Warnath, C. F. (1971). *Old myths and new old readings: College counseling in transition*. San Francisco: Jossey-Bass.

Watanabe, C. (1972). 1971 Asian studies report on composition and reading problems among Asian students. *Journal of Educational Change, 4*, 1, 3.

Watanabe, C. (1973). Self-expression and the Asian-American experience. *Personnel & Guidance Journal, 51*, 390-396.

Watanabe, C., & Gordon, F. (1977). *How to study chemistry*. University of California-Berkeley: Student Learning Center.

Watkins, A. E., Albers, D. J., & Loftsgaarden, D. O. (1993, Spring). A survey of two-year college mathematics programs: The boom continues. *The AMATYC Review (American Mathematical Association of Two-Year Colleges), 14*(2), 55-66.

Weigand, G. R. J. (1949). *Motivational factors associated with success and failure of a group of probational students*. Unpublished doctoral dissertation, University of Maryland, College Park, MD.

Weigand, G. R. J., & Blake, W. S. (1955). *College orientation*. Englewood Cliffs, NJ: Prentice-Hall.

Weinsheimer, J. (1993). *Turning point: Getting off probation and on with your education*. Belmont, CA: Wadsworth Publishing Company.

Weinstein, C. (1982). Learning strategies: The metacurriculum. *Journal of Developmental Education, 5*(2), 6-7, 10.

Weinstein, C. (1988). Executive control processes in learning. Why knowing about how to learn is not enough. *Journal of College Reading & Learning, 21*, 48-56.

Weinstein, C. E., & Rogers, B. T. (1985). Comprehension monitoring: The neglected learning strategy. *Journal of Developmental Education, 9*(1), 6-9. 28-29.

Wepner, G. (1987). Evaluation of a postsecondary remedial mathematics program. *Journal of Developmental Education, 11*(1), 6-11.

Whimbey, A. E. (1976). You can learn to raise your IQ score. *Psychology Today*, 27-29.

Whimbey, A. E., & Barberena, C. J. (1977). *A cognitive-skills approach to the disciplines*. Bowling Green, OH: Competency-Based Undergraduate Education Project, Bowling Green State University.

Whimbey, A., Linden, M. L., & Williams, E., Sr. (1992). Two powerful methods for teaching writing skills: Sentence combining and text reconstruction. *Review of Research in Developmental Education, 91*(1).

Whimbey, A., & Lochhead, J. (1981). *Developing math skills: Computations, problem solving and basics for algebra.* New York: McGraw-Hill.

Whimbey, A., & Lochhead, J. (1984). *Beyond problem solving & comprehension: An exploration of quantitative reasoning.* Hillsdale, NJ: Lawrence Erlbaum Associates.

Whimbey, A., & Lochhead, J. (1990). *Problem solving & comprehension: A short course in analytical reasoning.* (5th ed.). Hillsdale, NJ: Lawrence Erlbaum Associates.

Whimbey, A. E., & Whimbey, L. S. (1975). *Intelligence can be taught.* New York: Dutton.

Whipple, M. (1916). *How to study effectively.* Illinois: Public School Publishing Co.

White, W. G., Jr., & Schnuth, M. L. (1990). College learning assistance centers: Places for learning. In Hashway, R. M. (Ed.). *Handbook of developmental education.* New York: Praeger Press, 157-177.

White, W. G., Jr., Kyzar, B., & Lane, K. E. (1990). College learning assistance centers: Spaces for learning. In Hashway, R. M. (Ed.). *Handbook of developmental education.* New York: Praeger Press, 179-195.

Widdick, C. (1977). The Perry Scheme: A foundation for developmental practice. *Counseling Psychology, 6,* 35-38.

Wilding, S., & Shearn, E. (1991). *Building self-confidence in math: A student workbook.* (2nd ed.). Dubuque, Iowa: Kendall-Hunt Publishing Company. (Audio-tapes are available from the publisher to accompany this.)

Wiley, M., & Hegeman, J. (1990). Reflective practice in developmental education programs. In Atkinson, R. H., & Longman, D. G. (Eds.). *Celebrating our past: Creating our future.* Selected Conference Abstracts. National Association for Developmental Education, 14th Annual Conference, March 1-4, 1990, Boston, MA.

Winnard, K. E. (1991, Fall). Codependency: Teaching tutors not to rescue. *Journal of College Reading and Learning, XXIV:*1, p. 32-39.

Wirtz, W., & others. (1977). *On further examination: A report of the advisory committee on the Scholastic Aptitude Score decline.* Princeton, NJ: College Entrance Examination Board.

Witkin, H. A., & others. (1977). Role of the field-independent cognitive styles in academic evolution: A longitudinal study. *Journal of Educational Psychology, 69,* 197-211.

Wittrock (Ed.). *Handbook of research on teaching.* (3rd ed.). New York: MacMillan.

Wlodowski, R. (1985). *Enhancing adult motivation to learn: A guide to improving instruction and increasing learner achievement.* San Francisco: Jossey-Bass.

Wood, N. V. (1977). *College reading and study skills.* New York: Holt Rhinehart and Winston.

Wood, N. V. (1989, Winter). Reading tests and reading assessment. *Journal of Developmental Education, 13*(2), 14-16, 18.